Multinational Enterprises and Emerging Challenges of the 21st Century

Multinational Enterprises and Emerging Challenges of the 21st Century

Edited by

John H. Dunning

Emeritus Esmee Fairbairn Professor of International Investment and Business Studies, University of Reading, UK and Emeritus State of New Jersey Professor of International Business, Rutgers University, US

Tsai-Mei Lin

Professor of International Business and Dean of the College of Business, Chinese Culture University, Taiwan

Edward Elgar
Cheltenham, UK • Northampton, MA, USA

Published by
Edward Elgar Publishing Limited
Glensanda House
Montpellier Parade
Cheltenham
Glos GL50 1UA
UK

Edward Elgar Publishing, Inc.
William Pratt House
9 Dewey Court
Northampton
Massachusetts 01060
USA

A catalogue record for this book
is available from the British Library

Library of Congress Cataloguing in Publication Data

Multinational enterprises and emerging challenges of the 21st century /
edited by John H. Dunning and Tsai-Mei Lin.
    p. cm.
  Includes bibliographical references and index.
1. International business enterprises. 2. International economic
relations. 3. Investments, Foreign. 4. Globalization. 5. International
business enterprises—Taiwan—Case studies. I. Dunning, John H. II. Lin,
Caimei.
  HD62.4.M84225 2007
  658'.049—dc22

                                                        200701062

ISBN   978 1 84720 356 4

Printed and bound in Great Britain by MPG Books Ltd, Bodmin, Cornwall

Contents

List of contributors   *viii*
Acknowledgements   *x*

1 Introduction   1
   John H. Dunning and Tsai-Mei Lin
2 Three important trends in recent global economic development   7
   Jen-Hu Chang

PART ONE   FDI AND MNES: SOME RECENT
           DEVELOPMENTS

3 FDI, globalization and development   13
   John H. Dunning
4 Foreign direct investment and investor strategies in China   25
   Phillip D. Grub and Jiawen Yang
5 An econometric investigation of Chinese outward direct
   investment   55
   Adam Cross, Peter Buckley, Jeremy Clegg, Hinrich Voss,
   Mark Rhodes, Ping Zheng and Xin Lui
6 From the internationalization of R&D to a global
   R&D network   87
   Hiroo Takahashi

PART TWO   NEW DIRECTIONS OF THINKING IN IB
           RESEARCH

7 International business studies: episodic or evolutionary?   109
   Daniel P. Sullivan and John D. Daniels
8 Ignorant internationalization? The Uppsala Model and
   internationalization patterns for Internet-related firms   135
   Mats Forsgren and Peter Hagström
9 The value creation perspective of international strategic
   management   153
   Reid W. Click

10 Embedding the multinational: bridging internal and external
     networks in transitional institutional contexts   177
     Ray Loveridge

11 Managerial trust and leadership in global management:
     propensities to trust, the influence of national culture on
     trust and conditional trust – a cross-cultural study   201
     James J. Cavazzini and Min H. Lu

12 Cultural genes, the trust model and the specialization and
     internationalization of the management of Chinese family
     enterprises   223
     Donglin Song and Zheng Li

13 The subsidiary role of multinational enterprises and procedural
     justice   245
     Tai-Ning Yang and Chuan-Ling Kang

14 The history and prospects of international business education
     in Japan and in the Asian region   269
     Noritake Kobayashi

15 Globalization and higher education: some strategies adopted
     by Waseda University   277
     Ken'ichi Enatsu

16 Developing Singapore as a global education hub: opportunities
     and challenges   285
     Ah-Keng Kau

17 The global impact of American restaurant franchises: an
     international perspective   303
     Mahmood A. Khan and Maryam Khan

18 Sustainable tourism, industrial development and multinational
     corporations: a case of productivity spillovers in Malaysia   323
     Wong Kong Yew and Tom Baum

19 Managerial philosophies, peace culture and the performance
     of multinational enterprises' cross-cultural management   339
     Tsai-Mei Lin and Gun-Ming Chuang

PART THREE   SOME TAIWANESE CASE STUDIES

20 An empirical examination of the association between
     manufacturing decisions and performance evaluation:
     evidence from Taiwanese listed electronic firms   367
     Fujiing Shiue and Yi-Yin Yen

21 Domestic inter-firm networks and corporate
     internationalization: a cross-industry study of Taiwanese SMEs   389
     *Ku-Ho Lin, Isabella M. Chaney, Thomas C. Lawton and
     Meng-Chun Liu*

22 The influence of the Internet on the internationalization of
SMEs in Taiwan   407
Yi-Long Jaw and Chun-Liang Chen
23 Knowledge transfer and entry strategies of Taiwan
transnationals   435
Yung-Kuei Liang

Index   455

List of Contributors

Tom Baum, Professor of Tourism Studies, University of Strathclyde, UK

Peter Buckley, Professor of International Business, Leeds University Business School, UK

James J. Cavazzini, Instructor of Strategic Managment, Management and Marketing Department, Monmouth University, USA

Isabella M. Chaney, Senior Lecturer in Marketing, School of Management, Royal Holloway, University of London,UK

Jen-Hu Chang, Chairman, Board of Regents, Chinese Culture University, ROC

Chun-Liang Chen, Lecturer, Chinese Culture University, ROC

Gun-Ming Chuang, Lecturer, Chinese Culture University, ROC

Jeremy Clegg, Professor of International Business, Leeds University Business School, UK

Reid W. Click, Associate Professor, George Washington University, Washington DC, USA

Adam Cross, Senior Lecturer, Leeds University Business School, UK

John D. Daniels, Professor, Samuel N. Friedland Chair of Executive Management, University of Miami, USA

John H. Dunning, Professor Emeritus of International Business at Reading University, UK and Rutgers University, US

Ken'ichi Enatsu, Professor, Faculty of Commerce, Vice-President, Waseda University, Tokyo, Japan

Mats Forsgren, Professor, Department of Business Studies, Uppsala University, Sweden

Phillip D. Grub, Professor Emeritus of International Business, George Washington University, Washington DC, USA

Peter Hagström, Associate Professor and Director, Stockholm School of Economics, Sweden

Yi-Long Jaw, Professor, Graduate Institute of International Business, National Taiwan University, ROC

Chuan-Ling Kang, Associate Professor, Chinese Culture University, ROC

Ah-Keng Kau, Deputy Director, NUS Entrepreneurship Centre, and

Professorial Fellow, NUS Business School, National University of Singapore, Singapore

Mahmood A. Khan, Professor, Department of Hospitality and Tourism Management, Pamplin College of Business, Virginia, US

Maryam Khan, Director, Assistant Professor, Hospitality Management Program, Howard University, USA

Noritake Kobayashi, Professor Emeritus, Keio University, Japan

Thomas C. Lawton, Senior Lecturer, International Business Strategy, Tanaka Business School, Imperial College London, UK

Zheng Li, Lecturer, Department of Economics, Jilin University, PRC.

Ku-Ho Lin, Assistant Research Fellow, Chung-Hua Institute for Economic Research, ROC

Meng Chun Liu, Deputy Director, International Division, Chung-Hua Institute for Economic Research, ROC

Tsai-Mei Lin, Professor of International Business, Former President, Dean, College of Business, Chinese Culture University, ROC

Yung-Kuei Liang, Associate Professor, Tatung University, ROC

Ray Loveridge, Professor, Said Business School, University of Oxford, UK

Min H. Lu, Associate Professor of Marketing, Management and Marketing Department, Monmouth University, USA

Xin Lui, PhD student, Leeds University Business School, UK

Mark Rhodes, Lecturer in Economics, School of Management and Business, the University of Wales, Aberystwyth

Fujiing Shiue, Professor and Chairman, Department of Accounting, National Taipei University, ROC

Donglin Song, Professor of Economics, Jilin University, PRC

Daniel P. Sullivan, Associate Professor of Business, University of Delaware, USA

Hiroo Takahashi, Professor, Hakuoh University, Japan

Hinrich Voss, PhD Student, Leeds University Business School, UK

Tai-Ning Yang, Associate Professor, Chinese Culture University, ROC

Jiawen Yang, Professor of International Business and International Affairs, George Washington University, Washington DC, USA

Yi-Yin Yen, Assistant Professor, National Taipei College of Business, ROC

Wong Kong Yew, Lecturer, Universiti Putra Malaysia, Malaysia

Ping Zheng, Research Fellow, Leeds University Business School, UK

Acknowledgements

We would first like to recognize the vision and outstanding scholarship of Professor Itaro Irie. Professor Irie first came to Taiwan in 1979, and helped found the 'AIB in Taiwan'. He also assisted the Chinese Culture University in inviting many prestigious scholars to participate in the first International Conference in Taipei. These included Professors Noritake Kobayashi and Kenichi Enatsu from Japan; and Professors John Daniel and Phillip Grub from the USA. Over the years, these and other world renowned multinational business academics have been regular attendees at the eight conferences held so far.

In addition, we would also like to express our sincere gratitude to the Chairman, Board of Regents, CCU, Dr Jen-Hu Chang for his generous support over two decades. We are also most grateful for the interest and encouragement of the current president of CCU, Tien-Rein Lee.

With respect to the preparation of this volume for publication, we would like to thank all the contributors for permitting us to publish the papers presented at the 8th International Conference on Multinational Enterprises held on 14–16 March 2006. We would also like to thank most warmly the assistance given Dr Tai-Ning Yang, Dr Betty Teng and Ms De-Hui Chang. We would finally like to express gratitude to Rayming Painting Co., Ltd, and especially to Edward Elgar Publishing for promoting this book worldwide so that it might provide a valuable reference for IB researchers. We would also like to thank Alan Sturmer of Edward Elgar, for assisting us through the entire book publication process.

John H. Dunning
Tsai-Mei Lin

1. Introduction

John H. Dunning and Tsai-Mei Lin

This volume includes a selection of the papers presented at the 8th International Conference on Multinational Enterprises organized by the Chinese Culture University and held on14-16 March, 2006. Altogether 82 papers were delivered by Chinese scholars and those of other nationalities. In addition to the insightful and sensitive keynote address given by Dr Jen-Hu Chang of the Chinese Culture University, we have selected 22 of these papers for publication, which we believe best represent the main thrust of interest of the participants, and are of high scholarly quality. We regret we are unable to include many other excellent contributions, but space constraints prevent us from doing so.

The theme of the 2006 conference was The Management Strategies of Multinational Enterprises, and several of the papers presented dealt specifically with the impact of globalization, technological advances and the emergence of multinational enterprises from developing and transition economies on such strategies. But, as in previous conferences organized by the Chinese Culture University, the intellectual agenda was incredibly rich and varied. Topics ranged from the macro-economic and institutional implications of the evolving characteristics of twenty-first century MNE activity to an impressive array of carefully constructed and intriguing company case studies.

The geography of the issues covered by the conference was truly global. As might be expected, there was a concentration of interest of scholars on the determinants and impact of foreign owned MNE activity in China, Hong Kong and Taiwan, and that of outward foreign investment from those countries. However, several contributors viewed these and related issues from a broader Asian, European and North American perspective.

Several of the papers embraced topics at the cutting edge of international business research. These included the significance of institutions in influencing the location and strategic behaviour of MNEs; the increasing importance of services in the off-shoring activities of MNEs; the critical role of good corporate governance; the interplay between managerial philosophy and leadership in the public and private sectors; the influence of cultural factors on human resource management; the contribution of foreign direct investment to sustainable development in tourism; the ways in which e-commerce is challenging the internationalization strategies of MNEs, and, in particular, the operational management of small and medium sized MNEs.

In considering the contents of this volume, we decided to focus on three main issues and several sub-issues. In Part One we include four chapters which examine some of the most significant developments in FDI and MNE activity over the last decade or so, and how these have affected the structure of inward and outward FDI into and out of China, and the strategies of the investing firms. The final chapter in this part by Hiroo Takahashi gives especial attention to the growing internationalization of innovating activities by MNEs[1], and to the role of global networks in facilitating both knowledge creation and learning among its participants. Each of the chapters in this section of the book offer new and insightful perspectives on how globalization and contemporary thinking about the purposes and modes of development are affecting the competitive advantages of MNEs and the locational attractions of countries.

Part Two begins with an important contribution by Daniel Sullivan and John Daniels who question the suitability of the mainstream theories and methodologies in explaining international business activity in a changing and uncertain economic environment. This chapter is followed by a reappraisal by Mats Forsgren and Peter Hagström of the influential Uppsala Model which seeks to explain the internationalization of firms in terms of incremental learning and overcoming psychic distance. The authors offer some short contemporary case studies of Internet-related firms and assert that the 'model's central tenet of incremental learning has been scrutinized and found wanting'. Partly, at least, they believe this is because it does not explicitly acknowledge the importance of investing in and upgrading business relationships among suppliers and customers in different cultures.

This chapter brings the volume nicely to a discussion of institutional developments both within and between firms. The concept of value creation and how this may be affected by the design and implementation of 'best practice' institutions by MNEs is explored and evaluated by Reid Click in Chapter 9. The importance of bridging internal and external networks in transitional institutional contexts is underlined by Ray Loveridge in Chapter 10, while in Chapter 11 James Cavazzini and Min Lu point to the critical role played by trust and leadership in the successful management of value added activities. In Chapter 12, Donglin Song and Zheng Li then consider the application of a trust related model to understanding the management structure of Chinese family enterprises, while Chapter 13 examines the strategic and differentiated role of MNE subsidiaries in determining the modalities and procedures involved in the decision making process.

The book then includes a number of studies on two important service sectors, namely education and tourism. The two chapters (14 and 15) on the internationalization of education from Japan are especially rich, and contain much information unfamiliar to the international business scholar of the West. The third study by Ah-Keng Kau on 'Developing Singapore as a global education hub' is particularly interesting as it examines both the strengths and weaknesses of that country in its attempts to attract foreign students to study at its educational institutions. It also evaluates Singapore's opportunities and marketing strategies to tempt more foreign schools and universities to set up in its midst, and to help it upgrade its capabilities as an educational hub of the Asia/Pacific region.

The tourism-related studies offer two perspectives on the subject. The case study of McDonalds written by Mahmood A. Khan and Maryam Khan, illustrating the cultural, economic and political impact of restaurant franchising, is absolutely fascinating. Here is a truly global company, yet to be successful it needs to be sensitive not only to the social and cultural mores of the countries in which it operates, but how its operations impact on indigenous human resources, technology and the local environment. By contrast, in Chapter 18 Wong Kong Yew and Tom Baum take a broader perspective in studying the impact of production spillovers of foreign owned or franchised hotels on the economic development of Malaysia. The authors observe that, while the Malaysian hotel industry is relatively mature, there is still some way to go in its attempt to benefit from productivity spillovers. To counteract these obstacles and ensure sustainable development, the authors recommend a more integrated approach to tourism planning by the Malaysian authorities.

In Chapter 19 Tsai-Mei Lin and Gun-Ming Chuang make a strong and persuasive case for a more responsible and ethically sensitive approach to the cross-cultural management of MNEs. Taking the case of US and Japanese MNEs in Taiwan, and adopting the proposed world peace solution of Dr Ikeda Daisaku, the authors recommend an integrated approach by MNEs among multiple cultures and ethnicities, if they are to improve their global performance. They believe that, as part of this approach, MNEs should adopt the management philosophy of peace culture and in so doing in their words 'make the world of the 21st century to be more friendly and peaceful, more considerate to the standpoints of others and more benevolent'.

The final part of the volume – Part Three – contains a series of case studies of the determinants and effects of Taiwanese inward and outward investment. First, in Chapter 20, Fujiing Shiue and Yi-Yin Yen present a perceptive and insightful case study of how the relationship between the extent and form of internationalization by Taiwanese electronics firms affects their performance. The authors conclude that, on the basis of the MNEs sampled, there were noticeable differences between their size and organizational structures compared to those of their first world counterparts. they speculate these differences might partly reflect the fact that most Taiwanese companies are relatively small or medium sized. This characteristic is taken up more fully in Chapter 21 by Ku-Ho Lin, Isabella, Isabella Chaney Thomas Lawton, and Meng-Chun Liu. In their study of these latter companies, they conclude that domestic inter-firm networks are a way for SMEs to acquire–non financial external resources without incurring of some the risks and uncertainties associated with the internationalization process.

Further consideration of the impact of the Internet on the internationalization of SMEs is given in Chapter 22. Here Yi-Long Jaw and Chung-Liang Chen find that the degree of internationalization is positively related to the degree of electronic commerce utilized by some 700 SMEs. At the same time, the authors believe that existing theories of the determinants of IB activity may need to be modified to take account of the particular strengths and weaknesses of SMEs, particularly those engaged in the non-manufacturing sector.

In Chapter 23 Yung-Kuri Liang examines the location and entry strategies of a group of 74 Taiwanese manufacturing MNEs. While his findings lend general support to previous research studies, they particularly emphasize the importance of the quality of absorptive capacity of subsidiaries in determining the degree to which knowledge transfer can be made effective.

In all, we believe these varied and distinctive contributions not only address themselves to the main theme of the conference, but fit together well in an integrated network of studies, and reflect much of the current interest of contemporary international business research. In particular, the focus on the changing human environment in which MNEs are operating, and the challenges of trying to overcome psychic and institutional distance in a world in which information and knowledge flows increasingly speed across national borders, is a very timely and welcome one. Several chapters in this volume explore some of the implications of these challenges for the managerial strategies of Taiwanese firms; and in particular identify how these strategies differ from those of other third world, or, indeed, of first world, MNEs.

On behalf of the contributors to this volume, we hope its contents will be of interest and value to all those seeking to understand better the changing role of MNEs in the 21st century, and thus to meet the key objectives of the 8th International Conference on Multinational Enterprises organized by the Chinese Culture University.

NOTE

1. See UN (2005) for a detailed examination of this phenomenon.

REFERENCE

UN (2005), 'World Investment Report: transnational corporations and the internationalization of R&D' New York and Geneva: UN.

2. Three important trends in recent global economic development

Jen-Hu Chang

Although the world economy has accelerated rapidly in the last few years, there are at least three important trends that deserve our attention.

The first trend is the failure of globalization to benefit the majority of the poor people of the world. According to the 26 December 2005 issue of *Business Week* magazine, of the largest 500 corporations in the world, the US had 227 (45.2 per cent), the European Union 147 (29.4 per cent) and Japan 56 (11.2 per cent). Together, they accounted for 85.8 per cent of the total. On the other hand, Africa had none and South America only 5 (1.0 per cent). Unbalanced patterns of foreign direct investment and trade are prime sources of political turbulence. In the developing world, most foreign direct investment is concentrated in only 12 countries. In our world of more than 6 billion people, the top 1 billion own 80 per cent of global wealth, while the poorest 1 billion struggle to survive on less than a dollar a day. The number of people earning less than 2 dollars a day has increased in recent years. The greatest benefits of 'globalization' have been garnered by a fortunate few. The gap between rich and poor has also widened within wealthy nations.

Some of the poorest nations in Africa, such as Burkina Faso, Chad, Mali and Benin, depending on cotton for much of their meager exports, have blamed heavy subsidies given by the US government to farmers for depressed world market prices. In September 2003, when the World Trade Organization met in Cancun, Mexico, there was a bitter row between representatives of the US and developing nations and the meeting broke up in acrimony.

In addition, foreign aid from the rich to the poor countries is far below the long-standing target of 0.7 per cent of GDP. The United States, in particular, is at the bottom, contributing only 0.1 per cent of her GDP.

The second trend is the emergence of China as a major economic power. Since 1978 China's annual GDP growth has averaged 9.6 per cent. It is no higher than previous emerging economies in Asia, but that of China is having a more dramatic effect because of her large population. In 2005, China's GDP of $2.26 trillion sent the country soaring to the world's fourth largest economy after the US, Japan and Germany.

For the low-income countries, GDP underestimates their actual wealth. After adjusting for purchasing power parity (PPP), the World Bank found that during the period 1995 to 2000, China accounted for 25 per cent of global growth, outranking the USA.

In 2004, China received $55 billion in foreign direct investment and had a trade surplus of $33 billion. About two-thirds of the export growth over the last ten years has come from subsidiaries of multinational enterprises headquartered in Japan, the US and Europe, and from their joint venture partners.

China's economy has moved up the value chain from simple manufactured goods like textiles, shoes and plastics to very sophisticated electronics. China has already overtaken the US as the world's biggest supplier of information and communication goods, including laptop computers, mobile phones and digital cameras. Recently, China unveiled a new supercomputer that is capable of performing 11 trillion calculations per second, making it among the fastest in the world.

China has about 250 000 engineering and science graduates a year, compared with 60 000 in the US and has an ample supply of less skilled labor force. However, China faces at least three major problems: (1) a fragile financial system, (2) inadequate natural resources including oil, natural gas, iron, copper, aluminum and water (in North China), (3) an increasing income gap between the urban and rural population.

The third trend is the important effect of oil prices on the world economy. Since the 1960s oil has become the major source of energy of the world. The fluctuation of oil prices has affected the prosperity of the world economy. The three major prices jumps in 1973-74, 1978-80 and 1989-90 were all followed by worldwide recession and rising inflation. Oil prices remained relatively low in the 1980s and 1990s when they averaged $30 a barrel. However, oil prices have exceeded $60 a barrel since 2005. The current episode has its origin in an increasing global demand. Oil consumption increased from 70 million barrels per day (bpd) in 1995 to over 82 million bpd in recent years. China has accounted for one-third of the growth in global demand since 2000. Over the next five years the emerging economies could account for three-quarters of the increase in demand.

According to a model developed by the International Monetary Fund (IMF), an increase of $10 a barrel in oil prices should knock three-fifths of a percentage point off the world's output in the following year. The International Energy Agency has estimated that if the $20 per-barrel increase in oil price were sustained, it would reduce economic growth in 2006 by 1.0 per cent in the US, 1.6 per cent in Europe, but 3.2 per cent in India and 5.1 per cent in some developing nations in Africa. One reason for the disparity is that the advanced global economy runs on brain power and microchips rather than on oil. In addition, developed countries use energy more efficiently.

Both the US and China import nearly 40-50 per cent of their oil consumption from more than ten countries throughout the world. The scramble for oil has generated frictions. Geopolitics and geoeconomics are intertwined. The effect of oil prices on the world economy will be even more acute in the near future when oil production is expected to reach a peak and then to decline gradually.

PART ONE

FDI and MNEs: Some Recent Developments

3. FDI, globalization and development[1]

John H. Dunning

1. INTRODUCTION

The main task of this chapter is to summarize the current state of thinking on the extent to which, and the ways in which, the increasing globalization of economic activity, and new ideas about the purposes and content of economic development, is affecting our understanding about the causes and effects of foreign direct investment by multinational enterprises (MNEs). Inevitably, I shall have to be selective in the issues I cover, and I shall also express a very personal view.

That being said, my primary focus will be on identifying general trends and their policy implications, rather than on those particularly relevant to any particular country. In doing so, I will highlight the main thrust and conclusions of scholarly research on three issues. First, I shall identify what, to my mind, are some of the critical characteristics of our contemporary world economy. Second I shall describe the interface between, and offer some contemporary facts about, globalization, development and FDI. Third, and perhaps most importantly, I shall offer some suggestions of what, to my mind, are the critical components of FDI policy which all governments – be they from developing or developed, or large or small countries, and be they concerned with inward or outward FDI – need to focus on in these early years of the twenty-first century.

Obviously, some of what I write will be especially apposite to the contemporary situation in countries such as Taiwan; but some more so to other developing countries who are now emerging as important players on the world economic stage.

2. THE EVOLVING WORLD SCENARIO

We live in a world characterized by the geographical spread of market based economic democracy, tempered, to some degree or other, by the intervention of national and supranational regimes to protect or enhance extra-market political or social objectives.

We live in a world in which there is increasing cross-border interconnectivity between human beings and organizations. While such interconnectivity offers huge potential for economic progress and social intercourse among the peoples of the world, it is frequently uneven in its content and outcome, and leads to more rather than less constrained human relationships.

We live in a world of economic and political turbulence, where change, volatility and complexity are among its endemic features.

We live in a world in which continuous advances in techno-knowledge and falling communication costs are dramatically reconfiguring our economic landscape; and the fabric of our daily lives.

We live in a world replete with paradoxes and tensions. Globalization brings with it its own 'yang' and 'yin': where convergence and divergence, uniformity and diversity, competition and cooperation, centralization and decentralization, and individualism and communitarianism go hand in hand.

We live in a world in which the goals and content of human development are being reappraised. Compared with the past, more attention is now being paid to the social, cultural and ideological well-being of individuals and communities; to issues of security and the environment; and to the moral dimension of development.

We live in a world in which the global competitive position of corporations and countries is increasingly dependent on their success in forming, and learning from, cross border partnerships, strategic alliances, and of being part of a network of related activities.

We live in a world in which the content and quality of incentive structures and belief systems of countries are increasingly influencing societal attitudes and policies towards development strategies, and to the social responsibilities of both firms and governments.

In short, we live in a world in which the human and physical global environment underpinning the wealth-creating activities of corporations, and the policies of national governments, is rapidly and fundamentally changing. And it is the corporations and governments that are best able to respond to and benefit from these changes, and that are best equipped to minimize or counteract the disruptive effects of them, that are the most likely to succeed in today's hugely competitive global village.

3. THE INTERFACE BETWEEN GLOBALIZATION, DEVELOPMENT AND FDI

What then is the relevance of these characteristics for globalization and for economic development? What role does FDI play in both fashioning and reacting to these characteristics?

The circles in Figure 3.1 demonstrate how these three concepts interface with each other. I shall concentrate my remarks on the shaded area. The rectangles surrounding the circles identify the main decision-taking entities in contemporary economies. As I have already said, the majority of economic transactions in most countries are undertaken through markets, but the extent to which, and the ways in which, these markets are supported, influenced or controlled by the actions of extra market actors varies considerably. Compare, for example, the governance and institutional structure of the US and China, or those of Brazil and Korea, in this respect.

In this chapter, I will focus primarily on the role of two of the key actors-firms (and particularly MNEs) and national governments.

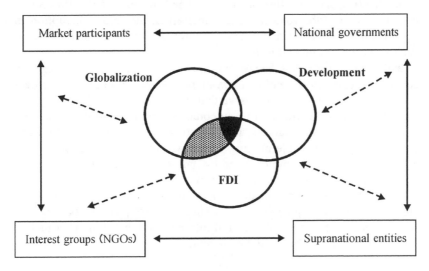

Figure 3.1   The globalization/development/FDI triad

3.1   Globalization

Let me now consider some of the main attributes and extent of twenty-first century globalization. Essentially this phenomenon is best thought of as the interconnectivity of people and organizations across the planet

(Figure 3.1). Such connectivity may be shallow or deep, short or long-lasting. It may be geared towards advancing personal or organizational interests, and to promoting economic, cultural or political goals. Its main outcome is an increasing and deepening interdependence between otherwise geographically segmented human and physical environments.

E-commerce and the Internet are the quintessential indices of globalization. But there are many others, such as the extent and geography of cross-border travel, the media (especially TV coverage), technology and financial flows, and people movement. At the same time, it is worth noting that few organizations, public or private, are fully global in their activities. Most large MNEs, for example, still confine the greater part of their value added activities to two of the five continents of the globe (Rugman and Verbeke, 2004).

Globalization, in and of itself, is a neutral concept. But it can be used to advance good or bad goals or to achieve good or bad effects. The 'yang' of globalization is that it can raise incomes, transfer ideas and knowledge, open up new markets, and promote more dialogue and understanding among different cultures. The 'yin' of globalization is that it can lead to more volatility and uncertainty, and more disruption in people's lives. It can also facilitate the international movement of 'bads' such as drugs, crime and terrorism.

In the maximization of the positive and the minimization of the negative consequences of globalization, extra-market organizations have a critical role to play. For example, I believe that the fact that globalization is not as inclusive or as equitable in its outcome as it might be is often due less to the inadequacies of markets, and more to differences in the institutions and cultural mores underpinning these markets, and of inappropriate policies designed and implemented by national governments.

One final point about globalization worthy of mention is the growing role of multi-stakeholders (notably NGOs, consumer activists, shareholders, labour unions), in influencing its content and consequences – particularly so in respect of the international and intranational distribution of its key resources and capabilities, and of its end products.

3.2 Economic Development

What next of the contemporary scholarly thinking among scholars about the purposes and content of economic development? Key among the new or revised ideas are those about the composition and determinants of development. No longer are crude and single measures of development such as GDP per head acceptable. Increasingly, those which emphasize quality of life measures, such as safety and security, good health, reduced infant mortality and education, are being factored in to any measurement of human well-being.

This reflects the increasing attention being paid by national governments both to the social needs and the cultural uniqueness of the individuals and communities for which they are responsible. In an age of global branding of many products, it also suggests the need for more local ownership of critical values, ideas and institutions; of more multi-stakeholder involvement in policy formation; and of more consensus-related decision taking.

All contemporary data point to the substantial progress which is being made in upgrading living standards and reducing levels of extreme poverty in most developing countries. According to the World Bank the share of the population of developing countries in abject poverty (defined as those living on less than a dollar a day) fell from one third in the mid-1980s to one quarter in the early 2000s. There have also been noticeable improvements in the quality of life, for example health provision, life expectancy, adult literacy and human rights, and in gender-related development.

At the same time, there are other areas of the life style of people which are giving more cause for concern. Along with (though not necessarily the result of) rising living standards and increasing behavioural freedom, has come more terrorism, crime, corruption, drug trafficking and social disorder, with all the disbenefits and uncertainties associated with those.

Development then, first and foremost, needs to be viewed as a holistic and multi-dimensional concept (Dunning, 2006a). To be successful, its contents and implementation need an input from a wide range of stakeholders. Its determinants are multi-causal; its effects are multi-faceted. To understand its determinants and effects, it needs a variety of disciplinary methodologies.

At the same time, although it is possible to identify many common elements in the design and implication of development strategies, especially among transition economies, each country has its own particular economic and social agenda and is a creature of its own special cultural heritage. Each country too has its distinctive institutions, economic priorities, forms of governance and cultural values. And it is from such varied perspectives as these that MNEs have to evaluate and choose between the investment opportunities offered by different locations.

3.3 FDI

What now of FDI as an instrument for upgrading national competitiveness and promoting structural change?

The recent growth in FDI stocks has closely paralleled that of globalization. According to UNCTAD (2005), between 1990 and 2004 the combined world inbound and outbound FDI stocks increased 4.4 times (from $3554 billion to $18 628 billion). Over the same period, outbound FDI stocks from Asian and Latin American developing countries rose by 7.0 times and inbound FDI stocks by 6.5 times.[2] FDI today is not only the most important component of trans-border economic activity, it is also one of the most critical shapers of the international division of labour, of economic restructuring and of life styles.

It is now estimated that MNEs currently account for three-quarters of all global innovating activity and spending on human resource development. Increasingly, they are decentralizing such higher value activities to their foreign affiliates (and particularly so within higher and middle income countries) (UNCTAD, 2005). In most instances, this is to be welcomed since the speed at which countries can move up their development ladders is increasingly resting on the quality of the human and physical assets, and the enterprise and vision of their firms and people.

However, as research over the last three years has indicated, the benefits which a particular country derives from the operations of the affiliates of foreign MNEs in its midst, and from the activities of its own firms outside their national boundaries, is highly contingent on the quality and content of its social capital, its institutions, and the values, belief systems and cultural preferences of its people.

4. FDI POLICY

Let me now turn to consider more specifically what I believe to be the most critical ingredients of FDI policy, in the light of the contemporary perceptions about economic development and globalization.

In doing so I shall offer 11 propositions. These are based upon my reading of the latest scholarly research on the subject, of the main sources of data such as those contained in UNCTAD's annual *World Investment Reports*, and of a variety of surveys about how they view the changing nature of determinants and effects of FDI into and out of developing economies.

I set out these propositions – each of which, I believe, should be considered as part of a coordinated and interactive system of FDI policies – as bullet points and in no particular order of importance. In any case, such ordering is likely to be highly contextual, and will vary according to the types of and motives for FDI and the particular situation of individual home and host countries.

1. In seeking to maximize the benefits of globalization and to promote the desired development, FDI policies are only as effective as the general macroeconomic and micro-management policies of which they are part. I shall term this the *holistic* proposition.
2. Inbound FDI policy must take account of the likely costs and benefits of different kinds and forms of MNE activity, as well as the effectiveness of any measures designed to attract new investments. In the early twenty-first century, most attention to the impact of inbound FDI is focusing on its 'spillover' effects and especially on the competitiveness of indigenous firms, and the promotion of the dynamic comparative advantage of the host country. This is the *effects* proposition.
3. FDI policy must be dynamic, flexible and appropriate to the particular characteristics of development of a country. It should be geared to ensuring that both inward and outward FDI help to upgrade the structural transformation of the country, in an efficient, socially acceptable and properly sequential way. This is the *structural transformation* proposition.
4. FDI policy needs to be aware of the changing locational needs of foreign investors, and in particular, the growing importance of the scope and content of host country incentive structures and regulatory mechanisms in fostering indigenous entrepreneurship, and assisting individuals and firms to cope with global change and its implications. This is the *institutions* proposition.
5. As knowledge embodied in human and physical assets becomes a more important ingredient of a country's economic welfare and growth prospects, so FDI policy must especially address itself to the best means of accessing, creating and enhancing physical and human resource capabilities. This is the *capability upgrading* proposition.
6. By the provision of appropriate incentives, inbound FDI policy should recognize the growing needs of foreign direct investors to form alliances with, and/or tap into, the assets of networks of indigenous firms. This is the *partnership* proposition.
7. FDI policy should take account of the increasing role of multi-stakeholder initiatives, such as those of consumer groups, labour unions, and civil society, which are affecting the goals, pattern and ownership of economic activity. This is the *stakeholder* proposition.
8. Inward FDI policy must accept that the global market economy often widens the locational options of many MNEs. This being so, it is all the more important for host governments to identify and promote the unique and sustainable comparative economic advantages of the resources and capabilities within their jurisdiction, as well as taking into account the FDI (and other) policies of competitor countries.

This is the *leveraging* proposition.

9. As countries move upwards along their development paths, the need for an integrated policy towards both outward and inward FDI becomes more imperative. Each has its own unique (but related) role to play in advancing structural change and upgrading domestic competitiveness. This is the *integration* proposition.

10. FDI policy should take note of the trend towards the decentralization of decisions taken within MNEs. It should show a better understanding of the role foreign affiliates may play in tapping into and learning about localized economic capabilities, and social and cultural preferences. This is the *localization* proposition.

11. While FDI policy – and particularly investment – should be as transparent, general and consistent as possible, there may be merit in tailoring the contents of particular aspects of this policy in order to target certain types of FDI or MNEs. This is the *targeting* proposition.

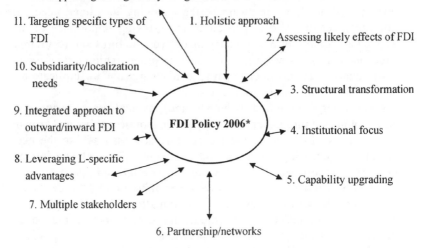

Notes: Such a policy will vary according to (a) type of FDI and strategy of individual MNEs, (b) country/region-specific characteristics affecting attitudes towards globalization and economic development.

Figure 3.2   Proposed ingredients of FDI policy

Figure 3.2 combines these various drivers and determinants of FDI policy into one diagram. As we have already suggested, the prioritization and importance of each is likely to vary according to the type of FDI and the strategies of individual MNEs. The costs of their implementation, and the specific characteristics of particular countries or regions may also affect the attitudes and actions of governments towards globalization and economic development.

5. CONCLUSIONS

What then may we conclude from this chapter? First that countries – both developed and developing – should consider globalization as an opportunity and challenge both to better promote the kind of economic and social development they desire, and to enhance their ownership of that development.

Second, that as development proceeds, inbound and then increasingly outbound FDI can·play an important positive role in exploiting these opportunities and challenges, provided that the appropriate societal institutions and the policies of national governments are in place and working well. Third, that in framing and implementing FDI policies, there are several issues specific to the needs of the global economy – and to particular countries and firms – in the twenty-first century which, I believe, should be accorded high priority.

Let me finally offer you three statements which, though seemingly obvious, I believe should guide any actions taken by national governments and international investing agencies seeking to gain the most from FDI.

1. *While both outward and inward FDI can help a country to benefit from globalization and foster economic development, it should not be regarded as a panacea for its economic ills.* With a few exceptions, a country's long-term economic success and social welfare must rest on its willingness and ability to upgrade its indigenous resources and capabilities. In pursuance of this objective, I believe that it is essential that a country should retain full ownership of its entrepreneurial vision, its critical institutions, its cultural identity and its belief systems.
2. *History and geography matter.* Policy makers should seek to learn from the successes and failures of the past, and from the experiences of other countries most similar to those of their own. However, they should not be bound by, or be slaves to, these successes, failures and experiences. In the light of the perceived contribution of FDI to economic development, and of the axiological changes now occurring in the global human environment, national administrations should (a) devise the macroeconomic and microeconomic strategies most suited to their own particular situation and needs; and (b) ensure that they have the appropriate institutional mechanisms to implement these strategies.

3. *Policy makers should be cautious about making easy generalizations about the economic and social consequences of FDI.* Its effects will vary not only according to the motive for, and kind of, inward and outward FDI undertaken, but also according to the values, attitudes and actions of the societal stakeholders most affected by it, and to the strategies and policies pursued by the decision makers most concerned.

One very last thought. In a speech given in London in 2005, the UK Chancellor of the Exchequer, Gordon Brown, set out his vision for the UK to become one of the most successful enterprise countries in the world. This vision was couched in the form of a challenge to Britain's corporations and workforce to (I quote) 'reform, liberalize, meet and master the high-tech value added competition'. To do so, he argued, the UK needed to become the world leader in education, science and creativity and to offer both foreign owned and domestic firms the most attractive location in which to do business and to create new businesses. The result of a more enterprising Britain, he suggested, would not only be the creation of new wealth but, equally important, the best way of opening up a life-enhancing opportunity for all, and particularly for those most economically deprived.

If this vision is to be embraced by the UK, how much more so is it of relevance for Taiwan – one of the worlds newest and most vibrant nations. I wish you well in this daunting, but most fulfilling and rewarding task.

NOTES

1. An earlier version of this talk was given at a conference, organized by Invest in Sweden Agency, in Stockholm in August 2005, and sequentially published in Passow and Runnbeck (2005). Part of this chapter is also incorporated in Dunning (2006b).
2. The equivalent multiples for developed economies were 5.3 and 4.6.

REFERENCES

Dunning, J. H. (1994), 'Re-evaluating the benefits of foreign direct investment', *Transnational Corporations*, **3**(1), 23-52.
Dunning, J. H. (2003a), *Making Globalization Good: The Moral Challenges of Global Capitalism*, Oxford: Oxford University Press.
Dunning, J. H. (2003b), 'The role of foreign direct investment in upgrading China's competitiveness', *Journal of International Business and Economy*, **4**(1), 1-13.
Dunning, J. H. (2004), 'Determinants of foreign direct investment: globalization

induced changes and the role of policies' in Tungodden, B., Stern, N. and Kolstad, I. (eds), *Towards Pro-Poor Policies and Institutions and Globalization, Annual World Conference and Development Economics (Oslo, 2003)*, Washington, and Oxford: The World Bank and Oxford University Press, 279-290.

Dunning, J. H. (2006a), 'Towards a new paradigm of development: implications for the determinants of international business activity', *Transnational Corporations*, **14**(1), 173-227.

Dunning, J. H. (2006b), 'Globalisation and development: Some implications for Korean economy and Korean firms', *Journal of International Business and Economy*, **7**(1), 1-19.

Dunning, J. H., C.-S. Kim and J.-D. Lin (2001), 'Incorporating trade into the investment development path', *Oxford Development Studies*, **29**(2), 146-152.

Dunning, J. H. and Narula, R. (2004), *Multinationals and Industrial Competitiveness*, Cheltenham, UK and Northampton, MA, USA: Edward Elgar.

Economist Intelligence Unit (2004), *World Investment Prospects, The Revival of Globalisation*, London: E.I.U.

North, D. C. (2005), *Understanding the Process of Economic Change*, Princeton, NJ: Princeton University Press.

Nunnenkamp, P. (2002a), 'Determinants of FDI in developing countries: has globalisation changed the rules of the game?' Kiel: Kiel Institute for World Economics, Working Paper No. 1122.

Nunnenkamp, P. (2002b), 'To what extent can foreign direct investment help achieve international development goals?' Kiel: Kiel Institute for World Economics, Working Paper No. 1128.

Passow, S. and M. Runnbeck (eds) (2005), *What's Next? Strategic Views on Foreign Direct Investment*, Stockholm: Invest in sweden Agency.

Rodrick, D. (1998), *Globalization, Social Conflict and Economic Growth, Geneva*, 8th Prebisch Lecture, UN.

Rondinelli, D. A. and Behrman, J. N. (2000), 'The institutional imperatives of globalisation', *Global Focus*, **12**(1) 65-78.

Rugman, A. M. and Verbeke A. (2004), 'A perspective on regional and global strategies of multinational enterprises', *Journal of International Business Studies*, **35**(1), 3-19.

Sen, A. (1999), *Development as Freedom*, Oxford: Oxford University Press.

Stiglitz, J. (2003), 'Towards a new paradigm of development', in Dunning, J.H. (ed.), *Making Globalization Good. The Moral Challenges of Global Capitalism*, Oxford: Oxford University Press, 76-107.

UNCTAD (1998), *World Investment Report: Trends and Determinants*, New York and Geneva: UN.

UNCTAD (1999), *Foreign Direct Investment and Development*, Geneva: UNCTAD, Series on Issues in International Investment Agreements.

UNCTAD (2005), *World Investment Report: Transnational Corporations and the Internationalization of R&D*, New York, and Geneva: UN.

UNDP (2004), *Human Development Report 2004; Cultural Liberty in Today's Diverse World*, New York: UNDP.

World Bank (2004), *World Development Report 2005*, Washington and Oxford: The World Bank and Oxford University Press.

Yuan, Z. (2005), 'Features and Impacts of Internationalisation of Transnational Corporations' R&D: China's Case', Paper presented at Expert Meeting on FDI and Development, Geneva, January 2005.

4. Foreign direct investment and investor strategies in China

Phillip D. Grub and Jiawen Yang

1. INTRODUCTION

To keep pace in this changing and increasingly competitive world economy, the challenge facing multinational corporate executives lies in developing an organizational climate within their firms whereby technological innovation thrives. This climate must also allow for creativity and resourcefulness leading toward optimization of resources of all types. In addition, organizational structures must be tightened and adjusted in order to be more responsive to cost factors as well as market sensitivities and needs. Finallly, emphasis must be placed on providing leadership that is truly global in its view, yet adapting to meet local conditions and needs. Foreign direct investment must be a significant part of any MNE's strategy.

During the past decade, China has become the largest foreign direct investment (FDI) recipient among developing countries. This is not surprising because, with global trade of $1.42 trillion, China is the world's third largest trading nation, surpassed only by the United States and Japan. According to a March 2006 report by Standard Charter Bank's Shanghai branch, China's per capita economic output – or GDP – jumped from $1,277 in 2004 to $1,738 in 2005. China's economy has also shown tremendous growth, growing at an average rate of 9 per cent a year since the late 1970s. This is a rate of sustained growth that has never before been seen in a major world's economy, making the China market even more attractive for investors.

By the end of 2004, the accumulated FDI in China amounted to $562.10 billion. FDI has been a major contributing factor to the high growth rate of the Chinese economy and China's exports. Foreign invested enterprises in China accounted for more than 57 per cent of China's imports, exports and total trade in 2004. Multinational enterprises (MNEs) have been the driving force of FDI in China. The purpose of this chapter is to take stock of FDI in China, analyze the FDI strategies of MNEs, and look into the future prospects of both FDI and MNEs in China and their impact on the world business environment.

The development of FDI and MNE strategies are analyzed in a number of important aspects.[1] First, by examining the industry distribution of FDI, an analysis has been made of how MNEs have formulated their strategies for their mode of entry into China. MNEs have thus far concentrated investments in the manufacturing sector, particularly in consumer products. Second, the geographical distribution of FDI in China is highlighted. FDI in China has been uneven in terms of geographical locations with areas along the east coast of China receiving unproportionally large FDI inflows over the past decades. Third, an analysis of the country/regional origins of FDI and MNEs in China reveals unique patterns of FDI and MNEs strategies in China. Hong Kong, Taiwan and Macao are by far the largest source of direct investment in mainland China. While the amount of investment from these areas is collectively large (more than 50 per cent of total FDI in China by end of 2003), the individual investment project sizes are relatively small. In contrast to FDI by MNEs from industrial countries, investments from these regions have been dominated by small and medium-sized enterprises (SMEs). This unique phenomenon challenges the traditional eclectic models of FDI and alternative modeling and explanations for FDI by SMEs are provided. Fourth, the roles of FDI and MNEs in the Chinese economy are analyzed. In some product areas, such as camera films, cell phones and carbonated beverages, it is shown that MNEs have obtained dominating market shares in China. Fifth, the linkages between the Chinese economy and world markets are highlighted, illustrating the roles played by MNEs in China's international trade and overall external economic relations.

Since China joined the World Trade Organization (WTO) in 2001, significant changes have occurred both in China's business environment and MNE strategies in China. First, MNEs through FDI are or will be allowed to enter selected industries including civil aviation, retail banking and other financial services. Thus, the industry distribution of FDI in China will be altered and so will MNE entry strategies. Second, as China promotes development of the inland areas that have received little or no FDI, MNEs will soon be, if they are not already, moving into these areas. The result will be to create a more even distribution of FDI in China geographically. Third, given that China has a comparative advantage in labor-intensive industries, China will continue to become an even greater leading manufacturing base for consumer products. Hence, it is believed that exports from China will account for over 50 per cent of the world's total exports by 2010 if the current trend continues.

To meet this challenge, MNEs need to formulate a series of different actions and strategic responses to such developments or their position in world markets will diminish because China will become an even more formidable competitor in the future. This is even more significant as it is estimated that China will need approximately 25 million new jobs a year just to keep up with population growth. And, as the domestic China market continues to grow, serving local market demand must be a part of MNE strategies, especially those firms producing quality consumer products.

2. FDI IN CHINA

The rich literature of contemporary theories offers many explanations as to why foreign direct investment takes place. The monopolistic advantage theory initiated by Stephen Hymer in the 1960s predicts that foreign direct investment occurs largely in oligopolistic industries in which the investing firm enjoys advantages in technology, marketing or financing capability that are not available to local firms. Caves (1971) expanded Hymer's theory to show that superior knowledge permitted the investing firm to produce differentiated products that the consumers would prefer to similar locally made goods and thus would give the firm some control over the selling price and an advantage over indigenous firms (Ball et al., 2006, p. 110). The International product life cycle theory posits that as products become mature and standardized, producers in advanced economies move production to other countries where production costs are lower. Other theories explain MNE behaviors such as following the leader, following the customer, seeking knowledge, seeking resources, and strategic alliances.

While all these theories help explain the phenomenal trend of FDI in China, there have been two significant factors that have contributed to the thriving of MNEs in China. They are preferential government policies toward foreign investment and a cost-efficient labor force. China's preferential policies toward foreign investment include tax holidays and favorable resource allocation for foreign investors. Foreign investors are exempt for income tax for the first two years starting from the year when they make profits. Then they pay only half of the income tax in the next three years. Foreign firms operating in China pay about 15 per cent income tax on average, while indigenous Chinese firms pay around 33 per cent. Foreign companies also enjoy preferential treatment in land allocation, local financing and administrative procedures for investment projects.

China has a very cost-efficient labor market that is very attractive for foreign investors. Labor cost should be measured not only in wages and salaries; it should also be based on marginal cost of production. Not only are wages and salaries low in China, Chinese workers are also hard working, reasonably skilled and easily trained. These three factors, together with internal political stability and an external peaceful environment, have made China one of the most attractive places in the world for MNEs and for foreign investment.

2.1   Industry Distribution of FDI in China

Foreign investment in China has thus far been concentrated heavily in the manufacturing sector. At the end of 2003, the accumulated value of contracted foreign investment in the manufacturing sector accounted for 63.66 per cent of the total accumulated value of contracted foreign investment. Table 4.1 shows the industry distribution of foreign investment in China from 1999 to 2003. The share of actually utilized foreign investment capital in the manufacturing sector increased from 56.06 per cent in 1999 to 69.03 per cent in 2003.

Within the manufacturing sector, consumer goods such as consumer electronics and processed food have been a major focus of foreign investment. In 2003, automobile-focused transportation equipment manufacturing and chemical raw materials and products manufacturing picked up speed noticeably (China Ministry of Commerce, 2004). Other sectors that received relatively large shares of foreign investment include real estate management (9.79 per cent in 2003), social services (5.91 per cent in 2003), electric power, gas, and water production and supply (2.42 per cent in 2003). In addition, foreign investment flows have gone into wholesale operations, retail trade and catering services (2.09 per cent in 2003).

These statistics, provided by the Chinese government, are highly consistent with the results of an annual survey conducted by the Fortune magazine (China edition). According to its 2005 survey (Fortune China 2005), 53.4 per cent of multinationals' operations in China are in manufacturing industries, 24.5 per cent in services, 12.8 per cent in diversified businesses, and 9.3 per cent in other sectors.

In a study of the regional distribution of FDI in China, Wei et al. (1999) found that there was a long-run relationship between the spatial distribution of FDI and a number of regional characteristics. It should be noted that provinces with higher levels of international trade, lower wage rates, more R&D manpower, higher GDP growth rates, and quicker improvements in infrastructure attract more pledged FDI. Other factors include rapid advances in agglomeration, more preferential policies and closer ethnic links with overseas Chinese.

Table 4.1 Foreign direct investment actually utilized by sector in China (1999-2003)

(US$ million)

Sector	1999		2000		2001		2002		2003	
	Value	%	Value	%	Value	%	Value	%	Value	%
National Total	40,319	100.00	40,715	100.00	46,878	100.00	52,743	100.00	53,505	100.00
Farming, Forestry, Animal Husbandry and Fishery	710	1.76	676	1.66	899	1.92	1,028	1.95	1,001	1.87
Mining and Quarrying	557	1.38	583	1.43	811	1.73	581	1.10	336	0.63
Manufacturing	22,603	56.06	25,844	63.48	30,907	65.93	36,800	69.77	36,936	69.03
Electric Power, Gas and Water Production and Supply	3,703	9.18	2,242	5.51	2,273	4.85	1,375	2.61	1,295	2.42
Construction	917	2.27	905	2.22	807	1.72	709	1.34	612	1.14
Geological Prospecting and Water Conservancy	5	0.01	5	0.01	10	0.02	7	0.01	18	0.03
Transport, Storage, Post and Telecommunication Services	1,551	3.85	1,012	2.49	909	1.94	913	1.73	867	1.62
Wholesale & Retail Trade and Catering Services	965	2.39	858	2.11	1,169	2.49	933	1.77	1,116	2.09
Banking and Insurance	98	0.24	76	0.19	35	0.08	107	0.20	232	0.43
Real Estate Management	5,588	13.86	4,658	11.44	5,137	10.96	5,663	10.74	5,236	9.79
Social Services	2,551	6.33	2,185	5.37	2,595	5.54	2,943	5.58	3,161	5.91
Health Care, Sports and Social Welfare	148	0.37	106	0.26	119	0.25	128	0.24	127	0.24
Education, Culture and Arts, Radio, Film and Television	61	0.15	54	0.13	36	0.08	38	0.07	58	0.11
Scientific Research and Polytechnic Services	110	0.27	57	0.14	120	0.26	198	0.37	259	0.48
Other Sectors	753	1.87	1,453	3.57	1,051	2.24	1,321	2.50	2,251	4.21

Source: China statistics Yearbook 2002 and 2004, National Bureau of Statistics of China
www.stats.gov.cn/english/statisticaldata/yearlydata/yb2004-e/indexeh.htm (last accessed 21 July, 2005)

Some researchers have shown concerns about the industrial distribution of FDI in China. Zhang (1999) observed that sectoral distribution of FDI has appeared to be of undesirable or irrational composition, with excessive concentration in simple processing and labor-intensive industries, real estate, hotels and services. Instead, he points out that there has been little FDI in the primary sectors, particularly technology- and capital-intensive manufacturing industries. This situation, however, is changing rapidly as the China market continues to expand.

2.2 Geographical Distribution of FDI in China

Most observers agree that the geographic distribution of foreign direct investment in China has been uneven. As shown in Table 4.2, shares of foreign investment in East China (mainly the coastal areas) were 88.02 per cent, 87.36 per cent, and 85.88 per cent for the number of new investment projects, contractual value, and actual utilization of investment capital respectively in 2003. The other two regional areas, the central and western regions, received less than 15 per cent in any measure.

Table 4.2   Regional distribution of FDI in China, 2003

	No. of Projects		Contractual Value		Actual Utilization of Foreign Investment	
	Numbers	Share %	Value	Share %	Value	Share %
Total	41,081		115,070		53,505	
East Regions	36,159	88.02	100,530	87.36	45,951	85.88
Central Regions	3,177	7.73	9,552	8.30	5,831	10.90
West Regions	1,745	4.25	4,988	4.33	1,723	3.22

Source: National Bureau of Statistics of China,
www.fdi.gov.cn/common/info.jsp? id=ABC00000000000016054 (last accessed 23 July, 2005)

A more detailed geographical distribution of FDI in China is provided in Table 4.3. It is clear that the coastal provinces and municipalities Jiangsu, Guangdong, Shandong, Shanghai, Zhejiang, Liaoning and Fujian ranked the top receivers of FDI in 2003, as they have always been since China began to receive foreign investment in the 1980s. Despite China's efforts to promote economic development in the inland areas during the past few years, foreign investment in these areas (central and western China) is still lagging behind the coastal areas, especially in the Special Economic Zones and Shanghai.

This situation appears to be changing as the costs of doing business in Beijing, Shanghai continue to mount. Smaller cities along the Yangtze river, as well as other smaller cities that have been overlooked as investment

Table 4.3   Geographical distribution of FDI in China, 2003

Locality	No. of Projects		Contractual Foreign Investment Value		Actual Foreign Investment Value	
	Number	Share %	Value (US$, Mil)	Share %	Value (US$, Mil)	Share %
Total	41,081	100.00	115,069.69	100.00	53,504.67	100.00
Jiangsu	7,182	17.48	29,781.30	25.88	10,563.65	19.74
Guangdong	7,039	17.13	13,485.18	11.72	7,822.94	14.62
Shenzhen	2,267	5.52	3,205.40	2.79	2,129.51	3.98
Shandong	5,208	12.68	12,430.13	10.80	6,016.17	11.24
Qingdao	2,179	5.30	4,439.82	3.86	2,626.41	4.91
Shanghai	4,462	10.86	10,751.15	9.34	5,468.49	10.22
Zhejiang	4,460	10.86	12,283.86	10.68	4,980.55	9.31
Ningbo	1,180	2.87	3,606.29	3.13	1,364.23	2.55
Liaoning	2,231	5.43	6,472.32	5.62	2,824.10	5.28
Dalian	871	2.12	2,277.53	1.98	815.71	1.52
Fujian	2,272	5.53	4,281.05	3.72	2,599.03	4.86
Xiamen	368	0.90	638.71	0.56	421.87	0.79
Beijing	1,539	3.75	5,999.59	5.21	2,191.26	4.10
Jiangxi	761	1.85	2,318.25	2.01	1,612.02	3.01
Hubei	510	1.24	2,329.66	2.02	1,568.86	2.93
Tianjin	957	2.33	3,053.38	2.65	1,534.73	2.87
Hunan	509	1.24	1,338.84	1.16	1,018.35	1.90
Hebei	610	1.48	1,672.53	1.45	964.05	1.80
Henan	304	0.74	1,055.50	0.92	539.03	1.01
Hainan	166	0.40	232.67	0.20	421.25	0.79
Guangxi	334	0.81	643.13	0.56	418.56	0.78
Sichuan	326	0.79	893.80	0.78	412.31	0.77
Anhui	425	1.03	967.62	0.84	367.20	0.69
Shanxi	242	0.59	760.02	0.66	331.90	0.62
Heilongjiang	239	0.58	487.85	0.42	321.80	0.60
Chongqing	205	0.50	423.57	0.37	260.83	0.49
Shaanxi	89	0.22	395.96	0.34	213.61	0.40
Jilin	340	0.83	658.40	0.57	190.59	0.36
Inner Mongolia	138	0.34	390.74	0.34	88.54	0.17
Yunnan	165	0.40	445.83	0.39	83.84	0.16
Guizhou	66	0.16	199.16	0.17	45.21	0.08
Qinghai	47	0.11	191.42	0.17	25.22	0.05
Gansu	59	0.14	252.21	0.22	23.42	0.04
Ningxia	28	0.07	537.59	0.47	17.43	0.03
Xinjiang	86	0.21	202.82	0.18	15.34	0.03
Tibet	49	0.12	47.76	0.04		

Source: National Bureau of Statistics of China,
www.fdi.gov.cn/common/info.jsp? id=ABC00000000000016051 (Last accessed 23 July, 2005)

sites, are making a pitch for firms to locate within their jurisdictions and not in the already highly developed areas. In March, 2006, a delegation of 75 business leaders and city officials made visit to Silicon Valley for this purpose.

One of the municipalities represented in this delegation was from Changzhou, a port city about 100 miles up the Yangtze river from Shanghai that is relatively unknown to foreigners. An industrial city of some 3.5 million people, it is best known for its production of textiles as well as a manufacturer of agricultural machinery and construction equipment. However, like other secondary neighboring cities such as Nantong and Wuxi, efforts are being placed on attracting high tech firms from the United States to assist in developing their information technology and biochemical industries. It remains to be seen if their efforts will come to fruition.

While foreign investment has helped economic growth and development in the coastal areas, it has also contributed to the regional disparity in China. According to Zhang (1999), China's location-based policies, such as preferential policies toward special economic zones, have resulted in a growing imbalance of regional investment distribution, and have contributed to regional inequality in income distribution. Zhou et al. (2005) examined 2,933 cases of Japanese investment in 27 provinces and regions in China. They found that special economic zones and opening coastal cities had a strong influence on Japanese foreign investment during the early years of China's economic reform, but that this effect diminished over time as other parts of China adopted similar preferential policies.

In their studies of locational choices of FDI, Fung et al. (2002, 2005) found that soft infrastructures, in the form of more transparent institutions and deeper reform, consistently outperform hard infrastructure in the form of more highways and railroads as a determinant of FDI across regions in China.

2.3   Sources of FDI in China

While China has been cited as the largest foreign investment recipient among developing countries, much of the recorded foreign investment is not really 'foreign' since the lion's share of these capital flows has been from Hong Kong, Taiwan and Macao. It should be noted that some of the investing firms from these three locations are firms that are headquartered elsewhere in the world but have set up a base of operations there, thus disguising the real country source of the investment. As illustrated in Table 4.4, Hong Kong investment in mainland China represented about one third of total FDI flows to China. Investment from Taiwan accounted for another 6.31 per cent in actually utilized capital in the mainland in that year. Table 4.5 provides the sources of China's accumulated FDI to the end of 2003. Investments from Hong Kong, Taiwan and Macao account for more than half of the total actually utilized FDI values.

Companies based in other Asian economies, such as Japan, South Korea and Singapore, have also been major investors in China. In 2003, investments from Japan, South Korea and Singapore accounted for 9.45 per cent, 8.39 per cent, and 3.85 per cent of China's total utilized foreign investment capital respectively. Investments from the ten Asian economies constituted 63.34 per cent of China's utilized FDI in 2003. In terms of accumulated utilization of FDI (Table 4.5), the top five Asian investors– Hong Kong, Japan, Taiwan, Singapore and South Korea – accounted for 68.6 per cent of the total.

Apart from Asia, the United States has been the largest investor in China. It invested about \$4.2 billion (actually utilized as shown in Table 4.4) in China, accounting for 7.85 per cent of China's utilized capital. The European Union together invested about \$3.9 billion (actually utilized), accounting for 7.35 per cent of China's total.

According to Schroath et al. (1993), the geo-cultural factor was particularly evident from their study of FDI in China. Hong Kong's companies' investment concentration in the southern region of China and Japan's in the north-eastern region, were clearly both a function of geographic proximity and the close cultural ties that Hong Kong and Japan have with each of the respective regions.

3. FDI STRATEGIES IN CHINA

United States firm's investments in China have shown several interesting characteristics that represent investor strategies. First, US investors in China span the business spectrum from the world's largest multinational companies to small firms and individual enterprises. Their investment projects range from large-scale development of China's natural resources to the establishment of amusement arcades and fast food ventures (such as McDonalds, KFC and Starbucks). This is a reflection of both the natural 'fit' between China's consumer needs and priorities and US industrial strengths. Second, US investors have a strong interest in forming equity joint ventures and wholly owned enterprises as compared to contractual joint ventures. This is due, in large part, to the relative interest of US investors in developing long-term manufacturing ventures aimed at the Chinese market. Third, US investment in China has fluctuated over time.

The literature on FDI has focused on multinational enterprises (MNEs), giving people the impression that only MNEs are involved in foreign direct investment. If this were true, then FDI in China has demonstrated some unique characteristics. While many large multinational enterprises, including those on the Fortune 500 list, have established a strong presence in China over the last two decades, the majority of 'foreign' investors are not MNEs.[2] Many of the Hong Kong and Taiwanese investors are small and medium-sized firms or individuals and are not qualified as MNEs by the standard definition. The average size of their investment projects in China is relatively small. In the following section, the strategies of two different types of investors, small and medium-sized firms and large multinational enterprises in China, are explored.

Table 4.4   FDI from selected countries/regions for 2003

Country/Region	No. of Projects	Share %	Contractual Value	Share %	Realized Value	Share %
Total	41,081	100.00	115,069.69	100.00	53,504.67	100.00
10 Asian Investors	29,010	70.62	73,870.75	64.20	33,889.76	63.34
Hong Kong	13,633	33.19	40,708.03	35.38	17,700.10	33.08
Indonesia	143	0.35	631.18	0.55	150.13	0.28
Japan	3,254	7.92	7,955.35	6.91	5,054.19	9.45
Macao	580	1.41	1,295.17	1.13	416.60	0.78
Malaysia	350	0.85	958.08	0.83	251.03	0.47
The Philippines	297	0.72	556.73	0.48	220.01	0.41
Singapore	1,144	2.78	3,418.73	2.97	2,058.40	3.85
Republic of Korea	4,920	11.98	9,177.16	7.98	4,488.54	8.39
Thailand	194	0.47	612.45	0.53	173.52	0.32
Taiwan Province	4,495	10.94	8,557.87	7.44	3,377.24	6.31
European Union	2,074	5.05	5,854.32	5.09	3,930.31	7.35
Belgium	67	0.16	168.09	0.15	110.59	0.21
Denmark	42	0.10	81.06	0.07	42.82	0.08
United Kingdom	438	1.07	1,209.49	1.05	742.47	1.39
Germany	451	1.10	1,390.92	1.21	856.97	1.60
France	269	0.65	722.68	0.63	604.31	1.13
Ireland	9	0.02	19.12	0.02	10.61	0.02
Italy	297	0.72	620.90	0.54	316.70	0.59
Luxembourg	16	0.04	47.50	0.04	175.43	0.33
the Netherlands	189	0.46	951.42	0.83	725.49	1.36
Greece	6	0.01	2.53	0.00	1.77	0.00
Portugal	13	0.03	16.29	0.01	4.15	0.01
Spain	129	0.31	316.75	0.28	91.81	0.17
Austria	64	0.16	128.11	0.11	94.50	0.18
Finland	26	0.06	68.18	0.06	32.39	0.06
Sweden	58	0.14	111.28	0.10	120.30	0.22
North America	4,961	12.08	11,771.19	10.23	4,762.02	8.90
Canada	901	2.19	1,609.72	1.40	563.51	1.05
United States	4,060	9.88	10,161.47	8.83	4,198.51	7.85
Some free ports	3,113	7.58	16,943.07	14.72	7,628.72	14.26
Cayman Islands	217	0.53	1,694.53	1.47	866.04	1.62
Virgin Islands	2,218	5.40	12,664.16	11.01	5,776.96	10.80
Western Samoa	678	1.65	2,584.38	2.25	985.72	1.84

Source: National Bureau of Statistics of China
www.fdi.gov.cn/common/info.jsp? id=ABC00000000000016798 (last accessed 23 July, 2005)

Table 4.5   Origin of FDI in China: accumulation to end of 2003

(Amount in US$ billion)

Country/Region	Number of Projects		Amount of Contractual Foreign Capital		Amount of Actual Utilization of Foreign Investment	
	Number	Percentage (%)	Amount	Percentage (%)	Amount	Percentage (%)
Total	465,277		943.13		501.471	
Hong Kong	224,509	48.25	414.514	43.95	222.575	44.43
America	41,340	8.89	86.443	9.17	44.088	8.8
Japan	28,401	6.1	57.487	6.1	41.394	8.26
Taiwan	60,186	12.94	70.029	7.43	36.488	7.28
Virgin Islands	8,877	1.91	62.012	6.58	30.165	6.02
Singapore	11,871	2.55	43.568	4.62	23.531	4.7
Korea	27,128	5.83	36.653	3.89	19.688	3.93
UK	3,856	0.83	20.842	2.21	11.438	2.28
Germany	3,504	0.75	15.713	1.67	8.851	1.77
France	2,302	0.49	7.915	0.84	6.148	1.23
Macao	8,407	1.81	12.087	1.28	5.19	1.04
Netherlands	1,254	0.27	9.926	1.05	5.064	1.01
Cayman Islands	923	0.2	11.175	1.18	4.669	0.93
Canada	6,941	1.49	11.987	1.27	3.921	0.78
Australia	6,073	1.31	9.993	1.06	3.421	0.68
Other	29,705	6.38	72.786	7.72	34.84	6.95

Source: National Bureau of Statistics of China,
www.fdi.gov.cn/common/info.jsp? id=ABC00000000000017510 (last accessed 23 July, 2005)

3.1   Small and Medium-Sized Investors in China

An examination of the data in Tables 4.4 and 4.5 reveals an interesting phenomenon relating to FDI in China. While the ten Asian investors accounted for 70.62 per cent of the new investment projects in 2003 (Table 4.4), the contractual value accounted for only 64.2 per cent. That is, the average value of the investment projects was smaller than that from other parts of the world. This situation is even more pronounced for Taiwan and Korea. In 2003, the number of new projects invested in by Taiwanese investors accounted for 10.94 per cent while the contractual value was only 7.44 per cent. In the case of Korea, the number of new projects was 11.98 per cent while the contractual value was merely 7.98 per cent. While surprising to some, this is not a new phenomenon. Yang (1997) documented this characteristic of Taiwanese investment in China

–collectively large but individually small. The same characteristic is evident for Hong Kong investment as well in the accumulated investment data. As Table 4.5 shows, the accumulated number of investment projects by Hong Kong investors was 48.25 per cent of the total investment projects in China, but the share of their contractual value was only 43.95 per cent.

While Taiwan allowed indirect investments in the mainland by the end of the 1980s, there have been restrictions on the size of individual investment projects in specific industries. In January 1996, the limit was set at 40 million New Taiwan dollars (NT$40 million). That was equivalent to less than US $1.5 million at the exchange rate of about NT$27 to the US dollar at that time. Even though the average size of the Taiwanese investment in the mainland did not exceed this limit until 1995, the restriction may well have curtailed otherwise large investments. While restrictions set by the Taiwanese authorities may represent one factor that contributes to the relatively small investment sizes of Taiwanese investment in the mainland, a more important factor is that many small and medium-sized Taiwan firms have invested in China.

Unlike multinational enterprises, the majority of Taiwanese investors in the mainland are small- and medium-sized firms or individuals with moderate capital commitments. As explained by Yang (1997), this phenomenon reflects an important aspect of the mainland's special investment environment and the ethnic and cultural affinities between the two sides. One distinctive feature of China's economic reform that differs from most other emerging markets is that there exist immense initiatives at the grass-roots level to vitalize local industries, particularly in the coastal areas. They need a lot of capital collectively, but in most cases each investment opportunity can only absorb a limited amount of capital. As these local projects do not require large investments, it is easy to get approval from the local authorities and they are easy to manage. Those local capital needs may not attract large multinationals from industrialized countries who usually aim at large projects that require significantly larger amounts of investment capital and higher level government approvals, sometimes at the very top.

On the other hand, small- and medium-sized investors from Taiwan are in a unique position to dovetail the needs of local industries in the mainland. In this regard, investors from Hong Kong are in a similar situation, where there are no authoritative restrictions on investment in the mainland, but the average investment size has also been relatively small. In a study of Korean direct investment in China, Kim (1995) finds that Korean investment in China has also been dominated by small- and medium-sized firms or individuals who regard investment in China as being more manageable than investment in other countries. Kim cites geographic/cultural proximities and the existence of ethnic Koreans in China as a possible explanation of such a perception for Korean investors.

The phenomenon that a large number of small and medium-sized firms invest in China defies traditional FDI theories. The 'eclectic approach' to foreign investment proposed by Dunning (1979) lists three key elements of direct investment: ownership advantage, internalization advantage and locational advantage. One implication of the eclectic theory is that the individual size of foreign investment should be reasonably large to make these advantages work. While this may be the case for foreign direct investment by large multinationals and occurring among industrial countries, small and medium-sized firms' investment in mainland China presents a noticeable exception.

3.2   A Theoretical Model of Investment Size

To bridge a gap in FDI theory, and to explain the unique pattern of Asian investors' investment strategy in China, the authors offer a simple theoretical model of investment size in this section.

Consider an investor who wishes to start a new project in a foreign land. Without loss of generality, assume that the project has a time horizon of two periods: the initial outlay, I, is made in the first period and net revenue, R, is generated in the second period. The initial outlay determines the production capacity, Q, such that $Q=Q(I)$.

In addition to the normal investment outlay, the investor is likely to incur some extra cost, B, to overcome entry barriers due to a new environment. Such a cost may occur before, during, or after the investment is made. This is one of the factors that distinguish domestic and foreign investment. That is, $B = 0$ for domestic investors. Examples of such a cost include cost of acquiring information about the host country or learning the new business environment, cost related to expatriates residing in the host country, and other expenses that do not normally arise for domestic operations.

In the meantime, the foreign investor may possess some comparative advantages over investors in the host country. Such advantages can stem from the various sources as described in Dunning's eclectic approach. These advantages translate into cost advantages in that they lower the production cost at any level of investment. Given the aforementioned assumptions, the second-period net revenue is defined as follows:

$$RI = PQ(I) - \frac{C[Q(I)]}{1 + \alpha} - B \qquad (4.1)$$

where $C[Q(I)]$ is the production cost function, and a ($a>0$) the advantage parameter. The second-period net revenue represents the total return for the investment, which is equivalent to

$$R(I) = I(1 + r) \tag{4.2}$$

where r is the marginal as well as the average rate of return on investment:

$$r = \frac{\partial R(I)}{\partial I} - 1 = \frac{R(I)}{I} - 1 \tag{4.3}$$

The investor's decision is to select an investment size to maximize the net present value (NPV):

$$NPV = R(I)(1 + c)^{-1} - I \tag{4.4}$$

where c is the investor's marginal as well as average cost of capital, which is assumed to be constant. Differentiating,

$$\frac{d\,NPV}{d\,I} = (1 + c)^{-1}\left[P\frac{d\,Q}{d\,I} - (1 + a)^{-1}\frac{d\,C}{d\,Q}\frac{d\,Q}{d\,I}\right] - 1 = 0 \tag{4.5}$$

Here the investor is assumed to face a constant market price, P. Rearranging terms, the first order condition becomes

$$r = c \tag{4.6}$$

That is, the marginal rate of return and the marginal cost of capital are equal. The second order condition requires that

$$\frac{d^2 R}{d\,I^2} = P\frac{d^2 Q}{d\,I^2} - (1 + a)^{-1}\left(\frac{d^2 C}{d\,Q^2}\left(\frac{d\,Q}{d\,I}\right)^2 + \frac{d\,C}{d\,Q}\frac{d^2 Q}{d\,I^2}\right) < 0 \tag{4.7}$$

Totally differentiating the first order condition,

$$\frac{d^2 R}{d\,I^2}d\,I + \frac{dQ}{d\,I}d\,P + (1 + a)^{-2}\frac{d\,C}{d\,Q}\frac{d\,Q}{d\,I}d\,a = d\,c \tag{4.8}$$

Equation (4.8) yields a number of relationships regarding the size of investment:

$$\frac{d\,I}{d\,c} = [d^2\,R/d\,I^2]^{-1} < 0 \tag{4.9}$$

$$\frac{d\,I}{d\,a} = -\frac{(1+a)^{-2}(d\,C/d\,Q)(d\,Q)}{d^2\,R/d\,I^2} > 0 \tag{4.10}$$

$$\frac{d\,I}{d\,P} = -\frac{d\,Q/d\,I}{d^2\,R/d\,I^2} > 0 \tag{4.11}$$

First, there exists an inverse relationship between the investment size and the cost of capital: investors with higher cost of capital will select a smaller investment size. Second, investors who possess comparative advantages in production will pursue larger investment projects. Third, investors will commit larger amount of funds in investment as the perceived product price increases.

There is one more important relationship embedded in this model that is not captured by the derivatives. That is the fixed cost of entry barriers, B, and investment. The fixed cost appears to have no effect upon the investor's investment decision as the fixed cost term vanishes upon differentiation. Yet the fixed cost does affect the investor's decision. This may be shown by an illustration. Suppose an investor has no advantage (so that $a=0$) and the optimal investment size obtained from NPV maximization, I^*, yields the following situation:

$$R(I^*) < I^*(1+c) < R(I^*) + B \tag{4.12}$$

That is, *NPV* is negative with the cost of entry barrier but positive without it. Here the fixed entry cost, B, plays a critical role. Consider two investors, investor X, the foreign investor, and investor Y, the domestic investor. Investor Y has a positive *NPV* while investor X has a negative *NPV* at the optimal investment level, I^*, as described in Equation (4.12). Since investor X has to bear the extra entry cost which makes the *NPV* negative at the margin, investor X will not enter.

However, if investor X possesses some comparative advantages (so that $a>0$) over investor Y such that

$$NPV_X = \left[PQ_X(I_X^*) - \frac{C[Q_X(I_X^*)]}{1+a_X} - B\right](1+c)^{-1} - I_X^*$$
$$= NPV_X = [P\,Q_Y(I_Y^*) - C[Q_Y(I_Y^*)]](1+c)^{-1} - I_Y^* > 0 \tag{4.13}$$

where $I_Y^* = I^*$ as in Equation (4.12), both investors will enter the market since *NPV* is positive for both. Yet investor X will incur a larger investment than investor Y: $I_X^* > I_Y^*$ since $dI/da > 0$.

Alternatively, suppose investor X enjoys a lower cost of capital (so that $c_X < c_Y$) but no comparative advantage ($a_X = a_Y = 0$). Setting *NPV* for both investors equal and greater than zero:

$$NPV_X = [P Q_X(I_X^*) - C[Q_X(I_X^*)] - B](1 + c_X)^{-1} - I_X^* > 0$$
$$= NPV_Y = [P Q_Y(I_Y^*) - C[Q_Y(I_Y^*)]](1 + c_Y)^{-1} - I_Y^* > 0 \qquad (4.14)$$

Again both investors will enter, but investor X will incur a larger investment than investor Y: $I_X^* > I_Y^*$ since $dI/dc > 0$.

The existence of an entry cost establishes a hurdle for the foreign investor. To overcome this hurdle, the foreign investor has to have a comparative advantage in either production cost (as represented by a) or an advantage in the cost of capital (c). Either will lead to a relatively larger investment.

This analysis helps to explain two stylized facts in foreign investment. First, due to entry cost, foreign investors will find it not worthwhile (NPV being negative) to invest in small projects in the domestic market. Thus, the size of foreign investment tends to be larger than the average of domestic investors. Second, foreign investors with limited investment funds (or small or medium-sized investors) are more likely to refrain from investing abroad due to entry costs. But entry costs generally do not hinder large investors who may not only possess the capacity to mobilize large sums of funds at a lower cost, but also enjoy advantages in production cost. Large multinational firms are, therefore, seen as more actively involved in foreign investment than small and medium-sized firms. Thus, our model leads to the following proposition: because of entry barriers for foreign investment, the average size of foreign investment is larger than that made by domestic investors in the domestic market.

But not all outside investors face the same entry costs, and entry barriers can change over time. Those who face smaller entry costs will find it economically viable to take on smaller projects. Reduction in entry barriers can afford small and medium-sized opportunities to trade or invest abroad. This analysis has a number of implications and empirical testable hypotheses.

First, familiarity breeds commercial exchange. Cultural bond and proximity provide to the Anglo-American groups share some common cultural heritage and corporate philosophies.[3] One may expect more SME trade and investment amongst these countries. Similarly, Mainland China, Taiwan, Hong Kong and other economies in the Asia area share a cultural bond or similarities. SMEs from regional areas are more likely to invest in each other's economies. Fan (1998) shows that the commonality of culture and language reduces the communication costs of business transactions and that is why overseas Chinese have been the dominant suppliers of FDI in China. Hayter and Han (1998) also state that, compared to Western and Japanese MNEs, Hong Kong-controlled FDI faces significantly lower spatial entry barriers because of cultural and geographical proximity.

Second, common borders or geographical adjacency permit more SMEs to trade between each other and invest in each other's economies. Geographical proximities make it easier to gather information and facilitate exchange, hence promoting trade and investment. For example, trade by SMEs between the United States and Canada should be larger than that between the United States and Japan. Similarly, more US SMEs invest in Canada than in Japan. Empirically, one expects the average size of US investment in Japan to be larger than that in Canada. For the same reason, we should see more US SME activities in Latin America, more Japanese SME activities in Asia, and more EU SME activities in Eastern Europe.

Third, international agreements that promote free trade and investment pave the way for SMEs to participate more actively in international trade and investment. Such agreements lower entry barriers for trade and investment across countries, thus allowing SMEs to overcome the hurdles of foreignness. The North American Free Trade Agreement (NAFTA) is one such example. One would have anticipated more SMEs involved in trade and investment across the borders of the United States and Mexico after 1994, when the agreement became effective, something that did not occur.

Fourth, domestic policies that encourage foreign investment can lower the hurdle for foreign SMEs. Since its economic reform started in 1978, China has adopted various policies to attract foreign investment. The preferential policies toward foreign investment not only lowers entry barriers, as denoted by B in our simple model, but also provides incentives such that being foreign itself becomes an advantage, thus increasing the parameter a in our simple model. Consequently, one should anticipate more foreign SME investment in China than elsewhere.

The investment model set forth in this chapter provides an explanation for the overwhelming presence of tens of thousands of small and medium-sized firms from Taiwan, Hong Kong, Korea and other Asian economies investing in mainland China.[4] They may not possess the various advantages that Dunning. (1979) proposed that multinationals should be equipped with to invest abroad. Yet they have the capital, albeit small in size individually, that the mainland local industries need. Their linguistic and cultural affinities to the mainland facilitate contacts and negotiation, and help them find appropriate investment opportunities in local industries.

3.3 Multinational Enterprises' Presence and Strategies in China

While small and medium-sized investors from some Asian economies are collectively large in investment value, as well as in the number of investment projects undertaken, it is the large multinational enterprises that have been the dominating force in terms of structural change within the industries in which they have invested. According to China's National Statistics Bureau, a total of 2,477 foreign-invested enterprises, with a contractual foreign investment of over US $10 million each, were set up in 2003 alone.

Many multinational companies have gained brand recognition and dominance in some consumer markets in China. For example, General Motors automobiles, Dell computers, Motorola cell phones, Kodak film, Coca-Cola and Pepsi-Cola soft drinks, McDonalds hamburgers and Marlboro cigarettes (to name just a few) have become household names and are popular in major Chinese cities. In fact, one can find almost all brand-name consumer products in major cities in China that one can find in other major cities around the world. According to a market survey for consumer products conducted in 32 major cities in China in October 1997, the market shares of Motorola, Coca-Cola and Kodak were already over 40 per cent of their respective markets in China (Yang, 1998).

According to Lardy (2002), at the turn of the twenty-first century foreign manufacturers, led by Motorola, Nokia and Ericsson, had captured 95 per cent of the market for cellular telephones. In addition, Coca-Cola was the dominant supplier of carbonated beverages with a market share 15 times that of its closest domestic competitor; McDonald's and KFC, with almost 900 outlets between them, dominated China's rapidly growing fast food market. Also, Kodak had captured half the market for film and photographic paper; and Proctor and Gamble had more than half of the shampoo market. On February 23, 2005, Jorma Ollila, CEO of Nokia, the world's foremost seller of mobile telephones, stated that he anticipates that the Chinese market will soon over take that of the United States, his firm's biggest market. In fact, citing the rapid growth of the economy and rising incomes within China, he added that that event may occur within the next three years!

Multinational investment strategies have evolved over the past two decades. According to Chen (1994), multinationals build their business presence in China in three stages: opportunistic experimenter, strategic investor, and dominant local player. In the first stage, they establish a small local presence and have simple operations with low asset commitment and exposure. Many multinational firms have gone beyond the first stage by now. In fact, many large corporations are beginning to set up their research and development facilities in China.

Large manufacturers are not the only ones to have taken advantage of China's low labor costs and large market. Many firms in the service and retail sectors have moved to China to expand their business horizon. Many hotel chains from the United States and elsewhere have a presence in major cities. Wal-Mart, the largest US retailer, has been sourcing its supplies from China to keep its 'everyday low prices'. In recent years, Wal-Mart has been setting up stores in China as well.

4. IMPACT OF FDI ON CHINA AND THE WORLD ECONOMY

Many theories may help explain the motives for foreign investment in China. However, the lower labor cost and huge consumer market have been the predominating considerations for the majority of foreign investors in China. Foreign manufacturers move their production facilities to China to take advantage of the low labor cost on the production side. On the marketing side, they serve both the Chinese consumer market and the international market through export. In fact, some apparel manufactures that set up shop in China as a base to produce for export to other markets already see China as a prime market for their goods. This is a result of the booming increase of the numbers of middle class citizens and their desire for western style garments. According to the *Wall Street Journal*, 'Hennes and Mauritz AB, the Swedish owner of the H&M fashion chain, said it will open its first Asian retail outlets in Shanghai and Hong Kong early in 2007. VF Corporation, owner of Lee jeans, Kellwood Co., maker of Phat Farm and baby Phat lines, Inditex ZA's Zara and Mango have opened, or are about to open, stores in China' (*Wall Street Journal*, June 23, 2006, page B1).

One of the most important impacts of FDI in China is export re-routing from China. That is, many manufacturers who used to produce and export from their own country/region now have moved to China to produce and export from China. Figure 4.1 depicts this export re-routing from China to the United States by foreign investors. Originally, producers in Taiwan, Hong Kong and South Korea produced domestically and exported to the United States. In recent years, many producers from these countries/ regions have moved to China and export from China to the United States. In fact, many US companies have production operations in China and sell their goods produced there in the US market. About 60 per cent of China's exports are produced by foreign invested enterprises and approximately 80 per cent of China's exports to the United States are produced by foreign invested firms.

Led by FDI, China has become a manufacturing base or workshop for the world market. As shown in Table 4.6, China's share of exports in the world's total export has increased steadily since 1980, from merely 1 per cent in 1980 to 5.84 per cent in 2003. China became the fourth largest exporter and the third largest importer in the world in 2003 (see Tables 4.7 and 4.8)

The export re-routing by producers from other economies has made the United States the major destination for exports from China. The top 10 destinations for China's exports are listed in Table 4.9. The total value of China's exports to the United States reached about $125 billion in 2004.[5] Relatively large exports to Hong Kong – about $100 billion in 2004 – reflect the unique position of Hong Kong as an intermediary in international trade between mainland China and the rest of the world.

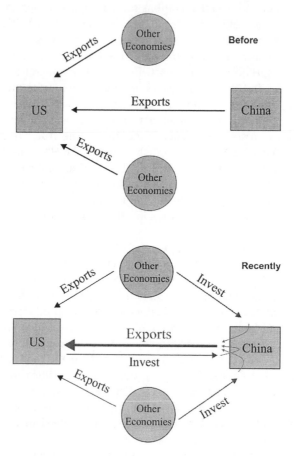

Figure 4.1   Export re-routing from China to the United States

Table 4.6   China's share in international trade

Units (US$billons)	China			
	Exports		Imports	
Year	Value ($ Billion)	Share of World's Total %	Value ($ Billion)	Share of World's Total %
1980	18.14	0.99	19.51	1.02
1981	21.48	1.12	21.63	1.08
1982	21.86	1.23	18.92	1.02
1983	22.10	1.28	21.31	1.18
1984	24.82	1.35	25.95	1.35
1985	27.33	1.46	42.48	2.15
1986	31.37	1.54	43.25	2.01
1987	39.46	1.63	43.22	1.72
1988	47.66	1.72	55.35	1.93
1989	52.91	1.77	59.14	1.90
1990	62.76	1.86	53.81	1.53
1991	71.97	2.06	63.87	1.76
1992	85.62	2.29	81.87	2.10
1993	91.69	2.46	103.62	2.73
1994	120.87	2.84	115.71	2.68
1995	148.96	2.93	132.16	2.57
1996	151.17	2.85	138.95	2.58
1997	182.92	3.31	142.16	2.54
1998	183.74	3.40	140.39	2.54
1999	194.93	3.44	165.72	2.85
2000	249.20	3.90	224.94	3.41
2001	266.70	4.34	243.57	3.81

Source: National Bureau of Statistics of China

5. PROSPECTS FOR FDI IN CHINA

Since China joined the WTO in 2001, the business environment in China for foreign investment has experienced further improvement. According to a survey, 70.3 per cent of multinationals operating in China believe that China has fulfilled most of the commitments stipulated in its agreement to join the WTO (Fortune China, 2005). Of those surveyed, 96.3 per cent

Table 4.7   The world's leading exporters, 2003

Rank	Exporters	Value ($billion)	Share (%)
1	Germany	748.3	10.0
2	United States	723.8	9.6
3	Japan	471.8	6.3
4	China	437.9	5.8
5	France	386.7	5.2
6	United Kingdom	304.6	4.1
7	Netherlands	294.1	3.9
8	Italy	292.1	3.9
9	Canada	272.7	3.6
10	Belgium	255.3	3.4
11	Hong Kong, China	228.7	3.0
	domestic exports	19.6	0.3
	re-exports	209.1	2.8
12	Korea, Republic of	193.8	2.6
13	Mexico	165.4	2.2
14	Spain	151.7	2.0
15	Taipei, Chinese	150.3	2.0

Source: The World Trade Organization

Table 4.8   The world's leading importers, 2003

Rank	Importers	Value	Share (%)
1	United States	1303.05	16.75
2	Germany	601.691	7.74
3	China	413.062	5.31
4	United Kingdom	390.774	5.02
5	France	390.528	5.02
6	Japan	382.93	4.92
7	Italy	290.811	3.74
8	Netherlands	262.816	3.38
9	Canada	245.021	3.15
10	Belgium	235.37	3.03
11	Hong Kong, China	233.194	3.00
	retained imports a	24.127	0.31
12	Spain	200.996	2.58
13	Korea, Republic of	178.827	2.30
14	Mexico	178.503	2.29
15	Singapore	127.934	1.64
	retained imports	63.526	0.82

Source: The World Trade Organization

Table 4.9   China's top 10 export destinations

($ million)

Rank 2004	Country	2004
1	United States	124,947.7
2	Hong Kong	100,878.0
3	Japan	73,514.3
4	South Korea	27,818.4
5	Germany	23,755.9
6	Netherlands	18,519.2
7	United Kingdom	14,968.3
8	Taiwan	13,545.2
9	Singapore	12,687.3
10	France	9,922.1

Table 4.10   China's top 10 import suppliers

($ million)

Rank 2004	Country	2004
1	Japan	94,372.1
2	Taiwan	64,778.6
3	South Korea	62,249.8
4	United States	44,678.6
5	Germany	30,368.4
6	Malaysia	18,174.3
7	Singapore	13,996.6
8	Russia	12,129.5
9	Hong Kong	11,800.4
10	Australia	11,552.5

view the Chinese market the extremely important, very important or important, while 79 per cent of the respondents plan to keep their current rate of investment or increase investment in China in the next three years. While foreign investment has fared well in China, there are a number of challenges that confront China and the FDI investors.

5.1   Internal Challenges

In addition to the attraction of efficient labor costs and a huge consumer market, foreign investment has benefited from two other very significant factors' tax incentives and favorable allocation of local resources. Foreign investors in general, and investors from Taiwan, Hong Kong and Macao in particular, enjoy tax holidays for the first five years after their operations in China become profitable. This includes two years of 100 per cent tax exemption and three years of 50 per cent tax reduction. In addition, these investors receive priority in local resource allocations including land usage, human resources and financial resources.

This preferential treatment for foreign investors has created an uneven playing field and has put domestic producers at a competitive disadvantage. There have been increasingly stronger complaints about this super-national treatment for foreign investments by researchers and domestic firms in China. FDI may be adversely affected once this preferential treatment is reduced or eliminated.

Recent studies have shown that many of the benefits resulting from foreign investment in China, including export sales, are absorbed by foreign investors. The average profit from a shirt produced by a Chinese firm is between $0.30 to $0.40. A Barbie doll that sells for $10.00 in the US renders only about $0.35 valued added for the Chinese producer. It has been calculated that the Chinese need to export approximately 0.8 billion shirts in order to buy one large airplane. The low value added situation is further aggravated by environmental damage. Many people in China are beginning to wonder about the real costs of being the world's foremost workshop.

One of the motivations for China to attract foreign direct investment is to encourage technology transfer to their various industries. Empirical evidence in the 1990s showed that the extent of technology transfer was indeed limited (Young and Lan, 1997). There has been limited evidence that such transfer has improved in recent years, with more and higher levels of technology transferred as a result of foreign direct investment.

To correct the situation whereby Chinese industry relies too much on foreign technology, the central government in China has called upon Chinese enterprises to increase research and development and technology innovation. In a separate study, Kinoshita (1998) found that foreign-owned firms in China are unlikely to invest in the education of local workers. On the contrary, they tend to maintain product quality by importing intermediate goods from their home countries and by transferring managers from their headquarters.

The question of how much China has benefited from foreign direct investment has surfaced in recent years. As Braunstein and Epstein (2002) state, given China's size and huge allure of its cheap labor force and customer base, one would think that if any country had the bargaining power vis-à-vis multinational corporations to benefit from FDI, it would be China. But does FDI really deliver these commonly perceived benefits? They found that, contrary to the conventional wisdom, inward FDI has had a relatively small positive impact on wages and employment, while having a negative impact on domestic investment and tax revenue.

Huang's study (2004) of FDI in China raises further doubts on FDI and the balance of China's economic development. He claims that the large absorption of FDI by China is a sign of substantial distortions in the country's economic and financial system. These economic and financial distortions have led to a weak domestic corporate sector, despite more than 20 years of continuous economic and export growth. According to Huang, FDI surged in part because of strong economic growth but also because of the failings of the domestic corporate sector to respond to and capitalize on the propitious macro conditions. Furthermore, market fragmentation constrains domestic firms more than foreign firms, which allows foreign firms to expand their investments and to respond to market opportunities more than domestic firms.

These factors and studies call for a change or improvement in China's policies toward FDI. One direction of change is to allow equal treatment of domestic firms with foreign-invested firms. But there are also calls for further deregulation toward foreign investment. Graham and Wada (2001) called for the dismantling of conditions and limitations placed upon foreign-invested enterprises and for allowing foreign takeovers of incumbent state-owned enterprises on terms that foreign investors can accept.

5.2   External Challenges

In recent years, there has been mounting pressure on China about the US trade deficit with China and the valuation of the Chinese currency. If the Chinese currency were to revalue significantly, it would increase the cost of doing business by foreign investors operating in China.

Political and historical factors are also at play in foreign investment in China. Rong (1999) documented that the growth of Japanese FDI in China had been overshadowed by the lingering historical experiences of the two nations since 1895, and had been disrupted by a series of political incidents between the two countries during past years.

While China is seen to be well on its way toward becoming 'the factory of the world', most of China's Asian neighbors appear to be very worried about such prospects, particularly the lesser developed economies

(Chantasasawat et al., 2004). Is China really taking direct investments away from other economies in Asia and Latin America? Chantasasawat et al. (2004, 2005) found that the China effect is not the most important determinant of the inward direct investment for these economies. Market sizes and policy variables, such as market stability, openness and corporate tax rates, tend to be more important.

6. CONCLUDING REMARKS

Without a doubt, the global balance of power is rapidly shifting decisively to Asia which, in the authors' opinion, will dominate the twenty-first century just as Europe and the United States dominated their respective eras. What the world is witnessing is an historic transfer of power that is taking place and multinational corporate firms and other investors will have to keep pace with changes taking place or suffer the consequences because the major player in this new era will be China.

Given the assumptions of internal stability and an externally peaceful environment, the Chinese economy is expected to continue to grow at a relatively high rate. According to Fung (2005), as a developing country China is unusual in playing two important roles for multinational enterprises as well as many small and medium-sized firms. It is a competitive, low-cost export platform and, at the same time, a large and rapidly growing market domestically.

Therefore, it is not at all surprising that China is attracting and will continue to attract foreign direct investment from companies around the globe. At the same time, China will continue developing her own multinational enterprises that, in turn, will invest elsewhere in the world. In a paper analyzing multinational enterprises in transition to the year 2000 and beyond, and FDI in China in particular, Grub (1995) forecast that China would emerge as one of the world's foremost trading nations by the year 2005. He also forecast that, in the latter part of that decade, China would overtake the United States as the world's leading economic power in terms of gross domestic product. Given China's comparative advantage in labor cost and vast consumer market, foreign direct investment in China will continue in the foreseeable future. Multinational enterprises and other foreign investors will play an even greater role in China's economic development than they have in the past, as well as in strengthening China's linkages with the rest of the world in the remainder of this decade and beyond. China's exports from the manufacturing sector will certainly take a leading position globally in the foreseeable future if the current trend continues.

Due to changes in the internal and external environments, foreign investors will have to formulate new strategies for doing business in China. First, more sectors of the Chinese market are being liberalized and open to foreign investment. Industries such as transportation and financial services (stock brokerage, insurance and banking) will receive an increasing share of private and foreign investment. Second, foreign investors will face increasing challenges from domestic firms who are becoming more vocal in demanding a level playing field with foreign investors. Third, as Chinese consumers are becoming increasingly aware of their rights and global standards, foreign manufacturers and service providers will have to constantly monitor and revise production and marketing strategies in China to provide higher quality goods and improved services. Fourth, China has become painfully aware that it still lacks core technologies in such key sectors such as telecommunications, automobiles, heavy equipment and computers. Therefore, the call for independence and self-reliance in technology development in China may exert pressure on multinational companies to increase their local R&D activities in those fields. Opportunities for MNEs are there if these firms can meet the challenges of investing and operating in China successfully.

NOTES

1. For a study of the earlier stages of foreign investment in China, see Grub and Lin (1991).
2. There are different definitions of a 'multinational enterprise or company'. It often refers to an enterprise that has widespread international operations or has a number of overseas operations. See Ball et al. (2006) for further discussions.
3. The Anglo-American group is defined to include the United States, United Kingdom, Canada, Australia, and New Zealand. See Eiteman, Stonehill and Moffett (2004) for discussions of the Anglo-American corporate and investor philosophies.
4. In 2003, there were 230,000 foreign-invested enterprises currently registered and operating in China, out of which 160,000 of them were industrial enterprises (China National Statistics Bureau).
5. The value of China's exports to the United States was even larger according to reports by the United States. There have always been disagreements on the statistics of imports and exports between China and the United States (see Yang 1998 for detailed descriptions).

REFERENCES

Ball, D.A., W.H. McCulloch, Jr., P.L. Frantz, J.M. Geringer, and M.S. Minor

(2006), *International Business: The Challenge of Global Competition* (10th edn), Boston: McGraw-Hill.

Braunstein, E. and G. Epstein (2002), 'Bargaining Power and Foreign Direct Investment in China: Can 1.3 Billion Consumers Tame the Multinationals?', working paper http://ssrn.com/abstract=343540 (accessed 13 June, 2005)

Caves, R. (1971). 'International corporations: The industrial economics of foreign investment', *Economica*, **38**, February, 1-27.

Chantasasawat, B.B., K.C. Fung, H. Iizaka, and A.K.F. Siu (2004),'The Giant Sucking Sound: Is China Diverting Foreign Direct Investments from Other Asian Economies?' working paper, http://ssrn.com/abstract =711224 (accessed 13 June, 2005).

Chantasasawat, B.B., K.C. Fung, H. Iizaka and A.K.F. Siu (2005),'FDI flows to Latin America, East and Southeast Asia and China: Substitutes or Complements?', working paper http://ssrn.com/abstract=711224 (accessed 13 June, 2005).

Chen, K. (1994), 'Giants in China build-up: Multinationals move to pre-empt entry by rivals', *South China Morning Post*, 16 February.

China Ministry of Commerce (2003) 'An overview of Chinese absorption of foreign direct investment in 2003', www.fdi.gov.cn/common/info.jsp? id= ABC00000000000017179 (accessed 23 July, 2005).

Dunning, J.H. (1996),'Explaining changing patterns of international production: In defense of the eclectic theory', *Oxford Bulletin of Economics and Statistics*, November, 269-96.

Eiteman, D., A. Stonehill and M. Moffett (2004), *Multinational Business Finance* (10th edn), Addison Wesley.

Fan, C.S. (1998), 'Why China has been successful in attracting foreign direct investment: A transaction cost approach', *Journal of Contemporary China*, 7(17) 21-32.

Fortune China (2005), *Fortune Iinvestment Survey*, 2005, May, 95-9.

Fung, K.C. (2005),'Trade and Investment Among China, the United States, and the Asia-Pacific Economies: An Invited Testimony to the US Congressional Commission', working paper, http://ssrn.com/abstract=721593 (accessed 13 June, 2005).

Fung, K.C., H. Iizaka, C. Lin and A.K.F. Siu (2002),'An Econometric Estimation of Locational Choices of Foreign Direct Investment: The Case of Hong Kong and US Firms in China', working paper, http://ssrn.com/abstract=379040 (accessed 13 June, 2005).

Fung, K.C., H. García, I.H. Alicia and A.K.F. Siu (2005),'Hard or Soft? Institutional Reforms and Infrastructure Spending as Determinants of Foreign Direct Investment in China' http://ssrn.com/abstract=710584 (accessed 13 June, 2005).

Graham, E.M. and E. Wada (2001), 'Foreign Direct Investment in China: Effects on Growth and Economic Performance', Institute for International Economics Working Paper No. 01-03,www.iie.com/publications/wp/2001/01-3.pdf (accessed 13 June, 2005).

Grub, P.D. and J.H. Lin (1991), *Foreign Direct Investment in China*, New York: Quorum Books.

Grub, P.D. (1995), 'The multinational enterprise in transition to the year 2000 and beyond', Presentation at the Sixth International Conference on the Multinational Enterprise, Taipei.

Hayter, R. and S.S. Han (1998), 'Reflections on China's open policy towards foreign direct investment'. *Regional Studies*, **32**(1),1-16.

Huang, Y. (2004), 'Economic fragmentation and FDI in China', William Davidson Institute working paper, http://ssrn.com/abstract=270322 (accessed 13 June, 2005).

Kim, S.J. (1995), 'Korean direct investment in China: Perspectives of Korean investors', in S.J.L. Croix, M. Plummer and K. Lee (eds), *Emerging Patterns of East Asian Investment in China*, Armonk: M.E. Sharpe.

Kinoshita, Y. (2005), 'Technology Spillovers through Foreign Direct Investment', working paper http://ssrn.com/abstract=157614 (accessed 13 June, 2005).

Lardy, N.R. (2002), *Integrating China into the Global Economy*, Washington, DC: Brookings Institution Press.

Rong, X. (1999), 'Explaining the patterns of Japanese foreign direct investment in China', *Journal of Contemporary China*, **8**(20), 123-46.

Schroath, F.W., M.Y. Hu and H. Chen (1993), 'Country-of-origin effects of foreign investments in the People's Republic of China', *Journal of International Business Studies*, **24**(2), 277-90.

Wei, Y., X. Liu, D. Parker and K. Vaidya (1999), 'The regional distribution of foreign direct investment in China'. *Regional Studies*, **33**(9), 857-67.

Yang, J. (1997), 'The emerging patterns of Taiwanese investments in Mainland China', *Multinational Business Review*, **1**(Spring), 92-9.

Yang, J. (1998), 'Some current issues in US-China trade relations', *Issues & Studies*, **34**(7), 62-84.

Young, S and P. Lan (1997), 'Technology transfer to China through foreign direct investment'. *Regional Studies*, **31**(7), 669-80.

Zhang, Z. (1999), 'A comparative study of foreign direct investment in China and Vietnam', *American Asian Review*, **17**(2), 117-51.

Zhou, C., A. Delios and Y.Y. Jing (2005), 'Locational Determinants of Japanese Foreign Direct Investment in China', working paper, http://ssrn.com/abstract=305346 (accessed 13 June, 2005).

5. An econometric investigation of Chinese outward direct investment

Adam Cross, Peter Buckley, Jeremy Clegg, Hinrich Voss, Mark Rhodes, Ping Zheng and Xin Lui

1. INTRODUCTION

This chapter is the outcome of an econometric investigation into the determinants of foreign direct investment (FDI) undertaken by Chinese multinational enterprises (MNEs) over the period 1991 to 2003. Research on China and its increasingly prominent role in the globalization of economic activity generally focuses on aspects concerning its position in world trade and inward investment flows and on its competitiveness as a manufacturing location (for example, Branstetter and Lardy, 2006; Buckley, et al., 2002; Buckley, 2004; Chen et al., 2002; Lall and Albaladejo, 2004; Lardy, 1998; OECD, 2002).[1] However, since the mid-1990s, a further and less well understood dimension to China's integration with the global economy has become increasingly prevalent – namely Chinese outward direct investment (ODI) flows. By 2004, China had become the eighth most important source country for FDI among developing countries, behind Hong Kong (SAR), Singapore, British Virgin Islands, Republic of Taiwan, the Russian Federation, Brazil and South Korea (in US$ million stock value terms; UNCTAD, 2006) and was a larger foreign investor nation than countries such as Israel, South Africa and India. By 2004, the value of Chinese-owned ODI stock was estimated to be US$38 825mn, more than a sevenfold increase on the figure of US$5368mn reported for 1991 (UNCTAD, 2006). A number of recent surveys point to this figure increasing as Chinese firms continue to expand their activities internationally,

Adam Cross, Peter Buckley, Jeremy Clegg, Hinrich Voss, Mark Rhodes, Ping Zheng and Xin Liu would like to thank Tim Rose for his supportive work. We would also like to thank the organizers of the 8th International Conference on Multinational Enterprises held in Taipei in March 2006 and the conference participants for their helpful suggestions.

especially to Africa and the Asia-Pacific region (UNCTAD. 2004, 2005). In short, there is good evidence to suggest that China will increasingly contribute to global FDI flows over the coming years.

Up to now, understanding on the determinants and drivers of Chinese ODI has generally been informed by in-depth case studies of a small number of high-profile Chinese MNEs (for example Warner et al., 2004; Zhang, 2003; Liu and Li, 2002). In this exploratory study we follow an alternative approach by analyzing official data published by one of the key government agencies involved in China's ODI approval process, namely the Ministry of Commerce (MOFCOM). In particular, we seek to identify the determinants of Chinese ODI using a panel data approach. Our focus is mainly on host country location-specific factors and, in particular, the extent to which FDI-influencing variables as identified in the literature for industrialized country investors have explanatory power when applied to outbound FDI from a developing economy such as China. We also incorporate a discussion on how government engagement and policy has helped to shape the investment decisions of Chinese firms.

The remaining chapter is organized as follows. In the next section, we review the general motivations for FDI as presented in the literature, and discuss their ability to explain patterns of outward FDI observed from a developing economy such as China, where intervention by the state in the development of the external sector has been strongly felt. We go on to describe a number of economic and policy variables that have been demonstrated to influence (industrialized country) FDI flows and discuss their ability to explain Chinese ODI patterns. These variables are then tested in a model of Chinese ODI using investment flow figures calculated from data published by MOFCOM. We reveal that standard explanations of FDI are important in the case of China, but that idiosyncratic explanations are evident too, especially concerning the attitude of Chinese firms to market risk. We conclude by suggesting some directions for future work.

2. OUTWARD FDI AND MOTIVATIONS

The OECD defines FDI as an 'investment (that) reflects the objective of obtaining a lasting interest by a resident entity in one economy ... in an entity resident in an economy other than that of the investor .... The lasting interest implies the existence of a long-term relationship between the direct investor and the enterprise and a significant degree of influence on the management of the enterprise' (OECD, 1996: 7-8).

Economic theories of the MNE generally assume FDI to be part of the process by which the net worth of firms and their shareholders is maximized (Barrell and Pain, 1996). MNEs are said to possess monopolistic ownership (O) advantages which enable them to out-compete local firms. These advantages typically take the form of proprietary technology, marketing capabilities, managerial skills and other intangible assets (Hymer, 1960; Dunning, 1993). Dunning's eclectic paradigm asserts that international production is undertaken when a firm combines O-advantages with immobile locational (L) advantages abroad (otherwise it would export) and when benefits associated with internalization (I) accrue from cross-border exchanges that take place within the firm rather than at arm's length with independent firms (otherwise it would license). The main motives for foreign direct investment are:

1. Market-orientated investment;
2. cost-orientated investment and
3. the acquisition of key inputs.

The first type of FDI occurs in situations where it is the optimum method of securing market access versus the alternatives of exporting or non-equity forms of operation. It may include production within markets of high growth potential, tariff-jumping FDI or even the use of a particular market as a further jumping off point for other markets (Dunning, 1993).

Cost-orientated FDI is often underpinned by the search for cheap labour. It also includes investment in tax havens and in locations that reduce transport costs. In the context of developing country ODI, especially Chinese ODI, the relative costs of operation between alternative locations may be important. A simple comparison of Chinese costs (especially labour costs) with the cost base of investment locations abroad may discourage purely cost-based investment (Fortin, 2005). However, relative cost differences between locations may play a part in the FDI decision of Chinese firms.

There are various types of inputs that investing firms may seek to obtain and control by FDI. These include raw materials and natural resource based inputs – minerals, energy and primary products. Asset-seeking FDI is also a potentially important motive. The assets that may be sought by investing firms include brands, specialized knowledge, access to capital markets and specialized skills such as design, R&D and know-how (Dunning, 1993).

In addition, we should not lose sight of 'push' factors driving ODI from the home economy. These can be both positive and negative. Positive push factors include the release of value through the employment of underutilized resources, the diversification of risk (including earning foreign exchange), the advantages of multiple sourcing and the ability to exploit abroad certain cost advantages and knowledge derived from spillover and demonstration effects in the domestic economy. Negative push factors include escape from an unfavourable domestic environment (perhaps in response to heightened levels of domestic competition), the avoidance of restrictions on business and the circumvention of constraints on growth.

The bulk of theorizing on the motivations of FDI is based on the understanding of industrialized country firms. However, there are a number of important reasons for suggesting that ODI from a developing country such as China may be motivated differently. Research suggests that FDI flow from a developing to an advanced country (South-North) and from one developing country to another (South-South) will have different rationales. The former will be market-seeking in those niches where the investor has a competitive advantage and may also be asset-seeking. The latter will be mostly natural resource-seeking and may have a sub-set that is concerned with serving markets or may be cost reduction-seeking (Wells, 1977, 1983; Lecraw 1977; Khan, 1986). Moreover, monopolistic advantage and other firm-specific advantages such as size arguably may not adequately explain the growth of MNEs from developing countries (Lall, 1983). This is because such firms generally command fewer technological and managerial resources and capabilities compared to industrialized country firms. In the case of China a number of authors, such as Nolan (2002) and Duan (1995), have highlighted the limited international competitiveness of state-owned Chinese MNEs.

Up to now, our analysis has assumed that the internationalization of firms is predicated upon rational, entrepreneurial decision-taking that is guided strongly by the objectives of profit-maximization and the maximization of shareholder value. However, there is good reason to believe that the firm-level strategic decision-taking within Chinese firms is predicated less upon profit maximization (and concomitant consideration of market and industry-related push and pull factors outlined above) and more upon the achievement of certain political and economic objectives as set by government. This is because the Chinese government, at both the national and sub-national levels, has long intervened in the development of China's external sector, both directly, through state ownership of various kinds, and indirectly, through economic policy and administrative control.

For many developing and transition countries such as China, the creation of MNEs has represented an important strand of economic development policy (Aggarwal and Agmon, 1990). Accordingly, objectives such as security in the supply of strategically important raw materials and other inputs can lead to the establishment of state-led MNEs (Warner et al., 2004). In the case of China, the government has actively encouraged FDI in the energy and minerals sectors for many years to meet growing needs at home (Lawrence, 2002). The national government has also stated its intention to see established 50 internationally competitive Chinese MNEs by the year 2010 (Sauvant, 2005) (although the mechanisms for doing so are unclear) in a process that mirrors, though arguably somewhat more ambitiously, the intentions of other Asian countries such as Singapore, South Korea and Malaysia in the past (Wang, 2002; Dicken, 2003; Heenan and Keegan, 1979). Indirect government support for developing country MNEs is typically reflected in privileged access to cheap capital, raw materials and other production inputs as well as preferential subsidies, skewed industry policies and other benefits designed to offset ownership and location disadvantages commonly found among indigenous firms (Aggarwal and Agmon, 1990). At the same time, preferential measures are often offset by highly bureaucratic and burdensome administrative outward FDI approval procedures, as governments attempt to shape the volume and direction of outward capital flows (with the main objective being to bolster domestic investment capital stocks and, in the case of China, to maintain control of state-owned assets). Such restrictions may lead to informal or illegal outflows of investment capital, especially in cases where particular industries and ownership forms (for example private firms) are targeted by government with discretionary and restrictive investment-related policies. In the case of China, preferential investment incentives implemented to promote inflows of FDI have seen outward investments being reinvested back into China in what has become known as the 'round-tripping' phenomenon (Sung, 1996; Wall, 1997).

The institutional framework of a developing country like China can therefore determine to a considerable degree the ability and willingness of indigenous firms to invest abroad and the subsequent investment decision-making processes of managers. In sum, supportive, coherent and liberal policies towards outward FDI will tend to encourage it, while discretionary and frequently amended policies which seek to maximize domestic over international investment may do the opposite. In the case of China, policy towards ODI has swung regularly between these two standpoints. At various times, a variety of government agencies (at both national and sub-national levels) have supported and constrained the development of Chinese MNEs, and not always in concert. This has been accomplished in a number of ways, including direct intervention through the corporate governance structures of state-owned firms, administrative regulations, investment approval procedures, foreign currency availability, economic policy, industrial policy and other measures intended to advance the country's economic development agenda (Buckley et al., 2006). This has led to different motivations driving the expansion of China's external sector over time. Key developments of the formal ODI approval process are presented in Table 5.1. Scholars generally assert that Chinese ODI in the 1980s and early 1990s was motivated primarily to support the export activities of state-owned manufacturers; to stabilize the international supply of domestically-scarce natural resources; to acquire foreign market information and to learn about conducting business on an international scale (Buckley et al., 2006; Ye, 1992; Zhan, 1995). At this time, Chinese ODI, and especially natural resources-orientated FDI, was distributed predominately among the developed countries (Buckley et al., 2006) (see Table 5.2). In the late 1990s, there was a perceptible shift in the investment behaviour of Chinese MNEs, which paralleled growth and marketization of the domestic economy. Today, Chinese MNEs are observed to be internationalizing in order to improve the access to strategic proprietary assets held abroad such as technology, brands and distribution channels, and to tap foreign capital markets. This is often accomplished by acquisition. Increasingly, Chinese MNEs are also developing new markets and diversifying business activities to improve their international competitiveness (Taylor, 2002; Deng, 2003; Zhang, 2003). This has led to Chinese ODI becoming more spatially dispersed, especially amongst the developing countries (see Table 5.2), with both defensive (import-substituting and quota-hopping) and offensive (developing new markets) market-seeking FDI increasingly undertaken (Buckley et al., 2006). At the same time, outbound natural resource-oriented FDI has continued to be important, especially after 1999 when a number of national oil companies began to become increasingly acquisitive, especially in the developing countries (Ma and Andrews-Speed, 2006).

The continued political, financial and other assistance provided by Chinese government, either through direct ownership or via other supportive mechanisms, arguably constitutes a firm-specific advantage (Ding, 2000). Such support has been articulated formally in the government-led 'Go Global' ('*zou chu qu*') initiative which was introduced in 1999. This has led to a steady liberalization of the outward direct investment approval process, the relaxation and removal of certain administrative controls and the reduction of foreign exchange restrictions. The ultimate aim of this programme is to promote the international competitiveness of Chinese firms. At the same time, however, doubts have been raised in the literature about the extent to which protective support and assistance by national and sub-national governmental agencies actually shape the internationalization of Chinese MNEs in practice. To illustrate, Wong and

Table 5.1   Key developments in China's ODI policy

1979-1985	*Stage One: Cautious internationalization* With the 'open-door' policy, Chinese state-owned firms start to set up their first international operations. Only state-owned trading corporations under MOFERT (later MOFCOM or Ministry of Commerce) and provincial and municipal 'economic and technological cooperation enterprises' under the State Economic and Trade Commission (SETC) are allowed to invest abroad. Only 189 projects were approved, amounting to around US$197mn.
1986-1991	*Stage Two: Government encouragement* The government liberalized restrictive policies and allowed more enterprises to establish foreign affiliates, provided they had sufficient capital, technical and operational know-how and a suitable joint venture partner. Approval was granted to 891 projects, totalling some US$1.2bn.
1992-1998	*Stage Three: Expansion and regulation* Encouraged by domestic liberalization, initiated by President Deng Xiaoping's journey to the South, sub-national level authorities rush into international business activities with companies under their supervision, especially in Hong Kong, to engage in real estate and stock market speculation. The Asian crisis in 1997 and the subsequent collapse of companies such as GITIC slows down this development. Latterly, concerns about loss of control over state assets, capital flight and 'leakage' of foreign exchange saw a tightening of approval procedures, notably for projects of US$1mn or more. Individual ODI activity declines, despite an increase of total ODI of US$1.2bn.
1999-2001	*Stage Four: The 'Go Global' period* Contradictory policies characterized this period. Further measures to control illicit capital transfers and to regularize ODI towards genuinely productive purposes are introduced. On the other hand, ODI in specific industries is actively encouraged with export tax rebates, foreign exchange assistance and direct financial support, notably in trade-related activities that promoted Chinese exports of raw materials, parts and machinery and in light industry sectors like textiles, machinery and electrical equipment. In 2001 this encouragement is formalized within the 10th five year plan which outlined the 'Go Global' or 'zou chu qu' directive. Total approved ODI rises by US $1.8bn, with an average project value of US$2.6mn.
Since 2001	*Stage Five: Post WTO period* Heightened domestic competitive pressures, due to the opening of once protected industries and markets to foreign and domestic competitors, forces some Chinese firms to seek new markets abroad. In the outline of the latest five year plan, the 11th, the Chinese government stressed again the importance of 'zou chu qu' for Chinese firms and the Chinese economy. Nevertheless, direct and proactive support of ODI continues to be limited, mainly to preventing illegal capital outflows and loss of control of state assets.

Sources: Wong and Chan (2003), Wu and Chen (2001), Guo (1984), Ye (1992), Ding (2000).

Table 5.2 Approved Chinese FDI outflows, by host region and economy, 1990-2003 (10 000 US dollars and per cent)

	Percentage Annual Average Stock (Investment Project Number)				
	1990-1992	1993-1995	1996-1998	1999-2001	2002-2003
TOTAL CHINESE OUTWARD FDI (US$ 10 000)	133,847.53 (1057)	176,010.77 (1765)	235,466.77 (2173)	377,761.70 (2855)	1,038,208 76 (7214)
Percentage distribution by area:					
DEVELOPED COUNTRIES	69.44 (384)	64.12 (574)	49.95 (652)	36.11 (759)	22.60 (1818)
Western Europe	2.62 (81)	2.63 (108)	2.21 (122)	1.72 (141)	4.15 (430)
European Union (15 countries)	2.29 (71)	2.38 (97)	2.01 (110)	1.58 (129)	4.08 (412)
Denmark	0.02 (2)	0.02 (2)	0.01 (2)	0.01 (2)	2.22 (3)
Germany	0.52 (21)	0.48 (27)	0.42 (30)	0.36 (35)	0.61 (159)
France	0.58 (8)	0.52 (12)	0.41 (14)	0.26 (16)	0.32 (54)
Italy	0.22 (6)	0.17 (6)	0.13 (6)	0.22 (9)	0.25 (32)
UK	0.33 (6)	0.33 (8)	0.29 (10)	0.22 (13)	0.24 (55)
Other Western Europe (3 countries)	0.33 (11)	0.25 (11)	0.20 (12)	0.14 (12)	0.07 (18)
North America	41.59 (186)	39.86 (291)	31.25 (335)	23.67 (401)	12.82 (894)
USA	22.19 (137)	18.87 (217)	15.98 (256)	13.65 (311)	8.58 (745)
Canada	19.40 (49)	20.98 (74)	15.27 (79)	10.03 (90)	4.24 (150)
Other developed countries (4 countries)	25.22 (117)	21.63 (174)	16.49 (194)	10.71 (217)	5.62 (494)
Australia	23.34 (56)	18.39 (85)	13.93 (95)	9.03 (110)	4.31 (220)
Japan	0.71 (56)	0.78 (77)	0.68 (85)	0.46 (90)	0.83 (243)
New Zealand	1.18 (5)	2.46 (11)	1.88 (14)	1.22 (16)	0.47 (27)
DEVELOPING COUNTRIES	30.56 (673)	35.88 (1191)	50.05 (1521)	63.89 (2096)	77.40 (5397)
Africa	4.03 (111)	5.18 (173)	11.02 (259)	16 07 (401)	8.40 (612)
North Africa (6 countries)	0.20 (10)	0.10 (3)	0.37 (5)	0.70 (15)	0.50 (30)
Egypt	0.14 (3)	0.10 (3)	0.37 (5)	0.70 (15)	0.50 (30)
Morocco	0.003 (5)	0.05 (10)	0.04 (10)	0.07 (14)	0.07 (24)
Sudan	0.00 (0)	0.00 (1)	0.32 (6)	0.30 (8)	0.20 (14)
Other Africa (46 countries)	3.83 (101)	4.99 (156)	10.27 (235)	14.93 (358)	7.55 (524)
Zambia	0.24 (3)	0.20 (4)	0.91 (8)	2.77 (15)	1.29 (18)
South Africa	0.02 (1)	0.45 (14)	1.95 (39)	2.44 (76)	1.18 (103)
Mali	0.00 (1)	0.42 (2)	1.20 (3)	1.29 (5)	0.56 (5)
Nigeria	0.51 (11)	0.68 (18)	0.65 (21)	0.69 (27)	0.48 (56)
United Republic of Tanzania	0.15 (2)	0.19 (6)	0.69 (9)	1.02 (13)	0.40 (20)
Zimbabwe	0.19 (1)	0.14 (1)	0.88 (4)	0.85 (9)	0.34 (15)

	Percentage Annual Average Stock (Investment Project Number)				
	1990-1992	1993-1995	1996-1998	1999-2001	2002-2003
Congo, Democratic Republic	0.00 (1)	0.00 (1)	0.12 (3)	0.64 (7)	0.30 (10)
Mauritius	0.47 (14)	0.39 (16)	0.30 (18)	0.33 (20)	0.30 (26)
Kenya	0.05 (4)	0.07 (9)	0.33 (14)	0.42 (18)	0.22 (28)
Ghana	0.07 (1)	0.05 (1)	0.08 (3)	0.46 (14)	0.20 (21)
Gabon	0.22 (4)	0.19 (4)	0.32 (7)	0.40 (11)	0.19 (16)
Cote d'Ivoire	0.05 (4)	0.03 (4)	0.27 (7)	0.39 (12)	0.18 (22)
Cameroon	0.05 (5)	0.05 (6)	0.20 (9)	0.38 (14)	0.16 (18)
Mozambique	0.01 (1)	0.02 (1)	0.05 (2)	0.28 (5)	0.14 (6)
Liberia	0.14 (5)	0.42 (7)	0.31 (7)	0.20 (7)	0.12 (13)
Latin America & the Caribbean	4.87 (72)	4.96 (121)	10.04 (147)	13.83 (207)	7.13 (372)
South America (12 countries)	*3.64 (45)*	*3.19 (70)*	*8.40 (85)*	*8.89 (109)*	*4.18 (203)*
Peru	0.06 (2)	0.14 (6)	5.12 (8)	5.23 (11)	1.94 (22)
Brazil	0.83 (10)	0.72 (15)	1.38 (21)	1.78 (27)	1.20 (70)
Chile	1.60 (4)	1.24 (5)	0.93 (6)	0.55 (6)	0.24 (19)
Argentina	0.03 (6)	0.11 (10)	0.16 (13)	0.20 (18)	0.11 (28)
Guyana	0.32 (1)	0.26 (2)	0.20 (2)	0.46 (5)	0.17 (6)
Suriname	0.00 (0)	0.00 (0)	0.00 (0)	0.00 (1)	0.14 (3)
Other Latin America & Caribbean (18 countries)	*1.23 (27)*	*1.78 (52)*	*1.64 (62)*	*4.94 (98)*	*2.95 (169)*
Mexico	0.38 (9)	0.92 (27)	0.83 (30)	3.60 (35)	1.61 (46)
British Virgin Islands	(0)	(0)	(0)	(17)	(45)
Bermuda	0.37 (2)	0.28 (2)	0.33 (3)	0.36 (8)	0.78 (11)
Cuba	0.00 (0)	0.00 (0)	0.00 (0)	0.35 (3)	0.16 (9)
Honduras	0.00 (0)	0.06 (1)	0.06 (1)	0.30 (4)	0.16 (5)
Central & Eastern Europe (18 countries)	4.17 (114)	5.76 (251)	4.85 (280)	4.44 (344)	4.62 (690)
Russian Federation	4.09 (106)	5.43 (224)	4.14 (240)	3.09 (284)	3.63 (503)
Czech Republic	(2)	(3)	(3)	(4)	(14)
Georgia	0.00 (0)	0.00 (0)	0.01 (1)	0.24 (2)	0.25 (5)
Asia	16.61 (358)	18.71 (606)	22.22 (790)	27.87 (1090)	56.60 (3662)
West Asia (Middle East) (12 countries)	*1.09 (35)*	*1.17 (47)*	*0.98 (51)*	*1.61 (67)*	*1.46 (137)*
United Arab Emirates	0.32 (12)	0.38 (16)	0.33 (19)	0.44 (25)	0.47 (74)
Yemen	0.24 (7)	0.22 (8)	0.18 (8)	0.49 (9)	0.35 (10)
Central Asia (8 countries)	*0.09 (5)*	*0.26 (19)*	*0.49 (34)*	*1.50 (75)*	*0.91 (132)*

	Percentage Annual Average Stock (Investment Project Number)				
	1990-1992	1993-1995	1996-1998	1999-2001	2002-2003
Kazakhstan	0.01 (2)	0.08 (12)	0.16 (17)	0.80 (36)	0.40 (55)
Kyrgyzstan	0.02 (1)	0.06 (4)	0.16 (8)	0.46 (19)	0.29 (32)
Uzbekistan	0.04 (2)	0.09 (2)	0.12 (6)	0.17 (15)	0.17 (32)
South, East and SE Asia (20 countries)	*15.42 (319)*	*17.28 (540)*	*20.74 (705)*	*24.75 (948)*	*54.22 (3393)*
Hong Kong (China SAR)	8.12 (116)	8.08 (146)	9.35 (176)	8.83 (240)	40.53 (2062)
Thailand	2.94 (76)	3.15 (120)	2.83 (135)	2.96 (146)	2.30 (240)
Korea, Republic	0.23 (2)	0.39 (9)	0.39 (17)	0.35 (23)	1.98 (67)
Macao (China SAR)	1.19 (24)	1.02 (26)	2.11 (40)	1.55 (57)	1.92 (234)
Cambodia	0.00 (0)	0.11 (4)	1.17 (21)	2.40 (47)	1.37 (63)
Indonesia	0.16 (4)	0.78 (27)	0.96 (37)	1.45 (43)	1.12 (62)
Viet Nam	0.00 (0)	0.03 (2)	0.14 (8)	0.86 (27)	0.86 (82)
Singapore	0.65 (26)	0.81 (49)	0.87 (69)	0.86 (90)	0.82 (180)
Myanmar	0.02 (1)	0.06 (4)	0.18 (11)	0.93 (19)	0.64 (38)
Mongolia	0.07 (6)	0.14 (22)	0.12 (25)	1.28 (53)	0.63 (74)
Malaysia	0.82 (21)	1.21 (51)	1.17 (71)	0.85 (80)	0.36 (101)
India	0.00 (0)	0.00 (1)	0.04 (3)	0.41 (9)	0.20 (15)
Philippines	0.39 (12)	0.49 (25)	0.44 (29)	0.35 (31)	0.16 (40)
The Pacific (9 countries)	0.88 (18)	1.27 (41)	1.92 (46)	1.69 (55)	0.67 (62)
Papua New Guinea	0.45 (5)	0.56 (9)	1.31 (12)	1.16 (17)	0.43 (20)
Fiji	0.21(6)	0.29 (11)	0.26 (13)	0.24 (14)	0.10 (16)

Notes: The principal host countries of Chinese FDI are listed for each region. The total number of recipients of Chinese FDI is shown in the region heading. Regions are as per UNCTAD (1998). Countries are in declining rank order for the period 2002-2003.
Source: Calculated from MOFCOM, Almanac of China's Foreign Economic Relations and Trade (various years) and China Commerce Yearbook (2004)

Chan (2003) assert that, even though state-owned, the majority of Chinese MNEs are motivated primarily by profit maximization and, consequently, that they have 'more or less the same motivations as those in other countries' (p. 284). Similarly, Balfour (2005) reports that, despite being 50 per cent owned by Chinese authorities, the internationalization strategies and operations of the Chinese computer company Lenovo are based solely on commercial considerations. Moreover, greater openness of the Chinese economy and the technological upgrading that is occurring as a result of spillover and demonstration effects associated with inbound FDI to China, as well as improvements in China's stocks of human and intellectual capital, may have resulted in at least a proportion of the recent growth in Chinese ODI being attributable to enhancements of the competitiveness of Chinese firms through some genuine augmentation of firm-specific advantages rather than merely being a consequence of direct and indirect government support. This debate provides a rationale for the present study. Given these dynamics, it is now relevant to assess the extent to which the investment location decisions of Chinese MNEs, when considered in aggregate, are informed by firm-level strategic and market considerations (that is autonomous, discretionary decision-taking) or whether they are influenced by national economic imperatives and other similar pressures (that is decision-taking constrained by government). By evaluating the extent to which Chinese ODI is explicable by conventional FDI theory (which is founded mainly upon observations of profit-maximizing industrialized country MNEs) we can draw inferences about the degree to which outbound investment-related decision-taking in Chinese firms is shaped by government influence and fiat or, for example, by market forces.

In order for these interactions to be captured, it is important that modelling of the determinants of Chinese ODI draws on literature which provides a general theoretical understanding of why firms invest equity abroad, as well as that on developing and transition economy ODI, in addition to extant work specifically on the internationalization of Chinese firms. This we do in the following section.

3. TOWARDS A MODEL OF THE DETERMINANTS OF CHINESE ODI

In this section, we review the 'traditional' determinants of FDI established in the literature, and comment on the extent to which they are likely to influence the historical distribution of Chinese ODI.

3.1 Market Size

Market size, measured in GDP or GDP per capita, is generally recognized as a significant determinant of FDI flows from industrialized countries (Chakrabarti, 2001). Under the market size hypothesis, it is argued that opportunities for the more efficient allocation of resources and the generation of scale and scope economies through FDI increase with market size (UNCTAD, 1998). A number of studies demonstrate that FDI flow and absolute market size are positively associated (see Chakrabarti, 2001 and Pearce et al., 1992). Recent research argues for the growing importance of offensive market-seeking motives among Chinese MNEs (Buckley et al., 2006; Taylor, 2002; Deng, 2004; Zhang, 2003). It might be expected that this activity is increasingly being directed towards large markets. However, both theory and observation suggest that market size might not necessarily be a strong determinant of Chinese ODI.

Although developing country MNEs generally possess a limited set of ownership advantages relative to their industrialized country counterparts, research has established that they can achieve a competitive advantage over local and foreign firms in other developing countries because they are able to draw upon the skills and experience acquired as a consequence of their home country embeddedness: that is their familiarity with operating in a developing country milieu (Lall, 1983). Lau (2003), for example, argues that developing country MNEs often confront an institutional and political environment abroad comparable to that already experienced at home, with similar constraints, bureaucratic hurdles, customer needs, barriers to entry and so forth. In other words, developing country MNEs may enjoy fewer 'liabilities of foreignness' compared with industrialized country firms when they enter other developing markets. Also, developing country MNEs may be able to meet particular local demand and price conditions and quality needs in other developing countries because they are already skilled at innovating appropriate products and services. They may also be able to deploy or customize mature, discarded or redundant technologies they have previously acquired from industrialized country firms (perhaps via international technology licensing and joint venture agreements) but which are still marketable in less advanced countries (Monkiewicz, 1986; Lau, 2003; Lecraw, 1977). This might be done by downscaling, simplifying or substituting local inputs or increasing the labour intensity of production, for example (Shenkar and Luo, 2004). For all these reasons, market-seeking Chinese MNEs may be predisposed to exploit their firm-specific advantages by investing in relatively less advanced economies (with low GDP per capita ratios). If so, this strategy is at odds with the standard market size and market growth hypotheses.

On the other hand, developing country MNEs are also known to flourish in niche markets in industrialized countries overlooked by larger firms (Child and Rodrigues, 2005). In recent years, an expressed goal of state-motivated Chinese ODI is to improve access to advanced proprietary technology, immobile strategic assets and other capabilities abroad (Warner et al., 2004; Taylor, 2002; Deng, 2003; Wall, 1997; Zhang 2003), through both greenfield entry and acquisition. To illustrate, Wu and Sia (2002) report that a major reason why Haier, the Chinese household appliance company, established a new factory in the USA was to obtain new technology. Because location advantages like these are found predominantly in more advanced economies, asset-seeking Chinese ODI is likely to be positively associated with more advanced host countries. For these reasons, we cannot predict a priori the relationship between market size and Chinese ODI. However, we do note that, from our previous discussion of the evolution of government policy and the motivations of Chinese firms, changes in market-seeking and asset-seeking firm behaviour may be discernable over time.

3.2 Market Growth

Under the market growth hypothesis, it is posited that rapidly growing economies present more profit generating opportunities than those which are growing more slowly or not at all (Lim, 1983). Theory thus proposes that market-oriented, horizontal FDI will be positively associated with economic growth (Chakrabarti, 2001). However, caution should be exercised in assuming a priori that this will be the case for Chinese ODI. First, for many years Chinese ODI has been directed towards the acquisition of information and knowledge on how to operate at an international level, especially during the 1980s and early 1990s (Buckley et al., 2006; Ye, 1992; Zhan, 1995). Such ODI would not necessarily be directed to quickly growing markets but rather towards those economies with higher levels of human and intellectual capital. Second, in recent years, the strategic asset-seeking motive of improving access to foreign proprietary technology, brands and local distribution networks has seen Chinese MNEs become increasingly acquisitive (Warner et al., 2004). Amongst the most renowned and widely reported cases within the timeframe of this study are the purchases of Schneider Technology (Germany) by the Chinese consumer electronics company TCL in 2003, the acquisition of Meneghetti SPA's Italian refrigerator manufacturing plant by Haier in 2001 and the purchase in 2001 of the US-based company Universal Automobile Industries by the Wanxiang Group, the Chinese manufacturer of vehicle components. In many of these acquisitions, especially those involving European and

US firms, the target company at the time was ailing or insolvent. For these reasons, it may well be that low or declining economic growth rates in the host country are positively associated with Chinese ODI.

3.3   Exchange Rate

Theory asserts that the lower the exchange value of a country's currency, the more attractive it will be as an investment location (Aliber, 1970; Chakrabarti, 2001). This is because the home currency price of assets denominated in a foreign currency falls as the host currency weakens relative to the currency of the foreign investor. Stevens (1993) concludes that the weight of evidence for inward FDI flows into the US is that a dollar appreciation reduces US FDI inflows. Froot and Stein (1989) employ finance theory to propose that a firm's potential for financing a foreign acquisition is an inverse function of the target firm's net worth in host country currency. This would argue that appreciation of the host country currency relative to China would lead to a fall in Chinese outward FDI to that country.

3.4   Trade Intensity with China

As mentioned above, Chinese ODI during the 1980s and early 1990s was generally undertaken to assist Chinese exporting firms. The aim was to enable Chinese firms to generate foreign exchange earnings, to obtain market information, and for overseas affiliates and branch offices to provide international trade, transportation and financial services to the parent company (Wu and Sia, 2002; Ye, 1992; Zhan, 1995). In some cases, these small scale investment projects served as 'toe in the water' operations for more substantial investment later, a development which in part mirrors the Chinese government's 'trial-and-error' approach that generally characterized national economic reform in the 1980s and 1990s. In 1999, direct government support in the form of export tax rebates, foreign exchange assistance and financial support was introduced as part of the 'Go Global' policy to further foster FDI in trade-related activities and promote Chinese exports, especially in the textiles, machinery and electrical equipment sectors (Wong and Chan, 2003). We therefore expect a positive association between Chinese ODI and a country's position as a trading partner for China, especially after 1999.

3.5   Geography and Chinese ODI

A number of studies have identified an incremental, or stages, model to the internationalization of firms (Johanson and Vahlne, 1977). This model proposes that early investments are commonly placed by firms in locations that are geographically close to the home market and in countries where relationships and experience have already been established through prior trading relations. In the case of developing countries, this is observed in work on MNEs from Hong Kong (Lau, 1992, 2003), South Korea (Erramilli et al., 1999), India and Argentina (Ferrantino, 1992; Pradhan, 2003), Brazil (Villela, 1983) and among large enterprises from Malaysia (Zin, 1999). The model also proposes that early investments will occur in countries that have a similar cultural background to the home country (Johanson and Vahlne, 1977) and where ethnic or familial ties with a specific minority population in the host country can be exploited to reduce investment and commercial risk (Lau, 2003; Wells, 1983; Lecraw, 1977; Zhan, 1995). In the case of developing country MNEs, some research shows that subsequent investment decisions may be less influenced by cultural or ethnic ties, however (for example, Lau, 2003).

The Overseas Chinese are generally acknowledged to have contributed much to the integration of China into the world economy, especially in helping to facilitate inbound FDI from those Asian countries with a significant ethnic Chinese population, such as Singapore, Taiwan and Hong Kong (Yeung, 2000; Henley et al., 1999; Ng and Tuan, 2002; Yeung, 1999; Sikorski and Menkhoff, 2000).[2] It can be argued that the Chinese diaspora and the importance of *'guanxi'* relationships and networks have had a similar effect on the destination of outbound FDI (Standifird and Marshall, 2000; Luo, 1997; Tong, 2003). Ethnic and familial relationships may constitute a firm-specific advantage to Chinese MNEs because these can be used to reduce investment risk in host markets. In this way, established *'guanxi'* networks may compensate 'latecomer' Chinese MNEs (Sung, 1996; Braeutigam, 2003; Li, 2003). Such networks are especially prevalent in Asia, of course. Consequently, Chinese firms may reveal a propensity to invest in geographically proximate Asian countries. However, we also note that the high level of financial and political support provided to some state-owned firms by their supervisory agency may mean that network effects are of no consequence. To capture these interactions, we introduce a geographic distance variable to our model. On the one hand, Chinese ODI might be positively associated with the extent of the Overseas Chinese diaspora, the effect of which is likely to be stronger the closer a country is to China geographically. On the other, internalization theory asserts that market-seeking firms will export to geographically proximate countries and will serve more distant markets using FDI (Buckley and Casson, 1981). For these reasons, therefore, we do not make an a priori prediction about the relationship between geographic distance and Chinese

ODI.

3.6 Inflation

FDI is likely to be discouraged in those countries that have volatile and unpredictable inflation rates because this creates uncertainty and renders aspects of long term corporate planning problematic, especially with respect to price-setting and profit expectation. Moreover, high inflation rates generally constrain the export performance of both domestic and foreign firms because rising prices of local inputs reduces cost-competitiveness in third markets. Conventional wisdom would predict a negative association between Chinese ODI and inflation.

3.7 Political Risk

Internalization theory posits that market-oriented companies will demonstrate a propensity to operate in less risky countries through local production instead of arm's length modes such as exporting and licensing. Similarly, resources-oriented firms will generally limit their commitment to countries with high political risk levels because of the high levels of sunk cost, which this type of investment often entails (Buckley and Casson, 1981, 1999). Political risk involves government interference with business activities as well as factors which generally constitute a business risk such as government stability, internal and external violence and threat of expropriation (Kobrin, 1979). Thus, conventional wisdom asserts that higher levels of political risk negatively affect inbound FDI flow (Chakrabarti, 2001). However, there are a number of reasons why this might not hold true in the case of Chinese MNEs. First, China's political and ideological heritage may have led to Chinese ODI being preferentially directed to fellow Communist countries. These countries generally score high on standard political risk measures, which are designed and used primarily to inform on the decision-taking of industrialized country firms (World Bank, 2006). Second, natural resource-seeking Chinese ODI directed towards countries associated with high levels of risk, such as the Central Asian countries (for example for oil-related projects) and the African countries (for example for agricultural, oil and minerals-related projects) may have been facilitated by close political connections between them and China. This may have helped to ameliorate risk-related concerns for Chinese investors. Third, the level of direct and indirect support and assistance that Chinese firms receive from the Chinese government or their supervisory agency may enable them to invest in countries that might be regarded as risky by profit-maximizing firms. Finally, given the relative inexperience of many Chinese firms concerning the establishment and management of operations abroad, some FDI projects may have been made without full and proper consideration of attendant risk (Wong and Chan, 2003). The first three propositions would be revealed if we find a negative association between Chinese ODI and the measure of political risk employed. The fourth proposition would be revealed if we find no statistically significant association between our political risk variable and aggregate Chinese ODI since inadequate due diligence would lead to investment in risky and non-risky markets in equal measure.

3.8   Natural Resources Endowments

Research demonstrates that a prime objective of the Chinese government is to ensure the supply of domestically-scarce resources through ODI, an imperative which has grown in significance along with the Chinese economy (Buckley et al., 2006; Deutsche Bank Research [DBR], 2006; Ye, 1992; Zhan, 1995). Key commodities in short supply in China include crude petroleum, iron, ores and minerals, timber, fishery and agricultural products (DBR, 2006; Wu and Sia, 2002; Cai, 1999). The driver for FDI, which may or may not be state-initiated, is to circumvent imperfections associated with raw material markets. Examples of China's politically-motivated quest for natural resources within the timeframe of our study include the acquisition of Devon Energy's Indonesian petrochemicals operations by PetroChina and China National Petroleum Corporation (CNPC) in 2002; the sale of the Indonesian operations of Repsol-YPF SA to China National Offshore Oil Corporation (CNOOC) in 2002 (DBR, 2006), and the purchase of a controlling stake in Aktobemunaigaz Oil Production Company by CNPC in 1997. For these reasons, a positive association between the natural resources endowments of a host country and Chinese ODI is expected. However, issues of indivisibility and the small number of high value investments that are commonplace in natural resources investments may obscure clear trends.

3.9   Market Openness

Conventional wisdom suggests that the more open a country is to international investment, the more attractive that country is as a destination for FDI (Chakrabarti, 2001). Openness is included in our model for completeness. However, the incorporation of this factor presupposes that FDI is driven by market considerations and this may not hold for Chinese ODI, much of which may be influenced by government, as we discuss above.

3.10 Policy Direction

The above discussion points strongly to the fact that Chinese government policies towards outbound capital flows have greatly affected ODI patterns and trends. Although the policy dimension is an important component of any formal model of Chinese ODI, it is a difficult variable to operationalize. Lack of transparency concerning the relevant regulations and incentive policies renders opaque the institutional framework within which Chinese ODI is conducted, even for investing firms themselves (Wong and Chan, 2003). We therefore incorporate into our model one of the most obvious aspects of Chinese policy liberalization of recent years, namely the introduction in 1999 of the 'Go Global' (or 'zou chu qu') policy. This led to a significant period of domestic market liberalization, and numerous sub-national level authorities increasingly internationalized those enterprises under their supervision. To investigate the affect of liberalization on Chinese ODI, we introduce a time dummy for 1999 and subsequent years.

4. THE MODEL

The above discussion indicates that a well-specified model to explain Chinese ODI can be constructed as follows:

FDI = f (Market size, Per capita market size, Market growth,
Exchange rate, Exports, Imports, Geographic distance, Inflation,
Political risk, Natural resources endowment, FDI stock,
Time dummy)   (5.1)

We hypothesize a log-linear relationship, giving the following model (W[114] denotes the log operator):

$$LFDI = \alpha + \beta_1 LGDP + \beta_2 LGDPP + \beta_3 GGDP + \beta_4 LERATE$$
$$+ \beta_5 LEXP + \beta_6 LIMP + \beta_7 LDIS + \beta_8 LINF + \beta_9 LPOLI$$
$$+ \beta_{10} LOIL + \beta_{11} LINFDI + \beta_{12} TD + \varepsilon_{it} \qquad (5.2)$$

5. DATA AND METHOD

5.1 Data

The dependent variable we use in this study is annual outward FDI flow from China to individual host countries calculated as the difference between annual stock levels reported by MOFCOM for the years 1990 to 2003 in the *Almanac of China's Foreign Economic Relations and Trade* (various issues) and its successor volume, *China's Yearbook of Commerce* (MOFCOM, 2004). In common with standard practice we estimate a log-linear model and thus the dependent variable is the log of FDI outflows. Observations where FDI flows were reported as a negative figure are excluded.[3] Omitted observations account for less than 3 per cent of the total and are therefore not likely to have biased the findings. Data for more recent years are not available. Our dataset also excludes ODI not captured by MOFCOM in the formal approval mechanism, for whatever reason. This includes a relatively small but indeterminate number of official FDI projects permitted by national and sub-national government agencies which were not reported to MOFCOM. Such investments arise because discretionary local politics have at times contradicted national Chinese law and investment procedure, allowing local government agencies to permit or undertake outward FDI projects without any formal procedure and which were therefore not reported to the relevant national administration (Ding, 2000). Also excluded is a potentially much larger, but again indeterminate, number of illegal, fraudulent and unofficial capital transfers made abroad. Many of these are transfers intended for re-investment in China in order to benefit from fiscal and other investment incentives granted to owners of inbound foreign capital – the so-called 'round-tripping' phenomenon (Ding, 2000; Deng, 2004; Wu and Sia, 2002; Wall, 1997; Sung, 1996).

Data on our independent variables were extracted from the following sources. The World Bank's World Development Indicators (April 2005) provided us with data for the market size proxies, namely GDP (*LGDP*), GDP per capita (*LGDPP*) and GDP growth rate (*GGDP*), as well as for the exchange rate (*LERATE*). Although per capita GDP is the most commonly used proxy for market size, since it reflects income levels, it may introduce bias because it may underestimate the relative attractiveness of large population countries (Chakrabarti, 2001). On the other hand, the alternative market size proxy, absolute GDP, may also be a poor indicator of market potential, especially for many developing countries, since it reflects the size of an economy rather than income (Chakrabarti, 2001). Given the high level of Chinese ODI in developing countries, and the exploratory nature of this study, we decided to incorporate both measures in our model. *LERATE* is calculated as an annual average of local currency units relative to the US dollar (against which the Renminbi was pegged over the years under study), with a rising number indicating a weakening host country currency.

The variable *LOIL* is the annual worldwide export volume (in thousands of tonnes) of crude oil and liquid natural gas reported for the host country by the International Energy Agency. To capture trade intensity, we use the value of China's exports to (*LEXP*), and imports from (*LIMP*), the host country as reported by the Chinese National Bureau of Statistics in the *China Statistical Yearbook*. Geographic distance (*LDIS*) is the distance between capital cities as calculated using a web-based city distance calculator (www.geobytes.com). The annual inflation rate of the host country was obtained from the World Economic Outlook Database of the International Monetary Fund. For political risk (*LPOLI*) we use the International Country Risk Guide (ICRG) published by the PRS Group, a standard index used in this type of work as it comprises a comprehensive set of factors that constitute political risk (World Bank, 2006). The ICRG composite index ranges from 0 (for insecure and unstable) to 100 (for secure and stable) for countries. For a host country's FDI stock level (*LINFDI*), we use the ratio of inward FDI stock to GDP as reported in UNCTAD's online FDI database. All monetary data for the host country variables are converted into constant (2000) US dollars. Missing country level data necessitated the deletion of a small number of observations from our panel, the final version of which incorporates 53 host countries for Chinese ODI. Table 5.3 summarizes the data sources and expected signs for the independent variables. We report in Table 5.4 the correlation matrix for the full sample only and conclude that there are no significant correlations between explanatory variables. The same conclusions hold for the correlation matrices on the two sub-samples. We do not present these matrices here, but they are available on request. The full specification of the equations as indicated by theory is employed.

5.2 Method

Pooled ordinary least squares (POLS) and random effects estimators (REs) are used to estimate equation (5.2). A fixed effects (FEs) model cannot be used as the equation includes variables which are invariant with respect to country or time. A Lagrangian multiplier (LM) test was conducted to identify whether POLS or REs furnishes the better model. An LM test value significantly different from zero suggests that the REs estimation is preferable to that of POLS.

We investigate the impact of changes in the policy regime dating from 1999 using a time dummy that takes the value 1 for 1999 and proceeding years. Theory suggests that these policy changes might influence the decision making of Chinese investors. Second, and as our discussions indicate, China's preference to invest in less developed countries may

Table 5.3 The locational determinants of Chinese outward FDI by country

Variable	Proxy and Measure	Expected sign
Chinese outward FDI (dependent variable)	*LFDI*: Approved China's outward FDI calculated from MOFCOM data (see text)	
Market size (GDP)	*LGDP*: Host country's GDP	+/−
Market size (GDP per capita)	*LGDPP*: Host country's GDP per capita	+/−
Market growth	*GGDP*: Host country's annual GDP growth	+/−
Exchange rate	*LERATE*: Host country's official annual average exchange rate	+
Trade intensity with China	*LEXP* and LIMP: China's exports to and imports from the host country	+
Geographic distance from China	*LDIS*: Geographic distance between the capitals of the host and home country	+/−
Inflation rate	*LINF*: Host country's annual inflation rate	+
Political risk	*LPOLI*: Host country's political risk rating	−
Natural resources endowment	*LOIL*: Exports of oil and natural gas products worldwide	+
Inward FDI stock of host country	*LINFDI*: Ratio of inward FDI stock to GDP of the host country	+
Time dummy	*TD*: Time dummy to capture the years following the introduction of China's 'go global' policy from 1999 onwards.	+

Table 5.4 Correlation matrix for the full sample
(695 observations)

	LGDP	LGGPP	GGDP	LERATE	LEXP	LIMP	LDIS	LINF	LPOLI	LOIL	LINFDI
LGDP	1										
LGGP P	0.68 16	1									
GGDP	−0.0093	−0.0157	1								
LERA TE	− 0.31	− 0.4763	0.168 5	1							
LEXP	0.7716	0.5183	0.1464	−0.1087	1						
LIMP	0.7725	0.5330	−0.0141	−0.2023	0.8057	1					
LDIS	−0.0972	−0.0441	−0.0828	−0.2030	−0.3806	−0.3016	1				
LINF	−0.1273	−0.1282	−0.2679	−0.0915	−0.1853	−0.0415	0.0141	1			
LPOLI	0.4574	0.7098	0.0094	−0.3554	0.3957	0.3958	−0.0452	−0.1183	1		
LOIL	−0.0084	0.0912	−0.0928	−0.0911	−0.1146	0.0784	0.1932	0.1411	0.2426	1	
LINFDI	−0.0283	0.2307	0.2568	−0.0452	0.2528	0.0959	0.1659	−0.2922	0.3145	−0.0383	1

reflect a different model of investment behaviour arising from state policy. To investigate this, we distinguish between developed and less-developed host countries by classifying them as either members or non-members of the Organisation for Economic Cooperation and Development (OECD). The model described by equation (5.2) is therefore estimated across two sub-samples.

Table 5.5   Estimation results

	REs (1)	OLS OECD (2)	REs non-OECD (3)
LGDP	0.3116 (0.2256)	1.1746 (0.4312)***	0.2386 (0.2727)
LGDPP	−0.4995** (0.2141)	−0.1837 (0.2910)	−0.3286 (0.2605)
GGDP	0.0359* (0.0211)	−0.647 (0.0624)	−0.0199 (0.0214)
LERATE	0.1404* (0.0719)	0.7805 (0.1349)***	0.1424 (0.0813)*
LEXP	0.3869 (0.1471)***	0.0334 (0.2849)	0.3956 (0.1614)**
LIMP	0.2058 (0.825)**	0.4214 (0.1854)**	0.1874 (0.0843)**
LDIS	−0.0429 (0.3946)	1.4357 (0.6417)**	−0.3639 (0.4725)
LINF	−0.0001 (0.0003)	0.0052 (0.0276)	−0.0002 (0.0003)
LPOLI	−0.6935 (0.8329)	−0.3969 (2.4423)	0.2984 (0.8793)
LOIL	0.0554 (0.1236)	1.3774 (0.2821)***	−0.0529 (0.1284)
LINFDI	0.3685 (0.1698)**	0.6389 (0.3015)**	0.1821 (0.1981)
TD	0.5687 (0.2309)**	0.3496 (0.3790)	0.8363 (0.2839)***
Observations	695	274	421
LM Test	$X^2 = 125.62$***	1.17	52.68***
Adj R²	0.4529	0.4008	0.4585

Notes: 1. Standard errors are in parentheses.
2. ***, ** and * indicate that the coefficient is significant at the 1%, 5% and 10% levels, respectively.

6. RESULTS AND DISCUSSION

The empirical results obtained from the POLS and the REs equations are similar. The large value of the LM statistics indicates in favour of the

REs against POLS for the entire sample and also for the non-OECD country model. However, for the model confined only to OECD host countries, the LM test indicates that the POLS estimation is preferred, and these are the results we report.

From the RE model result for the entire sample, shown in column (1) of Table 5.5, the exchange rate (*LERATE*), Chinese exports (*LEXP*), Chinese imports from the host country (*LIMP*), market openness (*LINFDI*) and the time dummy (*TD*) all attain statistical significance at different levels and are positively signed. Market size measured on a per capita basis (*LGDPP*) and market growth rate (*GGDP*) are also statistically significant at different levels, but are negatively signed. The following variables do not attain statistical significance in this model: absolute market size (*LGDP*), geographic distance (*LDIS*), inflation (*LINF*), political risk (*LPOLI*) and natural resource endowments (*LOIL*). This is despite them having an important place in the theory of FDI. These findings draw attention to the possibility that Chinese investors are motivated differently from industrialized country investors over the period under study.

With respect to the positive association between the exchange rate (*LERATE*) and Chinese ODI, since the variable is constructed as the price of foreign exchange (for the Chinese investor) a rise in the variable represents a foreign currency depreciation relative to the Renminbi (which at the time was pegged to the US dollar). We find that a depreciation in the host currency leads to an increase in Chinese FDI, as hypothesized.

Our findings for the two trade-related variables, *LEXP* and *LIMP*, also follow conventional theory. The positive association between these two variables and Chinese ODI indicates that the more a country trades with China the more Chinese ODI that country receives. A 1 per cent increase in Chinese exports to a host country results in a 0.39 per cent increase in Chinese ODI. Likewise, a 1 per cent increase in imports from the host country to China leads to a 0.21 per cent increase in Chinese ODI. These results reflect conventional wisdom in that investment follows trade intensity. It conforms to the view that a key policy of the Chinese government has been the promotion of domestic exports through trade-supporting FDI. This corroborates the findings of Buckley et al. (2006), Ye (1992) and Zhan (1995), amongst others. The finding for Chinese imports (*LIMP*) suggests that at least a proportion of Chinese ODI has occurred 'upstream' in the supply chain in order to secure access to inputs for use in domestic production as well as consumption.

The findings for our measure of market openness to FDI (*LINFDI*) reveal that a 1 per cent increase in total FDI inflow to a host country is associated with a 0.37 per cent increase in Chinese ODI. This, again, is the conventional result. Its importance demonstrates that Chinese investors have targeted more open host economies over the time period under study. Also positive and significant is the time dummy (*TD*), which is designed to capture the effect of reforms undertaken as part of China's 'Go Global' policies introduced in 1999. Our finding provides some evidence to support the view that qualitative changes in Chinese policy from 1999 onwards did lead to an increase in Chinese outward FDI. One interpretation is that policy changes freed state-owned enterprises to invest abroad for reasons other than the promotion of exports alone; that is, for reasons that were not directly trade- and market-related.

Two of our market-related variables are found to be significant and negative. A 1 per cent increase in GDP per capita of the host country is associated with a 0.50 per cent decrease in Chinese ODI, while a similar increase in GDP growth is associated with a 0.04 per cent decrease. Chinese ODI is revealed to be preferentially directed towards low income countries and to markets that are growing slowly. Ostensibly, this suggests that market-seeking motives have only limited power to explain Chinese ODI. However, a second explanation is that, as reported for developing country firms in general (Lall, 1983; Wells, 1977), Chinese MNEs are demonstrating an ability to compete more successfully in other developing countries, perhaps because capabilities developed in their home market (that is, their knowledge of operating in a domestic context characterized by opacity and rapid changes to the regulatory, legislative and operations environments) are able to be transferred and exploited abroad, and where lower liabilities of foreignness are enjoyed. The association with low growth markets also hints to the fact that Chinese MNEs have proactively invested in low performing economies, perhaps because of the low investment costs associated with the purchase of under-performing firms (or sub-divisions of them) in those countries. However, a third explanation is that this finding is a reflection of an inability of Chinese firms to evaluate long term market conditions and economic risk accurately, or that such factors play only a limited role in decision-taking. Several reasons for this can be envisaged. First, access to cheap capital in China through state ownership, soft budget constraints, government initiated credit policies and other ODI incentives may mean that management decision-taking by Chinese firms is predicated upon attitudes to market-related risk that might be regarded as perverse in comparison with industrialized country firms. Second, home country experiences may help Chinese firms to manage and mitigate the risks associated with operating in an environment abroad that is comparable to that found in China. Third, close political connections between China and certain developing host countries may help to facilitate inbound Chinese FDI, irrespective of prevailing risk conditions, especially when politically-motivated natural resources seeking investments are involved. Fourth, for those information and technology-seeking Chinese MNEs, market-related factors such as limited growth potential may be of only limited importance to their investment decision.

Theory suggests that the level of development of the host country may affect the investment decisions of firms. As noted earlier, Chinese government policy towards investment in less developed as opposed to developed countries may also differ. An overview of the results for the two sub-samples of OECD and non-OECD countries in columns (2) and (3) respectively (Table 5.5) indicates that a different model of Chinese investment does indeed apply according to the level of development of the host country. Market size (*LGDP*) is a significant determinant of Chinese ODI within the OECD group. This indicates that Chinese investors preferentially seek out larger developed country markets. This finding accords with conventional wisdom and probably captures that element of Chinese ODI that is market seeking. The exchange rate variable (*LERATE*) is significant and positive for both OECD and non-OECD countries. Again, this is the conventional result and indicates that inbound Chinese FDI is attracted by host currency depreciations, irrespective of whether or not the country is of developed or developing status. The finding for Chinese exports to the host country (*LEXP*) is positive and significant for non-OECD countries only. This indicates that Chinese ODI follows exports among the developing, but not to the developed, countries. This may be an outcome of the export market-seeking motive of Chinese firms, which applies mainly to incremental internationalization towards developing host countries. The geographical distance variable (*LDIS*) is significant for OECD countries only. This result also accords with theory, often encapsulated by gravity trade and FDI models, which posits that the more remote are larger markets, the more likely FDI is to replace trade. The variable for Chinese imports from the host country (*LIMP*) is significant and positive for both OECD and non-OECD countries. Taken together, these results suggest that Chinese investors are attracted to both developed and developing countries that have strong trade relations with China. We find that natural resources endowment (*LOIL*) is positively associated with Chinese FDI but for OECD countries only. This indicates that Chinese investors are resource-seeking and that they preferentially invest in resource endowed countries. This variable is likely to be capturing the large variation between developed countries in respect to resource abundance, and the attractiveness of Chinese MNEs to resource-rich countries such as the USA, Canada and Australia. In contrast, this variable does not discriminate between developing countries on the grounds of resource abundance.

Of the two remaining variables, we find that openness to foreign investment (*LINFDI*) is significant and positive but for the OECD countries only, and that the time dummy (*TD*) is significant and positive for the non-OECD countries only. Both findings conform to conventional wisdom. The former reflects the liberal and progressive approach to inward FDI that is demonstrated by developed countries and this may also have facilitated inward investment by Chinese MNEs. The latter may reflect the earlier discussion that, as China's policy regime has not remained constant, there has been a significant change in the foreign investment behaviour of Chinese enterprises over time. This may have led to Chinese ODI becoming distributed more widely to encompass developing as well as developed host countries (a trend which Table 5.2 also reveals). This finding implies that investment decision-taking was highly constrained by government in the years prior to liberalization in the ODI-related policies and regulations that began in 1999 under the 'Go Global' programme.

7. CONCLUSIONS AND FUTURE RESEARCH

The aim of this study was to advance our understanding of the determinants of Chinese ODI and to investigate whether or not divergence from those known to influence industrialized country FDI can be detected. We find that exchange rate differences, trade intensity and market openness are positively associated with Chinese ODI, as they are in numerous studies of industrialized country ODI (Chakrabarti, 2001). However, we find that decision-taking in Chinese MNEs is more idiosyncratic with respect to relative market size and market growth. We attribute this partly to the possibility that Chinese firms do not perceive market-related opportunities and risk in quite the same way as do industrialized country firms. This may be a consequence of the relative inexperience of Chinese MNEs at host market assessment, or because of the low cost of capital they enjoy, or because they are able to extend abroad successfully their familiarity with operating in a highly regulated and controlled environment at home (that is, as a consequence of their home country embeddedness). Not surprisingly, perhaps, we are also able to detect contrasting determinants between developed and developing host countries, with Chinese ODI to the former being influenced positively by absolute market size, exchange rate, import intensity, geographic distance and natural resources endowments, and to the latter by exchange rate differences, trade intensity and policy changes in China. Therefore, we conclude that the pattern of Chinese ODI observed over the period 1991 to 2003 has been generated by factors that are in part distinctive to China and to China's status as an emerging economy.

Data limitations have meant that labour-related variables are not included in our model. However, this is defensible since, given China's state of development over the years in question, it is unlikely that Chinese ODI will have been driven by labour-related considerations to any great extent. However, further refinement of our model should incorporate more detailed policy and institution-related factors, such as the role of China's foreign exchange regime and the exchange rate policy of the People's Bank of China and the State Administration for Foreign Exchange, for example. Research on the contribution of those positive and negative 'push' factors that arise from market liberalization and other domestic economic reforms on the patterns, motivations and character of Chinese ODI would also be illuminating, as would a more detailed examination of industry effects and firm effects such as size and form of corporate governance.

NOTES

1. In this study and related work (for example, Buckley et al., 2006), the terms China and Mainland China are used interchangeably to refer to the People's Republic of China (PRC). For our purposes, the PRC excludes the special autonomous regions of Hong Kong and Macau, unless specifically stated. The Republic of China (Taiwan) is treated as an independent country. All our statistics and figures respect these distinctions. Regions with disputed borders (for example, the Spratly Islands and the Paracel Islands in the South China Sea) are excluded from our definition of the PRC, as are associated economic activities.
2. Overseas Chinese are defined by Poston et al. (1994, p. 633) as 'all Chinese living outside mainland China and Taiwan, including *Huaqiao* (Chinese citizens residing abroad), Huaren (naturalized citizens of Chinese descent) and Huayi (the descendents of Chinese parents)'.
3. Negative FDI outflow figures are reported in instances where net divestment, intra-company loans and repatriated earnings exceed inflows.

REFERENCES

Aggarwal, R. and T. Agmon (1990), 'The international success of developing country firms: role of government-directed comparative advantage', *Management International Review*, **30**(2), 163-80.

Aliber, R.Z. (1970), 'A theory of foreign direct investment', in C.P. Kindleberger (ed.), *The International Corporation*, Cambridge, MA: MIT Press: 17-34.

Balfour, F. (2005), 'The state's long apron strings', *Business Week*, 22-29 August: 52-4.

Barrell, R. and N. Pain (1996), 'An econometric analysis of US foreign direct investment', *The Review of Economics and Statistics*, **78**(2), 200-207.

Branstetter, L. and N. Lardy (2006), 'China's embrace of globalisation', NBER Working Paper 12373.

Bräutigam, D. (2003), 'Close encounters: Chinese business networks as industrial catalysts in Sub-Saharan Africa', *African Affairs*, **102**(408), 447-67.

Buckley, P.J. (2004), 'The role of China in the global strategy of multinational enterprises', *Journal of Chinese Economic and Business Studies*, **2**(1), 1-25.

Buckley, P.J. and M. Casson (1999), 'A theory of international operations', in P. J. Buckley and P.N. Ghauri (eds), *The Internationalization Process of the Firm: a Reader*, 2nd edn, London: International Business Thomson: 55-60.

Buckley, P.J and M. Casson (1981), 'The optimal timing of a foreign direct investment', *Economic Journal*, **91**(361), 75-87.

Buckley, P.J. and M. Casson (1976), *The Future of the Transnational Enterprise*, London: Macmillan.

Buckley, P.J., L.J. Clegg and C. Wang (2002), 'The impact of inward FDI on the performance of Chinese manufacturing firms', *Journal of International Business Studies*, **33**(4), 637-55.

Buckley, P.J., A.R. Cross, H. Tan, X. Liu and H. Voss (2006), 'An examination of recent trends in Chinese outward direct investment', Centre for International Business University of Leeds working paper.

Cai, K.G. (1999), 'Outward foreign direct investment: A novel dimension of China's integration into the regional and global economy', *China Quarterly*, **160**(December), 856-880.

Chakrabarti, A. (2001), 'The determinants of foreign direct investment: sensitivity analysis of cross-country regressions', *Kyklos*, **54**(1), 89-114.

Chen, X., R.L. Yung and B. Zhang (2002), *China Manufacturing*, BNP Paribas Peregrine Economics/Sector Update April 2002.

Child, J. and S.B. Rodrigues (2005), 'The internationalization of Chinese firms: A case for theoretical extension?', *Management and Organization Review*, **1** (3), 381-410.

Deng, P. (2003), 'Foreign direct investment by transnationals from emerging countries: the case of China', *Journal of Leadership and Organizational Studies*, **10**(2), 113-24.

Deng, P. (2004), 'Outward investment by Chinese MNCs: Motivations and implications', *Business Horizons*, **47**(3), 8-16.

Deutsche Bank Research (DBR) (2006), 'China's commodity hunger', Deutsche Bank Research–China Special, 13 June, Frankfurt a. M.: Deutsche Bank Research.

Dicken, P. (2003), *Global Shift: Reshaping the Global Economic Map in the 21st Century*, 4th edn, London: Sage.

Ding, X.L. (2000), 'Informal privatization through internationalization: The rise of nomenklatura capitalism in China's offshore business', *British Journal of Political Science*, **30**(1), 121-46.

Duan, Y. (1995), *Chinese Firms' Transnational Operations and Strategies*, Beijing: Chinese Development Press.

Dunning, J.H. (1993), *Multinational Enterprises and the Global Economy*, Wokingham: Addison-Wesley.

Dunning, J.H. (1999), 'Trade, location of economic activity and the transnational enterprise: A search for an eclectic approach', in P.J. Buckley and P.N. Ghauri (eds), *The Internationalization and the Firm*, London: International Thomson

Business: 61-79.

Erramilli, M.K., R. Srivastava and S.-S. Kim (1999), 'Internationalization theory and Korean transnationals', *Asia Pacific Journal of Management*, **16**, 29-45.

Ferrantino, M.J. (1992), 'Transaction costs and the expansion of Third-World transnationals', *Economic Letters*, **38**, 451-56.

Fortin, C. (2005), 'Opening speech', International Forum on Going Global of Chinese Enterprises, Ministry of Commerce, Beijing, 28th April.

Froot, K.A. and J.C. Stein (1989), 'Exchange rates and foreign direct investments: An imperfect capital markets approach', NBER Working Paper, No. 2914, National Bureau of Economic Research, Cambridge, MA.

Guo, H. (1984), 'On establishment of joint ventures abroad', in *Almanac of China's Foreign economic relations and Trade*, Beijing: MOFCOM: 652-4.

Heenan, D.A. and W.J. Keegan (1979), 'The rise of third world multinationals', *Harvard Business Review*, **57**(1), 101-9.

Henley, J., C. Kirkpatrick and G. Wilde (1999), 'Foreign direct investment in China: Recent trends and current policy issues', *The World Economy*, **22**(2), 223-43.

Hymer, S. (1960), 'The international operations of national firms: a study of direct investment', PhD thesis, Cambridge, MA: MIT Press.

International Energy Agency (2006), 'Oil Information 2006', ESDS International, (MIMAS) University of Manchester.

International Monetary Fund (IMF)(2005), 'World Economic Outlook Database', April, www.imf.org/external/pubs/ft/weo/2005/01/data/index.htm (accessed 13 October, 2006).

Johanson, J. and J.-E. Vahlne (1977), 'The internationalization process of the firm – a model of knowledge development and increasing foreign market commitment', *Journal of International Business Studies*, **8**(1), 23-32.

Khan, K.M. (1986), *Multinationals of the South*, London: Frances Pinter.

Kobrin, S.J. (1979), 'Political risk: a review and reconsideration', *Journal of International Business Studies*, **10**(1), 67-80.

Lall, S. (1983), 'The theoretical background', in S. Lall (ed.), *The New Transnationals: the Spread of Third World Transnationals*, Chichester: Wiley: 1-20.

Lall, S. and M. Albaladejo (2004), 'China's competitive performance: a threat to East Asian manufactured exports?', *World Development*, **32**(9), 1441-66.

Lardy, N.R. (1998), *China in the World Economy*, Washington, DC: Institute for International Economics.

Lau, H.-F. (1992), 'Internationalization, internalization, or a new theory for small, low-technology transnational enterprises?', *European Journal of Marketing*, **26**(10), 17-31.

Lau, H.-F. (2003), 'Industry evolution and internationalization process of firms from a newly industrialized economy', *Journal of Business Research*, **56** 847-52.

Lawrence, S.V. (2002), 'Going global', *Far Eastern Economic Review*, **165**(12), 28 March, 32.

Lecraw, D.J. (1977), 'Direct investment by firms from less developed countries', *Oxford Economic Papers*, **29**(3), 442-57.

Li, P.P. (2003), 'Toward a geocentric theory of transnational evolution: The implications from the Asian MNEs as latecomers', *Asia Pacific Journal of Management*, **20**(2), 217-42.

Lim, D. (1983), 'Fiscal incentives and direct investment in less developed countries', *Journal of Development Studies*, **19**(2), 207-12.

Liu, H. and K. Li (2002), 'Strategic implications of emerging Chinese multinationals: the Haier case study', *European Management Journal*, **20**(6), 699-706.

Long, G. (2002), 'A study of policies on encouraging investment abroad', *China Development Review*, **4**(3).

Luo, Y. (1997), 'Guanxi: Principles, philosophies, and implications', *Human Systems Management* **16**(1), 43-51.

Ma, X. and P. Andrews-Speed (2006), 'The overseas activities of China's national oil companies: rationale and outlook', *Minerals and Energy*, **21**(1), 17-30.

MOFCOM (various years), *Almanac of China's Foreign Economic Relations and Trade*, Beijing: Ministry of Commerce.

MOFCOM (2004), *China Commerce Yearbook*, Beijing: Ministry of Commerce.

Monkiewicz, J. (1986), 'Transnational enterprises of developing countries: some emerging characteristics', *Management International Review*, **26**(3), 67-79.

National Bureau of Statistics (NBS) (various years), *China Statistical Yearbook*, Beijing: NBS.

Ng, L.F.Y. and C. Tuan (2002), 'Building a favourable investment environment: Evidence for the facilitation of FDI in China', *The World Economy*, **25**(8), 1095-114.

Nolan, P. (2002), 'China and the global business revolution', *Cambridge Journal of Economics*, **26**(1), 119-37.

OECD (1996), *OECD Benchmark Definition of Foreign Direct Investment*, 3rd edn, Paris: OECD.

OECD (2002), *China in the World Economy: An OECD economic and statistical survey*, Paris: OECD.

Pearce, R.D., A. Islam and K.P. Sauvant (1992), *The Determinants of Foreign Direct Investment: A Survey of the Evidence*, New York: United Nations.

Poston, D.L., Jr., M.X. Mao and M.-Y. Yi (1994), 'The global distribution of overseas Chinese around 1990', *Population and Development Review*, **20**(3), 631-45.

Pradhan, J.P. (2003), 'Outward Foreign Direct Investment from India: recent trends and patterns', Jawaharlal Nehru University Working Paper Series.

Sauvant, K.P. (2005), 'New sources of FDI: The BRICs', *Journal of World Investment*, **6**(5), 639-709.

Shenkar, O. and Y. Luo (2004), *International Business*, Hoboken, NJ: John Wiley and Sons.

Sikorski, D. and T. Menkhoff (2000), 'Internationalisation of Asian business', *Singapore Management Review*, **22**(1), 1-17.

Standifird, S.S. and S.R. Marshall (2000), 'The transaction cost advantage of guanxi-based business practices', *Journal of World Business*, **35**(1), 21-42.

Stevens, G.V.G. (1993), 'Exchange rates and foreign direct investment: a note', International Finance Discussion Papers, April, No. 444, Board of Governors of the Federal Reserve System, Washington, DC.

Sung, Y.-W. (1996), 'Chinese outward investment in Hong Kong: Trends, prospects and policy implications', OECD Development Centre Technical Papers No. 113, Paris: OECD.

Taylor, R. (2002), 'Globalization strategies of Chinese companies: Current developments and future prospects', *Asian Business & Management*, **1**, 209-25.

Tong, S.Y. (2003), 'Ethnic Chinese networking in cross-border investment: the impact of economic and institutional development', Published in 2001 and revised in 2003, Hong Kong Institute of Economics and Business Strategy

(HIEBS) working paper, The University of Hong Kong.

UNCTAD (1998), *World Investment Report, 1998: Trends and Determinants*, New York and Geneva: United Nations.

UNCTAD (2004), *Prospects for Foreign Direct Investment and the Strategies of Transnational Corporations, 2004-2007*, New York and Geneva: United Nations.

UNCTAD (2005), *Prospects for Foreign Direct Investment and the Strategies of Transnational Corporations, 20050-2008*, New York and Geneva: United Nations.

UNCTAD (2006), FDI/MNE database, http://stats.unctad.org/fdi (accessed 11 October, 2006).

Villela, A.V. (1983), 'Transnationals from Brazil', in S. Lall (ed.), *The New Transnationals: The Spread of Third World Transnationals*, Chichester: Wiley: 220-49.

Wall, D. (1997), 'Outflows of capital from China', OECD Development Centre Technical Paper No. 123, Paris: OECD.

Wang, M.Y. (2002), 'The motivations behind Chinese government-initiated industrial investments overseas', *Pacific Affairs*, **75**(2), 187-206.

Warner, M., N.S. Hong and X. Xu (2004), '"Late development" experience and the evolution of transnational firms in the People's Republic of China', *Asia Pacific Business Review*, **10**(3/4), 324-45.

Wells, L.T. (1977), 'The internationalization of firms from developing countries', in T. Agmon and C.P. Kindleberger (eds), *Multinationals from Small Countries*, Cambridge, MA: MIT Press: 133-56.

Wells, L.T. (1983), *Third World Multinationals: The Rise of Foreign Investments from Developing Countries*, Cambridge, MA: MIT Press.

Wong, J. and S. Chan (2003), 'China's outward direct investment: expanding worldwide', *China: An International Journal*, **1**(2), 273-301.

World Bank (2005), *World Bank, World Development Indicators (WDI)*, April, ESDS International, (MIMAS) University of Manchester.

World Bank (2006), 'Indicators of Governance and Institutional Quality', http://www1.worldbank.org/publicsector/indicators.htm (accessed 16 January, 2006).

Wu, F. and Y.H. Sia (2002), 'China's rising investment in Southeast Asia: Trends and outlook', *Journal of Asian Business*, **18**(2), 41-61.

Wu, H.-L. and C.-H. Chen (2001), 'An assessment of outward foreign direct investment from China's transitional economy', *Europe-Asia Studies*, **53**(8), 1235-54.

Ye, G. (1992), 'Chinese transnational corporations', *Transnational Corporations*, **1**(2), 125-33.

Yeung, H.W.-C. (1999), 'The internationalisation of ethnic Chinese business firms from Southeast Asia: Strategies, processes and competitive advantages', *International Journal of Urban and Regional Research*, **23**(1), 103-27.

Yeung, H.W.-C. (2000), 'Economic globalization, crisis and the emergence of Chinese business communities in Southeast Asia', *International Sociology*, **15**(2), 266-87.

Zhan, J.X. (1995), 'Transnationalization and outward investment: the case of Chinese firms', *Transnational Corporations*, **4**(3), 67-100.

Zhang, Y. (2003), *China's Emerging Global Business: Political Economy and Institutional Investigations*, New York: Palgrave Macmillan.

Zin, R.H.M. (1999), 'Malaysian reverse investments: trends and strategies', *Asia Pacific Journal of Management*, **16**(3), 469-96.

6. From the internationalization of R&D to a global R&D network

Hiroo Takahashi

1. NETWORKS AND INTERORGANIZATIONAL RELATIONSHIPS

1.1 Networks and the Development of Information and Communications Technology (IT)

In this chapter, I would like to observe what kind of management innovation is required in research and development (R&D) activities amid the information network-oriented society.

First of all, what has brought about the new interorganizational relationship, that is the network, since the early 1990s is the recent progress of information and communications technology (IT). Thanks to the development of this communications net, the mutual conveyance of information has been made much easier both inside and outside the company, thus promoting closer interorganizational relationships. This was perhaps the real beginning of the age of the network. It was in the 1990s that the word 'net-work' began to become familiar in Japan, where the computer network emerged following the rapid increase of the widespread use of personal computers. The MITI (Ministry of International Trade and Industry) defined the concept of 'net-work' as follows: 'it carries out in different places various operations concerning information, including its processing, conveyance, etc., using either electrical or electronic instruments such as computers or communications circuits'. The linkage of information through computer networks will create new interorganizational relationships across conventional borders of different

This chapter benefited greatfly from the conference given at the Western Academy of Management (WAM) – Shizuoka, International Management Conference 2000, 7-12 July. Thanks are due to Professor Larence Rhyne, San Diego State University, and Professor Manuel Serapio, University of Colorado-Denver for their comments and advice.

organizations, groups and technologies.

The concrete forms of interorganizational linkage through the medium of IT include: linkage between corporations; linkage between corporations and universities; between companies and the government; or between domestic and overseas corporations. When we consider forming a network with some other organizations we naturally do not expect anything negative, but rather hope for something positive, say, mutually synergetic functions, from the new interfaces. In other words, we expect some synergetic effect will be created out of mutual exchanges between different organizations to be connected by a network.

Differing from the viewpoint of conventional management theory, the concept of the network attaches importance to interorganizational relationships rather than to static organizations. This new view of organization theory relating to networks in interorganizational relationships is the field of 'interorganization theory and management', which aims at studying networks among corporate organizations.

1.2   The Internationalization of Business Activities of Corporate Organizations and the Relationships among Them

Today, Japanese companies are expanding their tie-ups and cooperation with overseas organizations, not to mention with domestic organizations, in various forms. These interorganizational relationships seem to be entering the stage of so-called globalization, that is, global-scale linkage, which is a highly advanced form of internationalization.

Globalization of business activities involves all the divisions ranging from sales, production, R&D, and even to finance, procurement and human resource management. The main subject of our study is to find out how the globalization – as an advanced form of internationalization – of R&D activities should be related to the advancement of the information network.

Problems incidental to internationalization of R&D activities have been drawing attention since the 1980s, or more precisely since the early 1990s in Japan among advanced multinational corporations. Such problems are the inevitable results of internationalization which MNCs experience in the process of development as the next step after moving production abroad. With the advancement of their overseas production, it becomes important for MNCs to consider tailoring their production know-how and their product development (the operation corresponding to D) – which eventually deepens into research activities (R) – to the specific foreign country where their market is. Such research and development activities, as the next step after the establishment of manufacturing operations abroad, now need to be dealt with realistically by MNCs in Japan.

The focus of MNCs' discussion today is on how their research and development abroad can be integrated into their corporate R&D strategy. Matsushita Electric Industrial Co., Ltd, for instance, has already started building up a global R&D system by networking both development units (divisional laboratories) and research units (corporate laboratories), which are scattered throughout the world. Many other representative MNCs in Japan, including NEC Ltd, Canon Inc., and Toyota Motor Co. Ltd, are also beginning to feel their way toward a practical way of management leading to the structuring of such a global R&D network.

What is remarkable and sought after in the idea of the 'global R&D network' today, is not merely the establishment of research laboratories abroad as component units, but the linkage of those units by networking in various forms. There you will see trends of outsourcing, a positive use of outside resources including inter-business tie-ups, capital participation, joint ventures, M&A, and so on. M&A, for example, which recently is increasingly being adopted by Japanese enterprises as an effective way of expansion abroad, usually buys up a whole organization including the affiliated research laboratories. Other instances of outsourcing include cooperation with universities or research institutes in carrying out studies or setting up joint ventures. Thus the form of R&D is changing and evolving into a more diversified mode with a much wider range of options available. Under such circumstances, networks connecting these activities begin to take on an extremely important significance.

2. THE VIEWPOINT OF INTERNATIONALIZATION OF R&D

2.1 The Developing Process of R&D

When we consider the internationalization of research and development, what do we have in mind as the subject or as the stance? Usually, the internationalization of 'research & development' has been looked at from the viewpoint of functional tactics in the process of the internationalization of business activities which flows as follows: internationalization of sales, internationalization of production, internationalization of R&D. In other words, when internationalization takes place in a Japanese corporation, the export of products comes as the first stage, in which a sales unit will also be set up in order to secure the market for the export. The next step is the internationalization of production, which is characteristic of MNCs. As a result of further functional development of these activities comes internationalization of research and development.

Thus the acclimatization of R&D, as it is generally understood, in the process of the internationalization of business activities, implies the establishment of some kind of physical units abroad, with the corporate headquarters as the centre. In setting up such units, consideration needs to be given to the purpose, ownership policy and the siting of the laboratory as well as the form of its advancement. The developing process to be followed will also need to be considered in relation to the above items of discussion. This is based on the concept that the internationalization of R&D, like that of business itself, progresses following certain stages. Rondstadt (1977) classified the progressive roles of overseas laboratories as follows.

1. Transfer Technology Units (TTUs). R&D units established to help certain foreign subsidiaries transfer manufacturing technology from the US parent while also providing related technical services for foreign customers.
2. Indigenous Technology Units (ITUs). R&D units established to develop new and improved products expressly for foreign markets. These products were not the direct result of new technology supplied by the parent organizations.
3. Global Technology Units (GTUs). R&D units established to develop new products and processes for simultaneous – or nearly simultaneous – application in major world markets of the multinational organizations.
4. Corporate Technology Units (CTUs). R&D units established to generate new technology of a long-term or exploratory nature expressly for the corporate parent.

We see internationalization of R&D as having the following five stages of development: collection of technical information → product improvement/ product reform (applied development) → experimental /technological learning → development of new products → original research.

1. Collecting Technical Information: Internationalization of business activities begins with the export of products, and with the setting up of sales units abroad. The primary purpose at this stage is to expand the new overseas markets for the products developed in the home country. As regards R&D activities, the main element consists in the market research for export and sales of the company's products as well as in the collection of technical information concerning the technology level/trend of rival companies. Hence, often at this stage, a liaison office is set up as the first corporate outpost for collecting technical

information.

2. Improvement/Reform of Products (applied development): Overseas production follows the stage of exporting and setting up sales units abroad. In the case of Japanese companies, the establishment of overseas production units accelerated as a result of the rapid appreciation of the yen after 1985. Using overseas production units brings problems with technology, which is indispensable to the operation.

   Production activities require engineers and other experts with technical knowledge. The permanent residence of expatriate engineers from the home country (corporate headquarters) and their interface with local experts is a preliminary step for R&D abroad. If it turns out that home products (technology) are not well received in the foreign market, the products must undergo improvement, reform or modifications to adapt to the specific market. As a result, a technical division is set up at the same location as the production unit.

3. Experimental/Technical Learning: It is at this stage that a small-scale laboratory in the form of an experimental station is set up abroad. Such laboratories are not so much expected to pursue R&D itself, as charged with various roles as the first overseas outpost to carry out part of the corporate R&D strategy. In the case of an automobile company, such an experimental station may act as the base for technical evaluation and purchase of materials, while in some other industries, it may serve as the centre for preparatory work for introduction of techniques or cross-licensing. Such experimental stations are also the centre where medical research can be carried out.

4. Developing New Products: With the expansion of activities for overseas production, the privileged 'insider' companies closely connected with the specific foreign market are urged to develop new products at the request of the subsidiaries and local technical experts. At this stage substantial managerial resources fit for the overseas R&D base will be invested to reinforce this function. Under these circumstances, a certain number of researchers/technical experts are secured, and new products will be developed as the first output of their R&D operation on foreign soil. This is, as it were, the realization of the MNCs' good, namely, an integrated management of all functions from R&D to production/sales carried out in each of the key areas of the world. It is, so to speak, the emergence of partial clones of the corporate activities.

5. Original Research: This is the most advanced stage of the internationalization of R&D. Once local scientists and researchers have been secured, fundamental research begins to be conducted side by side with production development.

   The allocation of resources for R&D will be examined from a global point of view through which each overseas unit can take part in the corporate strategy by making use of the most advantageous resources to hand. This stage corresponds to Rondstadt's fourth stage, Corporate Technology Units (CTU). So far, global research activities have not been fully realized by Japanese companies, but you can see this stage of research activities among such representative American multinational giants as IBM, Ford, GE and Exxon.

We consider that the degree of internationalization of R&D can be measured by placing the content of R&D together with the accompanying expenses on the Y-axis and with the extent of acclimatization of resources – human resources in particular – on the X-axis; the degree of internationalization is supposed to increase in relation to the progress made along both axes.

The Y-axis represents the process of the evolution of the subject/content of R&D. What starts merely as an incidental function under the corporate laboratory eventually grows, following the five steps, into a fully-fledged laboratory. R&D expenses increase with the enhancement of the function of the laboratory. The X-axis represents the degree of acclimatization of managerial resources. The allocation of resources including talent, equipment, funds and so on, increases as the overseas R&D subsidiary acquires a greater role. As globalization of R&D advances, laboratories make better use of resources from all over the world and thereby can enhance the content of their research.

Rondstadt classified the established overseas laboratories by the types of their roles/characters. Yet, if you examine his classification in the light of a development process, it would look similar to our classification, with his 'types' roughly corresponding to our 'stages' as follows: TTU → improvement/reform of products; ITU → experiment/learning; GTU → development of new products; CTU → original research. This type/stage classification may apply to manufacturing industries in general, including the technology-oriented assembly makers such as electric appliances, automobiles, and machines, but not necessarily to every industry.

2.2 Dynamism in R&D

Now let us take a pharmaceutical company as an example to see whether the above-mentioned classification applies to it. When overseas laboratories are set up by a pharmaceutical company, they are most often intended, from the start, as research-oriented laboratories. The position of these laboratories might correspond, as it were, to the stage of original research – or Rondstadt's GTU or CTU – instead of TTU or ITU which is naturally supposed to come at an early stage. Whether the purpose of overseas R& D is to accommodate the foreign market (home-based exploiting laboratory) or to reinforce the corporate R&D (home-based augmenting laboratory) depends on the company. Some companies do not necessarily follow the fixed stages; they may bypass or even reverse the steps. Taking the Rondstadt classification for example, one overseas laboratory may jump from TTU to GTU. Or an overseas laboratory originally intended to pursue basic research on behalf of the home-based corporation may fail to attain the anticipated res ults, and consequently change into a unit whose mission is to develop products adapted to the foreign market. In another case, there may be a unit originally set up to conduct market-oriented R&D for the purpose of accommodating the specific foreign market needs; when it turns out, however, that the quality of the local researchers/ technical experts is higher than that of those available in the home country, the unit may be changed into a research-oriented 'home-based augmenting' laboratory which is supposed to reinforce the corporate R&D. On the other hand, there are opposite cases where a unit primarily established as a research-oriented institute changes into a market-oriented laboratory. Also, if the home-based parent company is bought by another company, the original purpose of the overseas R&D may be changed completely, according to the latter's strategy.

De Meyer of the INSEAD Business School, France, made the following interesting observations based on his positive study of 22 overseas R&D laboratories belonging to Japanese and European corporations:

> it appears to us that the traditional categorization of overseas laboratories does not lead to a satisfactory discrimination of the different subsidiary laboratories ... We have observed in a clinical study of 16 cases that most of the established laboratories in a sample of about 100 subsidiary laboratories fulfilled almost all roles predicted by the economics literature, and that the differences in the way these laboratories were managed were barely influenced by the primary mission of the laboratory (De Meyer, Management of International Network of Industrial R&D Laboratories, 'R&D Management', 23 February, 1993)

Namely, he pointed out that the in-depth study of established overseas laboratories revealed a management condition that was not necessarily in conformity with the primary mission, method and stage of each laboratory; and that their management style was actually quite dynamic due to changes in R&D strategy of the home-based company.

In other words, the management of overseas R&D is not anything fixed or universal in relation to its purpose/mission, method or stage, but actually it is conducted more flexibly, in accordance with individual circumstances.

Thus we observe many instances of dynamic management carried out in response to individual circumstances which include: the change of functions of overseas R&D due to the review of R&D systems by the home-based company; new R&D subjects requested or supported by overseas manufacturing subsidiaries; alterations in R&D policy owing to the change of executives at subsidiary laboratories and so on. These realities ought to be understood better not from a static point of view which presumes that there are certain purposes and stages/types of internationalization of R&D, but rather from a dynamic standpoint of how to build up a global R&D system that fits in (accords with) the corporate strategy.

3. THE VIEWPOINT OF A GLOBAL R&D NETWORK

3.1 How it should be Viewed

As has been illustrated, the conventional method of 'internationalization of R&D' fails to explain actual conditions. Such being the case, where should we look for a feasible explanation of the internationalization of R&D in today's world of information networks?

What we should like to recommend here is to reconsider 'internationalization of R&D' from the standpoint of 'globalization of R&D'. This involves seeing R&D bases scattered both at home and abroad not as separate units but as an integrated whole, engaged in activities and connected by a R&D network, although this idea may apply only to the circumstances where overseas R&D has been advanced to some extent. This concept is based on the 'Global management of technology development' by Westney of MIT (Westney, 1998). She regards the network of R&D bases/units created by the corporation both at home and abroad as a linkage of total activities which could contribute to the technical strategy essential to R&D activities. This idea of total linkage is not the monocentric way of thinking which assumes the home-based headquarters as the sole hub of all activities, but it is a polycentric point of view which allows every unit to act as the centre whenever it proves to be the optimum R&D unit situated in the optimum area/country. It is a conceptional change from internationalization to globalization. While the conventional study of overseas bases/units was conducted from the viewpoint of internationalization, now they are regarded as part of the global management of technological development which considers how such units should be related to each other in a dynamic linkage. While internationalization of R&D has been concerned with the study of various problems concerning the establishment of overseas units revolving around the home-based corporation, global management of technology development places emphasis on considering what kind of relations, with which unit, should be formed in pursuing corporate R&D operations from a global point of view. Today's globalized corporations have a wide range of options and choices for their R&D activities including the introduction of techniques, personal exchanges through joint research or technical tie-ups with foreign companies, dispatch of researchers to overseas universities, financial aid, and so on, apart from the establishment of bases for overseas R&D. Under such circumstances, a globalized corporation's R&D lies in the consideration of how and where the best possible linkage (net-work) can be obtained, making the most of its choices for their activities.

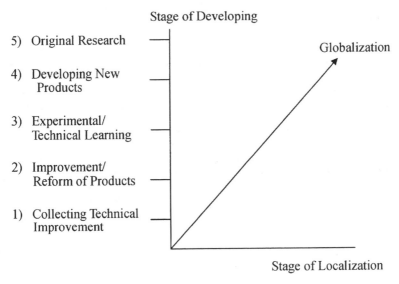

Figure 6.1   The developing processing internationalization of R&D

3.2   Viewpoints of Closed R&D and Network R&D

What are the contents of R&D viewed from the standpoint of network organization? The idea of a 'network organization' aims at incorporating in its own corporate strategy into their R&D resources adopted from a global stance. It aims to create efficient/productive ways of connecting laboratories and other related units at home and abroad by creating networks among them. The idea is not a of vertical structure based on the conventional pyramidal organization with the home-based corporation as the vertex, that is, the centre of all R&D activities; rather it is an interorganizational linkage-style of network organization, in which each unit can create mutual exchange relations both independently and creatively. With the traditional form of R&D in the pyramidal organization, information used to be centralized by the corporation under whose decision each unit was supposed to function. But in today's 'world of information networks' where networks are spreading all around us, a new system ought to be created in which information is dispersed and distributed to each and every unit which, in turn, is allowed to operate independently and creatively according to its circumstances.

I will distinguish the conventional idea of internationalization from the new concept based on a network organization, by calling the former 'closed R&D', and the latter 'network R&D'. Table 6.1 shows the differences between the two viewpoints.

Table 6.1   Comparison between closed R&D and network R&D

Closed R&D	Network R&D
Internationalization of R&D · monocentric/vertical way of thinking · static/orderly · high cost of maintenance · R&D style: in stages · development within the corporation · R&D resources concentrated at the home base · pyramidal organization (bureaucratic) · rigid structure · vertical organization · homogeneous management resource	Globalization of R&D · polycentric/horizontal way of thinking · dynamic/creative · low cost of maintenance · R&D style: project-based · internal development and tie-ups, joint research projects · dispersion of R&D resources · network organization (independent) · computer network · horizontal organization · heterogeneous management resource

The basic characteristic of 'closed R&D' is that the decision-making for R&D is in the hands of the top management of a pyramidal organization, under whose control information is conveyed to the middle and the lower divisions. Based on the 'seeds' of R&D discovered under the policy mapped out by the central corporate laboratory (home-based laboratory), each divisional laboratory moves ahead with its share of R&D which eventually leads to product development. Under such a framework, all the managerial resources necessary for R&D are obtained through homogeneous procurement within the corporation. As a result, both maintenance and personnel expenses required to maintain R&D operations would become costly. On the other hand, the basic aim of 'network R&D' is to create a linkage with each of the R&D units both at home and abroad which would not only compose the network but also act as a unit for innovation. Each unit makes an in-depth investigation of primarily project-based subjects, while also creating a closer network with other units. Managerial resources in this case are procured not only from within the corporation itself, but also by incorporating a wide range of external resources both at home and abroad.

As regards the siting of R&D laboratories from a global perspective, the primary consideration is where the 'knowledge cluster' is (Porter, 1998), and which of those areas of the knowledge cluster they should be linked with. If there are, in the world, any areas or regions (Europe, America, Asia or Japan, for instance) where relevant knowledge and managerial resources have accumulated and are consequently effectively available, the corporation will naturally intend to strengthen the network with these areas, even though its central R&D function remains in the home-based headquarters. Such a trend is observed among some advanced MNCs in Japan, which also promote mutual exchanges with foreign companies, universities, institutes, and so on, through tie-ups and joint research projects, in addition to establishing R&D laboratories in such regions as Europe, America, South-East Asia and China. While 'closed R&D' presumes the use of resources available within the corporation inside the home country, 'network R&D' considers the availability of managerial resources from a global point of view, and consequently creates networks with optimum organizations sited in optimum areas. Global R&D networks thus aim at an efficient and productive build-up of networks of excellent knowledge throughout the world.

3.3 The Basis for the Formation of Network R&D

The great impact for the promotion of network R&D is the progress of the information and communication network today. Being able to exchange information with anybody, any time, anywhere through a computer network can be an effective means of sharing the theme, contents and progress of research. Unexpected inspiration and new discoveries may emerge from such an exchange of information on the state of individual R&D through the computer network. The prevalence of email and Internet use today has made such sharing of information through mutual liaison even more convenient and efficient. Moreover, the potentialities of telecommunications have been greatly increased, thanks to the rapid strides made in communications technology based on the public data networks, satellite communications, and Integrated Services Digital Network (ISDN). Progress is also due to the 'electronics revolution', which has not only multiplied the progress of technologies but has also enabled the blending of existing technologies. For instance, the use of personal computers in the office has accelerated rapidly. Personal computers will facilitate communication through IT. Electronic mail is a means of communication whose cost, unlike other means of communication, does not increase in proportion to the distance it covers. For such reasons, the use of email and the internet in R&D units, both at home and abroad, is estimated to increase in the future. The merits of email include: a high transmission speed; easy time control (since the mailed document is stored by the server, the users can send or read messages whenever they like, and the time lag is negligible); easy document management. Also, voice recorders can reproduce spoken language with its accents and intonation, while video-conferencing which enables face-to-face communication, is carried out between or among laboratories inside and outside the country.

At IBM, for example, the exchange of information between laboratories is conducted through an in-house network called Notes Internet, a system which is almost directly accessible from a terminal unit on the desk of each researcher. IBM carries out various types of communication, exchange of information, reporting, and so on, by email 24 hours a day, seven days a week with any place in the world. In this way a vast range of services is provided, including the use of a data base, support for decision-making, guide or the internal standard for development, bulletin news, and notices of new books in the library. At the Tokyo Basic Research Institute, each employee is provided with at least one workstation. Thanks to this system, global time difference is no longer a problem. You could even take advantage of it, if you use the system cleverly, say, by sending a question abroad in the evening to receive the answer the next morning. Such a system could be a major tool in the development of globalized products throughout the world. As is expected of an institute engaged in basic research, IBM's Tokyo Institute has a system of receiving external scholars and scientists as visiting researchers regardless of their nationality. It is also keen to encourage technical exchange and cooperation through long- or short-term loans of employees. IBM is well known for adopting external resources in conducting numerous joint research projects in cooperation with universities or other research institutes not belonging to IBM.

4. THE HUMAN ASPECT OF GLOBAL R&D NETWORKS

4.1 The Significance of the Human Network

The word 'network' does not necessarily signify a computer network based on the use of IT. Various contacts and connections which we have or create through personal relationships in our daily life are the greatest resources of the network formation. While 'network' often denotes a 'hard network' based on IT, we should not forget, at the same time, the existence of 'soft networks' based on human relationships. Hard networks include both in-house and external (public) networks. A soft network, on the other hand, can be seen in terms of a human network spread both inside and outside the company. Both hard and soft networks spread across the boundaries of companies or countries and are the foundation of global R&D networks.

If what a computer network conveys is verbalized formal information, a human network is used to gather real or implicit information – tacit knowledge – created from communication between individual persons. Unlike a computer network which is structuralized and with which the users can share mutual information, a human network is perceived only through social contact or companionship which naturally cannot be structuralized.

R&D explores an unknown field, and it produces new values through 'knowledge creation' by individual persons. Knowledge creation is an inventive process consisting of the reading of formal information based on the use of IT on one hand, and the interpretation of implicit information – tacit knowledge learned from individual experience or personal communication – on the other. Unlike formal information, implicit information cannot be verbalized to be shared with others, since it is something unique, experienced or acquired by individual persons. Therefore, in order to cultivate implicit information, one needs to gain a variety of experience. Thus it becomes important to encourage researchers to have more international sense and experience. Implicit information (tacit knowledge) is acquired only through personal contacts and communication. Unlike formal information, implicit information cannot be obtained from anything structural, but only by means of a face-to-face network. Hence it is essential to strengthen the human network in the community of researchers and engineers both inside and outside the company. There are various forms of activity that can promote this purpose, including participation in research meetings, seminars and meetings for reading papers, and mutual visits to different laboratories, as well as other events.

Exchange of human resources is costly, but nothing can replace a human network, no matter how much progress is made in IT.

4.2   Autonomy and Control

Autonomy and control are important elements in constructing a global R&D network, although these two concepts are antinomic. The more autonomy each of the R&D units gains amid the trend of their global dispersion, the more important it becomes to control and steer them to the common goal of an integrated network. R&D is not produced through a fixed process under a given system, but is an accumulated collection of knowledge brought forth by the invisible creativity of individual persons. Therefore, there ought to be a mechanism in R&D to elicit creativity from each individual person. The kind of control or command given from above such as in the case of 'closed R&D' would only impair the originality/inventiveness of ideas. The part corresponding to the 'R' of R&D, namely, research, in particular, is an amorphous, creative process, which requires an atmosphere where the freedom of the individual is respected to the utmost degree. Development ('D'), on the other hand, is in the stage where the possibility of practical application is in sight, and consequently requires a certain degree of control in line with the goal. The problem here is that the more competent the scientist is considered, the more freedom and independence he or she tends to demand. The status and remuneration of the holders of a PhD (a doctorate conferred on a scientist or scholar) is clearly higher in the West than in Japan, and as a result, such persons often change companies or are targeted for promotion. Accumulating brilliant achievements in their career, they would choose to move to another company rather than to stay in the same position. Under such circumstances, it is extremely difficult to control the direction of research in conformity with the specific goal, while at the same time guaranteeing the freedom of researchers. A perception gap arises between the people in charge of the research divisions at the home-based corporation and those in the overseas laboratories. Local researchers must take part in the 'global R&D network' designed by the home headquarters. At the same time, they are also interested in exchanges with the local scientific community. Strengthening the interface with colleges and other research institutes that comprise the scientific community helps to awaken creativity in researchers but these relationships should essentially be regarded as no more than a part of a global R&D network. Perhaps the most important problem here is how to create a synergistic mechanism of control which could combine autonomous activities of each R&D unit with their motive for aiming at the global corporate goal.

4.3 Leadership

Generally speaking, R&D leaders (that is, those in charge of R&D) are assigned as follows: in the research-oriented case, a local scientist or researcher with worthy achievements in his or her particular field of studies will be chosen; in the development-oriented case, an engineer dispatched from the home-base is likely to be chosen. In either case, what is important is the leader's vision and management style at the starting point, since their R&D vision at the start-up stage becomes the culture of the whole laboratory and also the base for its management thereafter.

From the standpoint of 'network R&D', how each unit will be managed or how its research performance will be improved upon depends on the management style of the research leader who is responsible for daily decision making. Setting of research goals, hiring and carrying out of research, decisions on R&D expenditure and so on are left to the discretion of the leader of the autonomous unit who also acts as a part of the global R&D network.

The first requirement for the leader is naturally that he or she should have his own purpose, that is, the leader's vision of achieving the results of research in the future. They must be someone who can steer the research unit to expected goal with the clear understanding of what the future problems will be and what kind of transition will be required in the course of research, rather than having a vague idea of the objectives. In addition, they need the ability to communicate with the home-based corporation. Namely, they need to understand the top management's ideas and intentions as well as the corporate culture and characteristics. How can such a leader be obtained or brought up, then? According to my field studies of the actual conditions of Japanese companies in America, there are three ways of securing the leader: (1) public recruitment through advertisement in newspaper, and other mass media; (2) recruitment using head hunters (talent scouting agency); (3) recruitment by word-of-mouth communication with influential persons.

The first method (1) in which a large number of people apply for the position secures a wide range of talents, but it is not easy to find the most suitable person amongst so many unspecified persons just by evaluating applications and through interviews. Besides, in some countries there are restrictions on the questions that may be asked in selecting the applicants, according to equal employment opportunity law. The second method (2) by head hunters is employed by Japanese companies as well, but it is not a surefire way of finding the right person; the selected person may turn out to be unsuitable for the position of top management. It is thought that the third method (3) by word-of-mouth communication is the best. With this method, the right person is sought through the introduction by authorities in specific fields of studies (university professors, and so on) as well as through various contacts and connections created from long-standing personal relationships of those who have been concerned with the company. For instance, if an executive in charge of technology at the home-based corporation knew someone who was a close friend of theirs during the days when they were studying abroad, they could perhaps recommend them for the post. What is important here is that the leader of an overseas laboratory, although they are at the top of this part of the company, forms part of the corporate global R&D strategy, and that an understanding of the corporate culture and ability to communicate with the corporation's top management are essential requirements. In most cases, the laboratory leader is employed – selected – in his or her own native country, where other researchers and technical experts, in turn, are employed under his or her leadership and responsibility. The leader of a local laboratory is also expected to create an atmosphere where innovation of R&D is always encouraged and promoted. If overseas R&D operations are to be successful, those satisfying these requirements should be invited as leaders.

According to Kuemmerle (1997), R&D leaders ought to fulfill the following four qualities:

1. They are, at once, respected scientists or engineers and skilled managers.
2. They are able to integrate the new site into the company's existing R& D network.
3. They have a comprehensive understanding of technology trends.
4. They are able to overcome formal barriers when they seek access to new ideas in local universities and scientific communities.

5. CONCLUSION: NETWORKS AND THE CREATION OF KNOWLEDGE

Today, advanced MNCs intend to strengthen their R&D capacity by building their 'global R&D network'. Since the essence of corporate strategy of internationalized corporations consists in technological innovation, the productivity and speed of R&D gains importance as international technology competition intensifies. The intensification of international competition among corporations across borders suggests that we are now in an age of globalized competition, that is mega-competition, as it is called by today's industrial society. Large-scale

M&A and tie-ups taking place today among the world's leading corporations in such fields as automobiles, electrical appliances, chemicals, banks, insurances companies, and so on, indicate that these corporations are preparing themselves for survival in an age of 'mega-competition', which seems to require a globalized reorganization of industries.

In an era of such great worldwide competition, how should we proceed with corporate R&D strategies? Is it all right for Japanese companies to stick to the methods that they have so far, limiting their managerial resources to those available within their corporations or inside their own country in pursuing their R&D activities?

In light of what we have observed in this chapter, that is, that managerial activities of Japanese companies are now at the 'globalization' stage, such limitations ought to be reconsidered, and to be replaced by a new vision of the 'global R&D network'. The build-up of a 'global R&D network' aims at a dynamic use of knowledge available both at home and abroad by creating linkages not only with a company's own research laboratories inside or outside the country, but also with other organizations' research bases and units. What does knowledge mean in this context? The significance of knowledge in an organization has been attracting public attention in recent years due to the appearance of such words as 'knowledge management' or 'knowledge worker' (Nonaka, 1995).

Looking back over the history of civilization to this day, we realize that we have been developed by human wisdom and knowledge. Indeed, knowledge is an irreplaceable asset granted only to humankind, and this will never change. Is knowledge the same as information? Information is abundant everywhere, and if you wish to obtain it, it is always accessible anywhere in the world, thanks to what is called the 'revolutionary' progress of IT in recent years. Paradoxically speaking, is it because of the huge flood of information that people began to discuss the significance of knowledge, wondering what kind of information is truly required in the management of corporations or in pursuit of R&D? Knowledge is not information itself, but it is a part of 'knowledge creation' which utilizes information to create certain values or significance. Knowledge creation takes place only in a human head and is unlike the formalized information to be shared by others through an information network. Thus what will remain in the end is the knowledge creation by individual persons, and therefore, to invent a system to support this, we believe, is the significance of a network.

REFERENCES

Arimura, S. (1999), 'How Matsushita Electric and Sony manage global R&D', *Research Technology Management*, March-April.

Asakawa, K. (1996), 'External-internal linkage and overseas autonomy-control tension: the management dilemma of the Japanese R&D in Europe', *IEEE Transaction on Engineering Management*, **43**(1), February.

Bartlett, C. and S. Ghoshal (1990), 'Managing innovation in the transnational corporation', in C. Bartlett, Y. Doz and G. Hedlund (eds), *Managing the Global Firm*, London: Routledge.

Cheng, J.L. (1993), 'The management of multinational R&D: a neglected topic in international business research', *Journal of International Business Studies*, First Quarter.

Dalton, D.H. and M.G. Serapio (1998), 'Globalizing Industrial Research and Development', Technology Administration, US Department of Commerce, June.

De Meyer, A. (1993), 'Management of an international network of industrial R&D laboratories', *R&D Management*, **23**(2).

Florida, R. (1997), 'The globalization of R&D: results of a survey of foreign affiliated R&D laboratories in the USA', *Research Policy*, 26.

Grassmann, O. and M. Zadtwitz (1998), 'Organization of industrial R&D on a global scale', *R&D Management*, **28**(3).

Hayashi, T. (1994), 'Globalization of R&D and its implications', *R&D Management*, December, 75-87.

Hayashi, T. (1996), 'R&D fields and global R&D systems of IBM Corp', *Rikkyo Economic Review*, **50**(2), October.

Kuemmerle, W. (1997), 'Building effective R&D capabilities abroad', *Harvard Business Review HBR*, March-April, 61-70.

Nonaka, I. and T. Nishigaki (2001), *Knowledge Emergence*, Oxford University Press.

Pearce, R.D. and M. Papanastassiou (1996), 'R&D networks and innovation: Decentralized product development in multinational enterprises', *R&D Management*, **26**(4).

Pearce, R.D. and S. Singh (1996), *Globalizing Research and Development*, London: Macmillan.

Porter, M. (1998), 'Clusters and the new economics of competition', *Harvard Business Review*, November-December.

Ronstadt, R. (1977), *Research and Development by US Multinationals*, London: Praeger.

Rosenbloom, R.S. and W.J. Spencer (1996), *Engines of Innovation*, Boston: Harvard Business School Press.

Sakakibara, K. (1995), *R&D Management of Japanese Companies*, Tokyo: Chikurashobo.

Takahashi, H. (1996), *Actual Situation of Globalization of R&D*, Tokyo: Chuoukeizaisha.

Takahashi, H. (1997), 'Trends of overseas R&D strategies of the Japanese companies', *R&D Management*, December.

Takahashi, H. (1999), 'R&D siting in Silicon valley', *Hakuoh Business Review*, **6**, March.

Takahashi, H. (2000), 'Trends of Europe's R&D unit of Japanese companies', *Hakuoh Business Review*, **7**(1), March.

Westney, D.E. (1998), 'Research on the global management of technology management', *Business Review*, **46**(1).

Yamakura, K. (1993), *Inter-organization Theory and Management*, Tokyo: Yuhhikaku.

PART TWO

New Directions of Thinking in IB Research

7. International business studies: episodic or evolutionary?

Daniel P. Sullivan and John D. Daniels

1. INTRODUCTION

Buckley (2002) suggested that international business (IB) research, following decades of great accomplishment, is 'running out of steam'. Exploratory discussion of this supposition is apparent, for example the 2002 ANZIBA conference devoted a keynote panel to the theme (Nicholas, 2002; Welch, 2002). This chapter expands discussion of this issue by proposing that we reframe Buckley's episodic thesis to one on the philosophical evolution of IB studies. Doing so, we believe, identifies and develops the perspectives that promise to reenergize IB studies. First, let's summarize Buckley's thesis.

Buckley disaggregates IB studies into three specific episodes: the explanation of foreign direct investment (FDI) (post World War II-1970s); the forms and functions of the multinational firm (1970-1990); and the globalization of business (mid-1980-2000). He also notes a shadow area, comparative management, that has paralleled mainstream IB research. When each of the episodes emerged, scholars took their cue from the prevailing big empirical question to design, anchor and report research. Now, though, Buckley argues that the discipline lacks an apparent sense of purpose. The worrisome absence of a research path forward, or, as he puts it, the lack of a big empirical question which requires explanation, challenges the relevance and, ultimately, the legitimacy of IB studies. To preempt this threat, Buckley urges scholars to 'think of their future work in terms of the past achievements of their discipline'.

We support Buckley's call and understand the spirit of his premise – identifying past episodes of research and studying the specific issues and tasks of each in order to recognize how scholars developed new concepts,

The authors thank Peter Buckley, Gary Weaver and Frank DuBois for their helpful comments and suggestions.

theories, and methods to meet each episode's intellectual challenges. Ideally, this exercise enables us to generalize about the assorted theoretical challenges confronting IB and to develop the means to meet the intellectual challenges of the next 'big empirical question which requires explanation'.

2. CONCERNS

Several concerns lead us to break ranks with Buckley's thesis. To begin, we believe that Buckley's emphasis of episodic determinism downplays vital aspects of the cumulative knowledge of IB studies in helping us to interpret its evolutionary dynamic (Kuhn, 1970, 1990; Diamond, 1998). Partitioning IB into discrete episodes, taken to an extreme, requires that we await an emergent empirical question to guide our efforts rather than leveraging our existing literature to rethink past conclusions, refine current interpretations, and anticipate future developments. More pointedly, 'scientific development must be seen as a process driven from behind, not pulled from ahead ... as evolution from, rather than evolution towards' (Kuhn, 1990, p. 7). Second, categorizing research by topic or time-period is a shaky endeavor. Although we commend Buckley for specifying three broad topics that encompass primary facets of IB research streams, research often spills over into more than one category. Further, consolidating IB research into three or four discrete categories must perforce downplay significant research streams (such as the extensive literature on the effects of IB, mainly that of FDI, from various stakeholders'or agents' positions[1]) or overlook studies that preceded and followed particular episodes (for example current research on the liability of foreignness depends on explanations of direct investment for its theoretical foundation).[2]

In addition, Buckley's episodic structure seems likely to aggravate institutional biases. That is, compartmentalizing episodes of research in terms of specific content perpetuates the reductionism bias of IB research in ways that reinforce the constraint of intellectual and institutional factors (Dunning, 1989; Daniels, 1991; Toyne and Nigh, 1997). Unless arrested, these trends may unduly consign scholars to designing piecemeal studies – the infamous footnote to a footnote variety – that move us increasingly more slowly toward a supposedly more comprehensive account of IB.[3] Similarly, awaiting the next big empirical question risks that the IB discipline fails when called upon, scholars waste effort in the interim modifying inherently limited perspectives to novel realities, and we ultimately watch another discipline win intellectual leadership.[4]

Therefore, this chapter proposes reframing the interpretation of IB research from discrete episodes to evolutionary successions in order to improve our understanding of past research programs and to envision likely research agendas. Doing so, we submit, meaningfully frames the debate of the future of IB studies by sorting out historical research streams, linking the relevance of ongoing IB research to its philosophical evolution, and identifying a future path that leverages the cumulative accomplishments of IB studies. Importantly, we believe this approach complements and enhances Buckley's approach. That is, an evolutionary approach does not reject the possible emergence of important new questions. Instead, it engages the perspective to place those questions in a richer research context. Indeed, potential 'big empirical questions' may already be lurking in the business world or within the literature, simply awaiting 'discovery' by IB researchers – provided the latter can 'see' them within the context of the cumulative evolution of IB studies. For instance, FDI existed for centuries before any researchers considered it a 'big question'.

3. A POINT OF PERSPECTIVE

We agree with Buckley that newer and functionally superior ones typically displace older scientific theories. Further, we take as given that the refinement and extension of concepts and theories depend on the development of more robust explanatory perspectives. However, we disagree that one needs to await the cue of the next big empirical question to catalyze the inspiration for theory development. Rather, we see the task for IB scholars as one of moving ahead of the curve or else risking being left behind. Doing so requires that scholars move from reflecting on the characteristics of past episodes of IB studies to purposeful assessing, testing and debating ontological moderators of the ongoing philosophical evolution of IB studies.[5] Put differently, the challenge of 'interpreting' the IB research agenda becomes the challenge of showing how conceptual changes in scholarly perspectives steadily result in the synthesis of ideas that are better adapted to prevailing and emergent reality.

Meeting these goals, we believe, does not require conceiving a new-fangled model. Doing so would fail to heed pioneering works, notably Toyne (1989); Toyne and Nigh (1997, 1998, p. 14), and Mendenhall (1999), and their consistent call to address the question 'What knowledge do we seek, for what purpose, and why?' Therefore, we aim to reply to this by question, with regards to Buckley's assertion, by shifting debate from the epistemological character of the particular content of specific research episodes – the crux of Buckley's thesis – to the ontological principles of the evolution of IB research. That is, initially scholars must decide which philosophical perspectives are genuine possibilities for insightful and innovative interpretations of their research. They need to handle this preliminary sorting of initially plausible perspectives before then resolving epistemological questions of explanatory methods, analytical routines or empirical justification. A variety of literature, for example philosophy of science, evolutionary biology, cybernetics, provides rich material for studying the ontological evolution of IB studies. The literature also provides ample insights to assess and interpret both the discrete and cumulative perspectives that IB scholars have used to discriminate issues, classify variables, organize analysis, and anchor abstractions – or, in the shorthand for this chapter, to develop the ontologies of IB studies.

The social sciences in general and business in particular exhibit enduring perspectives that we use to frame our analysis. Specifically, we use the terms Scientific, Humanist and Chaos to delineate our ontological taxonomy. We apply this taxonomy to assess the cumulative IB research heritage, using it to partition different interpretative logics in ways that identify past points of divergence, recognize present points of convergence, and foresee likely future points of elaboration.

4. THE SCIENTIFIC ONTOLOGY

The scientific ontology (a.k.a., logical positivism, empiricism, the classical view) has precise standards: the rational value of research depends on the formal validity or logic of its arguments, the accuracy of testing the arguments/theories as true or false, and the ease of replicating conclusions through independent empirical observations. A fundamental premise is that conditions exist prior to the theories developed to explain them – essentially, Buckley's idea that theory development responds to a 'big empirical question'.

This ontology sees the world as a well behaved system of discrete parts operating in a consistent, systematic and predictable universe. It girds the idea that relationships between cause and effect are straightforward, for example if X, then Y. Within this context, scientists can assess objective data in order to predict the behavior, control for anomalies, and sustain system equilibrium. Taylor's (1911) scientific management perspective provides an application of the scientific ontology. Specifically, Taylor theorized, 'The best management is a true science, resting upon clearly defined laws, rules, and principles as a foundation ... those laws constitute an understandable, predictable, controllable system'. Essentially, this perspective sees business and, by extension its study, as an objective matter of optimization. Researchers are scientists who reasonably aspire to know and understand all. Fortified with a scientific outlook to 'search for general laws or rules', they search for the 'one best method' that optimizes performance, that is, Rugman's (1993, p.87) premise that MNEs have the 'single goal of efficient economic performance through a simplistic globalization strategy'.

Theoretical expressions of this philosophy abound. Positivists advocate 'methodological monism, mathematical ideals of perfection, and a subsumption-theoretic view of scientific explanation' (Von Wright, 1971, p. 9). Operationally, this philosophy spurs scholars to specify closed equilibrium models that delineate non-equivocating cause and effect relationships among a few key parameters that then anchor empirical testing of the derived propositions. The majority of social science theories conceived in the nineteenth and twentieth centuries were based upon positivistic assumptions. In the realm of IB studies, 'reductionistic, deterministic, and equilibrium-oriented perspectives' frame these sorts of analyses (Mendenhall,1999, p. 68).

Buckley's illustrations confirm that scientific ontology has helped make IB research more systematic, for example researchers have gained objective data and refined our understanding of IB by accepting the premise that agents – whether workers, managers, companies, institutions, or other stakeholders – can or should be rational systems that operate as efficiently as possible. Specifically, Buckley argues that these efforts showed up in 'Dunning's (1958) meticulous analysis of US FDI in the UK and on Bain's (1956) analysis on barriers to entry into industries, later refined by Caves (1971) in a paper which first systematised the industrial economics of foreign direct investment'. Further, the 2003 'Focused Issue' of the *Journal of International Business Studies* on 'The Future of the Multinational Enterprise: 25 Years Later' underscored the value of the scientific ontology to the evolution of IB studies as various authors focused on Buckley and Casson (1976). By and large, the reports in this issue not ed the foundation status of this work, due to its extensive use of systematic approaches and sophisticated statistical methods. Collectively, these reports note that this scientific perspective progressively refined research designs, measures and analytics, which, in turn, supported the development of clearly defined laws, rules and principles of IB.

The scientific perspective has endemic biases. Anomalies cannot be dismissed as 'noise' in the system, the result of human error or imprecise calculations; adherents must continually refine their measurement tools to explain them. This ontology's predisposition towards non-equivocating causality within a closed equilibrium system leads it to suppress other forms of reasoning that cannot be formally modeled (Hench, 1997; Safarian, 2003). It also encourages precise modeling methods and tools to fit the presumed characteristics of the phenomena – namely, parsimonious research designs that efficiently fit the prevailing 'big empirical question' rather than probing data mining to assess secondary and tertiary relationships. The quest to optimize may obsolesce existing ideas and methods, which may then not be revisited by scholars, even though they may have enduring merit. Finally, the scientific perspective is a closed rational approach, portraying agents in pursuit of preset ends, thereby disregarding possible connections to a wider environment.

These biases, we believe, show up in Buckley's positioning of comparative management studies, especially his characterization of culture, as a 'strand of work, parallel to and cross fertilizing 'mainstream' international business research' (Hofstede, 1983, 1991). This view, we believe, is open to debate. 'Comparative' studies have been an enduring and increasingly significant dimension of interest, seen early in Farmer and Richman (1965) and later in Hofstede (1991) and House et al. (2002). Rather than being tangential to 'mainstream' IB studies, studies of culture may be an underappreciated strand of its genetic code. For example, a bibliometric scan of the *Journal of International Business Studies* (JIBS) for articles including the keyword 'culture' yielded 410 citations between 1970 and Spring 2003 versus 486 for finance, 498 for export and 564 for economics. More tellingly, from Fall 1990 through Spring 2003, the JIBS published 53 articles in which the term 'culture' appears in the title, citation or abstract; the corresponding counts for finance, economics and export are 20, 22 and 41. Therefore, we take the position that studies of culture in terms of values, relativity, people, behavior, and so on, rather than being a tangential wildcard that runs parallel to the scientific stream of research, are examples of the ontology commonly referred to as humanism.

5. THE HUMANISM ONTOLOGY

Before describing the humanism ontology, it is helpful to assess Buckley's view of the bellwether status of Hofstede (1983). We propose that the humanist component of IB research, expressed early in Farmer and Richman (1965) and Negandhi and Prasad (1971) but conspicuously established with Hofstede (1983), steadily gained credibility because of the restrictive assumptions of the scientific ontology: (a) its treatment of culture – namely values, expectations and motivations – as either exogenous to models or undifferentiated among countries; (b) its premise that workers, managers, companies, institutions and stakeholders aspired to optimize absolute economic performance; and (c) its consequential neglect, if not rejection, of the human element of IB studies. Once these assumptions are questioned, as exemplified in Hofstede's conclusion that people with the same information might arrive at different decisions or behave dissimilarly because of their latent cultural values, the legitimacy or universality of direct deductive inferences from the scientific ontology are questionable. Thus, the idea of cultural relativity and its suggestion of behavioral and non-optimal decision-making challenged the premise that 'All agents rationally optimize performance', thereby challenging the closed equilibrium systems of the scientific ontology.[6]

Philosophically, humanism is freely applied to modern doctrines and non-scientific techniques that are based on the centrality of human experience – so-called anthropocentricity. Essentially, humanism champions the idea that people and, by extension, organizational and national cultures matter; hence, cultural relativity is a significant explanatory variable. Interestingly, Hofstede's study appeared around the same time that Peters and Waterman (1982) published their manifesto of humanism and its then heretical conclusion that successful business performance 'all comes from people'.

The ideas of humanism fundamentally affected interpretations in IB studies. Most immediately, they challenged ideas of human resource management. No longer could one assume that a well-performing procedure, tool, or even manager in New York would function in the same way in London or Tokyo (Ivancevich, 1969; Hays, 1974). Instead, humanism stressed that the effectiveness of a particular managerial procedure, tool or behavior is a function of its environment (Farmer and Richman, 1965). In following this reasoning, IB scholars have tried to assess if, when, how and why attitudes and values vary from one culture to another and what are the implications of variances to, for example, motivation (Abramson et al., 1993), nature of managerial work (Lubatkin, Ndiaye and Vengraff, 1997), expatriate performance (Black and Porter, 1991), joint ventures (Barkema and Vermeulen, 1997), management practices (Newman and Nollen, 1996), and strategic alliances (Tallman and Shenkar, 1994). Throughout this literature, scholars see coherence, not consistency, as the requirement for relevance and validity. This view then moves interpretation from the absoluteness of the scientifically optimal method to that of the relative effectiveness of various approaches.

To its fault, scant comparative management research has actually linked cultural differences between the effects of various approaches and international companies' performance, for example whether managers from cultures with norms of consultative management styles are likely to improve performance by being autocratic where autocratic management styles prevail. Consequently, the largely descriptive bent of comparative IB studies means that they are sometimes viewed skeptically by scholars and practitioners who prefer the prescriptive (albeit sometimes erroneous) conclusions from the scientific ontology. Nevertheless, as the number of comparative management studies proliferated, the ontology of humanism gained theoretical legitimacy.

6. ONTOLOGICAL INTERACTION: SCIENTIFIC HUMANISM

Despite the fuzziness of many humanist conclusions, humanist IB research has helped make scientific research even more 'scientific'. The increasing application of behavioral sciences, like anthropology and social psychology, to analyze the actions of and relationships among IB agents and stakeholders is improving the rigor of scientific interpretation. Much of the IB literature in the past decade contains examples of 'scientific humanism', in which scholars expanded their ideas of validity and considered additional variables to predict outcomes.

Notwithstanding the robustness of the scientific humanist ontology, we do not believe this integration is sufficient to study emerging issues in IB. Put simply, we question its robustness to improve significantly our understanding of emerging IB issues such as those Buckley identifies; 'mergers and acquisitions, knowledge management, geography, location, globalization, and new institutions such as NGOs (non-governmental organizations)'. While we agree that these sorts of phenomena possess both rational and behavioral properties, we see two risks in studying them only from scientific humanist perspectives. First, the use and refinement of these perspectives risk perpetuating the illusion that we can 'reasonably' predict the future, for example that models of the past will repeat in the future. Second, while many of these issues are within our historic perspectives, these emerging issues increasingly manifest properties and tendencies that challenge the design of a meaningful model.

For example, consider the issue of NGOs. Numbering just a few thousand in 1990, NGOs presently approximate between 50 000 and more than 250 000, and span local, national or international levels (van Tuijl, 1999).[7] Although this growth has occurred without central direction or institutional coordination, NGOs have materially and manifestly influenced international business-government-interactions on operating rules, norms and practices (Eden and Lenway, 2001; Doh and Teegen, 2002; Robinson,

2003; Kobrin, 2001). Matters get a bit more interesting when one considers the 'organizational' practices of NGOs. For example, autonomous but Internet-connected squads of demonstrators protested and temporarily shut down the World Trade Organization's Third Ministerial meeting in Seattle, as well as challenging subsequent meetings in Quebec City in 2001 and Cancun in 2003, by using 'swarming' tactics, mobile phones, websites, and laptops to create unprecedented alliances (for example labor coalitions with fringe eco-groups). Widespread technologies enabled loosely coupled, amorphous, and adaptive groups to mobilize into leaderless and self-organizing 'smart mobs' (Rheingold, 2002). More fundamentally, the fact that previously isolated groups could connect to one another through heterarchies meant that they could appeal to individuals and groups far outside the typical realm of social protest. Consequently, the activities of NGOs will likely grow in scale, scope and power in both vivid settings, that is ministerial meetings, and 'routine' processes, that is, hindering the distribution of genetically modified organisms or orchestrating the collapse of Multilateral Agreement on Investment (Kobrin, 1998; Eden and Lenway, 2001; Robinson, 2003). Thus, managers, companies and institutions will more often and in more places face groups that defy traditional notions of geography, time and organization but which, Eden and Lenway (2001, p. 16) conclude, could evolve into a 'global organization that could potentially threaten the continued liberalization of the global economy'.

The case of NGOs, we submit, confirms in general terms that Buckley is indisputably right: the research tools of preceding episodes of IB studies, although useful for many research agendas, lack the 'steam' to analyze the issue of NGOs (to say nothing of nascent forms of alliances,[8] processes of knowledge transfer, movements of globalization, or other phenomena in which order naturally emerges regardless of the complexity, loose connectivity, or non-linearity of the system). For example, again with respect to analyzing NGOs, whenever a new communications technology lowers the threshold for groups to act collectively, new kinds of institutions emerge. Rather than being defined in terms of conventional governance structures or administrative routines, these new institutions are defined more by network communications and social networks. Hence, reliance on traditional tools that can analyze the latter but not the former presents fundamental challenges that are not likely to be resolved by turbo-charging traditional ontological frameworks. Mendenhall and Macaomber (1997) amplify this point, contending that in complex, connected systems, the 'relationships of the parts within the system are so mutually intertwined that one cannot simply tear out a subsystem of a larger system and study it. It cannot be done because each element of the system is too richly interconnected with other elements of the system'. To put this directly in the context of this chapter, neither alone nor combined can the scientific or humanist ontologies be likely to analyze the unfolding complexity of NGOs meaningfully. Both frameworks tend to fall short when trying to discriminate issues, classify variables, organize analysis, and anchor abstractions of NGOs.

Kogut and Zander (1993) contend that the capacity to lead in knowledge production is the key to the ongoing success of firms. Effectively, their evolutionary approach warns against opportunistic behavior, such as waiting for the next big question to mobilize action. Similarly, Kuhn (1990, p. 7) sees scientific development 'as evolution from, rather than evolution towards'. Collectively, these views call for enriching, extending and checking the ontologies of science and humanism with that of chaos (Daneke, 1999; Lewin, 1999).

7. THE CHAOS ONTOLOGY

One may wonder, what is chaos, and why now? Theorists use chaos to signal something different from the conventional meaning of the word. Put simply, chaos refers to the particular zone between stability and instability, rather than 'out of control', or 'patternless'[9] (Pascale, 1999). As many agents' environments move toward more spontaneity and vibrancy, they search more intensely for positions and processes characterized by flexibility and adaptation.[10] For example, Buckley and Casson (2003) and Safarian (2003) note the need for a new research agenda that fits the volatility of the environment for IB – just as Buckley and Casson (2003, p. 219) noted in the 1970s that, 'a new framework was needed that would allow the statistics to reveal the underlying dynamics of multinational behavior'.[11]

Both scholars and practitioners routinely describe the need to analyze the environmental turbulence that confronts individuals, firms, institutions and countries because globalization, competition and technology require novel means to move from the static analysis of closed equilibrium systems to dynamic analysis of far-from-equilibrium systems. Increasingly, traditional methods are inadequate to fit agents' growing needs to be sufficiently flexible and adaptable in dynamic, far-from-equilibrium environments (de la Torre and Moxon, 2001; Child and Tse, 2001). The following discussion develops these ideas.

The ontology of chaos, also called complexity theory or non-linear systems, has demonstrated practical value in meteorology, ecology, quantum physics, mathematics, evolutionary biology, life sciences and statistics (Chin et al., 1996; Costantino et al., 1997; Iomin and Zaslavsky, 2002; Finkenstadt and Rootzen, 2003). Steadily, success shows up in the social sciences (Brier, 2000; van Staveren, 1999; Sterman and Wittenberg, 1999; Beinhocker, 1997; Martinez et al., 1999; Houston, 2001), affirming that the principles of chaos can effectively explain different system behaviors. Reports from cybernetics, biology, quantum physics and cognitive sciences outline the principles of the chaos ontology, most notably:

1. Everything in the world is interconnected with everything else; in an open, dynamic system, you cannot change an isolated facet without affecting another, which then affects another, ad infinitum.
2. Interactive agents make up each adaptive system such that when agents interact in a web of relationships, evolutionary changes by one agent will affect the evolution of others. This effect, known as coevolution, is seen in nature, and applies to the study of social sciences when an occurrence, such as trade liberalization, produces ripple effects throughout the global economy (for example FDI patterns, negotiating strategies, host government relations, operating forms, supply chains, knowledge diffusion, staffing practices, and so on).
3. Systems move toward more, not less, connectivity. When sufficiently complex and interconnected, the interaction among systems self-assembles them into a new, higher order; for example, evolution from the agreement among six European countries in 1952 to form the European Coal and Steel Community, to the adoption of regional trading groups worldwide.[12]
4. Self-organization emerges out of the dynamic interaction of agents, who individually may come and go without altering the pattern of self-organization, for example, NGOs.
5. Everything in the system is evolving simultaneously, affecting everything else. Consequently, change in just one part of the world can ultimately lead to radical transformations in the overall system – the so-called 'butterflies in China, hurricanes in the Caribbean' adage. More practically, the early application of quality circles in Japanese management eventually led to processes of self-organization, learning organizations, and radical forms of continuous quality improvement in American companies.

The principles of chaos have stark implications for the activity of agents. Their world is fundamentally unpredictable, uncertain and ultimately uncontrollable in ways that are routine (for example the progressive liberalization of trade through the GATT/WTO) or extraordinary (for example the terrorist attacks of 9/11). Certainly, agents may make a difference in the 'short term', developing useful positions and advantageous coalitions. Ultimately, though, an agent's fate is moderated by forces beyond its control.

The chaos ontology has significant research implications. First, its premise of dynamic connectivity shifts emphasis from the scientific cause-and-effect precision of Newtonian physics to the statistical estimate of probabilities of Einstein relativity in order to speak 'directly to the processes that created the phenomena under examination' (Toyne and Nigh, 1998; Mendenhall, 1999). Second, it incorporates the humanist perspective of non-optimal decision making so that researchers can generate new insights and path-breaking interpretations (Lewin, 1999). More pointedly, the chaos ontology spurs scholars to see the actions and behaviors of agents within an environment of multiple interdependencies and to acknowledge that these loosely-structured interdependencies are sufficiently unified to warrant use of the word 'system'. The ontology forces them to recognize that actions and reactions of individuals, small groups, dispersed coalitions, or even groups as large as nations or regional blocs fall within certain definable, more or less universal patterns of equilibrium and disequilibrium. Further, they must consider that the interdependence of roles, norms and functions is fundamental to the behavior of all types of agents in all sorts of systems.

The growing popularity of chaos ontology among scholars who profess its universal application can incite backlash (Sterman and Wittenberg, 1999). Thus, IB scholars must demonstrate its usefulness by developing and testing formal models; otherwise, their metaphorical use of concepts from non-linear dynamics or cybernetics, while provocative, will not be perceived as legitimate.[13] Rather than extolling the virtues of the chaos ontology, IB researchers must build rigorous theories, develop tools tailored for empirical situations, and conduct studies to test their theories and tools. Some IB research is already moving in this direction, such as Martinez et al.'s (1999) innovative application of non-linear 'phase planes' to analyze response adjustments in intervention strategies resulting from longitudinal changes in Mexican and Brazilian risk ratings;[14] Lisi and Medio's (1997) finding that non-linear systems were a better predictor of short-term exchange rate movements than the random walk hypothesis; Daneke's (1998) finding that ideas of chaos provide a better explanation of government policy toward industrial innovation than the entrepreneurial capitalist view; and Koza and Lewin's (1999) conclusion from the coevolutionary modeling of an international professional service network that networks may not necessarily foreshadow radically new forms of organization. This growing literature confirms the potential of chaos theory to IB studies.

There are ever-increasing research tools to apply the chaos ontology. Analytical techniques, advances in cognitive science and statistical techniques now permit much more realistic assumptions that can be translated into sophisticated simulations. In agent-based models, for example, any sort of agent can be modeled in an intelligent computer program to simulate learning, adapting and self-organizing. One can then program a group of agents into a simulated competitive market, unleash the forces of evolution, and view the unfolding of different futures. Other tools are also apparent: coevolutionary frameworks, decomposition of nested phenomena, models of multidirectional causalities, and options theory can advance theoretical and empirical research in IB studies. More importantly, situational contingencies stimulate experimentation with new methods that promise to help managers and scholars deal with the non-linear dynamics and adaptive complexity of chaos (Daneke, 1999). By using these tools, IB researchers ideally can develop experimental and field studies of individual, organizational and institutional behavior to build models that specify the decision rules governing the self-organization characteristics of systems of agents.[15]

8. THE DYNAMIC OF CHANGE

IB studies, like studies in almost any discipline, face the challenge of reaffirming their relevance or fading away. Fortunately, IB scholars have successfully met this challenge in the past. For example, reflections in the 2003 'Focused Issue' of JIBS on the 'The Future of the Multinational Enterprise: 25 Years Later' gives a sense of the likely dynamic of change. Throughout this issue, there is a sense of the Zeitgeist of IB 25 years ago. Specifically, Safarian (2003, p. 123) recounts that IB was a 'field in ferment' in the 1960s and 1970s, following 'two decades of experimentation with a variety of approaches'. Within this context, Buckley and Casson's (2003, p. 219) avowedly positivist approach to use statistics to 'reveal the underlying dynamics of multinational behavior' established 'the right theory [whereby] it would be possible to use the statistics to pass judgment on competing views'. These ideas evolved into the scientific ontology, whose 'unifying set of ideas, analytical power, institutional focus, and methodological accessibility' appealed to the then loosely related areas of IB studies (Safarian, 2003, p. 116). IB studies progressively gained legitimacy.

We believe this dynamic of change is set to replay – albeit under different intellectual circumstances. That is, we do not believe that reaffirming the relevance of IB studies hinges on awaiting the next big empirical question or, for that matter, trying to specify more sophisticated applications of the scientific and humanist ontologies. Rather, the relevance of IB studies depends on studying existing research streams and their evolutionary permutations by applying the precepts and procedures of new ontologies, such as chaos, and integrating these findings into mainstream IB literature.

Precedence suggests that IB scholars have the capacity to derive insights from chaos ontology. Recall IB's adoption of the humanist ontology and the adaptation of it to the scientific ontology. Synthesis was not a preordained outcome. Other fields, notably economics (Schnellenbach, 2002) and political science (Boylan and O'Gorman, 2003), continue to struggle with the humanist ontology's skepticism of rationality and optimization. Although we agree with Buckley that the concern should not be whether IB or functional scholars undertake IB research, we, nevertheless, believe that IB specialists may have a competitive advantage in undertaking research involving chaos theory simply because historically the field has been more cross-functional and cross-disciplinary than most others. Thus, IB researchers may intuitively understand connectivity more than many of their colleagues and may extract insights that are more powerful by applying a systemic perspective to IB (Daniels, 1991; Toyne and Nigh, 1997).

Historical accounts and applied simulations of the evolution of science underscore the peril of awaiting the next big empirical question and then studying it with the then best suited ontology (Sterman and Wittenberg, 1999). Disciplinary knowledge is marked by the ongoing emergence of many intellectual problems of many different types. While we agree with Buckley that emergence is sometimes a function of the topics being studied, it is typically more a function of the environment's and discipline's evolutionary stage (Kuhn, 1990). For example, Buckley notes that the 'Uppsala school whose "stages" model of internationalization became the foundation for the gradualist step-by-step internationalization model' was a significant element of the first episode of IB studies. Anchoring this model to a particular episode, however, downplays the striking evolution in our ensuing understanding of internationalization. That is, at one time, the model successfully predicted that companies expand abroad by following an incremental path from near to far geographic proximity and psychic distance (Johansson and Vahlne, 1977; Hornell et al., 1973). At a later time or stage, researchers found more exceptions and that companies become regional or global from birth (de la Torre and Moxon, 2001; O'Grady and Lane, 1996; Stottinger and Schlegelmilch, 1998; Singh and Kundu, 2002). Thus, inferring the future from the past may be less useful and relevant than researchers usually imply. Moreover, although historic perspectives help make sense of each situation, eventually they are inherently limited in providing a theoretically meaningful interpretation of everything. Finally, the historical evolution of any field generates a genealogy of varied problems (Kuhn, 1970), which inevitably necessitate different ontologies for different problems at different times.

9. THE MATTER OF COMMENSURABILITY

Given that the scientific, humanist and chaos ontologies differ in their philosophical assumptions, goals and methods, some may contend that engaging them simultaneously is theoretically flawed and intellectually perilous. After all, each ontology constitutes its own mutually exclusive perspective, such that representatives of various ontologies largely 'live in different worlds', hold mutually exclusive beliefs, use different vocabularies, and apply different approaches (Burrell and Morgan, 1979). Hence, arguably a discipline can only engage different ontologies sequentially (as Buckley implicitly suggests), rather than simultaneously (as this chapter proposes). If so, then some may contend that our call for IB studies to engage alternative ontologies simultaneously may bring about the 'theoretical hermeticism' (Hassard, 1988) and 'apartheid for paradigms' (Donaldson, 1988, p. 31) that precludes synthesis.[16]

Essentially, the issue is whether IB scholars can simultaneously engage different ontologies in ways that permit meaningful cross communication and fertilization. Theory and everyday practice suggest that such engagement is possible. For example, philosophers of science argue that incommensurability does not necessarily prevent the comparison of alternative ontologies. Whether incommensurability entails non-comparability depends on the cognitive and non-cognitive goals that we invoke for our scientific inquiries; success in achieving some pragmatic goals may be measurable apart from direct comparisons of the substantive content of different theories (for example Laudan, 1976; Weaver and Gioia, 1994). This line of reasoning suggests that, rather than debating notions of incommensurability, we ought to see competing ontologies as complementary means of ultimately understanding a unified picture in the sense that each contributes 'markedly different and uniquely informative theoretical views of events under study' (Gioia and Pitre, 1990, p. 590).

More practically, all of us in the intellectual and cultural melting pot of the IB field routinely manage to understand each other in a way that, although fallible, does not seem destined to failure. Granted, exchange may be taxing for, say, economists and behaviorists, but it is nonetheless the case that representatives of both groups manage to succeed reasonably well at it. More pointedly, Kuhn (1990, p. 300) asserts, 'anything that can be said in one language can, with sufficient imagination and effort, be understood by a speaker of another. What is a prerequisite to such understanding, however, is not translation but language learning'. The evolution of IB studies supports this interpretation; practitioners of the humanist ontology in IB studies have meaningfully communicated ideas, concepts and methods to their 'scientific' counterparts and, in kind, the latter have shared their worldview. It seems reasonable that reports grounded in chaos will yield similar dividends.

Therefore, this chapter takes as given the commensurability of ideas among the scientific, humanist and chaos ontologies – provided this thesis is framed in terms of the feasibility of communicating about and comprehending, though not necessarily wholly accepting, the arguments and views of each. Operationally, this statement suggests that the IB field can move toward a unified body of knowledge – presuming unification entails an ability to grasp the differences, similarities and interrelationships among the multiple approaches anchored in different ontologies – by dealing with the various aspects of a unified picture that is best grasped from different ontological perspectives.

10.   CONCLUSION

Buckley concludes, international business research has succeeded because it has focused on, in sequence, a number of big questions which arise from empirical developments in the world economy. The agenda has stalled because no such big question has currently been identified. His essay submits that the partitioning of IB research into discrete episodes, while provocative, downplays the more fundamental evolutionary dynamic of how questions progress and how we take different views about things international. Like others (for example Toyne and Nigh, 1997; Mendenhall, 1999), we contend that scholars need multiple perspectives to study different aspects of different questions at different times. They should decide which among all of the intellectually conceivable repertory of philosophical perspectives are genuine possibilities for insightful interpretations. Historically, the repertory in IB studies has included (1) the scientific ontology that championed the principles of rationality and optimization; (2) the humanist ontology that endorsed the ideas of culture, relativity, people and values; and (3) some combination of the two. We argue that while intrinsically powerful, these ontologies are limited in providing a theoretically meaningful interpretation of any and all phenomena.

Thus, we share Buckley's concern that the 'international business research agenda is running out of steam after a period of vibrancy'. However, we propose a radically different path forward. Whereas Buckley suggests the problem is not having a big question, we suggest there are big questions but that we're not engaging ontologies effectively to answer them. Instead, we propose that scholars reinvigorate IB studies by complementing traditional ontologies with that of chaos and its principles of self-organization, non-linearity and connectivity. The emergence of the ontology of chaos as a consistent and coherent theory, like that of the scientific and humanist perspectives, offers IB scholars new possibilities in discriminating issues, classifying variables, organizing analysis and anchoring abstractions. In effect, we submit that the ontology of chaos represents the natural progression of the evolution of thought in IB studies that can enrich and elaborate the scientific and humanist ontologies.

Like its counterparts, the chaos ontology is not fixed to a specific episode, but simply is part of the evolution of thought in IB studies. Hence, this chapter does not aim to profile a zero-sum contest, suggesting that scholars reflexively abandon a particular ontology in favor of another. In principle, the scientific, humanist and chaos ontologies can be fountainheads of ideas that separately and collectively improve the meaningfulness of IB research. Therefore, we endorse the idea of philosophical equifinality[17] in which no one ontology is suitable for all situations.

Finally, the adoption and integration of the chaos ontology into mainstream IB studies faces hurdles. Most immediately and perhaps most pernicious are institutional constraints. Generally, the historical development of science, for instance, shows that scholars have sometimes disregarded novel possibilities that later turned out to be basic for solving significant problems. Looking back, it is possible to reconstruct the rationale that might have been advanced at the time to explain this neglect. Even so, it sometimes appears that 'conventional and complacent' gatekeepers played key roles in suppressing new approaches (Buckley and Casson, 2003, p. 221; Clegg, 2002). Ultimately, reenergizing IB studies depends on leadership by confident and competent scholars in the belief that those with the best-trained minds can afford to give the freest rein to their intellectual imagination.

11. LIMITATIONS

This chapter has tried to identify the many ideas, consistencies, assumptions and expectations of the dynamic evolution of IB studies. Any such identification is inevitably less than what we tried to portray because we are unable to capture all the intricacies and subtleties of such a broad issue. Further, although we critique Buckley's attempt to partition all IB research into three, maybe four, categories, we are undoubtedly guilty as well of simplification by putting studies into specific ontologies. Still, when profiling a field historically and pointing to the future, we must resort to broad statements and tidy categorizations that often fall short of fully representing the specifics of a particular situation or sequence of events. We have tried, with the aid of several discussions and critiques, to minimize these sorts of distortions.

NOTES

1. Specifically, Robinson (1964), Polk et al. (1966), and Behrman (1974) highlighted the importance of economic and sovereignty effects on stakeholders in both home and host countries. Recent work, for example Prakash and Hart (1999) and Plender (2003) on questions of governance, confirm the ongoing vitality of this stream.

2. Since Buckley used the idiom of 'running out of steam', we will use a steam analogy to illustrate our point. Although James Watt's invention of the steam engine in 1769 to pump water from coal mines is said to have ushered in the age of steam, his work depended on Newcomen's 1717 steam engine invention, which depended on Savery's 1698 patent, which depended on Papin's 1680 design, and so forth. Further, research continued after Watt's invention by improving upon his work and by applying steam engines in cotton mills, locomotives and boats. A perusal of US patents registered in 2002 indicates that people are still finding new uses for steam engines and improving on existing models. To his credit, Buckley concedes this limit in one of his endnotes, stating, 'A great deal more could be said of the research which predated and foreshadowed Hymer's analysis, but that is for another paper'.

3. This approach has precedent; researchers in other social sciences areas have tried to reframe debate in ontological terms to resolve struggles with epistemological challenges (see, for instance, the modern-postmodern debate in *Organization Studies*: Chia, 1995; Cooper and Burrell, 1988; Burrell, 1988; Cooper, 1989).

4. We already see manifestation of this latter effect. Specifically, Gnemawat (2003), in a somewhat discouraging aside, surmised, 'International business has succeeded because it has focused on, in sequence, a number of big questions, which arise from empirical developments in the world economy. The agenda is stalled because no such big question has currently been identified. This calls into question the separate existence of the subject area. It raises the old problem of the relationship between international business and other functional areas of management and social science'.

5. We use the term ontology to signify an explicit specification of a conceptualization. We borrow the term from philosophy, where ontology is a systematic account of existence. The subject of ontology is the study of the categories of things

that exist or may exist in some domain. The product of such a study, called ontology, is a catalog of the types of things that are assumed to exist in a domain of interest from the perspective of a person who uses a language for the purpose of talking about the domain of interest. An ontology will thus analyze the most general and abstract concepts or distinctions that underlie every more specific description of any phenomenon in the world, for example time, space, matter, process, cause and effect, system, and so on.

6. Similar challenge and change took place in organizational theory. In the 1930s, the human relations movement emphasized the importance of social relations among organizational participants (Mayo, 1933). Subsequently, Simon (1947) proposed the idea of bounded rationality, whereby decision makers were not perfectly rational but actually had limited reasoning, perceiving and information-processing abilities. Related work showed the socio-technical systems view that stressed a work group is subject to social, psychological, technical and economic forces. In addition, in the mid-1950s, Argyris (1957) and McGregor (1960) developed their models of desirable organizations in which human needs would be more fully satisfied and more efficient use could be made of human capital. By and large, the human relations school has had many effects on scientific organizational theory – in the least, challenging many assumptions and in extreme, aspiring to reveal the inappropriateness of universal principles of organizations.

7. See, for instance, OECD Directory of NGOs, the United Nation Development Programme's (UNDP) Human Development Report, and the Yearbook of International Organizations. Whatever the souce, all report significant expansion of NGOs; the United Nations identified more than 6000 NGOs in 1990, 29000 NGOs in 1995, and 47 000 in 2000, the 2002 Yearbook of International Organizations identifies more than 250 000 NGOs, while informal estimates put the number of international NGOs at over one million.

8. Consider that intra-company alliances are an increasingly significant topic. Their numbers have grown by more than 30 per cent a year over the past decade. Similarly, their form has changed dramatically: the cross-border and technology agreements of the 1980s and the early 1990s have given rise to the much broader range of alliances seen today – R&D partnerships, outsourcing and offshoring agreements, consolidation ventures, start-ups, channel partnerships, and other co-branding and co-marketing deals. At many companies, a quarter or more of all revenues now come from alliances. Again, making sense of these aspects places increasing demands on scientific and humanist perspectives.

9. Pascale (1999, p. 85) explains that at this edge of chaos, 'the components of the system never quite lock into place, yet never quite dissolve into turbulence, either. These are the systems that are both stable enough to store information, and yet evanescent enough to transmit it. These are the systems that can be organized to perform complex computations, to react to the world, to be spontaneous, adaptive, and alive.'

10. Some may say that chaos is simply an extension of the well-established stream of research in contingency theory. In the realm of organizations, for example, contingency theory has examined organic forms adapted to highly complex and dynamic environments (Burns and Stalker, 1961; Duncan, 1972; Lawrence and Lorsch, 1967). Others, in the context of selection theories, relate the

emergence of new organization forms to environmental developments at the population level (Hannan and Freeman, 1989). Contingency and selection theories, however, purport to specify linear models that directly link specific form characteristics to environmental conditions whereas complexity theory begins with the assumption of non-linearity.

11. More specifically, Child and Tse's (2001) study of transitions in developing economies concluded: 'The inability to apply a simple linear model of transition means that international firms need new tools to function in dynamic and complex environments. ...The challenge for transition economies managers is how to model non-linear complexity and analyze its implications.'

12. Alternatively, for example, in the physical sciences, molecules to cells, cells to organs, organs to organisms, organism to societies.

13. A case in point is the routine caveat that we should engage aspects of chaos in future studies but chose not to do so in the present work. For example, Lovett et al. (1999), in a study of interlocking guanxi systems and the dynamic aspects of guanxi building, concludes with the caveat that however, as mentioned earlier, 'a research program must eventually expand beyond the single-period or static model presented in this paper in order to fully capture the dynamic guanxi process ... Depicting the resulting complexity of interlocking systems will make the model more realistic and more powerful, but also immensely more complex'.

14. The notion of phase planes is an element of so-called 'phase space' in which numerical values are transformed into geometrical representations by converting numbers into grid coordinates, thereby enabling graphical analyses of the behavior of particular phenomena over time.

15. To say the least, such techniques will challenge the epistemological techniques of the scientific ontology most dramatically. This ontology ultimately relies on mathematical proofs to model its theories. The benefit of this approach is that you can be confident of the logical rigor of your answer. The drawback is that proofs restrict you to simple assumptions such as perfect rationality. No matter how elegant or rigorous the model, if the assumptions do not reflect the real world, the answer will be irrelevant.

16. Or, as Burrell and Morgan (1979, p. 25) put it: 'A synthesis is not possible, since in their pure forms the paradigms are contradictory, being based on at least one set of opposing meta-theoretical assumptions. They are alternatives, in the sense that one can operate in different paradigms sequentially over time, but mutually exclusive, in the sense that one cannot operate in more than one paradigm at any given point in time, since in accepting the assumptions of one, we defy the assumptions of all the others.'

17. Equifinality is the observation that several or many different ways may exist to arrive at the same end state.

REFERENCES

Abramson, N., H. Lane, H. Nagai and H. Takagi (1993), 'A comparison of Canadian and Japanese cognitive styles: implications for management interaction', *Journal of International Business Studies*, **24**(3), 575-88.

Argyris, C. (1957), *Personality and Organization*, New York: Harper.

Bain, J.S. (1956), *Barriers to New Competition*, Cambridge, MA: Harvard University Press.

Barkema, H. and F. Vermeulen (1997), 'What differences in the cultural backgrounds of partners are detrimental for international joint ventures?', *Journal of International Business Studies*, **28**(4), 845-64.

Behrman, J. (1971), *US International Business and Governments*, New York: McGraw-Hill.

Behrman, J. (1997), 'Discussion of the conceptual domain of international business', in B. Toyne and D. Nigh (eds), *International Business: An Emerging Vision*, Columbia, SC: University of South Carolina Press.

Beinhocker, E. (1997), 'Strategy at the edge of chaos', *The McKinsey Quarterly*, **1**, 24-39.

Black, J. and L. Porter (1991), 'Managerial behaviors and job performance: a successful manager in Los Angeles may not succeed in Hong Kong', *Journal of International Business Studies*, **22**(1), 99-113.

Boylan, A. and P. O'Gorman (2003), 'Economic theory and rationality: a Wittgensteinian interpretation', *Review of Political Economy*, **15**(2), 231-45.

Brier, S. (2000), 'Trans-scientific frameworks of knowing: complementarity views of the different types of human knowledge', *Systems Research and Behavioral Science*, **17**(5), 433.

Buckley, P.J. (2002), 'Is the international business research agenda running out of steam?', *Journal of International Business Studies*, **33**(2), 365-74.

Buckley, P.J. and M. Casson (1976), *The Future of the Multinational Enterprise*, London: Macmillan.

Buckley, P.J. and M. Casson (2003), 'The future of the multinational enterprise in retrospect and in prospect', *Journal of International Business Studies*, **34**(2), 219-23.

Burns, T. and G.M. Stalker (1961), *The Management of Innovation*, New York: Oxford University Press.

Burrell, G. (1988), 'Modernism, postmodernism and organizational analysis 2: the contribution of Michel Foucault', *Organization Studies*, **9**, 221-37.

Burrell, G. and G. Morgan (1979), *Sociological Paradigms and Organizational Analysis*, London: Heinemann.

Capra, F. (1996), *The Web of Life*, New York: Anchor Books.

Caves, R.E. (1971), 'International corporations: the industrial economics of foreign investment', *Economics*, **38**, 1-27.

Chia, R. (1995), 'From modern to post-modern organizational analysis', *Organization Studies*, **16**(4), 579-604.

Child, J. and D. Tse (2001), 'China's transition and its implications for international business', *Journal of International Business Studies*, **32**(1), 5.

Chin, G., L. Senesac, W. Blass and J. Hillman (1996), 'Stabilizing lead-salt diode lasers: understanding and controlling chaotic frequency emissions', *Science*, **274**, 1498-501.

Clegg, S.R. (2002), 'Lives in the balance: A comment on Hinings and Greenwood's "Disconnects and Consequences in Organization Theory?"', *Administrative Science Quarterly*, **47**(3), 428-42.

Cooper, R. (1989), 'Modernism, post-modernism and organizational analysis 3: the contribution of Jacques Derrida', *Organization Studies*, **10**(4), 479-502.

Cooper, R. and G. Burrell (1988), 'Modernism, postmodernism and organizational analysis: An ntroduction', *Organization Studies*, **9**, 91-113.

Costantino, R., R. Desharnais, J. Cusing and D. Dennis (1997), 'Chaotic dynamics in an insect population', *Science*, **275**, 389-91.

Daneke, G.A. (1998), 'Beyond Schumpeter: nonlinear economics and the evolution of the US innovation system', *The Journal of Socio-Economics*, **27**(1), 97.

Daneke. G. (1999), *Systemic Choices: Nonlinear Dynamics and Practical Management*, Ann Arbor, MI: University of Michigan Press.

Daniels, J.D. (1991), 'Relevance in international business research: a need for more linkages', *Journal of International Business Studies*, **22**, 1776.

de la Torre, J. and R. Moxon (2001), 'Introduction to the symposium: E-Commerce and Global Business: The Impact of the Information and Communication Technology Revolution on the Conduct of International Business', *Journal of International Business Studies*, **32**(4), 617-40.

Diamond, J. (1998), *Guns, Germs, and Steel: The Fates of Human Societies*, New York: W.W. Norton.

Doh, J.P. and H. Teegen (2002), 'Nongovernmental organizations as institutional actors in international business: theory and implications', *International Business Review*, **11**(6), 665-85.

Donaldson, L. (1988), 'In successful defence of organization theory: a routing of the critics', *Organization Studies*, **9**, 28-32.

Dooley, K. (1997), 'A complex adaptive systems model of organization change', *Nonlinear Dynamics, Psychology, and Life Sciences*, **1**(1), 69-97.

Duncan, R.B. (1972), 'Characteristics of organizational environments and perceived environmental certainty', *Administrative. Science Quarterly*, **17**(3), 313-27.

Dunning, J.H. (1958), *American Investment in British Manufacturing Industry*, London: George Allen and Unwin.

Dunning, J.H. (1989), 'The study of international business: a plea for a more interdisciplinary approach', *Journal of International Business Studies*, **20**, 411-36.

Eden, L. and S. Lenway (2001), 'Introduction to the symposium: Multinationals: The Janus Face of Globalization', *Journal of International Business Studies*, **32**(3), 383.

Elliot, E. and L.D. Kiel (eds) (1996), *Chaos Theory in the Social Sciences: Foundations and Applications*, Ann Arbor: University of Michigan Press.

Farmer, R.N. and B.M. Richman (1965), *Comparative Management and Economic Progress*, Homewood, IL: Richard D. Irwin.

Finkenstadt, B. and H. Rootzen (eds) (2003), *Extreme Values in Finance, Telecommunications and the Environment*, London: Chapman and Hall/CRC.

Gnemawat, P. (2003), 'Semiglobalization and international business strategy', *Journal of International Business Studies*, **34**(2), 1383.

Gioia, D. and E. Pitre (1990), 'Multiparadigm perpectives on theory building', *Academy of Management Review*, **15**(4), 58402.

Gleick, J. (1987), *Chaos: Making a New Science*, New York: Viking Penguin.

Hannan, M.T. and J. Freeman (1989), *Organizational Ecology*, Cambridge, MA: Harvard University Press.

Hassard, J. (1988), 'Overcoming hermeticism in organization theory: an alternative to paradigm incommensurability', *Human Relations*, **41**(3), 247-59.

Hays, R. (1974), 'Expatriate selection: insuring success and avoiding failure', *Journal of International Business Studies*, **5**(1), 25-37.

Hench, T. (1997), 'The domains of international business: paradigms in collision', in B. Toyne and D. Nigh (eds), *International Business: An Emerging Vision*, Columbia, SC: University of South Carolina Press.

Hofstede, G. (1980), *Culture's Consequences: International Differences in Work-Related Values*, Beverly Hills: Sage Publications.

Hofstede, G. (1983), 'The cultural relativity of organizational practices and theories', *Journal of International Business Studies*, **14**, 75-89.

Hofstede, G. (1991), *Cultures and Organizations*, London: McGraw-Hill.

Hornell, E., J.E. Vahlne and F. Wiedersheim-Paul (1973), *Export och Utlandsetableringar (Export and Foreign Establishments)*, Stockholm: Almquist and Wiksell.

House, R. et al. (2002), 'Understanding cultures and implicit leadership theories across the globe', *Journal of World Business*, **37**, 3-10.

Houston, R. (2001), 'Participation as chaos: lessons from the principles of complexity theory for democracy', *World Futures*, **57**(4), 315.

Iomin, A. and G. Zaslavsky (2002), 'Quantum manifestation of Levy-type flights in a Chaotic System', *Chemical Physics*, **284**(1), 3.

Ivancevich, J.M. (1969), 'A study of American expatriate on-the-job performance failures', *Washington Business Review*, **2**(4), 33-38.

Johanson, J. and J.E.Vahlne (1977), 'The internationalization process of the firm', *Journal of International Business Studies*, **8**, 22-32.

Kobrin S.J. (1998), 'The MAI and the clash of globalizations', *Foreign Policy*, **112**, 97-109.

Kobrin, S.J. (2001), 'Sovereignty: globalization, multinational enterprise and the international political system', in T. Brewer and A. Rugman (eds), *The Oxford Handbook of International Business*, Oxford: Oxford University Press.

Kogut, B. and U. Zander, (1993), 'Knowledge of the firm and the evolutionary theory of the multinational corporation', *Journal of International Business Studies*, **24**(4), 625-45

Koza, M. and A.Y. Lewin (1999), 'The coevolution of network alliances: a longitudinal analysis of an international professional service network', *Organization Science*, **10**(5), 638.

Kuhn, T.S. (1962), *The Structure of Scientific Revolutions*, Chicago, IL: University of Chicago Press.

Kuhn, T.S. (1970), *The Structure of Scientific Revolutions* (2nd edn), Chicago: University of Chicago Press.

Kuhn, T.S. (1990), 'The road since structure,' *PSA: Proceedings of the Biennial Meeting of the Philosophy of Science Association*, **2**(7) 3-13.

Laudan, L. (1976), 'Two dogmas of methodology', *Philosophy of Science*, **43**, 5857.

Lawrence, P. R. and J. Lorsch (1967), *Organization and Environment*, Boston: Harvard School of Business Administration Press.

Lewin, A.Y. (1999), 'Application of complexity theory to organization science', *Organization Science*, **10**(3), 215-17.

Lisi, F. and A. Medio (1997), 'Is a random walk the best exchange rate predictor?', *International Journal of Forecasting*, **13**(2), 255.

Lovett, S., L. Simmons and R. Kali (1999), 'Guanxi versus the market: ethics and efficiency', *Journal of International Business Studies*, **30**(2), 231-47.

Lubatkin, M., M. Ndiaye and R. Vengroff (1997), 'The nature of managerial work in developing countries: a limited test of the universalist hypothesis', *Journal of International Business Studies*, **28**(4), 711-33.

Martinez, Z., H.R. Priesmeyer, R.A. Menger and M. Persellin (1999), 'Nonlinear systems theory: a more dynamic approach to international strategic management', *Managerial Finance*, **25**(2), 1-19.

Mayo, E. (1933), *The Human Problems of an Industrial Civilization*, London: Macmillan.

McGregor, D. (1960), *The Human Side of Enterprise*, New York: McGraw-Hill.

Mendenhall, M.E. (1999), 'On the need for paradigmatic integration in international human resource management', *Management International Review*, **39**(3), 65-87.

Mendenhall, M. and J. Macomber (1997), 'Rethinking the strategic management of expatriates from a nonlinear dynamics perspective', in Z. Aycan (ed.), *Emerging Perspectives in Expatriate Productivity*, New York: JAI Press, 41-62.

Mendenhall, M., J. Macomber, H. Gregersen and M. Cutright (1998), 'Nonlinear dynamics: a new perspective on international human resource management research and practice in the 21st century', *Human Resource Management Review*, **8**(1), 5-22.

Negandhi, A.R. and S.B. Prasad (1971), *Comparative Management*, New York: Apple-Century-Crofts.

Newman, K.L. and S. Nollen (1996), 'Culture and congruence: the fit between management practices and national culture', *Journal of International Business Studies*, **27**(4), 753-80.

Nicholas, S. (2002), 'Future for international business: running on empty?', speech presented at keynote panel of 2002 Australia New Zealand International Academy Brisbane, Australia, (8 November 2002).

O'Grady, S. and H. Lane (1996), 'The psychic distance paradox', *Journal of International Business Studies*, **27**(2), 309-34.

Pascale, R. (1999), 'Surfing the edge of chaos', *Sloan Management Review*, **40**(3), 83-94.

Peters, T. and R. Waterman (1982), *In Search of Excellence: Lessons from America's Best Run Companies*, New York: Harper & Row.

Plender, J. (2003), *Going Off the Rails: Global Capitalism and the Crisis of Legitimacy*, New York: John Wiley and Sons.

Polk, J., I. Meister and L.Veit (1966), *US Production Abroad and the Balance of Payments*, National Industrial Conference Board.

Prakash, A. and J. Hart (eds) (1999), *Globalization and Governance*, London and New York: Routledge.

Rheingold, H. (2002), *Smart Mobs: The Next Social Revolution*, New York: Pegasus Publishing.

Robinson, F. (2003), 'NGOs and the advancement of economic and social rights: philosophical and practical controversies', *International Relations*, **17**(1), 79-97.

Robinson, R.D. (1964), *International Business Policy*, New York: Holt, Rinehart and Winston.

Rugman, A. (1993), 'Drawing the border for a multinational enterprise and a nation state', in Lorraine Eden and Evan Potter (eds), *Multinationals in the Global Political Economy*, New York: St. Martin's Press.

Safarian, A. (2003), 'Internalization and the MNE: a note on the spread of ideas', *Journal of International Business Studies*, **34**(2), 117-26.

Schnellenbach, J. (2002), 'The new political economy, scientism and knowledge: a critique from a Hayekian perspective, and a proposal for an extension of the research agenda', *American Journal of Economics and Sociology*, **61**(1), 193-215.

Simon, H.A. (1947), *Administrative Behavior*, New York: Macmillan.

Singh, N. and S. Kundu (2002), 'Explaining the growth of e-commerce corporations (ECCs): an extension and application of the eclectic paradigm', *Journal of International Business Studies*, **33**(4), 679-98.

Sterman, J. and J.Wittenberg (1999), 'Path dependence, competition, and succession in the dynamics of scientific revolution', *Organization Science*, **10**(3), 322-44.

Stottinger, B. and B. Schlegelmilch (1998), 'Explaining export development through psychic distance: enlightening or elusive?', *International Marketing Review*, **15**(5), 357-73.

Sullivan, D. (1998), 'Cognitive tendencies in international business research: implications of a "narrow vision"', *Journal of International Business Studies*, **29**(4), 837-62.

Tallman, S.B. and O. Shenkar (1994), 'A managerial decision model of international cooperative venture formation', *Journal of International Business Studies*, **25**(1), 91-113.

Taylor, F. (1911), *The Principles of Scientific Management*, New York: Norton.

Toyne, B. (1989), 'International exchange: a foundation for theory building in international business', *Journal of International Business Studies*, **20**(1), 1-17.

Toyne, B. and D. Nigh (1997), *International Business: An Emerging Vision*, Columbia, SC: The University of South Carolina Press.

Toyne, B. and D. Nigh (1998), 'A more expansive view of international business', *Journal of International Business Studies*, **29**(4), 863.

Tse, D., P. Yigang and K. Au (1997), 'How MNCs choose entry modes and form alliances: the China experience', *Journal of International Business Studies*, **28**(4), 779-806.

van Staveren, I. (1999), 'Chaos theory and institutional economics: metaphor or model?', *Journal of Economic Issues*, **33**(1), 141.

van Tuijl, P. (1999), 'NGOs and human rights: sources of justice and democracy', *Journal of International Affairs*, **52**(2), 493.

Von Wright, G.H. (1971), *Explanation and Understanding*, Ithaca, NY: Cornell University Press.

Weaver, G. and A. Gioia (1994), 'Paradigms lost: incommensurability vs. structurationist inquiry', *Organization Studies*, **15**(4), 565-91.

Welch, L. (2002), 'International business research: running out of steam or getting up steam?', speech presented at keynote panel of 2002 Australia New Zealand International Academy at Brisbane, Australia (8 November, 2002).

8. Ignorant internationalization? The Uppsala Model and internationalization patterns for Internet-related firms

Mats Forsgren and Peter Hagström

1. INTRODUCTION

Firms invest abroad. Ever since Hymer's (1976) seminal study the research focus has very much been on how firms overcome their liability of foreignness vis-à-vis their competitors in overseas markets. The answer to the question of why firms can go abroad has fundamentally been put down to· such firms possessing a firm-specific competitive advantage (Buckley and Casson, 1976; Dunning, 1981, and Caves, 1982).

Another influential strand of research has instead occupied itself with the process of internationalization, that is how internationalization evolves over time. Traditional theories of internationalization behavior of firms take their cue from the historical experience of manufacturing firms. Carlson (1975) was one of the earliest scholars to make the observation that firms intending to invest abroad suffer from lack of knowledge about how to conduct business in a foreign market. His primary area of inquiry became the decision process itself after having formulated the hypothesis that firms tend to handle this risky problem by trial and error and by gradual acquisition of information about foreign markets. This empirically based reasoning gave rise to a what was to become the dominant internationalization process model with several variations. Essentially, this theory(-ies) makes two predictions: (1) firms internationalize through increasing commitments to foreign markets, and (2) firms choose new markets sequentially according to their perceived proximity.

The former is a story of incremental learning in a given foreign market. The latter builds on subjective perceptions (subject to the Chandlerian (1986) restriction of existing technology permitting the maintenance of relevant administrative structures across borders) determining the choice of which specific geographic markets to enter.

The resultant process has been seen to be slow and deliberate, seemingly flying in the face of recent experience, in particular as it pertains to the internationalization of Internet-related firms in the second half of the 1990s. Then, there was no shortage in the business press of accounts of how these firms expanded internationally and at what was a breathtaking speed. Although a more sober atmosphere has lately replaced the 'irrational exuberance' associated with rapidly expanding equity markets, the question still remains whether or not these new firms behaved differently when internationalizing from what the old models would have us expect. Anecdotal evidence often made Internet-related firms represent something totally different from traditional multinational enterprises.

The most well known model of internationalization behavior, the so-called Uppsala Model, has been claimed to be very general and therefore applicable to many different firms and different situations (Pedersen and Petersen, 1998). A reasonable task in order to develop the model, therefore, is to confront the model with data from more extreme cases, that is data from firms other than those firms through which the model was originally induced. In line with this, the purpose of this chapter is to scrutinize and discuss in more depth some of the basic assumptions behind the Uppsala Model of internationalization by confronting these assumptions with data from internationalization in some Internet-related firms.

The chapter first reviews the theoretical constructs associated with the Uppsala Model, focusing on the key concepts of learning and knowledge. Then, the internationalization experiences of selected Internet-related businesses are reviewed. Eight firms (two web design firms and six consumer retail firms) were singled out for a richer empirical setting. Interestingly, two of the firms, and probably the best known ones at the time, Boxman and Dressmart, have since gone bankrupt. This way we also avoid the standard empirical problem of only sampling successful, that is surviving, firms, which should add to the validity of our findings.

The third section of the chapter juxtaposes the predictions of the internationalization model with observed behavior. Some counterfactual experiences cast doubt over the continued relevance of the model, whereas other behavior can be accommodated within the realm of classical explanations. Since this inquiry does not constitute a 'test' of any propositions but is rather an inductive investigation, the chapter concludes with a brief discussion of possible new internationalization patterns.

2. THE ARDUOUS PROCESS OF INTERNATIONALIZATION

Carlson's (1966) reasoning laid the groundwork for what later has become known as the Uppsala Internationalization Process Model (Johanson and Wiedersheim-Paul, 1975; Johanson and Vahlne, 1977). It primarily deals, with knowledge acquisition, that is, learning. Central issues concern how organizations learn and how this learning affects their subsequent investment behavior (Johanson and Vahlne, 1977, 1990). A basic assumption of the model is that lack of knowledge about foreign markets is a major obstacle to internationalization, but that this obstacle can be overcome through learning about foreign market conditions. The firm's own current operations are the main source of this kind of learning. In turn, this reasoning leads to a second assumption of learning by doing (cf. Lindblom, 1959; Johnson, 1988). Investment decisions and actual investment commitments are made incrementally as uncertainty is successively reduced. The more the firm knows about a foreign market, the lower the perceived market risk will be and, consequently, the higher the actual investment by the firm in that market tends to be.

The core concepts of the model are market commitment, market knowledge, commitment decisions and current activities. All tangible and intangible assets that a firm accumulates in a specific geographical market make up its market commitment. This is a matter both of the sheer amount of resources committed and the degree to which they are committed to a specific market (cf. Johanson and Vahlne, 1990). The latter refers to the relative ease or difficulty of transferring resources to another market. For instance, well-established local customer relationships tend to be idiosyncratic to a particular geographic market.

Market knowledge is taken to stem from experience of foreign markets. Hence, the critical knowledge is on the whole tacit in nature. As such it is highly dependent on individuals and therefore difficult to transfer to other individuals or other contexts (cf. Johanson and Vahlne, 1977). This also constitutes a third, basic assumption of the model (cf. Forsgren, 2002). It is individuals, for example the sales subsidiary personnel, who learn about the problems and opportunities present in a particular market. Knowledge acquisition is then seen here as very much of a 'bottom-up' process. Learning is initiated when a problem is encountered in the current operations and ends when a satisfactory solution is found; a bounded rationality approach (cf. Cyert and March, 1963).

A given level of market knowledge and market commitment at a certain point in time will then affect the commitment decisions and how activities are carried out in subsequent periods. In turn, these decisions and activities will influence the later stages of market commitment and market knowledge in an incrementally evolving spiral.

On the basis of the three basic assumptions and four concepts above, the model predicts a pattern for firms' internationalization behavior. This pattern is characterized by two main aspects: (1) Investments in a given country are carried cautiously and sequentially as a result of incremental and concurrent local learning. (2) Firms start to (and continue to) invest in one or a few neighboring countries rather than investing in distant markets and/or several markets simultaneously. 'Closer' markets are those that are perceived to be close, that is, markets about which the extent of knowledge and the 'comfort level' are higher. These are markets located at a shorter psychic distance, which may diverge from straight geographic distance (cf. Johanson and Vahlne, 1990).

With the above terminology in place, the stage is set for a description of the internationalization process of young, Internet-related firms.

3. RECENT INTERNATIONALIZATION EXPERIENCE OF INTERNET-RELATED FIRMS

Eight Internet-related firms were investigated concerning their internationalization from the respective launch of the businesses to the end of year 2000. The sample of firms is by no means random as the relevant population was found to be impossible to identify. First, the phenomenon is new as postulated by our inquiry; a fact that implies that generally accepted groupings or listings of relevant firms have yet to emerge. Second, there is no officially accepted definition of this type of firms, making them hard to classify. Rather than using an arbitrary definition of the population, a decision was made to ensure variation in the sample, and to select firms that are known to have been actively engaged in internationalizing their businesses.

The firms under consideration are Bokus, Boxman, Buyonet, CDon, Dressmart, SEB, Framfab and Icon Medialab. The first six firms have sold consumer products or services over the Internet, and the last two firms are web-design consultancies. All businesses were launched in 1995 or later. Two firms, Boxman and Dressmart, have gone bankrupt since the investigation started and the consultancies have gone through major restructuring, in other words, downsizing. This is an advantage, as the common drawback of only studying successful firms is somewhat mitigated. Firms only needed to demonstrate short term survival instead of the long term staying power normally associated with firms drawn from official sources or the like.

Primarily for practical reasons, all the firms are of Swedish origin. Data collection was made easier. However, Sweden is also known for an exceptionally early and high Internet penetration rate (together with the US and other Nordic countries) although the top rankings may vary somewhat depending on source. The fact remains that Sweden is a good place to start since we are interested in a longitudinal study.[1]

Both primary and secondary data were collected. Much of the data gathering was carried out by Masters' students working under supervision on their final theses at the Stockholm School of Economics.[2] Both the sheer volume and overlap of data and of data sources have assured substantial triangulation. The reliability of the material is judged to be fairly high. The validity of the studies is clearly not very high, and that goes especially for the external validity. The findings are thus best interpreted as exploratory (cf. Yin, 1984), generating hypotheses instead of attempting to falsify them.

In view of space constraints, only highlights from the case study firms are presented below.

2.1 Bokus

The on-line bookseller Bokus went live in August, 1997. It was modeled on Amazon.com and the ambition was to become a regional alternative to the same Internet store. The first funding came from a couple of business angels.[3] The ambition to expand internationally required additional funding and Bokus turned to a High Street competitor (similar to Barnes and Noble). The parent company (KF Media) purchased 45 per cent of the stock in Bokus in March, 1997. The company outsourced its distribution and computer systems as well as all invoicing and payments. Bokus held no stock, but left that to the publishers. The hired Chief Executive Officer had extensive experience from the industry, but not from operating an international company. To a large extent, Bokus relied on external consultants for market knowledge. The board contributed with experience from logistics and mail order.

The first international subsidiary was established in Finland one year after commencing operations. A local office with local customer service was set up only to be withdrawn promptly when local fixed costs started to mount. All activities except for a single country manager were pulled back to Sweden. The leaner model was employed for subsequent establishments in Denmark (one month after Finland) and Norway (another nine months later). The company put down its choice of markets to enter as a function of first, the extent of Internet usage and second, the structure of the local markets.[4] Proximity, in a wide sense, was seen as a concern only after that. KF Media had bought another 47.5 per cent of Bokus in January, 1999, and their corporate strategy had a clear Nordic focus.

In the beginning of 2000, 50 per cent of Bokus was sold to Bertelsmann, and the company began to operate under the Bertelsmann trademark of bol.com. That foray into a larger international market never took off and the Bokus name was re-launched in May, 2002. That fall, KF Media repurchased Bertelsmann's shares and withdrew from all foreign markets.

2.2 Boxman

Boxman's Swedish website for selling CDs opened in December, 1997. A venture capital firm financed the startup with the explicit ambition of expanding the product range to also include videotapes and computer games. In addition, the company had an explicit strategy of internationalizing quickly in order to build a brand name and to exploit first-mover advantages. During the third quarter of 1998 Boxman placed a new tranche of shares with private investors and opened green-field subsidiaries in Norway, Denmark and Finland. The model was to hire a local country manager, who in turn hired around 4-8 people to man a local site for customer support, adaptation of the product range and payments. The computer systems and logistics were out-sourced as were some corporate payments. The choice of countries was first and foremost contingent on the degree of Internet maturity. These countries also served as trial markets before the larger markets of France, United Kingdom and Germany were entered in the period March-May, 1999. Less mature and bigger markets also meant heavy spending on marketing, not least since generic marketing activities were required. In August, 1999, the Dutch subsidiary opened for business.

Boxman went bankrupt and the trademark (only) was acquired by a new firm that was launched under that name in 2002. The 'new' Boxman operates in the Swedish market only and is in the business of renting movies over the Internet.

2.3 Buyonet

The *raison d'être* of Buyonet was a patented software that allows the company to track whether or not a customer has received a functioning copy software on-line. In June, 1997 Buyonet began offering standard software from its first, Swedish site in ten languages and accepting payments in ten currencies. By December, 1998 the number of languages had increased to 12 and currencies to 20. One year later, Buyonet handled 20 languages and 22 currencies for customers in around 120 countries. All major software companies have licensed their products to Buyonet except Microsoft, which has limited its licensing to the US market only. Buyonet's only foreign subsidiary was established in April, 1998 in Seattle, Washington. The main rationale for this was to avoid European value added taxes, since electronically stored and delivered services are exempt if they come from outside the European Union. The US office handles local customer support, while the rest of the world is dealt with from the head office in Got henburg. A US partner, Netsales, is responsible for storage and transport as well as for delivery of any complementary physical items.

Initial funding came from a local Gothenburg family. It was supplemented in 1999 by a fully-fledged venture capital firm, which with two purchases brought its share of the company up to 30 per cent by August. The internationalization strategy has largely been left up to management, subject to board approval. Buyonet has decided not to invest in any generic marketing. In fact, marketing expenses have been kept to a minimum.

Maintaining its Swedish link, from 1999 Buyonet has been operated by Mirror Image Internet out of Woburn, Massachusetts; a firm 99 per cent owned by Xcelera Inc. (formerly Scandinavian Company) incorporated in Grand Cayman, British West Indies.

2.4 CDon

The Swedish Media conglomerate Modern Times Group (MTG) founded and funded the on-line compact disk (CD) retailer CDon in February, 1999. It opened shops in Sweden, Norway and Denmark on the same day. The degree of Internet penetration and geographic overlap with MTG's other activities motivated the choice of markets to enter. The latter criterion meant that a Finnish site was delayed until a year later and was quickly followed by sites in the Netherlands and Estonia.

CDon has relied rather heavily on MTG for market knowledge and has outsourced distribution, invoicing and payments, logistics and web traffic to other MTG subsidiaries. The intention has been to keep fixed costs low and to spend primarily on marketing. Activities are clearly geared towards the respective local markets, and the green-field sites are adapted to local tastes and market conditions, for example price levels. The local subsidiaries are largely left to grow organically.

CDon pulled out of Estonia and the Netherlands and focuses on the four Nordic countries complemented by an 'EU site'. At the end of 2003 CDon was the second largest on-line retailer of CDs and DVDs in the

Nordic region and the most visited Internet retail site of all categories in Sweden.

2.5 Dressmart

The business idea behind Dressmart was to sell good quality, brand name clothes to young, middle-aged, male professionals. This target group was thought to consist of people with little time on their hands for shopping for clothes and who would not be very price sensitive. The company began operating in April, 1999, backed by SEK 6 million from a venture capital firm and a government pension fund. The financial backers had a very clear strategy of rapid internationalization and openly declared that they would change the management team if this strategy could not be implemented according to schedule. Consultants who had been involved in the internationalization of Boxman were extensively used by Dressmart. By August, 1999, Merrill Lynch had also invested in the company and was committed to helping Dressmart raise the money needed for its international expansion.

Dressmart prepared each market entry well with extensive help from outside consultants. The business idea hinged on shipping directly from the manufacturer/distributor who owned the brand name so it became very important to build up networks of supplying firms. Dressmart also adapted its product range to fit each market and had a strong local presence to offer what was felt to be vital customer support. From the beginning Dressmart spent a staggering 60 per cent of turnover on marketing, chiefly for building the brand. Other activities were outsourced to the greatest possible extent.

The choice of which countries to enter was guided by degree of Internet maturity and then by market size. From August to October, 1999, Finland, Norway, Denmark and the Netherlands established Dressmart green-field subsidiaries. The larger markets, the UK, Germany and France, followed between October, 1999 and January, 2000. A plan for entering the US was never implemented as the company's investors began to get restless during the late spring. A protracted battle to stay in operation ensued until finally Dressmart went bankrupt during the fall of 2000.

2.6 SEB

Financial services are commonly perceived to be an extremely internationalized business. However, this pertains mainly to business-to-business transactions. Retail banking, personal insurance and brokerage for individuals are still very much of a local business with local brands.

SEB is one of the major Swedish banks with about a fifth of the Swedish savings market. It was the first bank to launch an Internet banking site in the country in January, 1996. During the first couple of years SEB was typically identified in the press as the largest Internet bank in the world as measured by the number of accounts. SEB's vision for its e-bank is for it to become the leading player in Europe for on-line personal savings and investments. The strategy is to internationalize quickly by exploiting its 'first-mover advantage'. SEB has developed a proprietary platform for both fixed and mobile Internet, a platform they believe is ahead of anything the competition has. SEB handles its activities almost exclusively in-house.

The early internationalization strategy for the e-bank has in practice been derived from the corporate strategy. In practice, the SEB e-bank has entered geographic markets when the parent company made acquisitions that allowed the e-bank a local brand name. Thus, SEB has been operating e-banks in Estonia and Latvia since 1999 and in Denmark, Germany and the UK since 2000. Only the last market entry was not linked to a local acquisition. With a local physical presence, customers are seen as more likely to trust SEB and access to local payments systems, ATM networks and so on are made easier. This was also the reason for rather quickly pulling out of the UK. SEB's Internet customers in the remaining markets doubled from approximately 800 000 in 2000 to more than 1.6 million in 2003.

2.7   Framfab

Framfab was established as an Internet consultancy in 1995. They developed one of the main Swedish portals (Passagen) for Telia and were responsible for the first live Internet presentation of a new car the following year (Volvo's C70). The firm grew organically as well as through acquisitions. The international expansion began during 1999 during the last eight months of which Framfab grew from a domestic firm with 270 employees to one of Europe's biggest Internet consultancies, with 750 employees in four countries. It is listed on the stock exchange.

A key concept at Framfab is that of a cell. Company policy dictated that no single office should have more than 50 employees. Projects can, however, be staffed with people from more than one cell. Not surprisingly, the approach to integrating acquired firms was quite relaxed in that they were accepted as an additional cell among all the others.

Framfab went through one year of frantic internationalization largely relying on its own devices. In May, 1999, one firm with 49 employees was acquired in Denmark and one with 20 employees in the UK. One in

France (41 employees) followed in September. In December there were acquisitions in Germany (105 employees) and in the US (15 employees). The last acquisitions were in Norway (25 employees) in February, 2000 and in May in the Netherlands (135 employees). Framfab used its own shares as payment in all instances. This currency ceased to be viable after the fall in equity values in the late spring. One green-field site was established in Italy in February, 2000.

Frantic restructuring allowed the company to remain in business. In the beginning of 2004 Framfab had 420 employees in Sweden, Denmark, Germany, Switzerland, the Netherlands and in the UK.

2.8 Icon Medialab

Icon Medialab opened its first overseas office within months of its founding; in Madrid in August, 1996. It developed a rather strong corporate culture and took great care to integrate acquisitions. For instance, where possible, offices were laid out and furnished to look similar around the world. Icon Medialab used a matrix organization along the dimensions of physical location and competence areas. The company is listed on the stock exchange.

Internationalization proceeded both through acquisitions and the establishment of green-field subsidiaries. Icon Medialab did not use consultants or other advisors to any significant degree. From August, 1996 until October, 1999 Icon Medialab opened eleven offices[5] abroad. In parallel, from November, 1997 to April 2000 13 international acquisitions were made.[6] By 2001, Icon Medialab had wholly-owned subsidiaries in 19 countries. Icon Medialab's aggressive growth strategy was funded by a rising share price as long as that lasted. The subsequent financial pressure forced a merger with a Dutch consultancy, Lost Boys, in January, 2002. The Swedish main subsidiary went bankrupt. The new merged company operates under the umbrella of Icon Medialab, International incorporated in Sweden. Corporate headquarters are located in Amsterdam, the Netherlands. Of the 'old' Icon Medialab, subsidiaries in Sweden, Italy, Spain, Portugal, the US and Swizerland remained at the end of 2003. Subsidiaries in the Netherlands, the UK and Germany operated under other names.

4. NEW INTERNATIONALIZATION PATTERNS?

At first sight, the general predictions of the Uppsala Internationalization Process Model do not seem to hold up that well when confronted with the experience of eight Internet-related case companies. Rather than slow and incremental, the process seems to be fast and discontinuous. Regarding choice of markets, it appears as if most firms did enter markets at a relatively short psychic distance. However, rather than cultural affinity or reduced uncertainty, the main reason given was the maturity of markets in terms of Internet usage that determined which markets to enter. If we believe the firms, then the observed pattern is just spuriously correlated with psychic distance. Market potential (size) was also unanimously put before any notion of psychic distance when motivating market choice.

Even though we have seen substantial variation among firms, one thing that they do have in common is an explicit internationalization strategy. Whereas the prediction was one of firm growth 'spilling over' the home country borders irrespective of whether or not any such decisions had been made (cf. Johanson and Vahlne, 1990), every case firm not only claimed an internationalization strategy but that international growth was a top priority.

The case firms do exhibit substantial variation in other aspects of their internationalization behavior, however. Boxman and Dressmart stand out in terms of making market commitments among the six business-to-consumer firms. They also forced the pace of internationalization to a greater extent than the other consumer market firms. CDon and SEB displayed a more moderate expansion pattern; one that is more in line with the traditional predictions. It is noteworthy that these two cases represent Internet business within bigger, more established firms. Bokus seem to fall somewhere in between, also having been bought by an established firm during the period under scrutiny. Buyonet is arguably more similar to an exporter in that the only subsidiary outside Sweden owes its existence to the wish to avoid paying European value added tax.

The web consultancies made the greatest market commitments both in relative and absolute terms. The need to secure scarce resources/competencies was on the agenda in addition to international expansion. This is evident from Framfab's and Icon Medialab's propensity to use acquisitions as a means for their international growth. Rather than the more passive, reactive learning allowed for in the model, we can see how these case firms take a much more proactive stance.[7] By acquiring a local firm the slow process of personal, experiential learning (Johanson and Vahlne, 1977) can be replaced by grafting (cf. Huber, 1991) knowledge into the firm. Why wait if there is a unit that already possesses the required knowledge that can readily be acquired? Obviously there are alternatives to only learning from one's own, current activities. However, this is not to say that this is always a successful strategy. The ability of the acquiring firms to assimilate the knowledge inherited in the acquired firms can be limited, and therefore create difficulties in later stages of the internationalization process. Still, this strategy implies a faster internationalization process than predicted by the received model, at least in the beginning of the process.

In addition, there is a problem with assuming that experiential learning and incremental behavior necessarily go hand in hand as is done in the Uppsala model. Not only can firms learn through making acquisitions, experience of making acquisitions is likely to equip the firm to be able to move even more quickly than it otherwise would be inclined to do (cf. Barkema and Vermeulen, 1998). Hence, there may be a negative relationship between experiential learning and incremental behavior.

Another complication for the Uppsala Model relates to the basic feature that firms are said not to invest abroad if they assess the risk of investing as intolerably high (cf. Johanson and Vahlne, 1997). However, it is quite possible that the firm experiences not investing abroad as even more risky and intolerable. This can be the case when the general uncertainty about the future of the industry is high in combination with a feeling that a first-mover advantage is crucial. Such a situation can force the firm to invest abroad, even if it considers the adventure an extremely high-risk project due to lack of market knowledge. The action would then be based on a conviction that if the firm does not take the step now, there will be no second chance in the future (Forsgren, 2002). Consequently, the first step in the internationalization process can sometimes occur much earlier than predicted by the Uppsala Model.

The speed of internationalization is moreover fueled by the desire to exploit economies of scale (Shapiro and Varian, 1999). One of the salient features of Internet technology is its scalability. The production costs for serving an additional geographic market are very modest. Costly production activities such as, for instance, distribution and payments are typically outsourced, reducing the need for investment in those activities.

The marketing costs have been seen to be substantial. Building a brand is expensive, in particular in consumer markets when generic advertising is also required. Internet savvy may also have to be taught in some markets. A somewhat curious possibility is that firms may actually reduce their physical market presence once they have well established customer relationships, that is improved market knowledge can lead to less market commitment. Bokus pulled back from Finland, and Buyonet handles its international customer support out of Gothenburg. It is not too far-fetched to imagine a situation when, say, SEB closes the branch network after having acquired and reassured the local customer base. The importance of initial local presence is further underlined by SEB finding itself having to exit the UK market.

A different twist to the story is that some firms do not build up home market knowledge before they go abroad (Oviatt and Phillips-McDougall, 1994). Boxman is a good example of such a strategy. It had an explicit intention to establish operations abroad quickly in order to build a brand name presence and exploit first-mover advantage. This strategy has first of all an impact on the amount of time lapsed before first going abroad, but tells us less about the speed of the further internationalization process. It has been suggested, though, that the time of the first step and the speed of the internationalization process are related. The reason for that would be that investing abroad in fact requires de-learning of certain routines and procedures acquired in the home market that have little relevance abroad. Therefore, no or limited knowledge from operations in the home market could actually constitute an advantage as there is not much to unlearn (cf. Autio, Sapienza and Almeida, 2000).

Another way of reducing the uncertainty associated with investing abroad not allowed for in the Uppsala model is mimetic behavior (cf. DiMaggio and Powell, 1983). Firms may imitate actions taken by other firms if these actions are seen to have been successful and/or legitimized some other way (Levitt and March, 1988). The point is that both radical and quick action may be taken under these circumstances without having to wait for experiential accumulation of one's own knowledge. There is no good reason why this general mechanism should not be applicable to internationalization.

The standard interpretation of imitation is that firms tend to follow typically one leading firm in the industry in order to reduce uncertainty by imitating a successful recipe (Haunschield and Mimer, 1997). A closer look at the case firms instead reveals that there is no apparent leader to imitate. The Internet-based concept was relatively new and the industry not old enough for any single leading firm to emerge. Still, the cases give the impression of a more or less pronounced following-the-herd behavior among the firms. The firms feel that they need to internationalize, and internationalize fast, because that is what other Internet-based firms do or should do. So, here we seem to have an interesting case of imitation without any leading firm to imitate. It seems like some kind of nervousness, and expectations evolve among firms in a new industry that lead to a following-the-herd behavior like screaming jackdaws at dusk. Similar to follow-the-leader behavior, it is an attempt to reduce the uncertainty of the individual firm. The difference, though, is that the behavior is not based on experiential knowledge of any firm, only on expectations, and in that sense it deviates even more from the Uppsala Model. The consequence, though, is again a faster internationalization process, at least as long as this is what the herd, as a group, appreciates as the appropriate behavior. Indeed, the case firms themselves stressed the momentum that built up when explaining the commonly ferocious internationalization behavior of Internet-related firms.

The case firms also demonstrate another important aspect if we want to understand internationalization behavior. In the Uppsala Model the crucial actors in the firm are the ones that acquire and hold market knowledge. They shape the internationalization process of the firm in accordance with their own learning, risk and opportunity perception.[8] The cases show quite strongly, though, that other stakeholders can also shape the internationalization behavior. The 'forgotten' stakeholder category is the owners. In particular, venture capitalists demanded a more rapid internationalization process than that motivated by the level of market knowledge of the firm in order for them to be able to profit quickly and in rich measure from their investment. Unlike the grafting strategy above it is not primarily an attempt to avoid the experiential knowledge imperative, but rather to disregard it. The non-listed firms also put this factor at the top of their list when explaining their urgency in implementing internationalization strategies.[9] The situations for Framfab and Icon Medialab were not too dissimilar in that the value of their shares was contingent on continued international expansion. Any delay tended to lead to lower share values, in turn making acquisitions more costly as the preferred mode of payment were the same shares. There are strong incentives in both these cases for internationalization that cannot afford to wait for experiential knowledge to build up.

The Uppsala Model concerns prediction of firm behavior. This also means that to the extent the conditions prevail assumed in the model, it also has managerial implications. It is interesting to note, though, that the model was originally launched as understanding actual behavior of firms, rather than suggesting suitable norms for how to invest abroad. Paradoxically, though, one may argue that an important strength of the model is more related to its normative implications than to its predictions of what firms actually do. On one hand, the cases suggest that there are factors missing in the model that shape the internationalization process of firms. These factors must be considered if we want to build a more fuly-fledged model of internationalization behavior. On the other hand, at least some of the cases suggest that if the firm had applied a more cautious, incremental strategy based on successive building up of market knowledge it may have been more successful or avoided bankruptcy. It is also interesting to observe that the managerial dimensions of the Uppsala Model have been focused lately in research that actually tries to relate economic performance to incremental behavior (cf. Drogendijk, 2001).

Our concern here with Internet-related firms highlights another important aspect of internationalization not dealt with explicitly in the Uppsala

Model: namely the importance of establishing and developing business relationships. One crucial factor behind the reason for a firm taking on an incremental, time-consuming internationalization behavior is the fact that exploring foreign markets is actually about investing in specific customer (and supplier) relationships within a foreign business network rather than surmounting economic, institutional and cultural country barriers. Investing in relationships also means demands to manage these relationships by learning gradually about the counterparts' capabilities. These aspects are fundamental insights from business network theory that can be used to infuse new elements into the Uppsala Model. An interesting issue, then, is to what extent Internet-related firms, which extensively manage their customer relationships through the Internet, are condemned to follow the same rules or not. Or expressed otherwise, how easy is it for these firms to exploit the sheer size of their customer network (by avoiding too much investment in specific relationships) and therefore conduct a faster internationalization than would otherwise be possible? A reasonable answer to that question is that Internet-related firms also differ in that respect, for instance in the sense that a publishing firm has a higher possibility to conduct an arm's-length relationship with customers while a consultant needs to build up and invest in such relationships more carefully and on a one-to-one basis.

5.   CONCLUSION

The Uppsala Internationalization Process Model has been the subject of – and has withstood – much empirical testing during its quarter of a century existence (for overviews see, inter alia, Young et al., 1989; Johanson and Vahlne, 1990). There has, however, been less scrutiny of the basic theoretical tenets of the model (Hadjikhani, 1997; Forsgren, 2002).[10] This chapter has the ambition to do a bit of both. Far from conclusively proving anything, we have called the model into question on theoretical as well as on empirical grounds. Although the attractiveness of the model in large part has rested on its simplicity and incorporation of a dynamic view of internationalization, it seems less well suited to the context of Internet-related firms.

In particular, the model's central tenet of incremental learning has been scrutinized and found wanting. A tell-tale example is when a firm is ignorant about the market conditions. Then the risk if investing abroad is great, and the model predicts the firm is unlikely to want to follow through with the investment. If, however, the firm finds the risk associated with not investing abroad even greater, then the ignorant firm will invest. The cost of not investing would then be forgoing first-mover advantages of the kind discussed above.

The case firms that most closely resemble this scenario would be Boxman and Dressmart. Since they were the ones to go bankrupt, perhaps there is more to be said about incremental market learning after all.

NOTES

1. An additional benefit is the possibility of this experience having a trail-blazing quality, meaning that similar patterns may occur in other markets as they mature in terms of Internet usage.
2. Bergman (2000), *The Broadening of Competencies of Internet Consultancies*; Johansson and Lindblad (2000), *Border Breaking Bits – Internationalization of Virtual Distributors*; Mörn and Cedervall (2000), *The Internationalization Process of an Internet Retailer: A Case Study of Boxman*; and Tersmeden and Törnell (2000), *The Internationalization of Bokus, Boxman, Buyonet, CDon and Dressmart.*
3. The founders were Kajsa Leander and Ernst Malmsten, who later went on to start Boo.com.
4. Finland does not have minimum price rules for books as do Denmark and Norway.
5. Spain, US, UK, Malaysia, Denmark, Finland, Germany, Belgium, Germany, Germany, and Spain.
6. Finland (11 employees), Germany (7), Norway (25), Norway (25), France (16), Italy (20), UK (15), Netherlands (40), US (100), France (5), Norway (50), UK (80), and Spain (142).
7. Of course, there is a strong element of opportunism here as well, since there must be firms to acquire.
8. The Uppsala Model assumes that the holders of market knowledge are the same individuals as those responsible for, and having the ultimate influence over, investment decisions. For larger organizations this is a questionable assumption (Forsgren, 2002).
9. Recall the ultimatum put to the management team in Dressmart, see 2.5 above.
10. Some notable exceptions are Anderson (1993), Barkema et al. (1996), and Pedersen and Petersen (1998).

REFERENCES

Anderson, O. (1993), 'On the internationalization process of firms: A critical analysis', *Journal of International Business*, **24**(2), 209-32.

Autio, E., H.J. Sapienza and J.G. Almeida (2000), 'The effects of age at entry, knowledge intensity, and imitability on international Growth', *Academy of Management Journal*, **43**, 909-224.

Barkema, H. and F. Vermeulen (1998), 'International expansion through start-up or acquisition: a learning perspective', *Academy of Management Journal*, **41**(1), 7-26.

Barkema, H.G., J.H.J. Bell and J.M. Pennings (1996), 'Foreign entry, cultural barriers and learning', *Strategic Management Journal*, **17**, 151-66.

Buckley, P.J. and M. Casson (1976), *The Future of the Multinational Enterprise*, London: Macmillan.

Carlson, S. (1975), *How Foreign is Foreign Trade: A Problem in International Business Research*, Uppsala: Uppsala University.

Caves, R.E. (1982), *Multinational Enterprise and Economic Analysis*, Cambridge: Cambridge University Press.

DiMaggio, P.J. and W.W. Powell (1983), 'The iron cage revisited: Institutional isomorphism and collective rationality in organization fields', *Administration Science Quarterly*, **48**, 147-60.

Drogendijk, R. (2001), *Expansion Patterns of Dutch Firms in Central and Eastern Europé: Learning to Internationalize*, Tilburg University: Center Dissertation Studies.

Dunning, J.H. (1981), *International Production and the Multinational Enterprise*, London: Allen & Unwin.

Forsgren, M. (2002), 'The concept of learning in the Uppsala internationalization process model: a critical review', *International Business Review*, **11**, 257-277.

Hadjikhani, A. (1997), 'A note on the criticisms against the internationalization process model', *Management International Review*, **37**(Special Issue), 1-23.

Haunschield, P. and A.S. Miner (1997), 'Modes of interorganizational imitation: the effect of outcome salience and uncertainty', *Administrative Science Quarterly*, **42**, 472-500.

Huber, G.P. (1991),'Organizational learning. The contributing processes and the literatures', *Organization Science*, **2**(1).

Hymer, S.H. (1976/1960), *The International Operattions of National Firms: A Study of Direct Investmen*, Cambridge, Mass.: The MIT Press (previously unpublished doctoral dissertation, MIT, 1960).

Johanson, J. and J.E. Vahlne (1977), 'The internationalization process of the firm –A model of knowledge development and increasing foreign market commitments', *Journal of International Business Studies*, **8**, 23-32.

Johanson, J. and J.E. Vahlne, (1990), 'The mechanisms of internationalization', *International Marketing Review*, **7**(4), 11-24.

Johanson, J. and F. Wiedersheim-Paul (1975), 'The internationalizatioñ of the firm-four cases', *Journal of Management Studies*, **12**, 305-22.

Johnson, G. (1988), 'Rethinking incrementalism', *Strategic Management Journal*, **9**, 75-91.

Levitt, B. and J.G. March (1988), 'Organizational learning', *Annual Review of Sociology*, **14**, 319-40.

Lindblom, C.E. (1959), 'The science of muddling through', *Public Administration Review*, **19** (Spring), 79-88.

Oviatt, B.M. and P. P.-McDougall (1994), 'Towards a theory of international new ventures', *Journal of International Business Studies*, **25**, 45-64.

Pedersen, T. and B. Petersen (1998), 'Explaining gradually increasing resource commitment to a foreign market', *International Business Review*, **7**, 483-501.

Shapiro, C. and H.R. Varian (1999), *Information Rules*, Boston, Mass.: Harvard Business School Press.

Yin, R.K. (1984), *Case Study Research: Design and Methods*, Beverly Hills, CA: Sage Publications.

9. The value creation perspective of international strategic management

Reid W. Click

1. INTRODUCTION

Management is the process through which value is created by an individual or a group of individuals, and international strategic management is the process through which value is created by an individual or group operating across a national border. Since the meanings of 'international', 'management', and 'international management' are apparently in dispute, or are at least under-understood (see Boddewyn, 1999 and references therein), these simple introductory definitions require further examination.A dictionary definition of 'management' is the act, manner, or practice of managing, handling or controlling something (Morris, 1975, p. 192).

In recognition of a *raison d'être* for the individuals who manage something, a normative version of the definition is 'the act, manner, or practice of managing, handling or controlling something in order to create value or wealth'. Although the normative appendage is disputable, managers must recognize that the things worth doing are the ones that create value. This is the overarching message conveyed in modern business school curricula. As Harrigan, (1992) points out, 'Business schools exist to improve management practice. All scholarly research, development of teaching materials, testing of theories, and other activities carried on by faculties of business schools should help managers develop tools for coping with the problems of international value creation' (p. 251). The rest of this chapter tackles the essence of value creation, so the definition being offered is the starting point for discussion rather than a definitive

This chapter is reprinted from *International Financial Review* volume 7, pp. 101-26, 2007, with permission from Elsevier. An earlier version of this paper, entitled 'Strategic Management of Multinational Enterprises and Value Creation', was presented at the 8th International Conference on Multinational Enterprises at the Chinese Culture University in Taipei Taiwan, March 2006. I am glateful for comments from the conference participants.

statement.

Since 'international' is 'relating to, or involving two or more nations or nationalities' (Morris, 1975, p. 685), 'international management' is 'the act, manner, or practice of managing, handling, or controlling something involving two or more nations'. Hence, incorporating the normative element offered in this chapter, international management is the process through which value is created by an individual or group of individuals operating across a national border.

In attempting to circumscribe the domain of international management, the definition of international management provides guidance for two reasons. First, it distinguishes international management from general management with the phrase 'operating across a national border'. Second, it distinguishes international management, being focused on the 'process through which value is created' internationally, from international business, which encompasses anything related to international commercial activity (such as elements of the operating environment). The domain of international management – as opposed to the domain of management or the domain of international business – should therefore be identified based on the value created by managerial actions across national borders.

Without denying that domestic management is complicated, international management is often distinguished from domestic management by its additional complexities. For example, while domestic management requires a vast knowledge base in accounting, finance, production, human resources, marketing, economics, law, public policy, behavioral psychology and so on, international management requires a commensurately larger knowledge base as the traditional areas become internationalized (and thus become part of the domain of international business) to account for additional governments, legal systems, cultural orientations, languages and the like. In addition, international management requires knowledge of disciplines typically ignored in domestic business, such as international political economy, foreign affairs and geographic area studies, which are important components of international business. Hence, the complexities which distinguish international management from domestic management result from operating across borders and having to deal with multiple economies, societies and governments.

Mastering international strategic management can be a Herculean task if the domain is too broad, so some priorities must be set in order to focus on the most germane activities of international value creation. The focus on value-creating activities is in fact what distinguishes international strategic management from the broader concept of international business. This chapter adopts a strategy approach to international management by considering a back-to-basics framework in which international management is the aggregation of value created through international production, marketing and financial activities. The framework is not a simple internationalization of the functional areas of business, but is instead a broadening of the perspective to analyze production, marketing and financial activities in a larger global context.

Other elements of international business can be put into this framework if they create value. For example, foreign languages and geographic area studies are often included in the domain of international business. The framework presented here requires specification of the value created by having such managerial knowledge in order to be included in the more exclusive domain of international strategic management. If knowledge of a foreign language facilitates management-labor communication at a foreign plant and thereby increases sales revenue abroad, it creates value and is within the domain of international management. However, the importance of the knowledge is directly related to the value created, and foreign languages and area studies are not automatically part of the domain of international management.

The concept of value creation is used in this chapter to answer three questions pertaining to strategic management of multinational enterprises. After this introduction, section 2 broadly examines value creation and the question, 'How important is international strategic management?' Section 3 develops the strategy framework for analyzing international management and asks 'What is the domain of international strategic management?' Discussions of international production, marketing and financial activities suggest that international management requires an outward-looking perspective rather than an inward-looking perspective in order to maximize the value of the multinational enterprise (MNE), and reveal that the domain of international management is very broad. Section 4 ties the elements of value creation strategy together by asking, 'Does international strategic management make the whole multinational enterprise worth more than the sum of its parts?' Empirical evidence from US multinationals in the early 1990s indicates that the answer is yes.

2. VALUE CREATION AND THE RELATIVE IMPORTANCE OF INTERNATIONAL STRATEGIC MANAGEMENT

Production and marketing operations represent the two main areas of business activity. Porter described these as the 'primary activities' in the firm's 'value chain'. The production operations are the 'upstream activities', such as inbound logistics, operations and the initiation of outbound logistics, which represent the 'cost side' or 'supply side' of the firm. The marketing operations are the 'downstream activities', such as the distribution activities of outbound logistics, marketing and sales, and after-sales service, which represent the 'revenue side' or 'demand side' of the firm.

Often, the objective of managing the supply side is to minimize the costs of producing goods and services, and this requires analysis of competitors and industry structures. A firm with production advantages, such as a proprietary production technology that utilizes lower quantities of inputs than competitors, is a low-cost producer in the industry and is able to pursue a 'cost-based strategy'.

The objective of managing the demand side is to maximize the revenues from selling goods and services, which requires analysis of customers and markets. A firm with a marketing advantage, such as brand recognition or unique products, emerges with market power and is able to pursue a 'differentiation strategy' or 'revenue-based strategy'.

Production and marketing decisions clearly need to be mutually consistent in order to produce an equilibrium. For additional discussion, see Besanko et al. (2003).

Discussion of value creation in international strategic management must also distinguish international production and marketing from domestic production and marketing. In considering the internationalization of the value chain, Porter (1986a) more specifically asserts:

> The distinctive issues in international, as contrasted to domestic, strategy can be summarized in two key dimensions of how a firm competes internationally. The first is what I term the configuration of a firm's activities worldwide, or where in the world each activity in the value chain is performed, including how many places. The second dimension is what I term coordination, which refers to how like activities in different countries are coordinated with each other (p. 17).

Porter then considers various combinations of geographically dispersed or concentrated configurations versus high or low coordination of activities. By the end of the article, Porter (1986a) suggests that 'today's game of global strategy seems increasingly to be a game of coordination-getting more and more dispersed production facilities, R&D laboratories, and marketing activities to truly work together' (p. 36). These ideas are further developed in Porter (1986b) and Porter (1990).

In a variation on the issue of coordination, Kogut (1985) asserts that international strategic management is distinguished from domestic management by the importance of flexibility: 'the unique content of a global versus a purely domestic strategy lies less in the methods to design long-term strategic plans than in the construction of flexibility which permits a firm to exploit the uncertainty over future changes in exchange rates, competitive moves, or government policy' (p. 27). Kogut then considers coordination of activities internationally to reap the benefits of flexibility, not just to manage risk and uncertainty, but to profit from them as well. There has subsequently been considerable attention to pre-planned flexibility and international strategic investments; see, for example, de Meza and van Ploeg (1987), Kogut and Kulatilaka (1994), and Amran and Kulatilaka (1999).

The ideas presented in Porter and Kogut relating to configuration, coordination, and flexibility suggest that strategic management of multinational enterprises creates value. Many other articles have also made this assertion in one way or another, including seminal works of Hamel and Prahalad (1985), Prahalad and Doż (1987), and Ghoshal and Bartlett (1990). The subject raises the question, 'How important is international strategic management?' Although difficult to answer definitively, some simple statistics illuminate the importance.

A first way to consider the importance of international management relative to domestic management is to examine macroeconomic aggregates. Net domestic product (NDP), a measure of valued created by all factors in a particular country, amounted to $10.3 trillion in the US in 2004 (US Department of Commerce, 2005). Factor income from abroad, which is predominantly earnings on direct investment, was $53.7 billion, representing 0.5 per cent of NDP. Hence, the pure foreign value creation does not appear very large, but further examination suggests that international activities are in fact important. Table 9.1 shows the breakdown of NDP into its basic components, and corporate profits (before taxes) amount to $1161.5 billion. (Note that this figure is not a measure of economic value added because part of corporate profits represents the required rate of return to shareholders.) Factor income from abroad thus represents 4.6 per cent of total corporate profits.

In addition, these figures exclude the contributions of exports to domestic profits and the contribution of imported inputs in reducing production costs. Export receipts amounted to 11.4 per cent of NDP, and although the value created from these exports cannot be determined, the gross magnitude suggests that international management is indeed important. Some value is also created by using imported inputs to reduce production costs. Imports amounted to 17.5 per cent of NDP, and although the portion attributable to inputs cannot be determined, this gross magnitude again suggests that international management is important.

Table 9.1   Value creation in the US based on Net Domestic Product, 2004

Type of Income	Billions of Dollars	Percent of Total
Compensation of Employees	6,693.4	65.0
Corporate Profits	1,161.5	11.3
Proprietors, and Rental Income	1,023.8	9.9
Net Interest and Dividends	446.0	4.3
Net Taxes on Production and Imports, Net Business Current Transfer Payments, and Statistical Discrepancy	974.3	9.5
Net Domestic Product (NDP)	10,299.0	100.0
Factor Income from Abroad	53.7	0.05
Exports of Goods and Services	1,173.8	11.4
Imports of Goods and Services	1,797.8	17.5

Source: US Department of Commerce, Survey of Current Business, August 2005, pp. 36-172.

A second way to evaluate the relative importance of international strategic management is to examine firm-level data. Data are widely available for the subset of all firms that are publicly traded, and although this subset is likely to contain more MNEs than the subset of firms not publicly traded, the available data are useful in analyzing value creation. In the Compustat database (Standard and Poor's Corporation, 1997), 6345 non-financial US firms report operating profits for 1994 amounting to $503.1 billion. Of these firms, 1215 report operating profits of foreign operations in addition to total operating profit, and operating profits from foreign operations amount to $74.3 billion from total operating profits of $261.8 billion, or 28.4 per cent. The $74.3 billion in profits from foreign operations represents 14.8 per cent of the aggregate profits of $503.1 billion, although this understates the relative profits from foreign operations because not all firms with foreign operations report profits from foreign operations when they report total profits. In addition, the figure does not include profits from exports, licensing/franchising agreements, or any form of international business other than direct foreign investment.

A third way of capturing the importance of international strategic management is to more broadly consider the sales revenues of the US firms. A total of 6345 non-financial firms report sales for 1994 amounting to $5 trillion. Table 9.2 presents some decomposition of this, indicating that 1634 firms report export sales and 1341 firms report sales from foreign operations. Because only 563 firms report both export sales and sales from foreign operations, a total of 2412 firms report some form of foreign sales. Hence, 38 per cent of the 6364 firms are labeled MNEs, and 62 per cent appear to be purely domestic corporations. Since MNEs are larger, however, they account for 60 per cent of total sales and domestic firms account for 40 per cent. Foreign sales reported by the 6364 firms amount to $1 trillion, or 20 per cent of total sales. Among the 2412 MNEs, the foreign sales account for 34.3 per cent of total sales. Furthermore, the data are again understated because not all firms with exports or foreign operations report segment sales. Of course, the focus on sales highlights the marketing side of the business and ignores the production side, but comparable data on costs are much harder to get than the data on revenues so cannot be examined here.

Table 9.2   Sales of US Corporations, 1994

	Number of Firms	Millions of Dollars
Sales	6,364	5,124,123
Export Sales	1,634	49,430
Sales from Foreign Operations	1,341	899,993
Total Foreign Sales	2,412	1,049,423
Total Multinational Enterprise Sales	2,412	3,059,468
Total Domestic Enterprise Sales	3,952	2,064,655

Source: Compustat and author's calculations

Financial activities also create value, although these are a little more suspicious than value creation through production and marketing activities since financial management does not obviously contribute either to the sales revenues of the firm or savings in the production costs of the firm. Porter (1985; 1986a; 1986b) implicitly considers financial management as a 'support activity' rather than as a primary activity and hardly addresses the issue. However, some of the most interesting questions in management relate to whether value is created through financial advantages, debt capacity, risk management, and so on. In addition, there are firms that exclusively create value through financial activities – such as banks and brokerage houses. Recognizing the difficulty of subjecting these financial firms to the same 'supply side' and 'demand side' analysis as non-financial firms, this chapter considers the activities of financial firms in the category of financial activities. Hence, two categories of value created through financial activities are the financial activities of non-financial firms and the activities of financial firms.

One way to assess the importance of international financial activities is to examine the performance of US financial firms. In the Compustat database, the operating profits of 714 financial firms amount to $137 billion. Of these, 109 firms report profits from foreign operations at $4.6 billion from total profits of $61.1 billion, or 7.5 per cent, which also represents 3.4 per cent of total financial industry profits. Thus, international financial management might be marginally important, but this figure again understates the importance of profits on foreign involvement because it does not capture the profit on international capital flows booked at home – such as profits on foreign deposits in the US or profits on foreign loans made from the US, and similar transactions in the bond and stock markets. International capital flows in the form of intermediated investment and portfolio investment are quite important compared to direct foreign investment, and firms managing these international capital flows are likely to create value through financial activities.

Based on these simple statistics for the US, we can conclude that strategic management of multinational firms is indeed important. Although it is not true that 'all management is international' in the US, international management is important in terms of its contributions at the margin when compared to domestic management, and is therefore well worth investigating.

3. VALUE CREATION AND THE DOMAIN OF INTERNATIONAL STRTIGIC MANAGEMENT

Having discussed value creation in terms of production, marketing and financial activities, this section combines these three categories into a basic strategy framework designed to examine the domain of international strategic management. Discussion is particularly focused on identifying the additional complexities resulting from crossing national borders that distinguish international management from domestic management. Each one of these areas could constitute a paper (or book) on its own, so the discussion is general rather than exhaustive, and references to additional literature are provided to fill gaps.

A framework for analyzing strategic management of multinational enterprises is presented in Table 9.3. This summarizes the distinctive issues in international strategic management, elements in the domain of international strategic management, and some representative studies.

Table 9.3 A framework for analyzing strategic management of multinational enterprises

International Value Creation Activities	Distinctive Issues in International Strategic Management	Domain of International Strategic Management	Representative Studies
Production Activities	Source inputs domestically or internationally, including supplier relations Produce domestically or internationally International alliance (licensing, franchising, joint venture) versus wholly-owned DFI International site selection decisions, including number and size of plants Input mix abroad (capital, unskilled labor, skilled labor, raw materials) Foreign production technology and equipment selection Human resources management in foreign countries Inventory management and cross-border transportation logistics R&D in process technologies	International trade theory, including comparative advantage, analysis of transportation costs, tariffs, and non-tariff barriers International political economy and foreign affairs Geographic area studies International financial theory, particularly exchange rate behavior and risk analysis International law Sociology/anthropology/religion Psychology Languages	(Stobaugh, 1969a) (Stobaugh, 1969b) (Flaherty, 1986) (Flaherty, 1996) (Dunning, 1988) (Ferdows, 1997) (Karrenbrock, 1990) (Hofstede, 1984) (Adler, 1996) (Quelch and Bloom, 1999)
Marketing Activities	International market selection, including number of foreign markets Market service and distribution methods (choosing exporting, international alliances, or DFI) Development of product attributes in different markets, including R&D into product technologies Product pricing internationally, including currency effects Promotional activities internationally, including language translation	Cultural studies Geographic area studies Sociology/anthropology/religion Psychology International financial theory, particularly exchange rate determination and behavior Languages	(Levitt, 1983) (Quelch and Hoff, 1986) (Douglas and Craig, 1989) (Hout, Porter and Rudden, 1982) (Kashani and Quelch, 1990) (Ricks, 1983) (Knetter, 1994)
Financial Activities	Foreign project evaluation (international capital budgeting) International cost-of-capital analysis and capital structure decisions, including capital structure of foreign subsidiaries Risk management for foreign exchange risk and foreign interest rate/ inflation rate risk, including diversification and hedging strategies International financing and the debt denomination decision International tax management	International macroeconomics International financial theory, particularly exchange rate and international interest rate behavior and risk analysis International political economy and foreign affairs Geographic area studies International portfolio theory International financial markets International tax law	(Shapiro, 1983) (Kogut and Kulatilaka, 1994) (Adler and Dumas, 1984) (Lessard and Lightstone, 1986) (Dufey and Srinivasulu, 1983) (Aliber, 1989)

The table suggests that areas in the domain of international production are international trade theory (comparative advantage), international political economy, foreign affairs and geographic area studies (political risk), international financial theory (exchange rates and risk), and area studies, law, sociology, anthropology, religion, psychology and language (applied to human resources management).

Elements in the domain of international marketing are geographic area studies, sociology, anthropology, religion and psychology (cultural determinants of product demand, product attributes, and promotional programs), international financial theory (exchange rates and pricing in different currencies) and language (promotional activities)

The domain of international financial activities includes international political economy, foreign affairs and geographic area studies (political risk), international financial theory and international macroeconomics (exchange rates and interest rates), international tax law (focusing on financing) and international portfolio theory and international financial markets (risk management and hedging).

Clearly, the domain of international strategic management is quite broad even under the criterion of value creation. Indeed, the diversity of international management is one appealing aspect that draws many managers into the field. References to additional literature are provided since space limitations preclude additional discussion here.

4. DOES INTERNATIONAL STRATEGIC MANAGEMENT MAKE THE WHOLE MULTINATIONAL ENTERPRISE WORTH MORE THAN THE SUM OF ITS PARTS?

By this point, the notion that international management creates value in ways somewhat different from domestic management is firmly established. After the discussion of production, marketing and finance activities covered in the strategy framework of section 3, a return to the more general issue of value creation is now warranted. Rather than focus on specific tasks that distinguish international management from domestic management, recall that Porter and Kogut discuss the distinction in more generic terms focusing on coordination and flexibility. In addition to indicating that international management creates value, both imply that the whole of the MNE is worth more than the sum of its parts; having n international subsidiaries is worth more as an MNE than the summation of the separate values of the n subsidiaries, as long as they are coordinated and are flexible enough to profit from changes in the environment.

Several reasons why the whole may be worth more than the sum of its parts have been developed in the international management literature. Kogut (1985) identifies several 'arbitrage' opportunities for international management to create value: production shifting, tax minimization, financial market imperfections and information arbitrage. Kogut also identifies a couple of 'leverage'opportunities: coordination and political risk management. Profits from arbitrage result from 'moving' something from one place to another, but profits from leverage result from using a position in one national market to enhance a position in another market. For example, global coordination can build a coalition of suppliers in one country in order to improve the position of the firm with respect to a rival in another, and with regard to political risk the position of a subsidiary in one country is likely to affect the firm's bargaining power vis-à-vis the government in another.

A second, more strategic reason for the whole to be worth more than the sum of the parts is due to cross-subsidization of operations. Hamel and Prahalad (1985) provide the example of competition in the tire industry: Michelin attacked Goodyear's US market by financing an aggressive marketing campaign using the profits from its European market, but rather than confine the competition to the US, Goodyear attacked Michelin's European market by financing market expansion in Europe using the profits from its US market. International cash flows may thus create value, such that Michelin (or Goodyear) is worth more than a simple summation of its operations in Europe and the US would suggest, because one operation can be defended by the other. (Without the second operation, the first would have to sink or swim on its own.) Necessarily, the cross-subsidization must not entail throwing good money into an unprofitable situation, but must be a temporary response to a situation which retains a positive present value.

Economies of scope from global distribution systems and synergies from knowledge created in different environments provide additional reasons for an MNE to be worth more than the sum of its parts; see, for example, Ghoshal (1987) and Douglas and Craig (1989). Economies of scope create value due to an ability to share investments across products and markets, as when two products sharing one distribution channel have a lower cost of joint distribution than the total cost of distributing the two products separately. Synergy is the ability to make two operations work better together than they would separately, and can result from learning; a production operation in one country might be improved by knowledge developed in a second country, and simultaneously the production operation in the second country might be improved by knowledge from the first country.

Given all this theoretical discussion of the value of the whole in relation to the sum of the parts, a natural question to ask is whether there is empirical evidence that the whole of an MNE is worth more than the sum of its subsidiary parts. If so, this is further testimony to the importance of studying international management. Unfortunately, the question has not been extensively researched. In a purely domestic setting, empirical evidence in Berger and Ofek (1995) and Comment and Jarrell (1995) reveals that product diversification destroys value because conglomerates lose focus, but literature considering international diversification is relatively scarce (however, see Hitt, et al., 1997 and Quian and Li, 1998). One way to approach the question is to consider whether an MNE creates more value than otherwise similar domestic firms. If so, the additional shareholder value is most likely to be created through international strategic management, the activities that otherwise similar domestic firms do not undertake.

4.1   Data and Empirical Strategy

Data are widely available for the subset of all firms that are publicly traded. This study utilizes the Compustat database of publicly traded US firms to compare firms engaged in international business to their domestic counterparts. In particular, it relies on the geographic segment files to distinguish exports from sales of foreign operations and to identify the regions in which sales from foreign operations occur.

The Compustat data are likely to be the highest quality available for US firms. However, they understate the true importance of multinational operations because not all firms with exports or foreign operations report segment sales. Since there is no way to correct for this, analysis proceeds under the assumption that any understatement is small. Of course, the focus on sales highlights the marketing side of the business and ignores the production side, but comparable data on costs are much harder to obtain than the data on revenues so cannot be examined here.

Although there are many possible measures of firm performance, the most common measure in the field of finance is the total return to shareholders (capital appreciation and dividend payments). This return is construed as a summary measure of all the information available on the firm – including all other performance measures such as the return on assets (ROA) frequently studied in the management literature, as in Hitt et al. (1997).

In finance, the total return is typically described as an increasing function of the firm's 'beta' from the Capital Asset Pricing Model (CAPM). In a series of papers, Fama and French (1992; 1993; 1995) show that for

US data, beta in fact does not contain much cross-section information when firm size and the ratio of book equity to market equity are included as determinants of returns. Financial leverage may have additional explanatory value as well. This chapter therefore controls for all of these variables in the investigation of the effects of international business.

One way to determine whether an international enterprise has different performance than an otherwise similar domestic firm is to determine whether measures of international involvement are significant determinants of total return, controlling for other characteristics known to affect firm performance. This chapter specifically considers five variables measuring international involvement based on exports, sales from foreign operations, and the geographic diversification of sales, and considers their contributions to total returns in cross-section regressions controlling for beta, firm size, the ratio of book equity to market equity, and financial leverage.

The measures of international involvement are derived from the Compustat data described above. The simplest type of international involvement is to export some domestic output. Bernard and Jensen (1999) revealed that exporting firms have superior performance when compared to non-exporting firms. Based on this, the empirical analysis here considers the effect of exporting on firm returns by using the Compustat data on export sales to form both a dummy variable for firms reporting exports and the ratio of export sales to the firm's total sales (the 'export ratio'). The dummy variable will capture the differential return for exporting firms vis-à-vis non-exporting firms. If exporting firms have higher (lower) returns than non-exporting firms, the coefficient on the dummy variable will be positive (negative). The export ratio will indicate whether the relative magnitude of exports contributes to differential performance. If exporting firms have higher (lower) returns than non-exporting firms, returns might also be an increasing (decreasing) function of the proportion of exports in total sales.

A more complicated type of international involvement is to operate facilities in foreign countries, and this is what is typically studied to help assess whether 'multinationality' affects firm performance. The literature in finance is generally inconclusive with respect to the empirical effects of multinationality on total returns. One of the earliest studies, Mikhail and Shawky (1979), reports that multinational shares outperform domestic shares. However, Brewer's (1981) subsequent study reports no significant difference in returns between multinational and domestic firms. After that, Fatemi (1984) reports that returns are identical between multinational and domestic firms except when the multinational operates in competitive foreign markets, in which case shareholder returns are lower for multinationals than for domestic firms.Subsequent research is equally inconclusive, so there is no consensus in the profession on the effects of multinationality on shareholder returns.

Empirical analysis here uses the Compustat data on sales of foreign operations to form both a dummy variable for firms with foreign operations and the ratio of sales from foreign operations to the firm's total sales (the 'multinational sales ratio'). If multinational enterprises have higher (lower) returns than otherwise similar purely domestic firms, the coefficient on the dummy variable will be positive (negative). In addition, the degree of multinationality might be important, such that returns might be an increasing (decreasing) function of the proportion of sales from foreign operations in relation to total sales.

The dummy variable and ratio for sales from foreign operations capture basic information as to whether a firm is a multinational enterprise and the overall degree of its multinationality. However, the variables do not capture the degree to which the firm is diversified with respect to its multinational activities. The value of multinationality is often associated with an integrated empire of operations, such that the whole is worth more than the sum of the parts. To the extent that international involvement makes the whole of the MNE worth more than the sum of its parts, it is because there are many parts, in many geographic areas throughout the world. Hence, the degree of geographic diversification is potentially the single most important determinant of shareholder returns due to international involvement.

The most common measure of geographic diversification is the entropy measure associated with Theil (1967):

$$ENTROPY = \sum_{i=1}^{n} S_i \ln(1/S_i) = -\sum_{i=1}^{n} S_i \ln(S_i)$$

where S_i represents the share of operations in the ith region relative to total operations. Sales are typically used as the measure of operations.

Compustat reports 1994 sales data broken into seven geographic regions (US, non-US North America, South America, Europe, Asia, Oceania and Africa) for 1221 firms. With seven geographic regions, entropy theoretically ranges from 0, which represents sales entirely in one region, to a maximum of 1.95, representing sales equally distributed among the seven regions. For the 1221 firms reporting geographic segment data, entropy empirically ranges from 0 to 1.37 and has a mean of 0.567.

A central feature of the entropy statistic is that it contains information not contained in the multinational sales ratio, as distinctions can be made among firms at a particular multinational sales ratio based on the dispersion of the sales from foreign operations. Figure 9.1 plots entropy against the multinational sales ratio, revealing of an inverted U shape. A regression estimating entropy as a quadratic function of the foreign sales ratio reveals:

$$\text{ENTROPY} = 3.479 \text{ RATIO} \quad 3.271 \text{ RATIO2}$$
$$(0.260) \qquad\qquad (0.400)$$

with an adjusted $R^2 = 0.79$. This equation implies that on average entropy reaches a maximum at 53 per cent multinational sales.

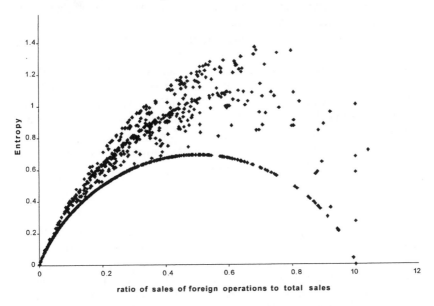

Figure 9.1   Entropy as a function of the ratio of sales of foreign operations to total sales

In order to determine the significance of international business the regressions control for other firm characteristics known to determine shareholder return, at least *ex post*. The first is the CAPM beta, measuring the risk of the stock against the market-wide portfolio. Compustat reports stock betas estimated by Standard & Poor's Corporation with five years of monthly data. As an independent variable, beta is expected to have a positive coefficient, such that riskier firms have higher returns. A lagged value of beta is used in order to reduce endogeneity.

Guided by findings from Fama and French, several additional control variables are included. Market size is the log of the lagged values of total market equity, which is expected to have a negative coefficient when small firms outperform large firms. The ratio of the book equity to market equity of the firm is the log of the lagged value, and is expected to have a positive coefficient since firms with high book equity in relation to market equity outperform firms with low book- to market-equity ratios. Financial leverage is the lagged value of the ratio of long-term debt to the sum of long-term debt and the market value of equity. The leverage variable is included in both level and squared form, which are expected to have positive and negative coefficients, respectively, suggesting that increasing leverage raises returns but at a decreasing rate and will even lower returns after some maximum.

Regressions also control for industry using a set of 13 industry dummy variables based on SIC code. This setup allows the constant in the regressions to vary by industry, since the industrial composition of MNEs is generally shown to be different from that of domestic corporations. The industries covered are: agriculture; mining and construction; food and tobacco; textiles and apparel; lumber, furniture and paper; chemicals; rubber, leather, stone and glass; metals; machinery, computers and electronics; transportation equipment; transportation and communications; wholesale and retail trade; and services.

4.2   Results

Tables 9.4 and 9.5 present cross-section regression results examining determinants of the return to shareholders of non-financial firms. Table 9.4 contains results using the return for 1994 in a sample of 3678 firms for which data are available. Table 9.5 contains results using the annual average return for the five-year period 1990-1994 in a sample of 2891 firms. The independent variables capturing international involvement are based on data for 1994. The dummy variables and ratios for export sales and foreign sales are as described above. Entropy is based on the formula given above; for any firms reporting zero sales from foreign operations, entropy is set equal to zero since all their sales therefore occur in the US

In order to conserve space, Tables 9.4 and 9.5 report fairly comprehensive equations containing the main combinations of the five variables representing international involvement. Many other combinations of variables were considered, but are not reported here because the results are consistent with these main combinations. Note that, as is typical in studies of returns, the adjusted R^2 of the equations is fairly low – at approximately 11 per cent for 1994 and 6 per cent for 1990-1994.

*Table 9.4   Determinants of shareholder returns, 1994
           (heteroscedasticity-consistent standard errors in parentheses)*

	1	2	3	4	5
Dummy for exports	8.258** (2.081)				
Dummy for multinational sales	5.899** (2.025)				
Export sales ratio		21.808** (8.417)	20.870** (8.408)		
Multinational sales ratio		0.366* (5.908)		9.361 (5.905)	
Entropy					12.531** (3.199)
Beta	−0.472** (0.133)	−0.433** (0.135)	−0.412** (0.136)	−0.424** (0.133)	−0.481** (0.128)
ln(market equity)	4.278** (0.519)	4.542** (0.508)	4.774** (0.477)	4.530** (0.508)	4.440** (0.587)
ln(book/market equity)	8.182** (1.572)	18.531** (1.572)	18.608** (1.567)	18.590** (1.573)	18.831** (1.758)
Leverage	10.833 (12.815)	14.150 (12.932)	14.822 (12.978)	11.068 (12.911)	11.597 (14.246)
Leverage^2	−25.315 (20.922)	−29.632 (21.015)	−30.175 (21.074)	−26.623 (20.996)	−30.294 (22.928)
Observations	3678	3676	3678	3676	2974
Adjusted R^2	0.11	0.11	0.11	0.11	0.12
SEE	50.340	50.440	50.460	50.487	50.552

Notes:
* Significant at 10% level
** Significant at 5% level
Regressions also include industry dummy variables.

In order to determine the significance of international involvement, the regressions control for other firm characteristics usually thought to determine shareholder return. Prominent among these variables is beta. For regressions in Table 9.4 using the 1994 return, beta is based on the period 1990-1994. For regressions in Table 9.5 using the 1990-1994 returns, beta is based on the period 1985-1989. The instability of coefficients on beta in cross-section regressions is reflected in the results presented in

Table 9.5 Determinants of average annual shareholder returns, 1990-1994
(heteroscedasticity-consistent standard errors in parentheses)

	1	2	3	4	5
Dummy for exports	1.177				
	(0.873)				
Dummy for multinational sales	1.515*				
	(0.886)				
Export sales ratio		4.033	3.630		
		(3.589)	(3.575)		
Multinational sales ratio		4.340*		4.146*	
		(2.408)		(2.398)	
Entropy					2.891**
					(1.149)
Beta	1.742**	1.755**	1.790**	1.794**	1.825**
	(0.778)	(0.778)	(0.779)	(0.779)	(0.871)
ln(market equity)	0.439**	0.459**	0.564**	0.451**	0.478**
	(0.199)	(0.195)	(0.185)	(0.195)	(0.230)
ln(book/market equity)	5.063**	5.078**	5.137**	5.088**	5.459**
	(0.608)	(0.607)	(0.608)	(0.608)	(0.696)
Leverage	13.472**	14.426**	14.041**	14.074**	12.565*
	(5.969)	(5.982)	(5.989)	(5.967)	(5.967)
Leverage^2	−25.519**	−26.743**	−26.320**	−26.495**	−26.399**
	(9.095)	(9.105)	(9.112)	(9.100)	(10.447)
Observations	2891	2889	2891	2889	2335
Adjusted R^2	0.06	0.06	0.06	0.06	0.07
SEE	19.749	19.744	19.759	19.745	20.002

Notes:
* Significant at 10% level
** Significant at 5% level
Regressions also include industry dummy variables.

Tables 9.4 and 9.5. Using the single-year returns for 1994, beta is shown to have a negative coefficient, which is an 'incorrect' sign according to the Capital Asset Pricing Model, and is statistically significant. For average annual returns for 1990-1994, however, the sign is positive, and significant. According to these results, 1994 was thus a year in which riskier stocks performed poorly, although the period 1990-1994 was generally one in which riskier stocks outperformed safer ones.

The Fama and French variables have consistent coefficients, but not necessarily conforming to earlier findings. The coefficient on size is positive in both tables, indicating that larger firms outperformed small firms during the early 1990s. This sign contradicts the Fama and French findings, although is not unusual because the effect of size on firm returns is the subject of some debate in the finance literature. The positive sign on the ratio of book equity to market equity is the 'right sign'. This ratio is typically regarded as a more robust determinant of returns in the finance literature, so the result somewhat reaffirms this robustness. The effect of leverage is also as expected: there is a positive coefficient on the variable and a negative coefficient on its square, and the variables are jointly significant. The maximum return occurs in the range of 19-27 per cent leverage.

The significance of international involvement as a determinant of shareholder returns is demonstrated by the results provided in the upper rows of Tables 9.4 and 9.5. Note that all of the signs are positive, indicating that shareholder returns are consistently positively related to international involvement. Nearly all of the coefficients in Table 9.4 are statistically significant at the 5 per cent level, and only the multinational sales ratio seems to be a relatively weak determinant. The coefficients in Table 9.5 are more often insignificant or are only weakly significant (that is, only at the 10 per cent level).

Exporting firms appear to have superior performance when compared to non-exporting firms for 1994, though not for the 1990-1994 period as a whole. For 1994, the dummy variable suggests that exporters had returns 8.25 percentage points above non-exporters. The export sales ratio suggests that returns were an increasing function of the proportion of exports, such that each percentage point of exports increased returns by 21-22 basis points.

Multinational enterprises appear to have superior performance when compared to domestic enterprises. The results for 1994 are stronger, both in magnitude and statistical significance, but the results for 1990-1994 still affirm the finding. For 1994, the dummy variable suggests that multinationals had returns nearly 6 percentage points higher than domestics, and the comparable figure for 1990-1994 is 1.5 percentage points. Although weaker than the results for the dummy variable, the coefficients on the multinational sales ratio suggest that returns were an increasing function of multinationality, such that each percentage point of sales from foreign operations increased returns by about 10 basis points in 1994 or 4 basis points during 1990-1994.

Among all the variables capturing international involvement, entropy might be the most important. The coefficient on entropy is statistically significantly positive at the 5 per cent level in both tables, suggesting that multinational diversification increases the total shareholder return. The average firm with an entropy value of 0.567 had a return 7.1 percentage points higher in 1994, and an average return 1.6 percentage points higher over 1990-1994, than an otherwise similar domestic firm, that is, a firm in the same industry, with the same beta, of the same size, with the same book- to market-equity ratio, and the same leverage). This is strong evidence that the value of international involvement is tied to the degree of diversification in the firm, such that a multinational enterprise as a whole is worth more than the sum of its subsidiary parts. Further discussion of this is provided in the summary.

5. SUMMARY

International strategic management is the process through which value is created by an individual or group of individuals operating across a national border. This definition thus distinguishes international strategic management from general management with the phrase 'operating across a national border', and distinguishes international management from international business by being focused on the 'process through which value is created' internationally. This chapter answers three questions from the premise that skills creating the most value in cross-border management are the most important elements in the domain of international strategic management.

First, how important is international management? The relative importance of international management is determined by the value created internationally compared to that created domestically, and section 2 presents several statistics that reveal the importance of international activities. Factor income from abroad, which is predominantly profits on direct foreign investment, represents 4.6 per cent of total corporate profits in the US. Among publicly traded non-financial firms, sales and profits from foreign operations amount to 34 per cent and 24 per cent of corporate sales and profits (respectively) for MNEs, and 20 per cent and 15 per cent of aggregate sales and profits of all US firms. In addition, financial firms create value from their international financial activities.

Second, what is the domain of international management? Since the domain is potentially unbounded under the definition provided here, this chapter considers a strategy approach in which international management is the aggregation of value created through international production, marketing, and financial activities. Section 3 develops this framework and uses it to define the core domain of international management. The conclusion is that the domain of international management is quite broad even under the criterion of value creation. Indeed, the diversity of international management is one appealing aspect that draws many managers into the field.

Third, does international management make the whole multinational corporation worth more than the sum of its parts? Effective management of production, marketing and financial activities is capable of creating more value in an MNE than in an otherwise similar purely domestic firm. section 4 presents some preliminary empirical evidence that this is indeed the case for US firms by showing that shareholder returns are positively related to measures of international involvement (and, by inference, the amount of international management). In particular, shareholder returns are positively related to the firm's geographic diversification; the average firm with an entropy value of 0.567 had a return 7.1 percentage points higher in 1994 (and an average return 1.6 percentage points higher over 1990-1994) than an otherwise similar domestic firm.

REFERENCES

Adler, M. and B. Dumas (1984), 'Exposure to currency risk: definition and measurement', *Financial Management*, Summer, 41-50.

Adler, N. (1996), *International Dimensions of Organizational Behavior*, third edition, South-Western College Publishers.

Aliber, R.Z (1989), 'The debt denomination decision', in R.Z Aliber (ed.), *The Handbook of International Financial Management*, Dow Jones-Irwin, 435-1.

Amran, M. and N. Kulatilaka (1999), *Real Options: Managing Strategic Investment in an Uncertain World*, Boston, MA: Harvard Business School Press.

Berger, P. and E. Ofek (1995), 'Diversification's effect on firm value'. *Journal of Financial Economics*, **37**, 39-65.

Bernard, A. and J. Jensen (1999), 'Exceptional exporter performance: cause, effect, or both?', *Journal of International Economics*, **47**, 1-25.

Besanko, D., D. Dranove, M. Shanley and S. Schafer (2003), 'Primer: economic concepts for strategy', in D. Besanko et al., *The Economics of Strategy*, New York: John Wiley & Sons, 1-37.

Boddewyn, J.J. (1999), 'The domain of international management', *Journal of International Management*, **5**, 3-14.

Brewer, H. (1981), 'Investor benefits from corporate international diversification', *Journal of Financial and Quantitative Analysis*, **16**, 113-26.

Comment, R. and G. Jarrell (1995), 'Corporate focus and stock returns', *Journal of Financial Economics*, **37**, 67-87.

de Meza, D. and F. van der Ploeg (1987), 'Production flexibility as a motive for multinationality', *Journal of Industrial Economics*, **35**, 343-51.

Douglas S.P. and C.S.Craig (1989), 'Evolution of global marketing strategy: scale, scope, and synergy', *Columbia Journal of World Business*, Fall, 47-59.

Dufey, G. and S.L. Srinivasulu (1983), 'The case for corporate management of foreign exchange risk', *Financial Management*, winter, 54-62.

Dunning, J.H. (1988), *Explaining International Production*, Boston, MA: Unwin Hyman.

Fama, E.F. and K.R. French (1992), 'The cross-section of expected stock returns', *Journal of Finance*, **47**, 427-65.

Fama, E.F. and K.R. French (1993), 'Common risk factors in the returns on stocks and bonds', *Journal of Financial Economics*, **33**, 3-56.

Fama, E.F and K.R. French (1995), 'Size and book-to-market factors in earnings and returns', *Journal of Finance*, **50**, 131-55.

Fatemi, A. (1984), 'Shareholder benefits from corporate international diversification', *Journal of Finance*, **34**, 1325-44.

Ferdows, K. (1997), 'Making the most of foreign factories', *Harvard Business Review*, March-April, 73-88.

Flaherty, T. (1986), *Coordinating International Manufacturing and Technology*, in M. Porter (ed.), *Competition in Global Industries*, Boston, MA: Harvard Business School Press, 83-93.

Flaherty, T. (1996), *Global Operations Management*, New York: McGraw-Hill.

Ghoshal, S. (1987), 'Global strategy: An organizing framework', *Strategic Management Journal*, **8**, 425-40.

Ghoshal, S. and C.A. Bartlett (1990), 'The multinational corporation as an interorganizational network', *Academy of Management Review*, **15**, 603-25.

Hamel, G. and C.K. Prahalad (1985). 'Do you really have a global strategy?', *Harvard Business Review*, July-August, 139-48.

Harrigan, K. R. (1992), 'A world-class company is one whose customers cannot be won away by competitors: internationalizing strategic management', in A. M. Rugman and W.T. Stanbury, *Global Perspective: Internationalizing Management Education*, British Columbia, Canada: Centre for International Business Studies, University of British Columbia, 251-63.

Hitt, M., R.E. Hoskisson, and H. Kim (1997), 'International diversification: effects on innovation and firm performance in product-diversified firms', *Academy of Management Journal*, **40**, 767-98.

Hofstede, G. (1984), *Culture's Consequences: International Differences in Work Related Values*, Beverly Hills, CA: Sage Publications.

Hout, T., M.E. Porter and E. Rudden (1982), 'How global companies win out', *Harvard Business Review*, September-October, 98-108.

Karrenbrock, J. (1990), 'The internationalization of the beer brewing industry', *Federal Reserve Bank of St. Louis Review*, November-December, 3-19.

Kashani, K. and J.A. Quelch (1990), 'Can sales promotion go global?', *Business Horizons*, May-June, 373.

Knetter, M.M. (1994), 'Exchange rates and corporate pricing strategies', in Y. Amihud and R. Levich (eds), *Exchange Rates and Corporate Performance*, Burr Ridge, IL; Irwin Professional Publishing, 181-219.

Kogut, B. (1985), 'Designing global strategies: profiting from operational flexibility', *Sloan Management Review*, Fall, 27-38.

Kogut, B. and N. Kulatilaka (1994), 'Operating flexibility, global manufacturing, and the option value of a multinational network', *Management Science*, 40, 123-39.

Lessard, D.R. and J.B. Lightstone (1986), 'Volatile exchange rates can put operations at risk', *Harvard Business Review*, July-August, 107-14.

Levitt, T. (1983), 'The globalization of markets', *Harvard Business Review*, May-June, 92-102.

Mikhail, A. and H. Shawky (1979), 'Investment performance of US-based multinational corporations', *Journal of International Business Studies*, **10**, 53-66.

Morris, W. (ed.) (1975), *The American Heritage Dictionary of the English Language*, Boston: Houghton Mifflin Company.

Porter, M.E. (1985), *Competitive Advantage: Creating and Sustaining Superior Performance*, New York: Free Press.

Porter, M.E. (1986a), 'Changing patterns of international competition', *California Management Review*, **28**, 9-40.

Porter, M.E. (1986b), *Competition in Global Industries*, Boston, MA: Harvard Business School Press.

Porter, M.E. (1990), *The Competitive Advantage of Nations*, New York; Free Press.

Prahalad, C.K. and Y.L. Doz (1987), *The Multinational Mission: Balancing Local Demands and Global Vision*, New York; Free Press.

Quelch, J.A. and H. Bloom (1999), 'Ten steps to a global human resources strategy', *Strategy & Business*, First Quarter, 18-29.

Quelch, J.A. and E.J. Hoff (1986), 'Customizing global marketing', *Harvard Business Review*, May-June, 59-68.

Quian, G. and J. Li (1998), 'Multinationality, global market diversification, and risk performance for the largest US firms', *Journal of International Management*, **4**, 149-70.

Ricks, D.A. (1983), *Blunders in International Business*, Cambridge, MA: Blackwell Publishers.

Shapiro, A.C. (1983), 'International capital budgeting', *Midland Corporate Finance Journal*, Spring, 26-45.

Standard and Poor's Corporation (1997), 'Compustat PC-Plus'.

Stobaugh, Robert B. Jr. (1969a), Where in the world should we put that plant?'. *Harvard Business Review*, January-February, 129-36.

Stobaugh, R. B., Jr. (1969b), 'How to analyze foreign investment climates', *Harvard Business Review*, September-October, 100-108.

Theil, H. (1967), *Economics and Information Theory*, Chicago: Rand McNally.

US Department of Commerce (2005), 'National income and product accounts of the United States', *Survey of Current Business*, August, 36-172.

10. Embedding the multinational: bridging internal and external networks in transitional institutional contexts[1]

Ray Loveridge

1. INTRODUCTION

The multinational enterprise (MNE) is often portrayed as both a major protagonist and an architect of integrated global markets. It thus becomes the site of a new concentration of authority within a 'trans-national social space' (Morgan et al., 2001). One source of its new found authority is to be found in the vast increase in foreign direct investment (FDI), that is to say, in assets located and operated within countries other than the one in which the MNE originated (UNCTAD, 2000). The reasons for the explosion of FDI in the final 20 years of the last century are complex (Dicken, 2003). They include both the search for new product markets and for newly exploitable resources. These include both the availability of cheaper recruits to a disciplined labour force or the appropriation of new knowledge in the form of localized technologies. This global search is seen to have given rise to a widespread 'locational tournament' in which national governments compete to demonstrate the attractiveness of locating foreign corporate activities within the territorial boundaries of their sovereign control (Mytelka, 2000).

The attractions of FDI for the host government can be seen as lying within an external source of job-creating capital combined with an often significant increase in export earnings. Of equal importance may be the perception held by the host government that the MNE is the carrier of 'modernizing' technological knowledge and attendant socializing disciplines. For many political leaders, as well as academic observers, the notion of national economic development through the alliance of local producers with MNEs has become a central tenet and aim of their acceptance of the ideology of globalization. In this sense, it is an extension of the much older 'doctrine of developmentalism' (Cowen and Shenton, 1996).

A central precept of the neo-liberal approach to globalization has been that successful governments must open their economies to external investment both as a source of energizing capital and of appropriative learning. This, in itself, represents a major shift from former notions of protecting 'infant industries' in the manner practised by the governments of Britain, USA, Continental Europe, Japan and South Korea at various stages of the industrialization of their economies. The best exemplars of the new thinking are often seen as the third wave industrializers of Pacific Rim Asia, namely Indonesia, Thailand, Malaysia and Singapore. In these countries national leaders have adopted a conscious strategy of attracting FDI through the institution of export processing zones (EPZ) and, especially in the latter two countries, through the creation of local development agencies and specialized institutes of higher education and technological research. The present study is located in the latter three countries together with Brunei, probably the wealthiest members of the Association of South East Nations (ASEAN) and certainly the fastest growing over the last quarter of a century.

In much of the business literature the comparative capabilities of nations and regions in this new mode of global tournament have been linked to the internal social cohesion of their institutional structure. In particular the existence of relational networks and of geographical clusterings of economic activities that are either complementary in form or draw off shared social and material resources are seen to have provided unique and non-replicable assets in this contest with 'outsiders' (Best, 2001). More widely the national societal setting of business institutions is sometimes seen as providing a unique 'institutional comparative advantage' within some sectoral markets (Hall and Soskice, 2001).

The term 'social capital' has entered the lexicon of prescriptive managerialist literature (Coleman, 1988) to describe the manner in which close relational ties can provide the basis for 'external economies' or 'commons'. There is, however, very little in the literature of international management to describe the manner in which the MNE relates to the prior existence of such local networks, or whether, indeed, the very nature of social closure exercised within these networks renders them unable to learn from any such externally defined 'knowledge'. Forsgren et al. (2005) are among those who ascribe a primary strategic importance to the creation of bridges into local networks as a means to achieving the advantages of locating overseas in the first place. In the study presented here I observe that the interfaces between the MNE and its host institutions take place at a number of layered levels of interaction between expatriate managers and their peers in host agencies. These transactions are shaped by actor interpretations of their situation in relation to a complex of local and more macro, sectorally related, perceived contingencies. Interaction along the socially and politically segmented networks that bridge boundaries between host and guest institutions have, then, to be seen both in terms of the micro-politics of symbolic interaction and the manner in which the separate worlds of the guest organization and the host community are perceived by the actors – a process made more problematic by shifting norms within both systems.

This leads me to propose that the manner in which technological or managerial knowledge is being 'transferred' from and to the guest MNE requires an act of translation along such operational networks (Callon and Latour, 1992). This can be seen to be driven by a mixture of actor interest and/or identity within events and situations which shape and colour the way ideas are conveyed and implemented (Czarniawska and Joerges, 1996). By the same token, the manner in which local 'market opportunities' are perceived and socially constructed can also be a product of realities negotiated between protagonists. On each side of the transaction the role of central office patronage or sponsorship and, with it, the clientelist status of the local affiliate or state agency tends to shape operational outcomes (Eisenstadt and Roniger, 1984). This analysis can be seen as an extension of a more discursive paper in ABM which derived from the same study (Loveridge, 2002).

2. THE REGIONAL AND NATIONAL CONTEXT

The four countries that provided the foci of the study had earned the title of 'New Tigers' by virtue of their average annual growth rate of 8 per cent over the decade preceding the 1997 financial crisis. The subsequent recovery of their economies has been interpreted in various and sometimes conflicting ways. Free market economists express doubt as to the reform of a banking system weighed down by so-called 'non-performing' loans, that is, loans that are not producing the anticipated return on investment. Other observers suggest that a lack of technically qualified labour was already, before the crisis, providing a ceiling to these economies' ability to advance technologically and to enter the premium league of product innovators (Jesudason, 1990). Both criticisms can be related to what Carney and Gedajlovic (2001) describe as nascent institutional conditions shaping the later developmental trajectory of their business systems. They see the family based conglomerate (FBC) as a continuing legacy of a colonial era. More recently these have been reinforced by the growth of newer forms of overseas Chinese family businesses, sometimes described as 'pariah capitalism' because of the manner in which host states discriminate against those labelled socially and, often, legally, as diaspora. Government Linked Enterprises (GLE) are, again, seen as a legacy of an era of post-colonial nationalist government devoted to state induced development in key industries. These authors are somewhat ambivalent about past and current linkages between GLE and FBC; others, especially local academic commentators such as Gomez and Jomo (1999) and Searle (1999) have been much more explicit in their criticism of these ties. They see a growing fusion of interest to have taken place between the dominant political coalition, the agencies of the state, including the financial institutions, and the personal wealth of a 'patrimonialist caste' who have gained their business ascendancy through personal political connection. In countries such as those in this study this convergence of interest has been justified by political leaders in terms of an outstandingly successful pursuit of national economic growth. But their critics see this goal as being undermined by the local business elite's lack of ability to learn from the MNEs who have been largely responsible for the vast inflow of capital that has fuelled the domestic growth of an 'ersatz capitalism' (Yoshihara, 1988).

In particular the tension is provided by official discrimination, particularly in Malaysia and Brunei, in favour of those seen as 'indigenous' within the labour market (Muslim Malay or Bumiputera), and against those labelled as 'diaspora' (Chinese and Indian Malay). This can be seen to work against meritocratic career criteria and, therefore, against the effective use of trained labour and investment capital. Jesudason suggests that in Malaysia the 'lack of co-operation between the state and Chinese capital has compromised the nation's ability to enhance its technological capabilities and develop a strong manufacturing sector' (Jesudason, 1990, p. 118). The more coercive policies of past Thai governments have, paradoxically, served to better integrate Chinese entrepreneurs into the social fabric of that country and a common religious affiliation (Buddhism) has ensured that this has not generally been a barrier to the formation of a national identity. However, in the case of Thailand, its critics, both internal and external, have seen popularly elected governments as being relatively weak and over-dependent on the Chinese family business (Kunio, 2004).

It is against this background of a state endorsed personal capitalism across the most successful ASEAN states that MNE management have to discover a relational basis for their commercial activities and for a supposedly technical-rational exercise of management techniques. For example, within at least three countries in the sample the labour market for the management occupations could be seen to be largely socially segmented. Within all of the MNE affiliates contained in the study most management and administrative positions were occupied by Chinese 'diaspora', in spite of regulations favouring the employment of Bumiputra.

In government agencies and in GLEs the reverse seems to be true. (This is confirmed in government produced labour market data.) In the latter, indigenously owned enterprises, management systems are likely to operate in a much more overtly paternalistically ascriptive manner than is likely to be found in the MNE (Searle, 1999). This is less likely in larger organizations in Singapore, but even there the dominance of SMEs tends to support a particularistic form of management control. It can, therefore, be seen that across the whole sample the MNE provided a very different mode of entry to professional socialization for local recruits from that offered by indigenous organizations.

3. THE STUDY SAMPLE

The study was an exploratory one sponsored by the ASEAN-EC Management Centre over a period from November 1997 to December 1999. Semi-structured interviews were conducted in 20 MNEs having their head offices in five separate European (EU) countries and having significant direct investment through affiliates in ASEAN countries. The sample was chosen on the basis of the size of participants (all but one firm had above 25 000 employees) and as representing a width of sectoral representation. A table combining country of origin, location of affiliate and dominant sector of operations is reproduced in Table 10.1. The interest of the sponsoring body was, of course, in how effective the presence of large European firms was in transferring technological knowledge to their ASEAN affiliates and how far the latter provided significantly to the design of local products and services.

Head office interviewees were senior executives responsible for corporate regional activities, together with the head of their R&D or product development activities. Interviews were also carried out in 23 affiliates located in Thailand, Malaysia, Singapore and Brunei Darussalam. These were normally with the local general manager, the test or quality control manager and, in some cases, with the HRM or training manager. I also visited local plants and had conversations with supervisors and operatives where they spoke English. (In the case of two auto electronic plants previous visits had been made from the mid-1980s onwards.) Interviews were held in the regional offices of the MNE where these were based in the country. Interviews were also held in regional or national development agencies with local public servants as well as with local university professors and science/technology park officials involved in technology

Table 10.1 Location of parent and affiliate organizations included in the sample by sector

Banking-Insurance	Aerospace/Aero-Components	Atomobile Components	Electrtcs/Electronics	Telecom	Glass Ceramics	Machinery	Food/Cosmetics	Petro-Chemicals	Specialist Chemicals
France/Brunei	Britain/Singapore	Germany/Malaysia	Britain/Singapore	Sweden/Malaysia	France/Singapore	Sweden Britain/Singapore	Netherlands Britain/Singapore	Netherlands Britain/Malaysia	Germany/Thailand
Britain/Thailand	Britain/Brunei	Britain/Malaysia	Brunei	Britain/Singapore		Malaysia		Brunei	Netherlands
								France/Singapore France/Brunei	Sweden/Malaysia
								Britain/Thailand	Britain/Malaysia

UK 9   All MNEs over 25, 000 employees, most over 50, 000.

FR 4   Local Asset Values: $US250 000 to 2 billion.

N   4   Local Employees: 30 to 3000

SW 3

G   2

182

diffusion. In all, 100 on-site interviews were held over that period. Subsequent research and teaching in the region has enabled me to keep in touch with my main informants and to follow their activities as reported in the local discourse.

4. SECTORAL FRAMES

In the initial research design I pursued two propositions. One related the extent of local mandate, or devolved authority within the MNE, to the perceived development of distinctive competences within the locally based affiliate. This assumption of a rationally assessed dependency relationship existing within the MNE between the centre of the organization and the management of its peripheral affiliates has been pursued in a number of studies by students of international business such as that of Birkenshaw and Hood (1998).

A second proposition that affected my choice of informant companies was that the structure and strategic recipe of the MNE vis-a-vis its overseas affiliates would reflect the institutional context of its national parent (Whitley, 1999). In a sense the latter proposition was a counter to the former. It was in part supported by the finding that, among solely British-owned firms within the same sector as Continentally based rivals, there appeared to be a much looser structure and style of communication with local affiliates than was discovered in the latter. This was perhaps typified in the remark made by the Singapore managing director of the British electrical MNE to the effect that he 'had to read the FT every week to find out what HQ was doing next'. It was, however, difficult to find a significant difference in the number or modes of formal communications passing between HQ and the local affiliate within the sample and, as described later, in many cases there were clear indications of greater reliance on a normative 'understanding' between the two in the shaping of their behaviours. In any case, the effect of national culture was difficult to establish in a small sample in which, for example, one German speciality chemist reverted to a totally decentralized holding group structure over the period of the study before announcing a merger with its major French rival. This was one example of the cross-border changes in ownership and drastic internal restructuring occurring in every European MNE in the sample over the period in which interviews were being conducted. A common thread running through the interview responses was that all informants reported the adoption of the concept of Economic Value Added (EVA) as a recently adopted guide to the firm's strategic investment.

(Over half the firms in the sample had changed their corporate identity within two years of the interviews in their head office. Most had existed for 80 or more years.)

In practice I discovered more uniformity of managerial views on style and strategic orientation within two main sectoral groupings of sampled firms, and in a manner that supported the power dependency argument contained in the first proposition (Pfeffer, 1992). The first of these groupings were long time investors in the region, generally having their origins in a colonial era. These were, or at one stage had been, in extractive or infrastructural sectors. Thus, the large Anglo Dutch and French mineral oil and gas MNEs and the Anglo Dutch food and cosmetics giant (formerly palm olive estate owner) were both long time residents. Others, like the British electrical firm and Swedish telecommunications provider, had been engaged in providing local infrastructural projects in Pacific Asia since the late 19th century. These firms now advertised their commitment to supplying local consumer and producer markets in their annual reports, as well as in the interviews reported here. The Asian Pacific markets were seen as their next big growth points when compared to satiated European and North American markets.

But their managers were essentially very different in their orientation from those of other MNEs using assembly or sequential batch production, that is in sectors like automobile or electronic components. By and large, the investment of the latter firms was in relatively footloose capital that had been attracted by generous fixed-term financial conditions for their initial investment and by the availability of disciplined but relatively lowly trained labour services. While important to the host state in terms of its appropriation of their modern technology, the local plants of such MNEs were seen by head office strategists as components in a global or regional supply chain that might well be moved to other locations in response to market changes. Nevertheless a preoccupation of managers within this group was with their inability to establish a reliable chain of local suppliers. The obvious nearby rival for all ASEAN states in this locational contest was named by both MNE managers and their host agencies as mainland China.

These two sectorally related positions shaped differences in the manner in which affiliates in the sample related to the agencies of the host state. In the first case early and present involvement in the industrial and political development of the host country had led to the incorporation of MNE management into the processes of national governance on a very different basis to that of the footloose global supplier. The latter tended to maintain an arm's-length relationship with national government, being much more concerned with the day-to-day interpretation of local regulations by local planning and development agencies in the management of their plant operations. In this activity they usually relied heavily on the presence of their (then) statutorily enforced local partner or director and other indigenous appointments to liaison roles such as that of personnel or HRM manager.

This contrasted with the heavy involvement with national civil servants and politicians by senior managers of the older ex-colonial firms. The nature of their activity was almost always directed at projects, often turnkey projects, seen to have a discernible long-term significance for the host economy and often being in the 'national interest' of their home government. For instance, over the course of the study the British defence manufacturer was negotiating to supply both attack planes and naval frigates to one of the national governments in the study. The contracts involved the construction of both a new harbour and a new airfield (by the same group) and the training of indigenous operational and support staff over a long period by British service personnel. In other cases generous export or aid-in-kind loans from the home government might underwrite the large amount of front-loaded investment required to undertake such projects. But overall such investments could 'capture' the MNE in a manner not found in the former, footloose manufacturers, making involvement in the strategic control of their environment seem somewhat more imperative.

Between these two poles business-to-business services were embedded, to varying degrees, in local business networks, often somewhat precariously. Banks who were not incorporated into the diplomatic network of national governance strove to enter the inner circle of lenders to the national debt. The French bank in the sample was negotiating to provide the national government with finance for the deal to buy the British arms described above. In this way its local managers hoped to elevate their status from that of providing local consumer branches, a loss-making strategy for entering the country, to one of membership of institutional incorporation into the local socio-political elite.

5. HIERARCHY, NETWORKS AND KNOWLEDGE ABILITY

All but five of the 23 affiliates visited in the survey had general managers who were European expatriates, though not all from the parent country. Most non-executive chairmen were of the locally dominant indigenous ethnic group, as were a majority of non-executive directors on the local board. Such local representation sometimes represented a financial interest, but most were chosen, with some advice from government agencies, during the period when the MNE was negotiating entry to the country. They were seen then, as now, as advisers on and representatives in the local structure of political influence (apparently known in the local community as 'Ali Babas'). Local government agencies were supposed to authorize such local appointments on the basis of the ability of incumbents to monitor the imposition of government set standards. Those relating to quotas of locally employed labour and to locally sourced materials were seen as particularly important by host agencies. In interviews, both HQ and local managers emphasized their intention to retain 'managerial control' over local operations. There did, indeed, seem many instances of relatively weak internal monitoring by external directors in a way which enabled expatriate mangers to violate the supposed quota rules. In the case of two companies in the sample they had obtained the agreement of the host government not to appoint local directors at all. (The statutory obligation has been relaxed in Malaysia and Thailand since the time of the survey.)

Within this largely expatriate population there appeared three very distinctive career groupings. The first was made up of a group of senior executives whose last series of appointments suggested a plateauing of their career as 'foreign service executives' (Desatnick and Bennett, 1977), or, as I have labelled them, 'diplomats'. Their role was largely that of global trouble-shooting or founding or nurturing new overseas ventures within the MNE. Within this sample they were generally located within regional or 'lead-nation' offices with wider regional responsibilities. I interviewed eight such executives, together with one former diplomat now overseas director of the MNE. In most other cases the existence of the role was brought into my interviews by HQ informants and plant mangers who saw such diplomats as important intermediaries within their global communications.

A second career category was that of the 'fast tracker'. These were managers moved from functional or plant responsibility in the home country to a role as general manager in an established Asian affiliate for a period of three to five years. There were seven such general managers in my sample. As in the Starkey and McKinlay (1989) study these managers were sometimes referred to as 'tourists' by their indigenous subordinates who were aware of the career expectations of their temporary boss. By way of contrast, the third category of career orientations among expatriates were of those who had gone 'local'. Their expectations had become shaped by marriage to a local partner, conversion to the local religion, or in other ways that had both motivated and enabled their social assimilation into the local community. These executives, of whom I interviewed four, saw their career as ending with relocation to a local retirement residence rather than a return to Europe. Interestingly, they are often referred to in the HRM literature, as in my HQ interviews, as a 'problem for international management' (Scullion, 1995). All three categories of career were present within each of the MNEs.

In spite of their prolonged absence from the parent country, diplomatic executives seemed highly regarded by HQ. Although not usually seen as candidates for chief executive they might, as in two of my HQ interviews, be appointed to specialized board positions as international directors. Their activities usually took place along networks containing local politicians, financial analysts, journalists and the heads of local business groups comprising regional and national commercial elites. They were regarded by HQ as important sources of strategic information as well as often being used to create the 'presence' needed to penetrate the elite networks of countries in which the MNE board was seeking to make an exploratory investment. The local head of the French bank referred to above was just such a figure. He had previously served in Uruguay, Cambodia, Vietnam and Thailand before being asked to create an opening for investment in the public expenditure of the Brunei government through the vehicle of a relatively small local office. Of the other interviews with diplomats, all but one were in the extractive/infrastructural sectors where the ex-colonial status of such MNEs often seemed to reinforce an institutionalized proximity to the local commercial/political elite. It was also among these firms that a more stable matrix of regional and product MNE structures was to be found. Among sequential supply chain manufacturers the location of regional diplomatic offices appeared more flexible. Most reported an expectation of their imminent move to the Chinese mainland.

While diplomats made frequent trips back home or to regional meetings of MNE management, theirs was a much greater sense of 'knowledge-ability' in their understanding of HQ intentions than those of colleagues. Goodall and Roberts (2003) borrow this term from Giddens (1979) to encapsulate the notion of a shared frame of reference between the HQ executive and the spatially distanced local manager within the MNE. Through prior experience of the way the other party works each is able to interpret the other's situational knowledge and is, therefore, likely to be better informed about the latter's intentions. For these high placed officials a common socialization in the company could be a resource upon which each could draw in their interpretation of a distant event. Nohria and Ghoshal (1997) report such homophilic relations as typical of successfully adaptive transnationals. Their importance was also brought out by Gupta and Govindarajan's (2000) large scale questionnaire survey of US and Japanese executives. Harzing (1998) emphasized the significance of such distant sources of self identity among MNE affiliate managers facing unfamiliar and apparently normless situations. These feelings were most explicitly recalled by one HQ overseas director in my study who had previously been a regional executive in many different overseas locations. More usually the general managers targeted their anxieties onto specific 'breakdowns in communication'. Goodall and Roberts ascribe importance to both material and cognitive factors in 'repairing the effects of distance'. Most important in their 'mantra of distance' is the retention of a 'co-presence' on the interpersonal network in the MNE and, in particular, the retention of an HQ patron with whom the expatriate retains 'a track record' of personal success. Thus a common understanding is likely to be shaped by the cognitive 'co-presence' of such patrons and with intermediaries in the network and by the constant refreshing of a positive common 'memory' and shared vocabulary of practice.

Fast trackers seemed likely to find this exercise much more fraught, if only because of the nature and career significance of their assignment and the judgemental position of their HQ sponsor. Unlike diplomats they were accompanied by both their spouse and children who were, therefore, part of the immediate work-leisure world of the expatriate. The latter attended local 'international' (normally English-French-German speaking) schools, unlike the children of diplomats who were usually in back-home private residential schools because of their parents' anticipated career mobility. The work-day of fast trackers was spent at the plant, as the German auto components manager put it 'From 7 to 7 weekdays – and often at week-ends too!'. In interviews and extended periods of observed behaviours, it was often possible to see their daily discourse as spanning the operational needs of their local plant in relation to its overall contribution to the much wider, but still relatively short term and explicit, needs of the global supply chains to which it contributed. Their leisure time was generally spent with expatriates from the housing enclaves in which they lived, but they also met indigenous managers, both business associates and others, at local chambers of commerce and social events. In all cases they spoke of their successors as possibly coming from their indigenous (Chinese) middle management. The reason they, and HQ informants, gave for this was one of cost, that is, by reference to the lower salaries paid to indigenous managers doing the same job as expatriates. There was little apparent consciousness of the importance of their cognitive affinity with others in their back-home network or of the potential cultural barriers for indigenous managers who lacked their networked knowledge-ability.

In fact, the third category of expatriate managers in my sample, the locals, were still being paid at a salary level comparable to that paid to their 'overseas' colleagues. But, unlike other groups of expatriates, the four locals in my study seemed to lack reliable sponsorship at HQ. They were sometimes described by HQ and regional colleagues as having 'gone native'. Visits from HQ representatives, or 'punctuated co-presences' to use Goodall and Roberts' phrase, seemed often to lead to encounters in which each party 'talked past each other'. The locals' isolation was made more difficult by the changes taking place in the parent company through restructuring consequent upon M&A. Hence new goals were often couched in an abstract and dislocated language, such as the adoption of models of EVA or TQM, which provided little immediate connection with work/ community networks along which they operated. Yet the weight of responsibility for explaining these strategically determined changes rested with them. As Goodall and Roberts observe, it was also they 'who had to struggle to preserve their contextual knowledge of the centre in order to be understood ... The condition and consequence of this synthetic corporate certainty is the anxious preoccupation with staying connected...' (Goodall and Roberts 2003, pp. 1169-70). Much the same anxiety was to be found among the five indigenous general managers in the sample. Their main complaint was that their advice on the unsuitability of both product design and workplace organization was persistently ignored in spite of their regular communication of these defects to both HQ and design and development. This awareness of social exclusion extended to their communications within HQ groups for the two indigenous general managers posted to positions in London prior to promotion to national lead-affiliates. They, quite independently, declared their HQ colleagues to be unwilling to reconsider corporate strategy on the basis of disconfirming evidence from those not on the networks of senior executives.

6. INNOVATION OR RE-EMBEDDING KNOWLEDGE ALONG NETWORKS

The importance of these socially layered networks within the MNE was reflected in the organizational level of their interface with that of the host business system and with wider society. Within the older colonial MNEs, the incorporation of their organization into the structure of the national economy and the social embeddedness of their diplomat executives often led to an apparent complementarity of goals with national politicians and civil servants. In such relations diplomatic expatriates occupied lead positions. This could readily be observed in the case of joint ventures such as those involved in the extraction and processing of mineral oil and gas and in the construction of infrastructural projects such as the Multi-Media Corridor to the south of Kuala Lumpur or the building of two new international airports and a new seaport in the region. In these ventures partnerships with indigenous business groups were a contractual requirement. But these collaborations could also lead to 'rent-taking' by the latter or by their sub-contractors, an experience rather ruefully shrugged off by the Swedish telecoms regional executive but regarded by the British electrics executive as a significant reason for his company's planned withdrawal from the region. This kind of collaboration was seen by national leaders as critical to the creation of long-term capabilities within their economies. The guarded comments of diplomat regional executives might be taken to support the more openly critical views of local academic observers quoted earlier (Gomez and Jomo, 1999).

In some cases this collaboration with host agencies extended to the introduction of new concepts of workplace management systems. This was evident in the large investment in training facilities for local technicians and operatives that was undertaken by firms engaged in infrastructural projects but opened to others in the same or related projects. Usually training was done in collaboration with local educational institutions but it could also involve the establishment of in-company academies, the most sophisticated of which was a management college run by the Swedish telecoms MNE in Malaysia. But, more directly, ideas for changes involving the introduction of new techniques, such as TQM, were often launched in collaboration with government ministries in both Singapore and Malaysia. Thus in the Anglo-Dutch petrochemical firm employee compliance to the new system of group working became propagated as part of a wider patriotic duty to contribute to national economic development. Programmes were launched by national politicians and 'cascaded' down the company with the endorsement of government leaders and wide coverage in the media.

In supply chain affiliates incorporation into the public governance structure was much more local, involving more day-to-day negotiation with regulatory and developmental agency representatives. Fast track expatriates or locally assimilated expatriates would be most prominent in conducting such transactions. As suggested above, the concerns of the former executives were focused on metrics that related their local performance to the global standards prevailing along the value chain. From time to time their relationship with their HQ network could be tested by local events which called for support from the centre. This was the case in the German auto-components firm when GM failed to open their planned assembly plant in Thailand for which the German manager had invested in new capacity. This fast-track executive was able to persuade his HQ superior to negotiate a rerouting of supplies from the Malaysian plant to the USA, which involved a further rerouting of the output from the MNE's Portugese affiliate to a different destination. In return for maintaining the local labour force in employment the German manager had recruited the support of the development agency in bringing about a change to much more demanding conditions for their employment: for example a 24-hour three shift cycle for the largely female workforce. Had the local trade unions and agency officials refused these changes they were threatened with the removal of production across the nearby border with Thailand. The opening of the GM plant one year after my original interview confirmed the success of the fast track manager upon his return home.

This was not an affirmation available to the locals in the sample. Indeed the overseas director of the British speciality chemist felt that expatriate managers who had not been moved within five years tended 'to go native and to lose their sense of judgement'. Generally they were portrayed as idiosyncratic individuals on the boundaries of corporate authority and often appeared as threatening archetypes for failed fast-trackers. In this sense they acted as an ever imminent other in 'the mantra of distance'. Yet in at least three instances locals in my sample had used their local networks to produce a significant recombination of the disembedded ideas contained in their organizational remit and those contained in the local community.

One such was the female manager of the health insurance provider whose local affiliate was intended to service expatriates among other MNEs in Thailand. She had discovered ways of creating new financial products for indigenous corporations and individuals. Another example was that of the general manager of the British auto-components affiliate who, prompted by a HQ campaign to 'diffuse' TQM throughout the group, had brought back older women who had trained with the plant before their marriage, to help train and to lead the new 'autonomous' groups of operatives. Most of the previously employed Malay Chinese male supervisors were concurrently set up as independent sub-contractors to supply specialized parts. The carrying out of this operation demanded a personal knowledge of the local community and of communally endorsed procedures gained from his 20 years' residence. His authority with his co-religionists also made it possible for him to justify employing a new chain of sub-contractors from outside that ethnic community.

A different kind of 'market' was produced by the Swedish adhesives local manager who sold his product by collaborating with a Singaporese entrepreneur in pioneering the production of hardboard made of reconstituted logs from nearby Malaysian palm oil estates. Unfortunately, at the time of my visit, his R&D laboratory had been visited over a six-month period by an HQ operations specialist attempting to introduce a highly detailed re-engineering of the laboratory. Of the three out of eight British trained graduate technicians I interviewed all were intending to leave because of what they saw as the breakdown of interpersonal collaboration brought about by adherence to the new system. Their feelings contrasted with the enthusiasm with which the visiting HQ re-engineering specialist described his impact on working arrangements in the laboratory. The attempt by the Swedish HQ to apply universalistically 'neutral' rules to this highly successful community of practice seemed, at that time, to be destructive of the creativity it was designed to bring about.

7. NETWORKS AND ROLE ORIENTATIONS

These last examples suggest that, in spite of their lack of resource along MNE networks and their precarious social position on the periphery of homophilic corporate communities, locals were often able to engage in much more exploratory relationships with their situational context than were either diplomats or fast trackers. In some cases the back-home career orientation of the fast track affiliate manager might be married to a perception of a footloose mode of investment that constituted the dominant strategic recipe within the global supply chain (Spender, 1989), as in the case of the German auto-component supplier. His primary referent was manifested in the performance metrics set by his head office patron. In this latter case the host network embeddedness of the manager was primarily shaped by the contractual obligations monitored by local regulatory agencies. The manager, like the organization, was 'incorporated' but not socially assimilated (Alexander, 2001). His community, and that of his family, was that of the larger, or closed social set of expatriates making up leisure clubs, international schools and so on. To some extent the social world of the diplomat was even more remote, but at the same time his inclusion in the political elite of the state and nation imposed a local identity and nexus of roles that might be seen as a kind of assimilation as well as formal incorporation at the very top of the social economic hierarchy.

By way of contrast with the 'exploratory' orientation ascribed to the embedded 'local' manager, we might use James March's (1991) description of an 'exploitative' approach to organizational learning to describe the manner in which the combination of career interest and sector recipe leads to a highly calculative approach to knowledge transfer in many such situations as those often facing expatriate managers. Geppert and Clark (2003) have usefully married this dichotomy in attitudes towards indigenous learning with that of Perlmutter's (1969) taxonomy of strategic orientations in MNE management. Thus they distinguish between Western MNEs having joint-ventures in Eastern European countries as having either polycentric-exploratory approaches to the venture or ethnocentric-exploitative ones. It might seem that within this sample such differences were also constituted by differences in networks that were socially segregated both within and across corporate boundaries. At the diplomatic level executives from 'Old Colonial' (that is, largely extractive/infrastructural) firms were often incorporated into local socio-political networks that led them to become important agencies in the wider governance structure of the host country. Similarly those who had chosen to become assimilated into local affective, sometimes ethnic, communities could, ipso facto, be more aware of local needs and of particularistic local translations of the universalistic rules of the MNE. Fast trackers were, by contrast, much more aware that their performance was to be judged according to the rules that held within the homophilic network of HQ. These rules, in turn, legitimated against the performance of a 'global system' as translated along local rules created by financial analysts and journalists in the bars and brasseries of Europe – and, of course, of Wall Street.

8. ABSORPTIVE CAPABILITY: FAMILIES AS ENTREPRENEURS OR RENTIERS?

As suggested in the introduction, the process of knowledge appropriation has become a central tenet of the developmentalist ideology that pervades business teaching. Developmental scholars have become increasingly aware of the need for an appropriative learning capability to be located within both specialized state sponsored agencies and within locally indigenous enterprises. The emergence of a small number of large family-owned business groups as major sources of technological innovation can be seen as a common feature of many successful industrial nations, most recently, Japan and South Korea (Okazaki and Okuno-Fujiwara, 1999). These are both countries taken as exemplars by the national leaders of their neighbours in the South. Increasing attention has also been given to the wider social infrastructure provided by past and current institutions as unique sources of comparative advantage in the global tournament.

Another thread in recent analytic approaches has been concerned with the role of informal trading relations along longstanding networks that shape, or even constitute, the accumulation of knowledge and its conversion into commercial practice. This process is usually seen to be related to the existence of trustful relations between networked actors (Coleman, 1988). However, the same type of collaboration within socially closed groups can, equally, be seen as collusion to gain an 'unfair' share of a wider distribution of gains and to monopolize knowledge inputs to the wider field of national business activity. Paradoxically, more egalitarian interpreters of the role of closed networks in the creation of social stratification, such as Bourdieu (1978) and Coleman himself, also speak of 'social capital' as a source of inequity within society, particularly when institutionalized in a self-reinforcive mode of elite education. There is evidently a tension in these disparate judgements on the role played by social closure in the process of the appropriation of scarce resources.

This tension is multiplied when deviancy from the dominant norms of conduct within the 'rules of the game' is labelled as 'corrupt'. This is the description most often used by global trading regulators using a free market, or neo-liberal, frame in judging the commercial practices of both MNEs and nation states whose activities are seen to be less than 'transparent'. As suggested above (The Regional and National Context) the Government Linked Enterprise has been seen by many local observers of economic development in ASEAN countries as giving rise to a form of rentier capitalism that will ultimately fail to provide the basis for technologically based growth. In a fairly narrow utilitarian manner, both Chandler (1990) and Mayer (1996) might be seen as suggesting that 'insider capitalism', or personally owned conglomerations, should be judged on their ability to sponsor both national growth and 'stake-holder' emancipation, in a word that they are driven by the ideal of 'stewardship'. Thus, the characteristic of family-run business groups within rapidly growing national economies, such as those of Germany and Japan, has been their willingness to re-invest profits in building the technological capabilities of their organizations, especially in technical education. In their very different ways, these family-owned concerns have contributed to the communally shared capacities of their contextual business systems. By contrast family- owned groups within ASEAN tend to use the resources provided by state institutions to accumulate personal wealth or to diversify their businesses in pursuit of low risk investments rather than in more uncertain technologically innovative sectors.

In applying these broad evaluative generalizations to the networks that could be traced through my interviews it became clear that many of the positions held by local directors of MNEs, and owners of local enterprises with whom MNEs had joint ventures, were not acting as informed conduits of technological transfer nor, indeed, were they sponsoring the work of local development agencies with any great effectiveness (Loveridge, 2005). That is not to say that the huge infrastructural projects undertaken by Old Colonials did not have the effect of creating large numbers of trained operatives and professionals. It is to say that the kind of knowledge multiplier projects sponsored by the government, such as the Multi-Media Super Corridor outside Kuala Lumpur, have spawned disappointingly few local entrepreneurs in spin-off ventures. The training provision of Footloose Supply Chain affiliates also provides an important alternative source of professional employment for minority ethnic groups such as Chinese and Indian graduates, alternative, that is, to the patrimonialism of local family businesses and the public sector. Unfortunately for the host country, many of these professionalized young managers and technicians join the outflow of migrants within and outside of the region.

Looking at the individual roles of expatriate managers, locally assimilated expatriates have an intimate knowledge of local labour markets and ability to exploit the skills present in the local community in a way that opens up new sources of enterprise and the establishment of stable and reliable supply chains. This role is not simply that of a conveyor of superior Western knowledge. On the contrary, very often the professionals sponsored by such figures were technically better qualified than the expatriate. He or she acted much more as go-between spanning networks, in a situation in which ethnic and corporate boundaries prevented the acknowledgement of such cross-communal expertise. It was known to exist, but, for socio-political reasons, could not be acknowledged; neither could the opportunities for innovation be officially recognized within the bureaucratic structure of the MNE. Perhaps, for the very reason that managers in such situations had become personally displaced and had often been through a process of transformative reinstatement of their personal identity, theirs was a more reflexive approach to their multiple roles within the corporate context and that of the local community.

9. CONCLUSION

In this chapter I have attempted to demonstrate the multi-layered nature of the socio-economic interfaces between the social systems that comprise the MNE and those of the political economy of the host. In doing so I have attempted to transcend the interpretations of these transactions that are offered by the discrete disciplines operating within management scholarship. In most cases these reflect the functional division of labour within the MNE and, indeed, the social biases that spring from these self-reinforcive frames of reference. Instead it is suggested that the enactment of power relations between the two systems translates technological knowledge in a way that shapes the ultimate legitimacy of its usage in ways that are often unrecognized or ignored by both practitioners and scholarly commentators. In attempting an understanding of this process of translation I have made use of both micro, or molecular, analysis of cultural politics and related this to a wider framework of career and wealth acc umulation that inspires and motivates actors, both individually and collectively.

Theoretically, this small study serves to balance the normative view within much of the business literature over the past decade or more which sees social networks in a wholly functional manner as aids to corporately legitimate innovation and creativity. As Lamont and Molnar (2002) have pointed out, social boundaries come into being for many reasons. Whilst fostering collaboration within the group they are often, by the same token, means to excluding those seen as not possessing the necessary characteristics of community identity. In many situations they can therefore provide obstacles to change and constitute sources of resistance to innovation, particularly when it threatens the very advantages enjoyed within the culture of the group. In both the corporate space of the MNE and the wider political economy of the host country, social networks provided means to the appropriation, or even expropriation, of status and career opportunities. These were likely to shape the views of their members as to the beneficial effects of suggested changes in institutionalized structures, or to the recognition of suggestions for change emanating from 'outsiders'. In this study managers who had 'gone native' represented just such a source of deeply felt anxiety for those within the homophilic frames of Fast Track careerists and, even more so, for the latters' patrons in HQ.

The existence of 'informal' structures has long been recognized in the analysis of organizational theorists. But often they, like scholars of international business and HRM, have tended to use a rational model of analysis which sees such informal modes of behaviour as giving way to the logic of the market. Thus, as in Perlmutter's (1969) model, MNE executives are seen to 'develop' from ethnocentric to polycentric approaches to business strategy through a rational learning process over time. (A little help from developmental trainers might speed the process.) Within this rational choice frame of analysis it is difficult to perceive the difficulties involved in the renegotiation of intra- and inter-organizational boundaries involved in a collective 'learning' process. Such perceptual difficulties are often married to methodologies that allow the formulation of general laws and of 'low context' explanations of corporate behaviour. These most often consist of a statistical analysis of aggregated data followed by a deductive surmising on their meaning (Child, 2000). Even at the macro level MNEs are generally seen to follow generalized patterns of entry to and exit from overseas markets, with little consideration of sectoral (or field) differences in the nature of socio-political relationships with host governments and firms. One of the key suggestions stemming from this research is that the operational significance of one form of expatriate network compared with another may be shaped by the sectoral field that provides the context for this interface. The framework emerging from this small study suggests that more work of an ethnographic, or 'high context' nature might produce a better informed analysis of the day-to-day construction of these interfaces by actors within the MNE and the agencies of the host nation state.

For the strategic managers of both MNEs and state agencies there may be a need to explore the unacknowledged creative behaviour of actors on the periphery of their organizations. Again, this is not a novel suggestion. Peters and Waterman in their epic work *In Search of Excellence* (1982) urged the acceptance of 'skunk works' in local plants as a form of illegitimate but creative behaviour. Whether these and other suggestions for 'schizophrenic' organization will succeed in reducing dysfunctional boundaries within the MNE is open to negotiation within the contingent boundaries of the managerial situation. More often than not the bonds that hold the corporation or nation state together in mature business systems cannot easily be de-institutionalized without traumatic disjuncture. In transitional or 'developing' economies this is not the case since traditional boundaries are in a state of flux. Management is therefore involved with the renegotiation of intra- and inter-organizational boundaries in the everyday enactment of those perimeters. Invasions of other corporate territories, such as those making up the surge of M&A activity among European MNEs that took place over the period of the study, may reveal unexpected intra-organizational terrains and pockets of resistance. But, of equal importance may be reconstruction of cross-boundary bridges into their host markets where the embeddedness of their new organization has critically depended upon the social assimilation of local management.

NOTES

1. Extracts from this paper formerly appeared in 'Embedding the Multinational: bridging internal and external networks in transitional institutional contexts', *Asian Business and Management*, 2005, 4 (389-409) by the same author.

REFERENCES

Alexander, J.C. (2001), 'Theorizing the "Modes of Incorporation"', *Sociological Theory*, **19**(3): 237-49.

Bartlett, C.A. and S. Ghoshal (1989), *Managing across Borders,* Boston, MA: Harvard Business School Press.

Best, M.H. (2001), *The New Competitive Advantage*, Oxford: Oxford University Press.

Birkenshaw, J. and N. Hood (1998), 'The Determinants of subsidiary mandates and subsidiary initiatives' in G. Hooley, R. Loveridge and D. Wilson (eds), *Internationalization: Process, Context and Markets*, Basingstoke, UK: Macmillan.

Bourdieu, P. (1978), 'Pouvoir et langue', *Communications*, **28**, 21-7.

Callon, M. and B. Latour (1992), 'Don't throw the baby out with the bath water!', in A. Pickering (ed.), *Science as Practice and Culture*, Chicago IL: University of Chicago Press, 343-68.

Carney, M. and E. Gedajlovic (2001), 'Institutional change and firm adaptation: toward a typology of South, East Asian corporate forms', Erasmus Research Institute of Management Report Series, ERS-2001-08-STR, January.

Chandler, A.P. (1990), *Scale and Scope*, Cambridge, MA: Belknap.

Child, J. (2000), 'Theorizing about organization cross-nationally', in J.L.C. Cheng (ed.), *Advances in International Comparative Management*, Stamford, CT: JAI Press, **13**, 27-75.

Coleman, J.S. (1988),'Social capital in the creation of human capital', *American Journal of Sociology*, **94** (suppl), s95-s120.

Goodall, K. and J. Roberts (2003), 'Repairing managerial knowledge – ability over Distance', *Organization Studies*, **24**(7), 1153-75.

Cowen, M.P. and R.W. Shenton (1996), *Doctrines of Development*, London: Routledge.

Czarniawska, B. and B. Joerges (1996), 'The travel of ideas', in B. Czarniawska and G. Sevon (eds), *Translating Organizational Change*, Berlin: de Gruyter.

Desatnick, R.L. and M.L. Bennett (1977), *Human Resource Management in the Multinational Company*, Farnborough: Gower.

Dicken, P. (2003), *Global Shift* (4th edn), London: Sage.

Eisenstadt, S.N. and Y. Roniger (1984), *Patrons, Clients and Friends*, Cambridge: Cambridge University Press.

Enderwick, P. (2005), 'What's bad about crony capitalism?', *Asian Business & Management*, **4**(2), June, 117-32.

Forsgren, M., U. Holm and J. Johanson (2005), *Managing the Embedded Multinational: a Business Network View*, Cheltenham UK and Northampton, MA, USA: Edward Elgar.

Geppert, M. and E. Clark (2003), 'The socio-political construction of transnational sites in post-socialist contexts', *19th EGOS Colloquium, Copenhagen*, 3-5 July.

Giddens, A. (1979), *Central Problems in Social Theory*, London: Macmillan.

Gomez, E.T. and K.S. Jomo (1999), *Malaysia's Political Economy: Politics, Patronage and Profits*, Cambridge: Cambridge University Press.

Gupta, A.K. and V. Govindarajan (2000), 'Knowledge flows within multinational corporations', *Strategic Management Journal*, **21**(4), 473-96.

Hall, P. and D. Soskice (2001), *Varieties of Capitalism*, Oxford: Oxford University Press.

Harzing, A. (1998),'Who's in charge?', University of Bradford Management Centre Working Paper, Series No. 9822, September.

Hedlund, G. (1986), 'The hypermodern MNC: a heterarchy?', *Human Resource Management*, **25**(1), 9-35.

Jesudason, J. (1990), *Ethnicity and the Economy*, Singapore: Oxford University Press.

Kunio, Y. (2004), 'The comparative performance of Malaysia: an analysis', *Southeast Asian Studies*, **42**(1), June, 3-25.

Lamont, M. and V. Molnar (2002), 'The study of boundaries in the social sciences', *Annual Review of Sociology*, **28**, 167-97.

Loveridge R. (2002), 'Incorporating the Multinational', *Asian Business and Management*, **1**, 153-87.

Loveridge, R. (2005),'Embedding the multinational: bridging internal and external networks in transitional institutional contexts', *Asian Business & Management*, **1**, 389-409.

Luo, Y. (2005), 'An organizational perspective on corruption', *Management and Organization Review*, **1**(1), 119-54.

March, J. (1991), 'Exploration and exploitation in organizational learning', *Organization Science*, **2**(1), 71-87.

Mayer, C. (1996), 'Corporate governance, competition and performance', Economic Working Paper 164, Paris: OECD.

Morgan, G., P.H. Kristensen and R. Whitley (eds) (2001), *The Multinational Firm: Organizing Across Institutional and National Divides*, Oxford: Oxford University Press.

Mytelka, L.K. (2000), 'Locational tournaments for FDI', in N. Hood and S. Young (eds), *The Globalization of Multinational Enterprise Activity and Economic Development*, London: Macmillan, Chapter 12.

Nohria, N. and S. Ghoshal (1997), *Differentiated Network: Organizing Multinational Corporations for Value Creation*, San Francisco, CA: Jossey Bass.

Orru, M., N.W. Biggart and C.G. Hamilton (1991), 'Organizational institutionalism in East Asia', in W.W. Powell and P. DiMaggio (eds), *The New Institutionalism in Organizational Analysis,* Chicago, IL: University of Chicago Press.

Okazaki, T. and M. Okuno-Fujiwara (eds) (1999), *The Japanese Economic System and its Historical Origins*, Oxford: Oxford University Press.

Perlmutter, H. (1969), 'The tortuous evolution of the MNC', *Columbia Journal of World Business*, **4**(1), 275-96.

Peters, T. and R.H. Waterman (1982), *In Search of Excellence*, New York: Harper & Row.

Pfeffer, J. (1992), *Managing with Power*, Boston, MA: Harvard Business School Press.

Scullion, H. (1995), 'International human resource management', in J. Storey (ed.), *Human Resource Management: A Critical Text*, London, UK: Routledge.

Searle, P. (1999), *The Riddle of Malaysian Capitalism: Rent-Seekers or Real Capitalists?*, Singapore: Allen and Unwin.

Spender, J.C. (1989), *Industrial Recipes: the Nature and Sources of Managerial Judgement*, Oxford: Blackwell.

Starkey, K. and A. McKinlay (1989), 'Beyond Fordism? Strategic choice and labour relatrions in Ford UK', *Industial Relations Journal*, **20**(2), 93-100.

United Nations Conference on Conference on Trade and Development (2000), *World Investment Report 2000: Cross-border Mergers and Acquisitions and Development, 2000*, New York: Oxford University Press.

Whitley, R. (1999), *Divergent Capitalisms*, Oxford: Oxford University Press.

Yoshihara, K. (1988), *The Rise of Ersatz Capitalism in South East Asia*, Singapore: Oxford University Press.

11. Managerial trust and leadership in global management: propensities to trust, the influence of national culture on trust and conditional trust – a cross-cultural study

James J. Cavazzini and Min H. Lu

1. INTRODUCTION

Trust has become an increasingly important leadership issue in current research. In the context of Enron, MCI Worldcom, Adelphia Communications, Tyco, Vivendi Universal, and so on, the confidence of employees has shrunk in terms of managerial trustworthiness. If employees do not trust their leaders, they will be unresponsive to a leader's effort to influence and motivate them. At the same time, we see a growing trend toward diversity and globalization characterized by the establishment of international strategic alliances, managing and hiring foreign workers, and entering new markets. Much of today's management theories (for example, transactional, transformational, and leader member exchange (LMX)) have their foundations laid on the bases of trust. The importance of firms being able to apply these management theories in different cultures has become a source of competitive advantage in the global marketplace. These trends suggest a need to examine the concept of trust from the prospective of national culture.

Today, even in Asian countries, a person can no longer depend on a job for life. P.R. China is regarded as a country where economic relationships are strongly dependent on trust (Fukuyama, 1995). At the same time, trust is difficult to build beyond well-defined relationships of kinship or a close social network. The nature of trust in China and its impact on leadership theory becomes an important consideration from a cross-cultural perspective.

Additional evidence suggests that although Japanese decision makers tend to think and plan for the long term and their American counterparts do so more for the short term (Neff, 1989), Americans feel less tense on the job (Lynn, 1982) and are generally happier (Inglehart and Rabier, 1985). There are numerous examples that could be cited reflecting differences between nations. It may seem obvious that these differences exist; however, understanding them is not as simple.

The benefits and importance of trust, and the emerging global and multicultural workplace, emphasize the necessity to understand how trust develops and the ways national culture impacts the trust-building process. Trust may form in numerous ways; however, whether and how trust is formed depends on the societal norms and values that guide people's beliefs and behaviors (Hofstede, 1980). Since each culture encompasses different norms and values, the processes people use to decide whether and whom to trust may be very dependent upon a society's culture. One of the greatest influences of culture is on how information is used to make decisions (Triandis, 1972).

This chapter examines a conceptual cultural framework of trust development and the extent to which cultural norms and values contribute to the formation of trust. It specifically considers the dispositional relationship of trust to gender, type of company, level of management, and length of time in the workforce. In addition, it examines the existence of conditional trust in the relationship between employees and managers. Participants have been invited with various corporate or non-corporate backgrounds from the United States and P.R. China.

2. LITERATURE REVIEW

2.1 Trust

Trust is important to organizational function in many ways. Trust has been viewed as an enabler of cooperative behavior (Gambetta, 1988), a promoter of adaptive organizational forms (Miles and Snow, 1992), a mediator of transaction costs and harmful conflict (Dore, 1983; Noordewier et al., 1990), and a facilitator of effective responses to crisis, thereby providing firms with a source of competitive advantage. Trust has received a great deal of attention from scholars in the disciplines of social psychology (Deutsch, 1960; Lewicki and Bunker, 1995; Lindskold, 1978), sociology (Lewis and Weigert, 1985; Strub and Priest, 1976), economics (Dasgupta, 1988; Williamson, 1991), as well as applied areas like marketing (Anderson and Weitz, 1989; Dwyer et al.,1987; Moorman et al. 1992) and management

(Gulati, 1995; Lane and Bachman, 1996). Although multidisciplinarity has contributed to the value of the construct, there have been few attempts to integrate the various prospectives on trust (Lewicki and Bunker, 1995; Mayer et al., 1995). Shapiro et al. (1992) proposed an integrative prospective proposing that trust has three bases: (1) deterrence-based trust emphasizes costs and benefits; (2) knowledge-based trust requires getting to know the target; and (3) identification-based trust forms on the basis of common values. Zucker (1986) proposed that trust may be based on: (1) the process of exchange; (2) characteristics of the exchange partners; or (3) societal institutions. Mayer et al. (1995) focused on the characteristics of the trustee, suggesting that a target's ability, benevolence and integrity are the primary factors leading to trust.

There have been many and varied definitions of trust. The most frequently cited definition is a willingness to be vulnerable. In order to establish clear boundaries to usefully inform research and theory, Rousseau et al. (1998) suggested that the most widely held cross-disciplinary definition of trust was: 'Trust is a psychological state comprising the intention to accept vulnerability based upon positive expectations of the intentions or behavior of another'.

There is a general agreement across disciplines that there must be two conditions present for trust to develop; risk and interdependence. Risk is the perceived probability of loss, as understood by a decision maker (Chiles and McMackin, 1996; Lewis and Weigert, 1985; Schlenker et al., 1973). There is a reciprocal relationship between risk and trust. The existence of risk creates an opportunity to trust; without risk there is no need for trust. Conversely, the existence of trust encourages risk taking and when the expected behavior materializes, trust is reinforced.

The second condition is interdependence. Interdependence is an environment where the interests (for example career advancement, salary increases, and so on) cannot be achieved without reliance upon another. If a manager is powerless to affect the interests of the employee either positively or negatively, there is little need for trust. The existence of this interdependence and its effect on the subordinate's cognitive attitude toward trust will be examined further in this study.

The definition of trust, therefore, can be expanded to include the willingness to be vulnerable under conditions of risk and interdependence existing in a psychological state of 'perceived probabilities', 'confidence', and 'positive expectations' (Rousseau et al., 1998). Rousseau et al. argued that trust should not be mistaken for either a behavior such as cooperation, or a choice such as risk taking, but a psychological condition that can cause (for example cooperation) or result from (for example risk taking) such actions.

Trust is as complex and dynamic as the human beings whose psychological state determines its existence. Often, trust is viewed as either present or absent, where one person completely trusts or completely distrusts another (Gabarro, 1990). Examination of this subject by several theorists proposed that trust is an evolving condition that gradually develops over time (Rempel et al., 1985; Zand, 1972). This perspective of trust would presuppose low levels of initial trust. However, McKnight et al. (1998), citing survey and experimental studies conducted by Berg et al. (1995) and Kramer (1994), found paradoxically high levels of initial trust in new organizational settings and proposed a model of specific relationships among several trust-related constructs and two cognitive processes to help explain this paradox.

The experience of trust is determined by the interaction of people's values, attitudes, moods and emotions (Jones and George, 1998). Values are principles or general standards that individuals consider inherently desirable ends (for example loyalty, reliability, integrity, competence). The value systems are the guiding principles that people use to determine which types of behaviors, events, situations and, most importantly, people are desirable or undesirable. Values contribute to the comprehensive experience of trust and can even create a propensity to trust (Mayer et al., 1995). Individuals also experience trust on a more specific mode as part of an attitude of evaluation toward other people and organizations (Butler, 1991). Moods and emotions are affective states or feelings about individuals or groups as people go about their daily business. Emotions are more intense and an affective state that interrupts continuing cognitive processes, while moods are less intense and not are linked to particular circumstances (Jones and George, 1998). People often decide if they can initially trust someone by examining the positive or negative feelings they have toward that person. A person's current mood or emotions may also color their judgment regarding another person. When a person's expectations of trust are broken, there can be a very strong emotional response to that violation of trust.

Jones and George (1998), in their model of the evolution of trust, propose a creation of conditional and unconditional trust. They propose that the development of trust depends on the degree of similarity between the values, attitudes, and moods and emotions of the two people. At the beginning of an encounter each person suspends belief that the other is not trustworthy, creating a state of conditional trust. This initial suspension of belief in untrustworthiness is also examined by McKnight et al. (1998), addressing the surprisingly high levels of early trust reported in both survey and experimental studies. They propose a model of initial trust formation based on one's disposition or propensity to trust, one's institution-based trust or the security felt reflecting an environment of guarantees, safety nets, and other structures, and cognitive-based trust that relies on the rapid cognitive cues or first impressions experienced by a person. They theorized that one's disposition to trust is based on a faith in humanity where people believe that others are generally well meaning and reliable and a belief that regardless of whether people are reliable or not, it serves their best interests to deal with people as though they are until proven otherwise by cues or experiences (McKnight et al., 1998).

Conditional trust, calculated trust and a 'trusting stance' are usually sufficient to make possible a broad range of social and economic exchanges. It is consistent with the idea that one of the bases for trust is knowledge (Lewicki and Bunker, 1996) or a positive expectation of another (Sitkin and Roth, 1993). Conditional trust is the most common form of trust existing in today's organizational environments.

Unconditional trust represents an experience of trust where people define their dyadic relationship as trustworthy. It is based on a confidence in the other's values that has emerged from empirical evidence from repeated behavioral interactions. In addition, positive affect increases as positive moods and emotions strengthen the affective bonds between parties and reinforce the experience of trust (Jones and George, 1998).

Much research has been conducted on the specific attributes and conditions promoting the evolution of trust. Butler (1991) conducted a research study to develop a content theory of trust conditions and derive scales measuring them. In his study he concluded that the literature on trust has converged on the beliefs that (a) trust is an important aspect of interpersonal relationships, (b) trust is essential to the development of managerial careers, (c) trust in a specific person is more relevant in terms of predicting outcomes than is the global attitude of trust in generalized others, and (d) a useful approach to studying trust consists of defining and investigating a number of conditions (determinants) of trust.

The ten conditions of trust identified were availability, competence, consistency, discreetness, fairness, integrity, loyalty, openness, promise fulfillment, and receptivity. Recent evidence has reduced this number to the following five: Integrity, Competence, Consistency, Loyalty and Openness (Schindler and Thomas, 1993). In addition, a substantial amount of research indicates that a leader being perceived as trustworthy leads to positive outcomes for organizations (Dirks and Ferrin, 2002). This meta-analysis indicates high specific relationships in the following areas: Job satisfaction, Organizational commitment, Turnover intentions, Satisfaction with the leader, and Favorable exchanges with the leader.

2.2 Leadership

The importance of trust can also be observed by its role in today's popular leadership theories. As mentioned previously, transactional leadership is one of the most prevalent forms of leadership today. It is built on a contingent reward factor between leaders and followers, whereby effort by followers is exchanged for rewards. The leader enters into an agreement with followers on what needs to be done (for example goals, objectives, performance levels, and so on) and what the payoffs (for example pay rises and promotions) will be based on performance of the followers. Bass (1985) referred to this form of exchange as contingent reinforcement. The amount of trust required in a transactional leadership environment would seem to be minimal considering the almost contractual nature of the relationship. However, even in a transactional environment leaders control a significant number of implied rewards such as the assignment of choice projects, office space, assistance and inclusion in important meetings, to mention only a few. These implied rewards are based on a conditional trust of the leader who dispenses these rewards based on an informal exchange of trust with subordinates. Transactional leaders wield influence because it is in the subordinate's own self-interest to do what the leader wants (Kuhnert and Lewis, 1987). Shamir (1990) proposed that transactional leaders build trust with their followers by behaving consistently in honoring agreements-formal or informal–with them. In a study by Podsakoff et al. (1990) it was found that there was a positive relationship between the leader's use of contingent reward behavior and the development of follower trust in the leader. Again, we can see the terms 'conditional trust', 'calculated trust', or a 'trusting stance' playing a significant leadership role.

Transformational and/or charismatic leadership theory is a category of leadership theories that has emerged over the last 20 years. Transformational leaders build more than an exchange or transactional relationship with their followers. Such leaders present a challenging vision for achievement while engaging an emotional involvement of their followers to build higher levels of identification, commitment and trust in the leader and the vision. This requires an alignment of the followers' personal values and interests with those of the organization (Bass, 1985). This abandonment of one's own self-interest for those of the organization is dependent on the leader's capability to build trust with subordinates and corresponds to Hofstede's collectivism dimension of collectivism and femininity. One of the factors of transformational leadership is charisma or idealized influence whereby followers identify with their leaders and want to emulate them. These leaders having high standards of moral and ethical conduct are deeply respected by followers, who place a great deal of trust in them (Northouse, 2004). However, Podsakoff et al. (1990) examined this relationship between a leader's role model and its influence on followers' organizational citizenship behaviors and found that it only influenced it indirectly; its influence was mediated by the amount of trust in their leader. Jung and Avolio (2000) conducted an experimental study that examined the effects of transformational and transactional leadership and the mediating role of trust and value congruence on follower performance. They found that transformational leadership had both a direct and indirect effect, mediated by trust and value congruence, on follower performance, while transactional leadership had only an indirect effect on performance through mediation by trust and value congruence. Implications of the study also identified the initial existence of conditional trust levels for both groups.

According to Leader-Member Exchange (LMX) theory, high-quality relationships are characterized by trust, respect and mutual obligation, generating mutual loyalty and influence between superiors and subordinates, and wide latitude of discretion for subordinates. LMX theory identifies this special dyadic relationship between a leader and certain subordinates as the formation of an in-group. This relationship could be described as a transformational component of an LMX organization. If subordinates are less compatible with the leader, they are characterized as being part of the out-group. The relationship between these subordinates and the leader are marked by formal communication based on job descriptions where they come to work, do their job, and go home. This relationship could be described as a transactional component of an LMX organization. The component of trust has been recognized as one of the three underlying dimensions of LMX (Graen and Uhl-Bien, 1995). Graen and Uhl-Bien found that leader-member exchanges produced such things as more positive performance evaluations, less employee turnover, greater organizational commitment, greater participation, and a number of other positive aspects that illustrate how much an organization gains from good working relationships. Cunningham and MacGregor (2000) studied the effect of trust in a way that distinguished it from LMX quality, and their findings suggest that perceptions of trust act independently of a job's motivational potential score (MPS) in affecting absence, intention to quit, satisfaction and performance. Trust was found to be as important as job design factors in predicting outcomes.

The presence of trust, or lack of trust, has been widely recognized to be vital in determining organizational outcomes. Trust is considered by many as the foundation of leadership. Whether an individual chooses to trust a leader has been a source of controversy in the literature. There are two prominent and contrasting schools of thought concerning choice; one that interprets choice in relatively rational, calculative terms and another that considers the social and relational foundations of choice as more important in trust choice situations (Kramer, 1999). Williamson (1996) argues that trust is justified by a rational expectation of positive reciprocal consequences and is another form of economic exchange. This perspective views trust from a conditional or transactional standpoint. Hofstede's dimension of individualism parallels this perspective. This views man as the traditional *Homo economicus*, the self-interested person of rational decision-making. On the other hand, Fichman (2003) has proposed that there are constraints on the study of trust such as cognitive adaptations, emotional regulation of trusting behavior, and a fundamental form of fairness, which underlies behavior in many types of social and economic exchange. Evidence also exists that individuals have a general predisposition to trust or distrust other people (Kramer, 1999). A person's gender, background, experiences and business environment all contribute toward their propensity to trust. The pivotal position of trust in organizational behavior, motivational constructs, and leadership theory make it an important area of study.

2.3   Cultural Norms

Cultural norms and values which establish appropriate behavioral standards and beliefs, facilitate or inhibit the application of the cognitive trust-building process. Researchers have suggested many different definitions of culture. Namenwirth and Weber (1987, p. 8) defined culture as a 'system of ideas' that provide a 'design for living'. Clark (1990, p. 66) in his review of national character, describes culture 'as a distinctive, enduring pattern of behavior and/or personality characteristics'. Hill (1997, p. 67) defined culture as 'a system of values and norms that are shared among a group of people and that when taken together constitute a design for living'. According to Hofstede (1984, p. 21), culture is 'the collective programming of the mind which distinguishes the members of one group from another'.

The label of national when applied to culture is used to distinguish it from other forms of culture (for example, corporate culture). In addition, Fukuyama (1995) has suggested that the cultural boundaries between nations are becoming increasingly 'fuzzy' due to the level of economic integration and there also may be significant cultural differences within countries. Researchers have taken two approaches in an attempt to define universal dimensions of national culture. Social scientists have developed a number of classification systems based on theory (for example, Clark,

1990; Inkeles and Levinson, 1969; Kluckhohn and Strodtbeck, 1961; Lynn, 1982). Other scholars have approached the dimensionalization of national culture based on empirical research (for example, Allport and Odbert, 1936; Hofstede, 1980; Peabody, 1985).

Culture is a characteristic that develops within any distinctive group lasting over time. For the purpose of this chapter, the values Hofstede uses to identify dimensions for his taxonomy make a particularly useful tool for studying the relationship between the cognitive trust-building processes and their underlying behavioral assumptions. Hofstede identified four 'value' dimensions on which countries differ:

1. Individualism/collectivism: refers to the relationship between the individual and the collectivity that prevails in society – a self versus group orientation. It reflects the extent to which people prefer to take care of themselves and their immediate families, remaining emotionally independent from groups, organizations and other collectivities. People with a high degree of individualism are self-oriented, value individual accomplishment, tolerate individual behavior and opinion, have low loyalty to other people and institutions, interact on an individual competitive basis, and have loose interpersonal ties. People with a high degree of collectivism have a group orientation, value joint efforts and group rewards, have norms for behavioral conformity, high loyalty, interact in a cooperative mode, and have strong personal ties.
2. Masculinity/femininity: this dimension concerns the dominant values in a society (Singh, 1990) and reveals the bias towards either 'masculine' values of assertiveness, competitiveness and materialism, or towards 'feminine' values of nurturing, and the quality of life and relationships. People with a high degree of masculinity value individual achievement, have a norm for confrontation, and independent thought and action. People with a high degree of femininity have norms for solidarity, service cooperation and honoring moral obligations.
3. Power distance: indicates the extent to which a society accepts the unequal distribution of power in institutions and organizations. People with a high power distance have norms for differential prestige, power, wealth, high degree of conflict, and authoritarian rule. People with a low power distance have egalitarian relationships, norms for cooperation, interdependence, solidarity and affiliation.
4. Uncertainty avoidance: refers to a society's discomfort with uncertainty, preferring predictability and stability. People with a high degree of uncertainty avoidance have a need for structure, norm for compromise, a strong faith in institutions, and a belief in experts and their knowledge.

3. RESEARCH PROPOSITIONS

The following research propositions consider how cultural norms and values, which establish appropriate behavioral standards and beliefs, assist or hamper application of the cognitive trust-building process. These propositions reference Hofstede's (1984) cultural dimensions, their associated norms and values, and the proposed relationships with the trust-building processes. The propositions also address the role of the dispositional nature of trust in determining the relationship between culture and the cognitive processes a person calls upon.

Comparing Hofstede's cultural dimensions for the United States and P.R. China reveals that the US has high individualism, high masculinity, a low power distance, and low uncertainty avoidance. On the other hand, P.R. China has high collectivism, high femininity, high power distance, and high uncertainty avoidance. The two countries seem to be at opposite ends of the cultural spectrum, which emphasizes the importance of understanding the comparable trust-building processes. The examination of these processes has important implications for the use of American leadership theories in China. Hofstede (1980) questioned whether American theories could be applied in certain other countries whose cultural norms and values were significantly different.

3.1 Individualism/Collectivism and Masculinity/Femininity

Two of Hofstede's (1984) dimensions encompass issues of personality and self-concept. These issues were addressed in Clark's (1990) conceptual domain as 'relation to self'. Individualism/collectivism refers to the relationship between people's individual rather than a group orientation. Individualism/collectivism reflect the norms and values associated with the way people interact, such as the importance of individual versus group goals, respect for individual accomplishment, the strength of interpersonal ties, and acceptance of individual opinions. Masculinity/femininity concerns the dominant values in a society (Singh, 1990) and assesses the degree to which 'tough' values, such as success, assertiveness and competition are more prevalent over 'tender' values, such as service, nurturing and solidarity. The individualism/collectivism and masculinity/femininity dimensions influence the probability that targets will act opportunistically (conditional trust), as well as the costs/rewards associated with such behavior. The probability that collectivists will act in opportunistic ways is low, since these people hold group values and beliefs and look for collective interests (Hofstede, 1984; Singh, 1990). Behavior of a self-serving nature is improbable since people are not motivated by self-interest (Earley, 1989; Ueno and Sekaran, 1992).

The motivation for self-serving behavior is improbable in feminine societies as well, since it is inconsistent with the value system. In feminine societies there is a tendency toward less aggressive, more cooperative behavior and a pattern of nurturing behavior, while in masculine societies, instances of opportunism are frequent and the price paid for opportunistic behavior is likely to be inexpensive. Societal norms in individualist societies encourage people to promote their own self-interest (Kale and Barnes, 1992; Singh, 1990; Ueno and Sekaran, 1992). The same can be said for masculine societies where evidence from anthropology, psychology and political science confirms a pattern of assertiveness and aggressiveness (Hofstede, 1984), which is fully consistent with a predisposition toward opportunism. Thus:

Proposition 1: *People in the US (individualist/masculine culture) are more likely to use a calculative process of trust-building than those in P.R. China (collectivist/feminine culture).*

Proposition 1a: *People in the US (individualist/masculine culture) are more likely to exhibit higher conditional trust than those in P.R. China (collectivist/feminine culture).*

The power distance dimension establishes acceptable levels of power and coercion which influences the probability that people will act opportunistically and the cost/rewards associated with opportunistic behavior. Opportunism may be less likely in low power distance countries, since there is a tendency towards a natural sharing of power and a more participative decision making process (Kale and McIntyre, 1991). In low power distance countries people are more willing to consult with others and to restrict the use of coercion and power (Kale and McIntyre, 1991).

On the other hand, the exercise of power and use of coercion are more frequent in high power distance countries (Kale and McIntyre, 1991). John (1984) states that increased perceptions of rule enforcement and controls lead to an increase in opportunistic behavior where high power distance societies will act opportunistically and fail to associate high cost with this behavior. Proposition 2a shows a conflicting influence on the use of the calculative trust-building process which should account for a certain level of conditional trust in China; however, the dominant values of the US individualist/masculine culture's influence on the calculative process should maintain an overall higher level of conditional trust than China. Thus:

Proposition 2: *People in the US (low power distance culture/weak uncertainty avoidance) are more likely to use a calculative process of trust-building than those in P.R. China (high power distance culture/weak uncertainty avoidance).*

Proposition 2a: *People in the US (low power distance culture/weak uncertainty avoidance) are more likely to exhibit higher conditional trust than those in P.R. China (high power distance culture/weak uncertainty avoidance).*

The importance of dispositional research has been addressed by House et al. (1996), who stated that 'Based on a review of studies of different populations in various settings and different assessments of dispositions, we conclude that the evidence presents a compelling argument for incorporating dispositional theory into explanations of behavior in organizations'. The following hypotheses were constructed to test the dispositional nature of trust and the relationship between trust and conditional trust in organizations in the United States and the P.R. China:

H1a: Females have a higher level of trust in their manager than males.
H1b: Levels of trust in managers are lower the longer a person has been in the workforce.
H1c: Higher level management positions within a company will exhibit higher levels of trust.
H1d: There is a relationship between the types of company a person works for and trust.
H2: There is a relationship between trust and conditional trust.

4. METHODOLOGY

A convenient sampling method was used to collect the data from two countries, the US and P.R. China, for this study. The survey in the US was performed with a group of MBA students who were employed full-time representing a diverse group of companies, government organizations, military and non-profit organizations. In addition, the survey questionnaires were mailed along with a self-addressed envelope to employees of various organizations including retail, service and manufacturing companies as well as an educational institution and charitable organization in the US. A total of 225 questionnaires were distributed and mailed. A total of 181 questionnaires were returned. Of the 181 participants there were 93 males (51.4 per cent) and 88 females (48.6 per cent). This corresponds to a response rate of 80.4 per cent.

A corresponding survey was also conducted in P.R. China. The survey questionnaire was first translated into Chinese and then independently translated back into English for verification of meaning. The survey was then mailed out from a major city in China with a return-postage-paid envelope to employees of various organizations inside China including schools, hospitals, trading companies, police stations, and so on. A total of 235 questionnaires were distributed, and a total of 189 of them returned. Among them, there were 95 males (50.26 per cent) and 94 females (49.74 per cent). This corresponds to a response rate of 80.42 per cent.

4.1 Data Analysis

4.1.1 H1a. Females have a higher level of trust in their manager than males

Trust levels were measured for the 181 US participants and 189 Chinese participants. The US sample indicates that females had an average level of trust of 5.075 as compared to males with an average trust level of 4.338. The average level of trust for females was compared to males using a t-test of two means. The results show that males had significantly ($t = -2.63$; $p = 0.009$) lower levels of trust in their manager than females. While the data from China shows that there is no significant difference between females and males in their levels of trust in their managers ($t = 0.150$; $p = 0.335$). As a result, H1a is accepted for the US sample but rejected for the Chinese sample(Table 11.1)

Table 11.1   H1a. Females have a higher level of trust in their manager than males

	US		China	
	Male	Female	Male	Female
N	93	88	95	94
Mean	4.33760	5.07500	4.97890	4.95320
Std. Dev.	1.88102	1.87845	1.09563	1.25481

$$t = -2.03 \qquad t = 0.150$$
$$df = 179 \qquad df = 187$$
$$p = 0.009 \qquad p = 0.335$$

4.1.2 H1b. Levels of trust in managers are lower the longer a person has been in the workforce

The average number of years in the workforce was 12.75 years in the US ranging from a low of 0.5 year to a high of 40 years. The sample in China shows a similar pattern. The mean number of years in the workforce is

17.35 years, ranging from 1 year to a high of 45 years. Since H1b does not meet the significance level of 0.05 for both samples, the hypothesis must be rejected (Table 11.2).

Table 11.2   H1b. Levels of trust in managers are lower the longer a person has been in the work fore

	US			China		
	Mean	Std. Dev.	Corr. Trust	Mean	Std. Dev.	Corr. Trust
Years in workforce	12.7459	9.94787		17.3466	11.12323	
Trust	4.6961	1.91062	−0.023	4.9661	1.17442	−0.034

p = 0.379   p = 0.644
n = 181   n = 189

4.1.3   H1c. Higher level management positions within an organization will exhibit higher levels of trust

There is a relatively even distribution of management levels within both samples. The largest group in the US sample is the Worker/Non Management positions (85 or 47 per cent), and the second largest group is the Middle Management position (52 or 28.7 per cent). The sample in China indicates a slightly different distribution. The largest group in Chinese sample is First Line Management (71 or 37.57 per cent) and the Worker/Non Management (67 or 37.01 per cent) group is the close second. The results of the AVOVA (f = 1.384, p = 0.249 for the US samples; f = 0.815, p = 0.487 for the Chinese sample) indicate that higher-level management positions within an organization do not significantly exhibit higher levels of trust. Therefore, the hypothesis for both samples is rejected (Table 11.3).

Table 11.3   H1c. Higher levels of management positions within a company exhibit higher levels of trust

	US			China		
	N	Mean	Std. Dev.	N	Mean	Std. Dev.
Worker/Non-Mgt.	85	4.77410	1.92695	67	4.80300	1.36737
1st Line Mgt.	26	4.00000	1.90158	71	5.01410	1.16291
Middle Mgt.	52	4.84230	1.83574	44	5.14550	0.85548
Executive Mgt.	18	4.91110	1.99791	7	4.91430	1.03187

f = 1.384   f = 0.815
p = 0.249   p = 0.487

4.1.4 H1d. There is a relationship between the types of organization a person works for and trust

The US sample indicates that the majority of participants (115 or 63.53 per cent) are in the For-Profit organizations, the second major group (32 or 17.68 per cent) is in the Non-Profit organization; while in the Chinese samples, 92 participants or 48.68 per cent are in the For-Profit organization and 58 or 30.69 per cent are in Non-Profit organizations. The groups working in the military organizations in both countries represent the smallest segment, 4 per cent in the US and 0.5 per cent in China. The results of the AVOVA indicate that the types of organization a person works for have a significant effect on trust for US samples ($f = 3.073$; $p = 0.029$ for U.S. samples). Therefore the hypothesis is accepted for the US sample. However, the Chinese samples ($f = 0.440$; $p = 0.725$) do not indicate that the types of organization a person works for have no significant effect on trust. For the Chinese sample the hypothesis is rejected (Table 11.4).

Table 11.4   H1d. There is a relationship between the types of organization a person works for and trust

	US			China		
	N	Mean	Std. Dev.	N	Mean	Std. Dev.
For Profit	115	4.54960	1.87314	92	4.90220	1.24229
Military	8	5.12500	2.18550	1	5.00000	.
Government	26	4.19230	2.15813	38	4.89470	1.00026
Non-Profit	32	5.52500	1.55231	58	5.11380	1.18476

$$f = 3.073 \qquad\qquad f = 0.440$$
$$p = 0.029 \qquad\qquad p = 0.725$$

4.1.5   H2. There is a relationship between trust and conditional trust

A reliability test was performed on the two constructs of trust in manager (TRUST) and the existence of conditional trust (CONTRUST) for both sets of data from the US and China. The five-item trust construct produced a Cronbach's alpha of 0.95 that was consistent with the previous research.

The three-item construct of the existence of conditional trust produced a Cronbach's alpha of 0.842 for the US sample and 0.697 for the Chinese sample. The constructs demonstrated reliability as both were above the commonly used threshold value of 0.70 (Sims, 2000).

The levels of trust for both US and Chinese participants were measured in the construct 'TRUST' representing the mean levels of questions 1-5.

The levels of conditional trust that represent self-interest in terms of protection by the manager, career advancement, and rewards or recognition were measure in the construct 'CONTRUST' by the mean levels of conditional trust of questions 6-8. The average level of trust for the US participants was 4.70 (SD = 1.911) and the corresponding levels of conditional trust were 4.37 (SD = 1.718). For the Chinese sample, the average level of trust was 4.97 (SD = 1.174) and the corresponding levels of conditional trust were 4.64 (SD = 1.167). The results of the correlation for both samples indicate that there is a significant relationship between trust and conditional trust (Table 11.5).

Table 11.5   H2. There is a relationship between trust and conditional trust

	US			China		
	Mean	Std. Dev.	Cor-Trust	Mean	Std. Dev.	Cor-Trust
CONTRUST	4.37020	1.71842	*0.842	4.64200	1.16666	0.697
TRUST	4.69610	1.91062		4.96610	1.17442	

$$*p = 0.000 \qquad p = 0.000$$
$$n = 181 \qquad n = 189$$

5. DISCUSSION

The results of this cross-cultural study indicate that the US and Chinese participants share the same stance in two hypotheses: there is no relationship between the length a person is in the workforce and their trust in their managers; and there is no relationship between the levels of positions and levels of trust. Therefore, we cannot prove that in both countries the longer a person works in an organization the lower the level of trust he/she will have. Neither can we say that the higher a person holds a position in an organization the more trust he/she will have.

Differences do exist between the two country samples in the other two hypotheses, gender and levels of trust, and types of organization and levels of trust. In the US, females tend to trust their managers more than males, while in China the gender difference is not there, which means men and women have the same level of trust in their managers in the workforce. There is a significant difference between the types of organization and the levels of trust between the US and Chinese samples. People in the US tend to have greater levels of trust working in non-profit organizations than any other types of organizations, while people in China do not show a significant difference working in various types of organizations. This lack of difference in these areas suggests that due to the basic cultural environment in China or subsequent years of education and training (brain wash) people have a basic level of trust regardless of their particular organizational working environment. Whether working in non-profit organizations or for-profit organizations, Chinese people do not indicate any differences in their levels of managerial trust. The results of the study also may suggest that even in today's environment of downsizing in US, employees becoming 'free agents', and corporate misbehavior, people seem to retain a certain level of trust no matter how long they have worked or what management level they have attained.

The research findings (H2) indicate that people in the US exhibit lower overall levels of trust than in China. However, people in China exhibit higher levels of conditional trust, which may suggest that a more calculative process in the development of trust exists in China than the US. Thus, China, with a high power distance and low uncertainty avoidance culture, may also have a higher level of conditional trust and is more likely to engage in a calculative process of trust-building. This may confirm Hofstede's (1991) conclusions that Asian enterprises resemble families, and subordinates have less formalized task roles and responsibilities. Furthermore, the high power distance in China seems to suggest that it is a significant factor in the level of conditional trust. In these organizations people play more of a social role and these organizations can be characterized as paternalistic. However, further study is needed to confirm these assumptions as suggested in Proposition 2.

6. LIMITATION AND FUTURE STUDY

The research findings demonstrate that the research objective to examine a conceptual cultural framework between two countries has been achieved. However, the research findings have also suggested that there are a number of limitations in this study that could be further examined in the future. The short timeframe, small size of samples, amount of background and attitudinal information have limited the scope of this research into a further in-depth study. The major concern and limitation of the study is the psychometric validity of the construct conditional trust. Dealing with the complex subject of trust is made even more complex when attempting to separate a component of this cognitive process. Developing valid and tested psychometric measures is vital to the future study of this subject.

The behavioral element of trust lends itself to a number of future research ideas. First, leadership researchers should examine the dispositional and cultural aspects of trust in the context of present leadership theories.

This will provide a better understanding of how leaders can inspire trust in their subordinates in the context of various dispositional environments.

REFERENCES

Allport, G.W. and H.S. Odbert (1936), 'Trait names: A psycholexical study', *Psychological Monographs*, **47**(211).

Anderson, E. and B. Weitz (1989), 'Determinents of continuity in conventional industrial channel dyads', *Marketing Science*, **8**, 310-23.

Bass, B.M. (1985), *Leadership and Performance Beyond Expectations*, New York: Free Press, 14-32.

Berg, J., J. Dickhaut and K. McCabe (1995), 'Trust, reciprocity, and social history', Unpublished working paper cited in McKnight et al. (1998), University of Minnesota, Minneapolis.

Butler, J.K. (1991), 'Toward understanding and measuring conditions of trust: Evolution of a conditions of trust inventory', *Journal of Management*, **17**, 643-63.

Chiles, T.H. and J.F. McMackin (1996), 'Integrating variable risk preference, trust, and transaction cost economics', *Academy of Management Review*, **21**, 73-99.

Clark, T. (1990), 'International marketing and national character: A review and proposal for an integrative theory', *Journal of Marketing*, **54**(4), 66-79.

Cunningham, J.B. and J. MacGregor (2000), 'Trust and the design of work: Complementary constructs in satisfaction and performance', *Human Relations*, **53**(12), 1575-91.

Dasgupta, P. (1988), 'Trust as a commodity', in D. Gambetta (ed.), *Trust: Making and Breaking Cooperative Relations*, New York: Basil Blackwell, 47-72.

Deutsch, M. (1960), 'The effect of motivational orientation upon trust and suspicion', *Human Relations*, **13**, 123-39.

Dirks, K.T. and D.L. Ferrin (2002), 'Trust in leadership: Meta-analytic findings and implications for research and practice', *Journal of Applied Psychology*, **87**(4), 611-28.

Dore, R. (1983), 'Goodwill and the spirit of market capitalism', *British Journal of Sociology*, **34**, 459-82.

Dwyer, F.R., P.H. Schurr and S. Oh (1987), 'Developing buyer-seller relationships', *Journal of Marketing*, **51**(2), 11-27.

Earley, P.C. (1989), 'Social loafing and collectivism: A comparison of the United States and the People's Republic of China', *Administrative Science Quarterly*, **34**, 565-81.

Fichman, M. (2003), 'Straining towards trust: some constraints on studying trust in organizations', *Journal of Organizational Behavior*, **24**, 133-57.

Fukuyama, F. (1995), *Trust: The Social Virtues and the Creation of Prosperity*, New York: Free Press.

Gabarro, J.J. (1990), 'The development of working relationships', in J. Gallagher, R.E. Kraut and C. Egido (eds), *Intellectual Teamwork: Social and Technological Foundations of Cooperative Work*, Hillside, NJ: Lawrence Eribaum Associates, 79-110.

Gambetta, D. (1988), 'Can we trust?', in D. Gambetta (ed.), *Trust: Making and Breaking Cooperative Relationships,* New York: Basil Blackwell, 213-37.

Graen, G.B. and M. Uhl-Bien (1995), 'Relationship-based approach to leadership. Development of Leader-Member Exchange (LMX) theory of leadership over 25 years: Applying a multi-level multi-domain perspective', *Leadership Quarterly,* **6**, 219-47.

Gulati, R. (1995) 'Does familiarity breed trust? The implications of repeated ties for contractual choice in alliances', *Academy of Management Journal,* **38**, 85-112.

Hill, C.W. (1997) *International Business: Competing in the Global Marketplace,* Chicago: Irwin.

Hofstede, G. (1980), *Culture's Consequences,* Beverly Hills, CA: Sage.

Hofstede, G. (1984), *Culture's Consequences: International Differences in Work Related Values,* Beverly Hills, CA: Sage.

Hofstede, G. (1991), *Cultures and Organizations,* Maidenhead: McGraw-Hill.

House, R.J., S.A. Shane and D.M. Harold (1996), 'Rumors of the death of dispositional research are vastly exaggerated', *The Academy of Management Review,* **21**(1), 203-24.

Inglehart, R. and J. Rabier (1985), 'If you're unhappy, this must be Belgium', *Public Opinion,* **8**(April/May), 10-15.

Inkeles, A. and D.J. Levinson (1969), 'National character: The study of modal personality and social systems', in G. Lindzey and E. Aronson (eds), *The Handbook of Social Psychology,* vol. 4 (2nd edn), Cambridge, MA: Addison-Wesly, 418-506.

John, G. (1984), 'An empirical examination of some antecedents of opportunism in a marketing channel', *Journal of Marketing Research,* **21**, 278-89.

Jones, G.R. and J.M. George (1998), 'The experience and evolution of trust: Implications for cooperation and teamwork', *The Academy of Management Review,* **23**(3), 531-46.

Jung, J.I. and B.J. Avolio (2000), 'Opening the black box: an experimental investigation of the mediating effects of trust and value congruence on transformational and transactional leadership', *Journal of Organizational Behavior,* **21**(8), 949-64.

Kale, S.H. and J.W. Barnes (1992), 'Understanding the domain of cross-national buyer-seller interactions', *Journal of International Business Studies,* **23**(1), 101-32.

Kale, S.H. and R.P. McIntyre (1991), 'Distribution channel relationships in diverse cultures', *International Marketing Review,* **8**(3), 31-44.

Kluckhohn, F.R. and F.L. Strodtbeck (1961), *Variations in Value Orientations,* Westport, CT: Greenwood Press.

Kramer, R.M. (1994), 'The sinister attribution error: Paranoid cognition and collective distrust in organizations', *Motivation and Emotion,* **18**, 199-230.

Kramer, R.M. (1999), 'Trust and distrust in organizations: Emerging perspectives, enduring questions', *Annual Review of Psychology,* **50**, 569.

Kuhnert, K.W. and P. Lewis (1987), 'Transactional and transformational leadership: A constructive/developmental analysis', *Academy of Management Review,* **12**(4), 648-57.

Lane, C. and R. Bachman (1996), 'The social constitution of trust: Supplier relations in Britain and Germany', *Organization Studies,* **17**, 365-95.

Lewicki, R.J. and B.B. Bunker (1995), 'Trust in relationships: A model of development and decline', in B.B. Bunker and J.Z. Rubin (eds), *Conflict, Cooperation, and Justice*, San Francisco: Jossey-Bass, 133-73.

Lewicki, R.J. and B.B. Bunker (1996), 'Developing and maintaining trust in work relationships', in T.R. Kramer and T.R. Tyler (eds), *Trust in Organizations; Frontiers of Theory and Research*, Thousand Oaks, CA: Sage, 114-39.

Lewis, D.J. and A. Weigert (1985), 'Trust as a social reality', *Social Forces*, **63**, 967-85.

Lindskold, S. (1978), 'Trust development, the GRIT proposal and the effects of conciliatory acts on conflict and cooperation', *Psychological Bulletin*, **85**, 772-93.

Lynn, R. (1982), 'National differences in anxiety and extroversion', in B.A. Maher and W.B. Maher (eds), *Progress in Experimental Research*, **11**, New York: Academic Press, 259-71.

Mayer, R.C., J.H. Davis and D. Schoorman (1995), 'An integrative model of organizational trust', *Academy of Management Review*, **20**, 709-34.

McKnight, D.H., L.L. Cummings and N.L. Chervany (1998), 'Initial trust formation in new organizational relationships', *The Academy of Management Review*, **23**(3), 473-90.

Miles, R.E. and C.C. Snow (1992), 'Causes of failure in network organizations', California *Management Review*, Summer, 93-72.

Moorman, C., G. Zaltman and R. Deshpande (1992), 'Relationships between providers and users of market research: the dynamics of trust within and between organizations', *Journal of Marketing Research*, **29**, 314-28.

Namenwirth, J.Z. and R.B. Weber (1987), *Dynamics of Culture*, Boston: Allen and Unwin.

Neff, R. (1989), 'And now, another form of Japanese hardball: Lowball pricing', *Business Week*, (20 November), 50

Noordewier, T.G., G. John and J.R. Nevin (1990), 'Performance outcomes of purchasing arrangements in industrial buyer–vendor relationships', *Journal of Marketing*, **54**(4), 80-93.

Northouse, P. G. (2004), *Leadership Theory and Practice* (3rd edn), Thousand Oaks, CA: Sage Publications, 163-5.

Peabody, D. (1985), *National Characteristics*, Cambridge, UK: Cambridge University Press.

Podsakoff, P., S. Mackenzie, R. Moorman and R. Fetter (1990), 'Transformational leader behaviors and their effects on followers' trust in leader, satisfaction, and organizational citizenship behaviors', *Leadership Quarterly*, **1**, 107-42.

Rempel, J.K., J.G. Holmes and M.P. Zanna (1985). 'Trust in close relationships', *Journal of Personality and Social Psychology*, **49**, 95-112.

Rousseau, D.M., S.B. Sitkin, R.S. Burt and C. Camerer (1998), 'Not so different after all: A cross-discipline view of trust', *The Academy of Management Review*, **23**(3), 393-404.

Schindler, P.L. and C.C. Thomas (1993), 'The structure of interpersonal trust in the workplace', *Psychological Reports*, October, 563-73.

Schlenker, B.R., R. Helm and J.T. Tedeschi (1973), 'The effects of personality and situational variables on behavioral trust', *Journal of Personality and Social Psychology*, **25**, 419-27.

Shamir B. (1990), 'Calculation, value, and identities: the sources of collectivistic work motivation', *Human Relations*, **43**, 313-32.

Shapiro, D., B.H. Sheppard and L. Cheraskin (1992), 'Business on a handshake', *Negotiation Journal*, **8**, 365-77.

Sims, R.L. (2000), *Bivariate Data Analysis: A practical guide*, Huntington, NY: Nova Science Publishers, Inc., 61.

Singh, J. (1990), 'Managerial culture and work-related values in India', *Organizational Studies*, **11**, 75-101.

Sitkin, S.B. and N.L. Roth (1993), 'Explaining the limited effectiveness of legalistic "remedies" for trust/distrust', *Organizational Science*, **4**, 367-92.

Strub, P.J. and T.B. Priest (1976), 'Two patterns of establishing trust: The marijuana user', *Sociological Focus*, **9**, 399-411.

Triandis, H.C. (1972), *The Analysis of Subjective Culture*, New York: Wiley.

Ueno, S. and U. Sekaran (1992), 'The influence of culture on budget control practices in the USA and Japan: an empirical study', *Journal of International Business Studies*, **23**, 659-74.

Williamson, O.E. (1991), 'Calculativeness, trust and economic organization', *Journal of Law and Economics*, **26**, 453-86.

Williamson, O.E. (1996), 'Economic organization: the case for candor', *The Academy of Management Review*, **21**(1), 48-57.

Zand, D. (1972), 'Trust and managerial problem solving', *Administrative Science Quarterly*, **17**, 229-239.

Zucker, L.G. (1986), 'The production of trust: institutional sources of economic structure, 1840-1920', in B.M. Staw and L.L. Cummings (eds), *Research in Organizational Behavior*, **8**, Greenwich, CT: JAI Press, 55-111.

12. Cultural genes, the trust model and the specialization and internationalization of the management of Chinese family enterprises

Donglin Song and Zheng Li

1. INTRODUCTION

Whether China can achieve brilliant success in the twenty-first century and becomes a world giant in economic terms as expected is, to a great extent, dependent on whether the source of economic growth can be shifted from the traditional companies to the newly-rising medium- and small-sized companies and whether they can start and expand their businesses successfully. If the present medium- and small-sized companies and family enterprises cannot expand appropriately, it will be hard to maintain the rate of economic growth. Although there is no final conclusion about which are more healthy – the large enterprises or the medium- and small-sized companies – for some product sectors, such as automobile manufacturing, aviation, semiconductor manufacturing and so on, large enterprises are not the only form that can be highly efficient and beneficial (Fukuyama, 1995). This is also true of small companies which can also make generous profits, and needn't expand; but for China, if the large enterprises lose competitive advantage, economic development will be greatly influenced, not to mention China's success in terms of global competition.

As to the normal modes of organization of companies, and seen from the history of economic development both in China and abroad, the state-owned and state-controlled large enterprises have not been able to solve the problem of low efficiency, and are not able to act as a major force in global competition. At the same time, although the family enterprise is the original and most fundamental mode of industrial organization (Lee,

2001), few have grown up to be large-scale enterprises; the highly-efficient and long-standing big groups, almost without exception, are private companies with professional management that have evolved from family enterprises (Zheng, 2001).

The private companies on China's mainland sprang up and grew after the Open-up in the late 1970s; 90 per cent of these are family owned or controlled (He 2003), and even now, all of them are still medium- or small-sized. With the coming of the new century, these family enterprises are experiencing a period of sensitivity and turbulence (Li 2002) because the management is being handed over, in one company after another, from the old generation to the new. Each company exists as a result of twenty years of hard work and struggle, so who will be qualified to take the relay baton? Will these companies be willing to accept a professional executive and successfully change themselves into modern executive-run companies as Chandler (1977) has already described? These questions are not only vital to the companies themselves – the transformation of China's private companies and the process of specialization and socialization of the management – but they are also influential in the outlook of China's economy and development of its society.

As crucial variables in the evolvement of family enterprises, professional management, and the distribution of power and human resources are hot topics in the studies of family enterprise theories in the west (Su Qilin and Ou Xiaoming, 2002). Many foreign researchers have devoted themselves to these fields (for the previous field we have Chandler, 1977; Hayes and Abernathy, 1980; Meek, Woodworth and Dyer, 1988; Lansberg, 1983; for the latter, Christen, 1953; Mc-Givern, 1974; Trow, 1961; Herson, 1975; Barnes and Hershon, 1977; Tashakori, 1977; Ward, 1987; Dyer, 1986; Rosenblatt, deMike, Anderson and Johnson, 1985), but few of them have studied family enterprises on China's mainland.

Chandler's (1977) findings revealed that even in the United States, where the notion of family culture was relatively weak, it took 100 years for those family enterprises to evolve into modern executive-run companies, which made the management itself become the source of the company's permanence, power and sustained growth. The management revolution in America was along the lines of executive capitalism replacing family capitalism and finance capitalism. Bukart (2002) made a systematic generalization about the inheriting modes of management in family enterprises of different countries and areas. He said that the founders of American family enterprises normally hired an executive at a very early stage. When he retired, he and his successors only kept the lowest level of ownership. That is also the case in the findings of Berle and Means (1932). But for west European counterparts, ownership quite often remains inside the family itself; their successors either hire an executive, as in BMW and Fiat, or run the company themselves as Peugeot did. But in less-developed countries, the ownership was mainly handed down to their offsprings; if they needed an executive, they would normally strengthen the relationship by marrying a female member of the family to him. But Berle and Means did not analyse this in any great depth.

Redding (1993) and Fukuyama (1998) once made a study on the problem of professional management in overseas Chinese family enterprises. Redding (1993) believed that 'There will be great difficulties to promote the overseas Chinese family enterprises to undergo the so-called management revolution, i.e, to hand over the management to the executive, and separate the management from the ownership.' That's also why Chinese family enterprises can't escape the family-dominated model. When faced with the question, 'why is it normally the case in Chinese family enterprises that close relatives often occupy very important positions and nepotism is highly valued?' he simply answered, 'because they do not trust anybody else'. Redding mainly made an analysis on the management of human resources from the angle of economic culture, which gave us a general idea about family enterprises as regards individuals and others, individuals and their relationships, and the company and society. However, as Redding concentrated entirely on to the relationship between the company and society and the source of the entrepreneurial spirit, he did not talk much about the organization of personnel and the reason why such an arrangement existed. Though Redding emphasized many times that Chinese entrepreneurs did not trust non-relatives, he did not clearly explain why. The only reason he quoted was Lin Yutang's words that 'Chinese lack Samaritanism'. As has been universally agreed, the Chinese don't trust outsiders.

Fukuyama (1995) has a similar viewpoint: 'Chinese family enterprises are often quite thriving and highly profitable, but when they want to systemize the company and form a long-term objective, not dependent on the financial power and influences of the family enterprises, great problems then arise.' Because of their utter distrust in outsiders, which often in turn prevents the institution of the enterprise, the owner of a Chinese family enterprise would rather split the company into a few small ones or even end the business than hand the company over to an executive (Fransis, 2001, p. 296). Both Redding and Fukuyama have pointed out the distrust problem in Chinese family enterprises. On one hand, because of the mainland's unusual history, there is a cultural gap (Fukuyama, 1995) with Taiwan and Hong Kong; overseas Chinese family enterprises are after all different from the mainland's. On the other hand, whether owners of Chinese family enterprises have no trust in non-relatives or have inherited 'a preference for centralization of power' (Chu, 2002), is still an issue in question.

Chinese scholars in Taiwan and Hong Kong applied the western trust theory to the studies of Chinese family enterprises relatively much earlier and have achieved brilliant results; among these Hwang (1988) is an important figure. Hwang argues that as the family enterprises develop to a certain level beyond the management competence of the family relatives, they then employ some non-relatives to be in charge of all kinds of production activities on the behalf of the owners. As the companies grow larger, more non-relatives are taken into the companies, and the distribution of work inside the companies becomes more and more elaborate, with owners having to make a choice between the man-ruled and the regulation-ruled management. In fact this is crucial to the modernization of family enterprises. Based on the social exchange theory, Hwang (1988) developed a theory model which is known as 'Human relationship and reputations: Games of power among Chinese'. The model fully displays, from sociology, the interaction between the owners of the Chinese family enterprises and the relatives, and the interactions between the owners and the non-relatives. The affection between the owner and the relatives, the affection between the owner and the non-relative employees, and the way of doing business according to these principles with staff outside the organization, fully show the characteristics of Chinese people's attitudes towards lives. Another important figure is Zheng (1995). He set up a model together with others claiming that Chinese bosses would like to classify their employees by the criteria of interrelation, loyalty and competence. As the model indicates, loyal staff are likely to be taken into the inner team by the bosses, and given more confidence. Competence is another factor, which has been proved by quality and quantity studies in the Taiwan area. But as Fukuyama (1995) has pointed out, the Chinese mainland has had an extraordinary history that caused an interruption in tradition, so the typical meaning of culture and tradition is not that strong compared with that in Hong Kong and Taiwan.

Up to now, the studies of mainland China's scholars in the field of professionalization of management and the mechanism of human resources in family enterprises are still weak. The findings have not come together in a systematic way, and have lacked the support of systematic theories; some of them have even gone too much into the dispute of the advantages and disadvantages of family enterprises and the direction of transformation (Su and Ou, 2002). As some scholars have indicated, the prevailing opinion in theory is that family enterprises should be transformed, and only through transformation can they escape their closed state and limitations (Wei, 2001). Many scholars in this field, through their studies of the structure of the standardized modern company, believe that in order to promote the development of Chinese family enterprises, we must depend on the establishment of the institution of a modern company, separating the management from the ownership. They also severely criticize the prevalence of family-styled management in Chinese private companies.

This can also be deduced from theory. With the expansion and development of the enterprise, the company is sure to develop more products, deal with more business, and expand into more fields. Consequently, the company will have to face more complicated environments and require the managing staff to take on more roles, especially more knowledge and skills. On one hand, the company is faced with the unlimited increase in the requirement of various skills in management; on the other hand, there is a rigid restriction in the number of managing staff, their knowledge, skills and learning capacity. So a 'scissor-like' difference arises. To make up the difference and achieve development, family enterprises have to import professional executives and set up a modern institution of enterprise management, separating the ownership from the management (Cao, 2002).

However, we should know that the basis for the fulfilment of this deduction is that we must have here in China a 'perfect' executive market and relative law and contract systems to regulate these executives. As Chu (2002) found out, many owners of family enterprises have seen the limitation of family-styled management and have begun to transform their company according to the model of modern companies, hiring executives to run the company, but they have experienced one failure after another. Therefore Zhang (2001) believed the growth of Chinese companies and the development of the Chinese private economy, to a great extent, depended on the morality of professional executives. 'We need not worry about the lack of entrepreneurs, instead, the risk-spirit and creativity consciousness are booming in China. What we should really worry about is that there is no professional morality good enough and insufficient qualified executives.' He also pointed out that the construction of a team of professional executives would be a very important and difficult issue after the property rights reform.

As can be seen superficially, the main contradiction which prevents the professionalization of management in Chinese family enterprises and that in turn affects the process of aggrandization of private companies is that there has not been a professional executive market which can back up the implementation of the modern company institution in the family enterprises (Cao, 2002). But as we look deeper into the history of the executive institution, even in western countries where the market economy is relatively complete, there are also insufficient qualified entrepreneurs and executives (Chu, 2002). Professional executives were born and grew up in the development of family enterprises. As to the professionalization of Chinese family enterprises, to own a pool of qualified executives is a necessary condition but not a sufficient one, therefore it is a result rather than a decisive factor.

But in my opinion, it is the cultural genes, the trust mode, and, to be more specific, it is the 'family culture' tradition, the kin and the special pattern of trust that determine the present level of the family nature of Chinese private companies and the stage of management professionalization. As a constituent of the transformation of the family enterprise institution, professionalization is associated with understanding in culture and is the process of adapting to the environment and the process of learning. From the viewpoint of system evolvement, the development of private companies has to be self-organized and route-dependent. To choose the best route, they have to change the original conditions, so it is an urgent prerequisite to set up an institution-based trust.

2. 'FAMILY CULTURE' AND THE MECHANISM OF HUMAN RESOURCES IN ENTERPRISES

After thousands of years of accumulation and deposition, Chinese 'family culture' has a similar impact in the minds of all Chinese, and the influence of this family culture in the institution of any organization and personnel is far-reaching and elaborate. As for family enterprises, the traditional 'family culture' has been inherited more specifically. The notion of the insider is just a very important part of the inheritance.

2.1 'Family Culture'

Home, to the Chinese, is a solid fortress; even the Great Wall is dwarfed in significance compared with it. Bodele said, 'in the whole world, home is the base of society, but in China, home is society. So we can say that Chinese society is the Chinese family institution' (Fan, 1995). In discussions about Chinese culture, no scholars will underestimate the influence of the family institution on Chinese society. So it is inconceivable to study Chinese family enterprises without taking 'family culture' as the core value system in Chinese culture.

As recorded in Chinese history and myths and legends, China evolved from a primitive society into a slave society, then into a class society. The original leaders in the tribe turned into the aristocrats in the slave society, and the family slave system developed into the clan system. This kind of evolution is quite different from the western one. In ancient Greece and Rome, the owners of the slaves broke the old clan system through a series of revolutions and transformation, which replaced the kinship clan system with countries formed around a certain region, replaced the family-centred clan society with the individual-centred society, and replaced the family-styled consanguinity government with the political government of the country. So the particularities of China's family system were already doomed from the very beginning by ancient history. Therefore when China's primitive society disintegrated, instead of replacing the patriarchal clan system, which took the clan kinship as the connection with a slave country, China evolved into a country with kinship as the hold and connection of the slave system. Then kinship became a basic relation in the society, helped form the prototype of the social relationships and established the kinship structure mode as the structure mode of all social relations, on the basis of which it set up a 'family and country as a unit' social system and structure.

And it is only in China that the word 'country' is translated as *guojia* which is a word that combines 'country' and 'family'. The family and home, which were originally different units of organization of society, are now so closely connected here and blended naturally into one. 'Family' is the prototype and matrix of 'country', 'country' is the expansion and enlargement of 'family', and the organizing principles of 'country' are the expansion of the organizing principles of 'family'. Family is not only the starting point of values, the choice of values, but also the ideal mode of all social relationships. The concepts: 'Brothers are all around the world', 'the whole world is under the roof of a family' just reflect this special kind of value ideal in Chinese culture.

As for the notion of 'family', although there are some differences in family regulations and family enterprises between China and the west, they share a number of characteristics such as affection, the differences between family members and outsiders and the authority of the older generation. But when the family concept, the family system and the rules of family activities are extended to various levels of society, there are completely different ideas in China and the west. The famous Taiwan scholar Yang Guoshu (Yang and Yu, 1993) once described the pan-family as the following:

> in the traditional society, the living experience and custom in the family is quite often the only team living experience and custom for Chinese, so they would naturally make the structure mode, the relation mode and way of doing things in the family, spread, generalize or bring into the non-family groups and organizations.

that is, the Chinese will take their family attitudes into groups and organizations outside the family.

2.2 The Influences of 'Family Culture' on Family Enterprises' Personnel Structure

The organization of family enterprises is a condensed image of Chinese family culture. In the medium- and- small-sized family enterprises, the structure of the family or the family group works as the basic construction of the business organization, and the basic relations in the family or the family group become the source of the power structure of the company. Family enterprises' personnel structure normally exhibit the following styles:

2.2.1 The patriarchal style

As the design of the organization is the shift of the family organization, the principal figures in the family and the family group then naturally become the figures of authority in the company. As Weber (1951) has pointed out, family authority belonged to the centre of power in the traditional organization while the authority of the bureaucratic organization was devised according to rationality and legality, which was the absolute result of the professionalization and specialization of modern society. However, the patriarch of the family enterprise naturally became the power centre of the company, and its rationality and legality would face no challenge from other members in the organization, in the same way as divine right of kings.

2.2.2 Personal favour supreme

As company structure mirrors family structure, the various relationships in the family and family group then permeate into the company. The relationships based on blood, marriage, common ancestry and home village, form the basic human relationships inside the family company, with various people swearing to treat each other like their own brothers and sisters and adopted relatives. These two categories of relationship together form the human relationships inside the family enterprises. 'Affection, reason and law' are three measures to deal with the relationships inside the family enterprises, with 'affection' as the major measure, 'reason' as the proof, and 'law' as the complement when there is no other option. The concept that 'a harmonious home is the basis of the prosperity of the family' is the principal ideology in the development of the enterprise.

2.2.3 Various grades and ranks

The relationship within the family results in the difference in the distribution of the power in the company. Appointment by favouritism is the most vulnerable in family enterprises. The owner's children are the absolute successors to them even though they may not make a good impression which is similar to the situation in feudal society. In the arrangement of top managers, combinations of relationship, loyalty and talent, relatives and friends have a short cut, especially in periods of stability. The situation will be better when the enterprises are in trouble or in intensive competition. Some of them are experienced seniors holding a high position, though they are few in number.

3. KINSHIP TRUST AND DISTRIBUTION OF CONTROLLING POWER OF CHINESE FAMILY ENTERPRISES

Influenced by family culture genes, the trust structure and appointment pattern in China can be distinguished in terms of family members, insiders and outsiders, but not absolutely. They are not completely separate entities. Chinese distrust in outsiders is not extreme or permanent, basically it is only an initial reaction. This trust structure and appointment pattern lead to the distribution of control power of Chinese family enterprises.

3.1 From Kinship Trust to Kinship-Based Trust

Traditional Chinese trust is based on the caring family. Children first have a relationship with their parents, brothers and sisters after their birth. This emotion deepens due to parents' unconditional devotion and care for their children as they grow up. Parents' love and children's filial duty form the core of trust based on kinship, therefore extending to grandchildren, sisters and brothers. This pattern of trust is similar to Confucian ethics, and is hierarchical. The family core gradually extends to brothers' independence, sisters' relationship by marriage through common ancestry, finally even to the same surname. Psychological identification beyond the family results in differences in relationship. Besides kinship, contact and location directly affect psychological identification of family members. In other words, the closer, the more intimate; the further, the more alien.

The Chinese psychological identification of family members is closely related to conflict with another family. Tradition believes that the same surnames are with one heart, one mind and one goal (Yu, 1988); on the other hand, different surnames mean a quite different cooperation with outsiders. Therefore though the distinction exists between trust and distrust in one family in terms of psychological identification, an outsider's involvement can make a distrusted family member trusted. Just as the saying goes: brothers quarrelling at home join forces against others' attack. That is what we call kinship trust.

Even so, modern Chinese society is not of a pure kinship trust, but a kin-like trust. It is not in the Chinese character and human nature to distrust outsiders, neither is this distrust extreme. In China a so-called outsider (not trustworthy) is different from both family members and insiders. But insiders (trustworthy individuals in some aspect) are a concept which reflects a special interpersonal relationship in Chinese society. Insiders are of kinship. Study shows that kinship and marital relationship are not the only criteria to identify insiders, especially with regard to marital relationships. That means family members are not equal to insiders, which is not a permanent situation. Some insiders will become outsiders in the future, and some will be insiders who were previously outsiders. In any case, insiders refer to those who are trustworthy, and relationship is more than kinship. The concept of the family makes Chinese family enterprises merge with social capitalism and grow much larger compared with the family enterprises of other civilizations. And it can lead to richer human and material resources being formed, leading to the development of enterprises on a larger economic scale.

Therefore, Chinese outsiders include those without any kinship or without psychological trust, even family members. The saying 'acquaintances look like strangers' is used to describe those who are psychologically estranged, like the relation between king and minister, wife and husband, 'strange bedfellows'. In this sense, outsiders are quite different from strangers in the English sense. Kinship trust is so complicated that the relationship between insiders, outsiders and others is changing constantly. Today's insiders may become the outsiders, or even enemies of tomorrow. The outsiders of yesterday may be the insiders of today. The dynamic evolution and vagueness of interpersonal relations characterize Chinese society. Distrust of outsiders is not exclusive to Chinese society. In contrast with intensive trust among family members, distrust of outsiders is more prominent.

3.2   Employment Patterns based on Kinship Trust in Chinese Family Enterprises

Family members, insiders and outsiders change constantly in Chinese family enterprises because of kinship and loyalty, and talent as well. The executives of Chinese family business employ mostly workers from their home town and select cadres among their family members. Meanwhile loyalty and talent are the main criteria for appointment. The relationship between leaders and subordinates in overseas Chinese enterprises seems contradictory to the filial piety of Confucian ethics. Redding (1993) found that a loyal subordinate would regard his leader as the family master and follow him without doubting or challenging the authority of the leader's management. Zheng (1995) also stressed that loyalty to a Chinese organization reflected a private loyalty and unselfish contribution to one's employer.

Employment in Chinese family enterprises begins with sensibilities including relatives, relatives' relatives and *laoxiang* (neighbours from the home town). Enlarging the scale of enterprises makes their membership more complex and they become open to graduates from universities and executive managers joining the company. In any case, outsiders' entry in to family enterprises signals the establishment of an employment relationship with the family. The connection depends on the loyalty and skill that the outsiders demonstrate in the cause of their work. Combinations of ability and character make it possible to enter the world of insiders. Traditional values cannot be understated when they are used to distinguish insiders from outsiders. Employment of insiders characterizes Chinese family enterprises in dominating key positions and heads of organizations.

Entrepreneurs' employment of employees, and the training and selection of staff for top positions, reflects the above two identification criteria of outsiders. Though entrepreneurs admit in their mind that there is a clear distinction between insiders and outsiders, problems occur when family members are removed from the group of insiders. Studies show that few hold that insiders are of kinship, most of them insist that insiders are trustworthy people and that is a flexible notion, corresponding to the multidimension about modern trust. It is natural that entrepreneurs' clear distinction between insiders and outsiders results in their appointment by favouritism. Furthermore, entrepreneurs' future is subject to the qualities and quantities of insiders whose mutual trust and general willingness are weapons with which enterprises can achieve success. The shortage of insiders is what the enterprises worry about most.

3.3. Distributing Test of Employment and Control Power Distribution Based on Kinship

3.3.1 Interviews and case studies

Among those interviewed, 30 entrepreneurs agree on a gradual understanding of outsiders who may become insiders if they have the necessary character and ability. In response to how to supplement managers as a result of enterprises' development, 66.66 per cent agree to choose from trustworthy individuals, former employees who have ability, which indicates that entrepreneurs' distrust of outsiders is not constant, but that it exists at the initial stage. After connection and communication with outsiders for a certain period, the character, ability and degree of trust will cause them to become insiders.

There are two family enterprises in Sichuan province which employ about 500 people. Their founders are husband and wife who act as chairman and vice chairman of the board, general manager and deputy general manager respectively. Others act as middle managers, a third of whom are relatives and two-thirds of whom are old friends or classmates of founders. Among friends, some are clerks or cadres of the state enterprises whom the entrepreneurs got to know when their business was in its early stages. They joined the family enterprises after their resignation or retirement, as the enterprises expanded. Their entry solved problems in basic management and systems, such as loss of cheque and falsification accounts that had occurred in the past, and which were later resolved by the appointment of a state enterprise manager in charge of store management. The entrepreneurs are less busy than before and receive fewer phone calls even after the expansion of business. One entrepreneur said he was good at running the business, while the state-owned enterprise managers did well in management.

3.3.2　Empirical tests

To further prove the conclusion from our theoretical analysis, we adapt survey data from the *Management Structure of Chinese Private Enterprises* from the Chinese Academy of Social Sciences. The project team surveyed 179 private Chinese enterprises and obtained data which to some extent show the general features of Chinese family enterprises (see Table 12.1).

In Table 12.1, among the family members, employers' relatives occupy a larger proportion of top management positions (general manager and deputy general manager) in 179 private enterprises, but outsiders, that is social employees, occupy less as management levels decrease. The percentage of the two sides changes in the opposite direction. In addition, based on the analysis of Chinese family culture genes and family enterprises, we have reason to think that managers from the basic level and employers' relatives working as managers are basically insiders who have a special relationship with the owners of family enterprises. The distribution of management control power of Chinese family enterprises is shown in

Table 12.2. Insiders form a large proportion of the top managers of family enterprises. The proportion decreases as the management levels decrease. The test result confirms the theoretical analysis (see Table 12.3).

Table 12.1 Distribution of importance of people mainly relied on by family enterprises (%)

	At initial stage			After development		
	No.1	No.2	No.3	No.1	No.2	No.3
Family members	63.8	6.8	5.7	52.4	8.4	8.4
Relatives	7.1	29.6	6.4	6.4	18.8	7.3
Spouse's relatives	4.3	10.2	15.6	2.7	10.2	11.2
Schoolmate	4.0	9.6	4.9	2.9	7.0	6.2
Friend from childhood	4.8	10.2	8.6	5.9	7.1	7.3
Previous colleague	5.1	12.9	7.2	4.3	13.7	11.1
Comrade in arms	1.4	5.2	7.2	4.5	5.4	6.8
Persons recommended by friends	2.0	7.9	13.6	3.6	12.3	12.9
Persons from society	3.6	7.6	26.8	16.9	17.9	29.0
others	1.0	0.1	1.1	1.5	0.2	1.0

Source: Zhang et al (2002)(2003)

Table 12.2 Human resources of private enterprises (%)

	Employment from society	Promotion from the basic level	Owner's relatives	Owner's relatives and friends	Government delegates	Others
Total number of management	43.8	29.24	11.67	8.59	0.58	6.11
General manager	16.00	25.00	42.00	3.00	1.00	12.00
Deputy general manager	29.33	23.55	24.23	11.05	1.50	10.30
General engineers	50.10	28.19	9.86	5.63	0.69	5.52
Financial manager	40.58	24.57	16.37	12.90	1.01	4.57
Purchase manager	36.16	36.45	15.85	6.79	0.75	4.01
Sales manager	41.87	35.60	13.59	3.89	0.46	4.60
Store manager	34.50	42.10	13.76	4.50	1.50	3.63
Ordinary managers	37.50	41.44	9.01	3.11	0.17	8.76

Table 12.3 Manager resources of private enterprises (%)

	Outsiders	Others	Family members	Insiders (including family members)
Total number of management	43.8	6.69	11.67	49.50
General manager	16.00	13.00	42.00	70.00
Deputy general manager	29.33	11.08	24.23	53.41
General engineers	50.10	6.21	9.86	43.68
Financial manager	40.58	5.58	16.37	53.84
Purchase manager	36.16	4.76	15.85	59.09
Sales manager	41.87	5.06	13.59	53.08
Store manager	34.50	5.13	13.76	60.36
Ordinary managers	37.50	8.93	9.01	53.56

4. INSTITUTION-BASED TRUST AND THE INTERNATIONALIZATION OF MANAGEMENT OF CHINESE FAMILY ENTERPRISES

4.1. The Bottleneck of the Internationalization of Family Enterprises' Management lies in the Special Trust Mechanism

Not only histories of China, but also developed countries' economic developments have shown that family enterprises play a very important role in early industrialization. In developed economies, professional skills increasingly determine salaries, and the criteria for employment lie in abilities rather than the special social network. As a result, along with the modernization and the internationalization of distribution and cooperation in work, family enterprises are breaking the closed family circles and kinship, and are adopting a non-personalized system. They are also changing from non-regulated management to modern management, which is very important to modern economic development. In this sense, Douglas North (1995) pointed out that the shift from a basis of personal trust to non-personal is the key point. We don't think it necessary to change family enterprises to non-family ones; in fact, numerous family enterprises are indispensable to the economic structure. In modern economic developments, however, family enterprises must integrate social resources to take part in internationalization.

The internationalization of Chinese family enterprises in essence is the growth of enterprises. Generally speaking, the development of companies mainly lies in the growth of capital, the improvement of systems and profit-seeking abilities. For family enterprises, the growth of capital implies breaking the restrictions of family capital and absorbing social financial capital. And the expansion of the organization structure shows that the enterprises' trust-agent chains are going to be lengthened, that the circle of family management will be broken and that professional managers and human resources will be integrated. The increasing ability of profit-seeking in the market shows that family enterprises need to establish an extensive business network or firms' alliance on the basis of effectively combining financial capital and human resources, so as to form the core competitiveness of a characteristic enterprise culture. In summary, family enterprises must absorb and integrate capital to ensure growth of the three factors pointed out. As a result, the key point of the growth of family enterprises lies in the successful integration of various capitals.

Generally speaking, if the family's internal resources such as capital and human resources can ensure the further development of an enterprise, its existence is sound and the management is effective. At the initial stage of a private enterprise, if the capital, human resources and factors of production meet basic requirements, family members' affinity and fidelity in the enterprise can be a boost and raise the cohesive force, which is sound management. Along with the initial set-up of the market economy, further development of private enterprise and the intensive competitive market, family businesses demand more and more technology, capital, professional management and scale economy. Limited funds and technology resources, poor management ability in family members, different treatment of insider and outsider employees, and the distribution system all have led to high management cost and low competitiveness, compared with those in non-family enterprises. At this time, the management in family enterprises is unreasonable and low in efficiency and it is urgent that they adjust management practice and innovating the institution.

The ability of self renewal in management is necessary for a really excellent enterprise (Peng, 2000), that is, the ability of management to evolve, in order to sustain the life of the enterprise. A family enterprise is bound to face the problem of absorption and integration of new management associated with the Penrose effect (Penrose, 1959). After 20 years of reform and opening to the outside, the supply of management in the human resource market is not as scarce as before. In fact, the shortage of management resources in the capital market has improved a great deal and should be promoted through the price mechanism. In fact, it is the resource of trust that restricts the growth of family enterprises, the lack of trust between the entrepreneur and the manager (Li and Hu, 2002). Without enough trust, the entrepreneur cannot obtain sufficient management resources from the market. And because of the asymmetric information and the lack of trust, entrepreneurs will possibly evaluate a high risk cost in the process of empowering managers. The financial restriction can illustrate this problem. The traditional family enterprises restricted development caused by funds in the stock market and other forms by holding stocks and controlling powers themselves.

What should be emphasized is that family enterprises and family-based management enterprises are two different concepts (Li, 2003). The definition of family enterprises mainly refers to family members' ownership, controlling powers and the inheritance of the enterprises. Family-based management is management behaviour carried out by family members or insiders, for example patriarchal style decision making, different policies for the appointment and promotion of insiders and outsiders, keeping the crucial positions under the control of the people on the inside. If an outsider makes some innovations in the enterprise it cannot threaten the ownership and power of the enterprise. The different meanings of the two types of enterprise provide a space for innovation in the internalization of the family enterprises.

4.2   The Efficiency Analysis of Pan Family Trust and the Institution-based Trust Mechanism

As a kind of human being's subjective prediction, trust has a deep relationship with society, history, culture and tradition. Different trust mechanisms can be produced by different conditions. The essence and character of trust can be distinguished as emotional private trust, institution-based trust and purpose-based trust. Family trust and pan-family trust produced in the kinship of Chinese social traditions are the typical mode of emotional private trust. Purpose-based trust is established on the basis of rational choice and is produced after the comparison of losses and gains in the exchange. According to the history of the development of western society, the institution has provided a basic support for the scale expansion of trust, which makes it possible for enterprises to further undertake the risk and trust. This kind of support can bring about better team and working performances in the organization; on the society level, legal institutions can be used more widely and more efficiently to protect personal property and the business rights of both parties. Institution-based trust includes the formal trust of legal contracts, and informal trust, such as the reputation mechanism and psychological contract concerning justice in the market-oriented economy. These two sides supplement and promote each other.

Family trust is a special personal trust system. The management of trust here is based on the character of personality. The core is family kinship, but it is not enough to solve all the problems that the family business encounters when it is necessary to absorb the outsiders of long-term contracts into the family circle. They are treated in the same way as family members in terms of ethics, emotion and payment. In the process of this special trust management, Confucianism plays a dominant role and is influenced and strengthened by the shortage of the society trust institution (Hamilton, 1991). It is not hard to see that compared with the general trust principle, the special trust institution of the family can not expand beyond a certain point as the enterprise grows, because it is restricted by the cost and value in establishing a long-term contract. Therefore, family trust actually restricts the internationalization of family enterprises.

To promote the family enterprises' institution-based management so as to solve the bottleneck problem of the trust mechanism, it requires 'regulation control' to replace 'human control' in the management of family enterprise. Choices between 'regulation control' and 'human control' are very important (Hwang, 1988) for the modernization of family enterprises. Many family enterprises in western countries tend to choose the 'regulation control' management to set up rational organizations. They depend on formal regulations to manage enterprises and then expand up to a giant scale in accordance with the requirements of modern production and distribution. In order to maintain the continuity of growth of family enterprises in the future, and so that some large-scale private enterprises can be major global competitiors, at least some family enterprises need to have professional management. But where? And how? According to scholars' analysis, professional management in family enterprises is dependent on the improvement of the external environment, especially the accumulation of social trust capital and the transformation of government administration. At present, the biggest obstacle is neither Chinese traditional culture itself, nor the executive manager market, but the special trust and trust model based on kinship. Therefore, it is urgent to set up a general trust mechanism.

4.3 Thoughts on Establishing the Trust Mechanism in Family Enterprises

Generally, the confidence needed to establish the trust mechanism comes mainly from two sources: the first source is social credit and the moral code. Social credit works through regulation legislation and its enforcement. The moral code creates a series of value criteria and behaviour standards. Both work through punishment and restriction systems. The second source is the categorization of the credit level according to the relationship with others developed in the long-term contract and the dynamic management or adjustment of the categorization. In most cases such trust management approximates an instinctive process. Comparatively, such a systematic mechanism of trust is not dependent on human characters without categorization; instead it is mainly based on social credit, and maintained through law and moral code. Here the construction of regulations and moral code is the social public product, whose economic values lie in the fact that it saves the cost needed in establishing individual trust. Individual trust is a private product, and has no effect on the scale economy (Li, 2002b).

Institution-based trust is a kind of result that people predict that their efforts will bring about in the future under a series of impersonal arrangements of institution. Institution-based trust can be divided into two types: (1) trust in the predictability of the institution; (2) trust in the guarantee of the institution. The trust in the predictability of the institution just reflects the 'form rationality', which regards the institution of the human world as 'a cause-and-effect mechanism' that can be controlled by precise calculation. The most representative example is Max Weber's 'ideal bureaucracy'. In the design of the organization, he emphasized the principle of being 'rational', 'purposeful', 'impersonal' and 'calculable', which enables the individual or the group under the system to predict the result of their activities. Predictability emphasizes method and programme. Everybody can use the same method and programme to pursue their own objective. There are many types of institution guarantee, among which the most popular are those tools with a deterrent force, for example, contract, regulations and lawsuit. Shapiro (1987) called them guardians of trust.

To run a family enterprise on the basis of a legal system means that the power of the entrepreneurs and their family is restricted, which is often unacceptable to many entrepreneurs. But as for sustained development, the first step is to restrict the power of the entrepreneurs and their family inside the enterprise and voluntarily take the revolution for control power. No institution is perfect. As a result, it is important to set up a sound trust and communication system between authorizer and authorizee. To enrol professional executives and specialists for key positions, some successful enterprises just turn the outsiders into their own men. The trust between them is the premise of good cooperation. Especially on the issue of succession, trust develops on the basis of long-term observation and mutual communication. As a result, both succession and the establishment of the institution take time; it is a process of establishing, adapting, implementing and adjusting to the new institution, and also a process of maturation and development of the new executive's leading style and trust cooperation culture. So it is of no use being eager for quick success and instant benefit.

As the function of the institution basically still lies in solving trust problems between individuals (Yamagishi and Yamagishi, 1994), the nature of institution-based trust, which includes trust in the professional group and trust in a common person in a specific society, is the trust in people generated by people's trust in the institution of society. In essence, firm trust lies in every detail of management activities. Trust is not a kind of independent resource, it is either included in the integrated cultural value system of society or comes into being as a result of long-term relation contracts and choice of tactics. The development of the enterprise is influenced by the integrated trust structure of society, which helps form the microenvironment belonging only to the trust structure through the business or connection with the firm organization. This is a process of mutual trust choice between the group staff. Besides, the mutual trust among the owner and the manager and the employees inside the company may affect the growth of the enterprise as well. According to the environments it depends on, the effective communication of inside information is the necessary condition for the smooth operation of the enterprise. To ensure a successful communication, information should not only be delivered but also understood. So the communication mechanism of the enterprise is also affected by the information structure. Talent, loyalty, virtues, charity and friendliness are the fundamental components that constitute trust. Talent only means that one has 'the ability to do such a thing' and the other four mean 'the willingness to do such a thing for me'. People can be only trusted on the condition that they are capable and of good virtue. So obviously the establishment and perfection of the trust mechanism inside the enterprise depend on the above components. So-called dependence refers to the following: (1) the staff have these qualities; (2) it is known that the staff have had them at the same time. The value standard and measures that the enterprise adopts, according to these two requirements, are basic methods where the enterprises develop a mutual trust mechanism, that is the mechanism of training, culture and inside information. As a result, institution-based trust can not only promote common trust in society and achieve prosperity in the country (Fukuyama, 1995), but also help achieve stratification of organizations and the standardization and legalization of management in the family enterprise.

REFERENCES

Berle, A. and G. Means (1932), *The Modern Corporation and Private Property*, New York: World, Inc.

Cao, D.J. (2002), 'Theoretical problems on the studies of family firms', *Finance and Economics*, (6), 55-60.

Chandler, A.D. (1977), *The Visible Hand: The Managerial Revolution in American Business*, Cambridge, MA: Belknap.

Chu, X.P. (2000), 'Research on family enterprises: a topic of modern meanings', *Sociology in China*, (5), 51-8.

Chu, X.P. (2002), 'Professional executives and the growing-up of family enterprises', *Management World*, (4), 100-108.

Chu, X.P. (2003), 'The development of family enterprises and integration with the social capital', *Economics Theory and Management*, (6), 45-51.

Fan, H.P. (1995), *Chinese Ethnic Spirits*, Taiwan: Taipei Wunan Publishing Company.

Fukuyama, F. (1995), *Trust: The Social Virtues and the Creation of Prosperity*, NewYork: Free Press.

Fukuyama, F. (1998), *The Great Disruption: Human Nature and the Reconstitution of Social Order*, New York: Free Press.

Hamilton, G. (1991), *Business Networks and Economic Development: East and Southeast Asia*, Centre of Asian Studies, Hong Kong University.

He, A.X. (2003), 'Review on the hot discussion about Chinese family business', *China Business Times*, 28 January.

Hwang, G.G. (1988), *Games of Power Among Chinese*, Taiwan: Taibei Juliu Publishing House.

Lee, K.H. (2001), 'The Chinese family business in S-E Asia', http://courses.nus.edu.sg/course/geoywc/publication/Star.html.

Lee, K.H. and C.-B. Tan (eds) (2000), *The Chinese in Malaysia, Shah Alam*; Oxford University Press.

Li, Jianli (2002), 'The succession problems and strategies of family business', *China Business*, (9), 30-35.

Li, X.C. (2002a), 'Trust and choices of developing modes', *Reform of Economy Institution*, (1), 51-5.

Li, X.C. (2002b), 'Trust, loyalty and the dilemma of clanism', *Management World*, (6), 87-156.

Li, X.-C.(2003), 'Trust and random choice on the firm's growth methods, *Reform of Economic Institutions*, (1).

Li, X.C. and J.Hu (2000), 'Restrictions of the control power on the growth of the company. *Nankai Business Review*, (3), 18-23.

North, D. (1995), 'Theoretical outlines of institutional evolution', *Reform*, (3), 52-6.

Penrose, E.T. (1959), *The Theory of the Growth of the Firm*, Oxford: Blackwell.

Redding, G. (1993), *The Thoughts of Management of Overseas Chinese Entrepreneurs –the Cultural Background and Style*, Shanghai: Shanghai Joint Publishing Company Limited

Shapiro, S.P. (1987), 'The social control of impersonal trust', *American Journal of Sociology*, **93**(3), 623-58.

Su, Q.L. and X.M. Ou (2002), The present situation of the studies of the family enterprises in the west', *Foreign Economies and Management*, (12), 6-12.

Weber, M. (1951), *The Religion of China: Confucianism and Taoism*, New York: Free Press.

Wei, Q. (2001), 'A general introduction to the recent studies of family enterprises and family-styled management in China', *Scientific Research*, (5), 14-18.

Yamagishi, T., and M. Yamagishi (1994), 'Trust and commitment in the United States and Japan', *Motivation and Emotion*, (18), 130-166.

Yang, G.S. and A.B. Yu (1993), *Chinese Psychology and Action – Ideas and Methods*, Taiwan: Taipei Guiguang Publishing Company.

Yu, Bo (1988), 'Psychological analysis on traditional family identification', *Research of History*, (4), 24.

Zhang, H.Y., L.Y. Ming and C.Y. Ling (2002, 2003), *A Report on the Development of Chinese Private Companies (2001, 2002)*, China: Sociology Literature Publishing House.

Zhang, W.Y. (2001), 'Strengthen the construction of executive teams', *Management and Fortune*, (2), 34.

Zheng, B.X. (1995), 'Different structure and Chinese organizational behaviors', *Research on Psychology*, (2), 78-93.

Zheng, Y.F. (2001), *Trust Theory*, Beijing: China Radio and Television Publishing House.

13. The subsidiary role of multinational enterprises and procedural justice

Tai-Ning Yang and Chuan-Ling Kang

1. INTRODUCTION

Significant changes to the corporate operational environment in past decades have prompted multinational corporations (MNCs) to pursue the foreign direst investment of strategic assets to strengthen and establish their ownership edge. Investments include those that are directed at accessing knowledge-intensive assets and learning experience (Dunning, 2001) and those that are aimed at enhancing competitiveness by acquiring specific technical capabilities (Wesson, 1999). However, all investment activities need to establish parent-subsidiary relationships and solve management issues such as the sharing of assets across borders, subsidiary autonomy, and the inter-organizational flow of resources (Kimberly, 2000). Roth, Schweiger and Morrison (1991) found that the sharing of management concepts within MNCs has a significant effect on the outcome of global strategy implementation. In addition, the organizational climate also affects the global strategy implementation result. Quelch and Hoff (1986) suggested that 'friendly persuasion, needs to be used to change the organizational climate to underpin the complex decision making process within MNCs. Empirical studies have proved the importance of the quality of communications between MNC headquarters and subsidiaries to the innovation process (Ghoshal and Bartlett, 1988; De Meyer, 1993) and to global marketing innovations (Kashani, 1990).

In Kim and Mauborgne's (1993a) research, procedural justice in the strategy planning process had positive effects on the work attitude, commitment, trust, and outcome satisfaction of the subsidiary's management team. This is a result of the subsidiary's top management's perception that headquarters exercised procedural justice by involving them in the decision planning process and higher levels of outcome control (Hundley and Kim, 1997; Gupta and Govindarajan, 1991). Organizational behavior researchers applied concepts from social psychology and law and established a positive relationship between procedural justice and organizational commitment (Dailey and Kirk, 1992; Konovsky et al. 1987; Sweeney and McFarlin, 1993). Other studies have also found procedural justice and job satisfaction, organizational citizenship behavior and work performance to be positively related (Colquitt et al., 2001).

Subsidiary units play different strategic roles in the MNCs'worldwide network based on differences in competition in the local environment, industry competition in the host country, importance of the host country, and the competitiveness and resources they possess (Bartlett and Ghoshal, 1986, 1989; Kim and Mauborgne, 1995; Gupta and Govindarajan, 1991). However, apart from work carried out by Kim and Mauborgne (1995) and Taggart (1997), little research has been done regarding the specific role subsidiaries play and how effective communication can be leveraged to enhance operational efficiency. This portends the cross-sectional nature of such research (Birkinshaw and Hood, 2000). It is also indicative of the conventional practice of seeing a subsidiary role as being allocated by the parent company.

MNCs are global network organizations (Chen and Chen, 1998; Birkinshaw, 1996; Dunning, 1996, 2001). More research needs to be done on how procedural justice contributes to the outcome of strategy implementation in the global network of multinational companies. Existing studies associated with the roles that subsidiaries play classify the latter according to the know-how involved in managing the multinational network (Gupta and Govindarajan, 1991) or subsidiary competitiveness in the host country (Bartlett and Ghoshal, 1989). However, such classification schemes fail to take into account subsidiaries that are set up to obtain strategic assets, or the significance of the industrial environment and technical standard in the host country regarding MNC competitiveness (Porter, 1990, 1998). Therefore, this study sets out to explore ways to identify the strategic roles of subsidiary units, exercise effective procedural justice principles, and enhance the effectiveness of corporate strategy implementation.

The organizational structure of multinational companies has changed from a superior/subordinate relationship between parent company and subsidiaries to a network of co-dependent relationships (Dunning, 1996, 1998; Furu, 2000). An organizational climate that induces value sharing and effective and sufficient communication has become a vital management issue (Taggart, 1997). The above are also critical factors in decision-making and implementation (Meschi and Roger, 1994; Hassard and Sharifi, 1989).

With respect to the global strategy planning process of MNCs, researchers have turned their academic focus from value sharing and communication to exercising procedural justice (Kim and Mauborgne, 1993a; Taggart, 1997; Birkinshaw, 2002). However, a consistent base for studies concerning the theoretical foundation and the principles of effective procedural justice during the strategic planning processes carried out by MNCs is lacking. Furthermore, as the MNC organizational structure differs in different countries due to location-specific features and operational motivations, there is a lack of existing literature covering the strategic roles of subsidiary units and procedural justice. Thus, this study hopes to complement relevant research in this field.

2. CONCEPTUAL BACKGROUND

2.1 Procedural Justice

Folger and Cropanzano (1998) defined procedural justice as an issue that is concerned with the methods, mechanisms and fair procedures involved in the decision making process. Procedural justice theories link procedural justice judgements to fairness of the rules and procedures adopted to distribute outcomes. This also suggests that the procedural effect is independent of its outcome (Cohn et al., 2000). The importance of relevant principles used to judge procedural justice differs with the nature of the forum (Brockner and Wiesenfeld, 1996).

Erdogan et al. (2001) pointed out that procedural justice is built on two theoretical bases, that is control theory and the group-value model. In control theory (Thibaut and Walker, 1975) it is assumed that individuals prefer to be in control over events that affect them, that is they want to be in control of decision making processes rather than being passive recipients. The group value model (Lind and Tyler, 1988) argues that group members want to be seen as valued individuals. The level of procedural justice is judged by a person's perceived status and respect within his or her group. Procedures are important because they are indicative of the relationship between an individual and his or her group.

Therefore, it follows that procedural justice is determined by the condition of such relationships. A fair procedure provides positive relationship data (Blader et al., 2001). Relationship elements of status recognition, neutrality and trust are typically used to assess the degree of justice of a given procedure (Tyler et al., 1996). The higher the elements, the better the perceived relationship between an individual and his/her organization. Process control as the core judgement criterion of procedural justice stresses the outcome, while the individual/group relationship as the core element of procedural justice emphasizes the influence of a collective group of people on individual identification with the group.

2.2   The Effect of Procedural Justice on the Subsidiary Strategy Implementation

Procedural justice as a universal value has already been established by existing studies (Lind and Tyler, 1988; Morris and Leung, 2000; Tyler et al., 1997). However, its application in the management of multinational companies went through a complex evolution process (Taggart, 1997). Garnier had already shown the importance of management theory with regard to the MNC headquarters/subsidiaries relationship back in 1982 (Garnier, 1982). Later, Roth et al. (1991) proved that an integrated mechanism that encourages sharing of management concepts bore significant results in the implementation of global strategies. Bartlett (1981) stressed the importance of changing the organizational climate to underpin the complex decision making process in MNCs. Quelch and Hoff (1986) described this process of change as 'friendly persuasion'. With regards to studies regarding the quality of communication between MNC headquarters and subsidiaries, Ghoshal and Bartlett (1988) and De Meyer (1993) claimed that effective com munication plays a significant role in innovation. Kashani (1990) found that communication has a similar effect in terms of the global marketing strategic innovations at MNC headquarters.

Existing research suggests that procedural justice enhances subsidiary compliance (Thibaut and Walker, 1975, 1978; Lind et al. 1973; Thibaut et al., 1974). This can be further elaborated from two aspects. The first is the long-term, self-interest perspective proposed by Lind and Tyler (1988). The subsidiary's top management trusts that their headquarters exercise procedural justice in the strategy making process. They are confident that subsidiary concerns, priorities and opinions will be taken into consideration. Hence subsidiary units believe that decision outcomes are not merely based on politics. Confidence in the long term that not only corporate interests but also subsidiary interests are advanced in the corporate decision making processes and by the outcomes motivates compliance with the strategic decisions (Kim and Mauborgne, 1993a, 1993b).

The second is based on the principles of interaction (Thibaut and Walker 1975, 1978) and the social exchange theory (Blau, 1964). According to Blau, the subsidiary's top management's belief that MNC headquarters exercise procedural justice in the strategy making process raises the former's perception of fairness of the resulting decisions. Satisfaction would make the subsidiary's top management more inclined to take responsibility and reciprocate with fair responses and behavior.

2.3 Subsidiary Roles

Overseas subsidiary units of MNCs assume different roles with the accumulation of resources, the development of specific capabilities, and differences in host country environment in the subsidiary evolution process as well as different investment objectives (Hedlud, 1986; Prahalad and Doz, 1981). Subsidiaries may also assume different responsibilities and play roles of varing importance in the multinational network (Bartlett and Ghoshal, 1986; Jarillo and Martinez, 1990; White and Poynter, 1984). Difference in the role of subsidiaries in the operational process and system of MNCs can be explained from three perspectives: the product life cycle (Vernon, 1966), the internationalization process of firms (Johanson and Vahlne, 1977), and the network model (Forsgren et al., 1992; Bartlett and Ghoshal, 1991).

The product life cycle model shows that overseas subsidiary roles shift with the stages through which individual products develop over time. Subsidiaries either introduce the products to overseas markets, or manufacture to export the goods back to the parent country, or engage in high value-added product research and development (Harrigan, 1984; Vernon, 1979). The internationalization process model is rooted in the behavior theory of the firm (Cyert and March, 1963). It elaborates the evolution through which multinational firms reached international markets (Agarwal and Ramaswami, 1992; Aharoni, 1966; Cavusgil and Nevin, 1980). The decision variables in this model include knowledge of foreign markets, commitment of resources to international markets, and commitment to future development (Johanson and Vahlne, 1977).

According to the internationalization process model, the subsidiary role is determined by the firm's commitment to invest. The market knowledge possessed by a subsidiary is indicative of its competitive advantages and disadvantages. Commitment to continued investment and learning enhances subsidiary development capability and affects the importance of subsidiaries in the organizational structure and the operational performance of MNCs (Birkinshaw, 1997).

The third theoretical base, the network model, asserts that it is possible for subsidiaries to become a leader within the MNC network or to reach a status on a par with the parent company. The core resources may be developed or acquired by subsidiary units and do not necessarily exist within the boundaries of the parent company (Rugman and Verbeke, 1992). The resources possessed and the competitiveness of subsidiaries affect MNC operations as MNCs are an interorganizational network (Bartlett and Ghoshal, 1991).

The classification scheme in existing studies regarding the subsidiary's strategic role varies. Some differentiate subsidiaries based at corporate level (Bartlett and Ghoshal, 1986) and some at subsidiary level (Birkinshaw and Morrison, 1995; Jarillo and Martinez, 1990). White and Poynter (1984) classified subsidiaries into five strategic roles with regard to the scope of product, market and value added activities. Their framework was applied at the subsidiary level as in subsequent studies by Birkinshaw and Morrison (1995) and Jarillo and Martinez (1990). The research findings offer sources of guidance in subsidiary development for its managers.

Bartlett and Ghoshal's (1986) analysis focused on the corporate level. They suggested an organizational model of differentiated subsidiary roles. Subsidiaries play four different types of roles based on the significance of their national environment to the company's global strategy and their local competence. Since this study follows the view that MNCs are an interorganizational network, our analysis is based on the corporate level. The significance of a subsidiary's national environment is determined by the importance of its national market, competitive positioning (Bartlett et al., 2003), and the spatial embeddedness of knowledge and learning (Porter, 1998). These are all strategic concerns of MNCs. In addition, subsidiaries' possession of strategic assets owned by MNC headquarters also reflects the former's significance within the global organizational network. Thus, this study identified the strategic roles played by subsidiaries in the MNC global network using two criteria: the core resources and capabilities possessed by subsidiaries and the importance of a subsidiary's national environment to the MNC's long-term operation.

3. RESEARCH HYPOTHESIS

3.1 The Relationship between Procedural Justice and Strategy Implementation Effectiveness

The exercise of procedural justice enhances the ability of MNCs to collect, interpret and judge the strategic information required to achieve strategic goals. Hence effective procedural justice contributes positively towards the formulation of global strategies (Kim and Mauborgne, 1993a, 1993c). The global strategic goals of MNCs are quite diverse. Drawing from relevant studies, Ghoshal (1987) listed three strategic goals: (1) global learning benefits, the creation, diffusion, sharing and re-creation of knowledge through the operational activities of the MNC global network; (2) global operational efficiency, developed through international scale economies, international scope economies, and organizational learning across national markets; (3) operational flexibility, to raise MNCs' capability to cope with unexpected problems through leveraging and cross-subsidiaries when operating across borders.

Kim and Mauborgne (1993a, 1993c) found that bilateral communication between headquarters and subsidiary top management helps the transfer of views, knowledge, professional skills and experience. This sharing of knowledge and ideas is conducive to the distribution of global experiences (Ghoshal and Bartlett, 1988). MNC headquarters are more inclined to pursue efficiencies from global perspectives while subsidiaries tend to respond to country-specific demands (Prahalad, 1976; Doz, 1980). Hence a high level of two-way communication is critical to balancing global operational efficiency and responsiveness to country-specific demands. The diversity of both sides in terms of background, experience and perspectives enhances the capability to cope with unexpected risks (Prahald and Doz, 1987).

The exercise of procedural justice allows subsidiary top management to legitimately challenge the strategic views of the headquarters, who can not pressure subsidiaries into following MNC practices. Thus both sides enjoy a balanced relationship. Also, the tendency to follow past experiences in the decision making process and to stick to existing strategic orientations will change as subsidiaries refute such practices. This expands the strategic flexibility needed to manage risks. Headquarters who are well informed about the local situations of subsidiaries are less likely to pursue global efficiencies at the cost of subsidiaries by making incorrect decisions that fail to identify national differences (Bartlett and Ghoshal, 1987). Thus, efficiency and responsiveness is balanced (Bartlett and Ghoshal, 1990).

In addition, if headquarters are consistent in making decisions across subsidiaries, subsidiary top management feels trusted, inspiring favorable attitudes towards cooperation and problem solution on both sides. Trust also fosters active commitment to contribute to the information required in the decision making process by sharing knowledge, skills and experiences. Thus, the scope of operation, organizational flexibility, as well as learning effects are expanded and strengthened. By obtaining detailed interpretation on the decision making process and decision outcome, subsidiaries are made aware of the head office management's concerns and why the latter's actions were not guided by subsidiary-level perspectives. Thus a process of organizational learning, or a feedback loop is formed to bridge mutual differences, allow headquarters to attend to subsidiary local situations, and enhance the capability and commitment to learn on both sides (Daft and Weick, 1984). In the meantime bilateral balance of strategic goals is achieved.

Based on the above, procedural justice should motivate subsidiary commitment to implement corporate decisions. Thus, it is conducive to global learning, operational efficiency and operational flexibility, three vital elements in MNC global strategies, and demonstrates positive effects on the effectiveness of strategy implementation at the subsidiary level.

Hypothesis 1. The exercise of procedural justice in the MNC strategy planning process has a positive effect on strategy implementation effectiveness

3.2   The Relationship between Subsidiary Strategic Roles, Procedural Justice and Strategy Implementation Effectiveness

The international environment within which corporates operate has witnessed substantial changes during past decades. Expansion into foreign markets has become the prerequisite for survival in certain industries as a consequence of emerging social, economic and technological trends. Continued survival and profit income for many firms can be best pursued by capturing new technologies and reacting positively to new market opportunities (Bartlett and Ghoshal, 2000). Interorganizational leveraging and cross-subsidizing are increasingly important for corporates to cope with fluctuations in national environments and to enhance competitive edge (Kogut, 1985b).

The MNC as an organizational network (Andersson and Forsgren, 2000) motivates the division of labor with each subsidiary unit attending to local situations and individual expertise. The subsidiary units are interdependent. One of the unique features of MNCs is that the complex and obscure resources and capabilities of each subsidiary are transferable (Kogut and Zander, 1996; Andersson et al., 2001). Dunning's (1993) eclectic theory also states that the competitive edge created by common governance is a ownership-specific advantage unique to MNCs.

The resource-based theory claims that the unique and heterogeneous core resource of a firm is critical to its continued existence and a vital factor in strategy selection (Prahalad and Hamel, 1990; Stalk, Evans and Shulman, 1992; Hamel and Prahalad, 1985). In addition to the core resources subsidiary units obtain from the multinational network, they must also possess the capability to respond to local environments for sustained existence (Nelson and Winter, 1982). Those who have to cope with harsh local conditions or complex situations develop advanced levels of capabilities and resources (Bartlett and Ghoshal, 1986, 1989; Ghoshal and Nohria, 1989). This, in turn, influences the progress of other group members through the interorganizational resource transference mechanism (Bartlett and Ghoshal, 1989). Thus the subsidiary with higher levels of capability emerges as the center of excellence in the multinational network (Surlemont, 1996).

Porter's (1990) diamond theory explains the conditions governing the performance of a specific economic region. To MNCs, the diamond theory highlights the importance of national positions in a given industry to innovation and technical advances. Bartlett and Ghoshal (2000) suggested that global learning of MNCs is one of the strategic goals in creating corporate competitive advantages. Other concerns associated with MNC investments in specific countries or markets include developments of key technology, advances in the industry, and the major rivalries. In addition to the above, MNCs also give thought to location-specific characteristics such as natural resources, other vital resources required for operation, market scope, and productivity.

Based on the above discussions, this study classifies the subsidiary units of MNCs into different strategic roles. Based on the model developed by Bartlett and Ghoshal (1986) and the two variables, the importance of host country environment to MNCs and the level of MNC core resources possessed by subsidiary, we differentiate subsidiaries into strategy leaders, innovators, detectors and implementers.

Strategic leaders are played by subsidiaries located in a strategically important market and possess a high level of core resources. They are granted a high degree of autonomy (Gupta and Govindarajan, 1991) and play critical roles in the formulation of global strategies (Ghoshal and Nohria, 1989). MNCs must take care not to hamper the unique competitiveness of this type of subsidiary by limiting its development. A positive environment that is favorable towards the inflow of knowledge from subsidiary to headquarters and a feedback loop must exist for the former to play its role well (Bartlett and Ghoshal, 1989). There should be bilateral communication, respect and a mutual sense of dependence. Subsidiaries can challenge or refute the strategic views of headquarters and express their own view. Hence, an environment in which a high degree of procedural justice is perceived should be present in the strategy formulation process (Kim and Mauborgne, 1993a, 1995).

In contrast, implementers are subsidiaries that do not possess any of the MNC core resources and that are located in strategically unimportant markets. Therefore, the effect of procedural justice on their strategy implementation results is not as high as strategic leaders. Innovators are subsidiaries that possess MNC core resources but that are not located in strategically important markets. Subsidiaries are knowledge exporters. Detectors are subsidiaries that are located in strategically important markets but import core resources from the headquarters.

Hypothesis 2. *The subsidiary's strategic role has a moderating effect on procedural justice exercised in the MNC strategy planning process and strategy implementation*

4. RESEARCH METHOD

4.1 Research Variables

The variables employed in this study include procedural justice, the subsidiary role, and strategy implementation effectiveness. They are defined and measured as follows.

Procedural justice is the extent to which an MNC's strategy planning process is perceived to be fair by subsidiary top management. The model developed by Kim and Mauborgne (1993a) was used in this study. Each of the two variables, process control and group relationship, were associated with three items. Strategy implementation effectiveness was measured by the extent to which the following corporate strategic goals were satisfied: global learning, overall operational efficiency, corporate operational flexibility and responsiveness to location-specific demands. The classification criteria suggested by Bartlett and Ghoshal (1986) and the model developed by Yip (1995) were adapted for use by this study. The three variables were global learning, overall operational efficiency and corporate operational flexibility, with a total of nine items. The subsidiary role referred to the strategic roles subsidiaries play within the MNC organizational network. The roles were measured through two variables: the possession of MNC core resources and the strategic importance of the host country environment. The model developed by Roth and Morrison (1992) and Birkinshaw and Hood (2000) were refined for this study. Respondents were asked to assess the extent to which (1) subsidiaries were responsible for product development and innovation; (2) corporate product experts were present at the subsidiary; (3) subsidiary managers were actively involved in the decision making process at headquarters; (4) subsidiary managers attend closely to the flow of technology and products within the organizational network. The strategic importance of the subsidiary host country environment to the MNC was measured using four items: source of industry technology, major product market, competitive interaction, and important production site. Responses to these questions were rated on a 7-point Likert scale with scale anchors 1 for 'strongly disagree'and 7 for 'strongly agree'. An aggregate index and indices for each of the variables were computed by summing the responses using factor analysis and principal component analysis.

4.2 Sample and Data Collection

Fifteen firms with foreign investments from the Hsinhu Science Park were selected for pre-testing using the convenience sampling method. The completed questionnaires were assessed for content, reliability and validity using statistical methods. The pre-tested and amended questionnaires were used for the full study. Firms with corporate headquarters based in Taiwan, Japan and the US were solicited using the purpose sampling method. Eight hundred questionnaires were distributed to subsidiary executives in Singapore Industrial Park in Suzhou and Kunshan Industrial Park in Shanghai with assistance from park administrations. Overall 390 were returned, 42 of which contained invalid or incomplete information. A total of 358 valid surveys were received, giving an effective response rate of 44.75 per cent. Of all the valid responses, 25 had parent companies located in countries other than Taiwan, Japan and the US, leaving only 333 as the final set of data for analysis.

The information industry accounts for the largest proportion of respondent firms with 100 companies, or 27.93 per cent; the electrical machinery industry with 63 companies, or 17.60 per cent; the electric and cable industry with 40 companies, or 11.17 per cent; the plastic industry with 32 companies, or 8.94 per cent; the textile industry with 31 companies, or 8.66 per cent; the transportation industry with 32 companies, or 8.94 per cent; the food industry with 24 companies, or 6.7 per cent; the construction industry with 2 companies, or 0.56 per cent; the chemical and pharmaceutical industry with 10 companies, or 2.79 per cent; the glass and ceramic industry with 9 companies, or 2.51 per cent; and 15 companies from other industries, making up the final 4.19 per cent. As to the nationality of the parent companies, 237 are Taiwanese, accounting for 66.20 per cent of total respondents. Japan comes second with 65 companies or 18.16 per cent; the US, 31 companies or 8.66 per cent. The remaining 25 companies, or 6.98 per cent of all those surveyed had parent companies based in other parts of the world.

4.3 Data Validity and Reliability

The confirmatory factor analysis method was applied to examine construct validity (Hair et al., 1995). Cronbach's alpha was used to test reliability and to observe the cognitive manifest behavior of the subsidiary and parent company under the latent factors. The index of intensity score of each variable was constructed through principal component analysis. The scores were used to measure the variables for subsequent analysis as well as to re-examine the validity of the models.

The dimensions of the variables were used as latent factors and the items in the models as explicit variables to construct the measurement model. The model fitness was measured by the GFI (goodness of fit) value and AGFI (GFI adjusted for degrees of freedom) values, which were both above the lowest acceptable value of 0.7 (Hair et al., 1995). The chi-square values for the models were significant, indicating overall fit was acceptable. Statistical results indicate high reliability. Cronbach's coefficient alpha for the variables was all above 0.8, revealing satisfactory levels of reliability (Nunnally, 1978). Results provide evidence that the models are accepted as valid and reliable in presenting the latent factors.

4.4 Subsidiary Roles

The variables of interest in this part were the level of MNC core resources possessed by subsidiaries and the importance of host country environment to MNCs. The values of the responses were transformed into principal component scores, which were then compared with the sample mean. The respondent firms were classified into four different groups according to the result of the comparison. The first group, strategic leaders, was composed of subsidiaries that possess higher levels of core resources owned by the parent company and operate in host country environments that are strategically important to the parent company. Innovators were characterized by subsidiaries with higher levels of core resources but located in strategically less important countries. Detectors were subsidiaries with lower levels of core resources but located in strategically important countries. Implementers were subsidiaries with lower levels of core resources and located in strategically less important countries. The number of firms in each of the four categories was 51, 65, 46 and 171, respectively.

5. ANALYSIS AND DISCUSSION

5.1 The Relationship between Procedural Justice and Strategy Implementation Effectiveness

Regression analysis was used to explain the effect of procedural justice on the result of strategy implementation and the three associated items: global learning, overall operational efficiency, and corporate operational flexibility. The results are shown in Table 13.1. The regression coefficient of procedural justice is 0.298, positive and significant ($p<0.01$). Results support Hypothesis 1. The exercise of procedural justice in the strategy planning process at the corporate level exerts a positive significant influence on the effectiveness of strategy implementation at the subsidiary level.

Table 13.1   Regression analysis of procedural justice and strategy implementation effectiveness

Dependent variable: Strategy implementation effectiveness	ß	t	R^2	F
Independent variable: Procedural justice	0.298	2.254**	0.209	45.42**

Notes: ** P<0.01

The next step tests the effect of procedural justice on strategic goals including global learning, overall operational efficiency and global operational flexibility. Table 13.2 demonstrated the regression coefficient for global learning effect and overall operational efficiency, which are statistically significant at 0.168 and 0.315, respectively (P<0.001). Results show that the exercise of procedural justice during the corporate strategy planning process exerts a significant positive influence on encouraging global learning and increases overall operational efficiency. However, the coefficient for corporate operational flexibility was not significant at 0.087 (P>0.05). Results show that the level of influence that procedural justice exerts on corporate operational flexibility was not significant during the corporate strategy planning process.

Global learning in MNCs transfers the knowledge and skills developed by a specific unit to the entire organizational network. Its benefits are now critical strategic assets (Bartlett and Ghoshal, 1986; Dunning, 1996). Knowledge and skills are intangible assets that are uncodified and embedded into the organizational network. Hence a consistent attitude and subsidiary compliance are required to reap the benefits of global learning from operating in diverse international markets (Kim and Mauborgne, 1993a).

Results found that a two-way communication between corporate headquarters and subsidiaries fosters the exchange of management ideas, knowledge and technology as well as encouraging attention to comments from the other side. This promotes the building of consensus and consistent attitudes (Kerr and Slocum, 1987). The diffusion of ideas and knowledge enhances global learning. The pursuit of overall operational efficiency by achieving global economies of scale and scope and utilizing competitive edges to respond to differentiated markets requires subsidiary compliance and identification with the corporate objective. Therefore, the exercise of procedural justice has a positive and significant influence on the result of strategy implementation as it motivates subsidiary compliance with corporate decisions (Kim and Mauborgne, 1993b).

MNC headquarters that are well informed of the subsidiary's local conditions formulate strategies that are guided by location-specific concerns. Decisions that are guided by headquarters' subjective judgments and those that fail to respond to local differences will not be made. The sharing of knowledge and collaboration between organizational group members foster favorable results in balancing local responsiveness and operational efficiency. MNCs generate ownership advantage by adjusting the subsidiary's operational activities in accordance with major supplier or customer demands or react to moves made by main competitors under the common governance structure (Dunning, 1988). The effect of procedural justice in this respect was not supported by the findings of this study. The benefits of competitive positioning, leverage and cross-subsidy (Bartlett and Ghoshal, 1986; Kogut, 1985b) must overcome government policy restrictions. They are reaped by firms that face global competition (Bartlett and Ghoshal, 2000). The lack of support for this hypothesis could be because the respondent firms are located in mainland China, where government policy is still fairly restrictive. Also, the competitive environments within which the surveyed firms operate are not set in a global context. Nevertheless, MNC headquarters will need to promote further integration and coordination within the global competitive interaction in the long term.

Table 13.2   Result of regression analysis of procedural justice and global learning, overall operational efficiency, and corporate operational flexibility

Dependent variable: Global learning	ß	t	R^2	F
Independent variable: Procedural justice	0.168	2.122**	0.171	41.66**
Dependent variable: Overall operational efficiency	ß	t	R^2	F
Independent variable: Procedural justice	0.315	2.973***	0.272	51.98***
Dependent variable: Corporate operational flexibility	ß	t	R^2	F
Independent variable: Procedural justice	0.087	1.214	0.038	3.17

Notes: ** $p < 0.01$ *** $p < 0.001$

5.2 The Moderating Effect of Subsidiary Strategic Roles

The next phase of analysis explores the moderating effect of the different strategic roles (as strategic leaders, innovators, detectors and as implementers) that subsidiaries assume on the link between procedural justice and strategy implementation effectiveness.

Following the recommendations of Baron and Kenny (1986), the moderating effect caused by the moderating variable on the relationship between the dependent and independent variables is assumed to be linear. The roles are used as dummy variables to test the influence of moderating variables and their strength on subsidiary roles. First, strategic leaders are taken as the base, followed by innovators, detectors and implementers, with values of 1,0,0; 0,1,0; 0,0,1. Second, implementers as the base group, followed by strategic leaders, innovators and detectors with values of 1,0,0; 0,1,0; 0,0,1. Lastly, innovators as the base, followed by strategic leaders, detectors and implementers, with values of 1,0,0; 0,1,0; 0,0,1.

Table 13.3 shows that when a subsidiary's strategic role changes from strategic leader to innovator, detector and implementer, the regression coefficients changed from 0.253 to –0.193, –0.177 and –0.223, respectively. The coefficients are all negative and statistically significant. This shows that subsidiary strategic roles exert a moderating effect on procedural justice and strategy implementation effectiveness. The exercise of procedural justice generates a greater degree of positive influence on the strategy implementation effectiveness of strategic leaders when compared to implementers, innovators and detectors.

Table 13.3   The moderating effect of subsidiary strategic role on procedural justice and strategy implementation effectiveness (base: strategic leader)

Dependent variable: Strategy implementation effectiveness	ß	t	R^2	F
Independent variable: Procedural justice	0.253	2.447**	0.264	61.45***
Procedural justice × Innovator	–0.193	1.976*		
Procedural justice × Detector	–0.177	1.872*		
Procedural justice × Implementer	–0.223	2.271**		

Notes: *** $p<0.001$,** $p<0.01$,* $p<0.05$

Table 13.4 shows that when a subsidiary's strategic role changes from implementer to strategic leader, innovator and detector, the regression coefficients changed from 0.137 to 0.223, 0.157 and 0.166, respectively. The coefficients are all positive and statistically significant ($p<0.05$). This shows that subsidiary strategic roles exert a moderating effect on procedural justice and strategy implementation effectiveness. The exercise of procedural justice generates a greater degree of positive influence on the strategy implementation effectiveness of innovators and detectors when compared to implementers.

Table 13.4 *The moderating effect of subsidiary strategic role on procedural justice and strategy implementation effectiveness (base: implementer)*

Dependent variable: Strategy Implementation effectiveness	ß	t	R^2	F
Independent variable: Procedural justice	0.137	2.117**	0.279	59.87**
Procedural justice × Strategic leader	0.223	2.097**		
Procedural justice × Innovator	0.157	1.762*		
Procedural justice × Detector	0.166	1.624*		

Notes: ** $p<0.01$,* $p<0.05$

Table 13.5 shows that when a subsidiary's strategic role changes from innovator to strategic leader, detector and implementer, the regression coefficients changed from 0.131 to 0.193, 0.032 and –0.157, respectively. Only the second (detector) is not statistically significant ($p<0.05$). This shows that the moderating effect exists, but no significant difference was found between the transformation from innovator to detector. Hence the results support Hypothesis 2.

Table 13.5 *The moderating effect of subsidiary strategic roles on procedural justice and strategy implementation effectiveness (base: innovator)*

Dependent variable: Strategy implementation effectiveness	ß	t	R^2	F
Independent variable: Procedural justice	0.131	2.256**	0.215	58.33***
Procedural justice × Strategic leader	0.193	1.976*		
Procedural justice × Detector	0.032	0.675		
Procedural justice × Implementer	–0.157	1.762*		

Notes: *** $p<0.001$,** $p<0.01$,* $P<0.05$

Numerous published works have suggested that the core knowledge and technical capabilities of MNCs are embedded in specific locations (Porter, 1990; Chen and Chen, 1998; Wesson, 1999; Holm et al. 1995; Furu, 2000). Competitive interaction and rivalry in a global setting means that firms attach special importance to major markets, major competitors, or major clients (Bartlett and Ghoshal, 2000). Therefore, the strategic roles played by subsidiaries may be location-specific. Taggart's (1997) study on autonomy and procedural justice indicated a strong relationship between the degree of autonomy a subsidiary enjoys and the level of perceived procedural justice it demands. The findings of this research support that subsidiaries of different strategic roles exert different levels of influence on the link between procedural justice and the effectiveness of strategy implementation. Evidence supports the importance of bilateral communication and the effect of strategic roles on communication content.

6. CONCLUSION

The objective of this study was to explore the relationship between independent variable (procedural justice) and dependent variable (strategy implementation effectiveness). The strategic role of subsidiaries is employed as the moderating variable to clarify the relationship between independent and dependent variable.

Findings support the hypothesis that the exercise of procedural justice during the strategy planning process of multinational corporations improves the efficiency of strategy implementation. According to our data, subsidiary top management's perception of procedural justice in strategy formulation at corporate headquarters leads to compliance with strategy implementation. Organizational commitment is inspired and so are feelings of trust in head office management. Social harmony between subsidiary and head office is generated. These are all vital elements and the basis for effective strategy implementation within the mutually dependent relationship of the multinational organizational network (Kim and Mauborgne, 1993a).

In other words, the exercise of procedural justice during the strategy formulation process generates subsidiary commitment and compliance to the decision outcomes. Subsidiary managers are inspired to identify with corporate strategic objectives and achieve those objectives. Therefore, it pays for corporate headquarters to attend to procedural justice in the strategy-planning process to enhance the effectiveness of strategy implementation across borders. Subsidiary managers pay close attention to the 'fairness' perceived in the strategy planning process and respond accordingly.

The current study started by suggesting that subsidiaries play different strategic roles according to the strategic importance of their national environments and their possession of core resources. They are classified into strategic leaders, innovators, detectors or implementers. Their differentiated roles indicate multiple tasks and dispersed responsibilities. Therefore, corporate headquarters should communicate with subsidiary managers to build consensus regarding the long-term development strategies. Research results found that the strategic roles exert varying levels of moderating effect on procedural justice and the effectiveness of strategy implementation. Perception of subsidiary units as merely strategy implementers and failure to apply appropriate communication approaches to subsidiaries of different strategic goals will hamper the effectiveness of strategy implementation. Hence, in order to generate more satisfactory strategy implementation results, corporate headquarters should retain less direct control, attend more closely to strategy formulation procedures, and grant more flexibility by adopting different management measures and communication approaches in accordance with the strategic roles of the subsidiaries.

REFERENCES

Agarwal, S. and S.N. Ramaswami (1992), 'Choice of foreign market entry mode: impact of ownership, location and internalization factors', *Journal of International Business Studies*, **23**(1), 1-27.

Aharoni, Y. (1966), 'The foreign investment decision process', *Interna-tional Executive*, **8**(4), 13-17.

Andersson, U. and M. Forsgren (2000), 'In search of centre of excellence: Network embeddedness and subsidiary roles in multinational corporations', *Management International Review*, **40**(4), 329-50.

Andersson, U., M. Forsgren and U. Holm (2001), 'Subsidiary embeddedness and competence development in MNCs: Multi-level analysis', *Organization Studies*, **22**(6), 1013-34.

Baron, R.M. and D.A. Kenny (1986), 'The moderator-mediator variable distinction in social psychological research: Conceptual, strategic, and statistical considerations', *Journal of Personality and Social Psychology*, **51**(6), 1173-82.

Bartlett, C.A. (1981), 'Multinational structural change: Evolution versus reorganization', in L. Otterbeck (ed.), *The Management of Headquarters – Subsidiary Relationships in Multinational Coporations*, Aldershot, UK: Gower, 138-46.

Bartlett, C.A. and S. Ghoshal (1986), 'Tap your subsidiaries for global reach', *Harvard Business Review*, **64**(6), 87-94.

Bartlett, C.A. and S. Ghoshal (1987), 'Managing across borders: new strategic requirements', *Sloan Management Review*, **28**(4), 7-17.

Bartlett, C.A. and S. Ghoshal (1989), *Managing across Borders: The Transnational Solution*, Boston: Harvard Business School Press.

Bartlett, C.A. and S. Ghoshal (1990), 'Matrix management: Not a structure, a frame of mind', *Harvard Business Review*, **67**(4), 138-45.

Bartlett, C.A. and S. Ghoshal (1991), 'Global strategic management: Impact on the new frontiers of strategy research', *Strategic Management Journal*, **12**(4), 5-16.

Bartlett, C.A. and S. Ghoshal (2000), *Transnational Management: Text, Cases, and Readings in Cross-Border Management* (3rd edn), NewYork: McGraw Hill.

Bartlett, C.A., S. Ghoshal and J. Birkinshaw (2003), *Transnational Management: Text, Cases, and Readings in Cross-Border Management* (4th edn), NewYork: McGraw Hill.

Birkinshaw, J.M. (1996), 'How multinational subsidiary mandates are gained and lost', *Journal of International Business Studies*, **27**(3), 467-95.

Birkinshaw, J.M. (1997), 'Entrepreneurship in multinational corporations: The characteristics of subsidiary initiatives', *Strategic Management Journal*, **18**(2), 207-30.

Birkinshaw, J.M. (2002), 'Managing internal R&D networks in global firms: What sort of knowledge is involved?', *Long Range Planning*, **35**(3), 245-67.

Birkinshaw, J.M. and N. Hood (2000), 'Characteristics of foreign subsidiaries in industry clusters', *Journal of International Business Studies*, **31**(1), 141-55.

Birkinshaw, J.M. and A.J. Morrisons (1995), 'Configurations of strategy and structure in subsidiaries of multinational corporations', *Journal of International Business Studies*, **26**(4), 729-54.

Blader, S.L., C.C. Chang and T.R. Tyler (2001), 'Procedural justice and retaliation in organizations: Comparing cross-nationally the importance of fair group process', *International Journal of Conflict Management*, **12**(4), 295-311.

Blau, P.M. (1964), *Exchange and Power in Social Life*, New York: Wiley.

Brockner, J. and B.M. Wiesnfeld (1996), 'An integrative framework for explaining reactions to decisions: Interactive effects of outcomes and procedures', *Psychological Bulletin*, **120**(2), 189-208.

Cavusgil, S., N. Tamer and R. John (1980), 'Internal determinants of export marketing behavior: An empirical investigation', *Journal of Marketing Research*, **18**(1), 114-19.

Chen, H. and T.J. Chen (1998), 'Research in international business: Problems and prospects', *Journal of International Business Studies*, **29**(1), 5-20.

Cohn, E.S., S.O. White and J. Sanders (2000), 'Distributive and procedural justice in seven nations', *Law and Human Behavior*, **24**(5), 553-679.

Colquitt, J.A., M.J. Wesson, O.L.H. Christopher, D.E. Porter, K. Conlon, Yee Ng, and E. Donald, (2001), 'Justice at the Millennium: A meta-analytic review of 25 years of organizational justice research', *Journal of Applied Psychology*, **86**(3), 425-45.

Cyert, R.M. and J.G. March (1963), *A Behavioral Theory of the Firm*, Englewood Cliffs, New Jersey: Prentice-Hall.

Daft, R.L. and K.E. Weick (1984), 'Toward a model of organizations as interpretation system', *Academy of Management Review*, **9**(2), 284-95.

Dailey, R.C. and D.J. Kirk (1992), 'Distributive and procedural justice as antecedents of job dissatisfaction and intent to turnover', *Human Relations*, **45**(3), 305-17.

De Meyer, A. (1993), 'Management of an international network of industrial R&D laboratories', *R&D Management*, **23**(2), 109-20.

Doz, Y.L. (1980), 'Strategic management in multinational companies', *Sloan Management Review*, **21**(1), 27-46.

Dunning, J.H. (1988), *Explaining International Production*, London: Unwin Hyman.

Dunning, J.H. (1993), *The Globalization of Business*, London and New York: Routledge.

Dunning, J.H. (1996), 'The geographical sources of competitiveness of firms: The results of a new survey', *Transnational Corporations*, 5(3), 1-29.

Dunning, J.H. (1998), 'Location and the multinational enterprise: A neglected factor?', *Journal of International Business Studies*, 29(1), 45-66.

Dunning, J.H. (2000), 'The eclectic paradigm as an envelope for economic and business theories of MNE activity', *International Business Review*, 9(1), 163-90.

Dunning, J.H. (2001), 'The eclectic (OLI) paradigm of international production: Past, present and future', *International Journal of the Economics of Business*, 8(2), 173-90.

Erdogan B., M.L. Kraimer and R.C. Liden (2001), 'Procedural justice as a two-dimensional construct: An examination in the performance appraisal context', *Journal of Applied Behavioral Scence*, 37(2), 205-22.

Folger, R. and R. Cropanzano (1998), *Organizational Justice and Human Resource Management*, Thousand Oaks, California: Sage.

Forsgren, M., U. Holm, and J. Johanson (1992), 'Internationalization of the second degree: The emergence of European-based centers in Swedish firms', in S. Young and J. Hamill (eds), *Europe and the Multinationals*, Aldershot UK and Brookfield, US: Edward Elgar.

Furu, P. (2000), 'Integration of technological competence in the MNC: The role of the subsidiary environment', *Management International Review*, 40(1), 7-27.

Garnier, G.H. (1982), 'Context and decision making autonomy in the foreign affiliates of US multinational corporations', *Academy of Management Journal*, 25(4), 893-908.

Ghoshal, S. (1987), 'Global strategy: An organizing framework', *Strategic Management Journal*, 8(5), 425-40.

Ghoshal, S. and C.A. Bartlett (1988), 'Creation, adoption, and diffusion of innovations by subsidiaries of MNCs', *Journal of International Business Studies*, 19(3), 340-42.

Ghoshal, S. and N. Nohria (1989), 'Internal differentiation within multinational corporations', *Strategic Management Journal*, 10(4), 323-38.

Gupta, A.K. and V. Govindarajan (1991), 'Knowledge flows and the structure of control within multinational corporations', *Academy of Management Review*, 16(4), 768-92.

Hair, J.F., R.E. Anderson, R.L. Tatham and W.C. Black (1995), *Multivariate Data Analysis*, Englewood Cliffs, New Jersey: Prentice Hall.

Hamel, G. and C.K. Prahalad (1985), 'Do you really have a global strategy?', *Harvard Business Review*, 63(4), 139-48.

Harrigan, K.R. (1984), 'Innovation within overseas subsidiaries', *Journal of Business Strategy*, 4(4), 47-55.

Hassard, J. and S. Sharifi (1989), 'Corporate culture and strategic change', *Journal of General Management*, 15(2), 4-19.

Hedlund, G. (1986), 'The modern MNC: A heterarchy', *Human Resource Management*, 25(1), 9-35.

Holm, U., J. Johanson and P. Thilenius (1995), 'Headquarters' knowledge of subsidiary network contexts in the multinational corporation', *International Studies of Management and Organization*, 25(1,2), 97-106.

Hundley, G. and J. Kim (1997), 'National culture and the factors affecting perceptions of pay fairness in Korea and the United States', *International Journal of Organizational Analysis*, **5**(4), 325-41.

Jarillo, J.C. and J.I. Martinez (1990), 'Different roles for subsidiaries: The case of multinational corporations in Spain', *Strategic Management Journal*, **11** (7), 501-12.

Johanson, J. and J.E. Vahlne (1977), 'The internationalization process of the firm: A model of knowledge development and increasing foreign market commitments', *Journal of International Business Studies*, **8**(1), 23-32.

Kashani, K. (1990), 'Why does global marketing work – or not work?', *European Marketing Journal*, **8**(2), 150-55.

Kerr, J. and J.W. Slocum (1987), 'Managing corporate culture through reward system', *Academy of Management Executive*, **1**(2), 99-108.

Kim, W.C. and R.A. Mauborgne (1993a), 'Effectively conceiving and executing multinationals' worldwide strategies', *Journal of International Business Studies*, **24**(3), 419-48.

Kim, W.C. and R.A. Mauborgne (1993b), 'Making global strategies work', *Sloan Management Review*, **34**(3), 11-27.

Kim, W.C. and R.A. Mauborgne, (1993c), 'Procedural justice, attitudes, and subsidiary top management compliance with multinationals' corporate strategic decisions', *Academy of Management Journal*, **36**(3), 502-26.

Kim, W.C. and R.A. Mauborgne (1995), 'A procedural justice model of strategic decision-making: Strategy content implications in the multinational', *Organization Science*, **6**(1), 44-62.

Kimberly, M.E. (2000), 'Strategic content, knowledge flows and the competitiveness of MNCs: A procedural justice approach', *Competitiveness Review*, **10**(1), 9-24.

Kogut, B. (1985a), 'Designing global strategies: Comparative and competitive value-added chains', *Sloan Management Review*, **26**(4), 15-28.

Kogut, B. (1985b), 'Designing global strategies: Profiting from operating flexibility', *Sloan Management Review*, **26**(1), 27-38.

Kogut, B. and U. Zander (1996), 'What firms do? Coordination, identity, and learning', *Organization Science*, **7**(5), 502-19.

Konovsky, M.A., R. Folger and R. Cropanzano (1987), 'Relative effects of procedural and distributive justice on employee attitude', *Representative Research in Social Psychology*, **17**(1), 15-24.

Lind, E.A. and T.R. Tyler (1988), *The Social Psychology of Procedural Justice*, New York: Plenum.

Lind, E.A., J.W. Thibaut and L. Walker (1973), 'Discovery and presentation of evidence', *Adversary and Nonadversary Proceedings*, **71**, 1129.

Meschi, P.X. and A. Roger (1994), 'Cultural context and social effectiveness in international joint ventures', *Management International Review*, **34**(3), 197-215.

Morris, M.W. and K. Leung (2000), 'Justice for all? Progress in research on cultural variation in the psychology of distributive and procedural justice', *Applied Psychology: An International Review*, **49**(1), 100-132.

Nelson, R.R. and S.G. Winter (1982), 'The Schumpeterian tradeoff revisited', *The American Economic Review*, **72**(1),114-33.

Nunnally, J.C. (1978), *Psychometric Theory*, New York: McGraw-Hill.

Porter, M.E. (1990), *The Competitive Advantage of Nations*, New York: Free Press.

Porter, M.E. (1998), 'Clusters and the new economics of competition', *Harvard Business Review*, **76**(6), 77-90.

Prahalad, C.K. (1976), 'The strategic process in a multinational corporation', Unpublished doctoral dissertation, Harvard, University, 67-78.

Prahalad, C.K. and Y.L. Doz (1981), 'An approach to strategic control in MNCs', *Sloan Management Review*, **22**(4), 5-13.

Prahalad, C.K. and Y.L. Doz (1987), *The Multinational Mission-balancing Local Demands and Global Vision*, New York: Free Press.

Prahalad, C.K. and G. Hamel (1990), 'The core competence of the corporation', *Harvard Business Review*, **68**(3), 79-91.

Quelch, J. and E. Hoff (1986), 'Customizing global marketing', *Harvard Business Review*, **64**(3), 59-68.

Roth, K. and A.J. Morrison (1992), 'Implementing global strategy: Characteristics of global subsidiary mandates', *Journal of International Business Studies*, **23**(4), 715-36.

Roth, K., D.M. Schweiger and A.J. Morrison (1991), 'Global strategy implementation at the business unit level: Operational capabilities and administrative mechanisms', *Journal of International Business Studies*, **22**(3), 369-402.

Rugman, A.M. and A. Verbeke (1992), 'A note on the transnational solution and the transaction cost theory of multinational strategic management', *Journal of International Business Studies*, **23**(4), 761-71.

Stalk, G., P. Evans and L.E. Shulman (1992), 'Competing on capabilities: The new rules of corporate strategy', *Harvard Business Review*, **70**(2), 54-65.

Surlemont, B. (1996), 'The influence of strategic centers of excellence in MNCs: The role of the organizational context', dissertation abstracts, *Journal of International Business Studies*, **27**(4), 823-24.

Sweeney, P.D. and D.B. McFarlin (1993), 'Workers' evaluations of the ends and the means: An examination of four models of distributive and procedural justice', *Organizational Behavior and Human Decision Processes*, **55**(1), 23-40.

Taggart, J.H. (1997), 'Autonomy and procedural justice: A framework for evaluating', *Journal of International Business Studies*, **28**(1), 51-76.

Thibaut, J.W. and L. Walker (1975), *Procedural Justice: A Psychological Analysis*, Hillsdale, New Jersey: Erlbaum.

Thibaut, J.W. and L. Walker (1978), 'A theory of procedure', *California Law Review*, **66**(3), 541-66.

Thibaut, J., N. Friedland and L. Walker (1974), 'Compliance with rules: Some social determinants', *Journal of Personality and Social Psychology*, **30**(4), 792-801.

Tyler, T.R., R.J. Boeckmann and Y.J. Huo (1997), *Social Justice in a Diverse Society*, Boulder, Colorado: Westview.

Tyler, T.R., P. Degoey and H. Smith (1996), 'Understanding why the justice of group procedures matters: A test of the psychological dynamics of the group-value model', *Journal of Personality and Social Psychology*, **70**(5), 913-20.

Vernon, R. (1966), 'International investment and international trade in the product cycle', *Quarterly Journal of Economics*, **80**(3), 191-207.

Vernon, R. (1979), 'The product cycle hypothesis in a new international environment', *Oxford Bulletin of Economics and Statistics*, **41**, 255-67.

Wesson, T. (1999), 'A model of asset-seeking foreign direct investment driven by demand conditions', *Revue Canadienne des Sciences de l'Administration*, **16**(1), 1-10.

White, R.E. and T.A. Poynter (1984), 'The strategies of foreign subsidiaries: Responses to organizational slack', *International Studies of Management and*

Organization, **14**(4), 91-106.

Yip. G.S. (1995), *Total Global Strategy:Managing for Worldwide Competitive Advantage*, New Jersey: Prentice-Hall Inc.

14. The history and prospects of international business education in Japan and in the Asian region

Noritake Kobayashi

1. EARLY HISTORY

It was in the late 1950s when business school type executive education was first introduced in Japan by faculty members of the Harvard Business School. I was told then that in the expanding cold-war situation between Western and Eastern countries and the attendant confrontation of capitalist and socialist ideologies, Harvard felt it would be very important to develop a cadre of managers of free enterprises as a bulwark against the onslaught of communism. The first top management seminars were held in 1957 in both Tokyo and Manila. These endeavors led to the establishment and development of Keio University Business School in Tokyo and the Asian Institute of Management in Manila, which became the first professional business schools in Asia.

An international business management course was added to the curriculum of the Keio Business School in 1962 and I was asked to teach this course. It was the first time that a course with this title was officially offered at a Japanese university. Before that time there were only courses related to international business (IB) activities including courses focusing on international economics and international trade issues.

The 1970s and 1980s were the golden years for the development of a board-based IB education in Japan. The Japanese business community and the government became richer as a result of rapid economic growth, and both gained confidence in extending international endeavors.

In the Japanese government, the Ministry of International Trade and Industry (MITI) established an expert research workshop (MITI workshop) in the early 1970s to study and research issues related to MNCs. This was due to the MITI realization that world markets would be controlled by MNCs and that Japanese businesses had to develop into MNCs before it became too late. The workshop had undertaken extensive questionnaire surveys and field research in Japan, the US as well as European and Asian countries. I served as the chairman of the workshop for nearly ten years and our efforts resulted in the publication of my book, *The Japanese Multinational Corporation* (Kobayashi, 1980). For some years this book served as a standard data book for the study of Japanese multinationals.

Almost at the same time MITI also established the Institute for International Studies and Training (IIST) at the foot of Mount Fuji. MITI tried to respond to the expanding demand for the development of Japanese managers versed in dealing with international activities. I had participated in the planning and early implementation stages of this institution. It is noteworthy that in the formative years of the Institute, a number of Academy of International Business (AIB) members assisted the Institute in developing its curriculum. AIB members who taught at the Institute included John Fayerweather, Richard Farmer, Lee Nehrt, Richard Robinson and Hans Schollhammer.

In the meantime, in 1972, an interdisciplinary group of scholars and practitioners interested in MNC study and research organized the Workshop for the Study of Multinational Enterprises. This workshop still exists and its initial membership of 30 has grown to more than 150. For more than ten years I served as the chairman of the workshop. In the 1990s, a second IB study group was organized. This group relies more on members of the academic community and they focus on a wide range of IB issues.

2. IB EDUCATION IN JAPAN AND ASIA

For my investigation of IB education in Japan I chose six business schools, including the Keio University Business School, the International University of Japan, Aoyama University, Hitotsubashi University, Kobe University and Waseda University. Keio and the International University have 30 to 40 years of history, whereas the other IB programs were launched in the late 1990s in response to the demand for MBA-type professional executive development.

My teaching experiences in Asia are limited to the position I held at AIM in Manila. But by doing research on the web I subsequently added several other reputable Asian business schools to my sample, including the China European International Business School (CEIBS), the Chinese University of Hong Kong, Nanyang Technical University in Singapore, Sasib Business School in Chilongkorn, Thailand and Yonsei University in Korea.

3. APPROACHES TO IB EDUCATION IN ASIA

In general, many of the business schools in Asia, including Keio and AIM, modeled their programs on those of Western business schools, the Harvard Business School and the business school in Asia in particular, have more or less followed a similar approach. I have found that the earlier the founding of an Asian business schools, the stronger is the influence of the program from which ideas were imported.

4. MISSION STATEMENT OF JAPANESE AND ASIAN BUSINESS SCHOOLS

Many Japanese and some Asian business schools have expressed at the preparation of students for the internationalization age is a very important aspect of their mission. However, it must be noted that there is frequently a disconnect between what is proclaimed in the mission statement and what is actually done with regard to curriculum development to support the stated goal.

5. THE ORGANIZATION OF IB EDUCATION IN JAPAN

Some Japanese business schools, including the International University, Hitotsubashi, Aoyama and Waseda, emphasized their international orientation by labeling the school or a department with the prefix 'international business'. In contrast, at many other schools IB consisted of nothing more than a simple survey course and at best offering a major or minor IB concentration without offering at the same time a reasonably comprehensive course program.

6. INTEGRATION AND POSITION OF IB COURSES IN THE BUSINESS CURRICULUM

Initially many Asian business schools recognized IB as the core course in their curriculum; they established an independent academic area and offered IB as a major or minor area of concentration. But after Harvard abolished IB as an independent area in its curriculum, many business schools in Asia adopted an 'infusion approach' by incorporating international business issues in a spectrum of functional courses.

When I taught at the Keio Business School, I had a serious discussion with my colleagues about whether or not IB should be retained as one of the core areas and maintained as a major or minor field of concentration. Some of my colleagues contended that business is business everywhere, implying that there is not really a need for a separate IB curriculum. They argued that in the age of globalization, many businesses operate across borders and thus the retention of courses focusing solely on international business issues would be old fashioned and out of date. In return I maintained that if they were correct in assuming that IB had become perfunctory and its importance diminished, then we should be seeing fewer international trade disputes and intra-company management difficulties related to doing business across borders. But this is not the case. If anything, international issues are more prevalent than ever. Until I retired from Keio several years ago, IB was kept intact as a major and minor field of concentration. But now I am somewhat disappointed to see that the only course bearing the IB name is a survey course in the doctoral program. It is some consolation, however, that IB-related matters are still taught at Keio using the 'infusion approach', incorporating IB material in the basic functional courses, and almost all the functional courses have same international content.

7. NEW APPROACH TO DEFINE THE IB AREA

Japanese universities such as Hitotsubashi, Kobe and Aoyama have recently offered courses in an interdisciplinary, composite form with titles such as 'global innovation and knowledge sharing', 'global entrepreneurship' and 'global corporate governance and socially responsible management'. I think this is a much better concept than the 'infusion approach', which incorporates IB materials in the basic functional courses. By adopting certain current topics as course titles the focus is clearer and, in addition, the solution of any recent IB problems requires a broader understanding of issues surrounding the main issue.

8. FURTHER DIRECTION OF RESEARCH IN IB EDUCATION

On the occasion of the 30th Anniversary of the Workshop for the Study of MNCs, I examined the opinion of IB scholars inside and outside Japan concerning what will be necessary for international business research and education in the twenty-first century. The issues discovered seem to be centered on a series of questions that can be summarized as follows:

1. Do the theories and practices developed in the 'internationalization age'continue to work in the 'age of globalization'?
2. How do we promote the creation and utilization of knowledge assets on a cross border basis?
3. All the new problems related to 'globalization' need to be reconsidered; for example, how can we adapt management to the requirements of 'new economy countries'?
4. What is the role of strategic alliances, mergers and acquisitions?
5. How do MNCs develop clear 'global standards' and a more effective corporate governance system in order to deal with the complexity associated with global management?

9. CONCLUDING REMARK

About 40 years ago, when a structured approach to IB education was introduced at a few Japanese universities, the initial effort was aimed at addressing three concerns: (1) to survey and to some extent emulate educational endeavors in some western countries, foremost the United States; (2) to examine the possibility of guiding the evolution of Japan-centered multinational firms; (3) to integrate existing concepts that deal with international business activities as reflected in international trade theories and theories of foreign direct investment.

During the early years of IB education in Japan, prominent topics to dealt with are: (a) the relationships between the firms' headquarters in Japan with their overseas operating units; (b) the operating conditions in the 'triad countries', that is the United States, Western Europe and Japan; (c) the internationalization in the manufacturing industries with gaining market access and improving the firms' overseas market position as dominant objectives.

In more recent years, the issues to be dealt with in IB education (and the related research endeavors) have broadened significantly. For example, a good deal of attention centers now on: (a) how to manage the integrated global business network activities; (b) how to develop business in the 'new economy countries', particularly in China; (c) the internationalization and management of firms in the financial sector and in service industries; (d) the management of strategic alliances, mergers and acquisitions; (e) the optimization of synergy effects from regional or global business activities; (f) the behavior and social responsibilities of internationally operating firms. In addition, there exists a broad-based recognition that Japanese businesses, which have long relied on the homogeneity of the workforce as a source of competitive strength, must change to a new policy of working with managers and employees of diverse origins as a result of progressing globalization. It requires a big change of the traditional Japanese mindset.

As international business education evolved, various theories, paradigms and conceptual frameworks have been advocated that were designed to explain the reasons for foreign direct investments and the peculiarities of managing foreign operations. For example, Ray Vernon's product life cycle theory and John Dunning's eclectic paradigm come to mind. These conceptualizations have been very useful for analyzing and explaining a wide range of IB issues. However, the ever-changing conditions and the dynamics of international business activities will require new theories and conceptualizations that will shape international business education. A major concern in the evolution of new conceptual approaches will have to center on an explanation and prediction of successful business performance in an international business context.

In the past, Japan has been successful by evolving a holistic and integrated strategy towards its industries, foreign trade and outward investment. I use the term 'holistic' because it was built on a collaborative effort between business, the government and the society at large to achieve the most effective results. Although the days of 'Japan Inc.' are gone, there is still a need to form and implement a renewed holistic approach. This conceptualization cannot be based on the traditional function-specific approach that merely leads to sub-optimization of outcomes in one business area or another. The challenge is to develop a new approach that incorporates environmental, behavioral, structural and institutional perspectives that will lead to an optimization of outcomes that serves the interests of business, the government and society as a whole.

In my view, future IB education must aim to provide Japanese business with a clear strategic orientation, emphasizing a global mindset and a recognition of the interdependence of various perspectives – the sum of which can be characterized as a 'holistic approach'. If and when IB education is successful in meeting this challenge, then international business courses and international business areas will form the core and be at the center of business school curricula.

NOTES

1. MITI is now reformed and renamed as METI (The Ministry of Economy, Trade and Industry).
2. This article was prepared by the author on the basis of his presentation which was prepared and presented for session:2.3.5-panel (The Birth of the Field of International Business Education) at the 2004 AIB Stockholm Conference.

REFERENCES

Business Week, 'B-School applications are MIA', 18 April 2005.

Dunning, J. (2000), 'The eclectic paradigm as an envelope for economic and business theories of MNE activity', *International Business Review*, **9**, 163-90.

Fortune, 'The trouble with MBAs', 30 April 2007.

International Business Education in the 1990s: A Global Survey (1993), sponsored by the Academy of International Business, The American Assembly of Collegiate School, of Business Education and Research University of South Carolina.

Kobayashi, N. (1980), *Nihon no Takokuseki Kigyo (the Japanese Multinational Corporation)*, Tokyo: Chuo Keozaisha.

Kobayashi, N. (1985), 'The pattern of management style development in Japanese multinationals in Japanese multinationals in the 1980s, in S. Takamiya and K. Thurley. (eds), *Japan's Emerging Multinationals*, Tokyo University Press.

Kobayashi, N. (2007), Japanese International Corporation, Tokyo: Chuo Keozaisha.

Kobayashi, N. (ed.) (1997), *Management: A Global Perspective*, Tokyo: The Japan Times.

Kobayashi, N. (2005), *Beikojuniokeru Takokusekikigyo no Kenkyu Kyouiku no Genjyou* (The Present Status of Research and Education on Multinationals in the United States), Sekaikeizai Hyouron, August.

Kobayashi, N. et al. (ed.) (2003), *New Dynamics of Multinationals in the 21st Century*, Tokyo: Diamond International Management Institute.

Loustarinen, R. and T. Pulkkinen (eds) (1991), *International Business Education in European Universities in 1990*, Helsinki School of Economics and Business Administration.

Nehrt, L. (1977), *Business and International Education*, A Report submitted by the Task Force on Business and International Education to the Government/Academic Interface Committee, International Education Project American Council of Education, Occasional Paper No.4.

Robook, S.M. and L. Nehrt (eds) (1964), *Education in International Business*, Bloomington, Indiana: Graduate School of Business, Indiana University.

Skipchandler, Z.E. (ed.) (1976), 'International directory: schools of business administration', *The Academy of International Business*.

Thanopoulos, J. and J.W. Leonard (eds) (1986), 'International business curricula: a global survey', *Academy of International Business*.

Vernon, R. (1966), 'International investment and international trade in the product cycle', *Quarterly Journal of Economics*, **80**(2), 190-207.

15. Globalization and higher education: some strategies adopted by Waseda University

Ken'ichi Enatsu

In this contribution, I would like to discuss the impact of globalization on higher education, with particular reference to some strategies adopted by Waseda University.

As all of you may agree with my observation, the effects of globalization (or internationalization) are not limited to the business sector. They are clearly and drastically influencing the world of education as well. The universities around the world today are facing an era of intensive competition beyond national borders. In this 'age of hyper competition' in the borderless twenty-first century society, the competition among universities involving education, research and management is moving well beyond the domestic arena.

In its 10 September, 2005 issue, the prestigious British business journal *The Economist* ran a special feature on 'the brains business'. In it, the article compared the symbolic significance of today's inter-university competition with that of globalization in the world of business.

Globalization in business originally began with an enterprise starting with import/export activities and licensing, and setting up service centers and production/sales facilities overseas, and the location of R&D and of head office functions. Internationalization has been regarded as something that then is developed from point to line to plane in a three-dimensional effort. This analogy could also be applied to the globalization of higher education.

Essentially, the internationalization of universities is synonymous with the international academic exchange, and networking between students and faculty members, through study abroad programs as its main objective. Increasing the number of overseas partner institutions represents 'point internationalization'. Waseda University, for example, currently boasts exchange agreements with over 450 institutions in more than 70 countries around the world.

Yet this kind of international exchange could easily become inactive, being individual, random and spontaneous in nature. To avoid such risks, we at Waseda University have been complementing our international programs for the past 15 years with overseas campuses in Bonn, Germany, and Portland, Oregon, USA. More recently, we have set up outposts with diverse functions in Seoul, Beijing, Shanghai, Singapore, Bangkok and Paris. Through these endeavors, Waseda has achieved 'line internationalization', serving the needs of both students and faculty.

The age of hyper competition requires not only the business but also the academic sector to conduct quality-based internationalization in education and research, based on specific strategies and vision. As Waseda University pursues its vision to become 'the top University in Japan, one of the top ten in Asia, and one of the top 100 in the world' in the near future, it will also contribute to the 'symbiotic creation of knowledge in the Asia-Pacific region' by 'investigating and constructing a practical framework for internationalization' based on this mission. This requires our engaging in strategic collaborative action with outstanding universities around the world.

To make the most of its university brand value in China, Waseda University started out with joint student recruitment, then joint lectures, and then moved on to launching an undergraduate double-degree program and graduate-level collaborative education with Peking University. It is now implementing similar joint programs with Fudan University, National Taiwan University and Nanyang Technological University, thereby promoting 'plane internationalization'.

In addition, Waseda University is committed to enhancing worldwide collaboration, with top-class research exchanges with Italian researchers, and membership in an international consortium of higher education based in Italy; and with joint educational projects between the industry, government, and academia and the management of a multinational research center in Singapore, in pursuing a 'three-dimensional internationalization'. This has required a common passion for the Waseda University system, where not only the International Affairs Division but also the Academic Affairs, Research Promotion, Finance Divisions, and other related university officers are holistically contributing to these efforts.

In Japan, globalization presupposes increased competition among universities, in order to overcome demographic decline, the increasing porosity of national borders and of international competition between institutions of higher education. Universities could not survive such an age without taking the appropriate measures to accommodate changes and challenges.

The big question for Waseda University is, inevitably, 'What is the core competence for our university in internationalization?' It is my belief that the schematic road map for a university to win totally in the global contest lies in these five keywords: vision, mission, action, passion and succession.

The 'university power' or international academic competence primarily consists of the following three abilities:

1. Educational competence, or the readiness to provide attractive curricula that are competitive with major universities around the world, for students both from Japan and other countries; and to cultivate and produce leaders able to think and act globally;
2. Research competence, or the power to conduct and promote joint research with international research organizations and major institutions of higher learning, while, at the same time, acquiring external funding, with a high profile of third-party evaluation;
3. Managing competence, or establishing proper governance for internationalization projects, and implementing educational goals as a business enterprise.

There is currently public demand for universities to create and enhance their involvement in 'the brains business' that caters to the evolving needs/wants of the global research and education markets.

Let me turn to consider some facts about Waseda University. The University was founded in 1882, and today is one of the oldest private universities in Japan. It consists of 11 undergraduate schools, 17 graduate schools, two high schools, three affiliate high schools and two schools of arts and architecture. It caters for about 54 000 students, with around 5000 faculty and 750 administrators. Waseda is the second largest university in Japan.

Waseda University is proud to have nearly half a million alumni worldwide. Over its long history, it has produced seven Prime Ministers in Japan, and many famous politicians, business leaders, scientists, artists, novelists and other influential persons in various fields all over the world.

As I have already mentioned, Waseda University has signed agreements with more than 450 universities around the world. This had been beneficial in creating mutual networks for the students and faculty going to and coming from abroad.

While international exchange has been conducted individually and spontaneously, a more sophisticated approach toward internationalization, based on the unique strategies and vision of the university, is becoming increasingly necessary.

For this purpose, we have targeted the following issues as the focal points in promoting internationalization, namely:

- To enhance intercultural exchange on a daily basis
- To establish a new School of International Liberal Studies
- To promote more educational projects overseas
- To promote joint education and research programs with overseas institutions
- To encourage the acceptance of international students, and the sending of Waseda students abroad, and
- To encourage the recruitment of researchers from overseas universities

The objective of a daily international exchange of students and faculty is to nurture global citizens, That is to say, to make 'a practical effort to cultivate active intellectuals with global competence'.

Waseda University believes that global competence is made up of the following five components.

- Acquiring applicable strategic skills
- Forming diverse, resourceful human networks
- Establishing a focused system of education for Asian students (specific to language, custom, religion, tradition, and so on)
- Developing a globally competent frame of mind (positive thinking, can-do spirit, intercultural communication skills)
- Moving toward knowledge-creating education and training

The formation of a Cyber University Consortium (CUC) is one practical attempt to achieve this goal. This is a consortium of universities in Asia and the Pacific region, promoting mutual exchange in joint lectures, research, students and researchers. One of the most interesting features of the CUC is that it is supported by two of Waseda's affiliated commercial companies, WUI (Waseda University International) and WLS (Waseda University Learning Square).

Waseda University has also established another consortium called DCC (Digital Campus Consortium): this is a corporate consortium for realizing a new university model for the twenty-first century, based on information networking in which major companies like NTT Comware, Sony BB Solutions, IBM Japan, NEC, NEC Soft, Panasonic and YOKOGAWA are participants.

The concrete educational program for this intercultural exchange on a daily basis is joint seminars with overseas partner institutions, and lectures by distance learning. We have named it Cross-Cultural Distance Learning

(CCDL) in which we offer cyber lectures and seminars with partner institutions to carry out discussions on fields of specialization in foreign languages. It is also a place for improving practical international communication skills through a common foreign language (English, Chinese, Russian, and so on).

In this connection, we have developed three practical tools for the intercultural exchange.

i. Method 1 (Tutorial Language Learning): includes approximately 10 000 Waseda students participating in the academic year 2005. In order to develop English negotiation techniques, we provide rigorous training to a small group of students to improve their speaking skills. The class size is four students with one native teacher.
ii. Method 2 (Online Chat): Real-time online chatting with overseas partner institutions on the World Wide Web, this is undertaken at least once a week (for about 45 minutes), on a wide range of topics such as current affairs, fashion, lifestyles, campus life, culture, education and social values.
iii. Method 3 (Video Conferencing): Real-time, two-way joint seminars which make use of the teleconferencing system, for lectures in specialized subjects, as well as language learning.

Waseda's second strategy for promoting international exchange is the newly established School of International Liberal Studies launched in 2004.

This school has two major missions. One is for arts education, for acquiring a fundamental knowledge of a wide range of subjects, and encouraging academic thinking by studying contemporary issues by exposure to advanced, updated learning.

The second one is to nurture global leaders with vision. This mission caters for a student body of 30 to 40 per cent international students. The classes are conducted in English. There is a one-year study abroad requirement; foreign language courses in 21 languages (besides Japanese and English) are offered as well as diverse internship programs at companies, local administrative offices, NGOs, and so on.

As I mentioned before, the university is aiming to strengthen the following three competences to cope with global hyper competition. Namely,

1. *Academic Competence*, with an attractive and competitive curriculum not only for the Japanese, but also for students all over the world. Such a curriculum should nurture and produce graduates able to succeed globally.
2. *Research Competence*, which includes collaboration with international

organizations and leading universities around the world, able to attract external funding such as from multinational corporations.

3. *Administrative Competence*, with firmly established financial governance in global enterprises; and the acceptance that higher education should be regarded as an industry.

Waseda is earnestly pursuing each of these goals through its internationalization programs.

Our goals concerning international student exchange are as follows:

- *Outbound*: To promote Waseda students studying abroad: we hope to send 3000 students abroad in 2007.
- *Inbound*: To recruit skilled human resources from foreign countries: our goal is to accept 3000 international students in 2007.

To realize these goals, Waseda University has set out the following requirements.

- *For Inbound Students*: all required coursework should be completed in English; research/office space should be secured, and the information environment maintained/provided; more scholarships to be offered; appropriate housing and accommodation to be secured.
- *For outbound students*: better information to be provided about available study abroad destinations.

Needless to say, promoting acceptance of visiting researchers from overseas is the most important issue Waseda University needs to challenge. In short, its basic strategy for enhancing global competence is in one phrase: 'Exposing Waseda's research and education to the global market'.

Waseda University is now trying to move on to the third stage of plane internationalization. In pursuing this stage, it has established various bases around the world to fulfill the following four areas of activities.

1. *Developing and offering academic programs for recruiting good students from overseas*; encouraging short-term study abroad programs: preparatory training, twinning programs, double-degree programs;establishing overseas degree programs: undergraduate, postgraduate.
2. *Developing and offering academic programs for nurturing students with international competence*; developing long-term and short-term study abroad programs; double-degree programs with partner institutions.
3. *Collaborative research, promoting industry-academia joint projects (such as with multinational corporations), securing external funding*;

promoting unique, specialized research; promoting collaboration between the industrial and academic sectors.

4. *Student recruitment and public relations activities*; dissemination of information for increasing public recognition for the Waseda brand name;recruitment activities conducted throughout the year; part of the student admission (candidate selection) from overseas.

Lastly, I would like to touch upon the three-dimensional internationalization approach of Waseda University. For this purpose, the university has initiated a variety of overseas educational projects. These include:

i. An Affiliated Senior High School – Waseda Shibuya Senior High School (established April 2002) in Singapore.
ii. A Preparatory program for studying in Japan – Waseda Education (Thailand) (established April 2003). This program has provided mainly Japanese language instruction.

The University has also promoted various joint academic programs abroad. These have included:

- Dual degree programs with partner universities.
- Joint doctoral program with Peking University (since September 2002).
- Double-degree programs with Peking University and Fudan University (since September 2005).
- Joint MOT (Management of Technology) program with Nanyang Technological University, in Singapore (from July 2006).

The University also has a joint bioscience research venture with Olympus Corporation in Singapore, and has begun a joint research organization with Peking University.

To accomplish its goals for promoting overseas enterprises, the University appreciates that there is need for the strategic concentration of its limited human and financial resources, and for its priorities to be carefully decided upon. It also needs: to set up a system for promoting overseas enterprises and enhancing university management; to increase collaboration with other administrative divisions (for example the Academic Affairs, Research Promotion, and Finance) within the university system. It must promote an integrative management of overseas campuses; and finally it must secure the necessary funds for these plans and their fulfillment.

These are just some of the strategies Waseda is trying to adopt in its attempt to be competitive in the global market place. Both the opportunity and challenge for universities like our own are very considerable indeed;

and as in the business world, only those with vision and an international perspective can hope to succeed.

In conclusion, to what extent, we might ask, are Waseda University's internationalization experiences consistent with the received paradigms and theories of MNE activity? The answer is very much so. Let us briefly illustrate with reference to the dynamic version of John Dunning's eclectic paradigm. Dunning (2002) has described some of Waseda University's ownership (O) specific advantages, in terms of its size, experience and academic excellence. Yet we have also argued that to benefit fully from being part of the global educational system, it must set up campuses outside Japan, and also encourage more foreign students into its domestic education system. It is also actively seeking learning institutional advantages with presence in foreign locations (L advantages.) Finally in its mode of foreign entry, it has both internalized (I) some of the O specific educational advantages, and is also engaging in a range of collaborative alliances with foreign universities in order to augment these advantages, and by so doing become one of the truly great global universities of the twenty-first century.

REFERENCES

Dunning, J.H. (2002), *Theories and Paradigms of International Business Activity*, Cheltenham, UK and Narthampton, MA, USA: Edward Elgar.

16. Developing Singapore as a global education hub: opportunities and challenges

Ah-Keng Kau

1. INTRODUCTION

Singapore, being a small country without any natural resources, has always viewed its 4.17 million residents[1] as its most important resource. The government believes that it has provided its people with quality education that is needed to facilitate Singapore's transformation into a knowledge-based economy. And as early as 1985, the Economic Committee, then led by Minister of State (Trade and Industry) BG Lee Hsien Loong, had already identified education as one of the 18 services sectors to be nurtured and promoted.[2]

Today, at least 1.8 million international students pursue higher education outside their home countries. About 45 per cent of these students are from Asia, mostly China, India, Japan, South Korea and Malaysia. Singapore has been a popular choice for students from countries like China and India.[3] Singapore sees Southeast Asia, China and India – countries within a seven-hour flight radius of Singapore – as a hinterland of hundreds of millions of people with rising incomes and aspirations who will demand good-quality education.[4]

In 1997, the Singapore government entrusted the Economic Development Board (EDB) with the task of establishing Singapore as a world-class education hub by attracting at least 10 world-class institutions to Singapore, and building a cluster of top-notch professional education and training centers to complement the world-class institutions.[5] In 2003, EDB's goal to attract at least ten leading education institutions to Singapore under its World Class Universities program was also achieved with Stanford University's partnership with NTU (Nanyang Technological University) in Environmental Science and Engineering.[6] As at 2002, the education service industry accounted for 1.9 per cent of Singapore's Gross Domestic

Product (GDP) and Singapore's government is aiming for the education service to contribute 5 per cent of GDP within ten years' time.[7] According to the latest CNA (Channel News Asia) report dated 18 July 2005, the Singapore Tourism Board aims to increase the number of foreign students to 150 000 in the next few years.[8]

This chapter therefore aims to identify key factors that Singapore must possess in order to realize its goal of becoming a global education hub, and presents an analysis of the Singapore education service industry. Finally, the challenges facing Singapore in this respect will be discussed.

2. SINGAPORE AS EDUCATION SERVICE PROVIDER

The Strengths, Weaknesses, Opportunities, Threats analysis framework will be used to analyze the education service sector of Singapore.

2.1   Strengths

2.1.1   Reputation for educational excellence

Over the years, Singapore has evolved from its traditional British-based education system to one that endeavors to meet the needs of individuals and seeks to nurture talents. The strength of Singapore's education system lies in its bilingual policy (English with Malay/Mandarin/Tamil) and a broad-based curriculum where innovation and entrepreneurship command a premium. Individuals acquire the relevant skills and abilities to survive in competitive environments and are equipped for a brighter future.[9]

Singapore's public schools have a distinctive record of high standards in teaching and learning, illustrated by international comparative studies such as the Third International Mathematics and Science Study that showed the majority of students from Singapore schools regularly outperforming the international average in Mathematics and Science.[10] Singapore students have also excelled in competitions such as world English debating championships and International Olympiads (Mathematics, Physics, Chemistry and Biology), ousting counterparts from other countries to clinch top prizes and distinctions.

At the tertiary level, the more established National University of Singapore (NUS) has been rated 18th in a new global ranking of universities by *The Times*, a highly influential national UK newspaper. The report was published in *The Times Higher Education Supplement* (*The Times Higher*) on 5 November 2004. In it, the World University Rankings lists showed the top 200 universities around the world. The other university, the Nanyang Technological University (NTU), was ranked 50, a still remarkable ranking considering the fact that it was established only in 1955. The newly established Singapore Management University (SMU) was not included in the ranking. In addition to boasting three locally grown universities, Singapore has attracted ten world-class institutions with strong industry links to set up centers of excellence in education and research. Among them are respected names such as the leading French university, INSEAD, the renowned Massachusetts Institute of Technology, and leading US business schools such as the University of Chicago Graduate School of Business.

2.1.2 Stable political and economic system

Despite Singapore being a small country with a population of only 4.17 million, it has enjoyed political stability and economic growth since independence in 1965. It has become a reputable financial center, a key regional trading center, the world's busiest port, and a top location for investment. Singapore has earned recognition from around the world and is often cited as a model for transparency, efficiency and political stability.[11]

The latest 2002 survey by the Economist Intelligence Unit (EIU) involving 60 economies, won Singapore the title of having the best business environment in Asia. The Swiss-based World Economic Forum (WEF) also rated Singapore as the most competitive economy, possessing great innovative ability and a solid macro-economy in the world. It has also been rated as the least corrupt country in Asia. In the Transparency International 2004 report, Singapore ranked fifth in the Corruption Perception Index, after Finland, New Zealand, Denmark and Iceland.

2.1.3 Infrastructure and accessibility

In terms of infrastructure and accessibility, Singapore is definitely of a comparable standard to most highly developed countries. Singapore is well connected via sea, air and telecommunications to all parts of the world. Singapore Changi International Airport serves more than 60 airlines, which fly to over 145 cities, and has for many consecutive years been nominated as the best airport in the world.[12] Therefore foreign students would find Singapore extremely accessible from their home countries. Given the vast number of airlines serving Singapore, foreign students would also find it very easy and convenient to get air tickets for home visits during holidays.

Singapore is located within eight hours' flying time of 2.8 billion of the world population. In particular, it is strategically located close to top source countries for international students.[13] Singapore is also strategically located at the heart of Asia and can be a hub to explore the Southeast Asian region.

Singapore is also probably the most wired country in Asia, with an Internet penetration rate of 42 per cent.[14] The high Internet penetration rate means that students studying in Singapore would be able to access the Internet easily and conveniently. This would certainly aid students in their projects and research, as the Internet provides them with a wide, reliable and convenient source for information. Most tertiary schools in Singapore also have wireless Internet access throughout the school compound.

2.1.4   A multicultural nation – a cosmopolitan city

The nation's rich multicultural heritage is highlighted through the various ethnic groups (Chinese, Malays, Indians, Eurasians) living together harmoniously who have gradually acquired a distinct identity as Singaporeans whilst still maintaining each race's traditional practices, customs and festivals. In addition, with more than 90 000[15] professional expatriates living and working in Singapore, they too bring their unique cultures and perspectives, adding color and vibrancy to cosmopolitan Singapore. Singapore, being a multicultural society, also makes it extremely easy for the foreign students to integrate and blend into the society. English is the language medium for instruction in schools and tertiary institutions. That proves to be an important factor when students consider studying abroad. In addition, English is widely spoken by the population, thus making communications extremely easy for most visitors.

2.1.5   High standards of living

Singapore's high standard of living is also something that students can be assured of. In a survey reported in *The Economist* in March 2002, Singapore's quality of life surpassed that of London or New York. Thirty-nine factors were considered, including political stability, personal freedom, air pollution and the quality of healthcare, schools, restaurants and theatres.[16]

Although a high standard of living can sometimes be considered as a disadvantage in the eyes of foreign students from poorer countries, the high standard of living in Singapore also presents them with a new experience, which they might not have experienced before in their home countries. As for the wealthier students, Singapore's high standard of living would guarantee the students and parents that they would be well taken care of in Singapore.

2.1.6 Variety of education services providers

The private education sector is already a vibrant industry, with a total of 110 000 students from both home and abroad, enrolled in more than 300 private commercial, IT, fine arts and language schools in Singapore.[17] Due to the nature of the courses offered by the private education organizations, which do not require heavy infrastructure investments, the barriers to entry are low. The low barrier of entry is likely to result in the entry of more private education providers in the coming years, as demand for quality education services intensifies further when more people from developing Asian countries (especially India, China and Vietnam) join the middle-income band.

2.2 Weaknesses

Singapore has a number of weaknesses that could thwart its efforts in attracting more foreign students to study in its educational institutions. These are described below.

2.2.1 Relatively higher costs of living compared to other Asian countries

Singapore is a relatively expensive city to live in, especially for international students from poorer countries, which happens to be the main source of international students. With a per capita income of about US$28 000 a year, it is one of the highest among Asian countries, with the exception of Japan.

2.2.2 Negative perception as a state with low freedom of expression

Singapore has earned a reputation as a country with tough social controls and pervasive censorship.[18] All these are at odds with the ideals of academia and the notion of a free-thinking campus full of intellectuals. The tough and restrictive rules and regulations set by the Singapore government also inhibit creativity and entrepreneurial spirit, which the government has been trying to promote in recent years. However, there are signs that a certain degree of relaxation has been initiated. More changes in policy will be gradually introduced.

2.2.3 Singapore's education system

Although Singapore's school system has won international praise, its elements of education continue to draw criticism. Many educationists criticize the Singapore education system for being too examination-oriented and focused too heavily on rote learning. Therefore, Singapore's record of producing creative and innovative students is poor. A comparative study conducted by a University of London Institute of Education researcher also pointed out that Singapore's education system is still weak compared to the standards of advanced countries in terms of leading-edge technological innovation and R&D. The study also states that Singapore's education system is well-attuned to supplying the skills for jobs at an operational and technical level, but less so in key areas where creativity and innovation are required.[19]

2.3   Opportunities

Owing to the different characteristics of the target market, the market for education services can be segmented into a few groups. This would mean that the opportunities for the different segments would be different; hence the opportunities analysis would be presented according to each different segment identified.[20]

2.3.1   Huge pool of local and foreign students

There is an estimated 1.8 million international tertiary students globally, and Singapore has captured only 1 per cent of the market share.[21] Since the National University of Singapore (NUS) and Nanyang Technological University (NTU) have already established a good regional reputation (for example NUS is constantly rated as one of the top five multi-disciplinary universities in Asia by *Asiaweek*), the Singapore government can increase the number of international students and retain more local students by capitalizing on the good reputation of Singapore universities.

However, due to the stringent admission criteria and limited vacancies of the existing universities, a sizable number of foreign and local students (mostly local students) are often refused admission by these local universities. The rejected applicants who are not attracted by private education then often choose to go overseas. This is evidenced in the huge outflow of Singapore students to Australia, Britain and the United States. Therefore, the finding of an alternative arrangement for this group of students represents an opportunity for the Singapore government.

Singapore would be able to capture a larger share of paying international students and reduce the leakage of local students by setting up more universities. The new universities do not need to be of equal standard to the existing ones but at least of an acceptable standard. As long as an effort is made to differentiate the new universities from the existing ones, the disparity in standards among the universities would prevent the brand erosion of the existing universities.

2.3.2   Branch campuses of foreign universities

Many reputable universities have set up branch campuses either singly or jointly with local institutions. For instance, the University of New South Wales will establish its first overseas campus in Singapore and enroll its first students in 2007. Many other universities, notably from Australia, have teamed up with local education providers to offer certificate, diploma, degree and post-graduate programs in Singapore. Students can choose to complete part of the programs in Singapore and the remaining segments in Australia. Alternatively, such programs can be completed wholly in Singapore. For instance, many of the MBA programs can be completed on a part-time basis in Singapore, but students obtain degrees conferred by their Australian partner universities.

2.3.3   Private education and specialty schools

The market opportunities for this segment are also excellent.[22] The schools can leverage on Singapore's branding and reputation in selected disciplines such as finance and logistics. Many of the more established private education organizations such as Informatics and TMC have been very aggressive in exploring overseas markets, in terms of attracting more foreign students to Singapore. Many of these schools are also actively developing overseas partnerships by setting up overseas campus and capitalizing on e-learning for scalability. Non-profit-making institutions like the Singapore Institute of Management, Management Development Institute of Singapore, Marketing Institute of Singapore and so on have found university partners from Australia, the UK and USA to offer programs in Singapore.

2.3.4   Corporate training centers and executive education

EDB has always been very proactive in attracting MNCs to establish offices here. There are approximately 6000 MNCs in Singapore, of which at least half have regional responsibilities that include training of manpower for their regional operations.[23] As companies have realized the importance of human capital as a source of competitive advantage, training has become a key strategic and important investment.

The global corporate training market was estimated at US$280 billion in 1999, and is expected to grow to US$365 billion by 2003 according to the Merrill Lynch 1999 report. The products that are needed by this segment are mainly more short term and flexible enrichment courses and postgraduate studies. Since they are already well-provided by the private education organizations, world-class institutions that have been invited to offer programs in Singapore and the government-supported universities, there should not be any serious difficulties for Singapore to capture a larger share in this segment. With a more aggressive marketing effort, Singapore should be able to better capitalize on the opportunities presented in this segment.

2.4. Threats and Challenges

2.4.1   Strong competition from other countries

Singapore encounters intense competition from other countries. Owing to increases in the standard of living in most countries and recognition of the importance of education, many countries, including emerging countries such as China, are trying to gain a larger share in the US$2.2 trillion education industry. In recent years, numerous countries have announced plans to expand their education service sector. They include Asian countries such as China,[24] Japan,[25] Malaysia,[26] Thailand,[27] Vietnam[28] and the Philippines.[29] According to a report in the *Straits Times* dated 11 May, 2005 (p. 3), even Japanese universities are also courting students from China as a result of Japan's low birth rate which has resulted in fewer university-going students.

Beijing has been a major teaching base for foreign students in China, with over 30 000 foreign students from 156 countries and regions.[30] As of May 2003, Japan also has a total of 109 500 foreign students,[31] which is roughly twice as many as Singapore. As for Malaysia, as of March 2003, it also reported a total of 39 796 foreign students, with the Chinese being the largest group at a figure of 18 482.[32] Malaysia is also expanding its education services industry very aggressively with the ambition of being the regional centre of education excellence.[33]

Besides the Asian countries, Singapore also faces strong competition from Australia, New Zealand, Britain and the United States. Despite the recent negative publicity, Britain's universities remain attractive to foreign students, especially to the Chinese students. Figures as at 2001 show that there were around 18 000 Chinese students in higher education in Britain and of the total of 143 000 foreign students, the Chinese represented the largest group.[34] The figures represented an increase of 71 per cent from the year 2000. US universities, with their state-of-the-art research facilities and good reputation have always been the top choice for foreign students. For 2002 alone, 583 000 foreign students were enrolled in American universities and colleges, contributing US$12 billion to the US economy.[35]

The number of foreign students studying in Australia has been rising by 20 per cent or more annually in recent years.[36] According to Department of Education, Science and Training figures, in 2003 there were more than

170 000 foreign students studying at Australian universities (which included students enrolled overseas through distance learning programs), compared with almost 146 000 in 2002, with most choosing to study in central Sydney or Melbourne.[37] However, the growth is likely to slow down due to the appreciation of the Australian dollar against major currencies. Despite that, Australia is still Singapore's strongest competitor in the region, grabbing a large chunk of the Asian market,[38] including Singaporean students.

2.4.2 Supply of good and experienced faculty members

As a result of the proliferation of education services, top faculty members are very much in demand; this problem is especially serious for business schools due to a decline in the enrollment in business PhD programs.[39] Coupled with the increase in the number of business schools, the problem of attracting quality faculty members for business schools would be an extremely challenging task.

As Professor Ronald Frank, outgoing president of SMU, remarked in a recent interview with Channel News Asia, finding good and experienced faculty members will be a challenge. He even pointed out that SMU has problems attracting older and more distinguished faculty members.[40] Furthermore, he commented that if the universities were to increase their capacities, there is no way that Singapore, or even Asia itself, would be able to supply enough quality faculty members.[41]

The fact that the teaching profession does not attract the best talents in Singapore, and Singapore has a mere population of 4.17 million, are the main reasons why Singapore is unable to produce sufficient high quality and experienced faculty members to meet the demand of the growing education services sector. Hence Singapore has to rely heavily on foreign academics to meet the demand for quality faculty members. However, foreign top academics are often reluctant to give up their lucrative consultancies elsewhere to move to Singapore and they also have doubts over the issue of freedom of expression in Singapore. Without good and experienced faculty members, the Singapore education services sector would have problems sustaining the quality of the courses it offers.

2.4.3 Overly ambitious goal

Professor Ronald Frank, who has previously taught at Harvard and Stanford, also commented on Singapore's goal to be a global education hub. He said that the best-known centers of higher learning across the world—from Cambridge to Harvard—took entire generations to cement their reputation and, in contrast, Singapore is trying to attain its world-class tag at the speed of thought.[42]

Without proper management and good judgment, the current growth rate would easily lead to over-capacity. The excess capacity would then lead to price wars and compromised quality. Ultimately, it would not only be detrimental to new entrants and smaller players, it would also cause the government's hard work in building Singapore as a hub of excellence to go down the drain.

2.4.4   Availability of employment opportunities

As noted by Dr Cham Tao Soon, NTU founder and now a distinguished professor at NTU, foreign students who go overseas to study are not just looking for qualifications, but also for jobs.[43] Therefore, the Singapore government's ability to create jobs would have an effect on Singapore's goal to be a global education hub. Apparently, it seems that the Singapore government is relying on attracting large R&D companies to take part in joint projects with Singapore universities to create jobs for Singaporeans and to create jobs through the development of the education services sector.

However, if both fail to create enough jobs for both the local and foreign students, the unemployment rate is likely to shoot higher. With a higher unemployment rate, foreign students would find Singapore less appealing. Given that Singapore's unemployment rate still stands at 4.5 per cent[44] currently and that economic recovery is still weak, the Singapore unemployment rate is unlikely to reduce drastically any time soon.

3.   DEVELOPING MARKETING STRATEGIES

It is essential to consider the marketing of educational services from the conventional '4Ps' perspective, namely, product, price, promotion and place. These are described below.

3.1   Product

In order for Singapore to attract more foreign students to Singapore for their education, it is necessary for Singapore education providers to offer a greater variety of courses. The courses offered should also be flexible and mass-customized in order to attract more post-graduate students and executives.

EDB has succeeded in wooing an established foreign institution, which offers a comprehensive curriculum from liberal arts to engineering, to set up a campus in Singapore. Unlike the existing three universities,

National University of Singapore (NUS), Nanyang Technological University (NTU) and Singapore Management University (SMU), the new fourth university (the University of New South Wales from Australia) will be privately funded. With the establishment of the fourth university, international students will have a wider array of choices; this strategy is expected to help to triple the number of foreign students in Singapore to 150 000 by 2012.[45]

Besides the establishment of the fourth university, the Economic Development Board (EBD) of Singapore has also successfully convinced ten top-ranked institutions to offer a diverse variety of programs here. The ten institutions are (i) Johns Hopkins, (ii) INSEAD, (iii) Massachusetts Institute of Technology (MIT), (iv) Technische Universiteit of Eindhoven, (v) University of Chicago Graduate School of Business, (vi) University of Pennsylvania's Wharton School, (vii) Georgia Institute of Technology, (viii) Stanford University, (ix) Technische Universität München and (x) Shanghai Jiao Tong University.[46] These ten world-class institutions offer a great variety of post-graduate courses, ranging from medicine, engineering and logistics, to business, finance and arts.

The private education providers in Singapore also offer a wide array of courses, ranging from short-term enrichment courses to diploma and degree programs from various established universities from overseas. Such courses include tourism management, business, engineering, nursing and so on. With the establishment of the Singapore Quality Class Award for private education organizations, foreign students can be assured that the quality of the courses offered by private education organizations would be of a certain standard.

3.2 Price

The government-supported universities such as NUS and NTU charged tuition fees of less than S$24 000 (approximately US$14 300[47]) for an MBA program. And according to Dr Neo Boon Siong, former Dean of NTU's Nanyang Business School, this total amount is under-priced.[48] An MBA program at an Australian university could be as high as S$55 000[49] and one by INSEAD would cost approximately US$100 000.[50]

For an undergraduate course, with the exception of medicine, dentistry and music courses, NUS and NTU charge international students $6220[51] (approximately US$3700[52]) per annum. This amount is much lower than the US$4500 charged by American universities and the S$10 500 to S$16 000 (approximately US$6200 to US$9500) charged by Australian universities.[53] Britain's government also intends to pass a bill allowing English universities to charge up to £3000 in tuition fees, instead of the current flat rate £1125.[54]

The prices charged by government-supported universities would also have an effect on the prices charged by private education organizations, as they are likely to use the prices as a benchmark. Therefore, the private organizations are less likely to set a price much higher than the government-supported universities as it would make their programs relatively more expensive and less appealing.

Ultimately, the lower prices charged by government-supported universities would serve as a deterrent for private education organizations charging high prices; the programs offered by the private education organizations would therefore be more affordable. In fact, the effect is already reflected in Singapore's private education organizations fee structures. A private education in Singapore, costing S$7000 to S$12 000 a year in fees, is much cheaper than a boarding-school stint in the US or Britain, which can exceed S$60 000.[55]

It is evidenced that Singapore offers more competitive prices compared to its main rivals. And since Singapore's main target markets are from poorer Asian countries, the lower prices charged by Singapore universities would be an added advantage to the foreign students, as this makes the courses more affordable for them.

However, one of the drawbacks of competitive pricing is that people sometimes tend to associate low prices with low quality, therefore the institutions have to make more effort to fight off this perception, and prove that they offer value for money, and are not inferior.

3.3 Distribution

Foreign students can easily apply for Singapore education services via the Internet or through the offices that are set up by the Education Services Strategic Tourism Unit (STU) in the respective countries. Singapore private education providers have also set up representative offices in various countries such as China, India, Thailand, Indonesia and Malaysia.[56]

In Singapore, the Bras Basah area is designated as the education hub of Singapore. The area is home to about 30 private schools, including well-known names such as Stansfield Group of Schools, Informatics and Management Development Institution of Singapore (MDIS).[57] Private education organizations such as Informatics and MDIS have several learning centers that are 'strategically located islandwide'.

3.4 Promotion

On 16 August 2003, the Singapore Tourism Board (STB) announced the launch of 'Singapore Education'; the umbrella brand that will spearhead Singapore's image as a premier education hub overseas.[58] STB will provide authoritative and comprehensive information channels for education in Singapore. This includes the development of a full range of publicity materials to market and promote Singapore's education services and the establishment of information centers in key markets such as China, India and Indonesia.[59]

STB has also developed a Singapore Education brand logo, which depicts a butterfly. The butterfly symbolizes the diverse education services Singapore offers and the transformation process that individuals will experience as they go through the learning journey in Singapore.[60] Besides that, the STB has also set up the Education Services Strategic Tourism Unit (STU) to promote Singapore education services to foreign students. The STU is made up of three departments, each focusing on their respective education services, namely (i) basic education and higher learning, (ii) enrichment courses and (iii) corporate education.[61]

As part of its promotional campaign, STB will also participate in education fairs, work with institutions to provide pastoral care for students and provide transparent course and enrolment information through STU.[62] Besides that, STB can also consider organizing field trips for potential students to tour Singapore and the schools at discounted prices.

In addition, a website containing information on courses, facilities and other information pertinent to studying in Singapore will provide a valuable and reliable resource for our target audience. Partnering Singapore educational institutions, STB will also participate in education fairs and embark on publicity efforts to convince more people in the overseas markets to further their education and training in Singapore.

3.5 Provision of Services

Another element of crucial importance in the marketing of education is the provision of excellent service. Being aware of the needs for such assistance, some government and non-government organizations have been tailoring measures to address these problems. The plans that are undertaken by the various organizations will be further elaborated in the following:

3.5.1 Establishment of a 'one-stop info centre' for foreign students

STB has announced plans to set up a 'one-stop info center for foreign students' in Singapore by the end of 2004,[63] a place that will provide information and handle complaints for foreign students. This move will further assist Singapore to achieve its goal to triple the number of foreign students to 150 000. The center will not only provide information regarding education services, it will also provide other information such as housing, getting around Singapore and air ticket prices. A travel agent will also be housed there to enable a more seamless and hassle-free assistance for the foreign students. STB will also locate the center in a more considerate and easily accessible location although it has not finalized its location.

Officers at the center will also handle complaints for foreign students by investigating and mediating in any complaints it receives from the students about their school or services. This service is especially valuable to foreign students as they are often quite helpless when problems occur. Besides that, the center will also organize orientation programs and social activities to assist students to adjust to life in Singapore.

As Mr John Conceicao, STB's assistant director of student services, has said, the services offered by the one-stop center will be especially beneficial and useful for private foreign students, as private students often do not have the privilege of making use of similar services offered by the public school and tertiary institution. Furthermore, the information and assistance offered by this one-stop center will be more comprehensive and unbiased compared to those that are offered by the educational institution. Since the center will be run by STB instead of by a private organization, the information that it provides will have more value in the eyes of the foreign students, as nothing is better than having a trusted and reliable organization that will provide them with unbiased assistance in a foreign land.

3.5.2   New accreditation scheme

The Consumer Association of Singapore (CASE) is also working on a new accreditation scheme to protect the interest of students, after receiving numerous complaints from them about private education centers. CASE is working with the government to launch its first island-wide accreditation scheme for private education centers by the end of 2004. The new scheme also aims at protecting foreign students from being misled by private education agencies.[64]

3.5.3   Government support of educational institutions

The Singapore government has demonstrated its commitment and sincerity in developing Singapore as a global schoolhouse in various ways. In order to attract world-class institutions to offer programs in Singapore, EDB offer them lucrative research funding. Dr Arnoud De Meyer, Dean of INSEAD's Asian campus, says the S$10 million that EDB will give as research funding over four years is a plus factor in their decision to invest S$60 million in Singapore.[65]

However, the funding for each university varies. For example, the Design Technology Institute, an NUS and Technische Universiteit of Eindhoven collaboration, cost EDB, the Education Ministry, NUS and industrial partners $28 million. To indicate an example of how doors are now swinging, it was reported that an EDB team visited seven top European universities recently in just one week.[66]

The government is also working to help Singapore education services providers to venture abroad. Several private schools as well as public schools are offering education services in the region, including China, where Singapore education service providers are seen as doing well due to their bilingual advantage. The swift action of the Economic Review Committee to correct the weaknesses or constraints of the Singapore education service industry reflects the commitment of the government in the development of Singapore as a global education hub.

4. CONCLUSION

Elevating the status of Singapore as an educational hub in Asia is an ambitious endeavor. Singapore is in possession of certain strengths which are not easily duplicated by other countries in this part of the world. However, there are also inherent weaknesses that Singapore must try to rectify or overcome. On the horizon there are also good opportunities for Singapore to take advantage of. For instance, it has been reported in the *Straits Times* (22 December, 2004, p. 14) that the United States, the leading educational hub in the world, has suffered a slip in its status as a result of visa processing delays and competition from other nations. The other English-speaking countries with reputable educational institutions such as Canada, the United Kingdom, Australia and New Zealand will be formidable competitors for Singapore. Nevertheless, it is anticipated that Singapore, with its commitment of resources, both financial and human, will be able to create a niche for herself in this increasingly competitive industry.

Other efforts include the following. EDB is working closely with SPRING Singapore (Standards, Productivity and Innovation Board) to develop an accreditation system that will create an upgrading path for local private education institutions and a reference point for prospective students about the quality of institutions. This initiative will be complemented by EDB's efforts to work even more closely with local private schools that plan to increase their international student enrollments by providing assistance in the areas of regulation, finance and infrastructure such as offering them access to state properties for the school's establishment or expansion.

In 2004, EDB succeeded in securing a project to set up Singapore's first private university and to welcome a greater diversity of educational offerings. These will include two or three private secondary schools and a range of specialist schools for fine arts, media, design, culinary arts and hotel management.[67] With all the effort put in by the government and private sector into the development of educational services, it is conceivable that the ambition of developing Singapore as an educational hub in the Asia Pacific region can be realized in the not-too-distant future.

NOTES

1. www.singstat.gov.sg.
2. Singapore Ministry of Trade and Industry, *The Singapore Economy: New Direction*, February 1986.
3. www.sedb.com/edbcorp/sg/en_uk/index/in_the_news/press_releases/2004/services_industry.html.
4. 'Singapore's Education System: Adjusting to a knowledge-based economy'. http://singapore.usembassy.gov/ep/2002/Education2002.html.
5. 'Singapore's Education System: Adjusting to a knowledge-based economy'. http://singapore.usembassy.gov/ep/2002/Education2002.html.
6. www.sedb.com/edbcorp/sg/en_uk/index/in_the_news/press_releases/2004/services_industry.html.
7. *The Straits Times*, 17 August 2003, 2003 Singapore Press Holdings Limited.
8. http://sg.news.yahoo.com/050718/5/singapore158358.html/.
9. www.singaporeedu.gov.sg/htm/sis/sis01.htm.
10. *The Economist*, 31 December 2003, **369**(8354), 37-8.
11. www.channelnewsasia.com/cna/parliament/erc/edu.pdf.
12. www.channelnewsasia.com/cna/parliament/erc/edu.pdf.
13. www.channelnewsasia.com/cna/parliament/erc/edu.pdf.
14. www.singaporeedu.gov.sg/htm/sis/sis01.htm.
15. www.channelnewsasia.com/cna/parliament/erc/edu.pdf.
16. www.singaporeedu.gov.sg/htm/sis/sis01.htm.
17. www.channelnewsasia.com/cna/parliament/erc/edu.pdf.
18. www.cnn.com/2003/EDUCATION/10/13/singapore.education.reut.
19. 'Singapore's Education System: Adjusting to a knowledge-based economy', http://singapore.usembassy.gov/ep/2002/Education2002.html.
20. The different segments identified for the education service market are adapted from an article from Channel News Asia, www.channelnewsasia.com/cna/parliament/erc/edu.pdf.

21. www.channelnewsasia.com/cna/parliament/erc/edu.pdf.
22. www.channelnewsasia.com/cna/parliament/erc/edu.pdf.
23. www.channelnewsasia.com/cna/parliament/erc/edu.pdf.
24. Xinhua News Agency, 'Beijing universities plan to enroll 10,000 more foreign students', 5 February 2004.
25. Kyodo News, 'Panel calls for policy to attract "quality" foreign students', 16 December 2003.
26. *Malaysian Business*, 'Exporting Education', 16 August 2003, 2003 New Straits Times Press (Malaysia) Berhad.
27. *The Economist*, 31 December 2003, **369**(8354), 37-8.
28. *The Economist*, 31 December 2003, **369**(8354), 37-8.
29. *The Economist*, 31 December 2003, **369**(8354), 37-8.
30. Xinhua News Agency, 'Beijing universities plan to enroll 10,000 more foreign students', 5th February 2004.
31. Kyodo News, 'Panel calls for policy to attract "quality" foreign students', 16 December 2003.
32. *Malaysian Business*, 'Private education at work', 16 January 2004, 2004 New Straits Times Press (Malaysia) Berhad.
33. *Malaysian Business*, 16 August 2003, 2003 New Straits Times Press (Malaysia) Berhad.
34. *The Economist* Print Edition, 'Western promise', 27 March 2003.
35. *The Economist* Print Edition, 'Beware students', 21 August 2003.
36. *The Australian Financial Review*, 'Degree of financial freedom', 29 February 2004.
37. *The Australian Financial Review*, 'Regional Unis take city trail', 20 March 2004.
38. http://quickstart.clari.net/qs_se/webnews/wed/cf.
39. *The Economist Global Executive*, 'The hunt for good professors', 8 May 2003.
40. www.todayonline.com/articles/9285print.asp.
41. www.todayonline.com/articles/9285print.asp.
42. www.todayonline.com/articles/9285print.asp.
43. *The Straits Times*, 17 August 2003, 2003 Singapore Press Holdings Limited.
44. www.mom.gov.sg/MOM/CDA/0,1858,1271--------4698----,00.html.
45. *The Straits Times*, 17 August 2003 s 2003 Singapore Press Holdings Limited.
46. www.sedb.com/edbcorp/sg/en_uk/index/industry_opp/education_services.html.
47. Based on 18 April 2004 exchange rate, www.economist.com/markets/currency/md_conv.cfm.
48. 'Executive Education: Singapore strives to become a world-class education destination', *The Asian Wall Street Journal*, 1 Dec 2003.
49. www.australian-universities.com/resources/study-costs.php.
50. *The Economist Global Executive*, 'INSEAD at a crossroad', 8 March 2004.
51. The full tuition fee is approximately S$20 000 annum for most courses; however, the Singapore government does offer tuition grants for international students, www.nus.edu.sg/registrar/undergraduate/fees.html.
52. Based on 18 April 2004 exchange rate, www.economist.com/markets/currency/md_conv.cfm.

53. www.australian-universities.com/resources/study-costs.php.
54. *The Economist* Print Edition, 'Pay or decay', 22 January 2004.
55. *The Straits Times*, 'School daze for foreign students', 22 September 2002.
56. *The Hindu*, 'Going west? Try East', 26 January 2004, 2004 Kasturi & Sons Limited.
57. *The Straits Times*, 'One-stop info centre for foreign students soon', 26 March 2004, 2004 Singapore Press Holdings Limited.
58. http://app.stb.com.sg/asp/common/print.asp? id=162&type=2.
59. www.singaporeedu.gov.sg/htm/mis/abo.htm.
60. www.singaporeedu.gov.sg/htm/mis/abo.htm.
61. www.singaporeedu.gov.sg/htm/mis/abo.htm.
62. *New Straits Times* (Malaysia), 'Singapore weighs in', 24 August 2003.
63. *The Straits Times*, 'One-stop info centre for foreign students soon', 26 March 2004, 2004 Singapore Press Holdings Limited.
64. *Channel News Asia*, 13 April 2004, 2004 MediaCorp News Pte Ltd.
65. *The Straits Times*, 'Campus courtship', 24 June 2001, 2001 Singapore Press Holdings Limited.
66. *The Straits Times*, 'Campus courtship', 24 June 2001, 2001 Singapore Press Holdings Limited.
67. www.sedb.com/edbcorp/sg/en_uk/index/in_the_news/press_releases/2004/services_industry.html.

17. The global impact of American restaurant franchises: an international perspective

Mahmood A. Khan and Maryam Khan

1. INTRODUCTION

Franchising has become one of the most dominant forces in the method of doing business by prominent multinational corporations. In order to fully understand the multinational significance of franchising, it is essential to know its fundamentals and mode of operation. According to a report by the Committee on Small Business, United States Congress (1990), 'franchising is essentially a contractual method for marketing and distributing goods and services of a company (franchisor) through a dedicated or restricted network of distributors (franchisees)'. The International Franchise Association, the major franchising trade association, defines franchising as a 'continuous relationship in which the franchisor provides a licensed privilege to do business, plus assistance in organizing, training, merchandising, and management in return for a consideration from the franchisee'. In short, franchising is designed to provide a symbiotic and mutually beneficial relationship between the franchisor and franchisees. The same guidelines work when it is related to multinational corporations. The major difference between other types of business compared to a franchise business is the legal agreement and bonding between a franchisor and a franchisee for the conduct of specific business, after meeting prearranged sets of legal requirements. This bonding is carried to wherever the multinational enterprise operates, either as a sole franchise-granting corporation or as wholly owned subsidiary. In franchising, the business is conducted under the terms of the franchise contract, where a franchisor grants the right and license to franchisees to market a product or service, or both, using the trademark and/or the business system developed by the franchisor. The entire process of franchising starts with a concept, which may be based on an idea, innovation, process, product, service format, or a combination of all these. The franchisor grants a license to another party to use this concept with very precise and approved changes based on the operational requirements in various countries. Due to the legal agreement there is strictly limited room for flexibility, which leaves a distinct impact wherever that concept is carried. It poses different challenges in different countries where the basic concept in its totality has to survive within the cultural, social, economical and political environments. In other words, a fairly rigid concept has to flourish in variable environments based on the country to which it is being transferred. It involves a major strategic decision for multinational enterprises since there is a need for major adjustments, resulting in positive as well as negative impacts.

An effort is made in this chapter to highlight these impacts, which has multifaceted consequences for multinational enterprises and the host countries. Restaurant franchises are used to analyze these impacts, primarily because of their prominence across the globe and also because they are the most common mode for the spread of franchising. Restaurant franchises were often among the first types of American businesses to open in the emerging market economies of the former republics of Russia, Eastern Europe, China, and many of the Southeastern countries.

Despite temporary setbacks during the global downturn after the turn of the millennium, franchising is still expected to be the fastest-growing market-entry strategy (Ziedman, 2003). Most notable trends that favor the increase in international franchising include: (a) increased educational status of the local population; (b) technological advancement facilitating travel, intercultural cooperation, and instant dissemination of information; (c) exposure to different foods; and the willingness of the younger generation to try new products and unconventional types of foods; (d) rapid development of rural areas, construction of highways, improved transportation methods, and overall industrial development; (e) improved economies and increased disposable family income; (f) the increased numbers of women in the workforce and of two-income families; (g) the increased significance of convenience as a result of one or more factors mentioned earlier; and (h) the popularity of take-out or home-delivered meals (Khan, 1999).

Due to the enormous increase in demand worldwide, one of the most intriguing strategic responses to the marketplace comes from Yum Corporation and its efforts to develop multi-brand units across the globe. Yum envisages multi-unit concepts featuring KFC and Long John Silver's or Taco Bell and A&W and a number of other combinations (Cunneen, 2004). For many of the restaurant franchises, the products and services are limited and therefore their strategies are focused on image building through aggressive marketing. To attract consumers, they try to establish a clear and unique image of their brand.(Lan and Khan, 1995).

2. METHODOLOGY

Qualitative assessment and case studies were used in this study for analytical purposes from very limited published studies on this subject. Several models were examined both for presumptive as well as comparative purposes. The primary intent of this chapter is to outline cultural, social, economical, legal, technological and environmental impacts of restaurant franchises when located in different parts of the world. Both positive and negative angles were considered in reviewing these impacts. The intent of this study is purely exploratory in nature due to very limited available published information, and we will delineate aspects that can lead to future empirical studies. Also, McDonald's Corporation is primarily used for case study examples since it has the largest number of franchise units worldwide and has a very distinct impact on aspects highlighted in this chapter.

3. MCDONALD'S STUDY

It is important to understand the global impact of multinational corporations. As mentioned earlier, McDonald's restaurants are cited as illustrative of the impact, which can be transposed to other restaurants. Table 17.1 and Figure 17.1 illustrate McDonald's restaurants system-wide present in different world regions by segment. McDonald's has more than 31 000 restaurants in 119 countries, serving 47 million customers a day. In the 1990s, when the company was adding 1500 to 2000 restaurants per year, it was growing at the rate of 7.5 per cent to 10 per cent. Although the rate has been scaled back there are some countries where much greater growth rate is evidenced. For example in China, the store base grew almost 20 per cent in 2004. McDonald's owns and operates about 30 per cent of its brand's restaurants worldwide; franchisees and joint ventures run 70 per cent, compared to the United States, where about 85 per cent of outlets are franchised. The ten largest markets within the McDonald's system are in Australia, Brazil, Canada, China, France, Germany, Japan, Spain and the United Kingdom and of course the United States. These markets represent approximately 24 000 McDonald's restaurants and account for approximately 72 per cent of their business. McDonald's generated a record $3.9 billion in cash from operations in 2004, which is $600 million more than in 2003. Comparable store sales for 2004 rose

9.6 per cent in the United States, 2.4 per cent in Europe and 5.6 per cent in the Asia/Pacific, Middle East and Africa region. China and Malaysia are two countries in the region that are targeted for expansion since both markets are developing at a rapid pace. McDonald's is operating in more than 100 cities in China with plans to open 500 stores in the next five years. For McDonald's, Latin America leads the international sales growth with the highest comparable sales increases in the system, of more than 13 per cent growth. Although McDonald's is used as an example, the aspects discussed apply in general to all foreign franchise restaurants. Also, McDonald's is widely considered to be one of the forerunners of global brand multinational expansion (Anonymous, 1997).

Table 17.1   2004 McDonald's system-wide restaurants by segment

Segment	Restaurants	Per cent
US	13,673	43
Europe	6,287	20
APMEA	7,567	24
Latin America	1,607	5
Canada	1,362	4
Other	1,065	4
Total	31,561	100

Source: McDonald's Shareholder Report, 2004

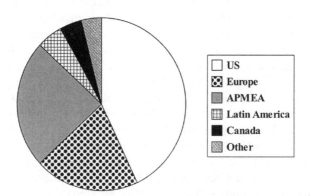

Figure 17.1   Graphic representation of the system-wide restaurants worldwide APMEA: Asia Pacific, Middle East, and Africa

3.1 Global Impact of Franchising

The global impacts of franchising can very well be examined by considering it from different angles. It requires an overall understanding of all factors in order to be successful in businesses in different countries. The experiences learned by US franchisors in Asia bear testimony to the importance of understanding foreign cultures' ways of doing business (Chan and Justis, 1992). For US franchisors seeking to expand globally, these include greater cultural universalism, a younger population willing to try new products, more women working, and thus, a higher percentage of two-income families with more disposable income. Franchisors must consider a number of strategic factors in making the decision to expand their franchising system globally, namely: (1) economic factors; (2) political-legal factors; (3) social-cultural factors; and (4) infrastructure. For example, US firms intending to franchise in Asia should be aware of the cultural, political, economic, and other infrastructure issues. More intricate involvement is needed rather than being aware of the situation. With the elimination of geographic and other barriers, consumers will have access to an increased variety of information and relevant data. The franchising concept, with its emphasis on trade-name/product recognition, quality control and uniformity, is well suited for several countries and is flexible to the demands and impacts of the situation in different countries; however, it demands action that is timely and pertinent to the particular situation. Global impacts viewed from different angles are shown in Figure 17.2.

3.2 Cultural Impact

According to Gilbert et al. (2004), in today's ever-increasing globalization of services and brands, service-oriented businesses need to attend to the satisfaction of their customers both domestically and abroad while transcending unique cultural differences from country to country. Their study reveals two empirically derived, cross-cultural fast-food customer satisfaction dimensions: satisfaction with the personal service and satisfaction with the service setting. Services involve people-to-people contact and thus culture plays a much bigger role in services than in merchandise trade. McDonald's require Polish employees to smile whenever they interact with customers, and such a requirement is considered by many employees as artificial and insincere (Cateora and Graham, 2005). It is very difficult, if not impossible, to distinguish the intricacies involved in any culture. One of the ways of examining some of the major dimensions of culture has involved a comparison of behavioral aspects. Most often used cultural dimensions are by Hofstede (1980), and primarily focus on

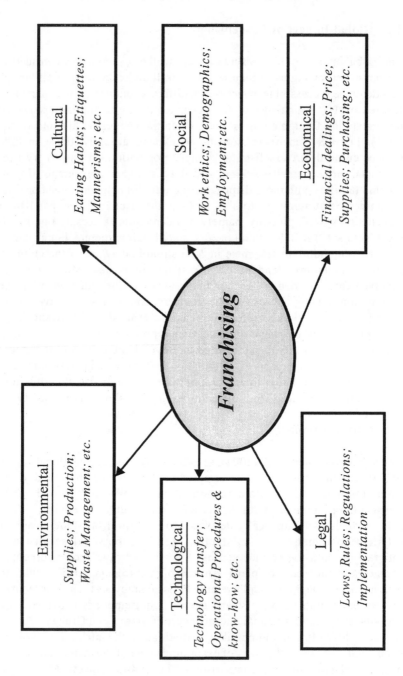

Figure 17.2   Global impacts of restaurant franchises

power distance, uncertainty avoidance, individualism-collectivism, and masculinity-femininity. Other cultural analysis by Trompenaars and Hampden-Turner (1998) is more recent and looks from a broader angle. There are few studies that have included these dimensions and their impact on different cultures. Restaurant franchising has certain distinct features which differ from independently owned restaurants. These features themselves have an impact when these restaurants move to multiple locations worldwide. The global impact of the basic features of franchise restaurants is shown in Table 17.2.

Manners and customs represent a culture's views of appropriate ways of behaving. It is important to monitor differences in manners and customs since they can have a direct effect on the service encountered (Zeithaml and Bitner, 2003). The most prominent and immediate impact on culture due to franchise restaurants is on food habits, etiquettes and mannerisms. Sandwiches, such as burgers, are alien to many cultures and do not resemble the staple foods and menus which have been followed traditionally for generations. The type of foods used, the method of preparation and choice of ingredients used varied from region to region even within a country. Now with franchising, standardization is taking place with very significant differences in the products and services compared to what populations have been used to for centuries. With few exceptions the franchise

Table 17.2   Global impact of the basic features of franchise restaurants

Franchising aspect	Primary global multi-dimensional impacts
1. Site selection	Social impact
2. Building and architecture	Environmental impact
3. Equipment and facilities	Technological impact
4. Training	Educational and cultural impact
5. Marketing	Economical impact
6. Communication link	Social and cultural impact
7. Territorial expansion	Economical impact
8. Purchasing	Economical impact
9. Operations	Technological impact
10. Management	Educational impact
11. Legal aspects	Legal and political impact
12. Research and development	Economical and cultural impact
13. Community development	Social impact
14. Financial	Economical impact

restaurant menu in most countries includes burgers, fries and colas (Watson, 2000). In many countries fast foods are traditionally served by vendors and mom-and-pop restaurants 'family businesses serving traditional home-cooked food'.

Lee and Ulgado (1997) studied the US and Korean fast-food customers, comparing their expectations and perceptions of McDonald's restaurants. In general, study results indicate that significant differences may exist between US and South Korean patrons in terms of their expectations and perceptions of fast-food restaurant services. To US consumers, low food prices are of paramount importance in their evaluations of fast-food establishments. In addition, assurance is also significantly important to Americans. On the other hand, to Korean customers, service dimensions other than low prices, such as reliability and empathy, increase in relative importance. However, for Koreans and other Asian cultures, service speed and low food prices may be important, but do not dominate their perceptions in the same way as other service features. McDonald's is considered in many countries as a prestigious dining restaurant symbolizing US culture and not necessarily as a fast-food restaurant with less expensive menu items. Features like air-conditioning, ambience, visual appeal and convenience are more important in many cultures in countries where franchise restaurants are currently expanding. For Koreans the expectations are higher and the product is not cheap, and it is imbued with the cultural messages of the richest country on earth. As a result, Lee and Ulgado (1997) find Koreans to be more likely to be disappointed by McDonald's. They look for a more complete experience, which includes the food, the speed of service and the association with American culture.

Drastic changes in preferences occur due to the introduction and exposure to products which are unfamiliar in a culture. For example, when Domino's Pizza went to Japan in 1985, the company discovered that no one knew what pepperoni is, and in fact there was no word for pepperoni. Domino's imported pepperoni until the Japanese were trained to make this product. After more than ten years, pepperoni pizza is the number-one-selling pizza in Japanese units. Restrictions on certain products also create situations where either changes have taken place or methods were devised to produce them locally. For example, in South Korea, pepperoni could not be imported because of the restriction on importation of pork products, which led to producing it locally. Special slaughtering restrictions such as Halal foods in Malaysia and Middle-Eastern countries, led to the development of products that meet those requirements. Thus franchising is not only accommodating local food preferences but is also developing new food choices, both of which have an impact on cultural modification and alignment.

Eating patterns are also influenced by the type of menus presented by franchise restaurants. The introduction of breakfast items has changed the way people select food and eat during breakfast. This is new for countries in the Middle East and other places where eating breakfast away from home is not the norm. Viewed from another angle, it can be said that the introduction of breakfast menu items and coffee are leading the way to a sort of homogenization of eating patterns and habits. Similarly eating styles and mannerisms have also been influenced. People in many countries do not like the idea of eating at a food stand or eating while standing. Holding sandwiches in one's hand, and not using a knife, fork or chopsticks to eat, is considered poor etiquette. Manners and etiquette have also been affected. For example, eating with chopsticks has been part of the culture in many Asian countries since ancient times; however, with the introduction of franchise restaurants practices such as eating with the hands/eating while standing have become part of the accepted norms. In Japan, it was taboo to eat while standing or with your hands, yet the Japanese have now embraced eating while holding food in their hand, although they still try to keep the wrapper on foods so as not to touch them. There is a gradual change, with people accepting more snacking with informal eating styles. One of the adverse effects noted is the erosion of the ritual of families eating together at home. Eating away from home or the habit of grazing has severely dented the opportunity of getting together at the dining table and interacting with each other. Also eating together with unfamiliar people or eating in front of others is not considered very polite in some cultures. This is also changing with the introduction of common seating areas and food courts, which are commonly seen in malls and shopping areas where a variety of restaurant franchises are present. In fact, these restaurants are strategically located in prime shopping areas to attract shoppers and weekend crowds. McDonald's in Japan publish McJoy, an information and entertainment magazine containing trends in fashion, sports and travel, which has helped it integrate with the mainstream society better than its competitors.

To many, the restaurants such as Golden Arches represent more than fast foods, to mean American, Western culture, capitalism, and a foreign competitor. Moreover, it is the homogenization of tastes and elimination or reduction of local cuisines that will have a slow but long-term impact. Although steps are taken to localize menu items, such as adding more spices in South America or Malaysia, the main items have to have the identity of the franchise. Some of the prominent examples of menu changes made by McDonald's restaurants worldwide include frankfurters, beer and a cold four-course meal in Germany; McLaks – a grilled salmon sandwich with dill sauce in Norway; Chicken tatsuta – a fried chicken sandwich spiced with soy sauce and ginger in Japan; McSpaghetti-Pasta in a sauce with frankfurter bits in the Philippines; Kiwi burger – a hamburger with a fried egg and a slice of beet in New Zealand; Samurai Pork burger – a sandwich marinated with teriyaki sauce in Thailand; Pechuga Crispy Thai – a long crispy chicken with Thai sauce, grilled onions and pickles in Argentina; and McHuevo – a hamburger with a poached egg on top in Uruguay. McDonald's makes heroic efforts to ensure that its food looks, feels and tastes the same everywhere. Consumers can enjoy Spicy Wings (red-pepper-laced chicken) in Beijing, kosher Big Macs (minus the cheese) in Jerusalem, vegetable McNuggets in New Delhi, or a McHuevo (a burger with fried egg) in Montevideo. It provides McArabia on its menu in the Middle East, which consists of tortilla sandwiches filled with spiced beef. Nonetheless, wherever McDonald's takes root, the core product – at least during the initial phase of operation – is not really the food but the experience of eating in a cheerful, air-conditioned, child-friendly restaurant that offers the revolutionary innovation of clean toilets (Watson, 2000). It is also argued that it is other conveniences provided by fast-food restaurants that establish their permanence. Also, one of the major impacts of franchising is developing food habits in children which will be hard to change for generations. From foods that children prefer, toys that they can obtain, to different marketing strategies, all have been affected worldwide in one way or another.

With all the adaptations that McDonald's makes to suit local tastes, the local culture seems to be changing rather rapidly as a result of its presence and business strength in different parts of the world. Recent additions include the McCafe coffee and dessert concept, developed in Australia and popularized in Latin America; a new line of toasted deli sandwiches, recently rolled out in Canada; home delivery in Egypt, Turkey, Hong Kong and throughout Southeast Asia. Regional products in the Middle East market include folded tortilla sandwiches filled with spiced beef, locally known as McArabia. In other markets in the Middle East and Pacific Rim, chicken is very popular. McDonald's restaurants in Indonesia, Malaysia and Thailand serve fried chicken. McDonald's restaurants in Latin America also offer such regional specialties as fried yucca sticks in Venezuela and an egg, rice, beans and chorizo platter for breakfast in Mexico. In addition to its branded restaurants, the company also operates 100 McCafe units in Latin America. The coffee and dessert cafe concept originated in Australia and has become popular throughout Latin America. Specialty items in Canada include the McLobster, a lobster salad sandwich offered in the summer months and Poutine, which features French fries topped with gravy and cheese curds. There are also different designs for its play-land concepts. McDonaldlandia in Mexico features an area for physical play as well as Nintendo video game stations. It also has a snack kiosk and a waiting area for parents. In France the Ronald Gym Club offers a variety of physical activity areas for kids, including basketball, dance and judo stations.

3.3 Social Impact

According to the McDonald's (McDonald's, 2002) plan, they pride themselves in having well trained employees that will proudly provide fast, friendly and accurate service with a smile, in a way that delights their customers. They have a responsibility to maintain a work environment where everyone feels valued and accepted for personal and professional growth, and to promote job satisfaction. This plan and responsibility have the positive impact of developing 'work ethics', particularly for younger workers who join the work force. The concept of having part-time workers, homemakers, the elderly and so on, which is practiced by many fast food restaurants at home in the US, is new and exciting for many prospective workers in different countries. In the United States, McDonald's alone have taught work ethics to millions of college students who are starting their professional career or who would like to support part or whole of their educational expenses. In a study carried out by Royle (1995) McDonald's workers in the UK and Germany were found to be fundamentally similar: largely deskilled owing to high levels of automation, and were part-time and shift workers. Usually only management had full-time contracts.

Working for McDonald's is considered to be highly desirable and prestigious by many in several countries. They receive a lot of applications from well-educated candidates. This is also true for other franchise businesses. Well structured training programs developed by franchise restaurants help in teaching teamwork, coordination, planning, synchronization and execution in a timely fashion. In addition to excellent training opportunities, stepwise promotion from line workers to managers were unheard of in many countries where only seniors based on age alone were given priority. The age-old requirement in some countries to work only for one corporation during one's lifetime has changed partly due to the influx and availability of jobs provided by franchise restaurants. According to Watson (2000), 'McDonald's opened in Beijing in 1992, a time when changes in family values were matched by a sustained economic boom. The startup date also coincided with a public "fever" for all things American-sports, clothing, films, food, and so on.' American-style birthday parties became key to the McDonald's expansion strategy. Prior to the arrival of McDonald's, festivities marking youngsters' specific birth dates were unknown in most of East Asia. In Hong Kong and India, for instance, lunar-calendar dates of birth were recorded for use in later life – to help match prospective marriage partners' horoscopes or choose auspicious dates. McDonald's and its rivals now promote the birthday party complete with cake, candles, and silly hats, in television advertising aimed directly at kids. Arranging birthday parties has become a very popular activity in most of the franchise restaurants, particularly in countries where celebrating birthdays was not known.

According to Watson (2000):

> given that most people in these cities live in tiny, overcrowded flats, the local Kentucky Fried Chicken or McDonald's is a convenient and welcoming place for family celebrations ... For the first time in Chinese history, children matter not simply as future providers but as full-scale consumers who command respect in today's economy. Until the 1980s, kids rarely ate outside the home. When they did, they were expected to eat what was put in front of them. The idea that children might actually order their own food would have shocked most adults ... In effect, the fast-food industry helped start a consumer revolution by encouraging children as young as three or four to march up to the counter, slap down their money, and choose their own food ... In Hong Kong, McDonald's has become so popular that parents use visits to their neighborhood outlet as a reward for good behavior or academic achievement.

Children are major target consumers and a driving force most in of the fast food restaurants worldwide. It is more than food that has made American restaurant franchises popular in other countries. It is a unique combination of cleanliness of restaurant, toilet facilities, quick service, value meals, air-conditioned atmosphere, different ambience, and the association of a super power. School and college kids go to fast food operations to socialize, enjoy the lighted atmosphere, and spend hours after school in those places. The elderly use these restaurants to get out of crowded living quarters, enjoy the openness and read the newspapers provided. Thus McDonald's is a place of socialization in many countries as opposed to being a fast turnover place in the United States. Sometimes social and religious dilemmas occur due to certain restrictions imposed by franchisors. For example the half-sleeve shirts worn by many in fast-food restaurants are frowned upon by people in countries such as Malaysia and the Middle East, where women normally follow a strict dress code. Women in Saudi Arabia are not allowed to drive or work freely in public places, which is very different for fast-food restaurants where females work on the front counter.

Another indirect or direct impact of fast foods is the creation of public civility, which was ignored in many countries. Crowded counters, customer rage, noisy atmosphere, breaking lines, discriminatory customers, and impatience were witnessed in many restaurants. However, with standard procedures, providing an attendant as well as with peer customer pressure, lines are well organized, and discipline is noted in little things like picking up and disposing of trash. In addition, the concept of self-service and self help is becoming popular in countries where such concepts were not prevalent traditionally.

Historically many family owned restaurants in Europe were closed on certain days of the week, on holidays, and for about two weeks during the late summer for family vacations. Most of the franchise restaurants including McDonald's are open on more days and hours than local businesses. This has affected the local restaurant practices as well as employees who would like to enjoy the former break periods. Also, drive-thrus, late night operations, delivery service, and 24-hour operations are new to many countries, which have their own implications on the social activities of the region. Problems faced by Canadian businesses stem from extreme weather during some months as well as their national bilingualism. Every document, voicemail and email has to be translated both into French and English simultaneously.

3.4 Economical

There is great interest in franchising because of the recent and projected impact of franchising on the world economy in the next decade. Franchising is one means of providing capital, needed services, and management training to businesses in communities that are experiencing rapid growth in their economy. Out of necessity and demand, many restaurants have to rely on growing their own products, thereby employing a local workforce. For instance, the demand for French fries in China and Russia encouraged local suppliers to provide varieties of potatoes with specific requirements. The technical and agricultural information for increasing crop productivity provided farmers with new tools and methods. Also, the logistics of managing the supply chain from field to restaurant provided a fresh insight into doing things differently and more productively.

Prices set by McDonald's restaurants worldwide are used as a barometer to measure the purchasing power of a country. The Big Mac index has become a comparative tool to assess certain financial parameters. The index is also an indicator of the pricing flexibility and differentiations that McDonald's allows for its products as well as an indication of local economy and purchasing power. *The Economist's* Big Mac index is based on the theory of purchasing-power parity (PPP), based on the notion that exchange rates should move to equalize the prices of a basket of goods and service across different countries. This differential is used for the comparative valuation of currency in respective countries. Table 17.3 shows a comparison of Big Mac prices in selected countries.

The concept of franchising is based on territorial expansion. This in turn results in a cycle of more sales, more use of resources and more overall purchasing. Also, prices have to be reasonable and well within the reach of an average person worldwide. Because of the standardization and ease of comparability, Big Mac indices were developed which provided an indication of the purchasing power of the country or region. Prices are based on the cost of resources needed, affordability by customers, competitors' prices, and value provided. Also the size of the population segments willing to pay offered prices is an important consideration for countries. Depending upon the country, the strategic decision is based on whether market penetration/share or competitive edge is desired. Similarly value pricing is carried out based on the country or region. McDonald's features the EuroSaver menu in several European markets and Amazing Value Menu in Asia, which parallels the Dollar Menu in the United States. In Russia, only hard currencies were accepted in many places, thereby restricting their use by common persons who only had the local currency of the people, Rubles. McDonald's broke that tradition by accepting only Rubles, which literally opened doors for common persons to visit restaurants. McDonald's focus on providing everyday low prices and value in their restaurants. Each restaurant has a 'branded affordability menu', which includes such low priced items as sandwiches, fries, drinks and desserts. These prices make products more affordable to local residents in every market.

The PLC or the product life cycle also becomes important in making decisions about the prices and how to compete with different products in the existing market. For some local businesses it may become very hard to compete, since franchising has collective power and can sustain losses when necessary. As is evident, many of the sandwich bakeries in the UK, soup and noodles shops in Thailand, and street vendors in most of the Asian countries were affected by the rise of franchise restaurants, where readily available hot food is sold at an affordable price in a relatively inviting atmosphere. Critics argue that McDonald's low prices force the local businesses out by undercutting them.

3.5 Political/Legal

For different political motives, franchise restaurants have been the targets of worldwide, sometimes violent, protests as seen in California, Mexico City, Taiwan, Beirut, France, and so on. McDonald's is often the preferred site for anti-American demonstrations even in places where the local embassies are easy to get at. McDonald's is more than a purveyor of food;

Table 17.3   Comparison of Big Mac prices in selected countries

Country	Big Mac Price $*	Under (–)/over (+) valuation against the US dollar, %
United States**	3.06	–
Argentina	1.64	–46
Australia	2.50	–18
Brazil	2.39	–22
Britain	3.44	+12
Canada	2.63	–14
China	1.27	–59
Denmark	4.58	+50
Egypt	1.55	–49
Euro area	3.58***	+17
Iceland	6.67	+118
Indonesia	1.53	–50
Jordan	3.66	+19
Lebanon	2.85	–7
Malaysia	1.38	–55
Morocco	2.73	–11
Norway	6.06	+98
Pakistan	2.18	–29
Russia	1.48	–52
Saudi Arabia	2.40	–22
South Africa	2.10	–31
South Korea	2.49	–19
Sri Lanka	1.75	–43
Switzerland	5.05	+65
Taiwan	2.41	–21
Thailand	1.48	–52
Turkey	2.92	–5
UAE	2.45	–20
Venezuela	2.13	–30

Notes:
*   At exchange rate (2005)
**   Purchasing-Power Parity
***Weighted average of member countries

it is a saturated symbol for everything that environmentalists, protectionists, and anti-capitalist activists find objectionable about American culture. McDonald's even stands out in the physical landscape, marked by its distinctive double-arched logo and characteristic design (Watson, 2000). Through successful global marketing of the McDonald's franchise, the 'Golden Arches' have come to symbolize American fast food and its related services such as convenience, quality, value and cleanliness. In Europe, anger behind the protests stems from a set of interrelated issues: escalating trade tensions and the importation of hormone-treated beef, dispute over the openness of the European Union markets to US goods, and French fears of the decay of their national culture as the US burrows deeper into French society (Kramer, 2000).

An area of great concern to franchising relates to laws governing the franchisor-franchisee relationship. Laws, rules and regulations vary from country to country. The very success of franchising is based on sound laws, which can be defended when necessary. In some countries either there is a complete lack of such laws or there is a problem with their implementation. Major differences exist even between the US and the EC systems. Whereas the United States has detailed state and federal laws regulating the franchisor-franchisee relationship, the EC has regulated it only through the general antitrust provisions in the Treaty of Rome and the competition law of each member state. The antitrust provisions of the treaty prohibit anything that tends to prevent or restrict competition between member states, which in franchising terms means exclusive territories and price controls. Problems in many countries also relate to the copyright and patent laws. Franchising concepts are closely guarded by franchisors, and any infringement leads to unfair competition. Thus the impact of franchising has been on either development of franchising laws or modifications in existing laws.

Laws affecting health and safety have a distinct impact on the functioning of chains in different countries. The widespread outbreak of avian flu in Southeast Asia in the past few years has had an impact on poultry sourcing for various franchise chains. Countries banned importation of products from affected areas which limits the sources available for importation.

McDonald's restaurants in many Middle Eastern markets have continued to operate despite the history of conflict. They have localized all the McDonald's in those countries by providing local ownership of restaurants in the region and the employment of local workers. All restaurants in the region are halal-approved, meaning that food is prepared and handled according to the tenets of Islamic law.

3.6 Impact on Human Resources

As a franchise operation, there is no more successful model than McDonald's Corporation, with more than 30 000 locations worldwide. In Europe alone, McDonald's has approximately 4850 locations, and the number keeps increasing. The effect of this one company on the service industry has been profound, from marketing and sales approaches to quality control, management methods, training and pricing. Arguably one of the company's most pervasive influences has been in the area of human resources, recruitment, training and particularly wages. It is not uncommon for McDonald's to be the employer of first resort for young people just entering the workforce, older workers desiring extra income, or for those planning on transferring from one corporation to another. The first Russian McDonald's located at Pushkin Square in Moscow received more than 27 000 applications in response to a single advertisement. McDonald's has become the trend setter in many aspects in different countries. For example, throughout all countries in Europe, it has become commonplace to look to the fast-food giant for trends in wages at entry level. In fact, in Europe there is now what is generally referred to as the 'McDonald's factor', a financial guide on worker wages that is published in the financial pages of major newspapers throughout the region. It is a commonly used economic indicator and a guide for other service sector businesses as to what the trends in worker wages are in their area. Other corporations and governmental agencies have used the information as a benchmark for entry-level employment and wages. For example, McDonald's places much emphasis on employee training to attain a standard level of service, regardless of the restaurant or the country they are in. Most training programs, which are an integral and mandatory part of the franchise agreement, are very carefully designed and cover all operational aspects. McDonald's has traced a number of other benefits to ongoing training – particularly in terms of improved morale and productivity. Apart from operational competence, training leads to personal development and creates a sense of achievement and belonging, which are highly valued in many countries.

3.7 Technological

Every franchise restaurant concept is based on specific operational and management criteria, which include technology in one form or another. The use of equipment, special control devices, temperature regulators, point-of-sales systems, inventory upkeep, financial information and communications are all linked to different technologies. Thus major technology transfer takes place when one franchise concept moves into another country. Both tangible and non-tangible technological aspects are transferred, which is necessary to provide standard quality of products and services. Constant communication links between the franchisor and franchisees are essential for maintaining a healthy relationship. Technology is used for this communication, which may range from day-to-day operation to occasional problem solving activities.

Biotechnology is also a major factor, which is becoming one of the major issues confronting franchise restaurants. In order to meet demands of the growth of restaurants and for quality reasons, biotechnology is being used increasingly.

One of the major positive impacts of franchise restaurants moving to different countries is the technology transfer that takes place. Transition from old-fashioned cash registers to computerized point-of-sale systems, computerized controls in equipment, and touch-screen counters introduced by corporations is conveyed to franchisors in different countries, whereby a uniform and simultaneous technology transfer takes place. For example, McDonald's emphasis on standardization provides the chain with the ability to roll out new technology worldwide. Also, it is planning to provide wireless Internet access to employees and franchisees, thereby improving communications.

3.8 Environmental

Rapid development of restaurant franchises worldwide will also have an impact on external and home environments. The continuous and enormous use of natural resources can disturb the balance in the ecosystem. McDonald's has a Rain Forest Policy, which declares its commitment to beef purchasing practices that do not contribute to tropical deforestation. Natural habitat can be disturbed by extensive deforestation and over-cultivation. Soil erosion and fertility can also be affected if appropriate measures are not taken. Other environmental concerns include water use efficiency, water being a very scarce and valuable resource in many countries. Harmful by-products may be released into the air, which may be due to the functioning within the restaurant or due to the harvest and transportation of needed supplies. Fertilizers and pesticides used for raising crops for animal feeds also add to the environmental concerns. In addition, energy use and sources used for energy become a very major impacting factor in many countries. Heavily populated cities such as Taipei and Jakarta do not have the infrastructure to handle large quantities of waste generated by processes and turnover from franchised restaurants.

Another major impact is related to the amount of waste produced from pre-production practices, leftover items, detergents and cleaning agents, garbage, and packaging materials. Millions of tons of plastic and paper packaging are used per year, which in turn uses chemicals and forest products. McDonald's alone is the largest consumer of beef products in many countries and some of the cattle were raised on ex-rainforest land. Deforestation not only removes vegetation, but also adds to the moving of communities into the cleared areas thereby multiplying the impact. The environmental impact varies from country to country. For example, Japan has limited land and therefore waste reduction becomes a priority, whereas in countries like Brazil and India, energy resources are scarce and need to be controlled. Thus the impact has to be evaluated based on the country where franchise restaurants are operating.

McDonald's is also the biggest purchaser of products such as napkins, clamshells, carryout bags, tray liners and so on. Although it purchases recycled products as well as practicing recycling, there are regions where there are no recycling facilities, where products might affect the environment in an adverse way. Also, McDonald's works with suppliers to incorporate socially responsible practices into their operations. This includes animal handling practices, use of antibiotics, the quality and safety of products and restaurant environments, conservation of natural resources and suppliers' employment practices. Cleaning compounds, insecticides, antibiotics and pesticides can have an impact on human, animal and environmental health. The use of foam materials or materials which do not decompose easily has also become a major concern. Thus recycling becomes extremely important to minimize the impact of waste on the environment. Franchise restaurants have to adopt social, environmental, and animal welfare actions in order to address most of the above-mentioned concerns.

4. CONCLUSION

An effort was made in this chapter to illustrate the global impact of restaurant franchising when viewed from a multinational point of view. McDonald's corporation was used as an example, since it is growing rapidly worldwide. Considerable positive and negative impacts are taking place which can be related to cultural, social, economical, environmental, political/legal and technological consequences. Since very little has been researched and published in this area, there is a considerable lack of empirical data on this subject. The intent of this chapter is to bring attention to the fact so that further studies can be conducted.

REFERENCES

Anonymous (1997), 'McDonald's focuses on similarities', *HR Magazine*, **42**(7), 107.

Cateora, C. and J.L. Graham (2005), *International Marketing* (12th edn), Boston: McGraw-Hill Irwin.

Chan, P.S. and R.T. Justis (1992), 'Franchising in the EC: 1992 and Beyond', *Journal of Small Business Management*, **30**(1), 83-9.

Cunneen, C. (2004), 'Recipe for success: Fast-food bigwigs vary strategies, menus to make it in 2004 market', *Nation's Restaurant News*, **38**(2), 30.

Gilbert, R.G., C. Veloutsou, M.M.H. Goode and L. Moutinho (2004), 'Measuring customer satisfaction in the fast food industry: a cross-national approach, *The Journal of Services Marketing*, **18**(4/5), 371.

Hofstede, G. (1980), *Culture's Consequences: International Differences in Work Related Values*, Beverly Hills, CA: Sage.

Khan, M.A. (1999), *Restaurant Franchising* (2nd edn), New York: John Wiley & Sons, Inc.

Kramer, G. (2000), 'McDomination', *Harvard International Review*, **22**(2), 12-14.

Lan, Li and M.A. Khan (1995), 'Hong Kong's fast-food industry: an overview', *Cornell Hotel & Restaurant Quarterly*, **36**(3), 34-42.

Lee, M. and F.M. Ulgado (1997), 'Consumer evaluations of fast-food services: a cross-national comparison', *The Journal of Services Marketing*, **11**(1), 39-52.

McDonald's restaurants (2002), 'Report', URL: www.mcdonalds.com.

Royle, T. (1995), 'Corporate versus societal culture: A comparative study of McDonalds', *International Journal of Contemporary Hospitality Management*, **7**(2,3), 52-7.

Trompenaars, Fons and Charles Hampden-Turner (1998), *Riding the Waves of Culture: Understanding Diversity in Global Business* (2nd edn), New York: McGraw-Hill.

United States Congress (1990), Special Report by the Committee on Small Business, *United States Congress*, Washington, DC.

Watson, J.L. (2000),' China's Big Mac attack', *Foreign Affairs*, **79**(3), 120-35.

Zeidman, P.F. (2003), 'The global brand: asset or liability?', *Franchising World*, May/June, 4.

Zeithaml, V.A. and M.J. Bitner (2003), *Services Marketing* (3rd edn), Boston: McGraw-Hill Irwin Publishing.

18. Sustainable tourism, industrial development and multinational corporations: a case of productivity spillovers in Malaysia

Wong Kong Yew and Tom Baum

1. INTRODUCTION

In many developing countries, the most important reason for a country to attract tourism foreign direct investment is perhaps the prospect of acquiring modern technology, interpreted broadly to include product, process and distribution technology, as well as management and marketing skills, which are often scarce or unavailable in developing countries. There are various ways in which nations can benefit from the presence of tourism multinational affiliates. For example, local firms may be able to improve their productivity as a result of forward and backward linkages with tourism multinational affiliates; local hotels may imitate or benchmark their operation with tourism MNC operation strategies; or they may hire workers trained by tourism multinationals. The increase in competition that occurs as a result of foreign presence may also be considered a benefit, in particular if it forces local firms to increase productivity and improve efficiency. This form of benefit can be categorized as 'productivity spillovers'. Another group of benefits that contribute to the more positive attitudes towards tourism FDI can be categorized as 'market access spillovers'. Tourism MNCs often possess strong competitive advantages from their image as international brands, experience and knowledge from previous international operations, established affiliation with other sectors within and between the industry, and existing loyal customers (Dunning and McQueen, 1982). As a result of their own international tourism marketing operations, tourism MNCs may pave the way for local firms to enter the same markets. For example, a new schedule or an increase in frequency of flights to the host country may be created by a tourism MNC; or when a tourism MNC fails to retain the business of its own customer's next visit or recommendation. However, it is worth noting that these processes are desirable for developing countries, but not necessarily desirable for multinational tourism firms.

The diffusion of proprietary knowledge to local hotel companies and hotel personnel is inevitable unless there is complete refusal to have any local business partner or total exclusion of locals in management (Go and Pine, 1995). In many cases, this can only be desirable in the short run. As noted by Kuin (1972) and Livingstone (1989), total exclusion of locals in management is very disadvantageous to the long-term development of the firm in the local environment.

After all, employment of locals in management and establishing local supply networks both backward and forward bring benefits to foreign multinational firms. This is because local managers are more aware of the domestic operational environment. This includes the local authority, community culture and business networks. Similarly, using local suppliers enables goods and services to be imported or obtained and delivered with minimum interruption. This is important because by nature many tourism products have a relatively short elapsed time from production to delivery. As a result, multinational firms will experience greater customer satisfaction, lower operational costs and greater local support, which contribute to a more sustainable long-term profitable operation.

Academic research, both conceptual and empirical, has confirmed the need for foreign multinational involvement in tourism destination development, its significant impact (Berhman, 1974; Billet, 1991; Dunning, 1993; Caves, 1996). Researchers also identify the changing pattern of non-equity involvement as opposed to the equity type of involvement (Rugman, 1982; Dunning and McQueen, 1982; Go and Pine, 1995). This indicates the importance of diffusion of technology (Pine, 1992; Armstrong and Taylor, 2000). It is the objective of this chapter to advance this body of knowledge by examining the degree of productivity spillovers in local industry.

Diffusion of technology or 'technology transfer' by itself will not lead to sustainable industrial development. It is hypothesized that evidence of strong positive productivity spillovers is an essential criterion for long-term sustainable industrial development. In addition, from the perspective of industrial policy, to achieve sustainable industrial development one should match the appropriate policy strategy to stimulate or prevent negative productivity spillovers. This critical point was broadly discussed by Dunning and McQueen (1982), Jenkins and Henry (1982) and Britton (1982) in the early 1980s and was further revisited by Dunning (1997), Dieke (2000) and Kusluvan and Karamustafa (2001). However, it remains conceptual and less specific in term of policy implications.

2. WHAT ARE PRODUCTIVITY SPILLOVERS?

Before further discussion on the productivity spillovers effect, it is important to introduce the term conceptually and analytically so that it gives operationable quality to the study. When companies establish affiliates abroad, they differ from existing firms in the host country for two reasons. One is that they bring with them some amount of the proprietary technology that constitutes their firm-specific advantage, and allows them to compete successfully with other MNCs and local firms that presumably have superior knowledge of local markets, consumer preferences and business practices.

In industries with rapidly changing technologies (and, more generally, in developing host countries) the competitive assets of MNCs are likely to be related to new products and processes. In mature industries, MNCs may base their competitiveness more on marketing skills or organizational advantages, such as the ability to specialize across international borders, in order to exploit the local comparative advantages of various host countries. Another reason is that the entry and presence of MNC affiliates disturbs the existing equilibrium in the market and forces local firms to take action to protect their market shares and profits. Both these changes are likely to cause various types of spillover that lead to productivity increases in local firms.

Generally, productivity spillovers are said to take place when the entry or presence of MNC affiliates leads to productivity or efficiency benefits in the host country's local firms, and the MNCs are not able to internalize the full value of these benefits (Blomstrom et al., 2000).

2.1 Identifying Spillovers from MNC Activities

This section discuss contagion and demonstration effects that result from the presence of international hotel chains in host destinations. Activities by MNC affiliates in a host country with potential productivity spillovers can be broadly classified into two categories, (1) within the host destination and (2) between destinations.

2.1.1 Within the host destination
Within the host destination, MNC affiliates engage in internal operations as well as external linkages with suppliers both forward, for example, coach operators, local travel agents, theme park operators, MICE (meetings, incentives, conferences, exhibitions) operators, and backward, for example, food and beverage (F&B) suppliers, sanitation service providers, hotel

architects. The uniqueness of the tourism industry or, more specifically, the hotel industry, is where both forward and backward linkages are of equal importance (Dunning and McQueen, 1982).

Therefore, more often than not, high quality goods and services are expected by the MNC from its supplier, because the MNC's major competitive advantage is its established brand name that is associated with a perceived international quality standard by international travelers. Therefore, local suppliers will have to meet these detailed specifications of products, produce and services set by international chain hotels. It is from these rigorous processes and requirements that we would expect to have initial evidence of productivity spillovers.

The evidence can be witnessed when, for example, local suppliers that have increased their goods and service quality according to 'international standards' are able to supply identical goods and services to local hotels. This new technology that a local supplier obtains as a result of its affiliation with international chain hotels is therefore available to the local industry and may also experience economies of scale (Go and Pine, 1995; Blomstrom et al., 2000). This may not have been possible earlier for a number of reasons; the costs could have been too high for local hotels to initiate use, the technology may not have been required given the competitive environment before the presence of foreign multinational hotels, and local firms have limited information about costs and benefits of new technology. However, as a result of the presence of multinational hotels, the industry competitive equilibrium has been disturbed (Caves, 1996) and local firms have more information about new technology from MNC affiliates (Blomstrom et al., 2000). Therefore, adaptation or change becomes necessary and less risky at the same time (Caves, 1996).

When local hotels' market position is being threatened by the presence of foreign hotels, this implies that existing technology used by local hotels is relatively inferior to that of their foreign counterparts. Local hotels are believed to be weaker in relative terms in their knowledge of international travelers' wants and needs, international affiliation with tour operators, airlines and also other foreign international hotel chains, and possibly experience in operating in and developing a destination (Dunnings and McQueen, 1982). Foreign multinational hotels enter the host industry with the technology that they already own and have established, and expect to yield additional returns (Caves, 1996; Rodgriguez, 2002). This is also known as rent-seeking activities by multinational firms (Chrystal and Lipsey, 1997).

However, what this study is interested in is how the local hotel industry or the wider tourism industry can potentially benefit from the presence of this superior technology. First of all, multinational affiliates' operations in the host industry will create opportunity for local employees to learn and to be trained in international hotel management skills that eventually will add value to their career development (Go and Pine, 1995). As Pine (1991) suggests, specifically in relation to the hotel industry, this process is known as technology transfer. However, unless this employee leaves the multinational firms and successfully utilizes his or her skills and knowledge in a local hotel, the industry will not experience productivity spillovers.

2.1.2   Between destinations

On the other hand, multinational affiliates in the host industry will closely link their corporate operational activities with the corporate home or regional office. Activities such as central purchasing units, sales and marketing promotion, reservation systems, corporate training, and corporate alliances and affiliations, give them a leading edge or comparative advantage in both technology know-how and cost efficiency (UNCTAD, 1997). These activities will directly and indirectly benefit the host industry and the destination. An example of a direct benefit is activities such as sending local employees offshore for corporate training programs or to a new assignment in another destination (Go and Pine, 1995).

Another dimension of how an MNC's activities could potentially benefit the host nation is that it develops the host nation as an international destination. This means that the host destination becomes more accessible, gaining positive publicity and welcoming international trade of goods and services. Multinational corporations are influential in establishing new air and sea routes to destinations. Besides, tourism promotion has the tendency to boost the positive aspects of a destination rather than projecting negative attributes. Destinations will begin to develop links with international distribution networks for goods and services. Once this is in place, the destination's industrial environment will become more conducive to trade and therefore will attract more foreign investment and trading partners. This means that more international brand hotels will establish operations as well as international food chains, tour operators, airlines and car rental companies. Within the wider service sector, we should also expect to see new international ventures such as banking, finance and insurance in the destination.

This industrial multiplier effect, whether intentional or unintentional, will occur in time. This also explains how a destination gains its equity over time. Destination equity, used in this study, refers to the significant level of knowledge and information that a traveler has about a particular destination in making his/her choice and whether international brands are essential for a comfortable and safe stay. This is based on the argument that 'foreign hotel accommodation as an "experience good" often purchased in an unfamiliar environment where the trademark of the MNE hotel chain guarantees a standard of service with the characteristics demanded by tourists (principally business tourists) from the principal tourist generating countries' (Dunning and McQueen, 1982, p. 89).

This level of knowledge and information can be accumulated by a traveler's own experiences, recommendations by friends and relatives, and information gathered from mass media such as television, printed material, the Internet and so on. Therefore, if there is evidence that suggests that an increasing positive level of destination equity is occurring, one should expect greater spillover presence in the industry. This suggests that the destination is relatively less dependent on the presence of foreign international hotel chains.

2.2 Competition Effect

It does not matter which specific determinant is in place, in terms of ownership, location and internalization advantages as described in Dunning's (1979) eclectic theory of international production, for an MNC to enter a host industry. Whichever determinant applies, it will create competitive disequilibrium in the host industry (Caves, 1996). It raises the level of market concentration in the host industry or spreads oligopolistic markets from the developed industry (home country) to the less developed industry (host country) (Hymer, 1960). The presence of rent-seeking MNCs imposes pressure on local firms to increase productivity and to improve efficiency either by using existing technology, acquiring new technology or by innovation.

Of course, foreign entry may also force local firms out of the industry or to take over existing local oligopolistic firms and, thereafter, monopolize the industry. Hence, the presence of competition-related spillovers between local and foreign multinationals is essential in any industry. Hypothetically speaking, the level of competition-related spillovers can be determined by technology gaps that exist between local and foreign operations and vice versa.

However, since the hotel industry serves various categories of guests, whether segregated by social, economic or geographical criteria, there may not be direct competition between hotels in a destination. Some scholars argue that luxury hotels often attempt to establish a unique market position in an effort to stay competitive, which includes branding and promotional efforts. This means allowing them to operate in an enclave environment (Jenkins, 1982; Blomstrom et al., 2000) and establishing both vertical and horizontal integration to sustain this position (Claves, 1996). Thus, since competition exists only when two or more hotels are targeting the same segment of the market, there will not be any direct competition. Other explanations of the need for market positioning will be the presence of competition so that hotels of a different class are forced to focus on other specific markets (Dev and Klein, 1993). This could means that, in this study, local hotels have no alternative but to forgo the market segment that they used to enjoy before the advent of direct competition from or presence of a foreign multinational hotel chain.

From the traveler's point of view, the pull factor, it could be that brand and perceived international quality will influence the choice of a specific brand, regardless of which geographical region they are from. These travelers are either non-frequent travelers or are price-insensitive and luxury oriented (Dev and Klein, 1993). Therefore, hotels in a destination have to establish their brand equity to attract this specific group of travelers. This means that competing on the grounds of brand equity is unavoidable.

As a result, it is problematic to attempt to draw a line between hotels in order to segregate the competition environment in the market. Therefore, in this study, competition-related spillovers are indicated by the level of productivity of local hotels as a result of productivity spillovers from foreign hotels. This is based on the assumption that hotels are competing based on productivity, which is determined by efficiency in production.

2.3 Market Access Spillovers

This study next discusses a conceptual phenomenon where empirical evidence is scarce. However, the acceptability and validity of this phenomenon should not be jeopardized by the lack of empirical evidence alone. The barrier that prevents the collection of empirical data related to this factor is caused by the complexity of the tourism industry and limited and non-standardized statistical data between nations.

The concept of market access spillovers refers to the direct and indirect efforts by multinational firms to transfer technology and establish networks, at international level, in the host industry (Kusluvan and Karamustafa, 2001). This leads to increases in international visitors that would not have been possible without the presence of the multinational's affiliates in the host country (Dunning and McQueen, 1982). As Blomstrom et al. (2000) suggest, being competent in manufacturing is not enough to become a successful exporter. Companies need to learn to manage international marketing, distribution and servicing of its products. Because these tasks are often associated with high fixed costs, few local firms, particularly those in developing countries, have the skills and resources to take on all these challenges on their own (UNCTAD, 1997).

In the context of the tourism industry, the statement above still fundamentally holds. A majority of tourism firms in many developing destinations have no technical know-how with which to break into international markets (Jenkins and Henry, 1982). The issue of penetrating new international markets is a complex discussion topic. It involves questions of who pays, or how the cost should be shared; doubts between tax receiver and tax payer, and between sectors; questions of which market segment – regions, social classes, interest groups and so on; what tourism product should be offered; the issue of sustainable tourism, alternative tourism, and so on (Burns and Holden, 1995).

For the purpose of this study, the focus is on how the presence of foreign multinational hotels impacts on local hotels positively in term of the number of foreign guests. If the assumption of superior knowledge of international tourism markets possessed by foreign multinational hotels holds, the time dimension is important in discussing the impact. Initially, a destination needs international brand hotels to attract tourists from abroad. Presumably, international hotels will disproportionately attract tourists from their home country, for example Nikko Hotel will attract Japanese tourists and Hilton will attract North American and European tourists. As more international hotels open and there is an increase in international tourist arrivals to the destination, the local industry will have exposure to the technology in providing service to and accessing various market segments by geographical boundary (country and regional), class of travelers (business, leisure and so on), and tourism products (shopping, adventure, nature and so on). International tourists and travelers are now aware of the standards of local hospitality service providers, and therefore will depend less on international brands (Dieke, 1993). Local hotels will use technology know-how from the distribution network established by international multinational hotels to access these markets.

This process take time, and the length of time is highly dependent on the rate of productivity spillovers of both contagion and demonstration effects, as well as competition effects. Therefore, one may suggest, market access spillovers are a product or evidence of positive productivity spillovers. This is a characteristic of developing host industries.

3. ABSENCE OF PRODUCTIVITY SPILLOVERS

Primarily, it is important to emphasize that productivity spillovers are not what multinational firms would like to see or at least are not their objectives in operating in the host industry. Unlike technology transfer, productivity spillovers do not benefit multinationals in terms of operational efficiency or productivity and in fact can be a threat to multinational affiliates. The lesser the competition and the larger the technology gap between foreign and local hotels, the lower the pressure for foreign hotels to be innovative in securing their rent-seeking behavior (Blomstrom et al., 2000; Harvey and Taylor, 2000). As a result, it is in the interest of foreign multinational hotels to secure competitive advantage in advantageous positions by reducing the rate of productivity spillovers. Evidence to support this is that foreign multinational hotels often pay higher wages and benefits to reduce turnover of management personnel, especially with respect to locals (Go and Pine, 1995).

Low productivity spillovers may also come from within the attributes of the host industry. When the technology gaps between two firms are too large, they form a barrier for local hotels to imitate the newest and most profitable technologies used by their international counterparts (UNCTAD, 1997; Blomstrom et al., 2000). High barriers can be explained by high market concentration, scale economies, high initial capital requirements, intensive advertising and advanced technology (UNCTAD, 1997).

Absence of productivity spillovers is a cause of considerable economic development loss and disadvantage. As Dieke (1989) highlights, the danger of the industry being dominated by foreign firms could lead to a loss of development direction. Other issues involve leakages and poverty issues (Britton, 1982). Large and powerful multinational firms are able to avoid taxation through transfer pricing, and repatriate significant amounts of profit from the host industry. This is when local governments have little control due to industry over-dependence on foreign inputs. This is raised by Held et al. (2001) as the phenomenon of corporate power versus state power.

To summarize, it is clear from the above discussion that there are a number of important tourism industrial attributes, which are necessary for positive productivity spillovers. These are labor skills, linkages within and between sectors and industry, competitiveness of local firms and destination equity. Labor skills refer to the basic skills that local employees must have in order to learn and to be trained successfully. This may involve language proficiency and level of education or vocational training. In addition, strong backward and forward industry linkages are essential for productivity spillovers, especially contagion and demonstration type of spillovers. The ability to compete and to secure a market share in a competitive environment is by no means the most important criterion that local hotels must have to achieve sustainable industrial development.

Lastly, destination equity is an asset that a destination can build upon over time, and will serve as a lubricant to stimulate the overall process of productivity spillovers.

As a result, quality knowledge of the state of development of such variables in the host industry is essential in policy decision processes. However, a precise indication of such information is often vague. In this chapter, we have adopted a qualitative approach to capture evidence of productivity spillovers in the Malaysian hotel industry. An elite group of interviews were conducted with key officers and personnel in government institutions, hotel associations and other related organizations.

4. SETTING THE SCENE

The hotel industry in Malaysia is different from that in many developing countries, in that monetary capital is not merely a barrier to development. The majority of the hotels in the country are privately owned by Malaysians. More often than not, hotel investors' core business is not primarily tourism-related. Over the last two decades, developers have seen the opportunity of building and owning hotels merely for their financial potential (that is operation profit, appreciation of property value, goodwill) rather than growth of the hotel industry's resources per se. There are negative implications of such motivations, which involve an influx of foreign managers into the industry and mismatch of policy and industrial development direction.

Because of the potential of the Malaysian tourism and hospitality industry, large corporations have been attracted to build luxury hotels. They invite established hotel brands and management groups to fill in the technology capital gap as a partner (equity form of involvement) or contractual base arrangement (non-equity form of involvement). This is by no means the fastest way to obtain superior technology and, thus, competitive advantage against its local counterpart. The technology that multinational hotel corporations (MNHCs) have to offer includes their international brand image, skilled personnel, production knowledge (that is purchasing, servicing, hotel architecture, and so on), alliances and customer base.

Without doubt, it would be expected that an MNHC would want to live up to its technology and be assured of its effective implementation. This point is particularly true in the initial stage, when a MNHC will send a group of managers to its foreign affiliate to act merely as a bridge of information and control. The owner is not greatly concerned by this practice as long as the financial objectives are delivered. However, as in many other countries in the developing world, requirements were also set that all hotels should involve more locals in middle and top management positions.

It is generally accepted that international managers monopolize key positions in the hotel sector in many developing countries, at least in the infancy phase. It is also a hypothesis that as the industry develops, more local managers will learn and develop and replace the role of foreign international mangers. This is achieved as more locals are employed in foreign MNHCs and receive the training and experience needed for its daily operation of the hotel.

All interviewees agreed that this is the way forward. However, there was still significant evidence of the domination of foreign international managers in the Malaysian hotel industry after almost three decades of growth. This case study reviews some of the reasons that contribute to the continuing reliance on foreign managers. Figure 18.1 represents the various actors that are directly and indirectly responsible for this, and is derived from the interviews undertaken for the research.

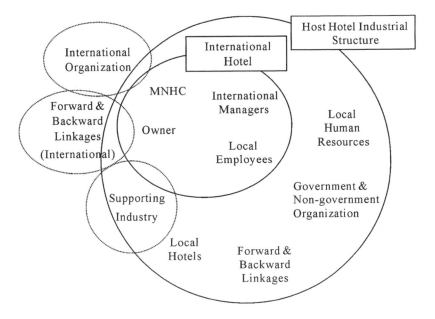

Figure 18.1   Host hotel industrial structure

5. FINDINGS

To engage in the hotel business, especially luxury hotels, involves high initial monetary capital. Owners turn to financial institutions (supporting industry in Figure 18.1) to capitalize their project. The financial institution will then assess the feasibility of the project. It is well known to the industry, as expressed by interviewees, that an important criterion that financial institutions consider as an indication for future success is the operating management group and brand. Not surprisingly, international management hotels with a strong brand and management score highly in this evaluation process. This would seem to indicate a lack of recognition from financial institutions and a clear indication of the lack of confidence in local management skills in the hotel industry.

Even though there are pressures from the OECD (1992) and also initiatives from MNHCs themselves to move towards polycentrism, its implementation is ineffective. Human resource capital in Malaysia has reduced in real terms. Human resource capital is arguably of a lower standard than in the 1980s and early 1990s. The number of local managers in the industry may have increased over time but this does not necessarily indicate higher capability of local managers. As indicated by the President of the Malaysian Hotel Association, over-promoting is an issue that the industry has to acknowledge and rectify. This issue is largely due to significant numbers of jobs at the managerial and supervisory level, which were available during the early to mid-1990s, when many new hotels were built. Since the skills to run a hotel are possessed by the rank and file and are developed through time, it is difficult for MNHCs to find suitable local managers in a pool of 'over-promoting' managers for key positions.

An issue such as English language proficiency among the Malaysian workforce is something that needs addressing. What used to be an advantage is increasingly a disadvantage in the Malaysian hospitality industry. As noted by Gladwin and Walter (1980), the American MNCs have been more successful in engaging locals in higher positions due to ease of finding locals who are fluent in English. The workforce in Malaysia, especially in the 1980s, was known for its English proficiency. However, the medium of education was changed from the English language to the Malaysian language (national language) in the mid-1980s. The resulting decline in English proficiency has led to many problems in training and development of local human resources.

Another concern, as expressed by interviewees, is the willingness of international managers to train local managers. This is particularly the case when local managers are perceived as a threat to their organizational position. This is consistent with Go and Pine's (1995) view that where local managers excelled and demonstrated potential, MNCs would retain these local managers by offering promotion opportunities which are often positions in larger operations of the MNCs in other host countries.

What is surprising is that despite the lower level of English proficiency, the local workforce prefers to be trained by foreign managers. The skills delivered by international mangers are perceived to be international. However, according to an interviewee of an MNHC, there is no doubt that language is the biggest barrier when it comes to the issue of training and development. In addition, the work ethic has changed immensely. The young workforce is less service-oriented than before. The friendly and hospitable culture is missing in the younger generation. The Malaysian hotel industry's previous success was mainly due to its service-oriented culture. Today, however, the workforce is less keen to work at operational levels, while attention is increasingly focused on promotion opportunities from within or amongst other hotels, which are abundant.

A final issue to consider is that while government is known for its role in imposing pressure to have more local managers in key positions, which indirectly contributes to the issue of 'over-promoting', government is also responsible for the pronounced use of international managers in hotels. An example would be the policy to promote local culture and arts in hotels. Hotels are encouraged to employ local artists to perform on their premises. As there was resistance from hotels in the implementation process who argued that the choice of performance should be customer driven, local authorities approached individual hotels. Local hotels or local managers were the initial point of approach in the process. Perhaps they are local and, therefore, should have the initiative and responsibility to promote local culture and arts. This is one example of pressure on local managers, which causes more hotels to use international managers in the process.

6. CONCLUSIONS

The findings in this chapter exhibit the learning process and maturity of the Malaysian hotel industry, particularly in human capital. There was evidence to suggest various forms of obstacles facing the industry in promoting higher degrees of productivity spillovers. However, the indications for potentially positive productivity spiilovers in the industry are relatively strong. Thus, this chapter draws attention to the need for a more integrated tourism planning approach to ensure sustainable tourism industrial development.

REFERENCES

Armstrong, H. and J. Taylor (2000), *Regional Economics and Policy*, Oxford; Blackwell.

Behrman, J.N. (1974), *Decision Criteria for Foreign Direct Investment in Latin America*, New York: Council of the Americas.

Billet, B.L. (1991), *Investment Behavior of Multinational Corporations in Developing Areas: Comparing the Development Assistance Committee, Japanese, and American Corporation*, New Brunswick: Transaction Publishers.

Blomstrom, M., A. Kokko and M. Zejan (2000), *Foreign Direct Investment: Firm and Host Country Strategies*, Basingstoke, UK: Macmillan Press Ltd.

Britton, S.G. (1982), 'The political economy of tourism in the third world', *Annals of Tourism Research*, **9**, 331-58.

Burns, P. and A. Holden (1995), *Tourism, A New Perspective*, Harlow: Prentice Hall.

Caves, R.E. (1996), *Multinational Enterprise and Economic Analysis* (2nd edn), Cambridge and New York: Cambridge University Press.

Chrystal, K.A. and R.G. Lipsey (1997), *Economics for Business and Management*, Oxford: Oxford University Press.

Dieke, P.U.C. (1989), 'Fundamentals of tourism development: a third world perspective', *Hospitality Education and Research Journal*, **13**(2), 7-22.

Dieke, P.U.C. (1993), 'Tourism and development policy in the Gambia', *Annals of Tourism Research*, **20**, 423-49.

Dieke, P.U.C. (2000), *The Political Economy of Tourism Development in Africa*, Elmsford, New York: Cognizant.

Dunning, J.H. (1979), 'Explaining changing patterns of international production: in defence of the eclectic theory', *Oxford Bulletin of Economics and Statistics*, **41**, 269-96.

Dunning, J.H. (1993), *The Globalization of Business: The Challenge of the 1990s*, London and New York: Routledge.

Dunning, J.H. (1997), *World Investment Report, Transnational Corporations, Market Structure and Competition Policy*, New York and Geneva: United Nations.

Dunning, J.H. and M. McQueen (1982), 'Multinational corporations in the international hotel industry', *Annals of Tourism Research*, **9**, 69-90.

Gladwin, T.N. and I. Walter (1980), *Multinationals Under Fire*, John Wiley & Sons.

Go, F.M. and R. Pine (1995), *Globalization Strategy in the Hotel Industry*, London and New York: Routledge.

Held, D., A. McGrew, D. Goldblatt and J. Perratan (2001), *Global Transformations: Polictics, Economics and Culture*, Oxford: Blackwell Publishers Ltd.

Hymer, S.H. (1960), 'The International Operations of National Firms: A Study of Direct Foreign Investment', PhD Dissertation, MIT, Cambridge, Mass. (Published by MIT Press, 1976).

Jenkins, C.L. (1982), 'The effects of scale in tourism projects in developing countries', *Annals of Tourism Research*, **9**, 229-549.

Jenkins, C.L. and B.M. Henry (1982), 'Government involvement in tourism in developing countries', *Annals of Tourism Research*, **9**, 499-521.

Kuin, P. (1972), 'The magic of multinational management', *Harvard Business Review*, November/December, 92-100.

Kusluvan, S. and K. Karamustafa (2001), 'Multinational hotel development in developing countries: an exploratory analysis of critical policy issues', *International Journal of Tourism Research*, **3**, 179-97.

Livingstone, J.M. (1989), *The Internationalization of Business*, Oxford: Macmillan.

OECD (1992), *The OECD Declaration and Decisions on International Investment and Multinational Enterprise: 1991 Review*, Paris: Organization for Economic Cooperation and Development.

Pine, R.J. (1991), 'Technology Transfer in the Hotel Industry', PhD Thesis, The University of Bradford.

Pine, R.J. (1992), 'Technology transfer in the hotel industry', *International Journal Hospitality Management*, **11**(1), 3-22.

Rodríguez, A.R. (2002), 'Determining factors in entry choice for international expansion. The case of the Spanish hotel industry', *Tourism Management*, **23**, 597-607.

Rugman, A.M. (1982), *New Theories of the Multinational Enterprise*, London & Canberra: Croom Helm.

UNCTAD (1997), *World Investment Report 1997: Transnational Corporations, Market Structure and Competition Policy*, New York and Geneva: United Nations Conference on Trade and Development, United Nations.

19. Managerial philosophies, peace culture and the performance of multinational enterprises' cross-cultural management

Tsai-Mei Lin and Gun-Ming Chuang

1. INTRODUCTION

The developments of multinational enterprises (MNEs) have increased dramatically, for instance, the total outward investments of MNEs all over the world were up to US$8000 billion in 2004, which was more than six times as great as in 1990 (US$1330.7 billion). In 2004, the US MNEs reached the world's largest outward investment of US$1788.9 billion, followed by the UK MNEs (US$988.6 billion), and the Japanese MNEs (US$915.6 billion). These statistics demonstrate not only the noteworthy contribution of the economic development of their home and host countries but also the development of the global economy. However, over the last two decades, two forces have led MNEs to change the areas in which they invested. The first force is the trade protection policy of the United States of America against the countries with which the US has a trade deficit, through Section 301 of the Trade Act, which has resulted in severe international trade friction. The second force is the European Union (EU), which is the largest market in the world and includes 25 countries and 4800 million citizens, and also contains high tariffs against non-member countries. MNEs can launch foreign direct investment (FDI) strategies to eliminate the restrictions of the US and EU markets, and to increase their international competitiveness. Nonetheless, the performances of MNEs' business strategies are mainly based on the consistencies of cross-cultural management. In addition, the managerial philosophies of the MNEs' leaders are even more important with all the confrontations caused by Eastern and Western political conflicts, the economic gap between North and South, historical hatred, and frictions between different races and religions.

According to the theory of the MNEs' cross-cultural management (Tsai-Mei Lin, 2003), the performance of MNEs' cross-cultural management is based on the excellence of MNEs' business strategies (S). In turn, the success of these business strategies depends on the superiority of the managerial culture of subsidiaries (M). And, most importantly, the managerial culture of subsidiaries is highly influenced by the MNEs' leaders, with their philosophies of life, society and the world (P). Nevertheless, there is little research concerning this issue. Therefore, the main purpose of this study is to investigate which managerial culture should be adopted by MNEs to increase the subsidiaries' business performances, and which managerial philosophies should be adopted by MNE leaders to increase the global subsidiaries' business performance.

2. CROSS-CULTURAL MANAGEMENT AND BUSINESS PERFORMANCE OF MULTINATIONAL ENTERPRISES

The performance of MNEs' business strategies is positively correlated with the consistence of MNEs' cross-cultural management. The evolution of management thought started with the scientific management theory of Frederick K. Taylor, who considered that the effects of tasks or work mainly rely on the efficiency of scientific management (Taylor, 1967). His follower, Elton Mayo, has amplified that management should be focused on human behavior, which is called behavioral science (Mayo, 1933). Later came McGregor's X theory and Y theory, concerned about employees' moral and group needs (McGregor, 1966). The super Y theory, presented by Morse and Lorsch (1970), stated the importance of humanity. Ouchi's Z theory amplified the basic managerial philosophies, being concerned with the relationships among mankind, tasks and enterprises, and the long-term benefits of employees, customers and societies (Ouchi, 1981). However, these theories do not take cross-cultural differences into account. Over the last 30 years, because of the rapid developments of MNEs, the casual comparative studies of cross-cultural management have received more attention. Nonetheless, little research has empirically analyzed the effects of the differences, such as social cultures, organizational cultures and values, between the home countries and the host countries, on the performance of business management of MNEs' subsidiaries.

2.1 MNEs' Cross-Cultural Management

The theory of MNEs' cross-cultural management (Tsai-Mei Lin, 1994) is concerned with the consensus of different cultural management styles

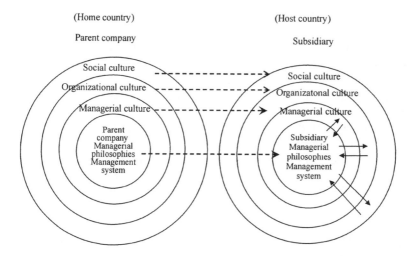

Source: Tsai-Mei Lin (1994)

Figure 19.1   Organizational culture and managerial philosophies

between two countries (M). It explains what kinds of management systems across cultures, expatriated managers should be adopting in order to better the business performances of subsidiaries in the host countries, and to strengthen their competitive power in the international market after considering the differences of social cultures, organizational cultures, managerial philosophies and managerial systems between these two countries (see Figure 19.1). This is the main issue that expatriates should pay more attention to. There are three types of cross-culture management, namely, the first culture management, the second culture management, and the third culture management (Tsai-Mei Lin, 1994).

In the first culture management, representing the home country's managerial culture, the managers of the parent company apply the social culture of their home country and the organizational culture and managerial philosophies of the parent company in the subsidiary to map out the management systems of the parent company. The parent company's management system philosophy is manifested through the knowledge system, the denotation system and the value system.

In the second culture management, representing the host countries' managerial culture, based on the social culture of the host country and the organizational culture and managerial philosophies of the subsidiaries, the managers of the subsidiaries map out the management system which is manifested through the knowledge system, the denotation system and the value system.

In the third culture management, integrating the advantages of managerial culture between home and host countries, the expatriated managers should fully understand the first culture of the parent company and be aware of the second culture indigenous to the host country. In order to enhance the management performance of the subsidiary in the host country, compared to other local companies, expatriate managers should integrate the advantages of the first culture and the second culture. This will be manifested in the new knowledge system, denotation system and value system and lead to the third culture management. The third culture will have a positive effect on encouragement and will improve management effectiveness for the employees under the management of the first culture and the second culture.

2.2   The Third Culture Management of the US and Japanese MNEs and their Business Performances in Taiwan

2.2.1   The consensus of cross-cultural management of the US and Japanese MNE subsidiaries in Taiwan

Based on the cross-cultural management theory, the author conducted a survey in 2004. A questionnaire was answered by 128 general managers of the Japanese and US MNE subsidiaries located in Taiwan. The results show that the US MNEs considered that the third culture management is the most important management system for human resources, recruitment, education and training, promotion, salary, compensation, rewards, pensions and redundancy. Similarly, besides recruitment, education and training, and promotion systems, which were considered best under the first culture management, the Japanese MNEs also considered that the third culture management is the most important system (see Table 19.1). This indicated that both US and Japanese MNEs, which implemented the third culture management as management systems, perform better than Taiwanese domestic firms.

2.2.2   The Comparison of Benefits in US and Japanese MNE Subsidiaries in Taiwan

Both the US and Japanese MNEs' subsidiaries in Taiwan all agree that the third culture management is the most important management system. Regarding the management systems adopted, US MNEs adopted the second culture management system, while Japanese MNEs adopted the first one. As a consequence, the benefits earned by employees of the Japanese MNEs such as travel expenses, bonuses and holidays, are more favorable than those of the US MNEs. For example, the annual bonus of most Japanese subsidiaries is more than three months'salary. On the other hand, few US subsidiaries give a lantern festival bonus or birthday vacation (see Figure 19.2).

2.2.3   The comparison of employee morale in US and Japanese MNE subsidiaries in Taiwan

Virtue is the most important employee promotion factor for the Japanese MNEs, compared the performance considered by the US MNEs. For instance, if facing an economic recession, the Japanese MNEs would reduce an employee's salary, and the US MNEs would tend to lay off the employee. Moreover, taking Taiwan as an example, employees do not want to be laid off as unemployment benefit is not universal (see Table 19.2). The frequency and amount of education and training provided by the Japanese MNEs is double that provided by the US MNEs. Owing to the fact that the Japanese MNEs use the first culture to educate and train their employees, the education and training in morale and skills is very rigorous. In addition, all of the benefit systems of the Japanese MNEs are much better than the US MNEs. As a result, the employee morale at the Japanese MNEs is much higher, the turnover rate is comparatively low, and the incidence of lateness or leaving work early is lower (below 3 per cent) than the US MNEs. In contrast, the turnover rate in the US MNEs is higher. Regarding quality control, most of the employees in Japanese MNEs would feel ashamed if they failed to perform well, and they would feel proud if they enhanced their capability. In comparison, most of the employees in the US MNEs lack a sense of quality control. As a result, the product quality of the Japanese MNEs is higher than that of the US MNEs, and the product price of the Japanese MNEs is much lower. As for the after-sales service, most employees of the Japanese MNEs are willingly to provide emergency service to customers after office hours, but most employees of the US MNEs insist that the time after work is their leisure time and are unwilling to provide maintenance services to customers; this may lead to higher customer loyalty to Japanese MNEs (see Figure 19.3).

2.2.4   The business performances of the third culture management of the US and Japanese MNE subsidiaries in Taiwan

Since most of the US and Japanese MNE subsidiaries adopted the third culture management as the most important management strategy, their inventory turnover rates, accounts receivable rates, fixed assets rates, operating profits, return on capital and return on fixed assets are higher

Table 19.1   Comparison between the cross-cultural management of US and Japanese MNEs in Taiwan in 2004

Origins of MNE management systems	US MNEs		Japanese MNEs	
	Majority	The next important style	Majority	The next important style
Human resources	3rd culture	2nd culture	3rd culture	1st culture
Recruitment	3rd culture	2nd culture	1st culture	3rd culture
Education and training	3rd culture	1st culture	1st culture	3rd culture
Promotion	3rd culture	1st culture	1st culture	3rd culture
Salary	3rd culture	2nd culture	3rd culture	1st culture
Benefits	3rd culture	2nd culture	3rd culture	1st culture
Reward	3rd culture	2nd culture	3rd culture	1st culture
Pension	3rd culture	1st culture	3rd culture	1st culture
Lay-off	3rd culture	1st culture	3rd culture	1st culture

Source: Survey by Tsai-Mei Lin (2004)

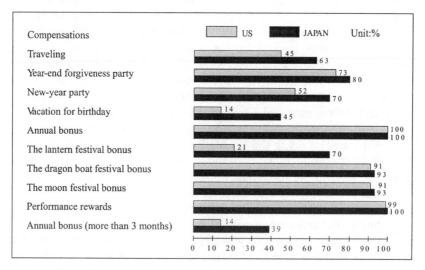

Source: Survey by Tsai-Mei Lin (2004)

Figure 19.2   Comparison of benefits in US and Japanese MNE subsidiaries in Taiwan in 2004

than the Taiwanese domestic enterprises. Because most US subsidiaries adopted the second culture management while most Japanese subsidiaries adopted the first and the third culture management, this may lead to better benefits, education and training, employee morality, product quality, lower

Table 19.2   Comparison of promotions and recruitment of general employees
in US and Japanese MNEs

	US MNEs		Japanese MNEs	
	Majority	Next important	Majority	Next important
Recruitment systems	Capability	Experience	Experience	Capability
Promotion systems	Performance	Personality	Personality	Performance
Lay off systems	Lay off	Salary reduction	Salary reduction	Job exchange

Source: As Table 19.1

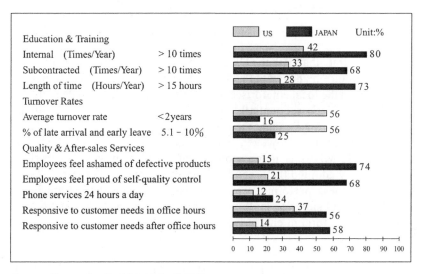

Source: Survey by Tsai-Mei Lin (2004)

Figure 19.3   *Comparison of employee morality in US and Japanese*
MNE subsidiaries in Taiwan in 2004

prices, and higher sales growth rates. Consequently, the accounts receivable
rates, the fixed assets rates, the operating profits, return on capital and
the return on fixed assets of the Japanese subsidiaries are better than the
US subsidiaries (see Table 19.3).

In sum, the US and Japanese MNE subsidiaries, which were primarily
considering the third culture management as their managerial culture,
have better business performances than the local enterprises. Our results

Table 19.3 Comparison between the financial performances in the US,
and Japanese MNEs, and Taiwanese companies in Taiwan

Unit: %

Financial Indices (%)	US MNEs	Japanese MNEs	Taiwanese Company
Inventory turnover rate	10.33	7.55	5.5
Accounts receivable rate	5.56	15.15	4.2
Fixed assets rate	1.95	10.56	2.2
Operating profits	3.65	6.58	2.3
Return on capital	17.29	207.93	3.1
Return on total assets	1.45	12.52	3.1
Return on fixed assets	7.11	69.48	4.6

Source: Investment Commission of Ministry of Economic Affairs, Taiwan (2003).

also demonstrate that both the US and Japanese MNE subsidiaries consider the third culture management as their managerial culture, and they have outperformed the local enterprises. In addition, our results also demonstrate that the US MNEs sequentially adopt the second management culture, and the Japanese MNEs adopt the first management culture as the sequential management culture. However, the first culture management adopted by the Japanese MNEs is much more suitable for Taiwanese enterprises, which mostly adopted the second culture management; hence the results that the business performances of the Japanese subsidiaries are better than the US subsidiaries in Taiwan. This result attracts the attention of Taiwanese and foreign enterprises.

3. MNES' MANAGERIAL PHILOSOPHIES OF A PEACE CULTURE AND GLOBAL BUSINESS PERFORMANCE

3.1 Managerial Philosophies

Managerial philosophies are the doctrines, beliefs and ideologies held by managers, which have a profound influence on the setting of business objectives, business actions, and the benefits of shareholders, employees and other interested parties. Managerial philosophies are manifested in a firm's doctrines and the behavior and attitudes of its managers. Managerial philosophies can be classified into three types: innovative, conservative and reactionary. They can also be classified into the typical type and modern type. The typical type is held by the owner-manager. The modern type is held by professional managers. In general, typical and reactionary types of managers believe that the purpose of a firm is profit maximization. On the other hand, the modern and innovative types of manager believe that the purpose of a firm is social responsibility. However, not all professional managers embrace the modern type of managerial philosophy. Consequently, it is the innovative type of managers who believe in social responsibility. The business performance of MNE subsidiaries is highly correlated with the managerial philosophies held by MNE leaders.

3.2 The Comparison between the Managerial Philosophies of Japanese and US Enterprises

3.2.1 The managerial philosophies of US enterprises
The history of scientific management started about one century ago. During the last century, scientific management developed fastest and most systematically in the US. The rigorous management systems created by Americans with exploration spirit, have resulted in considerable profits for US organizations. The US enterprises were based on the traditional spirit of individualism, efficiency and quantitative control and hence created a new era of mercantilism.

The American way of business management (Ouchi, 1981) is the product of American culture, with an emphasis on speed, the quest for quick results, immediate rewards, individual interests, high productivity for high returns, quantitative data as the standard for evaluation, material results and profits. The interests of shareholders are considered to be much more important than the needs of employees and society.

3.2.2 The managerial philosophies of Japanese enterprises
The characteristics of the Japanese style of management are team-culture featuring warm-heartedness, permanent employment and loyalty. Precise division of labor, high profit margins, low employee turnover, and excellent technology are not the main goals for managers. Japanese managers are proud of having these managerial philosophies whereby individuals can realize their philosophical ideals through the business operation. Japanese firms merge managerial philosophies with the enterprise in order to develop a common consensus as a family enterprise, with a trust and close affiliation that outsiders can never understand. Internally, the social life, work and livelihood of employees can be satisfied by this company philosophy. Externally, the long-term plan of the enterprise will not be affected by the pursuit of short-term profits, and can be achieved step by step. At the same time, Japanese companies have a kind of mentor-protégé

relationship whereby senior employees will pass their experiences and skills on to junior employees. They may have their job assignments individually, but they can also work as a team.

The managerial philosophies of the Japanese and US MNEs are quite different and both have their strengths and weaknesses. This study suggests that differences of social culture, organizational culture and managerial philosophies between home and host countries will greatly affect managerial performance.

3.3   The Managerial Philosophies of a Peace Culture in MNEs

In order to acquire consensus among multiple different cultures, ethnicities and countries (P), MNE leaders must break through the barriers between multiple different cultures, ethnicities, religions and countries. Only by obtaining the support of multiple different cultures, ethnicities and countries will MNEs increase the business performance of subsidiaries all over the world. This reveals the importance of further investigation of 'managerial philosophies of a peace culture'.

Tsai-Mei Lin (2006) has proposed the managerial philosophies of a peace culture in MNEs. Those who have lived in the twentieth century have experienced war and peace, East-West political confrontations, North-South economic differences, religious and cultural problems, and ethnic problems. As a result, MNEs must adopt 'managerial philosophies of a peace culture' to enhance business performance through cross-cultural management. For example, Buckley (1991) found that although products made by different countries had become similar in technology, the products still strongly reflected national features. Daniels (1991) suggests that MNEs should pay more attention to the management of cultural difference relating to different ethnicities in the twenty-first century. Dunning (1995) found that although the integration of economy and technology led to a massive homogeneous market, it also led to ethnic and religious problems between countries. In this chapter, although we have investigated the relationship between the third culture management and the business performance of MNE subsidiaries, it is very important to understand the impact of cross-cultural management of multiple ethnicities on the business performance of MNE subsidiaries.

3.3.1   The world peace philosophy of Ikeda Daisaku
Dr Ikeda Daisaku promotes the ideology of 'world peace and human well-being' to the whole world. He is an educationist, philosopher, religionist, and he is also the chairman of Soka Gakkai International (SGI). He has been conferred with an honorary doctoral degree and professorship by

more than 180 universities all over the world. He was awarded the UN Peace Award in 1983. Later, he was also awarded the United Nations High Commissioner for Refugees' (UNHCR) Humanitarian Award in Geneva in 1989. The purpose of the United Nations is to bring all nations of the world together to work for peace and world security, based on the principles of justice, human dignity and the well-being of all people. Like the United Nations, SGI addressed itself to respecting human dignity and the well-being of all people, and it is dedicated to world peace, culture, and education.

3.3.1.1 Dr Ikeda Daisaku's world peace philosophy

People living in the twentieth century have experienced 'war and peace', 'discrimination against equality', and 'poverty and affluence'. Dr Ikeda, the Chairman of SGI, takes a humanitarian position, based on Buddha dharma, and has broken the constraining influence of national boundaries through the philosophy of peace with the ideas of 'public priority' and 'people are the foundations'. Pursuing the idea of 'world peace', 'human intergrowth', and 'protection of the earth's environment', and so on, Dr Ikeda has initiated schemes to solve the international problems caused by a rapidly changing society. He has emphasized that the precondition for removing dispute among races and nations is to talk about 'mercy and liberality' with each other, and hence to make humankind look forward to a new century of humanity (Ikeda, 1999). The ideas about world peace and human well-being are simply as follows:

1. *Humanism*: this explains the limitless nature of the dignity of human life, there is 'mercy', to forgive people, and 'wisdom' to overcome all difficulties. This wisdom can not only expand the creativity of the human spirit, but it can also overcome any crisis, and create intergrowth and a peaceful society. Mercy means to relieve others' pain and unease, to offer happiness and hope, and to dedicate oneself to human well-being.
2. *Compassionate spirits*: with the idea of world citizens, compassionate spirits respect human rights, which is based on humanism. We should devote ourselves to the entire society and make some contribution to it. We should sincerely respect others, for instance, respect them as a prestigious guest or Buddha.
3. *Mercy, wisdom and courage*: the spirits of leaders should execute everything with mercy and wisdom, and should have courage, just as Mount Fuji towers impressively, and resolutely confronts the high wind, but enjoyed the owned 'justice' and brilliant victory to history.
4. *Buddhism 'five eyes sutra'*: the Five eyes are: 'Human eye', 'Divine

eye', 'Wisdom eye', 'Dharma eye', and 'Buddha eye'. MNE leaders should not evaluate others with a 'Human eye', but with a 'Divine eye' to observe others wisely, with a 'Wisdom eye' to take in evidence, and with a 'Dharma eye' to discriminate between goodness and evil and to treat others with mercy.

5. *The morality of intergrowth*: when people suffer from incurable disease in the twenty-first century, it is urgent and necessary to have reconciliation, unification and completeness instead of confrontation, distraction and selfishness.

6. *The earth of intergrowth*: rain fertilizes the earth, and helps grass and trees to germinate. All of us grow harmoniously on this nutritional land. Intergrowth means dependent origination, which reflects the fact that no one or nothing can exist alone; objects and humans are interconnected, interdependent and sequentially become one world.

7. *The principals of intergrowth among cherry blossoms, plums, peaches and prunes*: the cherry blossoms, plums, peaches and prunes bloom individually, and do not damage others or confront others. The idea of intergrowth is to cherish the differences among people and hence to establish a gorgeous spectacle of a life park together. There are different personalities, races and religions in the world, and the well-being of humans and world peace would be improved if these different cultures could intergrow harmoniously.

8. *Infinity of wisdom*: the origin of infinity of wisdom is the action of listening to people; with the idea of the nationalism of earth, to overcome the idea of 'ethnocentric enterprise' and to intergrow harmoniously. The purpose of education is the well-being of children.

9. *Mercy sutra*: to cultivate how to respect the 'intergrowth culture' of each person, to adjust the path of human history from discord to harmony, confrontation to cooperation, from war to peace, and hence to implement the action of Bodhisattva.

10. *The idea of the earth citizens*: the intelligent person with a deep understanding of life; the brave person who does not fear or is not against the differences of nationality, culture and races, and also who respects and understands these differences; the merciful person who can help and guide those who suffer hardship.

We look forward to the time when there will be a better peaceful world in the twenty-first century, where people show more consideration and mercy.

3.3.1.2   The consensus of the philosophy of peace between Dr Ikeda Daisaku and world leaders

Dr Ikeda cares greatly about human well-being and world peace, and after spending five decades visiting national leaders, educators and renowned artists all over the world (Ikeda, 1999) and investigating how to implement the 'philosophy of peace', he emphasizes that leaders should adopt a consensus concerning world peace and human well-being. The points are as set out below:

'The idea of popular benefits'. Working on behalf of other countries can also be a benefit to oneself. We should not wait for peace to come to us, but we should go out and take action to achieve it.[1] The wisdom of harmonious multinationality lies in a 'sincere heart', caring about other nationalities, and striving for peace, which could gain support from different nations, cultures and races.[2] Leaders should fully understand their colleagues' minds, which means that others' suffering is one's own, and should adopt the philosophy of 'share, stick together through thick and thin blissfully'.[3] Interpersonal relationships are based on 'the heart' and irrigation of trees is based on 'the root'.[4] 'Hearts' are more important than 'fighter planes'. Human beings' dignity would be destroyed if all communication among human beings was based on computer control.[5] The nation must be a moral nation, educational nation and humanitarian nation, which would be much more powerful than a military nation with a million armies.[6] The hopes of human beings are for world peace. It would be much better to integrate the European Union with human love than with military force.[7] Scientific progress should give children a healthy earth, and there should be no nationality in the dignity of life.[8] We should be world citizens, all human beings living in a global village, and we should respect each other's human dignity. People should not focus mainly on economic interests, but on the culture, humanity and democracy of the whole human being, and should coexist peacefully.[9] Each person is an instrument of his or her own mind; when the mind changes, everything will change. The essence is that the leadership culture is the kingcraft culture, which employees should obey not with 'strength' or 'authority', but with 'virtue'.[10] We should focus on the well-being of all humans, instead of focusing on our own happiness, which is based on the misfortune of others. Coexistence is the main way of economics and the leader's responsibility.[11] Lawyers should act with mercy. Law should be represented to rescue people rather than to judge them. Only the merciful person can conquer the world, and only the intelligent person can conquer destiny.[12] The importance of development depends on the 'Bodhisattva organization', which is a group combining the contributions of every Bodhisattva, who is an individual exhibiting mercy and morality.[13]

3.3.2   John H. Dunning's MNE globalization idea

Dunning (2003) has proposed that in the globalization era, MNEs should possess the following criteria in order to improve human well-being in reality:

1. Efficiency: Efficiency should be redefined as 'goods', 'service' and 'quality', and it will then improve real efficiency.
2. Equity: equity will improve world efficiency. Equity requires a basis of morals and ethics; a company will collapse if it has no ethics.
3. Participation: the enterprises and individuals should be eager to participate in order to avoid a puppet government or autocratic government.
4. Creativity: MNEs and international companies should create many opportunities to achieve equity, and hence improve the quality of life.
5. Risk adjustment: Enterprises will face a huge risk if they only work toward profit maximization, therefore, enterprises should not only focus on profit gathering, but more on ethics and laws.
6. Respect and human rights: Managers must respect others regarding different opinions, and should not discriminate against race, gender, religion or age. Many unnecessary conflicts would be avoided if we could learn how to forgive others. Moreover, more attention should be paid to human rights in the light of globalization.
7. Environment: An enterprise must guarantee environmental protection; we must hold the concept that the environment must be managed forever. Enterprises can not pollute the environment at will.

3.3.3   The managerial philosophies of Matsushita

The President of the Japanese Matsushita Company, Konoske Matsushita, is called the 'God of management'. The main idea of enterprise globalization is to 'concern people' and 'respect human dignity'. The managerial philosophies in practice by Kunosuke Matsushita are as follows (Matsushita, 1978):

a. The personal managerial philosophies of Matsushita Kunosuke
   1. Managers must have philosophies regarding 'life', 'society', and 'world'. The management should be like a reservoir, with autonomous management and responsibility, and it should emphasize the 'entire personnel management' and 'the harmony between labor and capital'.
   2. Managers must be 'sincere as the God', and keep to their own faith. The managers should fully realize the dramatic changes in the world, care about politics, incubate talents, benefit the masses, and coexist together.
   3. Managers must possess the virtue of patience, investigate universal philosophy, improve management performance, expand community responsibility, and promote world peace.

b. The managerial philosophies of Matsushita company
   1. Noble philosophy regarding life
   2. Recognize an accurate management mission
   3. Comply with the laws of nature
   4. The profit is the remuneration of rational investment
   5. Carry out the spirit of coexistence
   6. The justice society
   7. Faith in success
   8. Implement autonomous management
   9. Accomplish a reservoir type management
   10. Implement proper management
   11. Specialization
   12. Incubate talents
   13. Absorb all useful ideas, and the management of all personnel
   14. Harmonious relationship between labor and capital
   15. Management as creativity
   16. Adjustment regarding change
   17. Care of politics
   18. Sincerity

c. Important thinking for management
   1. Enterprises should fully understand popular feeling: no matter whether this is Western 'psychology', Eastern 'Buddha dharma life philosophy', Christian 'love' or, Buddhist 'mercy', all of them believe that managers should have 'concern for global people' and 'respect human dignity'. Enterprises should fully understand popular feeling and elaborate the idea of goodness, which could expand the world market (Matsushita, 1975).
   2. The success of enterprises is based on incubating talent: there is the 'ten realms sutra' in the Buddha dharma. Anyone may have worries like 'hell' and may also have goodness like 'Buddha'. In order to improve 'employee morale', it is important to forget one's worries and listen to customers and employees, like 'Shravaka' (sound hearer); to fully realize the truth, like 'Pratyekabuddha' (self-enlightened ones); to be merciful, patient, and to care for and assist others, like 'Bodhisattva'; to have a joyful life philosophy, like 'Buddha'. The most important message for enterprises is to incubate talent (Matsushita, 1975).
   3. The achievement of enterprises' globalization is based on the principle of intergrowth: Matsushita adopts 'the intergrowth principle' of cherry blossom, plums, peaches and prunes as the main mission to be harmonious and unified among different cultures and

nationalities, and to create a remarkable intergrowth to improve performance in terms of management and globalization (Kino, 2000).

3.3.4   The managerial philosophies of Toyota

Toyota Motor Corporation is known as a prosperous and powerful company, which is respected by its customers and the entire society. Toyota's managerial philosophies mainly emphasize the 'ethics of enterprises' and 'ethics of society'.

a. The guiding principles of Toyota: in 1992 Toyota established the basic development principles of international enterprises, by which the enterprise can be trusted by the host country and become a superior citizen. Later, in 1997, Toyota included the spirit of globalization in its managerial philosophy, respecting all legal systems and their spirit, and different cultures and customs (Nishimura, 2005).

b. The basic managerial philosophies of Toyota:
   1. All operational activities should comply with the domestic and international legal systems and their spirit, in order to nurture excellent enterprise citizens, who can be fully trusted by the international communities.
   2. Respect the cultures and customs of all countries. Enterprises located in a host country should make a greater contribution to the economy and society of the host country.
   3. The mission to offer safe products. To make a comfortable living environment and prosperous society from the corporate activities.
   4. To be dedicated to research and development in different advanced science and technology throughout the field, to satisfy global customers and to offer the most fascinating merchandise and service.
   5. There should be mutual trust and responsibility between labor and capital; an enterprise should be established that can increase personal creativity and strong teamwork.
   6. From the global management revolutions, enterprises should foster a harmonious relationship between the enterprise and local society.
   7. Business relationships should be dedicated to mutual research and innovations and long-term stable growth established to fulfill the coexisting relationship.

3.3.5   The theory of managerial philosophies of a peace culture

Based on Ikeda's thinking on world peace, the consensus of world peace and human well-being reached by national leaders, we also have taken the MNE managerial philosophies about globalization by John H. Dunning, Matsushita cooperation and Toyota cooperation as references, and have carried out a survey on the relationships between the managerial philosophies of MNE leaders and MNE business performance. Questionnaires were sent to managers of 186 Europe-, US-, and Japan-based subsidiaries in Taiwan. The research results show that all the managers agree that only the managerial philosophies of a peace culture can acquire support and collaboration from different cultures and races, resolve the above-mentioned problems, and increase the performance of subsidiaries all over the world.

The theory of the managerial philosophies of a peace culture of MNEs (P Theory) presented by Tsai-Mei Lin (2006) states that MNE leaders must adopt a managerial philosophy of a peace culture in order to enhance their management performances in the twenty-first century. Only the managerial philosophy of a peace culture can facilitate MNE leaders to reconcile the problems of animosity among nationalities, religions and races through history, and hence combine the cooperative power of cross-cultural ethnicity from different countries and increase the performance of international collaboration with subsidiaries located in different countries. This would assist the economic development of home countries and host countries and therefore increase human well-being globally, world peace and economic prosperity. The theory of MNE leaders' managerial philosophies of peace culture are presented by Tsai-Mei Lin (2006) as follows:

1. Enterprises should be run to maximize human benefit. The managerial philosophy of MNE leaders regarding profit maximization should not just consider corporate profits, but the profits of the employees in the parent company and subsidiaries, the consumer interests and social interests of the home and the host countries. Therefore, MNEs should not mainly emphasize the economic interests of the enterprise instead of the human livelihood and interests.
2. MNE leaders should have corporate ethics and glogal prospectives. The MNE leaders must embrace a philosophy regarding life, society, the world, respect for human dignity, concern for corporate morale and industrial morale.
3. The ability to act with mercy, wisdom and courage. MNE leaders must execute everything with mercy and wisdom. Therefore, the managerial philosophies of the MNE leaders must involve mercy, to tolerate others, and wisdom, to overcome all challenges. This kind of wisdom can not only develop the creativity of the human sprit, but also overcome any social crisis. With the spirit of justice, MNE leaders can implement anything bravely, resulting in peaceful, wealthy and coexistent enterprises for all the parent companies and subsidiaries

of the world.

4. Superior citizens of enterprises. The globalization of MNEs must follow each nation's laws and respect the culture and customs there. The enterprises located in the host country should make a greater contribution to the local economy and development of society, and become 'citizens of enterprises', who can be trusted by the international community; their main goal.

5. Emphasis on the high-tech products and local environmental protection. MNE leaders must be committed to research and development of different advanced science and technology throughout the field, in order to satisfy global customers and to offer the best service. Simultaneously, there must be concern for the protection of the local environment and for public health, while aiming for a comfortable earth and prosperous society.

6. Diffierent cultures exist harmoniously. MNE leaders are the persons who do not fear or oppose the differences of nationality, culture and race, and also respect and understand the differences and consider them as self-owned resources. The cherry blossoms, plums, peaches and prunes bloom individually, and do not damage others or confront others. The idea of intergrowth is to cherish the differences among people and hence to establish a gorgeous spectacle of a life park together.

7. The management thought of the kingcraft culture, and increased international competitiveness. The enterprise is the union of humans, and the human is the instrument of mind. The corporation may be considered as a convergence of human minds. MNE leaders need to apply the kingcraft management, which employees should not obey as a result of force or authority, but with virtue. This type of management not only concerns human dignity, but also the development of human nature through inspiration. Laws are not for judging people but rather to save them. In order to increase international competitiveness, MNE leaders should consider the importance of harmonious relationships with subordinates.

8. Building up sincere international friendships, and sharing a peaceful and prosperous society. The wisdom of harmonious multinationalities is based on a sincere heart. International consolidation and collaboration requires the foundation of respecting others as our esteemed guests or even as Buddha, with sincerity, and therefore this collaboration can result in sincere international friendships. The wisdom of MNE leaders in the harmony of different nations would be the mission for peace and creation of values. They should show their concern for other nations with mercy, build a foundation for uniting the different cultures and races, increase the performance of international

collaboration, and share a peaceful and prosperous society.

9. Concern for world citizens and respect for human rights. As world citizens, MNE leaders should have concern for the benefit of other nations or races, respect human rights and dignities, and possess the values of world peace and human well-being. MNE leaders should embrace the spirit of forgiveness, which considers no difference among religions, races and genders; establish and consolidate morals and ethics of enterprises; respect the 'intergrowth culture' of each person, adjust the path of human history from discord to harmony, from confrontation to merger, from war to peace. It is also necessary to create a merciful world, where different races can coexist harmoniously, and grow together to increase the power of the cooperation, and hence increase the MNEs' global business performance and economic development between home and host countries.

10. An enterprise with the organization of Bodhisattva. Bodhisattva is a person who is merciful and moral. The organization of Bodhisattva is a group combining the contributions of noteworthy management efficiency with every employee who possesses the ideas of Bodhisattva. MNEs should take the organization of Bodhisattva as their main objective. The employees of both the parent companies and subsidiaries have not only to be loyal to the company and perform their assigned duties properly, but also show their concern for worldwide consumer interests. They should strengthen their research and development of hi-tech products, and manufacture high quality products but for low prices with a detail-oriented and artisan mind and sense of honor. In post-sales services, they should be friendly and show their concern for customers, and provide prompt service. This is just the pyramid spirit of marketing. Thus, they must be able to give great satisfaction to consumers and gain their trust. The enterprise hence enhances its reputation in the international market and its international competitive power.

In sum, MNE leaders must embrace the 'managerial philosophies of a peace culture' to reduce the conflict among different races and religions resulting from cultural differences. This would enable them to collaborate better with different cultures and enhance their international management performance. Consequentially, MNEs will contribute more to the economic development of their home country and the host country, to world peace, human well-being, and world prosperity. MNEs should lead the twenty-first century into a better peaceful world where there is more consideration and mercy.

3.3.6   The comparison of managerial philosophy of a peace culture between American and Japanese MNEs

Table 19.4   The comparison of managerial philosophy of a peace culture between American and Japanese MNEs

Unit: %

Managerial philosophy of a peace culture	American MNEs	Japanese MNEs
Enterprises should be run to maximize human benefit	30	82
MNE leaders should have corporate ethics and global prospective	78	90
The ability to act with mercy, wisdom and just courage	31	82
Superior citizens of enterprises	82	91
Emphasis on the high-tech products and local environmental protection	80	82
Different cultures exist harmoniously	45	90
The management thought of the kingcraft culture, and increased international competitiveness	48	88
Building up sincere international friendships, and sharing a peaceful and prosperous society	85	90
Concern for world citizens and respect for human rights	76	88
An enterprise with the organization of Bodhisattva	51	92

Source: The empirical research of 162 American and Japanese MNEs in Taiwan by Tsai-Mei Lin in 2005

According to the above empirical research about the theory of 'managerial philosophy of a peace culture', it shows that these ideas have been highly emphasized by the American and Japanese MNEs (See Table 19.4). The analyses are as follows:

1. The common content of managerial philosophy of a peace culture between American and Japanese MNEs:
   • MNE leaders should have corporate ethics and global perspective
   • Superior citizens of enterprises
   • Emphasis on the high-tech products and local environmental protection
   • Different cultures exist harmoniously
   • Concern for world citizens and respect for human rights
2. The content of managerial philosophy of a peace culture that Japanese MNEs are more concerned related to American MNEs:
   • Enterprises should be run to maximize human benefit

- The ability to act with mercy, wisdom and just courage
- Different cultures exist harmoniously
- The management thought of the kingcraft culture, and increased international competitiveness
- An enterprise with the organization of Bodhisattva

According to the above analyses, Japanese MNEs are more concerned that enterprises should be run to maximize human benefit; the management thought of the kingcraft culture, and increased international competitiveness; different cultures existing harmoniously; an enterprise with the organization of Bodhisattva. It accommodates with the theory of MNE's managerial philosophy and cross-cultural management, which demonstrates the better managerial philosophy (P), the superiority of cross-cultural management (M) as the higher managerial strategic performance (S) would result. It also demonstrates the fact that Japanese MNEs place more emphasis on 'managerial philosophy of a peace culture', and this therefore results in better managerial performance, related to American MNEs.

4. CONCLUSIONS

In summary, the theory of MNEs' cross-cultural management concerning the subsidiaries of host countries suggests that the performance of MNEs' cross-cultural management depends on the excellence of MNEs' managerial strategies, which are determined by the adoption of the third culture management in the host country. Finally, the performances of cultural management are very much determined by the managerial philosophies of a peace culture by the MNE leaders (see Figure 19.4) (Tsai-Mei Lin, 2006). The conclusions of this study are as follows.

4.1 The Adoption of the Third Culture Management by the US and Japanese MNEs and Their Increased Management Performance

The best management system of MNEs' cross-cultural management is the adoption of the third culture management, which integrates the advantages of the first culture management and the second culture management, and increases the management performance of subsidiaries. The empirical study demonstrates that due to the fact that the US and Japanese MNE subsidiaries in Taiwan value the third culture management as the most important management system, their inventory turnover rates, account receivable rates, fixed assets rates, operating profits, return on capital, and return on fixed assets are much higher than those of the Taiwanese domestic enterprises. Next to the third culture management, most of the Japanese subsidiaries adopt the first culture management, and most of the US subsidiaries adopt the second culture management, which leads Japanese subsidiaries to have better performance than the US subsidiaries in all financial indicators. This indicates that the Japanese subsidiaries which launched the first culture management were more able to meet the needs of Taiwanese employees than the Taiwanese enterprises, which launched the second culture management. The empirical evidence is useful as a reference for Taiwanese enterprises.

4.2 MNEs' Managerial Philosophies of Peace Culture and Increased Global Business Performance

The major contribution of this study concern the managerial philosophies as consensus among multiple different cultures, ethnicities and countries. With the global problems of East-West political confrontations, North-South economic differences, nationalism, national interests, religious and cultural problems and ethnic problems, only the managerial philosophies of a peace culture can resolve them, and increase the performance of subsidiaries and the MNEs' business. As a consequence, MNE leaders should value the managerial philosophies of a peace culture even more from the current point of view, so that different races and cultures can work together, and therefore enhance the business performances of global subsidiaries. The key points of the theory of managerial philosophies of a peace culture (P Theory) are as follows:

1. Running enterprises is for the maximum benefit of all mankind.
2. MNE leaders shoud embrace a corporate morale and world philosophy.
3. The virtues of mercy, wisdom and courage.
4. Superior citizens of enterprises.
5. Emphasis on technology and the environmental protection of products.
6. The concept of the world citizen.
7. The management philosophy of kingcraft, and increased international competitiveness.
8. Building up sincere international friendship, and sharing a peaceful and prosperous society.
9. Concern for world citizens and respect for human rights.
10. An enterprise with the organization of Bodhisattva to increase business performances.

In other words, the global developments of MNEs depend on the degree of concerns that MNE leaders have for human well-being and for the national interests of other countries. Only after gaining support and strength from various countries, cultures and ethnicities, can MNEs therefore enhance the management performances of their subsidiaries, the prosperity of their home country, the host country and the global economy, the well-being of all mankind, and world peace. Therefore, P Theory needs to be adopted by MNE leaders.

Generally speaking, according to all the theories of managerial philosophies of a peace culture and MNEs' cross-culture management, the more ideal the managerial philosophy (P) is, and the more superior the management culture (M) is, the higher the performance of MNEs' business strategies(S) will be (see Figure 19.4). The framework suggests the following:

1. MNEs' leaders must embrace the managerial philosophies of a peace culture (P) to heighten the performances of global subsidiaries.
2. While dealing with cross-culture management in the host country, the performances of business strategies (S) of subsidiaries in host countries can be improved by using 'the third culture management' (M).

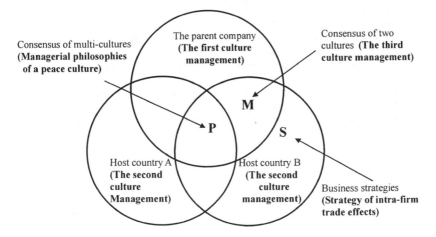

Source: Tsai-Mei Lin (2006).

Figure 19.4   The managerial philosophies of a peace culture and MNEs' cross-culture management

In other words, MNEs' leaders should embrace the managerial philosophies of a peace culture to gather support from different nations, races and cultures and consequently enhance their global business performances. As a result, MNEs will then make a greater economic contribution towards the home and host countries, having positive effects on human well-being and world peace. Based on this positive cycle, the global business performances of MNEs will therefore be enhanced. Therefore, MNEs should be responsible for creating a world with more friendship and peace, consideration and mercy in the twenty-first century.

NOTES

1. Ikeda, D. (1999), *Recollections of My Meetings with Leading World Figures*, Tokyo: Ushio Shuppansha. (Ikeda meeting with the former UN Secretary-General Boutros-Ghali, 1998.)
2. As in note 1. (Ikeda meeting with Sultan Azlan Shah, King of Malaysia, 1993.)
3. As in note 1. (Ikeda meeting with Kocheril Raman Naraynan, President of India, 1997.)
4. As in note 1. (Ikeda meeting with Chair Jiang Zemin of China, 1990.)
5. As in note 1. (Ikeda meeting with Franz Vranitzky, Austrian Prime Minister, 1989.)
6. As in note 1. (Ikeda meeting with President Oscar Arias Sanchez of Costa Rica, Nobel peace price laureate, 1996.)
7. As in note 1. (Ikeda meeting with the father of European integration, Count Coudenhove-Kalergi, 1970.)
8. As in note 1. (Ikeda meeting with Dr. Bernard Lown, the Prevention of Nuclear War, Nobel peace price laureate, 1989.)
9. As in note 1. (Ikeda meeting with Young-Seek Choue, founder of Kyung Hee University, Korea, 1997.)
10. As in note 1. (Ikeda meeting with Dr. Jen-Hu Chang, Chairman of Board of Regents of Chinese Culture University, 1994.)
11. As in note 1. (Ikeda meeting with Lin Chong Yah, economic scholar in Singapore, 1995.)
12. As in note 1. (Ikeda meeting with S. Mohan, Supreme judge of India, 1996.)
13. As in note 1. (Ikeda meeting with David W. Chappell, the Dean of Research Institute of the Eastern and Western religions, University of Hawaii, 1996.)

REFERENCES

Buckley, P.J. (1991), 'The frontiers of international business research', *Management International Review*, **31**, special issue, 7-22.
Daniels, J.D. (1991), 'Cross cultural studies: Some MNEs' needs for the twenty-first century', *The Fifth Multinational Enterprises International Conference*, Chinese Culture University, Taipei.
Dunning, J.H. (1995), 'Reconciling some paradoxes of the globalizing economy', *The Sixth Multinational Enterprises International Conference*, Chinese Culture University, Taipei.

Dunning, J.H. (2003), *Making Globalization Good: The Moral Challenges of Global Capitalism*, New York: Oxford University Press.

Ikeda, D. (1997), *The Proponents of Peaceful Century*, Hong Kong: Earth Publications.

Ikeda, D. (1999), *Recollections of My Meetings with Leading World Figures*, Tokyo: Ushio Shuppansha.

Ikeda, D. (2002), *The Conversation with Life in the Twenty-First Century*, Tokyo: SGI.

Kino, S. (2000), *Konosuke Matsushit*, Tokyo: Chichi.

Lin, T.M. (1994), *Multinational Enterprises*, 4th edn, Taipei: Wu-Nan.

Lin, T.M. (2003), *Multinational Enterprises*, 5th edn, Taipei: Wu-Nan.

Lin, T.M. (2006), 'Managerial philosophies, peace culture and the performance of multinational enterprises' cross cultural management', *The 8th Multinational Enterprises International Conference*, Chinese Culture University, Taipei.

Matsushita, K. (1975), *Real Leaders' Requirements*, Tokyo: Business Publications.

Matsushita, K. (1978), *Practical Managerial Philosophies*, Tokyo: Totsuham Painting Corporation.

Mayo, E. (1933), *The Human Problem of an Industrial Civilization*, NY: Mcmillan.

McGregor, D. (1966), *Leadership and Motivation*, Cambridge, MA: MIT Press.

Ministry of Economic Affairs (1992, 2003), *Overseas Activities of Japanese Business*, Japan.

Ministry of Economic Affairs (1991, 2001), *Trade White Paper*, Japan.

Morse, J.J. and J.W. Lorsch (1970), 'Beyond theory Y', *Harvard Business Review*, **48**(3), 61-68.

Nishimura, K. (2005), *Toyota Power*, Tokyo: Plazland Publication.

Ouchi, W. (1981), *Theory Z*, Taipei: Long River Publications.

Taylor, F.W. (1967), *The Principles of Scientific Management*, NY: Norton.

PART THREE

Some Taiwanese Case Studies

20. An empirical examination of the association between manufacturing decisions and performance evaluation: evidence from Taiwanese listed electronic firms

Fujiing Shiue and Yi-Yin Yen

1. INTRODUCTION

In the current trend of global supply chains, Taiwanese electronics companies have become active seekers of international resources, operating efficiency and consumer markets. In their global configuration, they learn fast and accumulate international expansion experience, engage in arbitrage transactions, and so on. As multinational operations result in higher costs associated with information gathering and transmission, execution and governance, which can neutralize the benefits of internationalization, it is therefore worthwhile to explore how the degree of internationalization influences a company's operating performance.

Previous research has generated mixed results on the association between the degree of internationalization and performance. In other words, contradictory findings include such relationships as positive linear, negative linear, U-curve, inverted U-curve, and even no relationship at all. Rather than using companies from developed nations as our research sample, this chapter applies the newly developed three-stage theory of internationalization expansion (Contractor et al., 2003; Lu and Beamish, 2004) and S-curve hypothesis to companies of newly industrialized countries. As the electronics industry of Taiwan is an integral and indispensable link in the global logistic and supply chain, this study therefore uses electronics companies listed in Taiwan to examine whether the relationship between the degree of international expansion and financial performance in the S-curve hypothesis exists.

This chapter is organized as follows: Section 2 discusses related literature and develops research hypotheses; section 3 stipulates research methods including variables definition, model specification, and sample collection. Section 4 covers data collection, section 5 presents empirical results and analysis, and section 6 presents conclusions and suggestions.

2. LITERATURE REVIEW AND RESEARCH HYPOTHESE

2.1 Internationalization and its Association with Performance

Since the 1960s, scholars have proposed an international product life cycle (IPLC) (Vernon, 1966) and have suggested that there are three stages in the life cycle of a product: introduction, maturation and standardization (Griffin and Pustay, 2002). From the 1970s to the 1980s, Dunning (1977, 1980) addressed the Eclectic Approach and asserted that enterprises would invest directly in order to enter the international market while they grasp location-specific endowments, ownership-specific endowments and internalization incentive advantages. The Eclectic Approach did provide a complete and systematic interpretation about enterprises' behavior regarding foreign direct investment (FDI).

Multinationality generally refers to the extent to which firms operate across national boundaries and can achieve economies of scale through product and geographical diversification (Kotabe et al., 2002). The advantages of multinationality include improving learning effects, enhancing international experiences, acquiring country-specific resources, aiming at competing targets, adopting price discrimination, and carrying out arbitrage activities (Contractor et al., 2003).

As for measuring the degree of multinationality for MNCs, past scholars have considered various methods of weighing the indexes such as the number of foreign countries in which foreign subsidiaries set up, the number of foreign subsidiaries, the ratio of the number of foreign subsidiaries to all subsidiaries, the ratio of foreign sales to total sales and export amount (Allen and Pantzalis, 1996; Delios and Beamish, 1999; Ruigrok and Wagner, 2003; Contractor et al., 2003; Chiou, Yu-Ching 2003; Lu and Beamish, 2004).

Allen and Pantzalis (1996) used two variables, breadth degree (the number of foreign countries in which the MNC has subsidiaries) and depth degree (the ratio of the sum of the subsidiaries in the two countries with the largest number of the MNC's subsidiaries as a fraction of the MNC's total number of foreign subsidiaries) of internationalization to evaluate the impact on operating flexibility. They found that the returns to multinationality are maximized for firms with high breadth degree (operations in more than ten countries), but low depth degree (concentration levels of less than 25 per cent).

As firms become more internationalized, they are more able to achieve resource-seeking efficiency, and meanwhile learn from international experiences to have the capability of global scanning of competitors, markets and other niches, such as adopting price discrimination and carrying out arbitrage activities. For MNCs, the benefits of multinationality could, on the other hand, be offset by higher political and economic risks as they would increase management costs. Therefore, such a controversial relationship between the degree of internationalization and performance gives rise to scholars' attention and discussion.

Regarding performance evaluation, most research focuses on two criteria: financial and operating performances. Financial performance is usually measured in terms of return on assets (ROA), return on sales (ROS), return on investment (ROI) or return on stockholders' equity (ROE) (Delios and Beamish, 1999; Kotabe et al., 2002; Ruigrok and Wagner, 2003; Contractor et al., 2003; Lu and Beamish, 2004). As for operating performance, sales/operating cost and Tobin's Q (Kotabe et al., 2002; Contractor et al., 2003; Lu and Beamish, 2004; Chiou, 2003) are among the most prevalent.

Previous research on the association between multinationality and performance has produced contradictory results such as positive linear, negative linear, U-curve, inverted U-curve, and even no relationship (Morck and Yeung, 1991; Gomes and Ramaswamy, 1999; Kotabe et al., 2002; Ruigrok and Wagner, 2003; Contractor et al., 2003; Chiou, 2003). As controversial arguments exist, some researchers have later incorporated the above concepts and proposed a three-stage theory of international expansion, that is, the S-curve relationships between multinationality and performance shown in Figure 21.1 (Contractor et al., 2003; Lu and Beamish, 2004). Here, internationalization is divided into three stages as performance is the dependent variable on the vertical coordinates; only stage 2 shows a positive slope while the other two are negative, shown as an S-curve.

The theory above claims that in stage 1, learning cost is a vital issue (Johanson and Vahlne, 1990) because at this stage companies are unfamiliar with foreign markets, culture and operating environments. Without achieving economies of scale, performance could be a negative relationship with the degree of internationalization (Contractor et al., 2003). However, learning effects, market-exploitation and resource-seeking would foster performance, so that at stage 2 of internationalization, a positive impact could be made on performance. But internationalization is over the optimum level in stage 3; soaring costs in coordination, management, trading

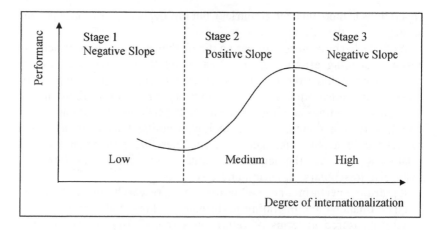

Figure 21.1   Three-stage theory of international expansion (S-curve)

and controlling would offset benefits and further influence performance, so the slope in the stage 3 changes to a negative one (Contractor et al., 2003; Lu and Beamish, 2004).

Compared with large multinational manufacturers from the US, Japan and Europe, the listed electronics companies in Taiwan are relatively small and medium-sized enterprises (SMEs). Like other MNCs, these SMEs also adopt strategies such as setting up subsidiaries abroad as a means of international expansion, exploiting any potential foreign markets and looking for resources to compete in global markets. This study attempts to test whether the internationalization expansion process of the electronic companies listed in Taiwan follows the pattern of the three-stage theory of international expansion (Contractor et al., 2003; Lu and Beamish, 2004). Two variables are used to measure the degree of internationalization, namely the breadth degree and the depth degree, as will be discussed later. Two hypotheses are proposed as follows:

Hypothesis 1: *As the breadth degree of internationalization for Taiwanese electronic companies enlarges, the financial performance will decrease first, then be followed by an increase, and finally decrease, demonstrating a non-linear S-curve relationship.*

Hypothesis 2: *As the depth degree of internationalization for Taiwanese electronic companies enlarges, the financial performance will decrease first, then be followed by an increase, and finally decrease, demonstrating a non-linear S-curve relationship.*

2.2 Resource-based View (Intangible Assets)

According to the resource-based view, while MNCs incur advertising and R&D costs, they will probably create more unique, valuable, rare and inimitable resources and help themselves to obtain competitive advantages (Kotabe et al., 2002). The capability of R&D could innovate the manufacturing process and product, upgrade quality, lower production costs, prolong the life cycle of products, and even create a competing niche (Delios and Beamish, 1999). The capability of advertising could build successful brands, differentiate products and services from competitors, attract consumers' attention and enhance firms' performance. To compete with MNCs worldwide, R&D and advertising has become more important in obtaining patents and increasing international brand exposures for electronics companies listed in Taiwan. Marketing and R&D intensity are two major measurements to capture the above capabilities in this study. The third hypothesis is proposed as follows:

Hypothesis 3: *Marketing and R&D intensity is positively related to the financial performance of Taiwanese listed electronic companies.*

2.3 Transaction Cost Theory

Transaction cost includes the total cost of completing the contract and governing the transaction (Huang, 1996). When the transaction cost is very high, companies will engage in foreign direct investment because they can internalize overseas production into inner operations. On the other hand, if the transaction cost is fairly low, companies will prefer a joint venture or franchise to achieve internationalization (Griffin and Pustay, 2002).

Besides the different strategies involved with entering foreign markets, the associated transaction costs include information transfer, execution, negotiation, delivery, governing, as well as financial and political risks (Hennart, 1991). Transaction costs result from the complexity, tacitness, specificity and uncertainty of trading objects (technology) or environments; and in addition, asset specificity is the core concept of transaction cost theory (Williamson, 1991; Lee, 2002). Previous studies have designed questionnaires to obtain data on transaction costs. This approach is subject to the traditional limitations of survey studies. In this study, we try to adopt a different approach and employ an appropriate proxy variable from secondary data, which of course has its own limitations in interpreting the results.

Disputes and litigation happen because of torts when enterprises try to enter international markets. If the enterprise loses a lawsuit, it will not only face paying compensation, but will also suffer the crisis of having to stop operations. On the other hand, if enterprises win a lawsuit, it will have a positive impact on performance. Potential transactional risk is measured by whether a firm is involved in disputes or lawsuits, and by how performance is affected. Hypothesis 4 is based on these presumptions.

Hypothesis 4: *Assuming that arguments or lawsuits happen on electronics companies listed in Taiwan, performance probably would be influenced.*

3. RESEARCH METHOD, VARIABLES DEFINITION AND MODEL SPECIFICATION

3.1 Research Method

Cross-section heteroskedasticity and time-series autocorrelation probably exist in the panel data of 396 observations of the 132 companies surveyed during the three years (2001-2003). To avoid loss of consistency and efficiency caused by these two problems, a GLS (Generalized Least Square) model was adopted when investigating internationalization and performance (Gomes and Ramaswamy, 1999; Kotabe et al., 2002; Contractor et al., 2003; Lu and Beamish, 2004; Chiou, 2003).

As for panel data, there are two kinds of model, fixed effect and random effect, used in GLS regression analysis (Greene, 2000; Huang, 2005). There are advantages and disadvantages to both models, so further testing needs to be done by the Hausman test (Hausman, 1978). If the result stays in the rejected region, then the null hypothesis will be rejected and the fixed effect model will be the correct one to choose; however, once the result moves to the accepted area, then the null hypothesis will be accepted and the random effect model could be the better choice (Greene, 2000; Huang, 2005).

3.2. Definition of Variables

3.2.1 Financial performance
Financial performance is used as the dependent variable of performance. Based on the previous studies, it was measured in terms of return on assets (ROA =[Net income after tax + interest expense after tax]/average

total assets) (Kotabe et al., 2002; Ruigrok and Wagner, 2003; Lu and Beamish, 2004).

3.2.2 Degree of internationalization

Although different methods were used to measure degree of internationalization, this research uses the variables which take into consideration research work by Allen and Pantzalis (1996) and the three-stage theory of international expansion (Contractor et al., 2003; Lu and Beamish, 2004). The degree of internationalization is divided into three stages and its association with the dependent variable of performance shows positive slope at stage 2 and negative slopes both at stages 1 and 3, as is shaped by an S-curve. Two variables are used in the measurement of internationalization:

1. BD (Breadth Degree): the number of foreign countries in which the MNCs have subsidiaries (own over 50 per cent of shares in the subsidiary).
2. DD (Depth Degree): the sum of the subsidiaries in the two countries with the largest number of MNC subsidiaries/the average number of foreign subsidiaries of all the sample companies.

The breadth degree of internationalization of stages 1, 2 and 3 are shown as BD, BD2 and BD3 respectively, while DD, DD2 and DD3 represent three stages of multinationality depth degree. The expected symbols of three stages are negative, positive and negative.

3.2.3 Marketing and R&D intensity

Enterprises could promote products successfully through marketing and R&D activities, which can differentiate markets from other competitors, so the higher the marketing and R&D intensity are, the better performance is (Allen and Pantzalis, 1996; Kotabe et al., 2002). Here, advertising expense/net sales is a proxy variable of marketing intensity; R&D expenditure/net sales is a proxy variable of R&D intensity. The expected impact of advertising and R&D intensity on performance is positive.

3.2.4 Potential transaction risk

It goes without saying that potential transaction risk will reduce performance when enterprises try to enter international markets and become involved in disputes and litigation because of unintentional torts. Information was obtained from annual reports and prospectuses in order to ascertain whether the sample enterprises are involved in disputes or lawsuits. A dummy variable is used, with 1 standing for yes and 0 otherwise. There is no predicted sign on this issue because it depends on the result of negotiation and the lawsuit.

3.2.5 Company characteristics

(1) *Firm size* Doubtless, the larger the company, the more abundant resources it owns (Kotabe et al., 2002; Contractor et al., 2003). It is easier to achieve economies of scale when a company is expanding overseas, or undergoing an investment configuration. A logarithm of total asset, a proxy variable for firm size, is regarded as a controlled variable in this study. (2) *Long-term debt ratio* Higher financial leverage, especially long-term debt ratio, would raise financial risk, increase expenses and further decrease performance (Allen and Pantzalis, 1996). Long-term debt/total assets, is regarded as a control variable and is expected to have a negative relationship with performance.

3.3 Model Specification

3.3.1 Fundamental model specification

Based on the viewpoints claimed by Contractor et al. (2003), this research aims to test whether the multinationality-performance relationship of electronic companies listed in Taiwan is an S-curve. The first regression model is specified as follows:

Model I: Testing S-curve hypothesis

$$ROA_{it} = b_0 + b_1BD_{it} + b_2(BD_{it})^2 + b_3(BD_{it})^3 + b_4DD_{it} + b_5(DD_{it})^2 + b_6(DD_{it})^3 + b_7LGSIZE_{it} + b_8LTD_{it} + \varepsilon_{it}$$

3.3.2 Testing the resource-based view

While MNCs incur advertising and R&D expenditures, they may give rise to specific competitive advantages such as products and manufacturing process innovation, quality improvement, cost reduction, image initiation, and even market segregation. In model II, we focus on the relationship between performance and marketing intensity as well as R&D intensity. **Model II:** Testing the resource-based view

$$ROA_{it} = b_0 + b_1BD_{it} + b_2(BD_{it})^2 + b_3(BD_{it})^3 + b_4DD_{it} + b_5(DD_{it})^2 + b_6(DD_{it})^3 + b_7ADV_{it} + b_8RD_{it} + b_9LGSIZE_{it} + b_{10}LTD_{it} + \varepsilon_{it}$$

3.3.3 Testing the potential transaction risk

Potential transaction risk will influence performance when enterprises enter international markets and become involved in disputes and litigation because of unintentional torts. Model III is set up to examine this.

Model III: Testing transaction risk

$$ROA_{it} = b_0 + b_1BD_{it} + b_2(BD_{it})^2 + b_3(BD_{it})^3 + b_4DD_{it} + b_5(DD_{it})^2 + b_6(DD_{it})^3 + b_7TRANRISK_{it} + b_8LGSIZE_{it} + b_9LTD_{it} + \varepsilon_{it}$$

ROA	Financial performance. ROA=(Net income+ interest expense after tax)/average total assets.
BD	Breadth Degree. BD=The number of foreign countries in which the MNCs have foreign subsidiaries (own over 50 per cent of shares in the subsidiary)
DD	Depth Degree. DD=The sum of foreign subsidiaries in the two countries with the largest number of MNC subsidiaries / the average number of foreign subsidiaries of all sample companies.
ADV	Marketing intensity, as a measure of marketing capability. ADV=Advertising expense/net sales.
RD	R&D intensity, as a measure of R&D capability. RD=R&D expense/net sales.
TRANRISK	Whether the enterprise is involved in disputes or litigation is shown in the prospectus, a dummy variable, 1-yes and 0-no.
LGSIZE	Firm size, measured as a logarithm of total assets, as a controlled variable.
LTD	The ratio of long-term debt to total assets, as a controlled variable.
i	Company i.
t	in time period t.
ε_{it}	Residual of Company i in time period t.

4. DATA COLLECTION

The samples in this study are selected from electronics companies listed on the Taiwan Stock Exchange with the first two security codes 14 and 16 (transfer into electronics industry), as well as 23, 24, 30, 54 and 61 during the period between 2001 and 2003. There are 223 samples in this database. By excluding 91 companies without foreign subsidiaries by the end of 2003, we obtain 396 panel observations of the remaining 132 companies. All the necessary financial information is derived from TEJ (*Taiwan Economics Journal*), including net profit after tax plus interest expenses after tax, total assets, net sales, advertising expenses, R&D expenses, long-term debt and common stock issued at the end of the year. The library of the Securities & Futures Institute provided the financial reports which contain information on foreign subsidiaries of listed electronic companies in Taiwan.

5. EMPIRICAL RESULTS AND ANALYSIS

5.1 Descriptive Statistical Analysis

Table 21.1 Descriptive statistics of variables

(panel data: n=396)

Variables[a]	Mean	The first quartile	Median	The third Quartile	Minimum	Maximum	Standard deviation
ROA	0.0631	0.0240	0.0671	0.1131	−0.3614	0.2673	0.0852
BD	4.0379	2.0000	4.0000	5.0000	1.0000	20.0000	2.4070
DD	0.7571	0.6181	0.7500	1.0000	0.3125	2.5000	0.2109
ADV	0.0030	0.0000	0.0007	0.0032	0.0000	0.0496	0.0066
RD	0.0413	0.0141	0.0254	0.0478	0.0000	0.5411	0.0565
T	0.3005	0.0000	0.0000	1.0000	0.0000	1.0000	0.4591
LGSIZE	6.7452	6.3689	6.6592	7.0180	5.8884	8.1871	0.4973
LTD	0.0898	0.0000	0.0706	0.1514	0.0000	0.4181	0.0918

Notes:
[a] ROA: Financial performance, (Net income+interest expense after tax)/average total assets; BD: Multinationality Breadth Degree, The number of countries in which MNCs have foreign subsidiaries (own over 50% share in the subsidiary). DD: Multinationality Depth Degree, The number of foreign subsidiaries in the two highest ranked countries/the average number of foreign subsidiaries; Marketing intensity, as a measure of marketing capability, Advertising expense/net sales; R&D Intensity, as a measure of R&D capability, R&D expense/net sales; TRANRISK: Whether the enterprises are involved in disputes or litigation is shown in the prospectus, a dummy variable, 1-yes and 0-no; LGSIZE: Firm size, measured as a logarithm of total assets, as a controlled variable; LTD: The ratio of long-term debt to total assets, as a controlled variable.

Table 21.1 presents descriptive statistics of both dependent and independent variables. From Table 21.1, the mean of ROA of all samples is 0.0631; the maximum is 0.2673 and the minimum is −0.3614. It is obvious that there is a performance difference among the sample companies. The mean, maximum and minimum of BD are 4.0379, 20 and 1 respectively. Obviously, there is a wide gap in the investment configuration for international expansion. Still, most companies adopt a policy where they invest in more than one subsidiary in the same foreign country, because the mean,

Table 21.2   All variables' Spearman's coefficient of rank correlation and Pearson's coefficient of correlation[b]

(panel data: n=396)

Variables[a]	ROA	BD	(BD)²	(BD)³	DD	(DD)²	(DD)³	ADV	RD	TRANRISK	LGSIZE	LTD
ROA	1.00	-0.03 (0.60)	-0.03 (0.60)	-0.03 (0.60)	0.09 (0.08)	0.09 (0.08)	0.09 (0.08)	0.03 (0.54)	0.04 (0.38)	-0.03 (0.51)	-0.10* (0.04)	-0.22* (0.00)
BD	-0.04 (0.47)	1.00	1.00**	1.00**	0.48** (0.00)	0.48** (0.00)	0.48** (0.00)	0.14** (0.01)	0.07 (0.17)	0.18** (0.00)	0.29** (0.00)	0.01 (0.81)
(BD)²	-0.01 (0.88)	0.93* (0.00)	1.00	1.00**	0.48** (0.00)	0.48** (0.00)	0.48** (0.00)	0.14** (0.01)	0.07 (0.17)	0.18** (0.00)	0.29** (0.00)	0.01 (0.81)
(BD)³	0.01 (0.83)	0.79** (0.00)	0.96** (0.00)	1.00	0.48** (0.00)	0.48** (0.00)	0.48** (0.00)	0.14** (0.01)	0.07 (0.17)	0.18** (0.00)	0.29** (0.00)	0.01 (0.81)
DD	0.10* (0.04)	0.54** (0.00)	0.48** (0.00)	0.39** (0.00)	1.00	1.00** (0.00)	1.00** (0.00)	-0.04 (0.40)	-0.08 (0.10)	0.11* (0.04)	0.42** (0.00)	0.05 (0.34)
(DD)²	0.10* (0.05)	0.50** (0.00)	0.47** (0.00)	0.39** (0.00)	0.93** (0.00)	1.00	1.00** (0.00)	-0.04 (0.40)	-0.08 (0.10)	0.11* (0.04)	0.42** (0.00)	0.05 (0.34)
(DD)³	0.09 (0.07)	0.41** (0.00)	0.39** (0.00)	0.33** (0.00)	0.77** (0.00)	0.95** (0.00)	1.00	-0.04 (0.40)	-0.08 (0.10)	0.11* (0.04)	0.42** (0.00)	0.05 (0.34)
ADV	-0.01 (0.90)	0.01 (0.84)	0.04 (0.42)	0.06 (0.26)	-0.07 (0.17)	-0.03 (0.51)	-0.01 (0.87)	1.00	0.31** (0.00)	0.02 (0.66)	-0.14** (0.01)	-0.04 (0.47)
RD	-0.07 (0.19)	-0.02 (0.70)	-0.04 (0.44)	-0.04 (0.44)	-0.08 (0.13)	-0.06 (0.26)	-0.04 (0.41)	0.37** (0.00)	1.00	0.01 (0.89)	-0.23** (0.00)	-0.05 (0.30)
TRANRISK	-0.07 (0.19)	0.17** (0.00)	0.15** (0.00)	0.11* (0.03)	0.18** (0.00)	0.19** (0.00)	0.17** (0.00)	0.08 (0.12)	0.00 (0.99)	1.00	0.21** (0.00)	-0.13* (0.01)
LGSIZE	-0.08 (0.13)	0.42** (0.00)	0.40** (0.00)	0.33** (0.00)	0.56** (0.00)	0.52** (0.00)	0.41** (0.00)	-0.05 (0.31)	-0.13** (0.01)	0.25** (0.00)	1.00	0.23* (0.00)
LTD	-0.18** (0.00)	-0.02 (0.68)	-0.03 (0.57)	-0.03 (0.53)	-0.04 (0.44)	-0.08 (0.13)	-0.09 (0.09)	-0.07 (0.15)	-0.04 (0.43)	-0.13** (0.10)	0.20** (0.00)	1.00

Notes:
[a] ROA: Financial performance, (Net income+interest expense after tax)/average total assets; BD: Multinationality Breadth Degree, The number of countries in which MNCs have foreign subsidiaries (own over 50% share in the subsidiary); (BD)² and (BD)³: Quadratic and cubic terms of BD respectively; DD: Multinationality Depth Degree, The number of foreign subsidiaries in the two highest ranked countries/the average number of foreign subsidiaries; (DD)² and (DD)³: Quadratic and cubic terms of DD respectively; Marketing intensity, as a measure of marketing capability, Advertising expense/net sales; R&D Intensity, as a measure of R&D capability, R&D expense/net sales; TRANRISK: Whether the enterprises are involved in disputes or litigation is shown in the prospectus, a dummy variable, 1-yes and 0-no; LGSIZE: Firm size, measured as a logarithm of total assets, as a controlled variable; LTD: The ratio of long-term debt to total assets, as a controlled variable.
[b] Those above and right of the diagonal are Spearman's coefficient of rank correlation, and below and left of the diagonal are Pearson coefficient of correlation; the values in brackets are two-tailed p-value; ** means significance level is 0.01 (two-tailed), significance; * means significance level is 0.05 (two-tailed), significance.

maximum and minimum DD is 0.7571, 2.5 and 0.3125. Regarding the ADV intensity, Taiwanese companies are relatively low at only about 0.3 per cent on average, compared with 2.34 per cent for the US and 2.4 per cent for Japan. R&D intensity is, however, at a relatively high average of 4.13 per cent compared to the international standard: American R&D is 2.49 per cent and Japanese 2.4 per cent. TRANRISK is 0.3005, which means that about one third of the companies have been involved in disputes or lawsuits before. Compared with big international firms, the LGSIZE of our sample companies is about 6.7452 (with the average total assets of NTD12.4 billion). As for the financial structure (LTD), the ratio of long-term debt to total assets has a mean of 0.0898, ranging from the maximum of 0.4181, and minimum of 0.0000, demonstrating a wide gap among sample companies. Spearman's coefficient of rank correlation (Spearman's p) and Pearson coefficient of correlation among all the related variables are presented in Table 21.2. Except for the higher correlation among breadth degree (BD, BD2, BD3), depth degree (DD, DD2, DD3), and LGSIZE, VIFs (Variance Inflation Factors) among other variables are between 1.142 and 6.023, less than 10, suggesting multicollinearity may not be a serious problem (Neter et al., 1990). With regard to the significant positive correlation between BD and DD at different stages, they are the focuses of this research.

5.2 Analysis of Empirical Study

5.2.1 Three-stage theory of international expansion

There are two kinds of model (Greene, 2000; Huang, 2005), fixed effect and random effect, used in the regression analysis of panel data. We adopt the Hausman test (Hausman, 1978), and find that test statistic -123.0159 is in the rejected region ($\chi^2(8)=15.51$, p<0.05) (Table 21.3), so the fixed effect model is the correct one. All the others also use the fixed effect model to analyze results because all Hausman test statistics are in the rejected area.

Table 21.3 indicates the relationship between degree of internationalization and ROA. We find that as BD increases, financial performance will increase first (coefficient 0.0286, p-value<0.01), decrease later (coefficient -0.0056, p-value<0.01), and increase finally (coefficient 0.0002, p-value<0.01), an inverted S-curve, contrary to the prediction of hypothesis 1. However, the relationship between DD and financial performance is not significant, and therefore hypothesis 2 is not supported. Possible reasons are as follows.

Table 21.3 Regression analysis: three-stage theory of international expansion

(panel data, n=396)

		Model I (Dependent Variable: ROA)		
		No fixed effects control	Fixed effects model	Random effects model
Variables[a]	Expected symbol	Coefficient (p-value)	Coefficient (p-value)	Coefficient (p-value)
Constant		0.2621 (0.0000)	−0.2306 (0.0119)	0.1400 (0.1537)
BD	−	−0.0166 (0.0002)	0.0286 (0.0000)	−0.0064 (0.2774)
$(BD)^2$	+	0.0015 (0.0109)	−0.0056 (0.0000)	0.0000 (0.4968)
$(BD)^3$	−	0.0000 (0.0626)	0.0002 (0.0000)	0.0000 (0.4240)
DD	−	0.0757 (0.0005)	−0.0091 (0.3517)	0.0400 (0.2006)
$(DD)^2$	+	−0.0280 (0.0691)	−0.0036 (0.4134)	−0.0165 (0.3092)
$(DD)^3$	−	0.0057 (0.1053)	0.0020 (0.2693)	0.0029 (0.3199)
LGSIZE	+	−0.0276 (0.0000)	0.0417 (0.0013)	−0.0095 (0.2552)
LTD	−	−0.0901 (0.0000)	−0.0445 (0.0016)	−0.0828 (0.0327)
F Value		160.0342	170.8576	1.0652
p Value		0.0000	0.0000	0.3868
R^2		0.7679	0.9893	0.0215
Adjusted R^2		0.7631	0.9835	0.0013
Hausman test		-123.0159	$\chi^2(8)=15.5073$	

Notes:
[a] ROA: Financial performance, (Net income+interest expense after tax)/average total assets; BD: Multinationality Breadth Degree, The number of countries in which foreign subsidiaries (own over 50% shareholders of the subsidiary) set up; $(BD)^2$ and $(BD)^3$: Quadratic and cubic terms of BD respectively; DD: Multinationality Depth Degree, The number of foreign subsidiaries in the ranking first two countries/the average number of foreign subsidiaries; $(DD)^2$ and $(DD)^3$: Quadratic and cubic terms of DD respectively; LGSIZE: Firm size, measured as a logarithm of total assets, as a controlled variable; LTD: The ratio of long-term debt to total assets, as a controlled variable.

The research results of Contractor et al. (2003) and Lu and Beamish (2004) are from MNCs from the US and Japan, which have an asset size much larger than that of our sample firms. Unlike those multinational firms which have overseas investment all over the world, samples in this research have on average invested in four countries. In addition, electronics companies in Taiwan have centralized their manufacturing arrangement, and have a relatively flexible organizational structure to be able to deal with contingent situations. Their products are more at a stage of maturity/growth in terms of product life cycle, compared with other international large firms (Wu, 2002).

Furthermore, in stage 1 of internationalization, the listed Taiwanese electronics companies face many adverse factors such as rising wages, surging land cost, and heavy taxes. Seeking resources, these companies would invest in Southeast Asia (including China and India) or other nations. Through cheap materials, low wages and land costs, these companies could lower their production cost and achieve their goal of efficiency-seeking. Thus, this stage shows a positive and statistically significant relationship between BD and performance, as shown in Figure 21.2.

In stage 2 of internationalization, the open market and rising income of Southeast Asia, especially China, have become the most lucrative and attractive markets. Companies with their own brands will actively penetrate these markets, while OEMs (original equipment manufacturing corporations) will try to build their own brands and explore the new markets. To further expand successfully, new knowledge and capabilities need to be acquired or developed (Lu and Beamish, 2001). It is therefore necessary for companies to have sufficient and complete information about the markets (Yu, 2000). If they lack knowledge of local markets, learning costs become very high. Performance drops with greater expansion of location, because of the increasing costs associated with coordination, management, trading and control. As a result, the costs of internationalization would exceed the benefits of international expansion, leading to a decline in performance. Therefore, a negative and statistically significant relationship between BD and performance is present in stage 2.

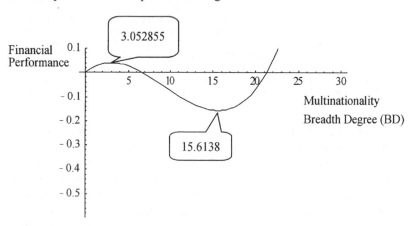

Figure 21.2   Relationship chart between BD and financial performance

In stage 3 of internationalization, companies overcome the barriers of learning and acquire information about local markets. Meanwhile, by building a good relationship with stakeholders such as customers, suppliers, employees, government officers and so on, companies are able to scan for market opportunities and enter the new markets successfully (Yu, 2000). Furthermore, companies could have their own strategic assets and strengthen their core competence by creating the high value-added specific resources of combining learning experiences, technical knowledge and management expertise. As internationalization expands, it is easier for companies to accomplish their goals in respect of resource and market diversification. When undergoing the integration of high industrial value-chain activities, they will be able to improve their core competence and performance. As a result, a positive and statistically significant relationship between BD and performance is seen in stage 3.

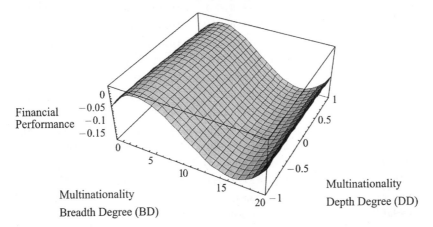

Figure 21.3   Three-dimensional picture of degree of breadth, degree of depth and financial performance

Although the depth degree (DD) is not statistically significant in relation to financial performance, the relationship among ROA, BD and DD in Figure 21.3 has demonstrated the existence of the same shape of the relationship between DD and financial performance. With regard to LGSIZE, the larger the company scale (LGSIZE=0.00417; p<0.01), the better is financial performance, because rich resources make it easier for companies to achieve economies of scale while they try to carry out internationalization. Regarding LTD, the higher ratio of long-term debt to total assets (LTD=-0.0445; p<0.01), the more financial risk will tend to have a negative effect on financial performance.

Based on the above analysis, it is therefore proposed that the S-curve relationship between internationalization and performance as proved in the MNCs from the US and Japan does not seem to exist in international firms of newly industrialized countries such as Taiwan. In this study, we have watched an inverted S-curve relationship between internationalization and performance.

Table 21.4 Regression analysis: resource-based view

(panel data, n=396)

		Model II (Dependent variable: ROA)		
		No fixed effects control	Fixed effects model	Random effects model
Variables[a]	Expected symbol	Coefficient (p-value)	Coefficient (p-value)	Coefficient (p-value)
Constant		0.2883 (0.0000)	−0.0440 (0.5808)	0.1713 (0.0841)
BD	−	−0.0141 (0.0012)	0.0246 (0.0000)	−0.0032 (0.3825)
$(BD)^2$	+	0.0013 (0.0263)	−0.0047 (0.0000)	−0.0004 (0.3977)
$(BD)^3$	−	0.0000 (0.1013)	0.0002 (0.0000)	0.0000 (0.3364)
DD	−	0.0595 (0.0047)	−0.0214 (0.1349)	0.0332 (0.2390)
$(DD)^2$	+	−0.0159 (0.2021)	0.0023 (0.4352)	−0.0124 (0.3498)
$(DD)^3$	−	0.0034 (0.2253)	0.0013 (0.3221)	0.0023 (0.3543)
ADV	+	0.1202 (0.2869)	−0.4970 (0.2519)	0.2807 (0.3725)
RD	+	−0.1102 (0.0000)	−0.9376 (0.0000)	−0.2939 (0.0025)
LGSIZE	+	−0.0311 (0.0000)	0.0207 (0.0397)	−0.0132 (0.1832)
LTD	−	−0.0859 (0.0000)	−0.0125 (0.2782)	−0.0762 (0.0411)
F Value		18.8458	267.1966	1.5818
p Value		0.0000	0.0000	0.1097
R^2		0.7553	0.9933	0.0395
Adjusted R^2		0.7490	0.9896	0.0145
Hausman test		-168.3662	$\chi^2(10)=18.3070$	

Notes:
[a] ROA: Financial performance, (Net income+interest expense after tax)/average total assets; BD: Multinationality Breadth Degree, The number of countries in which MNCs have foreign subsidiaries (own over 50% share in the subsidiary); $(BD)^2$ and $(BD)^3$: Quadratic and cubic terms of BD respectively; DD: Multinationality Depth Degree, The number of foreign subsidiaries in the two highest ranked countries/the average number of foreign subsidiaries; $(DD)^2$ and $(DD)^3$: Quadratic and cubic terms of DD respectively; Marketing intensity, as a measure of marketing capability, Advertising expense/net sales; R&D Intensity, as a measure of R&D capability, R&D expense/net sales; LGSIZE: Firm size, measured as a logarithm of total assets, as a controlled variable; LTD: The ratio of long-term debt to total assets, as a controlled variable.

5.2.2 Analysis of resource-based view

Table 21.4 shows the relationship between ADV, RD intensity and ROA. Results have shown that RD intensity has statistically significant influence on ROA (coefficient is -0.9376, p<0.01), yet ADV intensity is not statistically significant, contrary to our expectation. Therefore hypothesis 3 is not supported.

Possible reasons for the above findings are that only 24 per cent (32/132) of samples have their own brands, while most of them, about 70 per cent (93/132) are OEMs. OEMs are usually good at manufacturing, but American and Japanese MNCs are more skilled in marketing as is seen by the lower ADV intensity of 0.3 per cent in Table 21.1, less than that of American firms (2.34 per cent, Morck and Yeung, 1991) and Japanese firms (1.1 per cent and 2.4 per cent for large-size and small-to-medium size enterprises, Delios and Beamish, 1999; Lu and Beamish, 2001). Clearly, samples in this study do not meet the criterion. Regarding the average RD intensity of 4.13 per cent (Table 21.1), it is not less than the average of other international companies, for instance, American 2.49 per cent (Morck and Yeung, 1991), Japanese large firms 2.4 per cent (Delios and Beamish, 1999), and Japanese small-to-medium firms 1.4 per cent (Lu and Beamish, 2001). According to the generally accepted accounting principle of Taiwan, advertising and R&D expenditure are expensed, rather than capitalized, when incurred. Because their benefits may take a few years to the emerge, the required accounting treatment therefore has a possible negative impact on the current year's financial performance.

5.2.3 Analysis of potential transaction risk

Table 21.5 shows the relationship between TRANRISK and ROA. The findings show that when sample companies are involved in lawsuits or disputes while entering into the international market, there is an unfavorable influence on financial performance. In this study, lawsuits did have a negative impact on financial performance, but the influence was not significant (coefficient is -0.0055, p is 0.2992) enough to support hypothesis 4.

6. CONCLUSIONS

This study tries to explore the association between the manufacturing decisions and performance evaluation of Taiwanese multinational firms. Manufacturing decisions include the breadth and depth degree of internationalization, the marketing and R&D intensity, and potential

Some Taiwanese case studies

Table 21.5 Regression analysis: potential transaction risk

(panel data, n=396)

		Model III (Dependent Variable: ROA)		
		No fixed effects control	Fixed effects model	Random effects model
Variables[a]	Expected symbol	Coefficient (p-value)	Coefficient (p-value)	Coefficient (p-value)
Constant		0.2497 (0.0000)	-0.2586 (0.0081)	0.1169 (0.2381)
BD	−	-0.0116 (0.0096)	0.0270 (0.0000)	-0.0059 (0.2931)
$(BD)^2$	+	0.0010 (0.0860)	-0.0054 (0.0000)	0.0000 (0.4970)
$(BD)^3$	−	0.0000 (0.2087)	0.0002 (0.0000)	0.0000 (0.4240)
DD	−	0.0513 (0.0131)	-0.0085 (0.3662)	0.0349 (0.2321)
$(DD)^2$	+	-0.0107 (0.2895)	-0.0042 (0.4013)	-0.0138 (0.3378)
$(DD)^3$	−	0.0022 (0.3184)	0.0021 (0.2681)	0.0026 (0.3392)
TRANRISK	?	-0.0055 (0.1347)	-0.0055 (0.2992)	-0.0160 (0.1019)
LGSIZE	+	-0.0257 (0.0000)	0.0466 (0.0008)	-0.0052 (0.3607)
LTD	−	-0.0904 (0.0000)	-0.0369 (0.0645)	-0.0894 (0.0237)
F Value		25.8755	39.3925	1.2346
P Value		0.0000	0.0000	0.2721
R^2		0.7459	0.9558	0.0280
Adjusted R^2		0.7399	0.9315	0.0053
Hausman test		-186.3361	$\chi^2(9)=16.9190$	

Notes

[a] ROA: Financial performance, (Net income+ interest expense after tax)/average total assets; BD: Multinationality Breadth Degree, The number of countries in which MNCs have foreign subsidiaries (own over 50% share in the subsidiary); $(BD)^2$ and $(BD)^3$: Quadratic and cubic terms of BD respectively; DD: Multinationality Depth Degree, The number of foreign subsidiaries in the two highest ranked countries/the average number of foreign subsidiaries; $(DD)^2$ and $(DD)^3$: Quadratic and cubic terms of DD respectively; TRANRISK: Whether the enterprises are involved in disputes or litigation is shown in the prospectus, a dummy variable, 1-yes and 0-no; LGSIZE: Firm size, measured as a logarithm of total assets, as a controlled variable; LTD: The ratio of long-term debt to total assets, as a controlled variable.

transaction risks. The findings have shown the existence of an inverted S-curve relationship between multinationality and performance. Thus, the three-stage theory of international expansion, as is found in large international corporations in the US and Japan, is not suitable for MNCs of the newly industrialized countries such as the electronics companies listed in Taiwan. We suggest that one of the possible reasons is that the Taiwanese electronics companies are relatively small to medium sized. They have a centralized manufacturing arrangement and a flexible organizational structure, and are more capable of dealing with contingencies (Wu, 2002). Therefore, the characteristics of MNCs in developed countries and newly industrialized countries such as Taiwan are quite different.

This study does not consider the behavioral determinants such as motivation for the overseas investment, the timing and strategy of entering the foreign market, and so on. Also, it only focuses on 2001-2003 electronics companies listed in Taiwan. Therefore the external validity regarding different industries or longer periods of time needs to be reexamined. In addition, the expenditures from marketing and R&D may have deferred effects and the degree of internationalization could be further divided into high or low levels. These subjects constitute the avenues for possible future research.

NOTES

1. This formula is based on the regulations of the Taiwan securities market.
2. Allen and Pantzalis (1996) adopt the number of foreign subsidiaries to be the denominator when measuring the Multinationality Depth Degree of a company. Compared to the sample with ten subsidiaries set up in two countries, only one subsidiary sample got the same DD as the former one, but both samples have different intentions which cannot be seen from the DD index. That is why this research introduces the average number of subsidiaries of all the samples to solve the above problem.

REFERENCES

Allen, L. and C. Pantzalis (1996), 'Valuation of the operating flexibility of multinational corporations', *Journal of International Business Studies*, Fourth Quarter, 633-53.

Chiou, Y.C. (2003), 'The association among internationalization, product differentiation, and performance: the case of Taiwanese enterprises', Ph.D. Dissertation, Department of Business Administration, National Cheng-Chi University (in Chinese).

Contractor, F.J., S.K. Kundu and C.C. Hsu (2003), 'A three-stage theory of international expansion: the link between multinationality and performance in the service sector', *Journal of International Business Studies*, **34**, 5-18.

Delios, A. and P.W. Beamish (1999), 'Geographic scope, product diversification, and the corporate performance of Japanese firms', *Strategic Management Journal*, **20**(8), 711-27.

Dunning, J.H. (1977), 'Trade, location of economic activity and the MNE: a search for an eclectic approach', *The International Allocation of Economic Activity* (Proceedings of a Nobel Symposium held in Stockholm), The Nobel Foundation, 395-418.

Dunning, J.H. (1980), 'Toward an eclectic theory of international production: some empirical tests', *Journal of International Business Studies*, 11(1), 9-31.

Gomes, L.K. and K. Ramaswamy (1999), 'An empirical examination of the form of the relationship between multinationality and performance', *Journal of International Business Studies*, 30(1), 173-88.

Greene, W.H. (2000), *Econometric Analysis* (4th edn), New Jersey: Prentice Hall, Englewood Cliffs.

Griffin, R.W. and M.W. Pustay (2002), *International Business: A Managerial Perspective* (3rd edn), Prentice Hall.

Hausman, J. (1978), 'Specification tests in econometrics', *Econometrica*, 46, 1251-71.

Hennart, J.F. (1991), 'The transaction costs theory of joint ventures: an empirical study of Japanese subsidiaries in the United States', *Management Science*, 37(4), 483-97.

Huang, H.C. (1996), 'International joint venture', *Review of Taiwan Economics*, 2(2), 9-19 (in Chinese).

Huang, H.C., S.J. Wong and W.R. Lee (2005), *Management*, Taipei: Hwa Tai Publishing (in Chinese).

Huang, T.S. (2005), *Principles of Econometrics*, Taipei: Yeh Yeh Book Gallery (in Chinese).

Johanson, J. and J.E. Vahlne (1990), 'The mechanism of internationalization', *International Market Review*, 7(4), 1-24.

Kao, C. (2002), 'Globalization and the strategy of the division of labor of IT manufacturers across the Taiwan Strait', *Prospect Quarterly*, 3(2), 225-54 (in Chinese).

Kotabe, M., S.S. Srinivasan and P.S. Aulakh (2002), 'Multinationality and firm performance: the moderating role of R&D and marketing capabilities', *Journal of International Business Studies*, 33(1), 79-97.

Lee, W.R. (2002), 'Technology acquisition mode determinants of SMEs in Taiwan: a synthetic view of transaction cost economics, resource-based view of the firm, and behavioral decision theory', *Management Review*, 19(5), 873-900 (in Chinese)

Lin, Z.W., Y.C. Tsai and B.H. Ni (2003), 'The relation between marketing and R&D expenditure and management performance with enterprise's value: taking listed automobile industry as an example', *Journal of Contemporary Accounting*, 93, 18-26 (in Chinese).

Lu, J.W. and P.W. Beamish (2001), 'The internationalization and performance of SMEs', *Strategic Management Journal*, 22(6/7), 565-86.

Lu, J.W. and P.W. Beamish (2004), 'International diversification and firm performance: the S-curve hypothesis', *Academy of Management Journal*, 47(4), 598-609.

Morck, R. and B. Yeung (1991), 'Why investors value multinationality', *Journal of Business*, 64(2), 165-87.

Neter, J., W. Wasserman and M. Kutner (1990), *Applied Linear Statistical Models* (3rd edn.), Home wood, IL: Irwin.

Ruigrok, W. and H. Wagner (2003), 'Internationalization and performance: an organizational learning perspective', *Management International Review*, 43(1), 63-83.

Stern, C.W. and S.J. George (1998), *Perspectives on Strategy From the Boston Consulting Group*, New York: John Wiley and Sons, Inc.

Vernon, R. (1966), 'International investment and international trade in the product life cycle', *Quarterly Journal of Economics*, 80, 191-207.

Williamson, O.E. (1991), 'Comparative economic organization: the analysis of discrete structural alternatives', *Administrative Science Quarterly*, **36**, 269-96.

Wu, C.S. (2002), *International Business Management: Theory and Practice*, Taipei: Best-Wise (in Chinese).

Yu, J.M. (2000), *International Enterprises: Environment and Management*, Taipei: Hwa Tai Publishing (in Chinese).

21. Domestic inter-firm networks and corporate internationalization: a cross-industry study of Taiwanese SMEs

Ku-Ho Lin, Isabella M. Chaney, Thomas C. Lawton and Meng-Chun Liu

1. INTRODUCTION

The resource constraints of small and medium-sized enterprises (SMEs) have caused these companies to be underestimated and under-studied in international business research (Martinez and Jarillo, 1989; Oviatt and McDougall, 1999). Despite the resulting emphasis of international business literature on multinational enterprises (MNEs), the international market arena is not the exclusive preserve of large firms, together with a number of smaller, globalized high technology companies. In countries such as Taiwan, SMEs have, for some time, collectively accounted for the majority of international trade. Taiwanese SMEs have displayed a high – and growing – propensity to internationalize. Since the early 1980s, more than one in four Taiwanese SMEs have been involved in international trade, and 10 per cent have established overseas productions or business units (SMEA, 2002). Many internationalized in conjunction with their domestic networking partners and tended to duplicate the existing network structure in the host markets (Chung, 1997). Such an approach to internationalization, based on extended domestic inter-firm relationships, has become a major trend in the internationalization of Taiwanese SMEs.

In reviewing the international business literature, it is evident that numerous studies have been conducted on the effects of inter-firm networks on the internationalization process. However, most studies focus on the partnerships with already internationalized firms and relationships with firms and subsidiaries in foreign markets. Little is known specifically about the influence of domestic inter-firm relationships in the context of internationalization processes. Therefore, this chapter investigates this less explored research area and contributes a more comprehensive understanding of the role that domestic inter-firm networks play in the internationalization process of SMEs. We identify the determinants of domestic inter-firm network utilization in the internationalization process of Taiwanese SMEs in the automobile, electronics and textile industries. We argue that internationalizing through domestic inter-firm networks is positively correlated with firms' limited non-financial resources, perceived uncertainties and risks associated with internationalization, and dependence on home partners. The technology level of firms and deficiencies in local knowledge and experience do not have significant effects on firms' decisions to utilize domestic inter-firm networks in the internationalization process.

2. THE INTERNATIONALIZATION OF TAIWANESE SME INTER-FIRM NETWORKS

Due to a low degree of vertical production integration and a heavy dependence on subcontracting relations among firms, inter-firm networking has been an important characteristic of Taiwanese SME strategy (Hu and Schive, 1996). Such networking, embedded in the Taiwanese business system, is a key reason for the international success of Taiwanese SMEs. These stable inter-firm networks allow participating companies to gain reciprocal access to resources controlled by other network participants (Gerlach, 1992). Through the networks, Taiwanese manufacturers can efficiently coordinate their production, marketing and R&D activities with their suppliers and buyers. Based on this resource sharing and pooling and the coordination of production processes, firms can achieve economies of scale and scope and simultaneously avoid the disadvantages of full organizational integration, such as high integration costs and strategic inflexibility (Powell, 1990). In fact, these networks have proven so successful that Taiwanese SMEs are frequently involved simultaneously in more than one business network (Liu et al., 1994).

Among the various networking relationships, the center-satellite factory system (C-S system) is the main form of inter-firm network for Taiwanese SMEs (Yiu, 1997). This can be either a vertically or horizontally integrated production network. It is usually an association centered on one or several larger firms and containing multiple smaller satellite companies in the same industry (Su, 2003). Because of advantages accrued through inter-firm networks, many Taiwanese firms tend to extend their domestic network relationships when they invest abroad (Chung, 1997; SMEA, 2001). In terms of the unfamiliarity of local conditions and untested or unstable relationships with local suppliers and buyers in foreign markets, the replication of domestic networks tends to reduce risk – or at the very least, mitigate the perception of risk. In the internationalization of domestic networks, the C-S systems have been extremely successful in accelerating the internationalization of Taiwanese SMEs (Yeh, 1994; Wu, 1996; Ernst, 1997; Wu, 2003). When a member firm has internationalized to an overseas market, it exerts pressure on its C-S partners to follow suit and move their networks offshore (Lee, 2002). In Taiwan, more than half of the Taiwanese C-S systems have internationalized to overseas markets via such an approach (Yeh, 1994; Lee, 2002).

But when discussing the influences of inter-firm networks on corporate internationalization decisions, the literature tends to talk about the role of networks in terms of the complementarity of internal resources and knowledge and experience sharing (Johansson and Mattson, 1988; Axelsson and Johansson, 1992). Furthermore, most of the studies discuss only the development of inter-firm networks in foreign markets; domestic inter-firm networks are usually considered useful only in connecting networks in overseas markets (Johansson and Mattson, 1988). The influence of domestic inter-firm networks in the context of internationalization is still under-explored (Prashantham, 2003; Gemser et al., 2004). Some work has emphasized the importance of domestic inter-firm networks in the internationalization of SMEs. Holmlund and Kock (1998) surveyed Finnish SMEs and argued that the firm's domestic network impacts on the internationalization process by providing access to foreign market information and related resources. Ellis and Pecotich (2001) found that Australian and Hong Kong SMEs rely largely on social networks for internationalization opportunities. Other studies similarly suggest that domestic inter-firm networks can lead to positive externalities that facilitate the internationalization of SMEs (Brown and McNaughton, 2003).

3. INTERNATIONALIZATION MODELS AND THEIR RELEVANCE TO SMES

In the international business literature, several models have evolved to explain the internationalization process of firms. Traditionally, these models are grouped into two main categories: economic decision-based approaches and evolutionary behavioral approaches (Benito and Welch, 1994). The former include theories such as comparative advantage, internalization, exchange model and transaction cost and the resource-based model. The latter comprise two main streams – network dependency and organizational learning.

In the past, international business was considered inherently risky and only larger firms possessed the ability and the inclination to tackle the challenges of doing business in foreign markets (Cosset and Roy, 1991). Consequently, most of the theoretical models that developed focused on large, established multinational corporations (Oviatt and McDougall, 1999). Among these internationalization concepts, the stages model (Johansson and Wiedersheim-Paul, 1975; Johansson and Vahlne, 1977) and the network model (Johansson and Mattson, 1988) are most useful in examining the internationalization behavior of SMEs (Jones, 1999; Gankema et al., 2000).

The stages model (Johansson and Vahlne, 1977), sometimes referred to as the 'Uppsala process model', explains the internationalization of companies as a step-by-step process in which firms begin their international operations engaging in low commitment entry modes in nearby markets and, over time, target geographically and culturally more distant markets through higher commitment entry modes. The defining characteristic of this model is that the firm follows a sequential process of internationalization, switching operational modes at each stage of evolution. The network model (Johansson and Mattsson, 1988), on the other hand, illustrates how network relationships shape a firm's internationalization process. In this model, it is assumed that the individual firm is dependent on resources controlled by other firms (Johansson and Mattsson, 1988) and therefore a firm's internationalization decisions depend on both the firm's own international experience and its relationships in business networks (Johansson and Mattsson, 1998). In other words, a firm's internationalization is also a process of establishing and developing positions in its foreign network.

As the two most prominent behavior-based approaches to internationalization (Benito and Welch, 1994), both the stages model and the network model have focused on a firm's process of market knowledge acquisition and the way in which this process influences internationalization strategies. The stages model considers only the firm's experiential knowledge, and the network approach adds the firm's network relationships in host markets and explains a firm's internationalization strategies in terms of both internal and external factors. The main difference between these two models is that the stages model regards the internationalization as an outward extension of a single firm's current operations and the outcome of its decision-making (Johansson and Wiedersheim-Paul, 1975; Johansson and Vahlne, 1977). On the other hand, the network model views a firm's internationalization in terms of its existing inter-firm relationships, those that it may have to establish so as to operate in a new market and the acti ons of not only the firm, but also the other participants in the network. However, both models fail to provide a comprehensive framework to explain the whole process of corporate internationalization. Table 22.1 compares the two models in terms of the factors influencing a firm's internationalization decisions.

Table 22.1   Comparison of the stages model and the network model

Factors	Stages Model	Network Model
Motivations for internationalization	No	No
Knowledge accumulation	Yes	Yes
Firm's resources	Yes	Yes
Firm's international experience	Yes	Yes
Influence of domestic inter-firm networks	No	No
Influence of external organizations	No	Yes
Conditions in foreign market	Yes	No
Capabilities of the firm	Yes	Yes

Note:
Yes: The model considers the factor
No: The model does not mention the factor

As Table 22.1 illustrates, both models emphasize the importance of the firm's international knowledge and experiences. However, they do not discuss the factors that can trigger a firm's internationalization, that is they do not explain why and how the firm starts to internationalize. Furthermore, the stages model discusses the influences of both the external environment and internal capabilities in a firm's internationalization process, while the network model only emphasizes the influences of the firm's business relationships. Each model has different strengths in analyzing a firm's internationalization behavior, but also certain weaknees.

A number of studies suggest that integrating the internationalization models can improve our understanding of corporate internationalization, especially when studying the internationalization process of SMEs (Coviello and Munro, 1997; Coviello and Martin, 1999; Tayeb, 2000; Whitelock, 2002). This chapter adopts such an integrated view in examining the internationalization of Taiwanese SMEs in order to conduct a more realistic and comprehensive assessment of corporate internationalization decisions.

4. THE DETERMINANTS OF CORPORATE INTERNATIONALIZATION DECISIONS

A number of approaches have emerged to explain the determinants of SME internationalization. Traditionally, the internationalization models of SMEs explained the firm's internationalization decisions in terms of deficiencies in external resources (Chen, 1995; Crick and Spence, 2005) and internal resources (Ernst, 1997; Mentzer et al., 2000), or the lack of international experience and knowledge (for example Madhok, 1997; Petersen and Pedersen, 1999; Zaheer et al., 1999). However, each of these studies explains the firm's internationalization decisions through a specific perspective and tends to ignore other factors. All determinants should not be discussed separately, as they usually influence the firms' internationalization strategies in an interactive manner (Ahokangas, 1998). Our study incorporates the key factors addressed in the main internationalization models so as to present a more realistic and comprehensive overview of corporate internationalization decisions. Beginning with resources, we shall now treat the five key factors in succession, generating a set of related hypotheses.

4.1 Resources

In the resource perceptive it is pointed out that a firm's own internal resources and the external resources within the network determine the course of the firm's internationalization (Chen, 1995; Crick and Spence, 2005). As resource deficiency is a main characteristic of SMEs, we argue that internal resource constraints can be one of the main determinants of a firm's decision to internationalize through its domestic inter-firm networks. By internationalizing via its inter-firm network, the firm can acquire the external resources that are controlled within the network which, in turn, help the firm to reduce transaction costs in a new geographical market.

Hypothesis 1: Taiwanese SMEs with higher resource deficiencies (both financial and non-financial) internationalize through domestic inter-firm networks.

4.2 Knowledge and Experience

The role of domestic inter-firm networks in local and international knowledge acquisition has been under-addressed in prior studies because the network members are usually deficient in international experience and knowledge. This study argues that domestic inter-firm networks can be utilized as a vehicle for knowledge acquisition in host markets. By learning through inter-firm networks, firms can reduce the perceived uncertainties of foreign markets without having to wait until their own market knowledge has reached the required level (Forsgren, 2001). Sharma and Blomstermo (2003) argue that networks may influence the internationalization process of firms, as they can receive more, better and earlier knowledge compared to their competitors. The information benefits generated through participating in an inter-firm network are specific and difficult to imitate for firms outside the network. While internationalizing with other network members, a firm can obtain local knowledge by learning not only on its own but also from its network partners. Such an approach may help the firm accumulate local knowledge more effectively than when it internationalizes alone.

Hypothesis 2: *Taiwanese SMEs with higher deficiencies in international experience and knowledge of the local market internationalize through domestic inter-firm networks.*

4.3   Environmental Uncertainties and Risks

Some commentators argue that a firm does not internationalize if the perceived risk is higher than a pre-conceived tolerable level (Forsgren, 2001). Prior studies have pointed out that inter-firm networks could be an important way to help SMEs reduce the perceived uncertainties and risks of internationalization (Wu and Huang, 2002; Kirby and Kaiser, 2003). Lambe and Spekman (1997) argue that an uncertain market environment usually encourages foreign firms to form network partnerships in the market. Such relationships offer higher levels of coordination, greater stability and enhanced flexibility to cope with the uncertainties of the environment.

Hypothesis 3: *Taiwanese firms with a higher perception of environmental uncertainty and risk in the host market internationalize through domestic inter-firm networks.*

4.4   Technology Level

Internationalization can be an essential means by which firms with advanced or proprietary technology can achieve the necessary sales volumes before the technology becomes obsolete or is imitated by other firms. When facing a highly competitive environment in the overseas market, technological changes are usually uncontrollable for individual firms. Under this uncertainty, SMEs may utilize their domestic inter-firm networks in order to obtain more advanced technologies, or to keep their existing technologies within their organization or network (Mentzer et al., 2000).

Hypothesis 4: *Taiwanese firms with lower levels of technological sophistication internationalize through domestic inter-firm networks.*

4.5 Degree of Interdependence

Johnsen and Ford (2000) point out that the interdependence of relationships in business networks causes a firm to consider the impact and influences of external parties in the network when it designs and implements an internationalization strategy. The influence of the inter-firm network in shaping a firm's internationalization process has been discussed previously (Johansson and Mattson, 1988). However, the effect of the nature and level of inter-firm relationships (that is, the degree of interdependence) on the firm's internationalization decisions has had little attention. The degree of interdependence has a critical role in affecting a firm's intentions when forming strategic partnerships to pursue internationalization (Mentzer et al., 2000), as well as impacting on the firm's profitability in the host market (Blankenburg-Holm et al., 1996). We therefore propose that different levels of interdependence with domestic business partners will influence a firm's internationalization decisions.

Hypothesis 5: *Taiwanese firms with a higher degree of interdependence with domestic inter-firm networks internationalize alongside network partners.*

5. METHOD

This study examines the role of domestic inter-firm networks in the internationalization decisions and patterns of Taiwanese SMEs. To achieve this objective, a quantitative approach to data analysis was selected. We tested the hypotheses through a survey of internationalized Taiwanese SMEs in the automobile, electronics and textiles sectors. These three industrial sectors are selected by considering the representation and validation of the sampling. In foreign direct investment (FDI) activities in the Asian region, electronics, automobiles and textiles have been the most prominent manufacturing sectors (UNCTAD, 1995). Taken together, these sectors accounted for nearly 50 per cent of world merchandise trade in 1994 and 60 per cent of Asian exports (WTO, 1996). In Taiwan, electronics, textiles and automobiles (including their related manufacturing sectors) have also been the top manufacturing sectors for international business in Taiwan, accounting for over 30 per cent of the total amount of outward investment (Investment Commission, MOEA, 2004). Furthermore, annual export figures for the three sectors, taken together, account for almost 70 per cent of the total export of Taiwan (Department of Statistics, MOEA, 2004).

Among the various inter-firm relationships, the Taiwanese C-S system has been one of the most important networking types in the acceleration of SME internationalization since the 1970s (Ernst, 1997). Therefore, the C-S system is chosen to represent the domestic inter-firm networks of Taiwanese manufacturing SMEs in this research. In this chapter, those from the sample that internationalized with their inter-firm network partners are classified as the C-S group hereinafter, and those firms that internationalized in other forms are the non-C-S group.

Due to differences in the number of foreign markets that the sample firms have entered, we only examined the first market entered. By examining the first foreign market penetrated, we can also eliminate the effects of the firms' own experiential knowledge accumulated from previous investments.

The motivation of SME internationalization is examined in terms of both external and internal environmental factors as this helps identify the conditions that lead the SME to internationalize through the domestic inter-firm networks. The potential factors which influence a firm's internationalization decision are selected based on the literature review. The level of importance of each factor in internationalization decisions is ranked individually by the respondents.

We surveyed a sample of 1198 companies across the three sectors mentioned earlier. The total number of valid replies was 191, making a response rate of 15.9 per cent. In order to investigate the determinants using predictive powers, regression analysis is employed in this research (Field, 2000). A dichotomous categorical dependent variable is employed in this regression (that is to internationalize through the domestic inter-firm networks versus other forms of internationalization). As such, binary logistic regression is an appropriate approach for this analysis (Field, 2000). Such an approach has been adopted by prior internationalization studies (for example Pan et al.,1999; Andreson et al., 2004). In this binary model, firms internationalizing through domestic inter-firm networks (the

C-S systems) are coded as '1' and the others are coded as '0'.

The baseline model of the logistic regression can be written as follows:

P (internationalize through domestic inter-firm networks=1)=1/{1+e-y}

where: y=f (ownership type, firm size, firm age, degree of dependence with business partners, home market factors, host market factors, organizational factors, internal competence factors and internal constraint factors).

Several demographic variables and the other 22 possible influential factors obtained from the literature review are entered as explanatory variables in the regression model. In order to check if there are any possible problems of multicollinearity, a correlation analysis was conducted. Since the explanatory variables are ordinal level, Spearman's test is conducted for the correlation examination. The correlation matrix shows that several weak and moderate correlation relationships exist among several exploratory variables. None of the correlation coefficients in this test was greater than 0.50, while a correlation coefficient above 0.60 is considered rather high (Pallant, 2001). These weak or moderate correlations among the variables would not generate serious collinearity problems, indicating the results are not affected by these correlation relationships (Benito et al., 1999).

6. RESULTS

The overall regression model is shown in Table 22.2. The Wald statistic is used in this analysis as it can ascertain whether a variable is a significant predictor of the outcome (Field, 2000). The regression coefficient (ß) and significance (as determined by the Wald statistic) of each explanatory variable is shown in Table 22.2. When the coefficient (ß) of a predictor is significantly different from zero, the predictor can be assumed to make a significant contribution to the prediction of the outcome (Field, 2000).

Overall, the estimated model has a significant chi-square value (p= 0.000), which indicates a good level of fit, thus the null hypothesis can be rejected. The value of pseudo R^2 indicates the explanatory power of the set of predicting variables to the response variable. This pseudo R^2 is comparable to the R^2 in linear regression. The pseudo R^2 of the model is 0.343, which indicates that the explanatory variables explain a good level of the variation in the response variable.

Table 22.2 Overall model results: logistic regression estimation

Explanatory Factors	β	S.E.	Sig.
Ownership types	0.138	0.245	0.572
Firm size	0.176	0.294	0.549
Firm age*	0.716	0.216	0.001
Customer concentration*	0.666	0.236	0.005
Follow your existing customer/partners*	0.893	0.265	0.001
Follow competitor's move	0.310	0.286	0.278
Approach customers/suppliers in host market	−0.342	0.248	0.169
Encouraged by Taiwanese government's policy	−0.125	0.228	0.584
Encouraged by local governments	0.156	0.233	0.505
Recessions of domestic economic environment	0.407	0.326	0.212
Saturation in home market	−0.298	0.232	0.199
Explore potential market*	−0.770	0.297	0.009
Acquire lower cost of labour and raw material	0.236	0.316	0.455
Overseas market condition	−0.321	0.282	0.255
To achieve globalization	0.118	0.323	0.715
To achieve economies of scale	0.146	0.290	0.614
Possess more advanced technology	−0.316	0.246	0.199
Limited non-financial resources*	0.728	0.334	0.029
Lack of local and international knowledge	−0.137	0.366	0.708
Lack of international experience	−0.109	0.386	0.776
Unavailability of distribution channels	−0.207	0.463	0.654
Cultural distance as a barrier	0.056	0.367	0.879
Investment risks and uncertainties*	0.273	0.330	0.049
Lack of financial resources	−0.001	0.355	0.999
Difficulties in forming partnerships*	0.686	0.360	0.057
Assure demands from the existing customers	0.198	0.232	0.393
Constant	−8.437	2.341	0.000
Model indices			
Model Chi-square	69.067		
Significance	0.0000		
Nagelkerke Pseudo R²	0.343		
−2 log likelihood	172.172		

Note: * denotes that the coefficient is significant

The result of the logistic regression analysis supports several hypotheses advanced in this chapter. According to the regression coefficients (ß) of the model, limited non-financial resources (H1), perception of uncertainties and risks associated with internationalization (H3) and interdependence with home partners (H5) are positive to the firms' decisions to internationalize with domestic network partners. According to the regression coefficient, the factor 'possessing more advanced level of technology' (H4) has no significant association with the dependent variable. A prior study points out that a firm may utilize its existing inter-firm networks to obtain more advanced technologies through these networks (Mentzer et al., 2000). However, this function of the domestic inter-firm networks is not evident from our research.

On the other hand, the results found insufficient evidence to support the argument that the lack of international knowledge and experience (H2) and financial resources (H1) affect the firm's decisions to cooperate with domestic inter-firm networks in their internationalization. It has been pointed out that international knowledge can be derived from various sources and usually these are through external organizations rather than the firm itself (Bell, 1995; Pedersen and Peterson, 1998). Learning in an inter-firm network is another alternative approach to knowledge acquisition (Forsgren, 2001). This implies that deep and long-lasting business relationships facilitate the acquisition of market knowledge from different participants in the network (Andersson et al., 2001). Although previous studies have confirmed the mechanism of knowledge transformation within inter-firm networks, the knowledge transfer between firms sometimes does not occur as smoothly as the model predicts (Johansson and Elg, 2002). This could be because some firms may not be willing to contribute or obtain such knowledge and experience to or from other firms in the network. On the other hand, even when knowledge transfers are successful within the networks, the acceptors may not take the same decisions due to other influential factors, for example different capabilities and growth goals of the firms. Therefore, the role of inter-firm networks in knowledge transfers may not be as important as predicted by the previous model.

7. DISCUSSION AND CONCLUSION

This study confirmed that 'acquiring non-financial external resources' and reducing internationalization risks and uncertainties were the determinants that caused firms to internationalize through domestic inter-firm networks. High uncertainties about host markets encourage the firms to embed themselves in network partnerships, which may offer higher levels of coordination and greater stability and also flexibility to cope with the uncertainties of the environment (Lambe and Spekman, 1997). The survey result implies that cooperating with other firms can be an approach to managing internationalization risks and uncertainties. The higher the perceived risks and uncertainties, the more likely it is that firms will internationalize through the domestic inter-firm networks. In addition, strong dependency on business partners is also a significant factor in firms' internationalization decisions. The dependency within an inter-firm network leads a company to internationalize together with its domestic partners in order to maintain inter-firm relationships, reduce investment costs and avoid competition in the initial stage. On the other hand, internationalization opportunities provided by the domestic partners is also an important reason for firms to internationalize through the networks.

Previous work has illustrated that participating in an inter-firm network benefits a firm's internationalization process in several ways, for example acquiring external resources (Coviello and Munro, 1997), acquiring local knowledge (Gulati, 1999) and obtaining more advanced technologies (Mentzer, Min and Zacharia, 2000). We found no significant effect in respect of the firm's technology level and selection of internationalization approaches. Furthermore, internationalization knowledge and experience sharing, assumed by the network approach to be the main functions of inter-firm networks, were not sufficiently evident in our findings. The results reflected the fact that most Taiwanese SMEs internationalized in an unprepared manner (SMEA, 1999). These firms usually did not obtain sufficient local knowledge (social, economic, cultural, regulatory and so on) before they internationalized. Such an unprepared state may result from the unavailability of information channels and insufficient time to prepare for internationalization.

A group approach to internationalization is common among Taiwanese SMEs. In this research, the overall results showed the positive effect of domestic inter-firm networks on corporate internationalization. The study suggests that a firm and its environment should not be regarded as separate entities. SMEs may shape their firm's environment by interacting with other firms. Domestic inter-firm networks also play a certain role in creating a bridge between SMEs and the host market in terms of knowledge acquisition and the capturing of business opportunity. The competitive advantages generated within the networks – such as long-term cooperative relationships, lower investment costs, unsolicited contract demands and technical integration – lead the firms to internationalize with their existing domestic partners. These alternative advantages may provide an explanation for the firm's internationalization together with domestic partners who do not possess international knowledge and experience. Based on the findings of our research, we suggest that the top management teams of SMEs should not only focus on the firm's internal constraints to internationalization, but should also look to its network for resources and opportunities to internationalize. We further suggest that long-term relationships in domestic inter-firm networks can increase the internationalization capabilities of SMEs.

NOTES

1. Correlation is significant at the 0.05 level (2-tailed).
2. Correlation is significant at the 0.01 level (2-tailed).

REFERENCES

Ahokangas, P. (1998), 'Internationalization and Resources', www document, Vaasa University Digital Collection, available on: www.tritonia.fi/vanha/ov/acta64/acta64.html, (accessed 12 May, 2004).

Anderson, S., J. Gabrielsson and I. Wictor (2004), 'International activities in small firms: examining factors influencing the internationalization and export growth of small firms', *Canadian Journal of Administrative Sciences*, **21**(1), 22-34.

Andersson, U., M. Forsgren and T. Pedersen (2001), 'Subsidiary performance in multinational corporations: the importance of technology embeddedness', *International Business Review*, **10**(1), 3-23.

Axelsson, B. and J. Johansson (1992), 'Foreign market entry: the textbook versus the network view', in B. Axelsson and G. Easton (eds), *Industrial Networks: A New View of Reality*, London: Routledge, 218-34.

Bell, J. (1995), 'The Internationalization of small computer software firms: a further challenge to stage theories', *European Journal of Marketing*, **29**(8), 60-75.

Benito, G.R. and L.S. Welch (1994), 'Foreign market servicing: beyond choice of entry mode', *Journal of International Marketing*, **2**(2), 7-28.

Benito, G.R., T. Pedersen and B. Petersen (1999), 'Foreign operation methods and switching costs: conceptual issues and possible effects', *Scandinavian Journal of Management*, **15**, 213-29.

Blankenburg-Holm, D., K. Eriksson and J. Johansson (1996), 'Business network and cooperation in international business relationships', *Journal of International Business Studies*, **27**(5), 1033-54.

Brown, P. and R. McNaughton (2003), 'Cluster development programmes: panacea or placebo for promoting SME growth and internationalization?', in H. Etemad and R.W. Wright (eds), *Globalisation and Entrepreneurship: Policy and Strategy Perspectives*, Cheltenham, UK and Northampton, MA, USA: Edward Elgar.

Chen, T.J. (ed.) (1995), *Taiwan's Small and Medium-sized Firms' Direct Iinvestment in Southeast Asia*, Taipei, Taiwan: Chung-Hua Institution for Economic Research.

Chung, C. (1997), 'Division of labor across the Taiwan strait: macro overview and analysis of the electronics industry', in B. Naughton (ed.), *The China Circle: Economics and Electronics in the PRC, Taiwan and Hong Kong*, Washington, DC: Brookings Institution Press, 164-209.

Cosset, J. and J. Roy (1991), 'The determinants of country risk ratings', *Journal of International Business Studies*, **22**(1), 135-43.

Coviello, N.E. and A. McAuley (1999), 'Internationalization and the smaller firm: a review of contemporary empirical research', *Management International Review*, **39**(2), 223-57.

Coviello, N.E. and H. Munro (1997), 'Network relationships and the internationalization process of small software firms', *International Business Review*, **6**(4), 361-86.

Coviello, N.E. and K. Martin (1999), 'An integrated perspective of SME internationalization', *Journal of International Marketing*, **7**(4), 42-66.

Crick, D. and M. Spence (2005), 'The internationalization of high performing UK high-tech SMEs: A study of planned and unplanned strategies', *International Business Review*, **14**, 167-85.

Department of Statistics, MOEA, Taiwan (2004), online database, available on: http://2k3dmz2.moea.gov.tw/gnweb/statistics/ (accessed October, 2004).

Ellis, P and A. Pecotich (2001), 'Social factors influencing export initiation in small and medium sized enterprises', *Journal of Marketing Research*, **38**, 119-30.

Ernst, D. (1997), 'What permits David to defeat Goliath? The Taiwanese Model in the computer industry', International Business Economics Research Paper Series, No. 3, Farkas, AJ, Aalborg University, Denmark.

Field, A. (2000), *Discovering Statistics using SPSS for Windows*, London: Sage.

Forsgren, M. (2001), 'The concept of learning in the Uppsala internationalization process model: a critical review', *International Business Review*, **11**(3), 257-77.

Gankema, H.G., H.R Snuif and P.S. Zwart (2000), 'The internationalization process of small and medium-sized enterprises: an evaluation of stage theory', *Journal of Small Business Management*, **38**(3), 15-27.

Gemser, G., M.J. Brand, and A.M. Sorge (2004), 'Exploring the internationalization process of small businesses: a study of Dutch old and new economy firms', *Management International Review*, **44**(2),127-50.

Gerlach, M. (1992), *Alliance Capitalism: The Social Organization of Japanese Business*, San Francisco: University of California Press.

Gulati, R. (1999), 'Network location and learning: the influence of network resources and firm capabilities on alliance formation', *Strategic Management Journal*, **20**(5), 397-420.

Holmlund, M. and S. Kock (1998), 'Relationships and the internationalization of Finnish small and medium sized companies', *International Small Business Journal*, **16**(4), 46-63.

Hu, M.W. and C. Schive (1996), 'The market shares of small and medium scale enterprises in Taiwan manufacturing', *Asian Economic Journal*, **10**(2), 117-31.

Investment Commission, MOEA, Taiwan (2004), *Report of the Outward Investments of ROC Enterprises*, Taipei: MOEA.

Johansson, J. and L.G. Mattson (1988), 'Internationalization in industrial systems: a network approach', in N. Hood and J.E. Vahlne (eds), *Strategies in Global Competition*, reproduced in P.J. Buckley and P.N. Ghauri (eds) (1999), *The Internationalization of the Firm: A Reader*, London: Academic Press, 287-314.

Johansson, J. and L.G. Mattson (1998), 'Inter-organisational relations in industrial systems: a network approach compared with the transaction-cost approach', in C. John and D. Faulkner, *Strategies of Cooperation*, Oxford, Oxford University Press, 113-40.

Johansson, J. and J.E. Vahlne (1977), 'The internationalization process of the firm: a model of knowledge development and increasing foreign market commitments', *Journal of International Business Studies*, **8**, 23-32.

Johansson, J. and J.E. Vahlne (1990), 'The mechanism of internationalization', *International Marketing Review*, **7**(4), 11-24.

Johansson, J. and F. Wiedersheim-Paul (1975), 'The internationalization of the firm: four Swedish cases', *Journal of Management Studies*, **12**(3), 305-22.

Johansson, U. and U. Elg (2002), 'Relationships as entry barriers: a network perceptive', *Scandinavian Journal of Management*, **18**, 393-419.

Johnsen, R.E. and D. Ford (2000), 'Establishing an international network position: findings from an exploratory survey of UK textile suppliers', www document, IMP 2000 Conference paper, available on www.bath.ac.uk/imp/trackd.htm, (accessed 2 June, 2004).

Jones, M.V. (1999), 'The internationalization of small high-technology firms', *Journal of International Marketing*, **7**(4), 15-41.

Kirby, D.A. and S. Kaiser (2003), 'Joint ventures as an internationalization strategy for SMEs', *Small Business Economics*, **21**(3), 229-42.

Lambe, C.J. and R.F. Spekman (1997), 'Alliances, external technology acquisition, and discontinuous technological change', *Journal of Product Innovation Management*, **14**(2), 102-16.

Lee, W.H. (2002), 'Internationalization strategy of SMEs', in R.H. Lang et al., *Business Strategy of Small and Medium sized Enterprises*, Taipei: National Open University Press, 361-85.

Liu, P.C., Y.C. Liu and H.L. Wu (1994), 'Emergence of new business organization and management in Taiwan', *Industry of Free China*, November, Taiwan.

Madhok, A. (1997), 'Cost, value and foreign market entry mode: the transaction and the firm', *Strategic Management Journal*, **18**, 39-61.

Martinez, J.I. and J.C. Jarillo (1989), 'The evolution of research on coordination mechanisms in multinational corporations', *Journal of International Business Studies*, **20**(3), 489-514.

Mentzer, J.T., S. Min and Z.G. Zacharia (2000), 'The nature of inter-firm partnering in supply chain management', *Journal of Retailing*, **76**(4), 549-68.

Oviatt, B.M. and P.P. McDougall (1999), 'Accelerated internationalization: why are new and small ventures internationalizing in greater numbers and with increasing speed?', in R. Wright (ed.), *Research in Global Strategic Management*, Stamford, CT: JAI Press.

Pallant, J. (2001), *SPSS Survival Manual*, Buckingham: Open University Press.

Pan, Y., S. Li and D.S. Tse (1999), 'The impact of order and mode of market entry on profitability and market share', *Journal of International Business Studies*, **30**(1), 81-104.

Pedersen, T. and B. Petersen (1998), 'Explaining gradually increasing resource commitment to a foreign market', *International Business Review*, 7, 483-501.

Petersen, B. and T. Pedersen (1999), 'Fast and slow resource commitment to foreign markets: what causes the difference?', *Journal of International Management*, **5**(2), 73-91.

Powell, W. (1990), 'Neither market nor hierarchy: network forms of organization', *Research in Organizational Behavior*, **12**, 295-336.

Prashantham, S. (2003), 'The internationalization of small knowledge-intensive firms: leveraging foreign network relationships for international market entry and development', 30th AIB UK chapter Annual Conference, Leicester, UK.

Sharma, D. and A. Blomstermo (2003), 'The internationalization process of born globals: a network view', *International Business Review*, **12**, 739-53.

Small and Medium Enterprise Administration (SMEA), MOEA, Taiwan (1999), *White Paper on Small and Medium Enterprises in Taiwan*, 1999, Taipei, MOEA.

Small and Medium Enterprise Administration, MOEA, Taiwan (2001), *White Paper on Small and Medium Enterprises in Taiwan, 2001*, Taipei: MOEA.

Small and Medium Enterprise Administration, MOEA, Taiwan (2002), *White Paper on Small and Medium Enterprises in Taiwan*, 2002, Taipei: MOEA.

Su, G.H. (2003), *Synergy*, Taipei, Taiwan: Corporate Synergy Development Centre (CSDC) and the Commercial Press.

Tayeb, M. (2000), *International Business: Theories, Policies and Practices*, London: Financial Times Prentice Hall.

United Nations Committee on Trade and Development (UNCTAD) (1995), *World Investment Report*, Geneva: United Nations.

United Nations Committee on Trade and Development (UNCTAD) (2001), *FDI to Asia Booms, Fuelled by Hong Kong*, Geneva: United Nations.

Whitelock, J. (2002), 'Theories of internationalization and their impact on market entry', *International Marketing Review*, **19**(4), 342-7.

World Trade Organization (WTO) (1996), *Annual Report: Special Topic: Trade and Foreign Direct Investment*, Geneva: WTO.

Wu, R.I. and C.C. Huang (2002), 'Entrepreneurship in Taiwan, turning point to restart', research paper of Entrepreneurship in Asia program, The Maureen and Mike Mansfield Foundation, available on www.mcpa.org/programs/program_pdfs/ent_taiwan.pdf (accessed May 17, 2004).

Wu, U.M. (ed.) (2003), *Taiwanese Business Groups*, Taipei: National Open University Press.

Wu, W.I. (1996), 'The internationalization process of SMEs: a comparison study of Taiwan, Japan and South Korea', *Management Journal of Fu-Zen University*, **5**(2), 75-102.

Yeh Y.F. (1994), 'The internationalization of the Taiwanese companies in Asia', *Journal of Nan-Tai college Bulletin*, **19**, 47-52.

Yiu, G.M. (1997), 'The strategy of the internationalization of Taiwan enterprises: from the view network model', Research project report, National Science Council, Taiwan (NSC 86-2416-H-004-016).

Zaheer, S., S. Albert and A. Zaheer (1999), 'Time scales and organizational theory', *Academy of Management Review*, **4**, 725-41.

22. The influence of the Internet on the internationalization of SMEs in Taiwan

Yi-Long Jaw and Chun-Liang Chen

1. INTRODUCTION

SMEs have played a very important part in Taiwan's economic development; their strength has been the foundation for over 40 years of prosperity and growth. Many leading Taiwanese trading companies started out as SMEs, and these companies can be thought of as the forerunners in the internationalization of Taiwan's SMEs. However, since 1986 there have been major changes in the macroeconomic environment in Taiwan. The appreciation of the NT Dollar destroyed the price advantage that Taiwan's exports had previously enjoyed, wages rose, and the environmental protection and labor movements grew in strength. With production costs rising, Taiwanese products were no longer as competitive as those of Southeast Asian nations, mainland China and other Third World countries. Large numbers of Taiwanese SMEs moved their operations overseas to low-cost production destinations. This trend was not confined to manufacturing enterprises; trading companies also began to establish sourcing, purchasing and distribution facilities overseas as they adopted a transnational marketing model.

According to Parasuraman and Zinkhan (2002, p. 287), 'Internet technology has the potential to alter almost every aspect of business operations'. Developments like the Internet compel business researchers to re-visit the adequacy of existing conceptualizations. The sub-field of SMEs' internationalization is no exception (Dana, Wright and Etemad, 2004).

The role of the Internet in enhancing the internationalization of SMEs is supported by many scholars, such as Poon and Jevons (1997); Rialp and Rialp (2001); Knight and Liesch (2002) and Etemad (2004). They all argue that the commercialization of the Internet has created unpredicted opportunities for SMEs. The Internet will revolutionize the dynamics of international commerce and lead to more rapid internationalization of SMEs. SMEs can now access the same capabilities as large companies, and are able to engage in international markets that previously might have been unaffordable due to the considerable resources required. And it would also be interesting to analyze the extent to which the Internet has helped SMEs from developing countries to internationalize (Chrysostome, Beamish, Hébert and Rosson, 2004).

As indicated, the specific type of firm behavior of interest to this chapter is internationalization, the 'process of increasing involvement in international operations' (Welch and Luostarinen, 1988), with special reference to SMEs. However, internationalization theories, such as stage models, fail to recognize that use of the Internet for global business enables some firms to export from the outset and leapfrog the conventional stages of internationalization. Other scholars have also argued that the Internet is only a tool instead of strategy for SMEs. SMEs always have their own disadvantages compared with large companies, which have greater resources and network of operations. Although the cost of setting up a simple site is low and affordable for most SMEs, the cost of setting up comprehensive, high profile sites is prohibitive for SMEs (Samiee, 1998). Major search engines such as Yahoo and Google charge high fees for directing their Internet traffic to companies by leasing key words that reflect their business, which is clearly a disadvantage for SMEs (Svensson, 2003).

This research focuses on the use of the Internet as an instrument for SMEs to expand their operations beyond their national borders, and attempts to solve the following research problem: how does the use of the Internet influence the internationalization of SMEs in Taiwan? This research is conducted within the framework of Taiwanese SMEs and the following research questions are addressed in sequence: (1) How can the Internet enhancing the internationalization of SMEs? (2) How has the Internet affected SMEs' internationalization entry strategy? (3) What is the impact of the Internet in existing internationalization theories? By examining the relevant literature and case studies of SMEs, it can be proposed that SMEs that apply the Internet intensively tend to involve more extensively in their international operations. Preliminary support for this proposition is presented based on data from 700 SMEs.

This argument is explored here through the synthesis of relevant literature and the findings of an exploratory study comprising case studies that are supplemented by a preliminary quantitative study, conducted among SMEs in a developing economy context. Thus, the role of the Internet in the internationalization of SMEs has become such an issue that is vital both for practitioners and policy-makers seeking to understand how Internet technology can best be utilized to facilitate internationalization efforts.

The remainder of the chapter is structured as follows: the next section contains a review of relevant literature, followed by a brief discussion of the methodology employed in this study, after which findings are presented, and finally some conclusions and implications for academics, practitioners and policy-makers are drawn out.

2. LITERATURE REVIEW

In the first section, several scholars' popular theories including the internationalization process, entry modes, transaction cost analysis and network theory are presented; in the second section, existing findings concerning the Internet's general use for business, the Internet's applications to handling the internationalization process, entry modes and stage model for Internet commerce development are introduced.

2.1 Internationalization Theories

2.1.1 Internationalization process models

The internationalization process is conceptualized as the process of adapting firms' operations (strategy, structure, resources, and so on) to international environments (Johansson, 2000). Internationalization theories attempt to explain why companies choose to operate beyond their domestic market and the strategies and structures they develop to do this (Coviello and McAuley, 1999). Many theories have been advanced to explain the process of internationalization, such as the traditional marketing approach that focuses on the company's core competences combined with opportunities in the foreign environment (Penrose, 1959), the cost-based view that suggests that the company must possess a 'compensating advantage' in order to overcome the 'cost of foreignness' (Hymer, 1976; Kindleberger, 1969), Vernon's (1966) international product life cycle, Dunning's (1977) eclectic theory, and so on.

A useful starting point in the conceptualization of internationalization is Johanson and Vahlne's (1977) Uppsala model of internationalization, which essentially posits that firms' internationalization increases as its foreign market knowledge does, which has been confirmed as being crucial (Eriksson, et al. 1997). This behavioral view derived from case studies of internationalization paths taken by a number of Swedish companies (Johanson and Wiedersheim-Paul, 1975; Johanson and Vahlne,

1977). The stages theory posits companies as being either (1) a non-exporter, (2) an indirect exporter, having (3) overseas sales operations, or (4) overseas production units. Trade barrier reductions and global market growth have led to a quicker pace of company internationalization (OECD, 1998) than the stages theory would suggest. It has also led companies to follow paths that are at variance from the linear and predictable path of the stages theory. As a result, other approaches to internationalization have been widely discussed and examined.

There are three streams of and research focusing on (1) business networks, (2) 'born global' companies, and (3) international new ventures. Many scholars have drawn attention to the fact that companies exist within business networks and that these can profoundly influence the domestic and foreign market strategies and operations of single entities (Johanson and Mattson, 1988; Ford, 1997). Firstly, in the context of SMEs, network relationships are also known to influence and often accelerate their internationalization, resulting in a growing interest in this phenomenon among scholars (Coviello and Munro, 1997; Chetty and Holm, 2000). The basic assumption in the network model is that the individual company is dependent on resources controlled by other companies. Therefore a company must establish and develop positions in relation to counterparts in foreign networks to get external resources. A firm may receive useful information and knowledge about foreign markets and opportunities therein from customers, suppliers or other network relationships. Another advantage of the network model is that the relationships in a domestic network can be used as bridges to other networks in other countries. Also, when entering a network, the company's internationalization process will occur more rapidly. This is particularly advantageous for SMEs entering foreign markets and enables them to set up their own subsidiaries more quickly.

Secondly, research has also focused on those companies that are seemingly 'born global', those operate internationally from the first day (Knight and Cavusgil, 1996). There are two basic approaches for creating international inter-firm networks, the active approach in which the SME undertakes the investigation that results in finding partners and contracts, and the passive approach in which the SME is approached by foreign companies. SMEs can leapfrog early stages in the traditional internationalization process (McDougall et al., 1994; Reuber and Fischer, 1997). The extreme examples are the so-called 'born global' SMEs (Knight and Cavusgil, 1996). 'Born globals' are small, technology-oriented companies that operate in international markets from the earliest days of their establishment. The born global phenomenon suggests a new challenge to traditional theories of internationalization (ibid.).

Related is Oviatt and MacDougall's (1994a, 1996) research on international new ventures (INV). The nature of the product, industry norms and the orientation of the entrepreneur are primary components of the INV model. High R&D costs and shorter product life cycles force companies to recoup investments quickly and cover as large a market as possible. Converging international standards for some products have likewise created a global market where companies face global competitors. For instance, most computer components are interchangeable and can be sourced from many suppliers. To service this market, manufacturers must be capable of competing globally.

2.1.2 The transaction cost analysis

Coase made this model in 1937. He said, 'a firm will tend to expand until the cost for organizing an extra transaction within the company will become equal to the cost of carrying out the same transaction by means of an exchange on the open market' (Coase, 1937). It is a theory which predicts that a company will perform internally those activities it can undertake at lower cost through establishing an internal (hierarchical) management control and implementation system while relying on the market for activities in which independent outsiders have a cost advantage.

Arrow (1969) described transaction costs as the cost of running the economic system, and as distinct from production costs. Williamson (1996) defines transaction costs as the 'costs of contracting', and Cheung (1998) as institution cost. Searching for information, bargaining, monitoring, and contract enforcement are instances of such costs (John and Weitz, 1988). In transaction cost economics (TCE), attention is focused on economizing efforts that attend the organization of contracts – where a transaction occurs when a good or service is transferred across a technologically separable interface (Williamson, 1996).

2.1.3 Choice of entry modes

Extensive literature exists on the choice of entry mode (summarized in Root, 1987 and 1994). These choices include: export entry modes (indirect, direct agent/distributor, direct branch/subsidiary), contractual entry modes (licensing, franchising, technical agreements, service contracts, management contracts, construction/turnkey contracts, co-production agreement), and investment entry modes (direct entry, acquisition joint venture). Entry mode in this study is conceptualized as 'an institutional arrangement that makes the entry of a company's products, technology, human skills, management or other resources available in a foreign country' (Root, 1994).

The choice of foreign entry mode is a critical factor for success. Root

(1994) identifies three basic approaches to entry mode choice: (1) no explicit choice of market entry mode such as the case where SMEs receive unsolicited orders from foreign buyers; (2) a choice made in accordance with the existing market entry strategy; and (3) a choice that considers strategic rules and is based on a systematic comparison of the different possible modes.

2.2 SMEs' Internationalization and the Internet

A brief review of Internet-related literature on internationalization is offered below.

2.2.1 Internet applications for SMEs' internationalization

In some cases, the Internet will increase the pace of SME internationalization by eliminating or lessening the need for intermediaries (Quelch and Klein, 1996). These proposed effects of the Internet on the pace of the SMEs' internationalization have been confirmed in a study by Lituchy and Rail (2000) in which they stated that the use of a website propels SMEs into the internationalization process.

The Internet does not only help SMEs to begin to internationalize but also helps to maintain a strong position in foreign markets through activities such as marketing intelligence, global sales promotion and inter-firm R&D (Hamill, 1997). In fact, because it is a gateway to foreign markets, the Internet enables SMEs to become international whether this was planned or not (Lituchy and Rail, 2000).

Table 23.1 presents a conceptual framework for identifying strategic uses of the Internet in the context of SMEs' internationalization. Three main applications are identified namely, network communications, market intelligence, and sales promotion. Intended targets include all of the actors in the company's network including foreign customers, agents, distributors, partners, governments, R&D institutions etc.

2.2.2 Internet and network relationships

Prashantham and Berry (2004) argued that the Internet offers applications that facilitate network relationships, enabling firms to interact more widely and intimately with other actors, including customers, suppliers and collaborators. The Internet potentially lowers the cost of accessing and leveraging network relationships by facilitating the enhancement of firms' visibility, efficiency and intimacy, with respect to their network relationships (Prashantham and Berry, 2004). The Internet's ease of use, universal standards, and remote electronic access result in tools of communication

Table 23.1 Internet applications in SME internationalization

Communications
Tools: e-mail, Usenet, Listserv, voice mail, IRC, video conferencing, MUDS, etc.
Target: customers, suppliers, agents, distributors, partners, research centers, governments

Market Intelligence
Tools: WWW, information search and retrieval software – Netscape, Microsoft, Gopher, Archie, WAIS, Veronica, etc.
Target: country and market research reports, industry specific reports, trade contacts, agents and distributors, trade leads

Marketing and sales promotion
Tools: World Wide Web Site
Target: Global customers (actual and potential)

Source: Hamill and Gregory (1997)

and information-sharing (Morgan-Thomas and Bridgewater, 2004), enhancing visibility; collaboration and commerce (Tiessen et al. 2001), enhancing efficiency; and communities and privileged-access networks (Tapscott, 1999), enhancing intimacy.

The Internet provides SMEs with good opportunities to establish strategic alliances (Soliman and Janz, 2003). It stimulates collaboration between organizations (Aalst, 1999), and this is particularly true for SMEs that wish to internationalize.

2.2.3 Internet and born global

Hamill (1997) expects Internet-enabled companies to pursue international sales at earlier stages in their development. However, access to markets and customers is a double-edged sword. Sawhney and Mandal (2000) argue that the Internet exposes companies to global competition from the beginning. This puts pressure on companies to consider/pursue international sales very early in their development. As the Internet becomes more international, opportunities will increasingly lie outside of domestic markets, and companies must be able to respond.

Fillis (2002) found that United Kingdom and Irish exporting SMEs experienced substantial price and promotion challenges from competitors. SMEs have to face this competition at an earlier stage of their internationalization process, when they are typically not ready for such rivalry (Sawhney and Mandal, 2000).

2.2.4 Internet and transaction cost

It appears that the Internet can speed firm internationalization, particularly through reducing the costs incurred by SMEs (Petersen et al., 2002). The

Internet provides SMEs with considerable information that helps to reduce the uncertainties of foreign markets significantly, even though it does not eliminate risk (Petersen et al., 2002). E-business provides transaction speed, access to global markets, and mass customization (Littman, 2000). B2B allows the user to see the parts and products online, reach new customers, and provide better customer service. Through the use of the Internet, transaction costs can be dramatically reduced. The Internet allows for fewer data entry errors, creating time-savings and lower labor cost. Internal resources are reassigned and certain tasks are outsourced. Electronic procurement can cut purchase order costs to a third of those of conventional purchase orders (Martin, 1999).

2.2.5 Internet and entry mode

An SME with a website is in effect a global company, operating on the accessibility of its customers. This gives customers the opportunity to purchase, wherever they are, whenever they want (Rosson, 2004). A distinctive feature of the Internet then is that it makes it feasible for SMEs to position themselves instantaneously on many foreign markets (Petersen et al., 2002).

Craig and Thandarayan (2000) reported in their research on Australian and South African tourist firms that foreign marketing via the Internet failed in part because a standard product brochure was made available when, in fact, adjustments were needed in quality, price, language and culture. Furthermore, adjustments made by SMEs to serve one foreign market can often be transferred where indicated to others without major costs. Such transfers help make possible fast entry into successive foreign markets (Gareiss, 2000).

2.2.6 A stage model for Internet commerce development

Internet commerce is defined as: 'commercial activities associated with the Internet' (Bambury, 1998). Rao and Metts (2003) proposed that use of the Internet in a company's strategic development took place in four stages (Figure 23.1): presence, portals, transaction integration and enterprise integration.

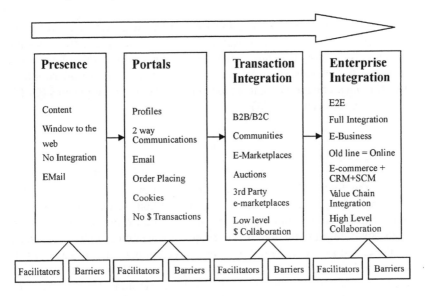

Figure 23.1   Stages of Internet commerce development and their characteristics

Stage 1: Presence Most companies make their first steps in electronic commerce by displaying their company brochure and product offer on a website (Timmers, 2000) and probably using email independently to communicate with customers, suppliers and employees. The presence stage involves the initial steps that organizations take to get involved in a digital environment.

Stage 2: Portals The main difference between this stage and the presence stage is the capability integration of two-way communications between the business and customers (B2C) and/or between businesses (B2B) through the Internet. The information provided in the presence stage can be coupled with facilities for ordering, product feedback, and product and/or quality surveys.

Stage 3: Transaction integration The transactions integration stage (TI) is differentiated from the portals stage mainly by the presence of transactions between partners. This in turn will require higher technical capabilities and IT infrastructure. Those at stage 3 have information-based websites operating and are developing on-line ordering facilities. The most advanced adopters may have online ordering in operation and are developing online payment capabilities.

Stage 4: *Enterprise integration* Enterprise integration (EI) refers to complete integration of business processes to the extent that old-line business is indistinguishable from online business. This level of integration involves high levels of collaboration between customers and suppliers by utilizing e-commerce systems to manage customer relationships (CRM) and the supply chain (SCM).

3. METHODOLOGY

While the Internet's potential benefit for firms based in developing economies has been suggested in the last section, few empirical studies appear to have been undertaken in a developing economy context. Most of the small firm internationalization theory focuses on developed economy contexts and may not readily hold in a developing economy context that has peculiar market- and policy-related problems (Maddy, 2000). There are two complementary methods employed in this study, briefly discussed below. The first method is comprised of case studies (Yin, 1994) of eight SMEs, which were selected across industries randomly and based on the potential respondents' willingness as well as experts' suggestions. Accordingly, the criteria for the sample selection in this study are: (1) small and medium-sized enterprises (by Taiwan Small and Medium Enterprise Administration's definition, i.e. employees less than 250, and with capital under NTD 80 million); (2) already involved in international business activities; (3) independent ownership – not a subsidiary of a large company. All interviews were conducted following a semi-structured format by the same interviewer to ensure consistency and comparability.

The second aspect of the research attempts to strengthen the main proposition of this chapter by analyzing the 700 SMEs Survey of 2005. The database is based on 4600 randomly selected Taiwanese SMEs, using the telephone to carry out the investigation, and the number of effective questioners was 700 (effective return rate is 15.21 percent). The number who had at least a corporate website on the Internet was 311.

Degrees of Electronic Commerce (DOEC) and Degree of Internationalization (DOI) are the major concepts adopted to test the propositions. Rao and Metts (2003) proposed that use of the Internet in a company's strategic development took place in four stages: presence, portals, transaction integration and enterprise integration. A score from 1 to 5 was assigned such that lower scores were given to brochure-ware type websites and higher scores for evidence of interactivity and the potential to leverage network relationships (through intranets and extranets). A score of 1 was awarded in the absence of a website, 2 for a brochure website that was displayed (presence stage), 3 for a website with the capability of two-way communications between the business and customers (B2C) and/or between businesses (B2B), that is, the portals stage. A score of 4 was awarded when financial transactions between partners were being made and is labeled as the transaction integration stage, meaning that interactions can be for selling as well as buying. This stage can include participation in virtual communities, which allows participants to share information of common interest. A score of 5 stands for the enterprise integration stage. This level of integration is e-commerce + CRM + SCM.

The DOI is measured by the proportion of revenue accruing from international business and the proportion of international assets. A score of 1 stands for 0-20 per cent of revenues accruing from international business and the proportions of international assets. A score of 2 represents 21-40 per cent, 3 is for 41-60 per cent, 4 is for 61-80 per cent, and 5 is for 81-100 per cent. The focus of this chapter is exploratory and tests the important proposition regarding whether the relationship between DOI and DOEC is positive, especially in a developing economy. Then the DOI is subsequently regressed against DOEC, as discussed in the subgroup analysis.

4. CASE AND BRIEFINGS

4.1   YFC-BonEagle Inc. (coding as Y Company, www.cables.com.tw)

Y Company began its operations in 1983 and has been proud to supply products worldwide. The company operates from its headquarters in Taiwan with two manufacturing facilities in Dongguan and one branch office in Shanghai, China. Their main products are cables, 3C plugs, patch cords and jacks, and optical devices. About 75 per cent of the company's products are distributed overseas, which includes North America and Europe. Its main customers include famous companies like IBM and ALCATEL. Regarding the company's computerization, the company has set up its own website and the electronic data interchange (EDI) system to manage the business and to share the information with its suppliers, such as Formosa Chemicals & Fiber Corporation. The company also uses email to communicate with customers, and provides an intranet for staff communication.

4.2   Kingcore Electronics Inc. (coding as K Company, www.kingcore. com.tw)

K Company has been in operation since 1986, with its headquarters in Taiwan and factory in Su-Zho, Jan Hsu Province, Shanghai, China. Its main products are cores for electronic products. About 42 per cent of the company's products are distributed overseas, including Asia, Australia, North America and Europe. Their main customers include famous companies such as Acer, Asus and Inventec, and the company is penetrating South-East Asia through a sales channel shared with its strategic partners. The company is also handling a quantity of OEM and ODM orders for Japanese customers. As to the company's computerization, the company has its own website and set up the electronic data interchange system to manage the business; it uses email to communicate with customers, and provides an intranet for staff communication.

4.3   Flytech Co. (coding as FT Company, www.flytech.com.tw/)

Since its foundation in 1984, FT Company has been dedicated to designing and manufacturing Book PCs, Net PCs and POS PCs. In the year 2000, FT Company relocated its headquarters in Hsi-Chih, Taipei County, Taiwan, expanding its capacity to provide the highest quality and service. Regarding global marketing, FT Company has established branch offices in Hong Kong, Germany, Japan, USA and China. Long-term cooperative distributors and agents around the world also provide its customers with the fastest and most direct support through channels that are close by and easy to access . About 30 per cent of the company's products are distributed overseas. Regarding the company's computerization, the company has its own website and set up the management information system (MIS) to manage the business, and it uses email to communicate with customers.

4.4   Fashionow Co. Ltd. (coding as FA Company, www.music.com.tw)

FA Company was founded in 1996 with 40 years of rich experience in the music industry. In 2000, FA Company transformed into an online music service provider and began to offer online music and entertainment services. By means of innovative R&D, FA Company has spearheaded its first innovative product, 'KURO', which has become the most popular music search and download application in both Taiwan and China. FA Company is not only a successful digital entertainment service provider, but it also became a pre-stock company in 2004, with its rapid revenue growth and profits. FA Company reached 500 000 subscribers in Taiwan and 300 000 subscribers in Mainland China, with a total annual revenue of over USD$10 million. About 15 per cent of the company's products are distributed overseas. KURO is a powerful music downloading browser based on cutting-edge P2P technology. It has gained a prominent role in the Chinese music industry, dominating the downloading and sharing field, with over 40 000 music fans online sharing its rich resources.

4.5   Tung Tzu Industrial Co. (coding as TT Company, www.babyace. com.tw)

The company was established in 1981, and is now becoming a professional toy manufacturer and exporter in Taiwan. The company's main products are baby walkers, strollers, high chairs, bath tubs, bath chairs, potties and safety gates, and so on. In addition, TT Company has also developed many baby products to match marketing demand and has won a good reputation worldwide. The company handles a number of OEM and ODM orders for overseas customers including famous brands such as Disney, Hello Kitty, etc. The company sets up its overseas production factory in Shanghai, China during 1992. TT Company develops its own branded name BabyAce to sell toys to Japan, South Asia, Europe and Latin America; these are primary markets representing over 95 per cent of sales. Regarding the company's computerization, the company has its own website and set up the enterprise resource planning (ERP) system to manage the business, and communicates with its customers via email.

4.6   Texma International Co. (coding as TM Company, www.texma. com.tw)

TM Company is an international manufacturer of women's textiles. It manufactures women's blouses, trousers, skirts, dresses, children's wear, and sleepwear. TM Company's main clients include well known companies such as Gap, JC Penny, Sears, Express Limited, Zara and Polo Ralph Lauren; these are spread across the United States, Canada, Europe and Japan. Its strategy is to concentrate on a smaller number of clients, which enables TM Company to provide more thorough services with its flexble capacity and resources to meet customers' needs. The company set up six overseas production factories in the Philippines, Indonesia, Vietnam, Cambodia and Mainland China. TM Company operates a triangle of trade, manufacturing in an overseas factory, selling to Europe and operating in Taiwan. Europe is currently responsible for approximately 20 per cent of sales, with the rest all coming from the US. Regarding the company's computerization, it has its own website, uses package software to improve its production process, and communicates with customers via email.

4.7   Ji Chyuan Enterprise Co. (coding as J Company, http://jichyuan. myweb.hinet.net)

J Company was founded in 1978. The company focuses on producing traditional auto parts, and is located in Tao Yuan County, Taiwan. The main products of J Company are: power steering hoses, assay tanks, stamping parts, tube-water bypass, oil strainers, partition bars, pedal assay brakes, accelerators and clutches. Currently, J Company has 168 employees and they created a turnover of NT 408 million in 2004. The company has invested in three manufacturing factories in Fujian, Sichuan, Kwangsi province, China. J Company has a technological cooperation with Preferred Technical Group (UK) and some other Japanese companies. The policy of J Company has been clear and consistent since it was founded, focusing on quality management in order to satisfy its customers. The company' s main customers are Ford Lio Ho, Yulon Nissan and Chinese Motor Company. About 42 per cent of the company's products are distributed overseas. As to the company's computerization, the company has its own website and set up the ERP system to manage the business, and uses email to communicate with customers.

4.8   Raytec Electronic Co. (coding as R Company, www.raytec.com. tw)

R Company began operation in 1991 with the goal of providing innovative solutions for cable assemblies as one of the international new ventures (INV). The R Company operates from its headquarters in Taiwan with five manufacturing facilities in Dongguan and Shanghai, China. Their main products are audio/video cables, computer cables, USB cables, Cat5e/6 cables, IEEE1394 cables, telephone cables and connectors/adapters for audio and video. When entering Mainland China, it decided to set up a joint venture with a local Taiwanese firm in order to reduce risk. The headquarters are in charge of taking orders, financial management and product testing, while the subsidiaries in mainland China are in charge of producing and distributing the products to both domestic and overseas market. As of now, 90 per cent of the company's products are distributed overseas, which includes Asia, Australia, North America and Europe. Its main customers include famous companies like ATI, Fujitsu, Sharp, SONY, Compaq and Xirlink. Regarding the company's computerization, the company has its own website and set up the ERP system to manage the business, and communicates with customers via email.

5. FINDINGS AND ANALYSES

Table 23.1 shows the relationship between internationalization and Internet usage for the case companies. Table 23.2 lists all the characteristics of the case companies' findings.

Table 23.1 Case companies' internationalization and Internet usage

Company name	Internationalization activities	Overseas sales percentage	Stages of Internet commerce development
YEC-BonEagle Inc.	Direct export, overseas production units	75	Portals
Kingcore electronics Inc.	Direct export, overseas production units, technical agreement	42	Transaction integration
Flytech Co.	Direct export, overseas sales operations	30	Transaction integration
Fashionow Co., Ltd.	Direct export, overseas sales operations, strategic alliance	15	Enterprise integration
Tung Tzu Industrial Co.	Direct export, overseas production units	95	Portals
Texma International Co.	Direct export, overseas sales operations	90	Enterprise integration
Ji Chyuan Enterprise Co.	Direct export, overseas production units	42	Portals
Raytec Electronic Co., Ltd.	Direct export, overseas production units, joint venture	90	Enterprise integration

5.1 The Internet and Internationalization

5.1.1 Internationalization paths

The Uppsala Internationalization School (Johanson and Vahlne, 1977) is a good stage-based explanation of how manufacturing SMEs move internationally. SMEs enter different foreign markets step by step, in terms of their knowledge of the level of entry modes, as shown in the example of Y Company, K Company, FT Company, and so on. Stage-based theories may be more applicable to traditional companies seeking to expand overseas than entrepreneurial INVs. The Internet has reduced the level of investment and resources required to operate, thus opening new avenues for companies to exploit. The Internet provides a direct channel to service customers and circumvents costly distributor arrangements. Direct interaction also leads to greater potential learning, since there are

Table 23.2 Summary of case companies' findings

Case firm name \ Item	Internet enhancing the internationalization of SMEs					Influences SMEs' choice of entry mode		Impact of the Internet in internationalization theories
	Internet applications in SME internationalization	Internationalization Process stage	Transaction cost	Network relationship	Choice of entry modes	Influences SMEs' choice of entry mode	Internationalization process model
Y Company	Communications, Market Intelligence, Marketing and sales promotion	Overseas production	Reduced	Domestic network	Contractual entry modes	unrelated	Uppsala model
K Company	Communications, Market Intelligence, Marketing and sales promotion	Overseas production	Reduced	Domestic network	Contractual entry modes	unrelated	Uppsala model
FT Company	Communications, Market Intelligence, Marketing and sales promotion	Overseas sales operations	Reduced	Foreign network	Export entry modes	unrelated	Uppsala model
FA Company	Communications, Market Intelligence, Marketing and sales promotion	Overseas sales operations	Reduced	Foreign network	Contractual entry modes	positive	
TT Company	Communications, Market Intelligence, Marketing and sales promotion	Overseas sales operations	Reduced	Global production network	Contractual entry modes	unrelated	Uppsala model
TM Company	Communications, Market Intelligence, Marketing and sales promotion	Overseas sales operations	Added	Foreign network	Contractual entry modes	unrelated	Uppsala model
J Company	Communications, Market Intelligence, Marketing and sales promotion	Overseas production	Reduced	Foreign network	Contractual entry modes	positive	Uppsala model
R Company	Communications, Market Intelligence, Marketing and sales promotion	Overseas production	Reduced	Global production network	Investment entry modes	positive	INV

no intermediaries to impede information flows. However, Bennett (1997) argued that the thing which cannot be justified by SMEs' practical business activities is the use of the Internet for global marketing might enable companies to leapfrog the conventional stages of internationalization. Even for the 'born globals' such as R Company, which aimed to develop its international business from the company's inception, its internationalization process still supported the Uppsala gradual development process. International expansion of its business progressed first from the neighboring countries to where it had subsidiaries, to some farther foreign markets. The Internet is not only used for enhancing communication and information exchange, but is also used to increase the speed of contact with potential foreign customers. Nonetheless, very few of the sample SME companies conduct their entire business process through the Internet.

Maloff (1995) similarly asserted that the Internet enabled SMEs to grow without expanding physically or incurring relocation expenses, and allowed them to advertise and promote themselves globally at minimal cost. Customers, according to Maloff, cared little about the physical size or remoteness of a supplier, as long as high quality products at fair prices were delivered. It becomes likely that the availability of the Internet removes a number of organizational and resource constraints associated with exporting. These standpoints sound fair, but very few of them have happened in our sample companies. Cultural and language barriers, customers' concerns about trying new products, and so on, have not disappeared after the proliferation of the Internet. Apart from the often cited benefit that money and time are saved when gathering information on the potential foreign market, the use of the Internet does not have much influence on SMEs' internationalization process. The only exception is the case company, FA Company, which surfs on the cyber world using the new digital music and entertainment business model.

5.1.2 Internet applications in Taiwan SMEs' internationalization

In our cases, the Internet provides such activities as marketing intelligence, global sales promotion and communications (Hamill, 1997). All our case firms involved in exporting suggest that firms' integration of Internet technology with their marketing activities has a positive impact on export performance when marketing orientation is leveraged. And they also agree that effective usage of even basic websites could lead to significantly higher international revenues.

5.1.3 Network relationship

The Internet facilitates exchange relationships among parties distributed in time and space. It also helps in the selection of local and foreign partners because it provides SMEs with relevant and timely information. This is particularly important when SMEs plan to internationalize through business networks rather than dealing directly with foreign customers, as in the case of J Company.

In these cases, the Internet helps to accelerate the process by saving the SME from high costs and by keeping its close person-to-person contacts with its partner. It is evident that SMEs can easily and quickly access information about their potential partners by visiting their websites and establishing contacts via costless email. They can also have access through the Internet to information regarding potential partners' past experiences in inter-firm relationships and the type of network links for further consideration.

As J Company stated, the Global Production Network (GPN) typically provides local suppliers with encoded knowledge, such as machinery that embodies new knowledge, blueprints, production and quality control manuals, product and service specifications, and training handouts. The Internet technology assists the suppliers in building capabilities that are necessary to produce products and services with the expected quality and price.

The Internet is equally important for finding downstream dealers when internationalization success is mainly dependent on selecting the right foreign market and local partner, and the quality of information that guides this process is critical. Most SMEs compete with niche products and the markets for these products necessitate multiple market entries. The Internet has moved SMEs into the world market, which can help them build the critical mass necessary for success.

5.1.4 Transaction cost

Transaction costs include the costs of searching for sellers and buyers; collecting information on products; negotiating, writing, monitoring and enforcing contracts; and the costs of transportation associated with buying and selling. For most of our cases, the Internet can reduce these costs. It reduces search costs because information on buyers, sellers and products can be obtained more easily through the web. For digital products like software, music and video, transportation costs are also greatly reduced since they can be shipped over the Internet.

One of the most important stages in creating inter-firm networks is to search for information on potential partners. This stage of internationalization is costly for SMEs since their limited resources do not allow them a large budget to search for foreign partners. With the Internet these costs have been reduced tremendously, as shown in the R Company and J Company.

For TA company, there are a wide range of Internet costs that internationalizing SMEs have to invest, ranging from website creation (including hardware and software), maintenance and updating, website translation and cultural adjustments, and specialized personnel. Continuous update and improvement of the application of the Internet is necessary to keep the interest of customers and to maintain a competitive edge, which incurs further cost. As a result, cost savings from the Internet are not assured for SMEs, as investment is also needed on a continuing basis.

5.1.5   International entry mode

SMEs that did not plan to internationalize may become active through the trigger of unsolicited orders from overseas resulting from the exposure provided by their website. Indeed, based on the case company FA Company, the Internet has radically changed the SME's traditional risk perception regarding foreign markets which provides more information to assess this risk and more opportunities to internationalize. SMEs can internationalize directly from their website by exporting the goods needed by their individual customers without intermediaries, and by negotiating contractual agreements for licensing, R&D contracts, or other alliances with foreign companies. The Internet speeds the pace of SMEs' foreign market entry. For many SMEs the barriers imposed by entry modes requiring investments, such as joint ventures and foreign direct investment, can be bypassed with the Internet, as experienced by the J Company. Consequently, the Internet makes it possible more often for SMEs to choose flexible non-equity entry modes and low resource requirements.

Among all entry modes, entering a foreign market by exporting entails the least risk and is the most flexible way as it requires a minimal commitment of resources or adjustment to a company's domestic operations. Because of SMEs' financial and managerial constraints, the exporting mode is the most common way for them to choose when considering international business (Jarillo, 1989; Oviatt and McDougall, 1994b). This viewpoint is supported in this study because direct export is adopted as the main entry mode by all of the sample companies.

After successfully exporting, some of the case companies like R Company set up their own foreign subsidiaries and leapfrog the intermediate entry mode stage. This shows that after the critical first step, there is no ideal mode path for SMEs to follow, and various entry modes may be adopted entering the same market and/or by the same company in different markets. Although the Internet reduces the barriers cased by physical distance, time and money when contacting potential customers, SMEs will not enter an unfamiliar faraway foreign country only because someone from that country has shown their interest by sending an online message.

Apparently, this is too risky, and careful study of the prospects is still necessary. Therefore, the adoption of the Internet has no direct effect on SMEs'selection of entry modes.

5.1.6 The degree of internationalization and Internet usage

Based on the 700 SMEs Survey 2005, other key findings presented above can be summarized as follows: the degree of internationalization (DOI) is positively correlated with the degree of electronic commerce (DOEC), as shown in Figure 23.2, where Pearson's correlation coefficient is 0.544. Cronbach's α is 0.724 which shows a good level of reliability. When we divided samples into two groups, manufacturing and services industry, we further found that DOI is positively and significantly correlated with DOEC in the manufacturing industry (R-square = 0.61), as shown in Figure 23.3, and where DOI is negatively correlated, insignificantly with DOEC in the services industry, as shown in Figure 23.4. It can be reasoned that the SMEs of the services industry are more domestic oriented, providing goods or services to local markets and customers.

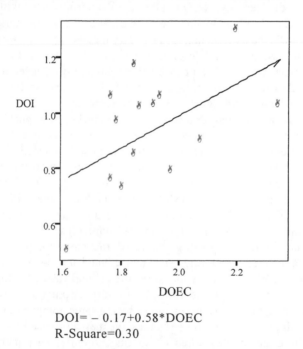

DOI= – 0.17+0.58*DOEC
R-Square=0.30

Notes: DOEC: Degrees of Electronic Commerce; DOI: Degree of Internationalization

Figure 23.2   Regression of the DOI and DOEC (all sectors, n=311)

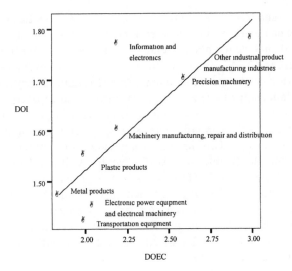

Figure 23.3 Regression of the DOI and DOEC (Manufacturing sectors, n=144)

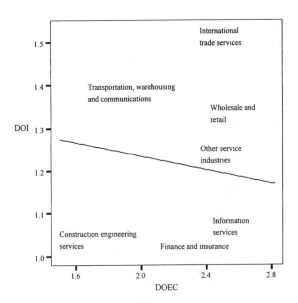

DOI=1.39-0.080*DOEC
R-Square=0.04

Figure 23.4 Regression of the DOI and DOEC (Non-manufacturing sectors, n=167)

When we subdivide the sample firms in the manufacturing industry more by the characteristics of whether or not they are knowledge intensive, we can find that Pearson's correlation coefficient for the knowledge-intensive group (0.247) is bigger than for the non-knowledge-intensive group (0.13). It can be conjectured that firms possessing stronger extensive network relationships have a stronger incentive, and capability, to apply the Internet more intensively; that is, they are using the Internet not merely to enhance their international activities but also to improve their network relationships. This implies that greater social capital might exist among the knowledge-intensive SMEs. Similarly, it can be conjectured that firms with a high level of Internet usage will enhance their involvement in international activities; this proposition can only be tested against large-scale quantitative research. An issue of concern is to establish whether the Internet encourages firms to be international from their inception, or whether global start-ups are able to internationalize more as a consequence of the Internet.

5.2 New Theories Required to Explain Internet Internationalization by SMEs

Classical theories regarding the internationalization of firms fail to explain the process followed by many SMEs when doing business through the Internet. The traditional theory of foreign direct investment does not seem appropriate to SMEs with limited financial resources and firm-specific advantages. Evolutionary theories that view internationalization as involving a gradual and incremental process have achieved wide acceptance in the literature and better represent the patterns for SMEs to expand internationally via the Internet (Johanson and Vahlne, 1977 and Cavusgil, 1980). However, this drawback is inevitable as these evolutionary theories were developed before the Internet changed the way of doing business. Employing Internet technology implies that SMEs today do not necessarily move through the internationalization process in a stage-by-stage manner. Learning about and entering foreign markets has been accelerated by the Internet as SMEs have become more flexible.

The other approach to firm internationalization is the network theory, which holds that through collaboration, non-competing firms can share knowledge and resources and, in the process, position themselves quickly on foreign markets. The network approach is particularly relevant for SMEs when they have specific advantages that are seen as complementary and non-competitive by their foreign partners. The limitation of this approach is the same as with the other internationalization theories: it was developed before the Internet diffusion boom and fails to explain how this technology interacts with the internationalization process.

Most of the cases studies seem to follow the Uppsala model for internalization. Besides the two exceptions listed in Table 23.2, more findings for the non-manufacturing sector in the 700 SMEs Survey 2005 have revealed the limitations of the theories.

6. IMPLICATIONS

Based on the previous analyses, findings and two avenues of suggestions, the agenda for SMEs and research are outlined below, namely, managerial implications for future study.

6.1 Managerial Implications for SMEs

This study might help manufacturing and services SMEs to reexamine the way in which they make good use of the Internet and websites. Entrepreneurs should give higher priority to involving the Internet in their business and follow best practice of how other SMEs conduct their Internet business in the international marketplace. In addition, the use of the Internet by companies involved in international trade raises a wide range of legal questions for which there are few answers at present. For example, how can the owner of an Internet home page take steps to ensure that he/she will not have to defend a lawsuit in a foreign court (Mykytyn, 2002)? Should the company have to comply with taxes (income tax, consumption tax, value added tax, and so on) in the countries of its customers? The vast majority of jurisdictions have not yet decided whether clicking on 'I agree' constitutes an enforceable agreement, although legal opinion seems to be moving in that direction (Weeks and Smith-Frisone, 1999). SMEs have to muddle through when conducting international transactions through the Internet in foreign markets in which legal systems are similar or underdeveloped (Newman, 2003).

6.2 Research Agenda

With the advent of the Internet, reduced barriers and time-to-market have cast questions on existing theories, the Uppsala model or Evolutionary theory in particular. In the cyber world, companies and SMEs are selling internationally over the Internet from their inception or at their current stage, often with no direct experience or resources. Further study and theorizing is called for; so are policies regulating international business activities.

Since this study is explorative in terms of scope and depth, future research should focus on comparing the internationalization paths for SMEs in the old and new economy. Also, the proposition that Internet application and international growth are strongly related is worth testing in future research. By the same token, analyses of returns on investment in setting up and maintaining Internet business are becoming urgent. SMEs are keen on financial performance in order to generate international revenue and to save operation costs. By matching costs against benefits, studies on the decision-making of investing and upgrading the Internet can be of good value both academically and practically.

REFERENCES

Aalst, Wil Van Der (1999), 'Loosely coupled interorganizational workflows: modeling and analyzing workflows crossing organizational boundaries', *Information and Management*, **37**, 67-75.

Arrow, K.J. (1969), 'The organization of economic activity: Issues pertinent to the choice of market versus non-market allocation. The Analysis and Evaluation of Public Expenditures: The PBB-System', Joint Economic Committee, 91st Congress, 1st session, and vol. 1, Washington DC: Government Printing Office.

Bambury, P. (1998), 'A taxonomy of Internet commerce', *First Monday*, **3**(10).

Bennett, Roger (1997), 'Export marketing and the Internet', *International Marketing Review*, **14** (5), 324-44.

Cavusgil, T. (1980), 'On the internationalization process of the firm', *European Research*, **8**(6), 273-81.

Chetty, S.K. and R.T. Hamilton (1993), 'Firm-level determinants of export performance: a meta-analysis', *International Marketing Review*, **10**(3), 26-34.

Chetty, S. and D.B. Holm (2000), 'Internationalization of small to medium-sized manufacturing firms: a network approach', *International Business Review*, **9**, 77-93.

Cheung W. (1998), 'The use of the world wide web for commercial purposes', *Industrial Management and Data Systems*, **98**(4), 172-7.

Chrysostome, E., P. Beamish, L. Hébert and P. Rosson (2005), *Management International*,. **10**(1), 1-18.

Coase, P.H. (1937), 'The Nature of the Firm', *Economica*, **4**(16), 386-405.

Coviello, N. and H. Munro (1997), 'Network relationships and the internationalization process of small software firms', *International Business Review*, **6**(4), 361-86.

Coviello, N. and A. McAuley (1999), 'Internationalization and the smaller firm: a review of contemporary empirical research', *Management International Review*, **39**(3), 223-56.

Craig, S. and V. Thandarayan (2000), 'The marketing of regional tourism via Internet: lessons from Australian and South African sites', *Marketing Intelligence Planning*, **18**(1), 45-9.

Dana, L.P., H. Etemad and R. Wright (2000), 'The global reach of symbiotic networks', *Journal of Euromarketing*, **9**(2), 1-16.

Dana, L.P., H. Etemad and R. Wright (2001), 'Symbiotic interdependence', in D.

Welsh and I. Alon (eds), *International Franchising in Emerging Markets*, CCH Publishing, 119-129.

Dana, L.P., R.W. Wright and E. Hamid (2004), 'Back to the future: international entrepreneurship in the new economy', in M.V. Jones and P. Dimitratos (eds), *Emerging Paradigms in International Entrepreneurship*, Cheltenham, UK and Northamption, MA, USA: Edward Elgar, 19-36.

Dunning, J.H. (1977), 'Trade, localization of economic activity and the MNE: the search for an eclectic approach', in Nobel Symposium (35th: 1976: Stockholm, Sweden) *The International Allocation of Economic Activity*, London: Macmillan Publishing.

Etemad, H. (2004), 'Marshaling relations: the enduring essence of international entrepreneurship', Chapter 13 in L.P. Dana (ed.), *The Handbook of Research on International Entrepreneurship*, Cheltenham, UK and Northanpton, MA, USA: Edward Elgar Publishing, 213-46.

Etemad, H. and H. Chu (2004), 'The dynamic impact of regional clusters on international growth and competition: some grounded propositions', in H. Etemad (ed.), *International Entrepreneur ship in Small and Medium Sized Enterprises: Orientation, Environment and Strategy*, Cheltenham, UK and Northampton, MA, USA: Edward Elgar Publishing, 39-58.

Etemad, H. and R. Wright (1999), 'Internationalization of SMEs: management responses to a changing environment', *Journal of International Marketing*, **20**(1), 13-28.

Etemad, H., R. Wright and L.P. Dana (2001), 'Symbiotic international business networks: collaboration between small and large firms', *Thunderbird International Business Review*, **43**(4), 481-500.

Eriksson, K., J. Johanson, A. Majkgard and D. Sharma (1997), 'Experiential knowledge and cost in the internationalization process', *Journal of International Business Studies*, **28**(2), 337-60.

Fillis, I. (2002), 'Barriers to internationalization: an investigation of the craft microentreprise', *European Journal of Marketing*, **36**(7/8), 25-44.

Ford, D. (1997), *Understanding Business Markets: Interaction, Relationships and Networks*, 2nd ed., London: Dryden Press.

Gareiss, D. (2000), 'Business on the world wide web', *Information Week*, **816**, 69-74.

Golinelli, R. and M. Monterastelli (1990), 'Un metodo per la ricostruzione di serie storiche compatibili con la nuova contabilita nazionale (1951-1989)', Prometeia, Bologna, Nota di lavoro n. 9001.

Hamill, J. (1997), 'The Internet & International Marketing', Scottish Exporters Virtual Community, available at: www.sevc.com/sevcab.html, Accessed 22 November, 2000.

Hamill, J. and K. Gregory (1997), 'Internet marketing in the internationalization of UK SMEs', *Journal of Marketing Management*, **13**(1-3), 9-21.

Hymer, S.H. (1976), 'The international operations of national firms: a study of direct foreign investment', Unpublished 1960 PhD thesis, Cambridge, MA: MIT Press.

Jarillo, J. (1989), 'Entrepreneurship and growth: The strategic use of external resources'. *Journal of Business Venturing*, **4**(2), 133-47.

John, G. and B.A. Weitz (1988), 'Forward integration into distribution: an empirical test of transaction cost analysis', *Journal of Law, Economics, and Organization*, **4**(2), 337-55.

Johanson, J. and L.G. Mattsson (1988), 'Internationalization in industrial systems: A network approach', in N. Hood and J.E.Vahlne (eds), *Strategies in Global Competition*, London: Croom Helm, 287-314.

Johanson, J. and J.E. Vahlne (1977), 'The internationalization process of the firm: A model of knowledge development and increasing foreign market commitment', *Journal of International Business Studies*, **8**(Spring/Summer), 23-32.

Johanson, J. and J.E.Vahlne (1990), 'The mechanism of internationalization', *International Marketing Review*, **7**(4), 11-24.

Johanson, J. and J.E.Vahlne (2003), 'Business relationship learning and commitment in the internationalization process', *Journal of International Entrepreneurship*, **1**(1), 83-102.

Johanson, J. and F. Wiedersheim-Paul (1975), 'The internationalization of the firm', *Journal of Management Studies*, **12**(3), 233-51.

Johansson, J.K. (2000), *Global Marketing; Foreign Entry, Local Marketing, & Global Management*, Second Edition, Irwin: McGraw-Hill.

Kindleberger, C.P. (1969), *American Business Abroad: Six Lectures on Direct Investment*, New Haven, CT: Yale University Press.

Knight, G.A. (2001), 'Entrepreneurship and strategy in the international SME', *Journal of International Management*, **7**(3), 155-71.

Knight, G. and T. Cavusgil (1996), 'The born global firm: a challenge to traditional internationalization theory', *Advances in International Marketing*, **8**, 11-26.

Knight, G.A. and P.W. Liesch (2002), 'Information internalization in internationalizing the firm', *Journal of Business Research*, **55**(12), 981-95.

Littman, M. (2000), 'Busy as a B2B', *Crain's Chicago Business*, **23**(11), 17, UMI Proquest Direct ABI/Inform.

Lituchy and Rail (2000), 'Bed and breakfast, small inns and Internet: the impact of technology on the globalization of the small businesses', *Journal of International Marketing*, **8**(2), 86-98.

Maddy, M. (2000), 'Dream deferred', *Harvard Business Review*, May/Jun2000, **78**(3), 56.

Maloff, J. (1995), 'The virtual corporation', *Internet World*, **5**, July, 46-50.

Martin, R. (1999), 'The new "geographical" turn in economics: Some critical reflections', *Cambridge Journal of Economics*, **23**, 65-91.

McDougall, P., S. Shane and B. Oviatt (1994), 'Explaining the formation of international new ventures: the limits of theories from international business research', *Journal of Business Venturing*, **9**, 469-87.

Morgan-Thomas, A. and S. Bridgewater (2004), 'Winners and losers in the Internet game: a study of British exporters', in F. Donald, M. Mayer and T. Buck (eds), *The Process of Internationalization: Strategic, Cultural, and Policy Perspectives*, Houndmills: Palgrave.

Mykytyn, P. (2002), 'Some Internet and e-commerce legal perspectives impacting the end user', *Journal of End User Computing*, **14**(10), 50-53.

Newman, M. (2003), 'E-commerce: the rules, so many countries, so many laws: the Internet may not have borders, but the legal system certainly does', *Wall Street Journal*, **28** April, R.8.

OECD (1998), *SMEs and Electronic Commerce*, Paris: OECD.

Oviatt, B. and P. McDougall (1994a), 'Explaining the formation of international new ventures', *Journal of Business Venturing*, **9**(6), 469-87.

Oviatt, B.M. and P.P. McDougall (1994b), 'Toward a theory of new international ventures', *Journal of International Business Studies*, **25**(1), 45-64.

Oviatt, B. and P. McDougall (1996), 'New venture internationalization, strategic change, and performance: a follow-up study', *Journal of Business Venturing*, **11**(1), 23-39.

Parasuraman, A. and G.M. Zinkhan (2002), 'Marketing to and serving customers through the Internet: an overview and research agenda', *Journal of the Academy of Marketing Science*, **30**(4), 286-95.

Penrose, E. (1959), *The Theory of the Growth of the Firm*, London: Basil Blackwell.

Petersen, B., L. Welch and L. Liesch (2002). 'The Internet and foreign market expansion by firms', *Management International Review*, **42**(2), 207-21.

Poon, S. and C. Jevons (1997), 'Internet-enabled international marketing: a small business network perspective', *Journal of Marketing Management*, **13**, 29-41.

Prashantham, S. and M. Berry (2004), 'The Internet and the internationalization of small knowledge-intensive firms: a conceptual approach', in M.V. Jones and P. Dimitratos (eds), *Emerging Paradigms in International Entrepreneurship*, Cheltenham, UK and Northampton, MA, USA: Edward Elgar, 192-216.

Quelch, J. and L. Klein (1996), 'The Internet and international marketing', *Sloan Management Review*, **37**(3), 60-83.

Rao S. and G. Metts (2003), 'Electronic commerce development in small and medium sized enterprises', *Business Process Management Journal*, **9**(1).

Reuber, R. and E. Fischer (1997), 'The influence of the management team's international experience on the internationalization behavior of SMEs', *Journal of International Business Studies*, **28**(4), 807-26.

Rialp, A. and J. Rialp (2001), 'Conceptual frameworks on SMEs' internationalization: past, present and future trends of research', *Advances in International Marketing*, **11**, 49.

Root, F.R. (1994), 'Implementing international countertrade: a dyadic approach', *Industrial Marketing Management*, **23**, 229-34.

Root, F. (1987), *Entry Strategies for International Markets*, Lexington, MA: Lexington Books.

Rosson, P. (2004), 'The Internet and exporting: Canadian success stories', in H. Etemad (ed.), *International Entrepreneurship: The Globalization of SMEs' Orientation, Environment and Strategy*, Cheltenham, UK and Northampton, MA, USA: Edward Elgar Publishing.

Samiee, S. (1998), 'Exporting and the Internet: a conceptual perspective', *International Marketing Review*, **15**(5), 413-26.

Sawhney, M. and S. Mandal (2002), 'Making the web world wide: a roadmap for globalization of ecommerce', Working paper, February 2002, Kellogg Graduate School of Management.

Soliman, K, and B. Janz (2003), 'An exploratory study to identify the critical factors affecting the decision to establish Internet based interorganizational information systems', *Information and Management*, October, 1-10.

Svensson, G. (2003), 'Consumer driven and bidirectional value chain diffusion models', *European Business Review*, **15**(6), 390-400.

Tapscott, D. (ed.) (1999), *Creating Value in the Network Economy*, Boston: Harvard Business School Press.

Tiessen, J.H., R.W. Wright and I. Turner (2001), 'A model of E-commerce use by internationalizing SMEs', *Journal of International Management*, **7**(3), 211-33.

Timmers, P. (2000), *Strategies and Models for Business-to-Business Trading Electronic Commerce,* Chichester: John Wiley & Sons.

Vernon, R. (1966), 'International investment and international trade in the product life cycle', *Quarterly Journal of Economics*, May, 190-207.

Weeks, A. and D.S. Frisone (1999), 'E-commerce: what legal issues does it present?', *Commercial Law Bulletin*, **14**(4), 13-15.

Welch, L. and R. Luostarinen (1988), 'Internationalization: evolution of a concept', *Journal of General Management*, **14**(2), 34-55.

Williamson, N.C. (1996), 'Gathering export market information using the Internet', *Multinational Business Review*, Fall, 1999, 73-80.

Wright, R.W. and H. Etemad (2001), 'SMEs and the global economy', *Journal of International Management*, **7**(3), 151-4.

Yin, R.K. (1994), *Case Study Research-Design and Methods*, Newbury Park, CA: Sage.

23. Knowledge transfer and entry strategies of Taiwan transnationals

Yung-Kuei Liang

1. INTRODUCTION

A transnational corporation builds its overseas subsidiaries according to the choice of entry mode and then transfers its resources and capabilities to them so as to continue its competitiveness. It is generally accepted that knowledge ranks first in the hierarchy of strategically relevant resources (Grant, 1996b). In the course of international expansion, entry mode choice, as a conduit of knowledge, plays a critical role in successfully transferring knowledge across borders. However, some knowledge characteristics, such as tacitness and complexity, make the transference uneasy and its outcome unpredictable. That is, if different knowledge characteristics matched a suitable knowledge transfer mechanism by way of the entry mode, the effectiveness of knowledge transfer would be encouraging and outstanding.

There is ample literature about knowledge transfer and its effectiveness, but an integrated approach is lacking and findings are mixed. Some studies research knowledge transfer from a transaction cost theory and resource-based view, whereas other studies explore knowledge transfer from each of the entry modes, such as direct investment, alliance and acquisition (Kogut and Zander, 1993; Inkpen, 1996; Bresman et al. 1999). But only a few research works explore and compare the influence of various entry modes upon knowledge transfer. This study explores the relationship among the transnational corporations' knowledge transfer, the entry mode, and effectiveness of knowledge transfer through the integration of transaction cost theory and the resource-based view of the firm. The main research questions include: first, how knowledge characteristics influence the choice of entry mode; second, how entry mode affects the transfer mechanism; and third, if the absorptive capacity of the knowledge recipient affects the transfer mechanism and the effectiveness of knowledge transfer.

2. LITERATURE REVIEW

2.1 Theoretical Perspectives

According to transaction cost theory, knowledge characteristics will have different characters and degrees of difficulty during the exchange of knowledge, and produce various transaction costs. When the cost of the market transaction is too high, the firm will lower the transaction cost and uncertainty by internalizing the transaction or through cooperation between organizations (Williamson, 1991). The tacitness of an asset in the transaction is an important factor when opting for an appropriate transaction mechanism. The higher the tacitness is, the more difficult it is for the buyer to recognize its value; therefore, the seller and the buyer need to pay more in negotiation, contract, and monitoring costs. As a result, the transaction cost will increase because of the tacitness of assets (Teece, 1977). In addition, the complexity and specificity of knowledge will influence the transaction and the choice of mechanism, and frequent transactions will oblige the firm to engage in horizontal or vertical integration (Hennart, 1988).

From the resource-based view of the firm, knowledge characteristics determine the resources, learning capacity and conditions that the firm must have. According to the degree of transfer, Winter (1987) classified knowledge characteristics into four spectra. First, tacitness (tacit articulated): tacit knowledge can not be expressed clearly, but articulated knowledge can be described clearly with any symbol. The degree of tacitness is determined as to whether knowledge can be taught and articulated. Second, observability (not observable in use/observable in use): this would influence the degree of imitation. The cooperation of the owner possessing knowledge and the observing cost would also influence the effectiveness. Third, complexity (complex/simple): complexity describes the amount of information which one kind of knowledge needs. The amount is about the variance of knowledge. Fourth, independency (module element in a system): one kind of knowledge that can be used alone is the module. Grant (1991) noted that the resources should have appropriability and durability. Besides, they should have four characteristics in order to bring competitive advantage for the firm: durability, transparency, transferability and replicability.

When Kogut and Zander (1993) explored knowledge of the firm, they used three continuous scales of the underlying dimensions of codifiability, complexity and teachability to measure knowledge. Furthermore, Grant (1996b) identified characteristics of knowledge as the following:

transferability, capacity for aggregation, and appropriability. Contractor and Ra (2002) noted that there are four principal knowledge attributes or characteristics of knowledge, including codification, newness, complexity and teachability. Tacitness and complexity of knowledge are the most important factors from a transaction cost and resource-based view. The former focuses on the characteristics of transaction asset, but the latter adopts a broader view to explore it. The resource-based view considers that not only the resources of transaction but also the relationship between the transaction and other resources in the firm will influence knowledge transfer.

2.2 Entry Strategy

A transfer can be successful if a suitable choice is made regarding the mechanisms and organizational arrangements of technology transfer (Grosse, 1996). For transnational corporations, the transfer mode is an organizational arrangement to achieve the goals of knowledge transfer, such as foreign direct investment, joint venture, turnkey operation, and licensing. The entry mode chosen is not only the way for transnational corporations to enter a foreign country but is also a mode for transferring knowledge to overseas subsidiaries. Many classifications of entry mode are discussed by scholars from the international business management perspective. Anderson and Gatignon (1986) divided the entry modes into three kinds according to the degree of control mode: high-control mode (dominant equity interests), medium-control mode (balanced interests) and low-control mode (diffused interests). Wu (2001) grouped the entry modes into four types: trade and counter-trade, contractual agreement, strategic alliance and foreign direct investment.

Some scholars discussed entry modes from the knowledge transfer perspective, as knowledge management is important. Grant (1996a) noted that the ability to integrate knowledge is the most important organizational capability in the dynamic competitive environment. He identified three fundamental ways of integrating external knowledge: internalization, market contracts, and relational contracts. Grosse (1996) identified the means that were often used for international technology transfer in services, including licensing and technical assistance contracts, training and turnkey contracts, representation and management contracts, franchising and R&D contracts, co-production agreements and subcontracting, exporting and foreign direct investment. Among these entry modes, only foreign direct investment belongs to equity-based relations; the others are contract-based relations. Mathews (1996) addressed five cooperative types: subcontracts, licensing, alliance, equity investment and joint ventures.

Contractor and Ra (2002) classified the entry modes into three types which included single contracts, alliances and wholly-owned subsidiaries, and according to four attributes – duration, breadth of contacts, intensity of interaction and contract completeness. These gave three archetypes of alliance: discrete repeated contracting and licensing, strategic supply chain partnership and equity joint venture.

2.3 Knowledge Transfer Mechanism

Dixon (2001) noted that knowledge transfer refers to applying knowledge that exists in one part of the organization in another part. The members of groups in the organization share knowledge using various kinds of tools and procedures, such as knowledge databases, best practice conferences, technology, cross-functional teams, email and social community software. For a start, the entry mode can be seen as a knowledge transfer mode as mentioned above. However, the entry mode is just one kind of transfer mode, and there are other studies discussing transfer modes. Dixon (2001) further divided knowledge transfer modes into five types: serial, near, expert, far and strategic.

The knowledge transfer mode shows the relationship and the degree to which two parties engage in knowledge transfer. However, the transfer mechanism is the practical instrument in the process of transference of knowledge. The transfer process entails technology sharing, joint venture (JV)-parent interactions, personnel movement, and linkage between parent and alliance strategies (Inkpen, 1996). From empirical study about international technology transfer in service industries, Grosse identified the following knowledge transfer mechanisms: hardware, software, personnel transfer, personnel training, documentation, communication and agreements. Orderd from the most important to the least are personnel training, manuals, visits from experts, and personnel rotation. The main type of knowledge in the service industry is tacit. Hence, the main mechanisms adopted are interpersonal, in addition to operations manuals.

Almedia and Grant (1998) have identified thirteen major mechanisms through which knowledge flows across borders. These mechanisms can be grouped into three main categories, i.e., personal communication, codified communication and embodied K-transfer. The first group, personal communication, includes the mechanisms such as personnel transfer, electronic mail, groupware, telephone, video conferencing, face-to-face meeting, training seminars and courses, and specialist knowledge transfer groups. The second group, codified communication, includes the mechanisms such as electronic data exchange, fax, written reports and manuals. The final group, embodied transfer, includes mechanisms such as product, equipment, rules, procedures and directives. Buckley and Carter (1999) noted that knowledge that could be transferred might be classified in three broad forms: personal communication (conversations, meetings, email, and so on), codified communication (reports, drawings, and so on), and embodied transfer (for example, as product or equipment).

2.4 Absorptive Capacity

The ability to exploit external knowledge is a critical component of innovative capabilities. Cohen and Levinthal labeled this capability a firm's absorptive capacity and suggested that it is largely a function of the firm's level of prior related knowledge. Thus, prior related knowledge confers the ability of a firm to recognize the value of new, external information, assimilate it, and apply it to commercial ends, and it is critical to its innovative capabilities (Cohen and Levinthal, 1990). Prior related knowledge influenced personal absorptive capacity when Cohen and Levinthal (1990) explored how the individual acquires new knowledge. The greater the related knowledge base in one's memory, the better the effectiveness of absorbing new knowledge. To conclude, the stock of prior related knowledge has critical influence on personal absorptive capacity.

An organization's absorptive capacity will depend on the absorptive capacities of its individual members. To this extent, the development of an organization's absorptive capacity will build on prior investment in the development of its constituent, individual absorptive capacities, and, like individuals' absorptive capacities, organizational absorptive capacity will tend to develop cumulatively. A firm's absorptive capacity is not, however, simply the sum of the absorptive capacities of its employees.

2.5 Effectiveness of Knowledge Transfer

Only when transferred knowledge is retained is the knowledge transfer effective. The capacity of institutionalizing new knowledge represents the recipient's retentive capability (Szulanski, 1996). Existing literature has discussed the effectiveness of knowledge transfer for a long time, but from various perspectives. Some scholars focused on transaction cost. Teece (1976) treated technology knowledge performance from the point of view of transaction cost. He thought that it could be determined from the cost of technology transfer. Three aspects of transfer cost would influence technology transfer: transfer experiences, newness of knowledge, and the number of companies using similar technology.

Some scholars discussed it from the effectiveness perspective. Satikarn (1981) studied technology transfer performance from this perspective, and thought that there were four dimensions in transfer performance: (1) the technology was used effectively in the environment, (2) the transferred knowledge could be absorbed completely, (3) the technology could be diffused to the same business, (4) according to specific needs or purposes, the recipient has the capability which could modify the technology. Mansfield (1982) thought that the success of technology transfer should be determined from three dimensions, including success in applying the technology, achievement of economic effect, and possession of skill in developing the product.

When exploring knowledge transfer in strategic alliances, Simonin (1999) used three measurements to judge the results of knowledge transfer: (1) the knowledge recipient learned a lot about the technology that its partner possessed, (2) after sufficient transfer of knowledge, the recipient reduced dependence on its partner for techology, (3) the recipient absorbed the partner's technology. Huang (1990) explored the effectiveness of technology transfer and used three variables to measure it, including productivity promoted performance, technological ability promoted performance and product market expanded performance. Another empirical test of performance of knowledge transfer in strategic alliances used four items to measure performance, including knowledge learning, reducing dependence, knowledge application and technology innovation (Chang, 2001).

2.6 Relationship between Knowledge Characteristics and Entry Mode

Transaction cost theory focuses on cost, and emphasizes that the choice criterion of governance is minimum transaction cost. Williamson (1979) addressed the relationship among transaction asset, transaction frequency and governance. When specificity of transaction asset and transaction frequency is higher, it is appropriate to use hierarchy governance. If the opposite is true, it is appropriate to use market governance. Hennart (1988) noted that complexity and specificity of knowledge and frequency of transaction would make the firm need horizontal or vertical integration. On the other hand, the incompleteness of the knowledge market also makes firms adopt a joint entry mode to foreign markets instead of licensing. The tacitness of assets involving the transaction is also an important factor in the selection of transaction mechanism. The higher the tacitness is, the more difficult it is for the buyer to recognize its value; therefore, the seller and the buyer need to pay more in negotiation, contract, and monitoring costs. This implies that the tacitness of knowledge will influence the entry mode choice.

On the other hand, the resource-based view focuses on promoting organizational capability in order to reinforce organizational competition.

The resource-based view also stresses the construction and utilization of resources, and the reservation of unique resources. Kogut and Zander (1993) found that the less codifiable, the harder to teach and more complex is the technology, the more likely the transfer will be to wholly owned operations. Mowery et al. (1996) found that equity joint ventures appear to be more effective conduits for the transfer of complex capabilities than are contract-based alliances such as licensing agreements. Contractor and Ra (2002) noted that the less the degree of codification and teachability, but the greater the degree of newness and complexity, the more likely it is that joint venture will be selected among alliance modes.

From the transaction cost theory and resource-based view, it is suggested that knowledge characteristics will exert influence on the choice of entry mode. Among these characteristics, tacitness and complexity are the most important factors. The higher the tacitness of knowledge is, the more likely it is that the equity-based entry mode, such as a wholly-owned subsidiary or joint venture, will be favored. In addition, the higher the complexity of knowledge is, the more likely it is that the equity-based entry mode will be chosen. In brief, the tacitness and complexity of knowledge increase the transaction cost of knowledge transference. The tacitness and complexity of knowledge will also raise knowledge transfer difficulties. Thus,

Hypothesis 1a: *The higher the tacitness of knowledge is, the more likely the equity-based entry mode will be chosen.*
Hypothesis 1b: *The higher the complexity of knowledge is, the more likely the equity-based entry mode will be chosen.*

2.7 The Relationship between Entry Mode and Knowledge Transfer Mechanism

Although the entry mode is an important issue for transnational corporations, and the transfer mechanism plays a critical role in knowledge transfer, few studies explore the relationship between the entry mode and the knowledge transfer mechanism. When a parent company uses contract as the entry mode, the interaction of the parent company and the overseas subsidiary will be less (Wang, 1998). Hence, the transfer mechanism will employ more documents and fewer personal contacts to transfer knowledge. When the entry mode is direct investment, the interaction of the parent company and overseas site will be greater. The transfer mechanism uses not only more documents, information and personal contacts but also many meetings, formal and informal information channels. To conclude, when the degree of involvement of the entry mode is higher, knowledge transfer is more likely to be the interpersonal transfer mechanism. On the other hand, when the degree of involvement of the entry mode is lower, such as through a contract, the knowledge transfer mechanism is less likely to be the interpersonal transfer mechanism. Thus,

Hypothesis 2a: When the transnational corporation adopts the contact-based entry mode, it will tend to use the codified transfer mechanism.

Hypothesis 2b: When the transnational corporation adopts the equity-based entry mode, it will tend to use the interpersonal transfer mechanism.

2.8 Knowledge Transfer Mechanism and Its Effectiveness

The knowledge transfer mechanism plays an important role in the process of knowledge transfer, because it is the instrument used to transfer knowledge. Different transfer mechanisms result in differences in effectiveness of knowledge transfer. Ounjian and Carne (1987) noted that the transfer mechanism included consultants, documents, training, demonstrations, cooperation, and so on. However, the most important factor influencing effectiveness of transfer was face-to-face communication. Another study had similar conclusions about the relationship between the knowledge transfer mechanism and effectiveness of knowledge transfer. Cutler (1989) compared knowledge transfer between universities, industries and senior research units of government in America with those in Japan by carrying out interviews. He found that the majority of researchers thought the people-intensive mechanism more effective than that of the paper-intensive mechanism. Thus,

Hypothesis 3: The transfer effectiveness of the interpersonal transfer mechanism is better than that of the codified transfer mechanism.

2.9 Absorptive Capacity, Knowledge Transfer Mechanisms, and their Effectiveness

Zander and Kogut (1995) noted that prior accumulated knowledge is the critical factor for understanding new knowledge. However, prior accumulated knowledge will influence individual absorptive capacity. An organization's absorptive capacity is based on individual absorptive capacity; therefore, an organization's absorptive capacity is a function of that organization's prior accumulated knowledge. Therefore, absorptive capacity will influence effectiveness of knowledge transfer. Teece (1976) asserted that codification of tacit knowledge has a direct relation to the degree of transferring knowledge. Even tacit knowledge can be switched to explicit knowledge by signs, but effectiveness of transfer depends on whether the recipient is familiar with the signs. Teece (1976) also noted that prior accumulated knowledge is important for knowledge transfer.

The empirical results of Mowery et al. (1996) provided some support for the importance of absorptive capacity in the acquisition of capabilities through alliances. 'A firm's ability to absorb capabilities from its alliance partner depends on the prevailing relationship between the two firms' patent portfolios.' When establishing his learning organization model, Goh (1998) especially emphasized that members' capability, knowledge absorption and organizational structure would promote effectiveness of knowledge transfer. The literature mentioned above shows that organizations' and individuals' absorptive capacity is important for effectiveness of knowledge transfer of organizations. Among these, prior related knowledge is also a critical factor. In other words, absorptive capacity will influence the transfer mechanism and effectiveness of knowledge transfer. Thus,

Hypothesis 4: *Absorptive capacity will affect the relationship between knowledge transfer mechanism and effectiveness of knowledge transfer.*

3. METHOD

3.1 Operational Definition and Measurement

Five constructs in the research are knowledge characteristics, the entry mode, the knowledge transfer mechanism, absorptive capacity and effectiveness of knowledge transfer. The operational definition of each variable is given according to the previous literature review. First, knowledge characteristics include tacitness and complexity that will influence the choice of entry mode. Second, the research explores two types of entry mode: contact-based and equity-based. On the other hand, the subject population is the manufacturing industry. Not every kind of entry mode occurs in the manufacturing industry, for example, franchising. So the researcher only chooses seven kinds of entry mode when designing the questionnaire. Third, the transfer mechanisms contain codified and interpersonal transfer mechanisms. Fourth, absorptive capacity incorporates organizational and individual absorptive capacity. Fifth, effectiveness of knowledge transfer includes four items: knowledge acquisition and dependence reduction, knowledge application and technology innovation. Apart from measurement of the entry mode, a 7-point Likert scale was adopted to measure each variable in the study and weights of 1, 2, 3, 4, 5, 6 and 7 were assigned to the answers 'completely disagree', 'slightly disagree', 'disagree', 'no opinion', 'agree', 'slightly agree', 'completely agree'.

3.2 Data Collection and Respondent Statistics

The subject of this study was the Taiwanese manufacturing industry, including food and cigarettes, textiles, shoemaking, paper-making, chemicals, and electrical machinery and electronic devices. The ranking directory for the top 5000 businesses provided by China Credit Information Service, Ltd was used as the sampling frame. This study sent out 500 copies of the questionnaire on 20 March, 2004. After two weeks, the telephone, fax, and email were used to encourage companies to response. By 16 May there were 83 responses, including 9 from companies without subsidiaries, and 74 from companies with overseas subsidiaries, representing a 14.8 per cent response rate. In addition to these surveys, a case study of one leading company, with more than 30 subsidiaries in 20 countries, was used to explore knowledge transfer in transnational corporations in more detail.

The best way to estimate the internal homogeneity of a set of items and concurrently to consider all items in the measurement scale is Cronbach's alpha, which is the most widely used when the summated measures have multiple-scored items. Generally speaking, the agreed upon lower limit for Cronbach's alpha is 0.70, but it may decrease to 0.60 or 0.50 in exploratory or basic research. In this research, all of the questionnaire items were above 0.70, ranking from 0.7345 to 0.8860, thus indicating acceptable reliability.

Of the 74 valid samples, the majority were from the electrical machinery and electronic device industry, accounting for 74.3 per cent of responses. About 43 per cent of the companies had been established over 21 years, 24 per cent for less than 10 years, and 32 per cent for periods in-between. On average, there were 1318 employees employed in the overseas subsidiaries, and their average foreign profit was NT\$3.3 billion during the previous three years. As for overseas operating experience, about 32 per cent of the companies had been involved in a foreign market for over 11 years. However, close to 39 per cent of the companies had been engaged in foreign investment for less than 5 years. Further, over 70 percent of the companies chose Asia when establishing their first overseas subsidiary.

The majority of overseas subsidiaries were also located in Asia.

When companies started to set up an overseas affiliate, they had a preference for a wholly owned subsidiary, the rate being 41.9 per cent. After having more experience, they still favored a wholly-owned subsidiary, the rate being slightly increased to 48.7 per cent. The number of companies adopting a contact-based and equity-based entry mode was 27 and 47, respectively. In the valid samples, 78.9 per cent of the most frequently interacting subsidiary with headquarters was in China, 8.10 per cent in Oceania, 6.76 per cent in Asia (except China), 5.41 per cent in America, and only 1.35 per cent in Europe. Additionally, 77.0 per cent of respondents' main value-added activity 'manufacturing' was carried out in the focal subsidiary.

ANOVA was employed to explore if there was a significant difference in research constructs among industries. The results revealed that tacitness and complexity of knowledge for industries were different. Furthermore, companies from different industries exhibited significant differences in the organization's absorptive capacity, knowledge learning and knowledge application. As to entry mode, all manufacturing industries favored an equity-based entry mode, except for the textile industry. Finally, the correlation coefficient of knowledge transfer mechanism and absorptive capacity was 0.292, at a 5 per cent significance level. As for that of knowledge transfer mechanism and effectiveness of knowledge transfer, the figure was about the same at 0.291. With respect to effectiveness of knowledge transfer and absorptive capacity, the coefficient was 0.662, significant at a 1 per cent level.

4. FINDINGS

4.1 Confirmatory Factor and Relationship Analysis

Confirmatory factory analysis was applied to the knowledge transfer mechanism, absorptive capacity, and effectiveness of knowledge transfer. According to the rotated factor loadings, two variables, interpersonal and codified transfer mechanisms, were extracted, accounting for 69.1 per cent of variance of knowledge transfer mechanism. As for absorptive capacity, this study retained 9 items and deleted 1 item, where rotated factor loading was below 0.5, and extracted two variables, an organization's and individual's absorptive capacity, which explained 73.9 per cent of variance. Finally, four variables – knowledge acquired, dependence reduction, knowledge application and technology innovation – were extracted which accounted for 83.4 per cent of variance.

Since knowledge characteristics and entry mode in this study were nominal-dichotomous variables, the contingency coefficient analysis was employed to determine if correlation between variables existed. The contingency coefficient between knowledge characteristics (tacitness and complexity) and entry mode (medium-level of control and equity-based) was positive, at 0.389, with a p-value below 0.05. This result suggested that H1 was supported.

4.2   Entry Mode and Transfer Mechanism

Because the p-value of Box's M (4.582) was greater than the critical level (0.05), the equality of the covariance matrices was supported, thus one-way MANOVA was employed to investigate the relationship between entry mode and transfer mechanism. In Table 24.1 the F value of the codified transfer mechanism was 3.100, with a p-value of 0.083. It indicated that the different entry modes adopted had slight differences in codified transfer mechanism selection, thus supporting H2a. Nevertheless, there was no significant difference in the interpersonal transfer mechanisms, thus rejecting H2b.

Table 24.1   ANOVA of entry mode and knowledge transfer mechanism

		Sum of Squares	df	Mean Square	F	Sig.
Between groups	mkm1	3.013	1	3.013	3.100	0.083
	mkm2	2.271	1	2.271	2.311	0.133
Within groups	mkm1	69.987	72	0.972		
	mkm2	70.729	72	0.982		
Total	mkm1	73.000	74			
	mkm2	73.000	74			

Notes: mkm1= codified transfer mechanism; mkm2= interpersonal transfer mechanism.

4.3   Knowledge Transfer Mechanism and its Effectiveness

From the outcome of the canonical correlation analysis shows that the first canonical function with correlation R (=0.520) and canonical R^2 (=0.270) is significant at 0.000 (see Table 24.2).

Table 24.2 Canonical correlation analysis of transfer mechanism and its effectivness

Canonical function	Canonical correlation	Canonical R²	Wilks' lambda	F statistic	Sig.
1	0.520	0.270	0.65507	4.00417	0.000
2	0.320	0.102	0.89753	2.62579	0.057

Dependent variables	Canonical loading		Independent variables	Canonical loading	
	1	2		1	2
Knowledge acquisition	0.656*	0.259	Interpersonal transfer mechanism	0.423*	−0.906
Dependence reduction	−0.388*	−0.475	Codified transfer mechanism	0.906*	0.423
Technology innovation	0.548*	−0.122			
Knowledge application	0.345*	−0.832			

The analysis demonstrates that the canonical loading of the codified transfer mechanism (0.906) is greater than that of the interpersonal mechanism (0.423). It implies that the codified transfer mechanism outperforms the interpersonal transfer mechanism in the effectiveness of knowledge transfer. It further suggests that the more the codified transfer mechanism is used, the more effective knowledge acquisition, technology innovation, and knowledge application will be, but the less effective the dependence reduction will be.

4.4 Absorptive Capacity, Knowledge Transfer Mechanism and Effectiveness

In Table 24.3, the result shows that the first two canonical functions are significant at 0.000 and are used as an interpretation lens for the relationship among absorptive capacity, transfer mechanism and effectiveness. In the first canonical function, the canonical loading of the interaction of the interpersonal transfer mechanism and individual absorptive capacity (0.789) is the highest, followed by the interaction of theh codified transfer mechanism and individual absorptive capacity (−0.690). This indicates that the more influence the interaction of the interpersonal transfer mechanism and individual absorptive capacity has, the less effective knowledge acquisition will be. Also, the less influence the interaction of the codified transfer mechanism and individual absorptive capacity has, the less effective knowledge acquisition will be. It indicates that an individual's absorptive capacity will affect the relationship between the knowledge transfer mechanism and the effectiveness of knowledge transfer. With absorptive capacity, an individual could transfer knowledge through the appropriate mechanism which in turn facilitates the other party to acquire and accumulate knowledge.

Table 24.3 Canonical correlation analysis of absorptive capacity, transfer mechanism and effectiveness of knowledge transfer

Canonical function	Canonical correlation	Canonical R²	Wilks' lambda	F statistic	Sig.
1	0.764	0.584	0.20831	4.44987	0.000
2	0.593	0.351	0.50105	2.79072	0.000
3	0.460	0.212	0.77230	1.79278	0.068
4	0.143	0.021	0.97947	0.34586	0.846

Dependent variables	Canonical loading				Independent variables	Canonical loading			
	1	2	3	4		1	2	3	4
Knowledge acquisition	−0.942*	−0.276	−0.192	0.018	mkm 1	0.028	−0.588*	0.091	0.660
Dependence reduction	−0.152	0.118	0.645	0.740	mkm 2	−0.287	−0.419*	−0.783	−0.178
Technology innovation	0.239	−0.331*	−0.635	0.656	mkm*abs	0.269	−0.433*	−0.240	−0.425
Knowledge application	0.181	−0.895*	0.380	−0.151	mkm 1* abs1	−0.228	−0.370*	0.046	−0.689
					mkm1* abs2	0.789*	0.049	−0.091	−0.222
					mkm2* abs1	0.274	−0.489*	−0.407	0.333
					mkm2* abs2	−0.690*	0.088	0.030	−0.052

Notes: mkm=knowledge transfer mechanism; mkm1=interpersonal transfer mechanism; mkm2=codified transfer mechanism; abs=absorptive capacity; abs1=a subsidiary's absorptive capacity; abs2=an individual's absorptive capacity.

In the second canonical function, the orders of the canonical loadings from the highest to the lowest are interpersonal transfer mechanism (−0.588), interaction of codified transfer mechanism and organization's absorptive capacity (−0.489), interaction of transfer mechanism and absorptive capacity (−0.433), codified transfer mechanism (−0.419), and interaction of interpersonal transfer mechanism and organization's absorptive capacity (−0.370). This suggests that the less that interpersonal and codified transfer mechanisms are used, the less effective knowledge application and technology innovation will be. In addition, the less influence the interaction of the knowledge transfer mechanism and absorptive capacity has, the less effective knowledge application and technology innovation will be. Also, the less influence the interaction of the codified transfer mechanism and organization's absorptive capacity has, the less effective knowledge application and technology innovation will be. Further, the less influence the interaction of the interpersonal transfer mechanism and organization's absorptive capacity has, the less effective knowledge application and technology innovation will be. Hence, an organization's absorptive capacity will affect the relationship between the knowledge transfer mechanism and the effectiveness of knowledge transfer.

In summary, absorptive capacity will affect the relationship between the knowledge transfer mechanism and the effectiveness of knowledge transfer. The effectiveness of knowledge acquisition from headquarters through interpersonal transfer mechanisms will be negatively influenced by an individual's absorptive capacity. Nevertheless, the same effectiveness through a codified transfer mechanism is positively reinforced by an individual's absorptive capacity. Furthermore, the effectiveness of knowledge application and technology innovation through both mechanisms is positively influenced by a subsidiary's absorptive capacity.

5. CONCLUSIONS AND SUGGESTIONS

5.1 Conclusions

This research showed that the majority (77 per cent) of transnational corporations from Taiwan, no matter how old they are, have chosen Asia as the location for their first overseas enterprise. The percentage is close to 77.03 per cent. After that, an increasing percentage (close to 88 per cent) established more subsidiaries in Asia, especially in China. The main value-added activities carried out in China are in manufacturing and marketing. Close to 50 per cent of the sample companies have adopted a wholly-owned subsidiary as an entry mode to further expand operations across borders.

In addition, knowledge attributes and entry mode are positively correlated. The higher the tacitness and complexity of knowledge is, the more likely the equity-based entry mode will be chosen. This reveals that transnationals tend to choose a higher-level control of entry modes to ensure effective transfer of knowledge when protecting them from imitation or piracy by potential competitors. Further, the research showed no significant differences either in the codified transfer mechanism or in the interpersonal transfer mechanism when different entry modes were adopted. It seems that the choice of entry mode and transfer mechanism is made individually without considering better possible alternatives when transferring valuable knowledge across nations. If this is the case, companies quite possibly do not generate the maximum potential rent from leveraging knowledge across countries in their transnational network. As for the effectiveness of transfer mechanisms, interpersonal transfer mechanisms were no better than codified transfer mechanisms.

Finally, absorptive capacity will affect the relationship between the knowledge transfer mechanism and the effectiveness of knowledge transfer. The effectiveness of knowledge acquisition from headquarters through interpersonal transfer mechanisms will be negatively influenced by an individual's absorptive capacity. Nevertheless, the same effectiveness through a codified transfer mechanism is positively reinforced by an individual's absorptive capacity. Furthermore, the effectiveness of knowledge application and technology innovation through both mechanisms is positively influenced by a subsidiary's absorptive capacity.

5.2 Managerial Implications

In the knowledge economy, while making an entry mode choice, apart from considering factors such as cost and market, a transnational corporation has to look at knowledge characteristics, both tacitness and complexity, in order to realize its economic and strategic return from transferring knowledge across nations. Since different manufacturing industries own different types and characteristics of knowledge, the same kind of entry mode will not be expected to provide equivalent results in the effectiveness of knowledge transfer. Further, transnational corporations have to consider specific knowledge transfer mechanisms and make a proper choice between codified and interpersonal instruments.

In the choice of entry mode, most Taiwanese manufacturing companies named cost as one of the most important factors while considering foreign expansion. This might explain why there are no significant differences in the selection of transfer mechanism when companies decide which entry mode to apply. If transnationals consider knowledge to be an important source of their competitiveness, they will think in-depth about the relevance of entry mode and transfer mechanism choices. The complexity of knowledge characteristics was seen to influence the decision of entry mode for transnational corporations. Although they are making decisions about entry mode mostly based on cost, they will be expected to pay more attention to the complexity of knowledge in the future in order to maximize their gain from leveraging organizational knowledge.

In addition, the influence of an individual's absorptive capacity upon the knowledge transfer mechanism is revealed in the fundamental aspect of an organization, such as knowledge acquisition. It was also found that the higher the absorptive capacity is, the more effective knowledge transfer will be. Indeed, successful knowledge transfer between countries needs the capabilities both of an individual and an entire organization. However, the effect of an organization's absorptive capacity on the knowledge transfer mechanism is shown in more respects, such as knowledge application and technology innovation, which involve broader aspects of an organization and can improve its competitive competence.

In summary, transnational corporations should discard their old-fashioned mindset – being afraid of losing their dominance over subsidiaries – and acquaint themselves with the absorptive capacity of subsidiaries in order to enhance the effectiveness of knowledge transfer. Generally speaking, if a transnational corporation realizes the importance of knowledge and defines the keys to effective knowledge transfer, they will attain and sustain their competitive advantage in the face of fierce competition.

5.3   Limitation and Suggestions

This study has explored the choice of entry mode and its effect from the knowledge transfer perspective without considering other important factors, such as global strategic factors and ownership and location advantages. Therefore, this research cannot give the complete picture regarding entry mode decisions. Further, it is very unlikely that all related variables have been taken into account while selecting entry modes. Future research can further explore the relationship between knowledge characteristics and entry mode by incorporating other important factors such as global strategic motives, ownership and location advantages.

On the other hand, the valid size of samples across different industries are not equal. The majority of the responses were from the electrical machinery and electronic device industries. To enlarge the sample size to include a similar number of companies from various industries would increase the findings' generalizability in a future study. Also, to expand the samples to include companies from other nations and services would also increase the validity and reliability of future studies. Finally, this study only investigated the relationship between knowledge characteristics and entry mode choices for Taiwanese transnationals. It would be useful to investigate if type of transferred knowledge is significant, and then further to explore the reasons behind the findings.

REFERENCES

Almedia, P. and R.M. Grant (1998), 'International corporations and cross-border knowledge transfer in the semiconductor industry', Available at http://cbi. gsia.cmu.edu/ newweb/1998WorkingPapers/grant/almedia.html.

Anderson, E. and H. Gatignon (1986), 'Mode of foreign entry: A transaction cost analysis and propositions', *Journal of International Business Studies*, **17**(fall), 1-26.

Bresman, H., J. Birkinshaw and R. Nobel (1999), 'Knowledge transfer in international acquisitions', *Journal of International Business Studies*, **30**(3), 439-62.

Buckley, P.J. and M.J. Carter (1999), 'Managing cross-border complementary knowledge', *International Studies of Management and Organization*, **29**(1), 80-104.

Chang, C.-Y. (2001), 'A study of the influence of knowledge attributes and strategic alliance types on the performance of knowledge transfer', Unpublished master's thesis, Graduate Institute of Business Administration, National Chengkung University, 2001.

Cohen, W.M. and D.A. Levinthal (1990), 'Absorptive capacity: A new perspective on learning and innovation', *Administrative Science Quarterly*, **35**(1), 128-52.

Contractor, F.J. and W. Ra (2002), 'How knowledge attributes influence alliance governance choices: A theory development note', *Journal of International Management*, **8**, 11-27.

Cutler, W.G. (1989), 'A survey of high-technology transfer practice in Japan and the United State', *Interfaces*, **19**(6), 67-77.

Dixon, N.M. (2001), *Common Knowledge: How Companies Thrive by Sharing what they Know*, Boston: Harvard Business School Press.

Goh, S.C. (1998), 'Toward a learning organization: The strategic building blocks', *Sam Advanced Management Journal*, **63**, 15-22.

Grant, R.M. (1991), 'The resource-based theory of competitive advantage: Implications for strategy formulation', *California Management Review*, **33** (spring), 114-35.

Grant, R.M. (1996a), 'Prospering in dynamically-competitive environments: Organizational capability as knowledge integration', *Organization Science*, **7**, 375-387.

Grant, R.M. (1996b). 'Toward a knowledge-based theory of the firm', *Strategic Management Journal*, **17**(winter), 109-22.

Grosse, R. (1996), 'International technology transfer in services', *Journal of International Business Studies*, **4**, 781-800.

Hennart, J.F. (1988), 'A transaction costs theory of equity joint ventures', *Strategic Management Journal*, **9**, 361-74.

Huang, J.-C. (1990), 'A study of the factors of introducing technology performance', Unpublished master's thesis, Graduate Institute of Business Administration, Chungyuan Christian University.

Inkpen, A.C. (1996), 'Creating knowledge through collaboration', *California Management Review*, **39**(1), 123-40.

Kogut, B. and U. Zander (1993), 'Knowledge of the firm and the evolutionary theory of the multinational corporation', *Journal of International Business Studies*, **4**, 625-45.

Mansfield, E. (1982), *Technology Transfer, Productivity and Economic Policy*, New York: W.W. Norton.

Mathews, J.A. (1996), *Organizational Foundations of the Knowledge-based economy: In the Knowledge Economy*, New York: Butterworth-Heinemann.

Mowery, D.C., J.E. Oxley and B.S. Silverman (1996), 'Strategic alliances and interfirm knowledge transfer', *Strategic Management Journal*, 17(winter), 77-91.

Ounjian, M.L. and E.B. Carne (1987), 'A study of the factors which affect technology transfer in a multilocation multibusiness unit corporation', *IEEE Transaction on Engineering Management*, 34(3), 194-201.

Satikarn, M. (1981), *Technology Transfer: A Case Study*, Singapore: Singapore University Press.

Simonin, B.L. (1999), 'Ambiguity and the process of knowledge transfer in strategic alliances', *Strategic Management Journal*, 20, 595-623.

Szulanski, G. (1996), 'Exploring internal stickiness: Impediments to the transfer of best practice within the firm', *Strategic Management Journal*, 17(winter), 27-43.

Teece, D.J. (1976), *The Multinational Corporation and the Resource Cost of International Technology Transfer*, Cambridge, MA: Ballinger Press.

Teece, D.J. (1977), 'Technology transfer by multinational firms: The resource cost of transferring technological know-how', *Economic Journal*, 87, 242-61.

Teece, D.J. (1998), 'Capturing value from knowledge assets: The new economy, markets for know-how, and intangible assets', *California Management Review*, 40(3), 55-77.

Wang, S.-T. (1998), 'International technology transfer of Taiwan service firms: The comparison of transaction cost theory and knowledge-based view', Unpublished master's thesis, Graduate Institute of International Business, National Taiwan University.

Williamson, O.E. (1979), 'Transaction cost economics: The governance of contractual relations', *Journal of Law and Economics*, 22, 233-61.

Williamson, O.E. (1991), 'Strategizing economizing and economic organization', *Strategic Management Journal*, 12(special issue), 75-94.

Winter, S.G. (1987), *The Competitive Challenge: Strategic for Industrial Innovation and Renewal*, MA: Ballinger Press.

Wu, C.-S. (2001), *International Business Management: Theory and Practice*, Taipei: Best-Wise.

Zander, U. and B. Kogut (1995), 'Knowledge and the speed of transfer and imitation of organizational capabilities: An empirical test', *Organization Science*, 6, 76-92.

Index

Aalst, Wil Van Der 413
Abramson, N. 115
absorptive capacity 439
Agarwal, S. 249
Aggarwal, R. 58, 59
Agmon, T. 58, 59
Aharoni, Y. 249
Ahokangas, P. 394
Albaladejo, M. 55
Alexander, J.C. 192
Ali Babas 186
Aliber, R.Z. 68
Allen, L. 368, 373, 374, 385
Allport, G.W. 209
Almanac of China's Foreign Economic Relations and Trade 73
Almedia, P. 438
Almeida, J.G. 147
Amran, M. 157
Anderson, E. 202, 437
Anderson, O. 150
Anderson, S. 397
Andersson, U. 252, 400
Andrews-Speed, P. 60
Aoyama University 270
arbitrage opportunities 163
Argyris, C. 127
Armstrong, H. 324
Arrow, K.J. 411
Autio, E. 147
Avolio, B.J. 207
Axelsson, B. 391

Bachman, R. 203
Bain, J.S. 113
Balfour, F. 65
Ball, D.A. 27, 51
Bambury, P. 414
Barkema, H.G. 115, 146, 150
Barnes, J.W. 211

Baron, R.M. 259
Barrell, R. 57
Bartlett, C.A. 157, 245, 246, 248, 249, 250, 251, 252, 253, 254, 257, 258, 261
Bass, B.M. 206
Beamish, P.W. 367, 368, 369, 370, 371, 372, 373, 379, 380, 383, 408
Behrman, J.N. 126, 324
Beinhocker, E. 119
Bell, J. 400
Benito, G.R. 391, 392, 398
Bennett, M.L. 186
Bennett, Roger 423
Berg, J. 204
Berger, P. 164
Berle, A. 224
Bernard, A. 165
Berry, M. 412
Besanko, D. 156
Best, M.H. 178
Big Mac index 315–16
Billet, B.L. 324
Birkenshaw, J. 183
Birkinshaw, J.M. 246, 247, 249, 250, 254
Bitner, M.J. 309
Black, J. 115
Blader, S.L. 247
Blankenburg-Holm, D. 396
Blau, P.M. 248
Blomstermo, A. 395
Blomstrom, M. 325, 326, 328, 329, 331
Boddewyn, J.J. 153
Bodhisattva 350–51, 353, 357–60
Bokus 139–40, 145–6
bol.com *see* Bokus
born globals 410, 413, 423
Bourdieu, P. 194
Boxman 136, 138, 140, 145, 147

see also Dressmart
Boylan, A. 122
Branstetter, L. 55
Braunstein, E. 49
Bräutigam, D. 69
Bresman, H. 435
Brewer, H. 165
Brier, S. 119
Britton, S.G. 324, 331
Brockner, J. 247
Brown, Gordon 22
Brown, P. 391
Brunei, official discrimination 180
Buckley, P.J. 55, 60, 66, 67, 69, 70, 71,
    77, 81, 109, 113, 118, 121, 125,
    135, 348, 439
Buddha eye 350
Bunker, B.B. 202, 203, 205
Burns, P. 330
Burns, T. 127
Burrell, G. 123, 126, 128
Butler, J.K. 204, 205
Buyonet 140–41, 145–6

C-S system (center-satellite factory
    system) 390
Cai, K.G. 71
Callon, M. 179
Canon Inc. 89
Cao, D.J. 227
capability upgrading proposition 19
CAPM beta 164–5
Carlson, S. 135, 137
Carne, E.B. 442
Carney, M. 179
Carter, M.J. 439
Casson, M. 69, 70, 113, 118, 121, 125,
    135
Cateora, C. 307
Caves, R.E. 27, 113, 324, 326, 328, 329
Cavusgil, T. 410
CDon 141–2
CEIBS (China European International
    Business School) 270
center-satellite factory system (C-S
    system) 390
Chakrabarti, A. 66, 68, 70, 71, 73, 80
Chan, P.S. 307
Chan, S. 61, 65, 68, 71, 72
Chandler, A.D. 224

Chandler, A.P. 194
Chang, C.-Y. 440
Chang, J.-H. 1
Changzhou 31–2
Chantasasawat, B.B. 50
Chaos ontology, and international
    business studies research 118–21
Chen, C.-H. 61
Chen, H. 261
Chen, K. 42
Chen, T.J. 261, 394
Chen, X. 55
Chetty, S. 410
Cheung, W. 411
Chia, R. 126
Child, J. 67, 118, 128, 197
Chiles, T.H. 203
Chin, G. 119
China
    cultural dimensions 210
    see also cultural norms, and
        trust-building
    environmental damage 48
    foreign investor preferential treatment
        27, 48
    graduates 8
    labor force 27–8
    MNE strategies 41–3
    recent growth 7–8
    trade surplus 8
    WTO membership 45, 47
China, FDI inward
    2004 levels 8
    geographic distribution 30–32
    impact 43–4
    overview 25–7, 50–51
    prospects 45–50
    reasons for 27–8
    sectoral distribution 28–30
    source company size 33–4
    source regions 32–3
China, FDI outward (ODI)
    determinants model
        data and method 72–6
        defined 72
        results 76–80
    motivations 56–60, 65
    overview 55–6, 80–81
    policy developments 60–61
    possible determinants

exchange rate 68, 77, 79
geography 68–9, 77, 79
inflation 70, 77
market growth 67–8, 77
market openness 71, 77–8, 80
market size 66–7, 77, 79
natural resource endowments 71,
    77, 79
policy direction 72, 78
political risk 70–71, 77
trade intensity with China 68, 77
China European International Business
    School (CEIBS) 270
China Statistical Yearbook 74
China's Yearbook of Commerce 73
Chinese University of Hong Kong 270
Chiou, Y.C. 368, 369, 372
Chrysostome, E. 408
Chrystal, K.A. 326
Chu, X.P. 225, 227
Chung, C. 389, 391
Clark, E. 193
Clark, T. 208, 210
Clegg, S.R. 125
Coase, P.H. 411
Coca-Cola 42
coevolution 119
Cohen, W.M. 439
Cohn, E.S. 247
Coleman, J.S. 178, 194
Colquitt, J.A. 246
Comment, R. 164
competition effect 328–9
complexity theory *see* Chaos ontology,
    and international business studies
    research
Conceicao, John 298
conditional trust 204–5
conditions of trust 205
Contractor, F.J. 367, 368, 369, 370, 372,
    373, 374, 379, 437, 438, 441
Cooper, R. 126
corporate identity 184
Corporate Technology Units (CTUs) 90
corruption, family-owned firms 194–5
Cosset, J. 392
Costantino, R. 119
Coviello, N.E. 393, 401, 409, 410
Cowen, M.P. 177
Craig, C.S. 163

Craig, S. 414
Crick, D. 394
Cropanzano, R. 247
Cross-Cultural Distance Learning
    (CCDL) 280–81
cross-cultural management theory
    339–42
    see also managerial philosophies;
        third-culture management
cross-subsidization 163
CTUs (Corporate Technology Units) 90
CUC (Cyber University Consortium)
    280
cultural impact, international franchising
    307–13
cultural norms
    literature review 208–9
    and trust-building
        research methodology 212–16
        research propositions 210–12
        research results 216–18
Cunneen, C. 304
Cunningham, J.B. 207
Cutler, W.G. 442
Cyber University Consortium (CUC)
    280
Cyert, R.M. 249
Czarniawska, B. 179

Daft, R.L. 251
Dailey, R.C. 246
Daisaku, Ikeda, world peace philosophy
    348–51
Dana, L.P. 407
Daneke, G.A. 118, 120, 121
Daniels, J.D. 110, 122, 348
Dasgupta, P. 202
DCC (Digital Campus Consortium) 280
de la Torre, J. 118
De Meyer, A. 93, 245, 248
De Meyer, Arnoud 298
de Meza, D. 157
Delios, A. 368, 369, 371, 383
Dell 42
Deng, P. 60, 66, 67, 73
Desatnick, R.L. 186
Deutsch, M. 202
development, contemporary thinking on
    16–17
Dharma eye 350

Diamond, J. 110
Dicken, P. 59, 177
Dieke, P.U.C. 324, 330, 331
Digital Campus Consortium (DCC) 280
DiMaggio, P.J. 147
Ding, X.L. 60, 61, 73
'diplomat'-type executives 186–8
Dirks, K.T. 205
Divine eye 349–50
Dixon, N.M. 438
DOEC (Degrees of Electronic
    Commerce) 416–17
Doh, J.P. 116
DOI (Degree of Internationalization)
    416–17
Domino's Pizza, in Japan 310
Donaldson, L. 123
Dore, R. 202
Douglas, S.P. 163
Doz, Y.L. 157, 249, 251
Dressmart 136, 138, 142, 145
Drogendijk, R. 148
Duan, Y. 58
Duncan, R.B. 127
Dunning, J.H. 17, 22, 37, 41, 57, 110,
    113, 135, 245, 246, 252, 257, 258,
    284, 323, 324, 326, 328, 329, 348,
    352, 368, 409
Dwyer, F.R. 202

Earley, P.C. 211
economies of scope 163
Eden, L. 116, 117
effects proposition 19
Eisenstadt, S.N. 179
Eiteman, D. 51
Elg, U. 400
Ellis, P. 391
employee benefits 342–3
employee morale 343
engineering graduates, China 8
entropy measure 166–7
entry modes 411–12
entry strategies 437–8
Epstein, G. 49
Erdogan, B. 247
Eriksson, K. 409
Ernst, D. 391, 394, 397
Erramilli, M.K. 69
Etemad, H. 407

EVA (Economic Value Added) concept,
    adoption 183–4
Evans, P. 252
expatriate executives, career types 185–9
export rerouting, through China 43–4
Exxon 92

FA Company *see* SMEs Internet and
    internationalization study, cases, FA
    Company
Fama, E.F. 164
family based conglomerates (FBC)
    179–81
family culture 228–31
family enterprises
    distinction from family-based
        management enterprises 238
    internationalization trust problems
        236–41
    management revolution problem
        223–8
    personnel structures 230–31
    power distribution 232–6
    trust structures 231–2
family trust 239
Fan, C.S. 40
Fan, H.P. 228
Farmer, R.N. 114, 115
Fashionow Co. Ltd *see* SMEs Internet
    and internationalization study,
    cases, FA Company
'fast-track'-type executives 188
Fatemi, A. 165
FBC (family based conglomerates)
    179–81
FDI
    and globalization 17–18
    investment size model 37–41
    outward (ODI)
        definition 56
        motivations 56–8
FDI policy
    critical elements 18–21
    objectives 21–2
femininity *see* masculinity/femininity
    dimension
Ferrantino, M.J. 69
Ferrin, D.L. 205
Fichman, M. 208
Field, A. 397, 398

Fillis, I. 413
Finkenstadt, B. 119
first-culture management 341
Fischer, E. 410
Flytech Co. *see* SMEs Internet and
    internationalization study, cases, FT
    Company
Folger, R. 247
Ford 92
Ford, D. 396, 410
foreign aid, globally below target 7
Forsgren, M. 137, 146, 149, 150, 178,
    249, 252, 395, 400
Fortin, C. 57
Framfab 143–4, 145, 148
franchising *see* international franchising
Frank, Robert 293
Freeman, J. 128
French, K.R. 164
Frisone, D.S. 429
Froot, K.A. 68
FT Company *see* SMEs Internet and
    internationalization study, cases, FT
    Company
Fukuyama, F. 201, 208, 223, 225, 226,
    241
Fung, K.C. 32, 50
Furu, P. 246, 261

Gabarro, J.J. 204
Gambetta, D. 202
Gankema, H.G. 392
Gareiss, D. 414
Garnier, G.H. 248
Gatignon, H. 437
GE 92
Gedajlovic, E. 179
Gemser, G. 391
General Motors 42
George, J.M. 204, 205
Geppert, M. 193
Gerlach, M. 390
Ghoshal, S. 157, 163, 187, 245, 246,
    248, 249, 250, 251, 252, 253, 254,
    257, 258, 261
Giddens, A. 187
Gilbert, R.G. 307
Gioia, A. 123
Gioia, D. 123
Gladwin, T.N. 334

GLE (Government Linked Enterprises),
    official discrimination 180–81
Global Technology Units (GTUs) 90
globalization
    attributes and extent 15–16
    and higher education 277–84
    and the poor 7
Gnemawat, P. 126
Go, F.M. 324, 326, 327, 331, 335
Go Global policy 61
Goh, S.C. 443
Gomes, L.K. 369, 372
Gomez, E.T. 180, 190
Goodall, K. 187, 189
Goodyear 163
Govindarajan, V. 188, 245, 246, 253
Graen, G.B. 207
Graham, E.M. 49
Graham, J.L. 307
Grant, R.M. 435, 436, 437, 438
Greene, W.H. 372, 378
Gregory, K. 413
Griffin, R.W. 368, 371
Grosse, R. 437
Grub, P.D. 50, 51
GTUs (Global Technology Units) 90
guanxi networks, and Chinese ODI 68
Gulati, R. 203, 401
Guo, H. 61
Gupta, A.K. 188, 245, 246, 253

H&M 43
Hadjikhani, A. 149
Haier 67
Hair, J.F. 255, 256
Hall, P. 178
Hamel, G. 157, 163, 252
Hamill, J. 412, 413, 423
Hamilton, G. 239
Hampden-Turner, Charles 309
Han, S.S. 40
Hannan, M.T. 128
Harrigan, K.R. 153, 249
Hart, J. 126
Harvard Business School, IB education,
    Japan 269
Harzing, A. 188
Hassard, J. 123, 246
Haunschield, P. 147
Hausman, J. 372, 378

Hays, R. 115
Hayter, R. 40
He, A.X. 224
Hébert, L. 408
Hedlund, G. 249
Heenan, D.A. 59
Held, D. 331
Hench, T. 114
Henley, J. 69
Hennart, J.F. 371, 436, 440
Henry, B.M. 324, 330
higher education
    and globalization 277–84
    see also Singapore, higher education
Hill, C.W. 208
Hitotsubashi University 270
Hitt, M. 164
Hoff, E. 245, 248
Hofstede, G. 114, 202, 208, 209, 210,
    211, 217, 307
Holden, A. 330
holistic proposition 19
Holm, D.B. 410
Holm, U. 261
Holmlund, M. 391
Hong Kong, investment in China 32
Hood, N. 183, 246, 254
Hornell, E. 122
House, R.J. 114, 212
Houston, R. 119
Hu, J. 238
Hu, M.W. 390
Huang, C.C. 395
Huang, H.C. 371
Huang, J.-C. 440
Huang, T.S. 372, 378
Huang, Y. 49
Huber, G.P. 145
Human eye 349–50
Humanism ontology, and international
    business studies research 114–16
Hundley, G. 245
Hwang, G.G. 226, 239
Hymer, S. 27
Hymer, S.H. 57, 135, 328, 409

IB (international business) education,
    Japan 269–74
IB studies research
    Buckley's episodes of 109–10

concerns with episodic approach
    110–11
dynamic of change 121–3
ontologies
    Chaos 118–21
    commensurability 123–4
    defined 111–12
    Humanism 114–16
    Scientific 112–14
    Scientific Humanism 116–18
    overview 124–6
IBM 92, 98
Icon Medialab 144, 145, 148
IIST (Institute for International Studies
    and Training) 270
Ikeda, D. 349, 351, 362
In Search of Excellence 197
Indigenous Technology Units (ITUs) 90
individualism/collectivism dimension
    209
    see also cultural norms, and
        trust-building
Inglehart, R. 202
initial trust 204–5
Inkpen, A.C. 435, 438
Institute for International Studies and
    Training (IIST) 270
institution-based trust 240–41
institutions proposition 19
integration proposition 20
International Conference on
    Multinational Enterprises, 8th 1–5
international franchising
    cultural impact 307–13
    economic impact 315–16
    environmental impact 320–21
    global issues 307
    human resource impact 319
    overview 303–5, 321
    political/legal impact 316, 318
    social impact 313–15
    technological impact 319–20
international product life cycle theory 27
international strategic management
    analysis framework 160–62
    definitions 153–5
    distinction from domestic 155–7
    importance 157–60
    overview 172–3
International University of Japan 270

internationalization
  and financial performance
  hypotheses 370–72
    literature 368–72
    model 374–5
    overview 367–8, 383–5
    research data 375–6
    research method 372
    research results 376–83
    variables 372–4
  process model, subsidiary roles 249
  resource-based view 371, 383
  three-stage theory 369–70, 378–82
  transaction cost theory 371–2, 411
internationalization process models
    409–11
  see also Uppsala Internationalization
    Process model
internationalization theories 409–12
Internet
  and born global 413
  commerce stage model 414–16
  and entry mode 414, 425–6
  and network relationships 412–13,
    423–4
  and SME internationalization
    applications 423
    degree 426–8
    literature 412–16
    overview 407–9
    paths 421–3
  and transaction cost 413–14, 424–5
Internet-related firms
  Uppsala Internationalization Process
    model (stages model)
    assessment against 138–44
    relevance for 135–6, 144–50, 429
INV (international new ventures) 411
Iomin, A. 119
IT, R&D networks impact 87–9, 97–8,
    102–3
ITUs (Indigenous Technology Units) 90
Ivancevich, J.M. 115

J Company *see* SMEs Internet and
    internationalization study, cases, J
    Company
Janz, B. 413
Japan
  IB education 269–74

managerial philosophies 347–8,
    358–60
Jarillo, J.C. 249, 250, 389, 425
Jarrell, G. 164
Jenkins, C.L. 324, 328, 330
Jensen, J. 165
Jesudason, J. 179, 180
Jevons, C. 407
Ji Chyuan Enterprise Co. *see* SMEs
    Internet and internationalization
    study, cases, J Company
Joerges, B. 179
Johanson, J. 69, 122, 137, 138, 145, 146,
    149, 249, 369, 391, 392, 396, 409,
    410, 421, 428
Johansson, J.K. 409
Johansson, U. 400
John, G. 211, 411
Johnsen, R.E. 396
Johnson, G. 137
Jomo, K.S. 180, 190
Jones, G.R. 204, 205
Jones, M.V. 392
Journal of International Business Studies
    114
Jung, J.I. 207
Justis, R.T. 307

K Company *see* SMEs Internet and
    internationalization study, cases, K
    Company
Kaiser, S. 395
Kale, S.H. 211
Karamustafa, K. 324, 329
Kashani, K. 245, 248
Keegan, W.J. 59
Keio University Business School 270
Kenny, D.A. 259
Kerr, J. 257
KFC 42
Khan, K.M. 58
Khan, M.A. 304, 305
Kim, J. 245
Kim, S.J. 36
Kim, W.C. 245, 246, 247, 248, 250, 251,
    253, 254, 257, 258, 261
Kimberly, M.E. 245
Kindleberger, C.P. 409
Kingcore Electronics Inc. *see* SMEs
    Internet and internationalization

study, cases, K Company
kingcraft culture 351, 356, 359–60
Kino, S. 354
Kinoshita, Y. 48
kinship trust, in family enterprises 231–2
Kirby, D.A. 395
Kirk, D.J. 246
Klein, L. 412
Knight, G. 410
Knight, G.A. 407
knowledge attributes 436–7
knowledge transfer
  absorptive capacity and transfer
    mechanism effectiveness 441–3,
    447–9
  ASEAN study
    context 179–81
    family-owned firms 193–5
    innovation 189–92
    management networks 185–9
    overview 195–7
    role orientations 192–3
    sample 181–3
    sectoral frames 183–5
  effectiveness 439–40
  entry mode and transfer mechanism
    441–2, 446
  knowledge characteristics and entry
    mode 440–41
  mechanism effectiveness 446–7
  mechanisms 438–9
  Taiwanese MNE study
    conclusions 449–50
    findings 445–9
    hypotheses 441–3
    implications 450–51
    literature review 436–43
    method 443–5
    overview 435
  as translation along networks 177–9
Kobayashi, N. 270
Kobe University 270
Kobrin, S.J. 70, 117
Kock, S. 391
Kodak 42
Kogut, B. 118, 156, 157, 163, 252, 258,
  435, 436, 441, 442
Konovsky, M.A. 246
Korea, investment in China 36–7
Kotabe, M. 368, 369, 371, 372, 373, 374

Koza, M. 120
Kramer, G. 318
Kramer, R.M. 204, 208
Kuemmerle, W. 102
Kuhn, T.S. 110, 118, 122, 123, 124
Kuhnert, K.W. 206
Kuin, P. 324
Kulatilaka, N. 157
Kundu, S. 122
Kunio, Y. 180
KURO 418–19
Kusluvan, S. 324, 329

labor force, China 27–8
Lall, S. 55, 58, 66, 78
Lambe, C.J. 395, 401
Lamont, M. 196
Lan, Li 305
Lan, P. 48
Lane, C. 203
Lane, H. 122
Lardy, N. 55
Lardy, N.R. 42, 55
Latour, B. 179
Lau, H.-F. 66, 69
Laudan, L. 123
Lawrence, P.R. 127
Lawrence, S.V. 59
Leader-Member Exchange (LMX)
  theory 207
leadership
  in global networks 101–2
  literature review 206–8
Lecraw, D.J. 58, 66, 69
Lee, K.H. 223
Lee, M. 310
Lee, W.H. 391
Lee, W.R. 371
Lenway, S. 116, 117
Leung, K. 248
leverage opportunities 163
leveraging proposition 19–20
Levinthal, D.A. 439
Levitt, B. 147
Lewicki, R.J. 202, 203, 205
Lewin, A.Y. 118, 120
Lewis, D.J. 202, 203
Lewis, P. 206
Li, J. 164
Li, Jianli 224, 240

Li, K. 56
Li, P.P. 69
Li, X.-C. 238
Liesch, P.W. 407
Lim, D. 67
Lin, J.H. 51
Lin, T.M. 340, 341, 344, 345, 348, 355, 359, 361
Lind, E.A. 247, 248
Lindblom, C.E. 137
Lindskold, S. 202
Lipsey, R.G. 326
Lisi, F. 120
Littman, M. 414
Lituchy, T.R. 412
Liu, H. 56
Liu, P.C. 390
Livingstone, J.M. 324
LMX (Leader-Member Exchange) 207
'local'-type executives 186–7, 188–9, 191
localization proposition 20
Lorsch, J. 127
Lorsch, J.W. 340
Loveridge, R. 179, 195
Lovett, S. 128
Lu, J.W. 367, 368, 369, 370, 372, 373, 379, 380, 383
Lubatkin, M. 115
Luo, Y. 66, 69
Luostarinen, R. 408
Lynn, R. 202

Ma, X. 60
Macao, investment in China 32
McAuley, A. 409
McDougall, P.P. 147, 389, 392, 410, 411, 425
McFarlin, D.B. 246
McGregor, D. 127, 340
MacGregor, J. 207
McIntyre, R.P. 211
McKinlay, A. 186
McKnight, D.H. 204, 205
McMackin, J.F. 203
McNaughton, R. 391
Macomber, J. 117
McQueen, M. 323, 324, 326, 328, 329
Maddy, M. 416
Madhok, A. 394

Malaysia
  hotel sector 332–3
  official discrimination 180
  tourism spillovers 334–6
Maloff, J. 423
managerial philosophies
  Ikeda Daisaku world peace philosophy 348–51
  Japanese enterprises 347–8, 358–60
  John H. Dunning 352
  Matsushita company 352–4
  peace culture 348, 354–62
  Toyota 354
  types 346–7
  US enterprises 347, 358–60
  see also cross-cultural management theory
Mandal, S. 413
Mansfield, E. 440
March, J.G. 147, 192, 249
market access spillovers 329–30
Marlboro 42
Marshall, S.R. 69
Martin, K. 393
Martin, R. 414
Martinez, J.I. 249, 250, 389
Martinez, Z. 119, 120
masculinity/femininity dimension 209
  see also cultural norms, and trust-building
Mathews, J.A. 437
Matsushita Electric Industrial Co. Ltd. 89
  managerial philosophies 352–4
Matsushita, K. 352, 353
Matsushita Kunosuke 352–4
Mattson, L.G. 391, 392, 396, 410
Mauborgne, R.A. 245, 246, 247, 248, 250, 251, 253, 254, 257, 258, 261
Mayer, C. 194
Mayer, R.C. 203, 204
Mayo, E. 127, 340
McDonald's
  brand recognition in China 42
  celebrating birthdays 313–14
  economic impacts 315–16
  environmental impact 320–21
  impact on entry-level employment 319
  Korean service expectations 310
  local menu accommodations 311–13

political/legal impact 316, 318
requirement to smile 307
targeting children 312, 314–15
teaching work ethics 313
technology transfer 320
McDonald's study, overview 305–6
McJoy 311
Means, G. 224
Medio, A. 120
Mendenhall, M. 117
Mendenhall, M.E. 111, 113, 120, 124
Menkhoff, T. 69
Mentzer, J.T. 394, 396, 400, 401
Meschi, P.X. 246
Metts, G. 414, 416
Michelin 163
Mikhail, A. 165
Miles, R.E. 202
Min, S. 401
Miner, A.S. 147
Ministry of Commerce (MOFCOM) 56
MNE
    advantages
        measurement strategy 164–8
        potential 162–4
        results 168–72
MOFCOM (Ministry of Commerce) 56
Moffett, M. 51
Molnar, V. 196
Monkiewicz, J. 66
Moorman, C. 202
Morck, R. 369, 383
Morgan, G. 123, 128, 177
Morris, M.W. 248
Morris, W. 153, 154
Morrison, A.J. 245, 250, 254
Morse, J.J. 340
Motorola 42
Mowery, D.C. 441, 443
Moxon, R. 118
Munro, H. 393, 401, 410
Mykytyn, P. 429
Mytelka, L.K. 177

Namenwirth, J.Z. 208
Nanyang Technological University
    (NTU) 270, 287
national culture 208–9
National University of Singapore (NUS)
    286

Ndiaye, M. 115
NEC Ltd. 89
Neff, R. 202
Negandhi, A.R. 114
Nelson, R.R. 252
Neter, J. 378
network model
    relevance to SMEs 392–3
    subsidiary roles 249
networks
    definitions 87–8
    electronic 97–8
    relationships and Internet 412–13,
        423–4
Newman, K.L. 115
Newman, M. 429
Ng, L.F.Y. 69
NGO analysis 117–18
Nicholas, S. 109
Nigh, D. 110, 111, 120, 122, 124
Nishimura, K. 354
Nohria, N. 187, 252, 253
Nokia 42
Nolan, P. 58
Nollen, S. 115
non-linear systems *see* Chaos ontology,
    and international business studies
    research
non-profit organizations, employee trust
    levels 216–17
Nonaka, I. 103
Noordewier, T.G. 202
North, D. 236
Northouse, P.G. 207
NTU (Nanyang Technological
    University) 270, 287
Nunnally, J.C. 256
NUS (National University of Singapore)
    286

Odbert, H.S. 209
Ofek, E. 164
O'Gorman, P. 122
O'Grady, S. 122
oil prices, impact on world economy 8–9
Okazaki, T. 193
Okuno-Fujiwara, M. 193
Ou, X.M. 224, 226
Ouchi, W. 340, 347
Ounjian, M.L. 442

outsiders 232
overseas laboratory roles 90
Oviatt, B.M. 147, 389, 392, 411, 425

Pain, N. 57
Pallant, J. 398
Pan, Y. 397
Pantzalis, C. 368, 373, 374, 385
Parasuraman, A. 407
partnership proposition 19
Pascale, R. 118, 127
Passow, S. 22
patriarchal style family enterprise 230
Peabody, D. 209
Pecotich, A. 391
Pedersen, T. 136, 150, 394, 400
Penrose, E.T. 237, 409
Pepsi-Cola 42
Perlmutter, H. 193, 196
Peters, T. 115, 197
Petersen, B. 136, 150, 394, 400, 413,
    414
Pfeffer, J. 184
Phillips-McDougall, P. 147, 389, 392,
    410, 411, 425
Pine, R.J. 324, 326, 327, 331, 335
Pitre, E. 123
Plender, J. 126
Podsakoff, P. 206, 207
Polk, J. 126
Poon, S. 407
Porter, L. 115
Porter, M.E. 97, 156, 159, 246, 250, 253,
    261
Poston, D.L., Jr. 81
Powell, W.W. 147, 390
power distance 209
Poynter, T.A. 249, 250
Pradhan, J.P. 69
Prahalad, C.K. 157, 163, 249, 251, 252
Prakash, A. 126
Prasad, S.B. 114
Prashantham, S. 391, 412
Priest, T.B. 202
procedural justice (in strategy planning
    process)
  definitions 247–8
  and subsidiary strategy success
    hypotheses 250–54
    literature 248

overview 245–7, 261–2
  research analysis 256–61
  research method 254–6
Proctor and Gamble 42
product life cycle model, subsidiary
    roles 249
productivity spillovers
  definitions 325
  between destinations 327–8
  disadvantages to MNE 330–32
  within host destination 325–7
  see also competition effect; market
    access spillovers
Pustay, M.W. 368, 371

Quelch, J. 245, 248, 412
Quian, G. 164

R Company *see* SMEs Internet and
    internationalization study, cases, R
    Company
R&D
  globalization, distinction from
    internationalization 94–5
  internationalization
    example 92–4
    stages 89–92
  IT networks impact 87–9, 97–8,
    102–3
  network R&D
    basis for formation 97–8
    distinction from closed R&D 95
    human aspects 99–102
Ra, W. 437, 438, 441
Rabier, J. 202
Rail, A. 412
Ramaswami, S.N. 249
Ramaswamy, K. 369, 372
Rao, S. 414, 416
Raytec Electronic Co. *see* SMEs Internet
    and internationalization study,
    cases, R Company
Redding, G. 225, 233
Rempel, J.K. 204
Reuber, R. 410
Rheingold, H. 117
Rialp, A. 407
Rialp, J. 407
Richman, B.M. 114, 115
Roberts, J. 187, 189

Robinson, F. 117
Robinson, R.D. 126
Rodrigues, S.B. 67
Rodrìguez, A.R. 326
Roger, A. 246
Rong, X. 49
Roniger, Y. 179
Ronstadt, R. 90
Root, F.R. 411
Rootzen, H. 119
Rosson, P. 408, 414
Roth, K. 245, 248, 254
Roth, N.L. 205
round-tripping phenomenon 59, 73
Rousseau, D.M. 203
Roy, J. 392
Royle, T. 313
Rugman, A.M. 16, 113, 249, 324
Ruigrok, W. 368, 369, 373
Runnbeck, M. 22

Safarian, A. 114, 118, 121
Samiee, S. 408
Sapienza, H.J. 147
Sasib Business School 270
Satikarn, M. 439
Sauvant, K.P. 59
Sawhney, M. 413
Schindler, P.L. 205
Schive, C. 390
Schlegelmilch, B. 122
Schlenker, B.R. 203
Schneider Technology 67
Schnellenbach, J. 122
Schroath, F.W. 33
Schweiger, D.M. 245
science graduates, China 8
Scientific Humanism ontology, and
    international business studies
    research 116–18
scientific management 347
Scientific ontology, and international
    business studies research 112–14
Scullion, H. 187
Searle, P. 180, 181
SEB 142–3, 146
second-culture management 341–2
Sekaran, U. 211
Shamir, B. 206
Shapiro, C. 146

Shapiro, D. 203
Shapiro, S.P. 240
Sharifi, S. 246
Sharma, D. 395
Shawky, H. 165
Shenkar, O. 66, 115
Shenton, R.W. 177
Shulman, L.E. 252
Sia, Y.H. 67, 68, 71, 73
Sikorski, D. 69
Simon, H.A. 127
Simonin, B.L. 440
Sims, R.L. 215
Singapore
    costs of living 289
    higher education
        as global hub 285–6, 299–300
        market strategies 294–9
        opportunities 290–92
        strengths 286–9
        threats 292–4
        weaknesses 289–90
    infrastructure and accessibility 287–8
    political stability 287
    standards of living 288
Singh, J. 209, 210, 211
Singh, N. 122
Sitkin, S.B. 205
Slocum, J.W. 257
smart mobs 117
SMEs (small and medium-sized
    enterprises)
    inter-firm networks 390–91
    international trade involvement
        389–90
    internationalization determinants
        hypotheses 394–6
        overview 400–402
        research method 396–8
        research results 398–400
    internationalization models
        literature 409–12
        relevance 391–3
    Internet and internationalization
        literature 412–16
        overview 407–9
SMEs Internet and internationalization
    study
    cases 417–20
        FA Company 418–19

FT Company 418
J Company 420
K Company 418
R Company 420
TM Company 419–20
TT Company 419
Y Company 417
findings 421–8
implications 428–30
methodology 416–17
Snow, C.C. 202
Soka Gakkai International (SGI) 348
Soliman, K. 413
Soskice, D. 178
Spekman, R.F. 395, 401
Spence, M. 394
Spender, J.C. 192
stages model *see* Uppsala
Internationalization Process model
stakeholder proposition 19
Stalk, G. 252
Stalker, G.M. 127
Standifird, S.S. 69
Starkey, K. 186
Stein, J.C. 68
Sterman, J. 119, 120, 122
Stevens, G.V.G. 68
Stonehill, A. 51
Stottinger, B. 122
Strub, P.J. 202
structural transformation proposition 19
Su, G.H. 390
Su, Q.L. 224, 226
subsidiary roles 249–50
Sung, Y.-W. 59, 69, 73
Surlemont, B. 253
Svensson, G. 408
Sweeney, P.D. 246
Szulanski, G. 439

tacitness 436
Taggart, J.H. 246, 247, 248, 261
Taiwan
investment in China 32, 35–6
third-culture management 342–6
see also knowledge transfer,
Taiwanese MNE study
Tallman, S.B. 115
Tao Soon, Cham 294
Tapscott, D. 413

targeting proposition 20
Tayeb, M. 393
Taylor, F.W. 112, 340
Taylor, J. 324
Taylor, R. 60, 66, 67
TCL 67
Teece, D.J. 436, 439, 443
Teegen, H. 116
Texma International Co. *see* SMEs
Internet and internationalization
study, cases, TM Company
Thandarayan, V. 414
Theil, H. 166
Thibaut, J.W. 247, 248
third-culture management 342–6,
359–60
Thomas, C.C. 205
Tiessen, J.H. 413
Timmers, P. 415
TM Company *see* SMEs Internet and
internationalization study, cases,
TM Company
Tong, S.Y. 69
tourism spillovers, overview 323–4
Toyne, B. 110, 111, 120, 122, 124
Toyota Motor Co. Ltd. 89
managerial philosophies 354
transaction cost theory 371–2, 411
Transfer Technology Units (TTUs) 90
Triandis, H.C. 202
Trompenaars, Fons 309
trust
appearance in leadership literature
206–8
definitions 203
importance as leadership issue 201–2
literature review 202–5
trust-building
and cultural norms
research methodology 212–16
research propositions 210–12
research results 216–18
Tse, D. 118, 128
TT Company *see* SMEs Internet and
internationalization study, cases, TT
Company
TTUs (Transfer Technology Units) 90
Tuan, C. 69
Tung Tzu Industrial Co. *see* SMEs
Internet and internationalization

study, cases, TT Company
Tyler, T.R. 247, 248

Ueno, S. 211
Uhl-Bien, M. 207
Ulgado, F.M. 310
uncertainty avoidance 209
unconditional trust 205
Universal Automobile Industries 67
Uppsala Internationalization Process
    model (stages model)
    anchoring in 1st episode of IB studies
        122
    Internet-related firms
        assessment against 138–44
        relevance for 135–6, 144–50, 429
    overview 137–8, 409–10
    relevance to SMEs 392–3
US
    cultural dimensions 210
    see also cultural norms, and
        trust-building
    foreign aid below target 7
    managerial philosophies 347, 358–60

Vahlne, J.E. 69, 122, 137, 138, 145, 146,
    149, 249, 369, 392, 409, 421, 428
value creation, definitions 155
van der Ploeg, F. 157
van Staveren, I. 119
van Tuijl, P. 116
Varian, H.R. 146
Vengroff, R. 115
Verbeke, A. 16, 249
Vermeulen, F. 115, 146
Vernon, R. 249, 368, 409
VF Corporation 43
Villela, A.V. 69
Von Wright, G.H. 113

Wada, E. 49
Wagner, H. 368, 369, 373
Wal-Mart 43
Walker, L. 247, 248
Wall, D. 59, 67, 73
Walter, I. 334
Wang, M.Y. 59
Wang, S.-T. 441
Wanxiang Group 67
Warner, M. 56, 59, 67

Waseda University 270, 277–84
Waterman, R.H. 115, 197
Watson, J.L. 310, 312, 313, 314, 318
Weaver, G. 123
Weber, M. 230
Weber, R.B. 208
Weeks, A. 429
Wei, Q. 226
Wei, Y. 28
Weick, K.E. 251
Weigert, A. 202, 203
Weitz, B. 202
Weitz, B.A. 411
Welch, L. 109, 408
Welch, L.S. 391, 392
Wells, L.T. 58, 69, 78
Wesson, T. 245, 261
Westney, D.E. 94
White, R.E. 249, 250
Whitelock, J. 393
Whitley, R. 183
Wiedersheim-Paul, F. 137, 392, 409
Wiesenfeld, B.M. 247
Williamson, N.C. 411
Williamson, O.E. 202, 208, 371, 436,
    440
Winter, S.G. 252, 436
Wisdom eye 350
Wittenberg, J. 119, 120, 122
Wong, J. 60, 61, 68, 71, 72
world economy, characteristics 13–14
Wright, R. 407
Wu, C.S. 380, 385, 437
Wu, F. 67, 68, 71, 73
Wu, H.-L. 61
Wu, R.I. 395
Wu, U.M. 391
Wu, W.I. 391

Y Company *see* SMEs Internet and
    internationalization study, cases, Y
    Company
Yamagishi, M. 241
Yamagishi, T. 241
Yang, G.S. 229
Yang, J. 35, 42, 51
Ye, G. 60, 61, 67, 68, 71, 77
Yeh, Y.F. 391
Yeung, B. 369, 383
Yeung, H.W.-C. 69

YFC-BonEagle Inc. *see* SMEs Internet
    and internationalization study,
    cases, Y Company
Yin, R.K. 139, 416
Yip, G.S. 254
Yiu, G.M. 390
Yonsei University 270
Yoshihara, K. 180
Young, S. 48
Yu, A.B. 229
Yu, Bo 231
Yu, J.M. 380, 381
Yum Corporation 304

Zacharia, Z.G. 401
Zaheer, S. 394

Zand, D. 204
Zander, U. 118, 252, 435, 436, 441, 442
Zaslavsky, G. 119
Zeidman, P.F. 304
Zeithaml, V.A. 309
Zhan, J.X. 60, 67, 68, 69, 71, 77
Zhang, H.Y. 235
Zhang, W.Y. 227
Zhang, Y. 56, 60, 66, 67
Zhang, Z. 30, 32
Zheng, B.X. 226, 233
Zheng, Y.F. 224
Zhou, C. 32
Zin, R.H.M. 69
Zinkhan, G.M. 407
Zucker, L.G. 203